Just Wars, Holy Wars, and Jihads

Just Wars, Holy Wars, and Jihads

Christian, Jewish, and Muslim Encounters and Exchanges

EDITED BY SOHAIL H. HASHMI

OXFORD
UNIVERSITY PRESS

OXFORD
UNIVERSITY PRESS

Oxford University Press, Inc., publishes works that further
Oxford University's objective of excellence
in research, scholarship, and education by publishing worldwide.

Oxford   New York
Auckland   Cape Town   Dar es Salaam   Hong Kong   Karachi
Kuala Lumpur   Madrid   Melbourne   Mexico City   Nairobi
New Delhi   Shanghai   Taipei   Toronto

With offices in
Argentina   Austria   Brazil   Chile   Czech Republic   France   Greece
Guatemala   Hungary   Italy   Japan   Poland   Portugal   Singapore
South Korea   Switzerland   Thailand   Turkey   Ukraine   Vietnam

Library of Congress Cataloging-in-Publication Data
Just wars, holy wars, and jihads : Christian, Jewish, and Muslim encounters
and exchanges / edited by Sohail H. Hashmi.
p.   cm.
Includes index.
ISBN 978-0-19-975503-5 (paperback) — ISBN 978-0-19-975504-2 (hardcover) 1. War—Religious aspects.
2. Just war doctrine. 3. Jihad. 4. War—Religious aspects—Christianity. 5. War—Religious aspects—Judaism.
6. War—Religious aspects—Islam. I. Hashmi, Sohail H., 1962–
BL65.W2J87   2012
201'.7273—dc23   2012003852

1 3 5 7 9 8 6 4 2

Printed in the United States of America
on acid-free paper

To the memory of
Omar Khalidi
(1953–2010)

CONTENTS

ACKNOWLEDGMENTS

This book began to develop many years ago when John Kelsay invited Martin Cook, James Turner Johnson, and me to join him in a study group on just war and jihad. I thank Jim, John, and Martin for their encouragement of this project from the start and their many valuable suggestions for how to improve this book.

The chapters in this volume benefited greatly from discussions at a colloquium held at Mount Holyoke College in October 2008. Financial support for this event came from the following sources at Mount Holyoke: the Purrington Fund and the Office of the Dean of the College, the Office of the Dean of Faculty, the McCulloch Center for Global Initiatives, and the Weissman Center for Leadership. Special thanks are due to Lee Bowie, Lois Brown, Penny Gill, Donal O'Shea, and Eva Paus. The following scholars generously offered their time and insights at the colloquium: Kavita Datla, Harold Garrett-Goodyear, John Grayson, Holly Hanson, Iza Hussin, David Perry, and Nadya Sbaiti. Administrative support was graciously provided by James Burke, Linda Fernandes, Bryan Goodwin, Anne-Laure Malauzat, and Marian Smith.

The production of this book was facilitated by the able editorial assistance of Andrea Reynolds. An anonymous reviewer for Oxford University Press offered many helpful suggestions, both substantive and stylistic. Doreen St. John produced the maps that accompany chapter 12. Finally, thanks to Theo Calderara, our editor at Oxford University Press, for his unflagging and patient support of this work.

This book is dedicated to the memory of our friend and colleague Omar Khalidi, who died just days after completing work on his chapter in this volume. Omar was a thoughtful mentor, a prolific writer, and a provocative public intellectual, tireless in his lobbying for justice for all of India's citizens. His untimely death stilled a restless mind and a generous heart.

SHH
South Hadley, Mass.

CONTRIBUTORS

Asma Afsaruddin is Professor of Near Eastern Languages and Cultures at Indiana University. She is the author or editor of four books, including *The First Muslims: History and Memory* and *Excellence and Precedence: Medieval Islamic Discourse on Legitimate Leadership*. She is currently completing a manuscript on a historical survey of jihad and martyrdom in Islamic thought and praxis.

Mustafa Aksakal is Associate Professor of Modern Turkish Studies and History at Georgetown University. His research interests focus on the political history of the modern Middle East and the region's role in international politics. He is the author of *The Ottoman Road to War in 1914: The Ottoman Empire and the First World War*.

Joshua C. Birk is Assistant Professor of History at Smith College, specializing in political history and identity politics across religious boundaries in the medieval Mediterranean world. He is currently writing a book titled *Baptized Sultans: The Norman Rulers of Sicily and Their Muslim Subjects*, which examines how the Christian rulers of Sicily co-opted and redeployed Islamic cultural tropes and administrative techniques to project their authority over Sicily in the eleventh and twelfth centuries.

Benjamin Claude Brower is Assistant Professor in the Department of History at the University of Texas at Austin. His research focuses on French colonialism and its impact on Algerian society. He is the author of *A Desert Named Peace: The Violence of France's Empire in the Algerian Sahara, 1844–1902*, a study of colonial violence in nineteenth-century Algeria. He is currently at work on a history of Muslim pilgrimage to Mecca and the Holy Places made from France's Mediterranean colonies, a project titled *The Mediterranean Hajj under French Rule, 1798–1962*.

Brinda Charry teaches early modern English literature and culture at Keene State College. Her area of specialization is early modern globalism and cross-cultural encounter, with a special emphasis on Anglo-Ottoman engagement as manifested in literary and cultural documents. She is the coeditor of *Mediating Worlds: Early Modern Emissaries, 1500–1700* and author of three works of fiction: *The Hottest Day of the Year*, *Naked in the Wind*, and *First Love and Other Stories*.

David Cook is Associate Professor in the Department of Religious Studies at Rice University. His interests include the study of early Islam, Muslim apocalyptic literature and movements for radical social change, dreams, historical astronomy, Judeo-Arabic literature, and West African Islam. His books include *Understanding Jihad*, *Contemporary Muslim Apocalyptic Literature*, and *Martyrdom in Islam*.

Martin L. Cook is Professor and Admiral James Bond Stockdale Chair of Professional Military Ethics in the College of Operational and Strategic Leadership at the United States Naval War College. His publications have explored a range of issues in theology and military ethics. His most recent book is *The Moral Warrior: Ethics and Service in the U.S. Military*.

G. Scott Davis is the Lewis T. Booker Professor of Religion and Ethics at the University of Richmond. Davis works in both philosophy of religion, where he specializes in theories and methods, and in ethics, where he divides his time between moral theory and the history of the just war tradition. He is the author of *Warcraft and the Fragility of Virtue* and the editor of *Religion and Justice in the War over Bosnia*. He is currently at work on *The Base of Design: The Pragmatic Turn in Comparative Religion and Ethics* and *Conscience and Conquest: The Discovery of the Americas and the Making of Modern Ethics*.

Sohail H. Hashmi is Professor of International Relations and Alumnae Foundation Chair in the Social Sciences at Mount Holyoke College. His work focuses on Islamic ethics and political theory, particularly as they relate to issues in contemporary international relations. He is the editor of *Islamic Political Ethics* and coeditor of *Ethics and Weapons of Mass Destruction: Religious and Secular Perspectives*. He is currently writing a book on Muslim responses to the rise of international law.

James Turner Johnson is Professor of Religion and Associate Member of the Graduate Department of Political Science at Rutgers—The State University of New Jersey. His research and teaching have focused principally on the historical development and application of moral traditions related to war, peace, and the practice of statecraft. His books include *Just War Tradition and the Restraint of War*, *The Holy War Idea in Western and Islamic Traditions*, *Morality and Contemporary Warfare*, and *The War to Oust Saddam Hussein: Just War and the New Face of Conflict*.

John Kelsay is Distinguished Research Professor, Bristol Distinguished Professor of Ethics, and Richard L. Rubenstein Professor of Religion at Florida State University. His most recent book is *Arguing the Just War in Islam*. Previous publications include *Islam and War: A Study in Comparative Ethics* and two volumes he coedited with James Turner Johnson: *Cross, Crescent, and Sword* and *Just War and Jihad*.

Omar Khalidi, at the time of his death in November 2010, was the Aga Khan Program Librarian at Massachusetts Institute of Technology and an independent scholar. He published extensively on the history and contemporary situation of Indian Muslims, including *Hyderabad after the Fall*, *Indian Muslims since Independence*, and *Muslims in Indian Economy*. He had recently completed an online guide to the architecture of Hyderabad and was working on similar resources for other Indian cities.

James E. Lindsay is Associate Professor in the Department of History at Colorado State University, specializing in premodern Middle Eastern history. He is the author of *The Intensification and Reorientation of Sunni Jihad Ideology in the Crusader Period: Ibn 'Asakir (1105–1176) and His Age* (with Suleiman A. Mourad) and *Daily Life in the Medieval Islamic World* and editor of *Ibn 'Asakir and Early Islamic History*.

Suleiman A. Mourad is Professor of Religion at Smith College. His research interests focus on medieval Islamic history and religious thought, including the Counter-Crusade jihad ideology. He is the author of *Early Islam between Myth and History: Al-Hasan al-Basri (d. 110 H/728 CE) and the Formation of His Legacy in Classical Islamic Scholarship* and coeditor of *Jerusalem: Idea and Reality*.

Michael Philip Penn is Associate Professor of Religion at Mount Holyoke College and a specialist in biblical studies and the history of early Christianity. He explores how early Christian communities forged their identity, especially in the context of religious and ethnic pluralism. He is the author of *Kissing Christians: Ritual and Community in the Late Ancient Church* and is currently writing two books on Syriac Christian reactions to the rise of Islam.

David Robinson is University Distinguished Professor of History, specializing in the history of Africa and Islam, at Michigan State University. His publications include *The Holy War of Umar Tal: The Western Sudan in the Mid-Nineteenth Century* and *Paths of Accommodation*, a study of Muslim movements in Senegal and Mauritania in the early colonial period. He recently authored a general study of Islam in Africa, *Muslim Societies in African History*.

Heather J. Sharkey is Associate Professor in the Department of Near Eastern Languages and Civilizations at the University of Pennsylvania. Her research and teaching focus on the history and politics of the Middle East and North Africa in the nineteenth century, including the cultural influences of Muslim, Jewish, and Christian communities on one another. She is the author of *Living with Colonialism: Nationalism and Culture in the Anglo-Egyptian Sudan* and *American Evangelicals in Egypt: Missionary Encounters in an Age of Empire*.

Paul Stephenson is Professor and Chair of Medieval History at Radboud University Nijmegen. His published work focuses on middle Byzantine history; the history and historiography of the Balkans, medieval and modern; and Byzantine warfare. He is the author of *Byzantium's Balkan Frontier: A Political Study of the Northern Balkans,*

900–1204, The Legend of Basil the Bulgar-Slayer, and *Constantine: Unconquered Emperor, Christian Victor.*

Suzanne Last Stone is Professor of Law at Cardozo School of Law and Director of Yeshiva University's Center for Jewish Law and Contemporary Civilization at Cardozo. In addition to teaching courses on Jewish law, she teaches civil procedure, federal courts, and law, religion, and the state. Her publications explore the intersection of Jewish legal thought and contemporary legal theory and include "In Pursuit of the Countertext: The Turn to the Jewish Legal Model in Contemporary American Legal Theory," "The Jewish Conception of Civil Society," and "Justice, Mercy, and Gender in Rabbinic Thought." She also serves as the coeditor-in-chief of *Diné Israel*, a journal of Jewish law.

George R. Wilkes is Director of the Religion and Ethics in the Making of War and Peace Project at the University of Edinburgh. He has published a series of articles on war in Jewish tradition and is currently writing a monograph on the subject. He has also published work on religion and politics in Israeli-Palestinian relations, the history of Jewish-Christian relations in the twentieth century, and contemporary European history.

A. Nuri Yurdusev is Professor of International Relations at Middle East Technical University. He is the author of *International Relations and the Philosophy of History: A Civilizational Approach* and the editor of *Ottoman Diplomacy: Conventional or Unconventional?* His current research interests include the theory and history of international relations, European identity, and Ottoman diplomacy.

Just Wars, Holy Wars, and Jihads

Introduction

SOHAIL H. HASHMI AND JAMES TURNER JOHNSON

This book is about the development of ideas of morally justified or legitimate war in Western and Islamic civilizations. These ideas have traditionally been grouped under three rubrics: just war, holy war, and jihad. A large body of literature exists exploring the development of concepts of just war and holy war in the West and of jihad in Islam. Yet until recently, the scholarship on just war and jihad has largely treated each tradition as separate and unrelated to the other. It is commonplace in histories of the evolution of just war thinking, for example, to trace a genealogy from Augustine of Hippo in the fifth century to Thomas Aquinas in the thirteenth century, with no mention at all of the rise and dominance of Islamic civilization in the Mediterranean during the intervening eight hundred years. Only a limited number of works deal comparatively with moral reasoning on war in Western and Islamic civilizations, and only a few articles explore the impact of contact among Christians, Jews, and Muslims on their respective views of war and peace. This book is the first to investigate in depth the interaction between just war and jihad thinking from the rise of Islam in the seventh century to the present. Two broad questions guide the discussion in each chapter: (1) What historical evidence exists—in treatises, chronicles, speeches, ballads, and other historical records or in practice—that Christian and Jewish writers on just war and holy war and Muslim writers on jihad knew of the other tradition? (2) Is there any evidence that Christians, Jews, and Muslims were influenced in their views on the ethics of war and peace through their mutual interaction? In other words, how did discourses on just war, holy war, and jihad influence one another?

Just War, Jihad, and Holy War

Moral reasoning on war is a human phenomenon perhaps as old and universal as war itself. All major civilizations have engaged in thinking about the justification of the resort to war and the proper means to prosecute it. This thinking is motivated by an intuitive or practical sense that the two ends of the moral spectrum—namely, pacifism (the rejection of all war) and total war (the acceptance of unrestrained warfare)—are unsupportable and that the right position is one that falls somewhere in the middle of the spectrum. We may label this activity in Western civilization as *just war thinking* and in Islamic civilization as *jihad thinking*. In both civilizations, such thinking on legitimate war historically has been grounded in a particular set of sources, has employed a generally consistent type of moral reasoning, and has yielded coherent sets of questions and answers that allow us to speak meaningfully of traditions of thought. In the West, it is the *just war tradition*; in Islam, it is the *jihad tradition*. Both traditions have tended to ask similar questions regarding the just causes or grounds for war (summarized in the Latin phrase *jus ad bellum*) and the just means or conduct of war (*jus in bello*). And for any given historical period, we can identify a broad consensus of scholarly opinion on the answers to these questions, on what the tradition says regarding the ethics of war of peace. In the just war tradition, we call this consensus *just war doctrine*; in the jihad tradition, it is *jihad doctrine*. Yet the scholarly consensus has been challenged and changed over time. Both just war doctrine and jihad doctrine have evolved significantly since the traditions began to develop, and each continues to do so today in response to new problems in international relations and the philosophical activity of contemporary theorists.

The origins of the just war tradition are commonly traced back to the writings of Augustine, the bishop of Hippo (d. 430). But there are two major problematic issues with this notion, and they are intertwined: chronology and thematic content. Augustine did not in fact elaborate a systematic conception of just war, and it is simply incorrect to treat the concept of just war as if it were already in well-defined existence by the time of his death. It would be better to say that Augustine is the source of various ideas that were put together in coherent form only centuries later. Even that is not quite correct, since much of what he said about the justified use of armed force traces back to earlier sources, notably the Old Testament of the Bible, Roman law and practice, and Cicero's philosophy. But in any case, the ideas from these sources were picked up and stated by Augustine, though never in the form of a coherent doctrine. By comparison, Augustine treated sexuality and marriage directly in four distinct treatises and as a prominent element in three others, while his comments on justified war were brief in scope, scattered over several different kinds of writings, penned in different contexts, and all directed by the purpose of whatever argument he was engaged in at the time.

Augustine's earliest thinking on war is found in the treatise *De ordine*, written to combat the Manichaean attack on earthly society as inherently evil. During this period, not long after his baptism, Augustine remained strongly influenced by Neoplatonism, and this is reflected in his depiction of justified war in this early treatise as a means by which a well-ordered society seeks to protect itself and conform with the cosmic law, put in place by God. Later, in midlife, his guiding concerns became more centrally Christian, and his thinking about war reflected this. In the treatise *Contra Faustum*, this time responding to the Manichaean attack on the Old Testament, he argued for the unity of God's saving work as revealed in both the Old and the New Testament, noting with reference to war that as described in the Old Testament, God had employed war as a means of combating evil. The message of the New Testament, meanwhile, is that death is not itself an evil, since Christians are promised eternal life. In this vein, Augustine wrote regarding war:

> What is it about war that is to be blamed? Is it that those who will die someday are killed so that those who will conquer might dominate in peace? This is the complaint of the timid, not the religious. The desire for harming, the cruelty of revenge, the restless and implacable mind, the savageness of revolting, the lust for dominating, and similar things— these are what are justly blamed in wars. Often, so that such things might also be justly punished, certain wars that must be waged against the violence of those resisting are commanded by God or some other legitimate ruler and are undertaken by the good.[1]

Thus, as a result of explicitly Christian thinking, Augustine shifted the ground on how to conceive of just war: the killing it may cause is not itself an evil, but rather the evil is in wrong intentions rooted in the disordered love (*cupiditas*) that results from sin. To combat such evil, just war "must be waged . . . by the good" on the authorization of God or a legitimate ruler, one responsible for the just ordering of his community. In this same vein, in his "Letter 138 to Marcellinus," Augustine counseled that even in war, "a spirit of benevolence must always permeate the will so as to avoid returning evil for evil."[2] During this same period, he also exchanged several letters with Count Boniface, a Christian who was the Roman official responsible for the province in which Augustine's episcopal seat, Hippo Regius, was located, stressing the justification of the use of armed force on public authority (in this instance, located in Boniface as the legitimate representative of the Roman government) to combat evildoing and protect the good.[3]

The middle period of Augustine's life coincided with the reign of the emperor Theodosius I (379–395), which many Christians, including Augustine, came to regard as an inbreaking of Christian society into history. But after Theodosius died, his heirs were emperors of a different sort. Accordingly, from about 400 on, Augustine's thinking shifted again. On war, he held to the conception of justified war defined earlier, but now (in *The City of God*, particularly book XIX) he understood it as a kind of bulwark against the threat of chaos all around, a means of holding to a limited "tranquility of order" within the "City of Earth" while awaiting the fullness of peace in God in the triumph of the "City of God."

The variability in Augustine's thinking on war has caught the interest of many recent commentators, but for the medieval canonists, it was the continuity in his thought that predominated. Although his scattered observations on war were generally known in centers of Christian learning through the early Middle Ages, it was not until the middle of the twelfth century, in the context of a broad reawakening of learning and knowledge, that they were pulled together and placed in a specific order as a guide for Christian conduct. This was what was accomplished by the canonist Gratian in his magisterial work, the *Decretum*, completed in 1148.

The *Decretum* was an ordered compilation of quotations from recognized Christian authorities together with relatively short comments by Gratian aimed at setting the interpretive context for the passages quoted. It was originally produced as a textbook for the study of canon law at the University of Bologna, where Gratian was on the faculty. Its authoritative nature was quickly recognized widely, and its use spread to the other schools of canon law in the Latin West. One entire section of this work, part II, causa 23, was devoted to the question of war. While passages from other authorities, including Ambrose of Milan and Isidore of Seville, appear here, causa 23 is dominated by extensive quotations of passages from Augustine. But in the *Decretum*, these passages, rather than appearing (as in Augustine) in scattered form in works on a variety of subjects, were ordered by being placed under specific "questions" defined by Gratian: question I, on who may resist violence, how it may be resisted, and what kind of violence may be resisted; question II, on the justifications (just causes) for resort to war; question III, distinguishing the use of force for the public good from that for private reasons; question IV, further on the difference between the use of force for personal reasons and for the public good; question V, on whether killing in war is homicide; and so on. The passage from *Contra Faustum* quoted above appears in question I; passages from *The City of God* appear in the context of question V; other passages from various places in Augustine's works appear in these questions and elsewhere.[4]

The *Decretum* not only connected Augustine powerfully to the issues addressed in the form of the various questions treated, but its widespread adoption as a text also ensured that the passages cited would be adopted by later authors as basic for defining the idea of just war. Nonetheless, even after the *Decretum*, there remained significant issues to be decided about the specific content of the idea of *justum bellum*, and these were the subject of extensive debate among canonical writers over the next century through two generations of canonists, the Decretists and the Decretalists. Partly because of the Crusades, there was considerable discussion among these writers of religious authorization and justification of war.

While particular commentators argued in various ways on these matters, a settled doctrine was reached by the mid-thirteenth century, the end of the era of the Decretalists. As for *jus ad bellum*, on this settled position, warfare is not justified to spread or coerce Christian belief, because it is impossible to coerce belief, but war may be fought to defend Christians from efforts to coerce their beliefs or practices, to defend church property, and to protect the lives and livelihoods of Christians in the face of attack. But the right of defense, *defensio*, was understood as given in the natural law, not as flowing from religion. As for authorization, the argument among the canonists had to do with whether church officials (particularly bishops) could legitimately authorize such war. The answer ultimately reached was that as a general rule, church officials did not have the right to authorize use of armed force. This right belonged specifically to princes, persons in the position of sovereignty, rulers with no temporal superiors. Both of these positions—the conception of jus. cause in natural law terms and the conception of authority to initiate use of force in terms of the responsibility of the temporal ruler—became part of the just war idea in its classic form.

Where the pope was concerned, the argument among the canonists produced no clear answer regarding whether he possessed the authority to initiate use of armed force. On the one side was the reasoning that the pope is not, as pope, a temporal lord, and thus he did not meet the test of temporal sovereignty. On the other side was the reasoning that as vicar of Christ on earth, the pope is superior to all temporal lords. The matter was effectively left open by the twelfth- and thirteenth-century canonists. But in practice, an answer did develop: a practical modus vivendi by which the pope might exhort the temporal princes of Christendom to make war for defense of Christians and Christendom, though not undertake war on his own authority. These temporal princes had to decide for themselves whether to do so in the case at hand. So even if the pope were considered to be able to authorize war, he did not in practice do so. This practical solution reflected the grounding of just war within the purview of temporal or secular government. But the solution reached nonetheless allowed popes to exhort temporal rulers to engage in warfare against non-Christians, Christian heretics and Jews in Europe, and Muslims abroad. Sometimes the temporal lords responded; sometimes they turned the call to crusade to their own uses; and at other times, and especially by the sixteenth century, they did not respond at all, because of their own reading of their obligations as temporal rulers.

We see a glimpse of the canonical argument over whether crusading is a form of just war, *justum bellum*, in Frederick Russell's discussion of the canonist Johannes de Deo (d. 1267), who argued that crusading is a type of just war.[5] While this was Johannes's position, his was only one contribution to an ongoing debate, and Russell offers it as such. Others took the opposite position, and the matter was still being disputed even as Johannes wrote. Russell turns to the men whose common position—and authority—effectively settled the matter, Pope Innocent IV (d. 1254; himself a canonist) and Hostiensis (d. 1271). Their answer was to define the idea of just war in terms of purely temporal reference points, so that the wars we now call the Crusades are just wars only if they satisfy the criteria for use of force by a temporal prince, whose duty is understood via a common proof-text, Romans 13:4: The prince "is the minister of God to come in wrath to punish those who do evil." The conception of just war first delineated by Gratian and effectively settled by Innocent and Hostiensis was memorably and influentially summarized by Thomas Aquinas (d. 1274) in *Summa theologiae* II/II, Q. 40, as including the requirement that *justum bellum* be authorized by one in sovereign (temporal) authority, that it be for the recovery of things wrongly taken or to punish evildoing, that it be undertaken so as to avoid the sort of wrong intentions summarized by Augustine in the passage from *Contra Faustum* quoted above, and that it be undertaken with the end of restoring or establishing peace.

Aquinas's question "On War" did not explicitly address the matter of right conduct in war; to use the terminology developed later, it had to do with *jus ad bellum*, not *jus in bello*. The canon law already set certain limits on conduct (a definition of noncombatant immunity and an effort to outlaw certain types of weapons), but Aquinas did not address them in this context. Later, in the era of the Hundred Years War (that is, in the last part of the fourteenth century and the first part of the fifteenth), certain writers, notably Honoré Bonet (d. ca. 1410) and Christine de Pisan (d. ca. 1434), accepting Aquinas's parameters for justified resort to armed force, fleshed out the idea of *jus in bello* by drawing from the chivalric code. The result was an idea of just war that included both a succinct *jus ad bellum* (drawn from Aquinas) and a developed *jus in bello* based on both the canon law and the chivalric code. This conception of just war passed intact into the modern era, where it can be found in the work of major theoretical writers such as Francisco de Vitoria (d. 1546), Francisco Suárez (d. 1617), and Hugo Grotius (d. 1645).

Grotius, though, transformed the understanding of just war from the tradition he received, reshaping it into a philosophical basis for a law of nations. Subsequently, theological thinking about just war declined; there is no creative theological work done on the just war idea from the time of the theologian Suárez, a contemporary of Grotius, until the recovery of just war as a theological concern in the last part of the twentieth century, beginning with the work of Paul Ramsey (d. 1988). During this period of roughly two and a half centuries, the tradition of just war was carried and developed as a part of a conception of international law. By the era of the American Civil War, the content of the idea of just war largely defined the accepted "laws and customs of war," although this was not explicitly recognized by the theorists and practitioners of those laws and customs. Similarly, as these "laws and customs" were codified into a positive law of war, ideas from just war tradition carried into the positive law treatment of noncombatant immunity and restraints on weapons and practices in war.

Recovering the idea of just war as a framework for moral discourse traces largely to the influence of three sources: Paul Ramsey's work in the 1960s, Michael Walzer's in the following decade, and that of the U.S. Catholic bishops in connection with their 1983 pastoral letter, *The Challenge of Peace*.[6] In subsequent years, forms of just war discourse have spread widely and proliferated in variety even as they have spread. Neither Ramsey nor Walzer nor the U.S. Catholic bishops sought to engage or recover the historical tradition of just war. Rather, they defined their own ideas of just war on the basis of their own sources: for Ramsey, largely a theological reading of Augustine highlighting his understanding of Christian love; for Walzer, largely a conception of human rights anchored in common human perceptions; for the Catholic bishops, an idea of just war framed in terms of a controlling "presumption against war" that may be overturned only if the just war criteria, as listed by the bishops, are fully satisfied. Forms of philosophical consequentialist understandings of just war have proliferated, and various political figures have invoked the term *just war* while giving their own particular content to the idea.

Such variety in moral discourse about war implies a certain vitality, at least vitality in interest in thinking morally about war, but James Turner Johnson's insistence that present-day uses of the term *just war* should be tested by reference to the classic historical content of the just war idea stands over against those contemporary conceptions of just war that have no connection to the historical just war idea.

When we consider the development of the jihad tradition, it is important to begin by acknowledging that the term *jihad* is not coterminous with war, or even a just war. The Arabic root *j-h-d*, from which *jihad* is derived, connotes a struggle or effort of any sort. In pre-Islamic Arabic literature, *jihad* seems to have not been used with any military connotation. Thus, the conduct of jihad "by the sword" appears to be an Islamic widening of the semantic field of this term.[7]

We may see this broadening of the concept within the Qur'an itself. In the Meccan period of revelation (610–622), *jihad* appears in the Qur'an in a purely metaphysical sense; there is no implication that it may be manifested as war. In fact, the specific word for war, *harb*, is nowhere to be found in verses believed to be from this period, and the few appearances of the word for fighting or combat, *qital*, are confined to nonmilitary contexts. *Jihad* in the Meccan period of the Prophet Muhammad's mission, it seems, meant only a nonviolent struggle to maintain faith and righteousness among the believers and to disseminate Islam to nonbelievers.

This situation changed dramatically following the Prophet's migration to Medina in 622 (the Hijra). In Medina, references to *jihad* increase in the Qur'an. While some of these verses continue employing the term in the sense of a spiritual or nonviolent physical struggle, a new dimension is added: physical force or fighting (*qital*). Qur'an 22:39–40, the focus of Asma Afsaruddin's discussion in chapter 2 below, are believed by many of the early commentators to signal the broadened semantic range of *jihad* in the revelation. It permits the Muslims to retaliate with force against those who continue to attack and persecute them. The reference to "monasteries, churches, synagogues, and mosques" suggests that violence undertaken for self-defense and for defense of religion is a legitimate cause not just in Islamic faith but in all faiths.

A subsequent series of verses (Q. 2:190–91) converts the permission of self-defense into an obligation, with the argument that "oppression is worse than killing." Then, after nearly eight years of warfare between the Muslims and their polytheist enemies, some of the Jewish tribes of Medina, and some of the southern outposts of the Byzantine empire, the Qur'an seems to enjoin a war of conversion against all remaining polytheist Arabs (Q. 9:5, known as the "sword verse") and a war of subjugation against Christians and Jews (Q. 9:29).

> But when the forbidden months are past, then fight and slay the polytheists [*mushrikin*] wherever you find them. Seize them, besiege them, and lie in wait for them using every stratagem. But if they repent, and establish regular prayers, and practice regular charity, then open the way for them. For God is most forgiving, most merciful. (Q. 9:5)

> Fight those who do not believe in God or the Last Day, nor hold for-
> bidden that which has been forbidden by God and his messenger, nor
> acknowledge the religion of truth, from among those who have been
> given the Book, until they pay the poll-tax [jizya] with willing submis-
> sion, having been subdued. (Q. 9:29)

For roughly two centuries after Muhammad's death in 632, Muslim thinking on
jihad remained largely inchoate, at least as far as we know from the dearth of sources.
The earliest surviving works on jihad, such as (in part) the *Muwatta'* of Malik ibn
Anas (d. 795) and the *Kitab al-jihad* (Book of Jihad) of 'Abdallah ibn al-Mubarak (d.
797), are not elaborations of anything resembling a doctrine but are compilations of
scattered sayings (hadiths) on jihad attributed to the Prophet and his companions.
More systematic discussions of the purposes and prosecution of war, such as the
work of the Syrian jurist al-Awza'i (d. 774), have survived only indirectly and piece-
meal through critical commentaries on them produced in later centuries.

It was not until the ninth century, following the consolidation of the Abbasid
caliphate in Baghdad, that a coherent tradition of scholarly thought on jihad began
to develop. Although *jihad* continued to be used broadly to mean both spiritual and
physical struggle—with early Sufis (Muslim mystics) emphasizing the former—the
term acquired a technical meaning through its appropriation by the jurists of the
classical period (roughly the ninth through the thirteenth centuries). In their efforts
to codify shari'a, which they understood as a comprehensive body of divine law, out
of the general precepts in the Qur'an and *sunna* (normative example) of the Prophet,
the jurists could hardly have avoided dealing with issues of war and peace. Thus, in
the major compendia of legal opinions of each of the four surviving schools of Sunni
jurisprudence, and also in the dominant Twelver Shi'i school, there is invariably a
section on jihad, understood as a just, legitimate, divinely commanded war.

At the heart of the classical jihad doctrine was the division of the world into two
contending spheres. One was *dar al-Islam* (abode or territory of Islam), a unitary
state made up of the community of Muslims, living by the shari'a, and led by the
just ruler (imam). *Dar al-Islam* also included non-Muslim communities, the *dhimmis* (protected people), whose separate communal laws and leaders were tolerated
by the Islamic state as long as they did not challenge Muslim sovereignty. Opposed
to *dar al-Islam* was *dar al-harb* (abode or territory of war), where Islamic law did not
prevail, leading presumably to anarchy and moral corruption.

The classical jurists' attention was focused on what may be called the expansionist jihad. The imam was obliged to undertake jihad whenever the conditions of
the Islamic state permitted him to reduce *dar al-harb* and bring its lands and peoples
into *dar al-Islam*. This was a collective duty of the Muslim community (*fard kifaya*),
one that required participation only from those financially and physically capable of
undertaking it.

The jihad in *dar al-harb*, in the view of the scholars, was aimed at bringing
Islam's higher civilization to those unaware of it, not territorial conquest, plunder,

or forcible conversion. Accordingly, they elaborated rules on what Muslim armies may or may not do in *dar al-harb*. Indeed, *jus in bello* concerns received far greater elaboration than *jus ad bellum*. The basis for such moral injunctions was the Qur'an's general command "Do not transgress limits, for God loves not transgressors" (Q. 2:190), which was given greater specificity by the practice of the Prophet and his first four successors. Before the start of any attack, enemies were to be offered the choice of accepting Islam, in which case no further action against them was permissible. If they refused, they were to be offered *dhimmi* status as an autonomous community within *dar al-Islam*. This option, deriving from Qur'an 9:29, initially pertained to Jews and Christians but was steadily expanded to include Zoroastrians, Hindus, and Buddhists as the Islamic frontiers expanded. Only the polytheist Arabs who had fought so bitterly against Muhammad and the early Muslim community were excluded from the *dhimmi* option and forced to convert according to Qur'an 9:5.

In fighting the enemy, Muslim soldiers were to avoid directly targeting women and children. Some jurists included old men, peasants, hermits, merchants, the insane, and other males who did not ordinarily take part in fighting on the list of prohibited targets. According to most scholars, all able-bodied adult males could, at the discretion of the imam, be killed, whether they were fighting or had been taken prisoner. The jurists permitted the use of all types of weapons or military tactics that were necessary to overcome the enemy, including laying siege to fortresses, firing incendiary devices, cutting off the water supply, or flooding. A few practices were categorically prohibited, based on injunctions attributed to the Prophet; these included killing by mutilation or torture, burning individuals alive, and violating oaths or grants of security to soldiers or envoys.

The second type of jihad may be termed the defensive jihad. It was commonly understood that Muslims had an individual obligation (*fard 'ayn*) to defend *dar al-Islam* whenever it was threatened by aggression from *dar al-harb*. When the classical jurists were developing this theory of war and peace, Muslims were already under attack and on the defensive throughout the northern Mediterranean. Yet this type of war received little explicit attention in chapters on jihad. Even when the Crusades forced Muslims into a protracted defensive posture, resulting in an upsurge of writings extolling the virtues of jihad, as discussed by Suleiman Mourad and James Lindsay in chapter 5 below, there was no clear acknowledgment that a different form of jihad was now necessary. The brief discussion that does exist focuses on the moral obligation of Muslims to fight the enemy and on whether Muslim populations who now found themselves behind enemy lines could legitimately remain within *dar al-harb*. The majority of jurists counseled that such Muslims should—as the Prophet and the earliest Muslims did—perform a *hijra*, that is, migrate out of *dar al-harb* and into *dar al-Islam* at the earliest possible occasion. The expectation was that the Islamic state would rush to their succor through a defensive jihad. Echoes of these debates would inform controversies centuries later, when, in the nineteenth century, European imperialism brought large Muslim populations under non-Muslim rule. David Robinson in chapter 12 below, for example, describes how jihad and *hijra* were negotiated by West African Muslims.

On the question of how a defensive jihad is to be waged, the classical jurists suggest—again without much specificity—that various restraints imposed on the expansionist jihad are relaxed. All able-bodied Muslims, male and female, are required to rush to the defense of the Muslim victims. If some Muslims are not close to the fighting and cannot travel to the battlefield, they are required to assist the Muslim defenders through material and moral support. Requirements relating to proper authority—that is, who may declare the jihad and under whose leadership it may be fought—become more ambiguous. If the leaders of the Islamic state are unable or unwilling to lead the defensive struggle, other Muslims must assume this responsibility. And finally, the normal constraints on how Muslims may fight to repulse the aggression are loosened under claims of necessity. This ambiguity in the classical theory gives an opening to modern-day Muslim militants, the subject of David Cook's analysis in chapter 18 below, to proclaim their violence as jihad.

All of the classical schools of jurisprudence accepted the validity of treaties that suspended (not eliminated) the jihad obligation. One school of Sunni jurisprudence, the Shafi'i, formalized the treaty relationship by interposing a third *dar*, *dar al-sulh* (territory of truce), between *dar al-Islam* and *dar al-harb*. The maximum duration of such a truce, according to most scholars, was ten years, although nothing prevented the imam from renewing the truce indefinitely if he deemed it in the Muslims' interest.

Whether wars within *dar al-Islam* constituted jihad was an issue that created ambivalence among Sunni jurists. Some preferred to treat such conflicts, including those against renegade apostates, highway robbers or pirates, and Muslim rebels, as a type of police action, not jihad strictly speaking. Rebels who claimed to be upholding a different interpretation of the Qur'an were in particular given special privileges, such as the right not to be pursued and killed during a rout and the right to retain their property if they surrendered.[8]

No such ambivalence is evident among Shi'i jurists. Jihad could be properly waged against all non-Shi'is, whether Muslim or not. The other major difference in Shi'i views on jihad was that only the righteous imam, a descendant of 'Ali, could lead the expansionist jihad. Since the line of imams ended with the disappearance of the twelfth imam in the ninth century, according to the dominant strand of Shi'ism, only a defensive jihad to repulse enemy aggression is theoretically possible.[9]

The classical theory described in broad outline above had its dissenters. Some early jurists challenged the validity of the expansionist jihad, arguing that only the defensive jihad was an obligation while the expansionist jihad was supererogatory, a praiseworthy but optional war.[10] In addition, the characteristics of *dar al-Islam* and *dar al-harb* were disputed, and writers frequently added many more types of *dars*. Such terms were open to dispute because they are found nowhere in the

Qur'an and hadith and thus were devoid of a textual "anchor," unlike the term *jihad*. Indeed, the worldview itself that emerges out of the *dar al-Islam/dar al-harb* bifurcation has no clear grounding in either Qur'an or hadith. Yet by the end of the classical period, the dissenters had been largely marginalized, so much so that their works are not extant.

The classical theory of a triumphant, expansionist, imperial Islam was simply that, a theory, as it was being formulated in the eighth, ninth, and tenth centuries. *Dar al-Islam* had fragmented, with Andalusia and North Africa breaking away from the Abbasid caliphate and the forward expansion of *dar al-Islam*'s frontiers giving way to protracted border wars with the Byzantines and internal threats from Persian, Kurdish, Turkish, and other warlords. Yet in the centuries that followed, no formal or systematic reelaboration of the classical jihad doctrine was undertaken. Throughout the nineteenth and into the early twentieth century, as European imperialism advanced in Muslim territories and as Muslim minority communities developed in remote parts of these empires, Muslims were debating whether they lived in *dar al-Islam* or *dar al-harb*, what was demanded of them in one territory or the other according to the shari'a, and how they should respond to the emerging *droit public européen*, the basis of modern international law.

Today the jihad tradition is still in the midst of transition. Two broad Muslim reactions to the political and intellectual dominance of the West in international relations may be identified: the modernist and the fundamentalist. The modernists' agenda is to reinterpret jihad in ways that make it compatible with the principles of modern international law. Thus, they challenge the classical theory's conception of a *dar al-Islam* in opposition to a *dar al-harb*. If the two basic sources for Islamic law and ethics, the Qur'an and hadith, are properly analyzed, they claim, jihad cannot be understood as a war to spread Islam or subjugate unbelievers. The idea of the expansionist jihad that was espoused by classical jurists either was the product of the early jurists' misreading of the Qur'an and the Prophet's practice or it was a historically limited theory that has no place in the modern world, where states agree to coexist peacefully on the basis of international law. Wars of religion are obsolete and morally unjustifiable. Jihad, therefore, can only be understood as a war waged in self-defense, in conformity with international law, when the lives, property, and honor of Muslims are at stake.

The fundamentalists also appeal to the Qur'an and hadith to challenge what they consider various false understandings of jihad. First, they refute the mystical strand of thought that emphasizes the superiority of the inner, spiritual jihad over the outer, physical jihad. Jihad, according to them, meant by the end of the Qur'anic revelation a struggle, through fighting if necessary, to establish the Islamic order over all unbelievers. In keeping with the argument of the majority of the classical jurists, the fundamentalists argue that the more tolerant and pacific texts relating to unbelievers were abrogated by the later, more belligerent verses. The sword verse (Q. 9:5), for example, is held by both old and new writers to have abrogated some 140 other verses.

For fundamentalist writers, un-Islamic regimes include those ruling in most Muslim countries. The immediate goal of the fundamentalist jihad is to replace hypocritical leaders with true Muslims. Only when this long and painstaking internal struggle has succeeded in reestablishing an authentically Islamic base can the external jihad resume. Thus, jihad is today largely synonymous with Islamic revolution within Muslim states—not a war of Islamic expansion into non-Muslim territory—in the works of most fundamentalists.

Jus in bello concerns have not elicited as much attention among modern Muslim theorists as *jus ad bellum*. Most Muslim theorists have been content to affirm that international humanitarian law conforms to Islamic requirements. During the past decade, however, *jus in bello* concerns have returned to the center of jihad thinking because of the upsurge in terrorism committed by groups claiming to be Muslim fighters. Although radical groups such as al-Qaeda have repeatedly justified targeting civilians, they have been careful to avoid suggesting that jihad countenances indiscriminate warfare. Rather, they have appealed to the notions of reciprocity and military necessity. Their tactics, they claim, are a permissible response to the unscrupulous means of their enemies.[11]

As the narrative above outlines, both the just war tradition and the jihad tradition demonstrate sustained, extensive, and continuous moral evaluation of war within certain commonly accepted philosophical parameters, at least among the systematic theorists within each tradition. Both ask questions about legitimate resort to war (*jus ad bellum*), addressing just cause, right intent, legitimate authority, and last resort. Both elaborate legitimate means in war (*jus in bello*), enjoining discrimination in targeting and proportionality of means. And both separate these two broad categories not only conceptually but also morally, by the so-called independence thesis: even if a belligerent meets the requirements of *jus ad bellum*, it must prosecute the war according to limits of *jus in bello*. In other words, neither just war nor jihad can be a total war.

The third broad category is that of holy war. Today it is commonly juxtaposed against just war as a different, rival system of moral evaluation of war in Western civilization. It is just as commonly identified with jihad by many non-Muslims and even some Muslims, while others strongly reject such association. In fact, the relationship between holy war and either just war or jihad is complex, confusing, and controversial, the result of the imprecise ways in which *holy war* has been defined and understood by Western writers. There is little by way of a "holy war tradition" or a "holy war doctrine," only broad characteristics outlined by a few modern scholars based on three historical contexts: the Israelites' wars against Canaanites in the Old Testament, the Crusades, and the wars of the Protestant Reformation.

What many accept today as the obvious meaning of *holy war* is the one popularized by Roland Bainton in *Christian Attitudes toward War and Peace*, published in 1960. In his introduction, Bainton outlines three Christian "attitudes": pacifism, just war, and crusade. The crusade, he writes, "arose in the high Middle Ages, a holy war fought under the auspices of the church or some inspired religious leader, not on behalf of justice conceived in terms of life and property, but on behalf of an ideal, the Christian faith."[12] Thus, with regard to the *jus ad bellum* categories of cause, intent, and authority, Bainton understands holy war to be grounded in religious ideals and purposes, and its authorization and leadership comes from clerical or other religious figures. Other prominent expositors of holy war generally agree with Bainton on these points, but they take exception to Bainton's view of just war and holy war/crusade as sharply delineated categories in the Middle Ages. LeRoy Walters, in a comparison of just war and crusade concepts, argues convincingly that early just war theorists such as Thomas Aquinas, Vitoria, Suárez, and Grotius viewed just war and religious war/crusade (he does not use the term *holy war*) as parallel, not opposed, concepts with regard to authority, cause, and intent. The difference between the two was that the former is grounded in secular and the latter in religious justifications.[13] James Turner Johnson posits "at least ten possible meanings" for *holy war*. Underlying all of these is the idea that a conflict is commanded by God, to defend God's community or to propagate God's laws, by means both violent and nonviolent, under the leadership of a godly authority.[14] On *jus ad bellum*, Johnson agrees with Walters's contention that just war and holy war are analogous, not antithetical.

Bainton continues his definition of "crusade" by claiming: "Since the enemy was without the pale, the code tended to break down."[15] We are left to infer from this terse comment that in Bainton's mind, because the *jus ad bellum* of holy wars is so exalted—nothing short of divine command or divine favor—*jus in bello* restrictions (the "code") quickly give way to unrestrained war. Holy war is total war. The seminal and paradigmatic holy wars for Bainton are the Old Testament wars of extermination that Yahweh commands the Israelites to wage against Canaanite idolators, mirrored in Christian history by the Crusades and the Catholic-Protestant bloodletting in the post-Reformation period.[16]

Bainton's claim that holy war collapses *jus in bello* under the weight of *jus ad bellum* is echoed by a number of other writers. For example, H. E. J. Cowdrey prefaces his study "The Genesis of the Crusades" by describing his topic as "total, ideological warfare, and the springs of its compulsion upon men." Cowdrey writes: "In the name of God, the participants sought to extirpate those whom they saw as aliens, both inside and outside Christian society."[17] Charles Kimball writes of the crusaders: "Those who used extreme violence to advance Christ's kingdom understood their actions in terms of 'holy war.' Horrific consequences resulted from the convergence of authoritative, charismatic leadership; absolute truth claims; and an end that justified the means."[18]

Bainton's claims have, however, been sharply criticized by other scholars. On the issue of means, Walters observes that "one searches in vain for any principled distinction" between just war and religious war in the early theorists' work. Both types of war were to be governed by rational moral standards of humane treatment of the innocent and good faith in honoring promises and treaties.[19] Johnson rejects Bainton's suggestion that holy war is characteristically "prosecuted unsparingly."[20] During the Crusades, *jus in bello* constraints were vaguely formulated in the emerging just war tradition, so there was no doctrine in place against which to contrast the unrestrained conduct of holy war. Johnson notes that the two sets of curbs on warfare—ecclesiastical limits, such as the Peace of God and the Truce of God, and chivalric codes—applied in theory only within Christendom and only to Christians. Jews and other non-Christians within Europe were not protected, and Orthodox Christians of the Byzantine empire and, of course, Muslims in Islamic territory were entirely beyond the pale. The Crusades were waged with ferocity against the infidels, but intra-Christian wars within Europe were no less wanton in their destructiveness, despite the church's efforts.[21] By the time of the second major case of holy war discourses in Europe, the wars of the Reformation, just war doctrine on *jus in bello* had developed appreciably, so there is a standard by which to compare holy war rhetoric. Johnson observes that during these conflicts, apologists for extreme measures against religious dissenters, whether Catholic or Protestant, tended to portray the enemy in political as much as in religious terms. They were rebels outside the legitimate authority of the sovereign and had therefore forfeited the right to humane treatment. The most ferocious bloodshed occurred in conflicts that were essentially civil wars; wars between sovereign powers tended to be more restrained. Finally, Johnson notes that the religiously charged conflicts of the Reformation also produced arguments for a righteous holy warrior, one more scrupulous and restrained than his secular counterpart.[22]

In short, Walters and Johnson refute Bainton's view of the crusade/holy war concept as distinct from just war. As Johnson argues, holy war has been a "sporadic theme" in the more developed literature on just war and is best viewed as a subcategory within just war tradition.[23] Its expositors did not see themselves as demarcating a different type of war from a just war but one that was complementary and parallel to it. Walters concludes that the view of religious war as antithetical to just war is the product of "contemporary typologists," not the early articulators of just war doctrine. As a modern, not historical, distinction, Walters welcomes it (in a surprising twist at the end), for the "crusade"—both religious and nonreligious—may usefully serve as an ideal type and a practical possibility of the "unjust war."[24]

Consider now the relationship between jihad and holy war. Clearly, the idea of the expansionist jihad developed by the classical jurists conforms in many important respects to the notion of holy war. The authority to wage this type of jihad belonged to the imam/caliph, who in Islamic theory combined political and religious leadership. The caliph was obliged to undertake jihad not as a "kingly" prerogative but as a divine injunction. The justificatory cause and intent of this war was religious; jihad was understood as a means to summon infidels to Islam. A legitimate cause for war arose when the infidel authority refused to embrace Islam or to accept *dhimmi* status. The expansionist jihad's immediate aim was to impose Islamic sovereignty over territory, with the long-term goal of thereby opening the

land to the propagation of the Islamic faith. But because the goal of jihad was ultimately to convert infidels, not to exterminate or plunder them, the classical jihad
doctrine contained restrictions on targets and tactics. If, as Bainton suggests, a
holy war is unrestrained warfare, then jihad is not holy war. Borrowing Walters's
terminology, it may instead be more useful and accurate to view holy war, jihad,
and just war as analogous, not antithetical or synonymous, concepts. The table
below summarizes the relationship among all three as they were understood in
their "classic" form, that is, by their premodern theorists.[25]

Three caveats should be made with regard to the discussion above. First, we have
outlined the *theory* of just war, holy war, and jihad. The theory, of course, was never
fully matched in practice. The authority for declaration of just war, holy war, and
jihad was frequently confused. In Muslim states, for example, sultans or warlords
quickly usurped the caliph's prerogative to initiate jihad, and instead of proper authority validating the waging of jihad, the waging of jihad came to be viewed as a
way of validating authority.[26] On the disputed issue of means, it is undeniable that
despite the theorists' efforts to limit the harm to innocents, just war, holy war, and
jihad were in many instances waged with abandon. But there is little evidence to
support the claim that religiously inspired wars are inherently less restrained and
more destructive than politically motivated conflicts. Ideological wars—"crusades,"
as Walters would have it—of all sorts tend to descend into total war.

Just War, Holy War, and Jihad: "Classic" Conceptions

	Just War	*Holy War*	*Jihad*
Cause	Offense against a sovereign, the state, and its people	Offense against Christians, the church, or God	Rejection of Islam or Muslim sovereignty; offense against *dar al-Islam* or Muslims
Intent	Defense of the state and the innocent; aid to allies; right of innocent passage; punishment of wrongs done to society	Defense of the Holy Land; aid to the Eastern church; right of missionaries to preach freely; defense of Christian converts; punishment of wrongs done to the church or to God	Establishment of Muslim sovereignty, thereby to propagate the Islamic faith; defense of Muslims and *dhimmis* in *dar al-Islam*
Authority	Prince	Pope or other religious leader	Imam/caliph
Means	Limited, tempered by military necessity	Limited, even against unbelievers, tempered by military necessity	Limited, tempered by military necessity

The second caveat is that the theory presented above represents the broad consensus of scholarly opinion in a given historical period. The "doctrines" are indicative of what could be called a "high culture" of moral reflection on war and peace. The mainstream just war and jihad traditions have always had their dissenters and challengers. This continues to be true today. Sometimes the challenge comes from other scholars, but it frequently arises from "popular culture," from people unschooled in the tradition or with limited knowledge of it who interpret the concepts for themselves and manage to gain followers. As several of the chapters on jihad in this book demonstrate, charismatic individuals and militant movements have arisen throughout Islamic history and have departed in dramatic ways from the jihad doctrine of their times. Sometimes their departure is justified as a return to the "more authentic" doctrine of an earlier era that had been modified significantly by contemporary scholars.

This brings us to the third caveat. Just war and jihad concepts have evolved significantly over time, and they are developing still. After the Peace of Westphalia (1648) brought to an end the wars of religion in Europe, the just war tradition by and large divested itself of any remaining holy war influences. Holy war rhetoric continued to be heard in the eighteenth and nineteenth centuries, particularly in wars of imperialism, but it was sporadic and marginal to official justifications.[27] Just war theory is pushing today into new areas, most prominently *jus post bellum*, or the ethics of ending war and peace building. Meanwhile, theorists of jihad are engaged in a century-old enterprise of reinterpreting jihad doctrine in light of the tremendous changes in international relations since the classical theory was formulated. The result, as Sohail Hashmi argues in chapter 16 below, is to bring jihad doctrine into conformity with just war principles and with international legal norms. Most important, authoritative Muslim scholars today generally disavow the expansionist jihad of the classical theory and limit jihad to purely defensive war.

Each chapter in this book highlights the diverse ways in which Christians, Jews, and Muslims have understood or implemented notions of just war, holy war, and jihad. So even while we speak of the just war and jihad traditions, we must acknowledge that just war, jihad, and holy war are polyvalent and polysemous concepts. This diversity of views is reflected in the title of this book: *Just Wars, Holy Wars, and Jihads*.

Encounters and Exchanges

This book surveys the period from the rise of Islam in the early seventh century to the present day. The encounter between Christendom and Islam over these fourteen centuries is marked by four phases of violent confrontation, in a back-and-forth pattern of one civilization's expansion at the expense of the other. The first phase is the Islamic conquests of the seventh and eighth centuries, the second is the Crusades and the Reconquista from the eleventh to the thirteenth centuries, the third is the rise of the Ottoman empire and its expansion into southern Europe from the thirteenth to the seventeenth centuries, and the fourth is the expulsion of the Ottomans from Europe and the progress of European imperialism in Muslim lands during the nineteenth and twentieth centuries. A fifth phase is the one we live in today, marked by the end of European imperialism, the emergence of independent Muslim states, and their accession to an international order aspiring to governance under the rule of law. Future historians will judge whether the current phase is characterized by peaceful coexistence or a "clash of civilizations."

The chapters of this book are divided roughly into these five historical periods. Each chapter considers how arguments on just war, jihad, or holy war were framed in its respective historical period and the intellectual, social, and political milieus in which these arguments were made. Each chapter advances the inquiry of the two central questions underlying the book, summarized in its subtitle: *Christian, Jewish, and Muslim Encounters and Exchanges*.

First consider the issue of "encounters." From the very beginning of Muslim contact with Jews and Christians, the encounter was far more complex than simple ideological or political contestation punctuated by periods of violent confrontation. Along the frontiers of Islam and Christendom, Muslims, Jews, and Christians intermingled and sometimes found themselves allied in war with infidels against their coreligionists. The questions we probe here are: What did Christians, Jews, and Muslims know about the others' views on war and peace and especially their views on legitimate or justified war? What were their sources? How accurate were their understandings? Why were they interested in such information?

The second issue is that of "exchanges" or mutual influences. What impact did knowledge of the others' views on war and peace have on their own conceptions of justified or legitimate war? Is there evidence of cross-cultural borrowing or adaptation of concepts and, if so, to what ends? These questions are, of course, notoriously difficult to answer, particularly as we move back in time. Tracing the genealogy of ideas or the influence of one theorist on another is difficult enough within any given intellectual tradition. It is vastly more difficult across cultural divides and when working with scant historical records.

Nevertheless, there are a number of reasons to undertake this enterprise. First, the comparative study of just war and jihad is in its infancy. This book aims to add to the literature and stimulate further discussion and study. The possibility of interactions and mutual influences has been taken up earlier by individual scholars who made, in most cases, limited and superficial forays into the historical record. There is, in other words, scope for much more sustained and serious exploration of this issue by scholars with the historical and linguistic training to pursue it intensively.

Second, although direct evidence of cultural influences and borrowing is difficult and may be impossible to unearth, especially for the premodern period, we can make educated inferences for such influences in the absence of any other plausible explanations. Careful scholarship can demonstrate the possibility and the probability that human beings borrowed ideas current in their environments and then adapted and applied them to their own purposes. Conversely, careful scholarship can contest or correct the sometimes glib assertions made by past writers of cultural influences where, in fact, the historical record does not permit such claims.

Finally, the comparative study of just war and jihad is important because it offers a corrective to popular attitudes and even much scholarly discourse on just war and jihad as two alien, opposed, and irreconcilable ethical theories. By glossing "jihad" as "holy war," many Western authors explicitly or implicitly separate it from just war concepts. Yet this separation is both inaccurate and, in our present age, harmful. Just war, holy war, and jihad are all interrelated—sometimes overlapping, sometimes differing—efforts by Peoples of the Book to subject war to ethical constraints.

Notes

1. Augustine, *Contra Faustum*, XXII.74, quoted from Gregory Reichberg, Henrik Syse, and Endre Begby, eds., *The Ethics of War* (Oxford, U.K.: Blackwell, 2006), 73.
2. Augustine, "Letter 138 to Marcellinus," in ibid., 73.
3. Augustine, "Letters to Boniface," in ibid., 74, 79, 88.
4. Gratian, *Decretum*, part II, causa 23, in ibid., 104–24.
5. Frederick H. Russell, *The Just War in the Middle Ages* (Cambridge, U.K.: Cambridge University Press, 1975), 199.
6. Paul Ramsey, *War and the Christian Conscience* (Durham, N.C.: Duke University Press, 1961), and *The Just War* (New York: Scribners, 1968); Michael Walzer, *Just and Unjust Wars* (New York: Basic, 1977); and National Conference of Catholic Bishops, *The Challenge of Peace: God's Promise and Our Response* (Washington, D.C.: U.S. Catholic Conference, 1983).
7. Ella Landau-Tasseron, "Jihad," in *Encyclopaedia of the Qur'an*, vol. 3 (Leiden: Brill, 2003), 36.
8. The most detailed study on this topic is Khaled Abou El Fadl, *Rebellion and Violence in Islamic Law* (Cambridge, U.K.: Cambridge University Press, 2001).
9. A. K. S. Lambton, "A Nineteenth-Century View of Jihad," *Studia Islamica* 32 (1970): 181–92; Etan Kohlberg, "The Development of the Imami Shi'i Doctrine of Jihad," *Zeitschrift der Deutschen Morgenlandischen Gesellschaft* 126 (1976): 64–86.
10. Chiragh 'Ali, discussed by Omar Khalidi in chapter 15 below, lists several such writers, including Ibn Shubruma (d. 761) and Sufyan al-Thawri (d. 778). Chiragh 'Ali, *A Critical Exposition of the Popular "Jihad"* (Karachi: Karimsons, 1977), 134–37.
11. See, for example, "A Statement from *Qaidat al-Jihad* [al-Qaeda] regarding the Mandates of the Heroes and the Legality of the Operations in New York and Washington," April 24, 2002, at http://web.archive.org/web/20031011102320/http://www.mepc.org/public_asp/journal_vol10/0306_alqaeda.asp (accessed August 27, 2010).
12. Ronald H. Bainton, *Christian Attitudes toward War and Peace* (Nashville, Tenn.: Abingdon, 1986), 14.
13. LeRoy Walters, "The Just War and the Crusade: Antitheses or Analogies?" *The Monist* 57, no. 4 (October 1973): 584–91.
14. James Turner Johnson, *The Holy War Idea in Western and Islamic Traditions* (University Park: Pennsylvania State University Press, 1997), 37–42.
15. Bainton, *Christian Attitudes*, 14.
16. Ibid., chap. 3.
17. H. E. J. Cowdrey, "The Genesis of the Crusades: The Springs of Western Ideas of Holy War," in Thomas Patrick Murphy, ed., *The Holy War* (Columbus: Ohio State University Press, 1976), 10–11.
18. Charles Kimball, *When Religion Becomes Evil: Five Warning Signs* (New York: Harper Collins, 2003), 164.
19. Walters, "The Just War and the Crusade," 591–92.

20. Johnson, *The Holy War Idea*, 33–34, 45; Bainton, *Christian Attitudes*, 148.
21. Johnson, *The Holy War Idea*, 103–12.
22. Ibid., 112–15.
23. Ibid., 43.
24. Walters, "The Just War and the Crusade," 592–94.
25. This table adapts and expands on two tables in ibid., 590, 592.
26. Fred M. Donner, "The Sources of Islamic Conceptions of War," in John Kelsay and James Turner Johnson, eds., *Just War and Jihad* (New York: Greenwood, 1991), 51.
27. See Jonathan Riley-Smith, *The Crusades, Christianity, and Islam* (New York: Columbia University Press, 2008), chap. 3.

PART ONE

THE EARLY ISLAMIC CONQUESTS

If the Qur'an is accepted as a historical record of Muhammad's prophetic career, then we can say that Muslims encountered Jews and Christians from the very formative period of Islam. As the Qur'an attests and later Muslim historians relate, the encounter was both peaceful and conflictual. Jewish tribes were formally incorporated into the Medinan community established by the Prophet Muhammad through the so-called constitution of Medina. There are records also of negotiations and agreements between the Muslims and the Christian communities of Arabia. But the Qur'an, as we have seen, contains verses that strike a belligerent tone also toward Jews and Christians, and Muslim historians recount numerous clashes between the Muslim community and certain Jewish tribes in and around Medina during the lifetime of Muhammad.

Soon after Muhammad's death, the Islamic empire began to push out of Arabia and within a century had established frontiers with the Byzantine empire in the east and the Frankish kingdom in the west, incorporating in the process large populations of Christians and Jews in the Middle East, North Africa, and Iberia. Recent historiography has emphasized secular motives, including the search for new and fertile lands for the growing population of Arabia, the channeling outward in foreign conquests of tribal energies that had previously led to internecine feuding, or the desire to secure commercial trade routes.[1] Some of these mundane factors may have played a role in the early Islamic conquests, as was acknowledged by Muslim historians themselves. The ninth-century chronicler al-Baladhuri writes that when the first caliph Abu Bakr called for jihad against the Byzantines in Syria, he appealed both to religious sentiment and to the desire for "obtainable booty from the Greeks. Accordingly, people, including those actuated by greed as well as those actuated by the hope of divine remuneration, hastened to Abu Bakr from all quarters."[2] What is certain, however, is that the early conquests occurred before any coherent theory of jihad had been formulated.[3]

When Muslim jurists began developing this theory in the ninth century, the expansionist jihad had more or less ground to a halt. The jurists' worldview of *dar al-Islam* locked in struggle against *dar al-harb* may have been prompted by the desire to revive a bygone era's sense of Muslim unity and outward focus instead of the internal dissension and disunity of their own times. What is particularly puzzling about the classical theory is the origin of the *dar al-Islam/dar al-harb* dichotomy at its core. These terms are found nowhere in the Qur'an or hadith. They seem to have entered Muslim parlance during the second Islamic century. Where did they come from? Were they coinages of the classical jurists, inspired perhaps by the loose Qur'anic division of people into believers and unbelievers? Or is it possible that, devoid of any precedents for imperial administration in Arab history, the jurists drew upon cultures that had long-standing traditions? The Byzantine empire, heir to Roman thought on conquest and governance, along with Sassanid Persia, may have provided the inspiration, if not the model.[4] But on this issue, as on those considered in the three chapters in this section, the scant source material from this period makes any suggestions for cross-cultural influences purely speculative.

Notes

1. See Fred M. Donner, *The Early Islamic Conquests* (Princeton, N.J.: Princeton University Press, 1981), 267–71.

2. Ahmad ibn Yahya al-Baladhuri, *Kitab Futuh al-Buldan: The Origins of the Islamic State*, trans. Philip Hitti (Beirut: Khayats, 1966), 165.

3. See Roy Parviz Mottahedeh and Ridwan al-Sayyid, "The Idea of the *Jihad* in Islam before the Crusades," in *The Crusades from the Perspective of Byzantium and the Muslim World* (Washington, D.C.: Dumbarton Oaks Research Library and Collection, 2001), 23–30.

4. See Fred M. Donner, "The Sources of Islamic Conceptions of War," in John Kelsay and James Turner Johnson, eds., *Just War and Jihad* (New York: Greenwood, 1991), 37, for a discussion of possible Byzantine and Sassanid influences.

1

Religious Services for Byzantine Soldiers and the Possibility of Martyrdom, c. 400–c. 1000

PAUL STEPHENSON

A dozen years ago, Robert Taft identified eleven liturgical topics relating to Byzantine views on war and peace that demand further study.[1] This chapter addresses just two of those topics (Taft's eleventh and eighth), which are closely related: (1) religious services performed for the Byzantine army and (2) indulgences, or spiritual rewards, including the promise of martyrdom, granted to Byzantines who fought. It is remarkable that these topics have been neglected, given how much attention has been paid recently to Byzantine warfare, notably to notions of "holy war."[2] The idea of earning spiritual rewards through fighting, as Taft implied, was not wholly absent from Byzantine thought,[3] and the possibility of battlefield martyrdom was raised, most clearly in the religiously charged wars of the seventh and tenth centuries fought in Syria, Palestine, and Mesopotamia. Ultimately, however, the martyr's crown was reserved for soldiers who were taken captive and who died refusing to abjure Christ; that is, it was awarded only to those who might fit within the category of neomartyrs elaborated by certain Christians, primarily monks who from the seventh century lived under Muslim rule.

Late Roman Military Services and the Purity of Soldiers

The religious life in the Roman army may best be understood in three categories. The first category is the official religious life of the army as a whole, which was distinct from the religious beliefs of individual soldiers. It was prescribed by the state and intended to sustain the link between the Roman people at peace, civilians, and the Roman people at war, the army. Over time, it evolved into a means to guarantee the link between the army and the emperors through cultivation of imperial cults, as is reflected in the *feriale*, the official calendar distributed by every new emperor to every unit in every part of the empire.[4] Soldiers were expected to worship the "divine quality," *numen*, of the reigning emperor and the divinity of his chosen forebears. The second category includes religious practices prescribed within each unit, with the state's sanction, which were intended to build morale and cohesion. Rituals were concentrated on the military standards and took place within army camps.[5]

The third category, by far the largest, embraces the private religious devotion of the soldiers, which generally took place beyond the limits of the camp. Soldiers recognized a multitude of gods and worshipped in a multitude of fashions, from private prayers to individual divinities to participation in the rites of hierarchical cults, which mirrored the structure of the army itself. At certain times, the veneration of particular gods was prescribed to serve the ends of the state as a whole—for example, the worship of the Syrian sun god by Elagabalus (218–222 C.E.)—but this was swiftly extirpated. Instead, thousands of surviving inscriptions suggest that individual worship was devoted primarily to private prayer and the consequent fulfillment of particular vows. A soldier would seek divine patronage for specific endeavors and give an offering of thanks if the prayer was answered.

Roman army religion, therefore, did not preclude Christianity. Indeed, it was perfectly possible for Roman soldiers privately to worship as Christians so long as this did not prevent participation in state rituals. It was when Christian leaders determined that they may not that conflict arose, either between more and less rigorous Christians or between rigorous Christians and those charged with enforcing participation in state rituals. Consequently, as long as each soldier obeyed his commanders and participated in prescribed ritual, his personal beliefs or individual spiritual purity were of little concern.

Nor did matters change suddenly when Constantine I (r. 306–337) identified the god of the Christians as the *summus deus* ("greatest god"), who granted him *felicitas* ("good fortune," i.e., victory) in return for his *virtus* (here best translated as "manly aggressiveness").[6] The Christian god was seamlessly integrated into the traditional "imperial theology of victory."[7] Constantine certainly encouraged his soldiers to worship his chosen god, but he did not demand it.[8]

It fell to Theodosius I (r. 379–395) to institute orthodox Christianity as the religion of the Roman state and to insist that all worship his god as their own. Yet victory remained the emperor's alone when he took the field against the pretender Eugenius. According to Rufinus of Aquileia (XI.33), Theodosius mandated public liturgical events before he departed Constantinople, and immediately before battle, he "prepared for war by arming himself not so much with weapons as with prayers and fast, guarded not so much by the night-watch but by nightly prayer vigils."[9] As matters went against the emperor at the Battle of Cold River, he lay prostrate and prayed, shouting that his campaign was undertaken for Christ in order to exact just retribution "lest the Gentiles ask, Where is their God? (Psalms 113:30)." Consequently, a wind blew up of such strength and direction that it blew the arrows unleashed by Eugenius's archers back against them. So inspired were Theodosius's officers that one of outstanding piety, a certain Bacurius, fought through Eugenius's bodyguard to kill him.

Orosius (d. 418), writing only shortly afterward, placed emphasis still more singularly on Theodosius, who was now deserted by his men but prostrated himself on the battlefield and maintained a vigil throughout the night, leaving "pools of tears which he had paid as the price for heavenly assistance." The following morning, he rose and threw himself into the thick of battle, certain of victory even if nobody else should follow him, and assisted by the whirlwind, the result was "determined from heaven between the party which without the help of men placed his faith humbly in God alone, and the party that most arrogantly trusted in its own strength and in idols."[10]

Rufinus's account of the public liturgical events that Theodosius had staged before he left Constantinople is, as David Bachrach observes, "the first surviving reference to an entirely Christian program of military-religious ceremonies."[11] Such ceremonies would grow ever more central to late Roman and Byzantine military preparations, most notably in the camps where the ritual life of the army was transformed. It is here that one might detect a shift from the traditional imperial theology of victory. In describing Theodosius's private actions, the authors placed emphasis not on his *virtus*, although this was manifest in his taking the field alone in Orosius's account, but rather on his personal piety.

Although Theodosius, with divine assistance, needed no help from his army, the new theology of victory that emerged at the end of the fourth century increasingly accommodated the purity of each individual soldier and his correct faith. Since all soldiers were now required to be Christians, their private religious devotion became fused with state-mandated ritual. It could, therefore, be controlled by the state, and increasingly it was, since soldiers were far easier to monitor and coerce than civilians. This change is clearly reflected in the adaptation of the *sacramentum*, the military oath that had caused consternation among earlier Christian commentators who regarded it as idolatrous. According to Vegetius (II.5.3), in the first half of the fifth century, the oath was sworn "By God, Christ, and the Holy Spirit, and by the majesty of the emperor, which second to God is to be loved and worshipped by the human race."[12] No longer was the *numen* of the emperor worshipped, but, rather, one swore loyalty to his "majesty," divinely given and guided.

In the reign of Justinian (527–565), we see the further elaboration of Christian liturgical celebrations in army camps. According to Corippus, in a panegyric celebrating John Troglita's campaigns in North Africa in 548–49, the enemy determined to attack on a holy day, perhaps simply a Sunday, when "The Roman soldiers, occupied with their customary rites, will fear no battle."[13] But the general John and his second Ricinarius anticipated the attack, and, like Theodosius at Cold River, they spent the night before in prayer and the spilling of tears. As the sun rose, their Christian soldiers trooped out with their standards to a tent in the center of the camp, a mobile chapel, where a priest draped the altar and conducted the regular service. The congregants wept and together wailed, "Forgive our sins and the sins of our fathers, we beseech You, Christ." John, the general, was with him on his knees, more tears "pouring from his eyes like a river" as he intoned a long prayer for victory. Once the priest had performed the eucharist, it was shown that "the gifts were acceptable to the Lord of heaven, and at once sanctified and cleansed" the army. Victory was ensured, and those who would die did so purified by their tears and the sanctified elements.

Two aspects of this account deserve closer consideration. The first is the rather straightforward adaptation of long-established practices to suit Christian needs. The mobile tent in the center of the camp had once been known as the *aedes*, the temple and treasury where the standards were stored and venerated. It was here that the units prayed together on holy days but also "on the actual day of battle before anyone goes out the gate," as is prescribed in Maurice's *Strategikon* of the later sixth century.[14] Maurice further required that the standards be blessed a day or two before battle; that the "Trisagion" ("Holy God, Holy Mighty One, Holy Immortal One, have mercy on us") be sung by each unit early in the morning and late at night, before and after all duties; and that as each unit marched out of camp, it should cry in unison, "God is with us" three times. Military religious services would become increasingly complex, as later military manuals reveal.[15] The second, more profound development is the expectation that soldiers would be spiritually purified by shedding tears and partaking in communion immediately before battle. No longer was military religion concerned simply with the external, the correct performance of rituals, but rather, the concern was with the internal, faith and contrition. There is no suggestion that those who had killed in battle would be denied communion, still less for three years, as Basil the Great, bishop of Caesarea, had advised in the 370s.[16] Indeed, quite the opposite is implied. The more tears spilled before battle, the less Christian blood would be spilled in battle.

The success of a unit had always depended on the efficacy of its weakest members, but now weakness was measured spiritually. Purity was demanded of all soldiers, for their moral flaws could lead to punishment for all. This is stated quite plainly in the *Ecloga*, a law book issued in March 741 by the first iconoclast emperors, Leo III and Constantine V: "Those who go to war against the enemy must protect themselves from every evil word and deed and keep their mind on God alone . . . for victory in battle depends not on the size of the army but strength comes from God."[17] "Beneficial tales" circulated promoting the virtue of chastity among soldiers. A notable story, rehearsed more than once, became associated with a battle of 811 (to which we shall return below). It draws its inspiration from the Book of Proverbs: a young man resists sexual temptation (by an older rich woman or the daughter of an innkeeper) and consequently finds Wisdom (an old man in white) and is saved from death in battle.[18] The soldier was encouraged to draw inspiration from Christ and from Christ's virginal mother, whose invincibility was predicated on her undefiled status.

According to Theophanes the Confessor, Heraclius (r. 610–641) sailed from Africa to Constantinople in 610 with "fortified ships that had on their masts reliquaries and icons of the Mother of God, as George the Pisidian relates."[19] But George of Pisidia, in his extant works, refers not to the Mother of God but to the *Parthenos*, "Virgin."[20] In George's *Bellum Avaricum*, an account of the Avar siege of Constantinople in 626, Mary is consistently addressed not as *Theotokos* (God-bearer) or *Theometer* (Mother of God) but as *Parthenos*. The Virgin is victorious because "she alone knows how to conquer nature, first by birth and then by battle." Her tears are both inspiration and salvation: "For the more you spread the flow of the eyes, the more you prevent the flow of blood."[21]

For all of this new emphasis on moral and sexual purity, the spilling of tears, not blood, one does not see the emergence of penitential discipline for soldiers as one does in the West.[22] Where disciplinary measures are incorporated into Byzantine military manuals, *taktika*, they are punitive and physical, not redemptive and spiritual. For example, in the *praecepta militaria*, which is assigned to the reign of Nikephoros II Phokas (r. 963–969), it is prescribed that "Whosoever is detected at the time of the litany attending to some other matter without thinking of putting all else aside to stand and offer his prayer in fear of the Lord, such a man is to be demoted from his office, is to be assigned to an inferior rank, is to be beaten, have his hair shorn and be publicly displayed."[23]

Prisoners of War and Neomartyrs

Through the elaboration of the liturgical life of the Christian Roman army and the increased emphasis placed on the moral and spiritual lives of individual soldiers, it became possible to contemplate that Christian soldiers might become martyrs not by resisting state-mandated ritual, as they had during the persecutions of the mid-third and early fourth centuries, but rather by defending their fellow Christians in battle.[24] These Christian martyrs of an age without Roman state persecution may be distinguished by the term *neomartyrs*.

There are indications, sparse but identifiable, that a protracted discussion about battlefield martyrdom took place between the late sixth and tenth centuries.[25] The earliest extant reference to an offer to Christian Roman soldiers of eternal life in paradise for death on the battlefield is by Theophylact Simocatta, who recorded a harangue delivered by the general Justinian, son of Germanus, before the battle of Melitene in 575. Troops about to engage in battle with the Persians are urged to "arm your spirits before your body. . . . Do not, by turning your backs on the barbarians, let your soul be affected by love of body. Death, this sweet thing which we daily assay, is a kind of sleep, a sleep that is longer than normal sleep, but is very brief when compared to the day that is to come."[26] Still clearer indications are preserved in an account of the wars fought by Heraclius against the Persians in the decade before the Islamic Hijra in 622. After Heraclius secured power in 610, his earliest struggles were against supporters of the deposed emperor Phocas (r. 602–610), which allowed Slavs and Avars to invade the Balkans and the Persians to launch the first of a series of invasions under Shahrbaraz, general of Khosrau II.[27] An attempt to stop the Persians at Antioch failed in 613, culminating in their capture of Jerusalem in 614 and the occupation of Egypt from 619. Heraclius made peace with the Avars to concentrate on the eastern front and shifted his European armies from Thrace to Anatolia. He withdrew to his winter palace to plan campaigns free from spies and there evidently read Maurice's *Strategikon*, which provided detailed information on the Persians, their temperament and tactics, weapons and armor, and also on the need for military religious services. Heraclius launched his counteroffensive in April 622, achieving several significant victories. Between March 624, when he set out for Armenia, and the end of 628, the emperor did not return to Constantinople, even as it endured the Avar siege.

Our principal historical source for the wars, the *Chronicle* of Theophanes the Confessor, was completed in c. 813 but drew extensively on earlier works, both extant and lost. Theophanes records that in 624, upon entering Persia, Heraclius exhorted his men to "fight to avenge the insult done to God. . . . Let us be inspired with faith that defeats murder." He concluded the harangue with a telling observation: "The danger is not without recompense; nay it leads to the eternal life. Let us stand bravely, and the Lord our God will assist us and destroy the enemy."[28] The exhortation worked, and the fortunate Romans won substantial victories. At the conclusion of a victorious campaigning season, the emperor "ordered that his army should purify itself for three days."

In the following year, according to Theophanes: "Heraclius gathered his troops and gave them courage by assuaging them with these words of exhortation: 'Be not disturbed, O brethren, by the multitude of [the Persian army]. For when God wills it, one man will rout a thousand. So let us sacrifice ourselves to God for the salvation of our brothers. May we win the crown of martyrdom so that we may be praised in future and receive our recompense from God.'"[29]

These passages are all derived from fragments of a lost work by George of Pisidia and therefore reflect ideas current and expressed in the 620s.[30] In Heraclius's harangues, we find a remarkable imperial guarantee of martyrdom to Christian soldiers fighting against the infidel, one that makes sense in light of the liturgical developments we have identified. However, it raises more questions than we can answer here. Would such a guarantee have been necessary were the army not "in a state of great sluggishness, cowardice, indiscipline and disorder"?[31] Were these sluggish soldiers sufficiently pure to merit such a guarantee? Why would Heraclius's soldiers trust his promise? Did the emperor have the spiritual authority to offer such a guarantee?[32] Should we imagine that the harangue was a final act of encouragement, by which the emperor echoed the preaching and ministering of military chaplains? Was such a guarantee more likely to influence soldiers in an expeditionary force, not defending their homes but encamped within hostile territory? Did the guarantee have an immediate effect? Did the offer of martyrdom influence the military thought of Heraclius's successors? Was it influenced by or did it influence the thought of his enemies?

This last question is particularly pressing, as Heraclius's success was ephemeral. He was confronted almost immediately by new enemies, the Arabs, who in 634 invaded Syria and in 636 defeated a Byzantine army decisively at the Battle of Yarmuk.[33] Byzantium remained on the defensive through the seventh and eighth centuries, a period for which there is an immense gap in contemporary Greek historiography. We remain reliant on Theophanes the Confessor, who was in turn largely reliant on a lost Syriac chronicle, the so-called *Syriac Common Source*, also known as the *Chronicle of 750* and attributed to Theophilus of Edessa (d. 785). From this source, we learn that the martyrdom of Christian soldiers remained a live issue, now within the broader context of Christian-Muslim relations in regions where Christians lived under Muslim rule.[34]

> In the same year [740] Isam [Hisham], the ruler of the Arabs, put to death the Christian prisoners in all the towns of his realm, among them the blessed Eustathius, son of the distinguished patrician Marianus, who did not abjure his pure faith in spite of much violence and proved to be a true martyr at Harran, a notable city of Mesopotamia, where his precious and holy relics work all manner of healing by God's grace. Many others too met their death in martyrdom and blood.[35]

The same episode, although apparently dated a decade earlier, is recorded by the Syriac author Dionysius of Tel-Mahre, as preserved in both the twelfth-century chronicle of Michael the Syrian and the anonymous Syriac *Chronicle of 1234*:

> In this same year Hisham [apparently 112/730], ruler of the Arabs, issued a decree that all Roman prisoners to be found in Arab hands were to be killed. He did this because he had heard it said that Leo [III, Byzantine emperor 717–740] had killed Arab captives, but this was not true. When Eustathius and his companions were killed at Harran, the question was raised of whether or not they should be recognized as martyrs.[36] Both Theophanes and Dionysius were drawing on the same lost Syriac chronicle.[37]

Dionysius's account was drastically condensed by Michael the Syrian, as was frequently the case, and slightly less so in the *Chronicle of 1234*. Consequently, Theophanes's account is the fullest, and he also provides an entry that records the capture of Eustathius, two years earlier.[38] The Constantinopolitan chronicler, therefore, preserves detail and local color from a Maronite source that was written only shortly after the martyrdom in question and about twenty-five miles from where it took place.[39] The healing miracles demonstrated, of course, that the debate over whether Eustathius was indeed a martyr was redundant.

Eustathius and his comrades are not recorded in the *Synaxarion* of Constantinople.[40] We cannot say, therefore, whether the "many others [who] met their death in martyrdom and blood" as prisoners of war were honored as martyrs outside the locale in which they died. However, between the two passages that Theophanes has culled from his sources, one Greek and one Syriac, both of which he has transmitted without comment, there is a clear distinction to be drawn. In the first, from George of Pisidia's metrical harangue, soldiers are promised martyrdom if they fall on the battlefield. In the second, taken from Theophilus of Edessa, soldiers are martyred after they have been captured and, under duress from their captors, refused to abjure Christ. The second situation, as one would expect, corresponds far more closely to the paradigm for becoming a neomartyr that was elaborated in the eighth and ninth centuries for those Christian populations now living under Muslim rule.

A body of tales of neomartyrs, composed in Syriac, Arabic, Armenian, Georgian, Coptic, and Greek, accompanied the expansion of Arab hegemony.[41] A common feature of many tales is that those celebrated by Christians as having been martyred for their faith were from the point of view of the Muslim authorities executed for apostatizing from Islam. Two involve violent Muslim youths who become pacific Christians, monks, in order to attain paradise. The *Life* of Anthony Ruwah was composed in Arabic at a time when those used to writing Syriac began to adapt to changed circumstances.[42] As a youth in Damascus, Anthony, a noble of the Quraysh, spent his time defiling the Christian sanctuary of the monastery of Saint Theodore. He drank the eucharistic wine, damaged the crosses and altar furnishings, and terrorized the priests. One day, however, he fired an arrow at an icon of Saint Theodore, and it bounced back "by the force of martyr" to pierce Anthony's own hand. Several days later, as priests celebrated Saint Theodore's Day, Anthony experienced a vision, where the bread and wine he had frequently stolen became a white lamb and a white dove. Later that night, Saint Theodore visited Anthony and persuaded him to convert. Baptized by two monks in the river Jordan, he himself adopted the habit of a monk and returned home to Damascus, where he was jailed as an apostate. His case was referred to the governor of Raqqa, who sought the judgment of Harun al-Rashid. Declining the caliph's offers of money and honor should he return to Islam, Anthony was beheaded on December 25, 799, and his body was hung on a cross on the banks of the Euphrates.

'Abd al-Masih an-Nagrani al-Ghassani set off as a twenty-year-old Christian to visit Jerusalem, but on the way, he fell in with a band of Muslim raiders. He joined them, and "he prayed with them, and became even more furious and hard of heart than they against the Romans [i.e., Byzantines]," so that for thirteen years, he raided "Roman territory." However, while visiting a church in Baalbek, he listened to a priest reading the Gospels, wept, and repented. Praying in the church, he threw down his sword and sold his horse and weapons to make alms, shortly afterward taking monastic vows at the monastery of Mar Saba (the Great Lavra of Saint Sabas) in the Judean desert. He rose to become superior of the monastery of Saint Catherine at Mount Sinai, where his life is preserved in an Arabic manuscript of the ninth century (*Sinai Arabic* MS 542). In that capacity, traveling to pay taxes, he was recognized by a former comrade in the raiding party, convicted of apostasy from Islam, and put to death.[43]

The edifying tales of Christian martyrs were intended to encourage converts to Islam to reembrace Christianity and to persuade those tempted to convert to Islam of the dangers and futility of apostasy. All would come to realize, the hagiographers imply, that Christianity is the one true faith, defended by Christ's spiritual warriors, the monks.[44] The tales were not concerned with those killed in battle with the infidel, because Christians in Syria and Palestine were no longer enrolled in the Byzantine army. Rather, those who renounced violence but to whom violence was done received the martyr's crown. We cannot, therefore, look to hagiography produced beyond the frontiers of Byzantium for evidence of battlefield martyrdom. Instead, we must turn to Greek texts produced at the imperial court and for the army camps, which begin to appear in increasing volume after a gap of two centuries. Here we find evidence that those who wished to persuade Christian soldiers to fight to the death and who were aware of the spiritual rewards being offered to Muslim warriors in this period considered battlefield martyrdom a possibility.

The *Chronicle of 811*

Several tales of Christian martyrdom in the late eighth and early ninth centuries, like that of al-Ghassani, have a connection with the Mar Saba monastery, which was a center for their production and dissemination.[45] Perhaps the most compelling story is the *Martyrion of the Twenty Sabaites*, the Greek version of which has survived (although it may have been composed in Arabic).[46] It commemorates the martyrdom in 797 (or 788, as Alexander Kazhdan has suggested) of twenty monks from the monastery by Arab raiders, who were intent on plundering the monastery. The monks, when it became clear that they could not pay the sums demanded by their attackers, were subjected to a variety of tortures, including beatings with cudgels, swords, and stones and burning. The monks had hitherto enjoyed good relations with Arab neighbors, and the attack caused them "anxiety, fear, distress and confusion."[47] Kazhdan has related the *Martyrion of the Twenty Sabaites* to another tale, the so-called *Chronicle of 811*. However, while both narratives are vivid and original, their protagonists and messages are quite different. The martyrs of Mar Saba were monks, spiritual warriors, who would not lift a hand to defend themselves (although several sought to save their brethren); those killed in the *Chronicle of 811* were soldiers.

The *Chronicle of 811* was composed from documentary material as a narrative before the 850s, but it survives only in a modification produced after 864/5 (the year in which the Bulgars were converted to Christianity).[48] There are indications within the text that betray this modification and suggest reasons for it. They center on the issue of martyrdom and a distinction that is drawn between those who died in battle and those who died as prisoners of war. Ivan Dujčev, who provided an edition and the most expansive commentary on the text, understood this distinction but failed to tease out the necessary connections, obscuring further discussion with his assertion that the fragment commemorated as martyrs "all the victims—with the exception of Nikephoros and probably some of those closest to him—who fell during the war of 811 or immediately afterwards."[49] In fact, the conclusion to the fragment quite specifically commemorates only those who were taken prisoner and refused to abjure Christ: "Many of the surviving Romans, after the battle ended, were forced by the impious Bulgars, who had then not yet been baptized, to renounce Christ and embrace the error of the Scythian pagans. Those who were preserved by the power of Christ endured every outrage and by various torments earned the martyr's crown." It is here that we find the most striking disparity between the information provided in the body of the text and its conclusion, therefore proof that the two were not written together.

The *Chronicle of 811* informs us at length of the various manners in which the Byzantine soldiers died. There is no mention whatever of prisoners being taken, who might later die in captivity, and thus the conclusion to the passage in its extant form is utterly incongruous, added to "clarify" how those who died in battle might be commemorated as martyrs. The unresolved tensions between the story told in the *Chronicle of 811* and its conclusion were evident to the compilers of later liturgical calendars, including the tenth-century *Typikon* of the Great Church of Hagia Sophia in Constantinople, where the event is commemorated thus: "26th of the month [July] . . . On the same day occurred, due to the carelessness and conceit of the emperor Nikephoros, his own death and the fall of many others."[50] Battle is not mentioned, perhaps deliberately to maintain ambiguity. However, this entry was greatly expanded and "clarified" in the *Synaxarion of Constantinople*, where we find reference to the martyrs of 811, who were celebrated on either July 23 or, correctly, July 26. The entry clearly summarizes the story presented in the 811 fragment, using remarkably similar vocabulary. However, it also elaborates, providing a story of survivors fleeing through densely wooded country, being taken alive, and subjected to countless tortures until, for refusing to abjure Christ, they are killed in several ways, including by beheading, strangulation, and wounding by missiles. "In this way they were wreathed with the crown of the martyr."[51] The modified version of the *Chronicle of 811* should be associated with the revised tale told in the *Synaxarion* and therefore might also date to the 960s. Consequently, although the *Chronicle of 811* is concerned with Christians who died at the hands of the infidel (Bulgarian pagans, not Muslim Arabs) in the ninth century, its "clarifications" project that discussion into the tenth century.

Leo VI's *Taktika*

Before c. 900, one finds strikingly little treatment in Greek literature of the Arabs as a fighting force and no substantial contributions to the corpus of military treatises. Matters change with the *Taktika* attributed to the emperor Leo VI (r. 886–912).[52] Leo's *Taktika* updates and expands Maurice's *Strategikon*. Whereas Maurice's first instructions "On the Day of Battle" are that the general should not "exert himself too much, become worn out and overlook some really essential matters,"[53] Leo advises the general to ensure first of all that his whole army is pure (καθαρὸν) and to offer fervent prayer through the night. He must ensure "that everyone is purified [or sanctified,[54] ἁγιασθῆναι] by priests, and that they believe completely in words and deed that they have divine help," so that they advance to battle in high spirits. A single military service has survived from this period, but one wonders how many have been lost.[55]

Where Maurice's *Strategikon* addresses the Persians, among other foes, the *Taktika* has a section devoted to the Arabs (called "Saracens"), addressing their nature and customs and how best to confront them.[56] It presents the clearest evidence that the Byzantines understood Islamic institutions and doctrines and how they underpinned the Arabs' war efforts. Moreover, and exceptionally, the Christian emperor, while offering the usual condemnation of the "barbarous and impious race," recommends that the Byzantines emulate the infidel. For the Arabs, Leo notes, there is no summons; they gather for war voluntarily. Moreover, warfare is a collective effort, whereby all members of society share in the expenses. By supplying the fighting men with arms and equipment, they also share in the rewards of warfare.[57] This passage demonstrates knowledge of Islamic *waqf* foundations[58] and perhaps an idealized notion of the efficacy of the *thugur* and *'awasim*, the two-tiered frontier structure on the caliphate's side of the border with Byzantium.[59] It reflects a desire to emulate the developing Arab system to assuage Byzantine problems associated with assembling troops and financing campaigns centrally.

Leo is aware that his foes are offered spiritual rewards for their efforts if they die in battle but also for supporting those who fight if they are unable to bear arms.[60] Leo calls the reward Muslims receive *misthos* (μισθὸς), which can mean "wage" but should here be translated more expansively as "the recompense given (mostly by God) for the moral quality of an action."[61] Consequently, it appears to correspond to the Arabic term *ajr*.[62] Earlier, Leo ordered that the general must be instructed in the correct faith of the Christians, as must his commander and all of his men, so that "all who fight through Christ our Lord and on behalf of their families and friends and country and for the whole Christian people will easily overcome the distress of thirst and the lack of food, and of excess cold or heat . . . and for their pains they will store up compensations [μισθῶν] from God himself and from his kingdom."[63] Leo goes still further:

If with God's help as an ally, properly armed and arranged, making an assault well and bravely against them, fighting for our spiritual salvation [ὑπὲρ τῆς ψυχικῆς ἡμῶν σωτηρίας ... ἀγωνιζόμενοι] just as for God himself, for our families and for our other Christian brothers, placing hopes unhesitatingly in God, we shall not fail but rather shall triumph completely against them.[64]

The key phrase is "fighting for our spiritual salvation." Contemporary documents record abundant donations to monasteries by those seeking "spiritual salvation."[65] Leo appears consciously to employ the language familiar to Byzantine donors, encouraging them to give not only to secure prayers for victory but also to secure arms and armor. The benefits of fighting for God will therefore be shared by those who fight and those who support them. It is striking, of course, that he anticipates that spiritual salvation will be a reward for those who fight, and although here he makes no mention of death or martyrdom, elsewhere Leo decrees:

It is your duty after the battle, O general, to console those soldiers wounded in it, and to honor those who fell in the battle with burial, and to consider them perpetually blessed [μακαρίζειν διηνεκῶς], since they did not esteem their own lives above their faith and their brothers. This blessed act enhances the zeal of the living.[66]

Those who die in battle should be considered perpetually blessed, *makarios*, a term used most frequently in patristic writings for "martyr."[67]

Tenth-Century Developments

The prescriptions in Leo VI's *Taktika* were a logical development of Christian practices, which had developed both before and since the emergence of Islam but also were a response to a particular set of Muslim doctrines and institutions with which Byzantine society was now confronted. Arabs all shared in the spiritual rewards of fighting the infidel, and Leo desired this for Christians. He wished to ensure that all involved in the struggle with the infidel received spiritual rewards, including those who fell in battle, who were perhaps the most deserving. A similar sentiment was expressed in a harangue composed and delivered for Leo's son, Constantine VII (r. 945–959), in the later 950s. Constantine wrote to those troops about to encounter the Muslim forces that cohered around Sayf al-Dawla, Hamdanid emir of Aleppo:

We will embrace you as victors appearing as triumphant conquerors against the enemy and receive you with joyful acclamations as you return. We will kiss your bodies wounded for the sake of Christ in veneration as the limbs of martyrs, we will pride ourselves in the defilement of blood, we will be glorified in you and your valorous accomplishments and struggles.[68]

A religious service for those killed in war, of the type that Leo VI prescribed, has survived from this period. It contains a unique version of the Triodion, the liturgical book for the Easter cycle, which records a service to be performed on Meat-Fare Saturday, the first of five All Souls Saturdays during Lent.[69] The first two verses of *stichera* may be translated thus:

> Let us gather together people of Christ
> And celebrate the memory
> Of our brothers who died in battle
> And those who perished in intolerable captivity.
> Let us entreat on their behalf.
> They were valiant until their slaughter
> Your servants, Lover of Man;
> They received
> Blows pitilessly,
> Persevering in fetters;
> Let it be that these men for these things
> Achieve atonement of their souls, Lover of Man.

This service failed to become established in the Orthodox calendar. It links, and treats as equally deserving of salvation, those who die in battle with those who die as prisoners of war, refusing to abjure Christ. That is, it juxtaposes the traditional notion of Christian martyrdom, revived and revised in lands where Christians lived under Muslim authority, with a second notion of battlefield martyrdom, articulated by Heraclius (or George of Pisidia) and implied in other contexts, including by Theophylact Simocatta, in the original version of the *Chronicle of 811*, Leo's *Taktika*, and Constantine VII's harangue.

But how many Christian prisoners of war were tortured by Arabs with the intent to enforce their conversion, in violation of a clear Qur'anic principle?[70] While in the earliest Islamic conquests, the Arabs enslaved enormous numbers of Christians, principally civilians whose lands had been overrun, whether they became Muslims was a matter of individual conscience or advantage, not of coercion.[71] The principle certainly was violated in the interests of particular regimes. During the reign of 'Umar II (717–720), according to Theophanes, "after a violent earthquake had occurred in Syria, 'Umar banned the use of wine in cities and set about forcing the Christians to become converted: those that converted he exempted from tax, while those that refused he killed and so produced many martyrs."[72] The reign of Mahdi (775–785) was punctuated with episodes of forced conversion recorded by the Syriac chroniclers and by Theophanes.[73] And in March 845, forty-two Byzantine soldiers who had been captured at Amorion more than six years before were publicly decapitated when they refused to pray with the caliph.[74]

However, the general principle was reiterated at exactly this time by the scholar Ahmad ibn Hanbal (d. 855): Christian children captured in raids without their parents might be regarded as Muslims, but no other Christians were to be forcibly converted.[75] Of course, Ibn Hanbal implies by his prohibition that he is well aware of the exceptions and also states that to his knowledge, some warriors operating across the frontiers were forcing conversion upon their captives. However, it would appear safe to conclude that Byzantine soldiers captured in war *generally* were neither tortured nor coerced to convert on pain of death. Nor were enslaved Christians manumitted and recruited into the Muslim army, as the Turks would be later. Rather, the martyred prisoner of war, like the apostate neomartyr, was an exemplar. His refusal to abjure Christ strengthened the faith of those faced with capture in war. But Christian soldiers, faced with an enemy promised paradise in the shadow of the sword, could not simply be encouraged to surrender and accept captivity. Those who would fight to the death also needed exemplars, and so those who had died in battle with the infidel were celebrated alongside tortured prisoners of war, in military services conducted for those in the army camps, in harangues, and in military treatises.

It was in the reign of Nikephoros II Phokas (d. 969) that the two paths to martyrdom for Christian soldiers diverged, and that which resulted from death on the battlefield was blocked. Nikephoros, unlike his imperial predecessors, sought clarification from the synod of Constantinople. According to the chronicler John Skylitzes, at an unspecified date, Nikephoros sought a ruling from Polyeuktos, patriarch of Constantinople, to ensure that "those who fell in battle be honored equally with the holy martyrs and be celebrated with hymns and feastdays."[76] He appeared to be asking simply that existing practices be sanctioned by the synod. But Nikephoros's request was denied, by reference to the thirteenth canon of Basil of Caesarea: "How is it possible to number among the martyrs those who fell in battle, whom Basil the Great excluded from the sanctified elements for three years since their hands were unclean?" There is no evidence that this canon had ever before been enforced. On the contrary, it would appear that the synod's ruling put an end to the practice that had endured for more than three centuries.[77] Consequently, the possibility of battlefield martyrdom for Christian soldiers did not survive the Byzantine reconquest of Syria and Palestine, under Nikephoros II and his successor, John I Tzimiskes (d. 976).

Conclusion

Up to and through the third century C.E., Roman soldiers were required to participate fully in public religious rituals, which ensured that the gods showed favor to the state and granted victory to the emperor and his commanders. At the same time, private worship outside the camps was both permitted and expected, and there were few bars on which gods might be venerated. Christianity was generally tolerated as one of many eastern cults, and in the early fourth century, the god of the Christians was identified as the greatest god, bringer of victory to the emperor Constantine. This was no deviation from the traditional imperial theology of victory. However, as Christianity developed from being a favored cult to being the only cult tolerated within the army camps, the distinction between a soldier's public and private religious worship was eliminated, and all were expected to participate in increasingly regular and elaborate Christian liturgies. While victory might still be afforded to the brave commander whose priests performed religious rituals correctly, correct belief was now essential for all, and defeat was seen as divine punishment for the sins of Christian soldiers of all ranks.

The inverse of divine punishment was spiritual compensation for material sacrifice, and those who made the ultimate sacrifice, death in battle, came to expect the ultimate spiritual reward, the martyr's crown. This was not denied them, and indeed, in the seventh century C.E., the promise of martyrdom was extended to Christian troops who fought against the Persians. Whether this promise was extended also to those Christians who fought the Arabs after 632 and whether it influenced early Muslim thought on martyrdom cannot be stated with any certainty, as we do not possess adequate Greek sources for the later seventh and eighth centuries. It is clear, however, that in those Roman lands occupied by Christians but now under Muslim rule, principally Syria and Palestine, a new paradigm for martyrdom was articulated that promoted nonviolent resistance to apostasy and forced conversion. Christian soldiers had a role to play in Syriac and Arabic Christian literature only as prisoners of war who might die refusing to abjure Christ. When Greek sources are again available, in the ninth and tenth centuries, Byzantine soldiers appear still to expect, and to be offered, spiritual rewards for fighting the infidel, and religious services are both commanded and performed to commemorate as blessed those who died in war or in fetters. Christian soldiers purified by prayer and the shedding of tears, who had sung litanies and the "Trisagion," whose battle standards were blessed before they marched out crying "God is with us," expected salvation if they died in battle.

Notes

1. See Robert F. Taft, "War and Peace in the Byzantine Divine Liturgy," in Timothy S. Miller and John Nesbitt, eds., *Peace and War in Byzantium: Essays in Honor of George T. Dennis, S.J.* (Washington, D.C.: Catholic University of America, 1995), 17–18. Taft treated his first neglected topic and noted the contribution to several others by Michael McCormick, *Eternal Victory: Triumphal Rulership in Late Antiquity, Byzantium and the Early Medieval West* (Cambridge, U.K.: Cambridge University Press, 1986). More recently, key areas have been covered by Eric McGeer, *Sowing the Dragon's Teeth* (Washington, D.C.: Dumbarton Oaks, 1995); Christopher Walter, *The Warrior Saints in Byzantine Art and Tradition* (Aldershot,

U.K.: Ashgate, 2003); Bissera Pentcheva, *Icons and Power: The Mother of God in Byzantium* (University Park: Penn State University Press, 2006).

2. Many responses were provoked by the publication of Athena Kolia-Dermitzaki, *O vizantinos "ieros polemos"* [Byzantine "holy war"], *Istorikes Monografies* 10 (Athens: Vasilopoulos, 1991). See Angeliki E. Laiou, "On Just War in Byzantium," in John S. Langdon et al., eds., *To Elle-nikon: Studies in Honor of Speros Vryonis, Jr.* (New Rochelle, N.Y.: A. D. Caratzas, 1993), 153–77; Nicholas Oikonomides, "The Concept of 'Holy War' and Two Tenth-Century Byzantine Ivories," in Miller and Nesbitt, *Peace and War*, 62–86; Tia M. Kolbaba, "Fighting for Christianity: Holy War in the Byzantine Empire," *Byzantion* 68 (1998): 194–221; John F. Haldon, *Warfare, State and Society in the Byzantine World, 565–1204* (London: Routledge, 1999), 13–33; George T. Dennis, "Defenders of the Christian People: Holy War in Byzantium," in Angeliki E. Laiou and Roy P. Mottahedeh, eds., *The Crusades from the Perspective of Byzantium and the Muslim World* (Washington, D.C.: Dumbarton Oaks, 2001), 31–39; Angeliki E. Laiou, "The Just War of Eastern Christians and the Holy War of the Crusaders," in Richard Sorabji and David Rodin, eds., *The Ethics of War: Shared Problems in Different Traditions* (Aldershot, U.K.: Ashgate, 2006), 30–43. Older literature includes Marius Canard, "La guerre sainte dans le monde islamique et dans le monde chrétien," *Revue Africaine* (1936): 605–23, reprinted in Marius Canard, *Byzance et les musulmans du Proche Orient* (London: Variorum, 1973), VIII; Vitalien Laurent, "L'idée de guerre sainte et la tradition byzantine," *Revue Histo-rique du Sud-Est Européen* 23 (1946): 71–98.

3. Kolbaba, "Fighting for Christianity," 204–7.

4. A version of the *feriale*, preserved at Dura Europos in Syria (the *Feriale Duranum*), is considered in great detail by Arthur Darby Nock, "The Roman Army and the Roman Religious Year," *Harvard Theological Review* 45 (1952): 187–252; J. F. Gilliam, "The Roman Military Feriale," *Harvard Theological Review* 47 (1954): 183–96. The full text is published in Robert O. Fink, Allan Spencer Hoey, and Walter Fifield Snyder, "The *Feriale Duranum*," *Yale Classical Studies* 7 (1940): 1–222.

5. John Helgeland, "Roman Army Religion," in *Aufstieg und Niedergang der Römischen Welt* [*ANRW*], (1979), II.16.2:1470–1555; Eric Birley, "The Religion of the Roman Army: 1895–1977," *ANRW*, II.16.2:1506–41; Michael P. Speidel and A. Dimitrova-Milčeva, "The Cult of the Genii in the Roman Army and a New Military Deity," *ANRW*, II.16.2:1542–55; A. H. M. Jones, *The Later Roman Empire, 284–602*, 3 vols. (Oxford: Blackwell, 1964), 1:97–100; 2:607–86; Ramsay MacMullen, "The Legion as a Society," *Historia* 33 (1984): 440–56; Allan Spencer Hoey, "Rosaliae Signorum," *Harvard Theological Review* 30 (1937): 15–35.

6. Myles Anthony McDonnell, *Roman Manliness. Virtus and the Roman Republic* (Cambridge, U.K.: Cambridge University Press, 2006). See also William V. Harris, "Readings in the Narrative Literature of Roman Courage," in Sheila Dillon and Katherine E. Welch, eds., *Representations of War in Ancient Rome* (Cambridge, U.K.: Cambridge University Press, 2006), 300–20.

7. Jean Gagé, "Stavros nikopoios: La victoire impériale dans l'empire chrétien," *Revue d'Histoire et de Philosophie Religieuses* 13 (1933): 370–400; François Heim, *La théologie de la victoire de Constantin à Théodose* (Paris: Beauchesne, 1992); Gilbert Charles Picard, *Les trophées romains: Contribution à l'histoire de la religion et de l'art triomphal de Rome* (Paris: E. de Boccard, 1957); J. Rufus Fears, "The Theology of Victory at Rome: Approaches and Problems," *ANRW* (1981), II.17.2:736–826. The term *theology* is used in a precise manner, to designate the interpretation and understanding of the nature of God, or the gods, and by extension his or their roles in delivering victory in battle. It does not refer to the study of religions generally or especially to that of Christianity.

8. Constantine, according to Eusebius, had "taught all the military to revere" Sunday, the Christian Sabbath, which was also the "Day of the Sun," and "to those who shared the divinely given faith he allowed free time to attend unhindered the church of God, on the assumption that with all impediment removed they would join in the prayers." See Eusebius, *Vita Constantini* IV.18–19; Eusebius, *Life of Constantine*, trans. Averil Cameron and Stuart G. Hall (Oxford: Clarendon, 1999), 159–60. I cover this at length in Paul Stephenson, *Constantine: Unconquered Emperor, Christian Victor* (London: Quercus, 2009).

9. *The Church History of Rufinus of Aquileia, Books 10 and 11*, trans. Philip R. Amidon (Oxford: Oxford University Press, 1997), 87–89. An excellent analysis upon which I have drawn is offered by David Steward Bachrach, *Religion and the Conduct of War, c. 300–1215* (Woodbridge, U.K.: Boydell, 2003), 12–14, which generally focuses on the Latin west.

10. Paulus Orosius, *The Seven Books of History against the Pagans*, trans. Roy J. Deferrari (Washington, D.C.: Catholic University of America, 1964), 345–46; Bachrach, *Religion and the Conduct of War*, 13–14.

11. Bachrach, *Religion and the Conduct of War*, 18. In fact, the competing rituals described are probably best treated with caution, in the manner commended by Philippe Buc, *The Dangers of Ritual* (Princeton, N.J.: Princeton University Press, 2001).

12. Vegetius Renatus Flavius, *Epitoma rei militaris*, ed. Michael D. Reeve (Oxford: Oxford University Press, 2004), 39; *Vegetius: Epitome of Military Science*, trans. N. P. Milner (Liverpool: Liverpool University Press, 1993), 35. The date for Vegetius's composition remains contested. See Michael B. Charles, *Vegetius in Context. Establishing the Date of the* Epitoma Rei Militaris (Stuttgart: Franz Steiner, 2007), 27–28, on the *sacramentum* and generally for assigning the work to the reign of Valentinian III (425–455), against those who prefer Theodosius I (379–395).

13. James Diggle and Francis Richard Davis Goodyear, eds., *Flavii Cresconii Corippi Iohannidos seu de bellis Lybicis libri VIII* (Cambridge, U.K.: Cambridge University Press, 1970), 173–78, for this and following quotations; *The Iohannis or De Bellis Lybicis of Flavius Cresconius Corippus*, trans. G. W. Shea (Lampeter, Wales: Edwin Mellen, 1998), 196–98. On the poem, see Averil Cameron, "Corippus' Iohannis: Epic of Byzantine Africa," *Papers of the Liverpool Latin Seminar* 4 (1984): 167–80; and now at greater length, Thomas Gärtner, *Untersuchungen zur Gestaltung und zum historischen Stoff der Johannis Coripps* (Berlin: Walter de Gruyter, 2008). On this passage, see McCormick, *Eternal Victory*, 245–46; Bachrach, *Religion and the Conduct of War*, 14–16.

14. Mauricius, *Strategicon*, ed. George T. Dennis (Vienna: Österreichischen Akademie der Wissenschaften, 1981), 138–40; *Maurice's Strategikon*, trans. George T. Dennis (Philadelphia: University of Pennsylvania Press, 1984), 33–34.

15. George T. Dennis, "Religious Services in the Byzantine Army," in Ephrem Carr et al., eds., *Eulogema: Studies in Honor of Robert Taft, SJ* (Rome: Editrice Anselmiana, 1993), 107–17; August Heisenberg, "Kriegsgottesdienst in Byzanz," in *Aufsätze zur Kultur- und Sprachgeschichte vornehmlich des Orients* (Breslau: M. and H. Marcus, 1916), 244–57; J. Viellefond, "Les pratiques religieuses dans l'armée byzantine d'après les traités militaires," *Revue des Études Anciennes* 37 (1935): 322–30.

16. Philip Schaff, ed., *Basil of Caesarea: Letters and Select Works*, Nicene and Post-Nicene Fathers, 2nd series, 8 (Edinburgh: T. and T. Clark, 1895), 323–28 (ep. XLVI), at 323–24.

17. Ludwig Burgmann, ed., *Ecloga: Das Gesetzbuch Leons III und Konstantinos V*, Forschungen zur Byzantinischen Rechtsgeschichte 10 (Frankfurt: Löwenklau, 1983), 244; McCormick, *Eternal Victory*, 250.

18. The tale appears first in the *Life of Nicholas of Stoudios*, for which see J.-P. Migne, ed., *Patrologiae cursus completus, Series graeca* 105, cols. 893A–897C. It is later retold, for which see J. Wortley, "Legends of the Byzantine Disaster of 811," *Byzantion* 50 (1980): 533–62; Paul Stephenson and B. Shilling, "Nicholas the Monk, Former Soldier," in E. Fisher, S. Papaioannou, and D. F. Sullivan, eds., *Byzantine Religious Culture: Studies in Honor of Alice-Mary Talbot* (Leiden: Brill, 2012), 421–38.

19. Cyril Mango and Roger Scott, eds. and trans., *The Chronicle of Theophanes Confessor: Byzantine and Near Eastern History, A.D. 284–813* (Oxford: Clarendon, 1997), 427–28, referring to George of Pisidia, *Heraclias*, II.15. But George refers here not to the "Mother of God" but to an icon of the uncorrupted Virgin (*Parthenos*), which Heraclius used against Phokas, "corrupter of Virgins." Agostino Pertusi, ed., *Georgio di Pisidia, Poemi*, I: *Panegirici epici*, Studia Patristica et Byzantina 7 (Ettal: Buch-Kunstverlag, 1959), 252. See also the comments by Mary Whitby, "A New Image for a New Age: George of Pisidia on the Emperor Heraclius," in Edward Dąbrowa, ed., *The Roman and Byzantine Army in the East* (Cracow: Drukarnia Uniwersytetu Jagiellońskiego, 1994), 209–10.

20. The only reference I find in George's oeuvre to Mary as Mother, not Virgin, is in a scene where she is cast as "Mother of the Judge," presiding over a case decided by battle: Pertusi, *Georgio di Pisidia*, I:193. See also Pentcheva, *Icons and Power*, 38–40, 44–46.

21. Pertusi, *Georgio di Pisidia*, I:176, 182–83. See also Pentcheva, *Icons and Power*, 64, 65–66, quoting Theodore Synkellos, *De obsidione Constantinopolitana sub Heraclio imperatori*, XIX: "It was proved most clearly that the Virgin alone fought this battle and won the victory."

22. Bachrach, *Religion and the Conduct of War*, 24–31; Michael McCormick, "The Liturgy of War in the Early Middle Ages: Crisis, Litanies, and the Carolingian Monarchy," *Viator* 15 (1984): 1–23.

23. *Praecepta militaria* VI, 2; trans. McGeer, *Sowing the Dragon's Teeth*, 56–57. On military manuals generally, see Alphonse Dain, "Les stratégistes byzantins," *Travaux et Mémoires* 2 (1967): 317–92; and now D. F. Sullivan, "Byzantine Military Manuals: Prescriptions, Practice, and Pedagogy," in Paul Stephenson, ed., *The Byzantine World* (London: Routledge, 2010), 149–61.

24. I have not here considered the tradition of suicide by soldiers, notably but not exclusively by officers and notables, which subject is addressed impressively in David Woods, "The Good Soldier's End: From Suicide to Martyrdom," *Byzantinoslavica* 66 (2008): 71–86.

25. Thomas Sizgorich, *Violence and Belief in Late Antiquity: Militant Devotion in Christianity and Islam* (Philadelphia: University of Pennsylvania Press, 2009), explores in rich detail the ways in which emergent Islam drew upon established late antique patterns of behavior and narrative reconstruction. Martyrdom is a key theme in this work but one of many. See also Thomas Sizgorich, "Narrative and Community in Islamic Late Antiquity," *Past and Present* 185 (2004): 9–42.

26. Theophylact Simocatta, *History*, 13.3; *The History of Theophylact Simocatta*, trans. M. Whitby and M. Whitby (Oxford: Clarendon, 1986), 126; J. D. Frendo, "The Armenian and Byzantine Foundations of the Concept of Jihad," *Byzantine Studies* 13 (1986): 241–50.

27. Walter Emil Kaegi, *Heraclius: Emperor of Byzantium* (Cambridge, U.K.: Cambridge University Press, 2003); G. J. Reinink and Bernard H. Stolte, eds., *The Reign of Heraclius (610–41): Crisis and Confrontation*, Groningen Studies in Cultural Change 2 (Leuven: Peeters, 2002).

28. Mango and Scott, *The Chronicle of Theophanes*, 438–39 Pertusi, *Georgio di Pisidia*, I:276–77, which, however, omits the reference to "eternal life." Pertusi conveniently reproduces the Greek text of Theophanes beneath the fragments in his edition.

29. Mango and Scott, *The Chronicle of Theophanes*, 442–43; Pertusi, *Georgio di Pisidia*, I:279. See also Kolbaba, "Fighting for Christianity," 206–7; Kaegi, *Heraclius*, 129, dates this episode to 624.

30. Mango and Scott, *The Chronicle of Theophanes*, xliii–lxiii. When reproducing material from extant works by George and others, Theophanes proves to be a reliable copyist. For the fullest commentary, see James D. Howard-Johnston, "Heraclius' Persian Campaigns and the Revival of the East Roman Empire, 622–30," *War in History* 6 (1999): 1–44; James D. Howard-Johnston, "The Official History of Heraclius' Persian Campaigns," in Dąbrowa, *The Roman and Byzantine Army*, 57–87; Mary Whitby, "George of Pisidia's Presentation of the Reign of Heraclius and His Campaigns: Variety and Development," in Reinink and Stolte, *The Reign of Heraclius*, 157–73; Whitby, "A New Image," 197–225.

31. Mango and Scott, *The Chronicle of Theophanes*, 436.

32. A strong case can be made that Heraclius believed that he had such spiritual authority, from his efforts to portray himself as a new David, the archetypal priest-king; from the rhetoric surrounding his recovery of Jerusalem and the True Cross; from his preference for the title *Basileus* over the established Augustus; and much else. On Davidic kingship and the Old Testament perspective of emperors, see Gilbert Dagron, *Emperor and Priest: The Imperial Office in Byzantium* (Cambridge, U.K.: Cambridge University Press, 2003). For reflections on the application of Dagron's thesis to war, see Paul Stephenson, "Imperial Christianity and Sacred Warfare in Byzantium," in James K. Wellman, Jr., ed., *Belief and Bloodshed: Religion and Violence across Time and Tradition* (Lanham, Md.: Rowman & Littlefield, 2007), 81–93.

33. Walter Emil Kaegi, *Byzantium and the Early Islamic Conquests* (Cambridge, U.K.: Cambridge University Press, 1992). As a character in early Islamic literature, Heraclius was treated rather well. See Lawrence I. Conrad, "Heraclius in Early Islamic Kerygma," in Reinink and Stolte, *The Reign of Heraclius*, 113–56; Nadia Maria El-Cheikh, "Muhammad and Heraclius: A Study in Legitimacy," *Studia Islamica* 89 (1999): 5–21, now integrated into her *Byzantium Viewed by the Arabs* (Cambridge, Mass.: Harvard University Press, 2004).

34. Mango and Scott, *The Chronicle of Theophanes*, lxxxii–lxxxvii, offer a detailed account of how Theophanes uses this "oriental" source, which in their English translation is identified by use of the font "Avenir Roman." For a full summary of the *Syriac Common Source*, see Robert G. Hoyland, *Seeing Islam as Others Saw It* (Princeton, N.J.: Darwin, 1997), 631–71.

35. Mango and Scott, *The Chronicle of Theophanes*, 573–74.

36. Jean-Baptiste Chabot, *Chronique de Michel le Syrien: Patriarche jacobite d'Antioche (1166– 1199)*, 5 vols. (Paris: E. Leroux, 1899–1924; reprinted Brussels: Culture et Civilisation, 1963), 2:501; Jean-Baptiste Chabot, *Chronicon Anonymum ad annum Christi 1234 pertinens*, Corpus Scriptorum Christianorum Orientalium, Scriptores Syri, 3rd series, 14 (Louvain: CSCO, 1937), 244, 313, which adds that Eustathius was the son of Marianus. Hoyland, *Seeing Islam*, 346.

37. Lawrence I. Conrad, "The Conquest of Arwad: A Source-Critical Study in the Historiography of the Early Medieval Near East," in Averil Cameron and Lawrence I. Conrad, eds., *The Byzantine and Early Islamic Near East*, vol. 1: *Problems in the Literary Source Material* (Princeton, N.J.: Darwin, 1992), 317–401, esp. the transmission chart on p. 326. The episode is not recorded in the Syriac *Chronicle of Zuqnin*, trans. Amir Harrak (Toronto: Pontifical Institute of Mediaeval Studies, 1999), written in 775, also called the *Chronicle of Pseudo-Dionysius of Tel-Mahre*.

38. Mango and Scott, *The Chronicle of Theophanes*, 570–71.

39. E. W. Brooks, "The Sources of Theophanes and the Syriac Chroniclers," *Byzantinische Zeitschrift* 14 (1906): 586–87, suggested that the Syriac account was translated into Greek by a Palestinian Melkite monk, c. 780, and subsequently was brought to Constantinople by those fleeing the destruction of monasteries before c. 813. Conrad, "The Conquest of Arwad," 336, sees no need to assign the monk to Palestine.

40. Hippolyte Delehaye, ed., *Synaxarium Ecclesiae Constantinopolitanae e Codice Sirmondiano* (Brussels: Apud Socios Bollandianos, 1902). However, he is commemorated as Saint Eustathius of Apsilia by the Orthodox Eparchy of Abkhazia.

41. Hoyland, *Seeing Islam*, 336–86. A brief overview is also offered by Sidney H. Griffith, *The Church in the Shadow of the Mosque* (Princeton, N.J.: Princeton University Press, 2008), 147– 51. See also references to two martyred Peters, from the *Syriac Common Source*, preserved in Mango and Scott, *The Chronicle of Theophanes*, 576–79.

42. Ignace Dick, "La passion arabe de S. Antoine Ruwah, néo-martyr de Damas (d. 26 déc. 799)," *Le Muséon* 74 (1961): 109–33, presents an edition of the Arabic text and French translation, with references to the subsequent Ethiopic and Georgian versions. A summary account is preserved in Chabot, *Chronique de Michel le Syrien*, 3:18–19.

43. Sidney H. Griffith, "The Arabic Account of 'Abd al-Masih an-Nagrani al-Ghassani," *Le Muséon* 98 (1985): 331–74; Hoyland, *Seeing Islam*, 381–83. There is no indication that al-Ghassani was forced to convert to Islam. Clearly, Christians (and Magians) might have been present in Arab war bands as late as the mid-ninth century, when they were entitled to a smaller share of the spoils than their Muslim comrades, according to Ahmad ibn Hanbal. See Sizgorich, *Violence and Belief*, 253.

44. On the phenomenon of "deserter monks" and the efforts made in ninth-century Byzantine hagiography to conceal culpability, see Cyril A. Mango, "The Two Lives of Ioannikios and the Bulgarians," *Harvard Ukrainian Studies* 7 (1983): 401–4. It was an abbot's responsibility to ensure that a postulant was admissible to his monastery, that is, that he was not a deserter from the army.

45. These are listed with brief commentary and full references by Robert Schick, *The Christian Communities of Palestine from Byzantine to Islamic Rule: A Historiographical and Archaeological*

Study (Princeton, N.J.: Darwin, 1995), 171–77. Remarkably, another monk of Mar Saba, named George, was martyred by Muslims while visiting a monastery in Cordoba, Spain, on which see Janna Wasilewski, "The 'Life of Muhammad' in Eulogius of Córdoba: Some Evidence for the Transmission of Greek Polemic to the Latin West," *Early Medieval Europe* 16 (2008): 333–53.

46. The Greek text is edited by Athanasios Papadopoulos-Kerameus, "Exegesis etoi martyrion ton agion pateron ton anairethenton to barbaron, egoun Sarakenon, en te Megiste Lavra tou Osiou Patrou emon Saba," *Pravoslavnyi Palestinskii Sbornik* 19/3 [57] (1907): 1–41. For analysis, see Alexander P. Kazhdan with Lee Francis Sherry and Christina Angelide, *A History of Byzantine Literature (650–850)* (Athens: Ethniko Idryma Ereunon, 1999), 169–81. There is also a Georgian version of the text: Robert Pierpont Blake, "Deux lacunes comblées dans la passion XX monachorum sabaitarum," *Analecta Bollandiana* 68 (1950): 27–43. The massacre is also referred to in Leontios, *Life of Stephen of Mar Sabas*, ed. John C. Lamoreaux, CSCO 571 (Louvain: Peeters, 1999), where Stephen is held to be the author of the *Martyrion*. Since Stephen died in 794, Kazhdan's date of 788 appears to be correct.

47. Papadopoulos-Kerameus, "Exegesis," 15. The slaughter of monks was not typical or widely condoned behavior, as Sizgorich, *Violence and Belief*, 232, notes: "Muslims and monks had a long history of mutual toleration. A century before [a ninth-century tale in the *Life of Timothy of Kakhushta*, recording a beneficial encounter between a Muslim and a monk] on the Syrian frontier with Byzantium, the Muslim *ghazi*/scholar al-Fazari had included in his work on the religious rules of warfare a pair of long entries forbidding the harming of Christian monks by Muslim raiders." The *Chronicle of Zuqnin*, trans. Harrak, 152–54, has a hagiographical interpolation into the entry for the year 720–21 which recounts a miracle of the bishop of Edessa, Mar Habib. A notable in the army of Maslama stops at the monastery of Mar Abel near Edessa and entrusts his gold to a monk: "Keep this for me. If I return alive, I will take what belongs to me; if you learn that I am dead, distribute it among the needy."

48. Paul Stephenson, "'About the Emperor Nikephoros and How He Leaves His Bones in Bulgaria': A Context for the Controversial Chronicle of 811," *Dumbarton Oaks Papers* 60 (2006): 87–109.

49. Ivan Dujčev, "La chronique byzantine de l'an 811," *Travaux et Mémoires* 1 (1965): 252–54.

50. Juan Mateos, ed. and trans., *Le Typicon de la Grande Église, Ms. Sainte-Croix n. 40, Xe siècle, I: Le cycle des douze mois* (Rome: Pontifical Institutum Orientalium Studiorum, 1962), 350–51. See also Wortley, "Legends of the Byzantine Disaster of 811," 545–46, n. 24. The story of the martyrs of 811 was conflated with that of the captives of a subsequent battle in 813, for which see E. Follieri and Ivan Dujčev, "Un' acolutia inedita per i martyri di Bulgaria dell' anno 813," *Byzantion* 33 (1963): 71–106.

51. Delehaye, *Synaxarium*, 850–51.

52. Since this chapter was written, a new critical edition and translation of this text has appeared. Because some pertinent chapters are numbered differently, I supply references to both new and older editions. The translations are my own. See George T. Dennis, ed., *The Taktika of Leo VI, Corpus Fontium Historiae Byzantinae* 49 (Washington, D.C.: Dumbarton Oaks, 2010); J.-P. Migne, ed., *Patrologiae cursus completus, Series graeca* 107 (hereafter PG, 107), cols. 671–1094. Rudolph Vári, *Leonis imperatoris Tactica*, 2 vols. (Budapest: Typis Regiae Universitatis Scientiarum Budapestinensis, 1917–22), covers only books 1–14. Several closely related textual studies were published by V. V. Kuchma: "Taktika L'va v istoricheskoi literature," *Vizantiiskii Vremennik* 30 (1969): 153–66; "Taktika L'va kak istoricheskii istochnik," *Vizantiiskii Vremennik* 33 (1972): 75–87; "Iz istorii vizantiiskogo voennogo isskustva na rubezhe IX–XV," *Vizantiiskii Vremennik* 38 (1977): 94–101.

53. *Maurice's Strategikon*, trans. Dennis, 69.

54. William F. Arndt and Felix Wilbur Gingrich, *A Greek-English Lexicon of the New Testament and Other Early Christian Literature* (Cambridge, U.K.: Cambridge University Press, 1957), 8–9. Since precise translations are vital here, I shall refer to the dictionary I have employed.

55. Agostino Pertusi, "Una acolouthia militare inedita del X secolo," *Aevum* 22 (1948): 145–68, which has been dated to the reign of Leo VI (886–912), but it could as easily be from the

joint reign of Constantine VII (945–959) and his son Romanos II. See also Kolia-Dermitzaki, *O vizantinos "ieros polemos,"* 252–60.

56. Gilbert Dagron, "Ceux d'en face: Les peuples étrangers dans les traités militaires byzantins," *Travaux et Mémoires* 10 (1987): 207–32; Gilbert Dagron, "Apprivoiser la guerre: Byzantins et Arabs ennemis intimes," in K. Tsiknakis, ed., *To Empolemo Vyzantio (9os–120s ai.): Byzantium at War, 9th–12th C.* (Athens: Goulandri Horn, 1997), 37–49.

57. Gilbert Dagron, "Byzance et le modèle islamique au Xe siècle, à propos des *Constitutions tactiques* de l'empereur Léon VI," *Comptes rendus des séances de l'année de l'Académie des Inscriptions et Belles-Lettres* (Paris, 1983), 224. See also Taxiarchis G. Kolias, "The Taktika of Leo VI and the Arabs," *Graeco-Arabica* 3 (1984): 129–35; Georges Michaelides-Nouaros, "O dikaios polemos kata ta Taktika tou Leontos tou Sophou," in *Mélanges Séfériadès/Symmikta Seferiadou* (Athens: Ecole des Sciences Politiques Panteios, 1961), 411–34.

58. Inalienable religious endowments for charitable purposes, here for supporting the jihad. See Claude Cahen, "Réflexions sur le waqf ancien," *Studia Islamica* 14 (1961): 37–56; Moshe Gil, "The Earliest *Waqf* Foundations," *Journal of Near Eastern Studies* 57 (1998): 125–40; Hugh N. Kennedy, "The Financing of the Military in the Early Islamic State," in Averil Cameron, ed., *The Byzantine and Early Islamic Near East*, vol. 3: *States, Resources and Armies* (Princeton, N.J.: Darwin, 1995), 361–78.

59. Michael David Bonner, "The Naming of the Frontier: 'Awasim, Thughur and the Arab Geographers," *Bulletin of the School of Oriental and African Studies* 57 (1994): 17–24, supplying full commentary on how the terms were understood, which cannot be conveyed in simple English translations; Michael David Bonner, *Aristocratic Violence and Holy War: Studies in the Jihad and the Arab-Byzantine Frontier* (New Haven, Conn.: American Oriental Society, 1996), 43–106.

60. Dennis, *The Taktika*, 482–83 (= XVIII.122); PG, 107:976 (= XVIII.128).

61. Arndt and Gingrich, *A Greek-English Lexicon*, 525.

62. Bonner, *Aristocratic Violence*, 8, 41–42, 122–25.

63. Dennis, *The Taktika*, 444–45 (= XVIII.19); PG, 107:949 (= XVIII.19).

64. Ibid., 484–85 (= XVIII.127); PG, 107:977 (= XVIII.133).

65. Hundreds of examples turn up in a *Thesaurus Linguae Graecae* (*TLG*) search.

66. Dennis, *The Taktika*, 306–7 (= XIV.31); PG, 107:859–60 (= XIV.35); Dagron, "Byzance et le modèle islamique," 230–31. Here ἀδελφῶν clearly means "[Christian] brothers-in-arms," whereas elsewhere it refers more generally to other Christians.

67. Arndt and Gingrich, *A Greek-English Lexicon*, 487–88.

68. Eric McGeer, "Two Military Orations of Constantine VII," in John W. Nesbitt, ed., *Byzantine Authors: Literary Activities and Preoccupations: Texts and Translations Dedicated to the Memory of Nicolas Oikonomides*, The Medieval Mediterranean 46 (Leiden: Brill, 2003), 132. McGeer's translations and insights are used by Stephenson, "Imperial Christianity and Sacred Warfare," 86–87.

69. Theoharis Détorakis and J. Mossay, "Un office inédit pour ceux qui sont morts à la guerre, dans le *Cod. Sin. Gr. 734–735*," *Le Muséon* 101 (1988): 183–211. The service is preserved in a tenth-century manuscript at Saint Catherine's Monastery on Mount Sinai and must date to the reign of Nikephoros II (d. 969) or slightly later, for which see Stephenson, "'About the Emperor Nikephoros,'" 107–8.

70. Qu'ran 2:256. See Michael David Bonner, *Jihad in Islamic History: Doctrines and Practice* (Princeton, N.J.: Princeton University Press, 2006), 90. A notable exception is highly suspect, especially since it took place at a time when Arab warriors were least inclined to increase the number of the faithful. See David Woods, "The 60 Martyrs of Gaza and the Martyrdom of Bishop Sophronius of Jerusalem," *Aram* 15 (2003): 129–50; and against Woods's view, Hoyland, *Seeing Islam*, 347–51; Schick, *The Christian Communities of Palestine*, 171–72.

71. Patricia Crone, *Slaves on Horses: The Evolution of the Islamic Polity* (Cambridge, U.K.: Cambridge University Press, 1980); Daniel Pipes, "Mawlas: Freed Slaves and Converts in Early Islam," reprinted in Robert G. Hoyland, ed., *Muslims and Others in Early Islamic Society* (Aldershot, U.K.: Ashgate, 2004), 277–322.

72. Mango and Scott, *The Chronicle of Theophanes*, 550.

73. Ibid., 624–25; and Hoyland, *Seeing Islam*, 1, for a Christian Arab tribe obliged to convert in c. 780.

74. Athena Kolia-Dermitzaki, "The Execution of the Forty-two Martyrs of Amorion: Proposing an Interpretation," *Al-Masaq* 14 (2002): 141–62, argues that the killings were a show of strength by the caliph, al-Wathiq, who was seeking to impose the Mu'tazila doctrine and had endured a series of uprisings. Consequently, he overruled an exchange of prisoners that had been agreed upon and staged his confrontation with the captives.

75. As noted by Sizgorich, *Violence and Belief*, 253.

76. John Skylitzes, *Synopsis historion*, ed. J. Thurn (Berlin: Walter de Gruyter, 1973), 274–75. This chronicler, working in the last decades of the eleventh century, had an agenda and peculiar working methods, on which see Catherine Holmes, *Basil II and the Governance of Empire (976–1025)* (Oxford: Oxford University Press, 2005). The ruling is mentioned for the second time in the early twelfth century by John Zonaras, *Epitome historiarum*, ed. Moritz Pinder and Theodorus Büttner-Wobst (Bonn, 1897), 3:506. It is noted again by Zonaras in a canonical commentary and by two further canonists: Theodore Balsamon in the twelfth century and Matthew Blasteres in the fourteenth, for which see Patrick Viscuso, "Christian Participation in Warfare: A Byzantine View," in Miller and Nesbitt, *Peace and War*, 37–39.

77. A detailed treatment of the developments of the tenth century is provided by McGeer, *Sowing the Dragon's Teeth*. See also Oikonomides, "The Concept of 'Holy War,'" 62–86; Stephenson, "Imperial Christianity and Sacred Warfare," 85–91.

2

In Defense of All Houses of Worship?

Jihad in the Context of Interfaith Relations

ASMA AFSARUDDIN

It is widely believed that Qur'an 22:39–40 were the first verses to be revealed allowing Muslims to engage in armed combat, repealing for them the earlier prohibition against fighting their Meccan persecutors. These verses state:

> Permission is given to those against whom fighting has been initiated [*yuqatalun*] because they have been oppressed, and God is able to help them [Q. 22:39]. These are they who have been wrongfully expelled from their homes merely for saying "God is our Lord." If God had not restrained some people by means of others, monasteries, churches, synagogues, and mosques in which God's name is mentioned frequently would have been destroyed. Indeed, God comes to the aid of those who come to His aid; verily He is powerful and mighty [Q. 22:40].

At first reading, Qur'an 22:39–40 clearly establish the reasons for engaging in armed combat (*jus ad bellum*) and, even more important for our purpose, transparently state that the objective of the combative jihad is to defend all houses of worship, and by extension all religious practitioners, when under attack. The combative jihad, according to these verses, may thus be understood to be undertaken in defense of a basic religious freedom to worship the one God, regardless of which religious group exercises it, when that freedom is violently curtailed by a hostile adversary. We will observe that although early commentators, such as Mujahid ibn Jabr (d. 720) and Muqatil ibn Sulayman (d. 767), stayed close to the actual signification of these verses and recognized their ecumenical potential, later commentators, starting with al-Tabari (d. 923), attempted to compromise and ameliorate this potential through a variety of hermeneutic and reading stratagems.

This chapter is a comparative study of early and late exegeses (*tafsir*), with a focus on what the changing hermeneutic trajectory that emerges might have to tell us about the complex relationships of Muslims with Christians and Jews, the so-called People of the Book, through time. Only Sunni works have been consulted in this study, in order to focus on majoritarian Muslim attitudes and because of space constraints. The main exegetical works used in this study are as follows, in chronological order:

(1) *Tafsir* of Mujahid ibn Jabr: This is the oldest published work of exegesis available to us by the Umayyad commentator Mujahid ibn Jabr, born in Mecca in 642. The extant published *Tafsir*, edited by al-Surta, is fragmentary and incomplete.[1] Mujahid was one of the most prominent students of Ibn 'Abbas (d. c. 687), the celebrated companion (belonging to the first Muslim generation) of the Prophet, and is said to have faithfully transmitted the latter's commentary on the Qur'an.[2] Mujahid displays rationalist and anthropomorphist tendencies in his exegesis, often resorting to *ra'y* (personal opinion), and is said to have made use of Christian and Jewish sources.[3] Although he was criticized by a number of scholars for these proclivities, he became widely recognized for his scholarship after his death in 722.[4]

(2) *Tafsir* of Muqatil ibn Sulayman: Another Umayyad commentator, Muqatil ibn Sulayman ibn Bashir al-Azdi al-Balkhi (d. 767) lived in Basra and then in Baghdad, where he achieved renown as a Qur'an commentator and a *mutakallim* (scholastic theologian). Like Mujahid, he, too, often relied on *ra'y* in his commentary and made use of the *Isra'iliyyat* (tales of the Israelites) attributed to Jewish and Christian sources. Muqatil made generous use of earlier commentaries without attribution, providing us with a valuable window into the opinions of the earliest exegetes from the first and second centuries of Islam.[5] He died in Basra at an advanced age.[6]

(3) *Tanwir al-miqbas*: The early *tafsir* work with the title *Tanwir al-miqbas min tafsir Ibn 'Abbas* and purporting to contain the exegesis of the same companion, Ibn 'Abbas, mentioned earlier, has been generally attributed to the later exegete and genealogist Muhammad ibn al-Sa'ib al-Kalbi (d. 763). This attribution to Ibn 'Abbas via al-Kalbi remains open to debate among modern scholars, however.[7] Since the tone and content of much of the exegetical material contained in this work often tend to agree with those of other certifiably early works, suggesting the genuinely early provenance of some of the views recorded in this work, the *Tanwir al-miqbas* is treated here as an early work (roughly before the end of the ninth century) but of undetermined date and authorship.[8]

(4) *Tafsir* of 'Abd al-Razzaq ibn Hammam ibn Nafi' al-San'ani: From the generation after Muqatil, this relatively early 'Abbasid *tafsir* contains important perspectives on jihad and martyrdom that have not always been preserved in later works. Its author (d. 827) was an important Yemeni scholar, who studied with some of the most prominent scholars of his time, initially in San'a and later in Syria and the Hijaz. These scholars included Ma'mar ibn Rashid (d. 770) in San'a, Ibn Jurayj (d. 767) in Mecca, Sufyan al-Thawri (d. 778) in Kufa, and Malik ibn

Anas (d. 795) in Medina. 'Abd al-Razzaq's *tafsir* is based on an earlier commentary by his teacher Ma'mar.[9]

(5) *Tafsir* of al-Tabari: The celebrated exegete, Abu Ja'far Muhammad ibn Jarir (d. 923), originally from Tabaristan, is the author of probably the most widely consulted work of Islamic exegesis, the *Jami' al-bayan fi tafsir al-Qur'an*, more simply known as *Tafsir al-Tabari*.[10] Along with the magisterial work of history that he compiled, this work showcases al-Tabari's encyclopedic knowledge of the various Islamic sciences. The *Tafsir* is notable for its emphasis on *ijtihad*, or independent reasoning. After meticulously referring to earlier sources and their theological and legal perspectives, al-Tabari characteristically weighs in with his opinion, providing well-crafted arguments to support his position. Besides religious dogma and law, al-Tabari also pays close attention to grammar and lexicography in his *Tafsir*. This work won immediate renown during the author's own lifetime and became the subject of a number of supercommentaries after it.[11]

(6) *Tafsir* of al-Wahidi: 'Ali ibn Ahmad ibn Muhammad al-Wahidi al-Nisaburi (d. 1076) is the author of several exegetical works, including the *Tafsir al-Wasit*, the work being used in this study.[12] As was customary, al-Wahidi was trained in grammar, lexicography, and rhetoric. He is said to have completed the *Wasit* around 1069, having started it five decades earlier. In comparison with his popular, shorter work, *Asbab al-nuzul*, the *Wasit* is more extensive in its commentary.[13]

(7) *Tafsir* of al-Zamakhshari: Abu al-Qasim Mahmud ibn 'Umar al-Zamakhshari (d. 1144), from Zamakhshar in Persia, was an accomplished grammarian, philologist, theologian, exegete, and litterateur, author of a highly regarded Qur'an commentary.[14] His Mu'tazili (rationalist) affiliation is evident in this work of exegesis, which has a strong linguistic focus and contains very little hadith (the Mu'tazila in general being skeptical of the probative value of hadith) in comparison with other exegetical works of a similar period.[15]

(8) *Tafsir* of al-Razi: Muhammad ibn 'Umar ibn al-Husayn Fakhr al-Din al-Razi (d. 1210) hailed from Rayy in northern Persia, where he was educated in grammar, philosophy, *kalam* (scholastic theology), and jurisprudence. He later went to Khwarazm, where he is said to have relentlessly debated the Mu'tazila, who eventually forced him to leave. After meeting the same fate in Transoxania, he returned to Rayy and finally settled down in Herat. He was acknowledged in his lifetime as a brilliant scholar, earning the title *shaykh al-Islam*, and as a formidable champion of Sunni orthodoxy in the theological controversies of his time. His *Tafsir* thus pays considerable attention to issues of theology and philosophy and attempts to justify his own views on the basis of specific Qur'anic verses.[16]

(9) *Tafsir* of al-Qurtubi: Muhammad ibn Ahmad ibn Abi Bakr al-Qurtubi (d. 1273), the well-known Andalusian scholar of Qur'an and hadith, is the author of the exegetical work *al-Jami' li-ahkam al-Qur'an*.[17] The *Jami'* makes considerable use of hadith and has a strong legal focus, while also paying close attention to the philological and rhetorical aspects of the Qur'anic language. Compared with a

number of his predecessors, al-Qurtubi is sparing in his use of the *Isra'iliyyat* in his commentary.[18]

Discussion of Qur'an 22:39–40

A majority of the exegetes surveyed believe that these were the first verses to be revealed giving the command to fight in the Medinan period, enumerating the specific reasons for resorting to physical combat at this specific juncture.

In his exegesis of Qur'an 22:39, Mujahid ibn Jabr in the late seventh century comments that the verse refers to the believers who emigrated from Mecca to Medina, pursued by the unbelievers from the Quraysh. Consequently, God gave them permission to fight the unbelievers through the revelation of this verse.[19] As for Qur'an 22:40, which begins with, "If God had not restrained some of the people by means of others," Mujahid understands it to mean that God had restrained some of them through others "in regard to bearing witness and with regard to truth" (*fi al-shahada wa fi al-haqq*). If this were not the case, then monasteries and all other houses of worship would have been destroyed. The *sawami'* mentioned in the verse refers to the monasteries or cells of the Christian monks (*al-ruhban*), along with all of the other places of worship "belonging to the People of the Book and to Muslims" (*li ahl al-kitab wa ahl al-Islam*) that were encountered along the way.[20]

Muqatil ibn Sulayman in the late eighth century explains that according to these verses, permission was given to Muslims to fight in the way of God because the unbelievers of Mecca (*kuffar Makka*) oppressed them and God helped them against these unbelievers after the prohibition, by which he presumably means a ban on fighting while the Muslims had been in Mecca. The verses explain the nature of this oppression: it consisted of being driven from their homes on account of the physical torture and verbal abuse to which many Muslims had been subjected. The pagan Meccans expelled the believers from their homes only because they acknowledged God and affirmed his oneness, he continues. If God had not constrained the polytheists through the agency of the Muslims, then the former would have prevailed and killed the latter. Subsequently, the monasteries of the monks, the churches of the Christians, the synagogues of the Jews, and the mosques of the Muslims would all have been destroyed. All of these religious groups (*al-milal*) mention the name of God profusely in their places of worship, and God defends these places of worship through the Muslims.[21]

According to the *Tanwir al-Miqbas*, these verses permitted the believers to fight against the unbelievers of Mecca on account of the fact that the former had been oppressed by the latter. God supports the believers against their enemy. The pagan Meccans had evicted them from their homes without due cause or any wrongdoing on their part (*bi la haqq wa la jurm*), except that they attested to the oneness of God and bore witness that Muhammad is the messenger of God. If God had not restrained certain groups of people by others—the believers by means of the prophets, the unbelievers by the believers, and the sitters-at-home without a legitimate excuse (*al-qa'idin bi ghayr 'udhr*) by those who fight (*bi al-mujahidin*)— then the monasteries (*sawami'*) of the monks, the synagogues (*biya'*) of the Jews, the fire temples of the Magians, and the mosques of the Muslims would have been destroyed. All of these are entrusted for their protection to Muslims (*kullu ha'ula'i fi ma'man al-Muslimin*), for in all God is much exalted and glorified. God aids the one who through jihad aids him and his Prophet, for God is invincible in his support for his Prophet and for those who support his Prophet. And God is mighty in exacting vengeance from the enemies of his Prophet, the *Tanwir* concludes.[22]

In his commentary, the relatively early exegete 'Abd al-Razzaq comments that these were the first verses revealed concerning fighting (*al-qital*), giving permission to the Muslims to engage in combat. He refers to the views of the successor (from the generation following the companions of the Prophet) Qatada ibn Di'ama (d. c. 735), who had stated that the *sawami'* belonged to the Sabians, the *biya'* belonged to the Christians, the *salawat* were the synagogues of the Jews (*kana'is al-yahud*), and the *masajid* were the places of worship of the Muslims, in which God's name is mentioned profusely. 'Abd al-Razzaq relates another Qur'anic verse (22:17) in this context, which states, "Those who believe, and those who are Jews, Sabians, Christians, and Magians, and those who are polytheists," as a reference to religious communities whose existence is recognized by the Qur'an. Once again, he refers to Qatada, who described the Sabians as those who worshipped the angels and prayed in a specific direction (*yasluna li qibla*) and recited the Zabur (the Psalms of David); the Magians were those who worshipped the sun and the moon; and the polytheists were those who worshipped idols. The religions are thus six in number; however, "five are for Satan and one is for the Merciful One [*al-Rahman*]," proclaims 'Abd al-Razzaq.[23] The very close attention paid to these specific Qur'anic terms for various religious communities indicates a general scholarly concern for defining the parameters and nature of interfaith relations by the early ninth century.

The late-ninth-to-early-tenth-century exegete al-Tabari has an extensive commentary on these two verses, recording a variety of views on their meanings. He states that there is a difference of opinion regarding the identity of those who were specifically granted permission in this verse to engage in fighting. Those who said that it referred to the Prophet and his companions included Ibn 'Abbas and Sa'id ibn Jubayr (d. 714). Through various chains of transmission, both are said to have affirmed that the verse refers to Muhammad and his companions at the time of the emigration to Medina from Mecca. In one report, Ibn 'Abbas related that when the Prophet departed from Mecca, Abu Bakr remarked, "They [the pagan Meccans] have evicted their prophet. Indeed we belong to God and to Him we return. May they perish!" At that, said Ibn 'Abbas, Qur'an 22:39 was revealed, and Abu Bakr knew that fighting was imminent. It was the first revelation concerning fighting. The successor Ibn Zayd (d. 798) commented that this verse permitted fighting after having prohibited it for the previous ten years.[24]

Other commentators maintained, continues al-Tabari, that the verse referred instead to a group of Muslims who wished to leave enemy territory and emigrate to Medina but were prevented from doing so by the pagan Meccans. Among those who subscribed to this view were some of the earliest exegetes known to us: Ibn Abi Najih (d. 748),[25] Mujahid, Ibn Jurayj (d. 767),[26] Qatada, and others. Thus, Mujahid is quoted as saying in exegesis of this verse, "Certain believers emerged [seeking to] emigrate from Mecca to Medina but were prevented [from doing so]. God therefore granted the believers permission to fight the unbelievers, and they fought them." Ibn Jurayj and Qatada remarked that this was the first time believers were given divine permission to fight. The rest of the verse affirms God's help for those believers who fight in the path of God, and that he will strengthen and elevate them, vanquish and humiliate their enemies.[27]

With regard to Qur'an 22:40, al-Tabari says that it refers to the believers who were evicted from their homes and subjected to physical torture and verbal abuse by the pagan Meccans for affirming their faith in God and his messenger, which forced them to emigrate. The pagans had no right to resort to such actions, remarks al-Tabari, for they were in the wrong, and the believers were in the right.[28]

With regard to the meaning of "If God had not restrained some of the people by means of others," al-Tabari points to the differences of opinion among the scholars. Some exegetes, such as Ibn Jurayj, said that it meant, "If God had not constrained the polytheists through the Muslims." Others, such as Ibn Zayd,[29] said that it meant, "were it not for fighting and jihad in the path of God" (*wa law la al-qital wa al-jihad fi sabil Allah*). Yet others said that its meaning was, "If God had not defended the successors [*al-tabi'un*] who followed by means of the companions of the Messenger of God, peace and blessings be upon him." Thus, according to Thabit ibn 'Awsaja al-Hadrami,[30] 'Ali ibn Abi Talib had remarked that this verse came down in regard to the companions, and therefore, the meaning of this part of the verse is that "if God had not defended the successors by means of the companions of Muhammad, the monasteries and churches would have been destroyed."[31]

Another group of exegetes were of the opinion that the verse had a much broader application and that it referred generally to those who are trustworthy witnesses in matters concerning the rights of some people over others and who prevent others who are not similarly trustworthy from committing wrongful acts, such as shedding blood, for example. Were this not so, then the oppressor would freely oppress people, and monasteries and so on would be destroyed. Those who subscribed to such views included Ibn Abi Najih and Mujahid.[32]

At this point, al-Tabari makes his preference known and says that it is most appropriate to understand this verse to mean that if God did not restrain some people by means of others, then the mention of God's name, for example, would cease; the polytheists are thereby prevented from doing so by the Muslims. The ruler who prevents his subjects from oppressing one another and the trustworthy individual who prevents the attrition of someone's rights through his or her truthful testimony also serve as examples of this kind of divine restraining of one group of people by another. Without this system of checks and balances, so to speak, people would wrong one another (*tazalamu*), "and the victors would destroy the monasteries and churches of the vanquished," in addition to the other places mentioned by God. Such a general interpretation is established not through transmitted reports but through reasoning and the obvious meanings of the words of this verse, states al-Tabari.[33]

Like earlier exegetes, al-Tabari focuses on the nature of the specific places of worship mentioned in Qur'an 22:40. The term *sawami'* has been interpreted in various ways, he notes. Those who said that it meant the monasteries of the Christian monks (*sawami' al-ruhban*) included the early exegetes Mujahid and Ibn Zayd, from whom numerous other narrators transmitted this interpretation. But others, primarily Qatada, said that it referred to the places of worship of the Sabians.[34]

The term *biya'* has also been explained in a number of ways by the exegetes. Some, such as Rufay',[35] Qatada, and al-Dahhak (d. 723),[36] understood it to mean the churches of the Christians (*li al-nasara*). Others, such as Mujahid, Ibn Jurayj, and Ibn Zayd, maintained that it referred to the synagogues of the Jews (*kana'is al-yahud*). Similarly, *salawat* was understood by a number of exegetes, such as Ibn 'Abbas, al-Dahhak, and Qatada, to refer to the synagogues of the Jews (*kana'is al-yahud*). Al-Dahhak specifically remarked that the Jews called their synagogue *saluta* (in Hebrew). But others, such as Abu al-'Aliya (d. 708 or 711)[37] and Rufay', said that it referred to the places of worship of the Sabians. A number of exegetes, primarily Mujahid, from whom Ibn Abi Najih, Ibn Jurayj, and others related, said that *salawat* referred in general to "the places of worship of the Muslims and the People of the Book." But Ibn Zayd maintained that it referred specifically to the places of worship for Muslims. And finally, there was a similar difference of opinion with regard to the *masajid*. Some exegetes, such as Rufay' and Qatada, said that it referred specifically to the places of worship for Muslims. Qatada added that it is specifically the *masajid* in which God's name is mentioned profusely. Others, such as al-Dahhak, said, however, that the word was used "for each one of these [places of worship mentioned in this verse] in which God's name is mentioned profusely, and did not specifically refer to mosques" (*wa lam yakhuss al-masajid*).[38] In this significant cluster of exegetical remarks preserved by al-Tabari, we observe a spectrum of views on the places of worship indicated by the specific terms in Qur'an 22:40. With the exception of *biya'*, which is universally understood to refer to non-Muslim Abrahamic places of worship, some exegetes, such as Ibn Zayd, Rufay', and Qatada, try to appropriate more general terms for houses of worship—*salawat* and *masajid*—for Islam alone. Others, however, such as Mujahid and al-Dahhak, underscore their broader, nondenominational signification, evidencing more inclusivist understandings of these Qur'anic terms in comparison with the former group of exegetes.

As for the final part of the verse, continues al-Tabari, it refers to God's assistance for those who fight in his path so that his word may reign over his enemies. God is formidable in his help for those among his supporters who strive in his path, powerful in his dominion, invincible and unvanquished in his might.[39]

Al-Wahidi in his *Tafsir* says that according to the exegetes, the Meccan polytheists used to torment the companions of Muhammad, inflicting both physical harm and verbal abuse on them. When they complained to the Prophet of this mistreatment, he would counsel them "to be patient for I have not been commanded to fight." This situation lasted until they emigrated to Medina and God caused this verse to come down there; it was the first verse ever revealed concerning fighting. The reason for this permission was that the Muslims had been subjected to persecution and aggression by the pagan Meccans which resulted in physical harm for the Muslims and expulsion from their homes. After granting the Muslims permission to fight, the verse also promised divine support for them on account of the fact that they had been evicted from their homes for no wrongdoing on their part except for having affirmed the oneness of God.[40]

Al-Wahidi then proceeds to discuss the differences of opinions regarding the meaning of the various places of worship mentioned in the verse. He mentions that according to Mujahid and al-Dahhak, *sawami'* refers to the monasteries of the Christian monks, while Qatada maintained that it refers to the places of worship of the Sabians. The *biya'* refers to the churches of the Christians, while the *salawat* are the synagogues of the Jews, a synagogue in Hebrew being known as *saluta*. The *masajid* are the mosques of Muslims from the community of Muhammad. Thus, the verse means, "If God had not restrained some people by means of others through fighting [*'an al-qital*], then the places of worship associated with the revealed law [*shari'a*] of every prophet would be destroyed." If it were not for this restraint (*law la al-daf'*), then synagogues in the time of Moses, monasteries in the time of Jesus, and mosques in the time of Muhammad would have been destroyed. Whoever bolsters God's religion and his revealed law, al-Wahidi continues, God will support him, for God is almighty over his creation, without peer in regard to his dominion and power.[41]

In al-Wahidi's time, we thus begin to see more stable meanings attached to specific terms for places of worship as compared with the earlier period, when a larger range of opinions existed about such references. Thus, *sawami'* and *biya'* are now commonly understood to refer to the monasteries and churches of the Christians, *salawat* to the synagogues of the Jews, and *masajid* to the mosques of Muslims. This stabilization in the meanings of these terms imposes certain temporal and chronological constraints on the understanding of the verse, however. Thus, non-Muslim houses of worship are understood to have been worthy of defense during the time of the prophets associated with prior Abrahamic religions, thereby potentially implying that they need not be defended after their time.

The twelfth-century exegete al-Zamakhshari says that the verse granted the companions of Muhammad permission to fight because they had been severely persecuted by the Meccan polytheists. After having suffered physical beatings and verbal humiliation, they used to come to the Prophet and complain to him of their mistreatment, and he would counsel them to wait until divine permission to fight was given. After the emigration to Medina, this verse was revealed, allowing fighting for the first time, after more than seventy verses had previously prohibited it. Others said that when a group of people attempted to emigrate to Medina and were stopped by the pagan Meccans, the verse came down giving the former permission to fight the latter. The verse also affirms God's mighty help for those who aid him and that the proclamation of the oneness of God does not warrant expulsion of believers from their homes.[42]

With regard to "If God had not restrained some people by others," al-Zamakhshari says that it means that God fortified the Muslims against the unbelievers through (armed) struggle (*bi al-mujahada*). If that were not so, then the polytheists would have gained control over the people of various religious communities ('*ala ahl al-milal al-mukhtalifa*) in their time and over their places of worship (*muta'abbadatihim*) and destroyed them. Thus, they would not have left standing the churches of Christians, the monasteries of the monks, the synagogues of the Jews, and the mosques of the Muslims. The verse may also be read as referring to the polytheists during the time of Muhammad, who would have (otherwise) triumphed over the Muslims and over the People of the Book in their protection and destroyed their various houses of worship. In this verse, continues al-Zamakhshari, a synagogue has been called *salah* because prayers are offered within it; it is an Arabized word derived from the Hebrew term *saluta*.[43] In comparison with al-Wahidi, al-Zamakhshari therefore allows for the verse to be understood as referring to Jewish and Christian places of worship both before and during the time of the Prophet Muhammad, with the implication that their defense remained an obligation for Muslims after the rise of Islam.

As for the last part of Qur'an 22:40, it refers to those who aid God's religion and his supporters. Al-Zamakhshari says that this is a reference to the Muhajirun, the Muslims who emigrated from Mecca to Medina, whom God established on earth and taught how to carry out religious obligations. Some read into this verse an indication of the legitimacy of the rightly guided caliphate (*sihhat amr al-khulafa' al-rashidin*) of Abu Bakr, 'Umar, 'Uthman, and 'Ali—all Muhajirun—"for God did not grant strength and successful execution of matters along with righteous conduct to any others besides the Muhajirun." The Ansar (the Muslim converts of Medina) and converts to Islam after the fall of Mecca (*al-tulaqa'*) had no part in this divine favor. In comparison with his predecessors, this is a new reading on al-Zamakhshari's part, conveying to us a probable heightened focus on the issue of legitimate leadership during the Sunni Seljuq military offensive against the Shi'i dynasties of his time.

The late-twelfth-to-early-thirteenth-century exegete Fakhr al-Din al-Razi understands *bi-annahum zulimu* ("because they were oppressed/tormented") to mean that permission was granted to the Prophet's companions to engage in fighting on account of the intolerable persecution they had been subjected to by the Meccan polytheists. The companions would come to the Prophet and complain of their mistreatment and suffering at the hands of the Meccan polytheists, and he would counsel them to be patient until a commandment from God came down. This verse, says al-Razi, was the first allowing Muslims to engage in fighting after more than seventy verses had prohibited it. According to others, the verse was revealed concerning a group of Muslims attempting to emigrate to Medina but who were prevented from doing so by the pagan Meccans, allowing the former to fight against the latter with the promise of God's help.[44]

The reason for this divine permission was that the Muslims had been persecuted in two ways: (1) they were expelled from their homes, and (2) their expulsion was on account of their affirmation of the oneness of God. Both of them constituted acts of great persecution, as indicated by the phrase *min ghayr haqq* (without just cause/wrongfully) occurring in the verse. Al-Razi refers to Qur'an 5:59 here, which states, "Do they seek revenge against us merely for believing in God?" God then makes clear in regard to "if He did not restrain certain people by means of others" that this is his way of "protecting His religion" (*an yahfuza dinahu*).[45]

What is the nature of this restraining? It consists of allowing the people of God's religion to fight the unbelievers. Were this not so—that is, if the polytheists were not reined in by the believers by granting the latter permission to fight the former and aiding the believers against their enemies—then the polytheists would be allowed the upper hand over the people of various religions (*ahl al-adyan*), and their places of worship would be destroyed. Permission is thus granted to believers to fight the enemies of religion so that the people of religion may be free to worship and construct their houses of worship (*li yatafarragha ahl al-din li al-'ibada wa bina' al-buyut laha*). It is in this context that the monasteries, churches, and synagogues are mentioned, even though they belong to non-Muslims (*li ghayr ahl al-Islam*). Al-Razi therefore states clearly what al-Zamakhshari had only implied, that Muslims as one of "the people of religions" may fight to defend the rights of other peoples of religion against the encroachments of those who oppose (monotheistic) religion in general.

Al-Razi further quotes here the eighth-century exegete al-Kalbi,[46] who had said that God restrains the believers by means of the prophets and the sitters-at-home (*al-qa'idina 'an al-jihad*) by means of those who fight. According to Abu al-Jawza',[47] reporting from Ibn 'Abbas, God restrains the evildoer (*al-musi'*) by means of the virtuous person (*al-muhsin*); the one who does not pray by the one who does; the one who does not give alms by the one who does; and the one who does not perform the pilgrimage by the one who does. Ibn 'Umar narrated a hadith in which the Prophet says that God restrains by means of the virtuous Muslim hundreds of his relatives and neighbors, after which he recited this verse. Al-Dahhak related from Ibn 'Abbas that God restrains the people of *dhimma* (non-Muslims under Muslim rule and protection) through the religion of Islam and its adherents.[48]

According to these different authorities, the verse therefore broadly suggests a moral hierarchy of sorts, which sets in motion a system of checks and balances whereby the morally superior agent acts as a restraint on the one who is assumed to be inferior.

Al-Razi then proceeds to answer the question "Why has God grouped the Jewish and Christian places of worship with those of the Muslims?" In response, he indicates that there are three schools of thought on this topic. First, al-Razi cites al-Hasan al-Basri (d. c. 728), who said that this verse collectively refers to the places of worship of all of the believers (*al-mu'minin*), even though their specific names vary. Second, according to the philologist al-Zajjaj (d. 923),[49] if God had not restrained certain people by means of others, then the specific places of worship associated with the revealed law of every prophet would have been destroyed. Synagogues, churches, and mosques in which people prayed according to the revealed law of Moses, Jesus, and Muhammad, respectively, would have been destroyed. All of these religious communities were thus protected as long as they observed the truth before the corruption of their scriptures and the abrogation of their creeds (*qabla al-tahrif wa qabla al-naskh*). Third, it is possible to say that the verse refers to the houses of worship belonging to the People of the Book[50] during the time of the Prophet, because "in any case, the mention of God the Exalted takes place in them and they are not houses for the worship of idols."[51] Worthy of note is al-Razi's introduction of the specific doctrines of *tahrif* and *naskh* into his commentary on this verse, the implications of which are further explored below.

What exactly is indicated by the various terms used for places of worship in this verse, asks al-Razi? Like a number of other exegetes whom we have already discussed, he indicates a variety of opinions regarding the identification of the specific houses of worship mentioned in this verse. Thus, according to Abu al-'Aliya, *sawami'* refers to the churches of Christians, *biya'* to the synagogues of the Jews, *salawat* to the Sabian places of prayer, and *masajid* to the mosques of Muslims. According to al-Zajjaj, both the *sawami'* and the *biya'* belong to the Christians, the former being built in the deserts and the latter in the cities, while the *salawat* belong to the Jews, reflecting the Hebrew term *saluta*. Qatada differed only in thinking that the *sawami'* belonged to the Sabians.

An interesting exegetical shift is next attributed to al-Hasan al-Basri. According to al-Razi, al-Hasan was of the opinion that all of these names for houses of worship referred to mosques, for the Muslims had taken control of the *sawami'* and the *biya'*, and these terms could therefore be considered an allegorical reference (*'ala sabil al-tashbih*) to mosques. *Salawat* refers to actual prayers, so that it may be said that if God had not restrained some people by means of others, prayers would have ceased, and mosques would have been destroyed.[52] If the question were to be posed consequently regarding how *salawat* can be described as subject to (physical) destruction if the meaning inferred is the prayers of the Muslims, then the answer would be that it refers to their cessation and the extermination of those who perform them, just as one may say that someone destroyed

(haddama) the charity (ihsan) of someone else if he were to receive it in ingrati-
tude. But even if one were to accept this interpretation, one could still say that
salawat metonymically refers to places of worship, which are susceptible to physical destruction, just as in Qur'an 12:82, where it is stated "Ask the village," when
what is intended is "Ask its people." Another rejoinder to such a question is that it
is possible to conjoin what can be physically destroyed to what cannot be physically destroyed in this case, in conformity, for example, with the expression
"sheathing his sword and spear," even though a spear cannot be sheathed.[53]

Al-Razi then deals with the question of whether the clause "in which God's
name is much mentioned" refers to mosques specifically or to all of the houses of
worship. According to al-Kalbi and Muqatil, the clause is a reference to all of the
houses of worship, for God is mentioned frequently in these places. But, al-Razi
says, it is more appropriate to understand the verse as referring only to mosques
"in special recognition of them" (tashrifan laha), for the profuse mention of God's
name occurs in them alone.[54] The contrast between al-Razi's exclusivist understanding of this verse as compared with more inclusivist understandings attributed to earlier exegetes is worthy of our attention.

In a similar vein, al-Razi continues, another question may be posed about why
the other houses of worship are mentioned before mosques. The answer, according
to him, is that because they are of an earlier provenance. Chronology, however, has
nothing to do with greater moral excellence, for, after all, "the Messenger of God,
peace and blessings be upon him, is the best among the messengers and his community is the best of communities, despite the fact that they are the last of them."
This is also the true import of another hadith, which states, "We are the last, [yet]
we precede" (nahnu al-akhirun al-sabiqun).[55] We should note once again that this is
a new concern on the part of al-Razi, not expressed by his predecessors.

The verse continues with God's promise of aid and support for those who support him and his religion by undertaking jihad, according to al-Razi. He acknowledges that others said, however, that it referred to those who carry out the (usual)
religious obligations. Al-Razi says that it is more appropriate to understand this
verse as containing the divine promise that God will help his servant by strengthening him against his enemies so that he may be victorious and in a position to
elucidate the proofs and evidences (that point to the truth of God's religion) and
by helping him in acquiring knowledge and carrying out the required duties. Included among these required duties is fighting in the path of God, in which God
has promised victory.[56]

In his exegesis of these verses, al-Qurtubi reiterates that they were revealed
after the emigration of the companions to Medina. Their revelation was in
response to the companions who had asked permission of the Prophet to fight the
pagan Meccans on account of the persecution they had suffered at their hands.
Significantly, al-Qurtubi says that this verse abrogates (nasikh) all other verses in
the Qur'an that advocate turning away from one's enemies and forgiving them,
and it was the first verse to be revealed concerning fighting, he asserts. Prominent

scholars such as Ibn 'Abbas and Ibn Jubayr had affirmed that the verse was revealed at the time of the Prophet's emigration to Medina. The two hadith scholars al-Nasa'i (d. 915) and al-Tirmidhi (d. 892) had also related from Ibn 'Abbas that when Muhammad was expelled from Mecca, Abu Bakr remarked, "They have evicted their prophet; they will suffer ruination!" Subsequently, Qur'an 22:39 was revealed, and Abu Bakr said that he knew that fighting was imminent.[57]

With regard to Qur'an 22:40, it refers to those who, on account of having affirmed the oneness of God, were wrongfully expelled from their homes by "the people of idols" (*ahl al-awthan*). According to "our scholars," the Prophet was not given permission before the pledge of 'Aqaba to wage war (*al-harb*) or to shed blood. Rather, he was commanded to pray to God, to show forbearance in the face of injury, and to forgive the ignorant for ten years, "so as to establish God's proof against them," as indicated in Qur'an 17:15, which states, "We did not punish until we had sent a messenger." The people thus continued to be persecuted by the Quraysh, some suffering banishment and some even renouncing their faith. Others fled to Abyssinia and later to Medina, while yet others continued to bear the torment patiently. When the Quraysh grew even more fierce and relentless in their opposition, God finally granted his messenger permission to fight and resist and win deliverance for the Muslims from their oppressors through the revelation of this verse.[58]

Thus, continues al-Qurtubi, if God had not commanded his prophets and the believers to fight their enemies, then the polytheists would have gained the upper hand and destroyed the places of worship for the various religions. Fighting was thus commanded to repel the polytheists and to allow the people of religion to worship freely. The command to undertake jihad had previously been given to past communities, thereby allowing for the restoration of God's laws (*al-shara'i'*) and for the congregation of believers. If it were not for fighting (*al-qital*) and *al-jihad*, then truth would have been extinguished in every community. Those among Christians and Sabians who shun jihad are in violation of their creed, for without fighting, religion would perish. The various places of worship mentioned in the verse refer to them before their corruption and transformation and before the supersession of these creeds (*al-milal*) by Islam. Thus, the verse means that if this restraint did not exist, then during the periods of Moses, Jesus, and Muhammad, synagogues, churches, and mosques would have been destroyed. The tenth-century Andalusian exegete Ibn 'Atiyya (d. 993)[59] said that the verse referred to the physical destruction of the houses of worship, while 'Ali ibn Abi Talib was of the opinion that the verse indicated that God had protected the successors by means of the companions. Al-Qurtubi agrees that one may read the meaning of protecting/restraining a group of people by another into this verse but says that it is more appropriate to understand it as referring to fighting. According to Mujahid, the verse referred to the restraining of unjust people with the witness of just people (*bi-shahadat al-'udul*). Others said that it means that God restrains the injustice of oppressors with the justice of rulers (*bi 'adl al-wulah*). The companion

Abu al-Darda'[60] said that the verse means that if God did not protect those who are not in mosques by those who are and those who do not take part in military campaigns by those who do, then they would be punished. Others said that it means that God averts punishment through the prayers of virtuous, upright people. The verse thus indicates in general, says al-Qurtubi, the protection and/or restraining of some people by others, and various commentators have added further details.[61] Like al-Razi, therefore, al-Qurtubi includes the duty of fighting as being indicated in the verse's reference to the restraint exercised by one group of people over another but stresses its prominence within the range of righteous actions to be carried out by the faithful.

Al-Qurtubi notes that according to Ibn Khuwayzmandad, a Maliki jurist of the tenth century, this verse prohibits the destruction of the churches, synagogues, and fire temples of the protected peoples, but they should not be allowed to add anything new to them or to increase the size and height of their physical structures. Muslims should not enter them or pray in them. If an addition is made, it should be dismantled. If such places of worship are encountered in hostile territory (*bilad al-harb*), they should be demolished, but similar places belonging to the protected people should not be demolished in Muslim territories, for their houses and property are under Muslim protection. But no additions may be made, "because in that there is display of the causes of unbelief." A mosque may be demolished, however, to rebuild it, as 'Uthman ibn 'Affan did with the mosque of the Prophet.[62]

Al-Qurtubi then engages in an extended description of the various houses of worship (and the possible etymologies of their names) mentioned in this verse. He says that according to Qatada, the *sawami'* before Islam belonged to Christian monks and the Sabian worshipers. *Biya'* referred to Christian churches, although al-Tabari mentions that it referred to Jewish synagogues, which explanation al-Qurtubi regards as an unnecessary interpolation emanating from Mujahid. According to al-Zajjaj and al-Hasan (al-Basri), the *salawat* are Jewish synagogues, going back to the Hebrew word *saluta*. According to Abu 'Ubayda (d. 825),[63] however, the *salawat*, Arabicized from *saluta*, are houses of worship erected on open stretches of land in which Christians prayed during their travels. Al-Qurtubi cites more authorities concerning their variant opinions regarding the specific identification of these places of worship, some of which have already been indicated above. Worthy of note are Ibn 'Atiyya's views, as recorded by al-Qurtubi, that these names for various houses of worship were shared by many of these religious communities and that the reference to all of them lends emphasis to the mention of the various worshipers. These names, according to Ibn 'Atiyya, refer only to those religious groups that had a revealed scripture (*laha kitab*) and do not include the Zoroastrians (*al-majus*) or the polytheists, "because they do not possess what must be protected, and the mention of God is not made except among the people of the revealed laws" (*'inda ahl al-shara'i'*).[64]

Al-Qurtubi also responds to the question of why mention of the other houses of worship precedes that of mosques. Like al-Razi, he says this is simply because the non-Muslim places of worship came into existence earlier. Others said that it was because they were closer to the occurrence of the word "destruction" in the verse, while "mosques" were the closest to "the mentioning [of God's name]." Those who morally precede (*al-sabiq*), reminds al-Qurtubi, may be mentioned last, as is evidenced also in Qur'an 35:32, which states, "There are among them those who are unjust to themselves, and those who are just, and those who precede with their good works."[65] Like al-Razi before him, al-Qurtubi, too, evinces a certain amount of concern lest Qur'anic syntax be construed in any way to imply a more favored status for confessional Christians and Jews over confessional Muslims and thus takes great pains to allay such potential anxiety. The final part of the verse provides assurance, he states, that God will aid the one who supports God's religion and his Prophet, for, according to al-Khattabi (d. 998), the verse says that God is strong (*qawiy*) and able to do so (*qadir*).[66]

Synopsis and Analysis of Qur'an 22:39–40: Tracing the Changing Conceptions of Jihad

According to a majority of the exegetes surveyed, Qur'an 22:39 was the first verse revealed permitting Muslims to engage in defensive armed combat against the pagan Meccans (in contrast with fewer exegetes who were of the opinion that Qur'an 2:190 was the first).[67] The reasons that emerge in these commentaries for sanctioning fighting at this stage are primarily twofold: first, because Muslims had been physically harmed by the pagans and expelled from their homes; and second, because such persecution was visited upon the Muslims merely on account of their monotheistic belief and not on account of any wrongdoing on their part. According to the first reason, the divine command to resort to fighting allowed Muslims to defend themselves against the aggression of the pagan Meccans, lifting a prohibition against physical retaliation imposed upon the Prophet and his followers during the twelve-year Meccan period. The second reason establishes the right of Muslims (and the People of the Book before them) to profess and propagate their religion peacefully without suffering molestation. Should such molestation occur, at least contingents from among these monotheistic groups have the right to retaliate militarily in order to defend their houses of worship. *Qital* (often conflated with jihad in exegeses) in this verse is thus defensive in nature and in response to prior persecution by the enemy, according to all of the exegetes surveyed. The right to profess belief in the one God and to resort to armed combat to defend this right when violently encroached upon is clearly stressed in all of the exegeses consulted.

The nature of the restraint to be exercised by one group of people over another as mentioned in Qur'an 22:40 is interpreted in various ways by our exegetes. Our earliest commentator, Mujahid, understands it to be a general restraint exercised by righteous people over unrighteous ones. His choice of language in this context is categorically nonconfessional, the righteous being defined not by their adherence to a specific religion or religions but by their testimony to the truth (*al-haqq*). Al-Tabari preserves a number of significant interpretations of this verse, ranging from 'Ali ibn Abi Talib's view that it referred to the companions of the Prophet who had successfully defended and preserved for the next generation all of the houses of worship (not just mosques) to Ibn Zayd's understanding that it was an exclusive reference to fighting in the path of God. Al-Tabari himself prefers the interpretation that the verse refers in general to virtuous people regardless of religious affiliation, who restrain those who oppress others through the offering of truthful testimony. In al-Wahidi's exegesis of the late eleventh century, we begin, however, to detect a change in tone whereby it is implied that the restraint is to be exercised by Muslims only in defense of their own houses of worship, not in defense of others. Restraint is simply and unequivocally equated with *qital* by him, clearly indicating to us that by the late eleventh century, the multiplicity of views concerning the nature of restraint/defense as recorded by al-Tabari had given way to a single, uniform understanding of jihad as primarily *qital*.

Al-Zamakhshari reverses this trend by adhering to the earlier view that Muslims must continue to defend all houses of worship against the onslaught of unbelievers. However, restraint/defense in this case is primarily military in nature (although we note that he uses the term *mujahada* rather than *jihad* to indicate the nature of restraint exercised in this context). It is also noteworthy that al-Zamakhshari understands the last part of Qur'an 22:40 as asserting the privileged status of the Muhajirun and hence by implication of a majority of the companions of the Prophet, thereby affirming the soundness of the Sunni position on the early caliphate. This interpretation is understandable against the backdrop of the Sunni resurgence in the Seljuk period, when there was more of a concern with containing internal dissension than with fighting external enemies.

Al-Razi's interpretation is similar to that of al-Zamakhshari—he, too, understands restraint/defense as fighting against the polytheists to protect "the people of religions" (*ahl al-adyan*), equated with monotheists. He goes further than al-Zamakhshari by unambiguously asserting that Muslims are obligated by this verse to continue to defend the houses of worship of (monotheistic) non-Muslims and that this command has not been abrogated by the advent of historical Islam. At the same time, al-Razi also records the opinions of early exegetes who more expansively understood the kind of struggle (*mujahada*/jihad) involved in restraining wrongdoers as being of a moral, ethical, and exemplary nature, in addition to being combative. However, as will be further discussed below, al-Razi then proceeds to set up a moral hierarchy among monotheistic believers. Al-Qurtubi's views parallel al-Razi's with two important distinctions: first, al-Qurtubi is more emphatic about the necessity of resorting to fighting to protect believers against unbelievers; and second, he maintains that the command to protect all houses of worship had lapsed after the advent of Islam because the prior monotheistic religions had suffered corruption and been superseded by Islam. In the waning days of Muslim rule in Andalusia in the late thirteenth century, al-Qurtubi's promotion of the combative jihad is not surprising in the face of a muscular Christian offensive against the Muslims there.

With regard to the various houses of worship mentioned in this verse in which the one God is revered, there is general agreement that they include the synagogues, churches, and mosques of Jews, Christians (and sometimes Sabians), and Muslims, respectively. Early exegeses are even more inclusive. Thus, the *Tanwir al-miqbas* includes the fire temples of the Magians/Zoroastrians among the houses of worship to be defended by Muslims, as does the early-eighth-century authority Qatada ibn Di'ama. Qatada additionally includes the polytheists among the religious communities recognized by the Qur'an, on the basis of Qur'an 22:17, as reported by 'Abd al-Razzaq. 'Abd al-Razzaq's disclaimer to the effect that only one of these six religious communities is to be deemed "for God" and the rest are "for Satan" is revealing of a heightened sense of confessionalism among Muslims during his period, that is, in the early ninth century, and the tendency to restrict salvation to Muslims alone, in contradistinction to Qatada's comment, which on the surface confers no such exclusive salvific status upon Muslims.

Al-Tabari refers to a number of reports from early authorities, such as Ibn 'Abbas, Rufay', Qatada, Mujahid ibn Jabir, and Ibn Zayd, who understood the various terms for houses of worship as references to places of worship for Jews, Christians, Sabians, and Muslims. Al-Tabari does not include, as does the *Tanwir al-miqbas*, any report referring to the fire temples of Zoroastrians. He includes additionally the testimony of al-Dahhak, who understood *masajid* as a general reference to all houses of worship in which God is praised abundantly, in contrast to Rufay' and Qatada, who interpreted *masajid* as specifically Muslim houses of worship. Qatada is also reported to have commented that only in the Muslim *masajid* (that is, to the exclusion of other houses of worship) was God mentioned profusely. In this significant cluster of reports from early authorities, we discern more inclusive and irenic interpretations juxtaposed with more exclusive and confessional ones, as particularly evident in comparing, for example, al-Dahhak's expansive understanding of *masajid* with Qatada's more restrictive one. In this rich cluster of exegeses preserved for us by al-Tabari, we find such exclusivist views vying for precedence with inclusivist ones already in the lifetimes of Qatada and al-Dahhak in the early eighth century during the Umayyad period. It is possible to speculate that continuing altercations between the Umayyads and the Byzantine empire are reflected to a certain degree in the progressively clearer demarcation of confessional boundaries as articulated by certain jurists and theologians, which clearly influenced the understanding of the nature and function of the combative jihad.

In the late eleventh century, al-Wahidi identifies the various houses of worship mentioned in the verse as those belonging to all of the monotheistic communities —Jewish, Christian, and Sabian, besides Muslim—but during the time of their respective prophets. Although he does not state this explicitly, the implication is that they were deserving of protection before the time of Islam but not after. The principle of *naskh* (abrogation/supersession) is implied in this understanding, but al-Wahidi makes no explicit mention of it. In the following century, al-Zamakh-shari leaves both possibilities open, allowing the verse to be understood as a reference to the pre-Islamic monotheistic houses of worship, both during the lifetimes of their prophets and during the lifetime of Muhammad, with their protection guaranteed by Muslims.

By the time we get to al-Razi and al-Qurtubi, new concerns have emerged, as reflected in their exegeses of Qur'an 22:39 in regard to the relation between Islam and the previous monotheistic dispensations. Three schools of thought jostle with one another, according to al-Razi, with regard to the interpretation of this verse. The first, more inclusivist understanding is attributed to al-Hasan al-Basri in the early eighth century, who understood this verse to be a reference to the houses of worship of all of the believers (*al-mu'minun*) collectively for all time without privileging any one religion. The second, more confessional understanding is attributed to al-Zajjaj in the early tenth century and asserts the inviolability of synagogues and churches before the advent of Islam, when the relevant religious communities had not corrupted their scriptures and their creeds were not abrogated (one assumes by Islam, although this is not explicitly stated). Here we have a specific articulation of the doctrines of *tahrif* and *naskh* in regard to pre-Islamic monotheistic religions, not encountered in the exegeses of the earliest commentators. As a comparison of the views of al-Hasan al-Basri and al-Zajjaj indicates, according to al-Razi's attribution, a major doctrinal shift thus seems to have occurred between the second and fourth centuries of Islam, the height of the 'Abbasid period, which allowed for a more exclusivist and confessional understanding of this verse to emerge gradually in this period. One is led to wonder if the famous jurist al-Shafi'i's legal division of the world into the "abode of Islam" (*dar al-Islam*) and the "abode of war" (*dar al-harb*) and the consequent formulation of the classical theories of jihad had influenced the formation of these changed perspectives in the ninth century after his death in 820.[68] It is also telling that al-Razi's predecessors consulted in this survey had not specifically invoked the terms *tahrif* and *naskh*, although a few hinted at them, as indicated above. It is possible that al-Razi is thus retrojecting his own perspectives back to an earlier period to establish a longer, and therefore more historically convincing, lineage for these terms.

The third school of thought holds that this verse refers to the houses of worship of the People of the Book even after the advent of Islam, since the one God, and not idols, is worshipped in them. This school still adheres to a more irenic perspective, in that it validates monotheism in general in opposition to associationism. Representatives of this school of thought are the late-eighth-century exegetes al-Kalbi (d. 763) and Muqatil (d. 767). Al-Razi expresses his dislike for this line of thinking, as we saw, for from his vantage point in the late twelfth to early thirteenth centuries during the Seljuq period and against the backdrop of the Crusades, this verse is to be more appropriately understood as an exclusive reference to mosques. This is so because God's name, he proclaims, is abundantly praised only in them. He is also eager to explain—a propensity not displayed by his predecessors—why non-Muslim houses of worship are mentioned before mosques in this verse. It is merely a fact of chronology, he asserts, since the former appeared earlier in history. In any case, the last can be the best, as is certainly the case with Islam. In contrast with the explicit wording of the verse and the understanding of several early authorities, al-Razi confidently discerns a divine privileging here of Islam and its houses of worship.

Like al-Razi, al-Qurtubi maintains that Qur'an 22:39 contains a reference to the non-Muslim monotheistic communities before their corruption and supersession by Islam. Both *qital* and jihad, he stresses, are necessary to preserve the right of the people of religion to worship freely. Since other religious communities have abdicated this responsibility, it has devolved upon Muslims to carry it out. Like al-Razi's commentary, al-Qurtubi's exegesis points to a progressively more narrowly confessional understanding of this verse over time. Thus, he reports that Ibn Khuwayzmandad in the tenth century understood this verse to prohibit the destruction of all houses of worship (including fire temples of the Zoroastrians), but he was also of the opinion that existing structures could not be repaired or augmented, an opinion not expressed by earlier exegetes. Like al-Razi, al-Qurtubi discounts any moral significance inhering in the mention of non-Muslim houses of worship before Muslim ones in the verse. It merely reflects historical chronology, he asserts.

Such views appear to have become de rigueur by the Mamluk period, as reflected in the fourteenth-century *tafsir* of Isma'il ibn Kathir (d. 1373). Ibn Kathir provides a range of hermeneutical opinions concerning the meaning of Qur'an 22:39–40, but like al-Razi and al-Qurtubi, he emphasizes the more exclusivist perspectives on the meanings of these verses. He shows a clear preference for the commentaries of scholars who consider the placement of the word *masajid* in Qur'an 22:40 as an indication that mosques and the Muslim faithful who flock to them outnumber non-Muslim houses of worship and worshippers.[69]

In comparison with those of their predecessors, the perspectives of al-Razi, al-Qurtubi, and Ibn Kathir clearly appear more exclusionary vis-à-vis the People of the Book and considerably attenuate the ecumenical potential of Qur'an 22:39–40. Their commentaries establish that by the Seljuq and Mamluk periods in the wake of the Crusades (and later the Mongol invasions) and, in the case of al-Qurtubi, by the time of the Spanish Reconquista, Muslims were increasingly fearful and on the defensive against non-Muslims. Such changing circumstances altered Muslim sensibilities, affecting the ways in which Muslims reimagined their relationships with other religious communities and found sanction for them in their readings of their holiest text. Such reimaginings are signaled by the changing conceptions of the purview of jihad/*qital* that emerge in these exegetical works.

Notes

1. Mujahid ibn Jabr, *Tafsir Mujahid*, ed. 'Abd al-Rahman al-Tahir ibn Muhammad al-Surati (Islamabad, n.d.).
2. See Ibn Kathir, *Tafsir al-Qur'an al-'azim* (Beirut: Dar al-Jil, 1990), 1:5.
3. Fuat Sezgin, *Geschichte des arabischen Schrifttums* (hereafter *GAS*) (Leiden: Brill, 1967), 1:29.
4. For example, al-Dhahabi, *Mizan al-i'tidal fi naqd al-rijal*, ed. Badr al-Din al-Na'sani (Cairo: Muhammad Amin al-Khanji, 1907), 3:9.
5. Muqatil ibn Sulayman, *Tafsir Muqatil ibn Sulayman*, ed. 'Abd Allah Mahmud Shihata (Beirut: Mu'assasat al-Ta'rikh al-'Arabi, 2002).
6. For whom see *GAS*, 1:36–37; *Encyclopaedia of Islam*, 2nd ed. (Leiden: Brill, 1960–2003; hereafter *EI²*), 7:508–9.
7. *Tanwir al-miqbas min tafsir Ibn 'Abbas* (Beirut: Dar al-Kutub al-'Ilmiyya, 1992). For this discussion, see Andrew Rippin, "*Tafsir Ibn 'Abbas* and Criteria for Dating Early *Tafsir* Texts," *Jerusalem Studies in Arabic and Islam* 18 (1994): 38–83; Harald Motzki, "Dating the So-Called *Tafsir Ibn 'Abbas*: Some Additional Remarks," *Jerusalem Studies in Arabic and Islam* 31 (2006): 147–63.
8. In this I am in agreement with Josef van Ess, *Theologie und Gesellschaft im 2. und 3. Jahrhundert der Hidschra: Eine Geschichte des religiösen Denkens im frühen Islam* (Berlin: Walter de Gruyter, 1995), 1:300–302; and Marco Schöller, "*Sira* and *Tafsir*: Muhammad al-Kalbi on the News of Medina," in Harald Motzki, ed., *The Biography of Muhammad: The Issue of the Sources* (Leiden: Brill, 2000), 42–44.
9. See "'Abd al-Razzaq al-San'ani," *Encyclopaedia of Islam*, 3rd ed., ed. Gudrun Krämer et al. (Leiden: Brill, 2011; online), 1:7–9.
10. *Jami' al-bayan fi tafsir al-Qur'an* (Beirut: Dar al-Kutub al-'Ilmiyya, 1997).
11. For more details, see "Al-Tabari," *EI²*, 10:11–15.
12. Al-Wahidi, *Al-Wasit fi tafsir al-Qur'an al-majid*, ed. 'Adil Ahmad 'Abd al-Mawjud et al. (Beirut: Dar al-Kutub al-'Ilmiyya, 1994).
13. "Al-Wahidi," *EI²*, 11:48.
14. Al-Zamakhshari, *Al-Kashshaf 'an haqa'iq ghawamid al-tanzil wa-'uyun al-aqawil fi wujuh al-ta'wil*, ed. Adil Ahmad 'Abd al-Mawjud and 'Ali Muhammad Mu'awwid (Riyadh: Maktabat al-'Ubaykan, 1998).
15. "Al-Zamakhshari," *EI²*, 11:432–34.
16. *Al-Tafsir al-kabir* (Beirut: Dar Ihya' al-Turath al-'Arabi, 1999).
17. Al-Qurtubi, *Al-Jami' li ahkam al-Qur'an*, ed. 'Abd al-Razzaq al-Mahdi (Beirut: Dar al-Kitab al-'Arabi, 2001).
18. "Al-Kurtubi," *EI²*, 5:512–13.
19. Mujahid, *Tafsir*, 169. This report from Mujahid is transmitted by 'Abd al-Rahman (ibn Zayd) from Ibrahim (al-Nakha'i) from Adam from Warqa' from Ibn Abi Najih.
20. Ibid., 170.
21. Muqatil, *Tafsir*, 3:130.
22. *Tanwir al-miqbas*, 353.
23. 'Abd al-Razzaq, *Tafsir*, 2:408.
24. Al-Tabari, *Tafsir*, 9:161.
25. 'Abd Allah ibn Abi Najih transmitted a recension of the Qur'an commentary of Abu Bishr Warqa' ibn 'Umar (d. 776), which was used by Mujahid ibn Jabr. See *GAS*, 1:37.
26. This is 'Abd al-Malik ibn 'Abd al-'Aziz ibn Jurayj, the author of a *Kitab al-tafsir* in which he quoted from early authorities such as Ibn 'Abbas 'Ikrima and Mujahid, among others. This *tafsir* was used by al-Tabari and by al-Tha'labi (d. 1035) in his *al-Kashf wa al-bayan fi tafsir al-Qur'an*. He was also a well-regarded scholar of hadith and jurist and the first Meccan to arrange hadith systematically. See *GAS*, 1:91.
27. Al-Tabari, *Tafsir*, 9:161–62.
28. Ibid., 9:162

29. 'Abd al-Rahman ibn Zayd ibn Aslam al-'Adawi al-Madani was the son of the well-known companion Zayd ibn Aslam, from whom the former transmitted hadiths. Ibn Zayd was known to have composed a Qur'an commentary, which was used by al-Tabari, and a work titled *Kitab al-nasikh wa al-mansukh*. See GAS, 1:38. Ibn Zayd's exegesis of specific Qur'anic verses frequently reveals a hawkish disposition, compared with a number of his contemporaries; see Asma Afsaruddin, *Striving in the Path of God: Jihad and Martyrdom in Islamic Thought* (Oxford: Oxford University Press, forthcoming). This section on the exegeses of Qur'an 22: 39–40 is derived from chap. 2 of the book.

30. I could not locate him in the usual sources.

31. Al-Tabari, *Tafsir*, 9:163.

32. Ibid.

33. Ibid., 9:163–64.

34. Ibid., 9:164.

35. This appears to be Rufay', father of the Umayyad caliph 'Abd al-'Aziz, who transmitted from 'Ali and Ibn 'Abbas. He was regarded by Ibn Hibban as one of the *thiqat* (reliable transmitters of hadith); Ibn Hajar, *Tahdhib al-tahdhib*, ed. Khalil Ma'mun Shiha et al. (Beirut: Mu'assasat al-Risala, 1996), 2:173.

36. This appears to be the well-known early exegete with the full name of al-Dahhak ibn Muzahim al-Hillali, whose *tafsir* was frequently consulted by later scholars. There are, however, a number of authorities by the name of al-Dahhak, and the specific referent is not absolutely clear here. For al-Dahhak ibn Muzahim, who related from Ibn 'Umar, Ibn al-'Abbas, Abu Hurayra, and Anas ibn Malik, see GAS, 1:29–30, and sources cited therein. Ibn Qutayba described him as a learned man/teacher (*mu'allim*); see his *Kitab al-ma'arif*, ed. Tharwat 'Ukkasha (Cairo: Matba'at Dar al-Kutub, 1960), 547.

37. His name is given as Rufay' ibn Mihran al-Riyahi al-Basri, who embraced Islam two years after the death of the Prophet and reported hadith from 'Ali, Ibn 'Abbas, Ibn Mas'ud, and 'A'isha, among others. He is generally regarded as a reliable transmitter and was a well-known Qur'an reciter. A Qur'an commentary known as *Tafsir Abi al-'Aliya wa al-Rabi'* (the latter a reference to al-Rabi' ibn Anas, d. 756) was used by al-Tabari and later by al-Tha'labi. See Ibn Hajar, *Tahdhib*, 2:172–73; GAS, 1:34.

38. Al-Tabari, *Tafsir*, 9:164–66.

39. Ibid., 9:166–67.

40. Al-Wahidi, *Wasit*, 3:273.

41. Ibid., 3:272–73.

42. Al-Zamakhshari, *Kashshaf*, 4:199.

43. Ibid.

44. Al-Razi, *Tafsir*, 8:229.

45. Ibid.

46. Muhammad ibn al-Sa'ib al-Kalbi was known for his commentary on the Qur'an and for his knowledge of history, genealogy, and geography. He was known to have pro-Shi'i proclivities. His *Tafsir* work draws heavily on Ibn 'Abbas's commentary but was not used by al-Tabari; cf. GAS, 1:34–35.

47. This is Aws ibn 'Abd Allah ibn al-Rab'i (death date not found), who reported from Abu Hurayra, 'A'isha, Ibn 'Abbas, 'Abd Allah ibn 'Umar, and others. His reputation as a transmitter is rather mixed; see Ibn Hajar, *Tahdhib*, 1:300–301.

48. Al-Razi, *Tafsir*, 8:229.

49. His full name is Abu Ishaq Ibrahim ibn al-Sari, author of the well-known commentary *Ma'ani al-Qur'an wa i'rabuhu*; see GAS, 9:81–82.

50. Al-Razi uses the term *al-sawami'* metonymically here to refer to all places of worship belonging to the People of the Book.

51. Al-Razi, *Tafsir*, 8:229.

52. Ibid., 8:229–30.

53. Ibid., 8:230.

54. Ibid.

55. Ibid.

56. Ibid.

57. Al-Qurtubi, *Tafsir*, 12:66, where he points out that al-Tirmidhi had deemed this hadith to be *hasan* (good). A variant of this hadith is transmitted without mention of Ibn 'Abbas, however, and ends with Sa'id ibn Jubayr.

58. Ibid., 12:67.

59. This is the early Syrian exegete, Abu Muhammad 'Abd Allah ibn 'Atiyya ibn 'Ali ibn Habib al-Dimashqi, who derives his name from having been born in the mosque of 'Atiya in Damascus; see *GAS*, 1:45. There is also the later Andalusian exegete named Ibn 'Atiyya (d. 1146). It is more likely that al-Qurtubi has the earlier exegete in mind rather than the later one, since he is citing mainly very early sources here.

60. He is 'Uwaymir ibn Malik/ibn Zayd or Ibn 'Amir or Ibn Tha'laba; other appellations are also given. He belonged to the Khazraj tribe among the Ansar and related hadith from Muhammad, 'A'isha, and Zayd ibn Thabit. He was described by the Prophet as "the wise man of my community" (*hakim ummati*) and died c. 652 (other death dates given); see Ibn Hajar, *Tahdhib*, 4:408–9.

61. Al-Qurtubi, *Tafsir*, 12:67–68.

62. Ibid., 12:68.

63. This is the famous grammarian Abu 'Ubayda, author of the *Majaz al-Qur'an*.

64. Al-Qurtubi, *Tafsir*, 12:69.

65. Ibid.

66. Ibid.

67. Cf. al-Tabari, *Tafsir*, 2:196. See my fuller treatment of this discussion in Afsaruddin, *Striving in the Path of God*, chap. 2.

68. For an extensive study of al-Shafi'i's major legal treatise, *al-Risala*, see Majid Khadduri, *al-Shafi'i's* Risala (Cambridge, U.K.: Islamic Texts Society, 1987).

69. See Ibn Kathir, *Tafsir*, 3:219.

3

God's War and His Warriors

*The First Hundred Years of Syriac Accounts
of the Islamic Conquests*

MICHAEL PHILIP PENN

An interesting aspect of the recent popular literature on jihad is the emphasis placed on the Islamic conquests of the seventh century. Author after author returns to the conquests as proof that Christian and Islamic civilizations are fated to clash, as justification for why conflicts ranging from the First Crusade to the invasion of Iraq are defensive wars, and as a harbinger for all future Christian-Muslim encounters.[1] The specific ways in which these twenty-first-century writers use the conquests are historically contingent. Nevertheless, these modern authors participate in a tradition dating back thirteen hundred years of seeing the Islamic conquests as a privileged moment that, once properly interpreted, reveals a transcendent truth.

Despite also having a strong interest in seventh-century history, the first generations of Christians under Muslim rule asked very different questions regarding the Islamic conquests. Much of this comes, of course, from the numerous differences between late antiquity and modernity. Much, however, stems from another cause. Contrary to the common maxim, history is not always written by the winners. Our earliest and our most extensive descriptions of the Islamic conquests were composed not by victorious Muslims but, rather, by defeated Christians, particularly by Christians from northern Mesopotamia who wrote in an Aramaic dialect called Syriac. These Syriac Christians lived in what are today Iran, Iraq, Israel, Lebanon, Palestine, Syria, and eastern Turkey. They composed our largest and our most diverse corpus of early Christian writings on Islam. When these Syriac Christians wrote about the Islamic conquests, the primary question they asked was not what the conquests taught about Islam but what they taught about Christianity.

Like many modern authors, early Syriac writers saw the Islamic conquests as a holy war. Their understanding of holy war, however, differed greatly from what we find in much of the current literature. For these modern writers, the term *holy war* is deployed pejoratively; the conquests were a holy war because Muslims wrong-fully claimed that they were justified by God. Syriac Christians also viewed the Islamic conquests as a holy war but in this case a legitimate one. That is, from the perspective of Syriac writers, the Arabs' destruction of the Persian empire, their capture of much of the Byzantine empire, and the subjugation of eastern Christians to Islamic rule were the outcome of God's war against Christians. Syriac writings thus present the unusual circumstance of a group interpreting not its victory but its defeat as the outcome of a holy war.

Attributing the conquests to divine intervention built on the Hebrew Bible's notion of war as an act of God's retribution, correction, or punishment. It gave Syriac Christians a convenient explanation for Arab military victory. But it also raised a very awkward set of questions: If the Islamic conquests were God's war, did this make the Arabs God's chosen warriors? And if the Arabs were God's warriors, what does this say about the legitimacy of their rule of Christian subjects? The result is a very different discussion about the seventh century from what we find in modern anti-Muslim writings. Make no mistake: ancient conversations among Syriac Christians regarding the conquests were neither homogeneous nor pacific. They represent neither a pinnacle of ecumenicism nor a role model for interfaith dialogue. Nevertheless, a better appreciation of the vast differences between the earliest Christian interpretations of the Islamic conquests and modern constructs of the same event can help problematize overly facile depictions of early Christian-Muslim interactions.

Particularly important for challenging the often reductionist character of modern discussions of early Christian-Muslim encounters is a better appreciation for the diversity found among our most ancient Christian writings about Muslims. Even a study limited to the first hundred years of Syriac conquest accounts quickly reveals that early Christian reactions to the rise of Islam were far from univocal.[2] Some of this diversity comes from the multiplicity of genres in which conquest accounts appear: chronicles, letters, apocalypses, scriptural commentaries, disputations, and vitae. Theological divisions among Syriac Christians made these reports even more varied. As a result of a series of theological controversies, especially those concerning how best to express Christ's divinity and humanity, from the fifth century onward, Syriac Christians were divided into a set of competing Christian factions. At the time of the Islamic conquests, the most prominent Syriac churches included those of Chalcedonian Christians, who were in theological agreement with the Byzantines;[3] Miaphysites, who emphasized Christ's single nature;[4] East Syrian Christians, who placed greater emphasis on Christ having a dual nature;[5] and Maronites, who initially supported the seventh-century doctrine of Christ having a single will. Each of these groups often combined its interpretation of the conquests with a polemic against other Christians. Syriac descriptions of the conquests also changed dramatically over the first century of Muslim rule as shifting historical circumstances affected the ways later Christians represented an increasingly distant past event. As a result, a chronological examination of Syriac references to the Islamic conquests reveals how a linguistically unified but theologically divided community employed a wide range of interpretive strategies to explain how Christians could lose a holy war.

The Earliest Reactions: Syriac Accounts in the Mid-Seventh Century

From the viewpoint of the twenty-first century, the Islamic conquests were a world-changing event. Few in the seventh century, however, saw them this way. This disconnection between modern and ancient assessments of the rise of Islam becomes especially clear in the earliest extant Syriac writings about the conquests. For most of the seventh century, Syriac authors do not speak about Islam as a religion, nor do they anticipate that their Arab conquerors will be around very long. Nevertheless, these first allusions to Arab military success lay the groundwork for the more involved and impassioned discussions that soon would follow.

The earliest reference to the Islamic conquests appears in very modest trappings. In 637, a writer used extra space at the front of a Gospel manuscript to compose what appears to be an eyewitness report of the conquests.[6] Even in its fragmentary state, the extant text clearly refers to Muhammad, to Arabs, to towns surrendering, and to substantial Byzantine casualties. This brief autographon, most likely written while the conquests were occurring, foreshadows many of the characteristics found throughout the first few decades of Syriac writings about the conquests. As in this note, the earliest strata of Syriac accounts report the conquests in an annalistic fashion. They document when and where battles were fought and often try to approximate Byzantine and civilian casualties. These early works do not speak of their conquerors as having any particular religion, nor do they suggest that Arab military expansion was religiously motivated.

Just three years after the *Account of 637*, a priest named Thomas composed a set of writings now called the *Chronicle of 640*.[7] Thomas's chronicle contains two brief references to the conquests. In an entry for the year 634, Thomas speaks of a battle in Palestine between the Byzantines and the "Arabs of Muhammad," in which the Arabs killed four thousand villagers and ravaged the region.[8] Immediately afterward appears an entry for the year 635/36 in which Thomas speaks of the Arab conquest of all of Syria, the invasion of Persia, and the killing of monks near Mardin, including Thomas's brother.[9] Particularly striking for someone who has lived through the conquests is how little Thomas has to say about them—in a twenty-eight-folio document, only five sentences. For Thomas, it was the Byzantine emperor Heraclius's defeat of the Persians twenty-five years earlier that was momentous, not the military conflicts of his own day.

In later decades, as Arab rule continued, Syriac writers felt increasingly obliged to present at least brief explanations for the conquests themselves. For example, among the extant letters of the East Syrian leader Isho'yahb III (d. 659) can be found one brief reference to the conquests. In a letter written sometime between 649 and 659, Isho'yahb notes that the "Arabs to whom God has at this time given rule over the world" are generally benevolent toward Christians.[10] Isho'yahb's statement that Arab rule has been divinely ordained is a claim that will become increasingly frequent and increasingly developed among later writers.

A few years after the death of Isho'yahb III, an anonymous East Syrian Christian composed a chronicle that modern scholars most often call the *Khuzistan Chronicle*.[11] Amid the several pages detailing the Islamic conquests appear only two brief sentences that try to explain the conquest's origins and the reason for Arab military success. Similarly to Isho'yahb III, the chronicler informs his readers that it was God who raised up the sons of Ishmael and God who gave them victory over the Persian and Byzantine empires, but he provides no further motivation for the Arabs' actions.[12]

Soon after the *Khuzistan Chronicle*, two Syriac authors provided much more partisan explanations for the conquests. A Miaphysite account now called the *Apocalypse of Pseudo-Ephrem* may be the earliest Syriac apocalypse that refers to Islam.[13] This seventh-century vision of the world's end depicts the conquests as the harbinger of the end times. According to *Pseudo-Ephrem*, the Islamic conquests were meant to punish Byzantine impiety, especially their persecution of Miaphysites.[14] But soon the Sons of Hagar became just as evil as their Christian predecessors. The Sons of Hagar "soak the earth with blood," impaling old men, trampling on infants they cast out of their mothers' arms, and enslaving all who somehow survive their onslaught.[15] In response to their wickedness, God will release the armies of Gog and Magog formerly imprisoned by Alexander the Great. The Antichrist will then come, soon to be followed by the eschaton and the last judgment.

Miaphysites were not the only Syriac Christians whose conquest accounts were shaped by intra-Christian conflicts. Around the early 680s, a Maronite bishop named George of Resh'aina wrote a brief biography of Maximus the Confessor.[16] Most Chalcedonian Christians approved of Maximus's opposition to the controversial doctrine of monothelitism, which claimed that although Christ had a divine and a human nature, he had only a single will. Bishop George disagreed. His text begins: "The history of the wicked Maximus of Palestine, who blasphemed against his creator and his tongue was torn out."[17] The extant text of this exposé begins with Maximus being born from the illegitimate union of a Persian slave woman and a Jew, and it cuts off in the midst of Maximus converting a convent of nuns to his beliefs. The intervening six folios make several brief references to the Arabs and their conquests but contain only a quick allusion to the Arabs being a God-sent punishment. More important for George is connecting the conquests with Maximus himself. George claims that once Syria was conquered by the Arabs, the Byzantine authorities no longer were able to combat Maximus's doctrines. After Maximus gained a following in Arab-controlled Syria, his influence moved into Africa, Sicily, and Rome. As Maximus's theology spread, so, too, did the Arabs who kept "following the wicked Maximus" as "the wrath of God punished every place which had accepted his error."[18] From George's perspective, the conquests had no connection to Islam, or really to the Arabs; rather, they primarily served as the catalyst and the punishment for Christian heresy.

A survey of the first few decades of Syriac conquest accounts suggests that their authors felt that they had much more pressing issues to address than the rise of Islam. Although the relatively little attention that these early authors gave to the conquests may surprise modern readers, it is perfectly understandable given their historical context. For the majority of seventh-century Syriac Christians, the most involved geopolitical changes came not with the Islamic conquests of the 630s but from Sassanian invasion of Byzantine territory in 602 and Heraclius's reconquest in 628. These Byzantine-Persian wars were much more destructive than the Islamic conquests.[19] In its first decades, Islam generally did not missionize to non-Arabs, and conversion rates among non-Arabs remained low.[20] Local governing structures were left almost completely intact,[21] and even the much-bemoaned poll tax (jizya) seems at first to have been more a continuation and gradual expansion of previous revenue structures than a radically new burden.[22] As a result, what we call the Islamic conquests were first described in terms where there was nothing "Islamic" about them, and what we see as one of the world's most important encounters barely received mention by its contemporaries.

The End Is Near: Conquest Accounts in the Late Seventh Century

Soon after *Pseudo-Ephrem* and the *Life of Maximus* were composed, the political situation of Syriac Christians changed drastically, forcing them to reevaluate the conquests and their aftermath. Of particular import were the changes brought about through the consolidation of Umayyad rule under the caliph 'Abd al-Malik ibn Marwan and his policies of Islamization. It is in this context that Syriac authors from the last decades of the seventh century began attaching a religious significance to the Islamic conquests that they previously lacked.

An increased emphasis on the conquests and their meaning first appears in the work of the East Syrian monk John bar Penkaye.[23] Around 687, John finished his *Book of Main Points*, a world history from creation to his own day.[24] John wrote his work during the second Arab civil war which began soon after the death of the caliph Mu'awiya II in 683. For the following nine years, the Umayyad caliphs Marwan (r. 684–685) and his son 'Abd al-Malik (r. 685–705) fought against a rival caliph, 'Abd Allah ibn al-Zubayr. To make John's situation even more precarious, when he composed the *Book of Main Points*, his region of Iraq was not under the control of either of these contending caliphs. Rather, a group

of non-Arab prisoners of war had just staged an initially successful anti-Arab rebellion and had recently taken the city of Nisibis, located about sixty miles southwest of the monastery John inhabited.[25] It was during this time of a local
rebellion amid a much larger civil war that John's abbot asked him to write his
history.

Unlike the previous generation of Syriac authors, John focuses not on what
happened during the Islamic conquests but on why the conquests occurred in the
first place. He could wait no more than a single sentence into his narrative before
launching into the explanatory framework that will dominate his understanding
of the rise of Islam:

> But it is not right that we should think of their coming in an ordinary
> way, for it was a divine deed. And before He called them, He previously
> prepared them to hold Christians in honor. In the same way, concerning
> our rank of solitaries, there was securely upon them some sort of com-
> mandment from God so that they would hold [it] in honor. And when
> these ones came, in accord with a divine commandment, they seized
> without battle and without fighting, so to speak, two kingdoms. Then in
> a contemptible way—as a brand is taken from the fire—without arms
> and without human trickery God thus gave victory into their hands so
> that what was written concerning them might be fulfilled: "one pursued
> a thousand and two put ten thousand to flight." How was it possible,
> then, that men who were naked and rode without armor and without
> shield would be victorious without divine aid [from] the one who called
> them from the ends of the earth to destroy with them a sinful kingdom
> and through them to humble the proud spirit of the Persians?[26]

Here we do indeed have a holy war. God called, prepared, commanded, and gave
victory to the Sons of Hagar in such a way that everyone could see that "the entire
world was handed over to the Arabs."[27] But why would God do this?

It is this question of theodicy that dominates much of John's work. John interprets the previous six centuries of church history as a cycle of Christians learning
from their tribulations, growing closer to God, and, once their situation improves,
falling back into error.[28] Applying this heuristic to his own time, John claims that
once Roman persecution of Christians subsided in the early fourth century, theological error overtook the church. It was the resulting Byzantine theology that led
to their defeat by the Arabs.[29]

Initially, God's new warriors did their job well. Nevertheless, according to John,
"It was right that the deeds done by the Sons of Hagar also should be avenged."[30]
Thus, the recent conquerors began to suffer exactly the same plight as the Christians before them. As soon as their military conquests were successfully concluded,
they, too, fell into laxity, resulting in internal divisions and civil war. Their first
civil war ended in the rule of Mu'awiya, whose peaceful reign induced another

cycle of laxity and disaster.[31] This brings us to John's own day, when, in the midst of the second Arab civil war, John and his contemporaries were suffering also from famine and plague.[32] So what will happen next? Here John again diverges from earlier seventh-century Syriac authors. According to John, humanity lost its last chance for reform during the peace under Mu'awiya. God has thus removed his heavenly care from the world, ushering in the beginning of the end.[33] As for the Sons of Hagar, according to John, it is the anti-Arab forces who just recently took control of Nisibis that will end their kingdom.[34] This victory, like that of the Arabs before them, will be short-lived, however, as John is "aware that the end of the ages has arrived for us."[35]

Although John dedicates only one book of his fifteen-book world history to discussing the Arabs, the *Book of Main Points* "was composed first of all as a Christian response to the rise of Islam."[36] John wrote his history backward.[37] Because of the tribulations that he and his community currently face, he is convinced that the eschaton will soon arrive. This motivates him to look back in time to establish an ongoing pattern of God's pedagogical relationship with humanity and to find a decisive moment, the Islamic conquests and their immediate aftermath, when this pattern was broken to the point of no return. Although his predecessors briefly alluded to God having given the Arabs military victory, John shows a level of theological engagement with the conquests not found in previous writers. Many of the questions John struggles with (why the conquests; what will happen to the Arabs; what will happen to us), along with his answers (we suffered because of our sins; God will defeat them; the world soon will end) dominate the writings produced in the following decade. Nevertheless, the rapidly changing political environment of the late seventh century will cause these slightly later authors to write very differently about such issues from how John did.

John ended up being wrong. The rebellion of former prisoners of war was easily put down, Ibn al-Zubayr was defeated in Mecca in 692, 'Abd al-Malik became the sole caliph, and his descendants would control the Umayyad caliphate until 750. The end of the second Arab civil war was not, however, an unmitigated blessing for Syriac Christians; as part of his consolidation of power, 'Abd al-Malik began a process of Islamization that drastically affected Christians under Muslim rule. The political stability following the second Arab civil war along with 'Abd al-Malik's substantial building program, the minting of his own coins, a census, and tax reform all suggested that the Arabs had established a successor state to the Byzantine and Persian empires that was not going away anytime soon.[38] As head of this state, 'Abd al-Malik took on the role of championing Islam.[39] Toward the end of the second Arab civil war, Muslim proclamations of faith and polemics against Christian theology begin to appear on mile markers,[40] coins,[41] and, most important, the newly constructed Dome of the Rock.[42] Built on the Temple Mount in Jerusalem and inscribed with Qur'anic passages decrying trinitarian theology, the Dome of the Rock clearly pronounced Islam's intent to be a successor religion to Christianity.[43] At the same time that 'Abd al-Malik was making

Islam increasingly prominent, he also began to regulate public displays of Christianity, especially of the cross.[44]

The immediate literary response to these changing circumstances was a series of Syriac apocalypses, the most popular being a document now called the *Apocalypse of Pseudo-Methodius*.[45] This text claims to have been written by Bishop Methodius (d. 311), to whom God revealed "the generations and kingdoms" from the time of Adam until the world's end seven thousand years later.[46] The real author, however, most likely wrote during the conclusion of the second Arab civil war in 690/91.[47] At this time, 'Abd al-Malik had just conquered Mesopotamia, and it became increasingly obvious that, contrary to the predictions of Christians such as John bar Penkaye, the civil war would not destroy the Arabs. 'Abd al-Malik had also just instituted tax reform, increasing the amount of revenue gathered by the Arab government, and he began constructing the Dome of the Rock.[48] In response to these developments, the author of *Pseudo-Methodius* adamantly proclaimed the invincibility of the Byzantine empire and the Arabs' imminent demise. Any day now, the last king of the Greeks would rise up, defeat the Sons of Ishmael in a holy war, reclaim Jerusalem, avenge persecuted Christians, punish apostates, hand over earthly rule to Christ, and help usher in the end of time.[49]

Like previous Syriac writings, *Pseudo-Methodius* stresses God's role in initiating the Islamic conquests. But in *Pseudo-Methodius*, as in the writings of John bar Penkaye before him, the present-day crisis is so great that these disasters serve not as a call for repentance but, rather, as a signal of the world's impending demise. *Pseudo-Methodius* assures its readers that "It was not because God loves [the Sons of Ishmael] that He allowed them to enter the kingdom of the Christians."[50] The Sons of Ishmael are simply God's tool to chastise Christians and to separate the truly faithful from the faithless. *Pseudo-Methodius* predicts that the seventh-century Arabs will rule for only seventy years, a period whose end had just about come when *Pseudo-Methodius* was written.[51] *Pseudo-Methodius*'s discussion of these last years of Christian servitude to the Sons of Ishmael corresponds to the author's own day. At this time, Christians will suffer even more through plagues, famine, and insatiable taxation, and the Sons of Ishmael will boast about their conquests, proclaiming that "the Christians have no savior."[52]

At this point in the narrative, *Pseudo-Methodius* introduces a new character into its eschatological drama, the last king of the Greeks, who launches a holy war against the blaspheming Sons of Ishmael in which he quickly defeats the Arabs and enslaves them a hundred times more bitterly than they did the Christians. The king next punishes Christian apostates and, from Jerusalem, reigns over a ten-year period of peace and prosperity. An invasion from the unclean people of the North follows, during which the king of the Greeks gives up earthly rule to Christ by placing his crown upon the True Cross as it ascends to heaven. The end of time concludes with Jesus's second coming and his defeat of the "Son of Perdition."[53]

Similarly to *Pseudo-Ephrem* and John bar Penkaye, the most likely Miaphysite author of *Pseudo-Methodius* considers the conquests as God's response to Christian sin, and, as do his apocalyptically bent predecessors, he predicts the brevity of Arab reign.[54] *Pseudo-Methodius*, however, represents "an important shift in the relation between apocalypticism and violence in the history of Christianity," especially in its depiction of Arab rule, its focus on Jerusalem, and its figure of the last Greek king.[55] *Pseudo-Methodius* presents a much more negative depiction of Muslims than that found in almost any other early Syriac text, and through emphasizing the role of a Byzantine emperor in overthrowing Jerusalem's erstwhile conquerors, in *Pseudo-Methodius* "Christian apocalyptic had, for the first time, issued a call for taking up arms against current foes."[56]

A year or two after *Pseudo-Methodius*'s initial composition, an author from the city of Edessa created an abridged and modified version of the work.[57] Modern scholars often refer to this slightly later text as the *Edessene Apocalypse*.[58] Although heavily dependent on *Pseudo-Methodius*, the *Edessene Apocalypse* makes several important changes to its apocalyptic schema. In the *Edessene Apocalypse*, the Sons of Ishmael's oppression of Christians results in the second Arab civil war. During this time, nature itself witnesses against the Arabs' infidelity through severe drought and famine. To foreshadow the final end of Arab rule, the *Edessene Apocalypse* draws on an earlier Syriac tradition, the *Judas Cyriacus Legend*, which has Constantine's mother, Helena, discover the True Cross in Jerusalem and make for Constantine a bridle from its nails.[59] According to the *Edessene Apocalypse*, in 692, an unridden horse will enter a church in Constantinople and place its head in this bridle, signaling that the "Kingdom of the Christians has come."[60] A king of the Greeks will then rise up and overthrow the Sons of Ishmael. This new Constantine will pursue the Sons of Ishmael to Mecca, where their kingdom will end. Unlike the case in *Pseudo-Methodius*, the eschaton does not soon follow the Arabs' demise. Rather, the kingdom of the Greeks will continue for 208 more years, and only then will the unclean nations previously vanquished by Alexander the Great invade. God will gather these nations in Mecca, and his angels will kill them with hailstones. Subsequently, the Son of Perdition will take control of all the world, except for the city of Edessa. When the Son of Perdition enters Jerusalem, another king of the Greeks will rise up and, as in *Pseudo-Methodius*, hand over his crown to Christ's cross on Golgotha. At this point, all living things will die, the world will end, and the last judgment will commence.[61]

The *Edessene Apocalypse*, like *Pseudo-Methodius* before it, uses a holy war to destroy the Sons of Ishmael quickly. But in the *Edessene Apocalypse*, this holy war is tied even more closely with sacred space. The text specifies that the defeat of the Sons of Ishmael and the unclean nations of the North will occur in Mecca, that the city of Edessa will remain inviolate, and that the victories of the now two kings of the Greeks will both follow reconquests of Jerusalem. The text's appropriation of the *Judas Cyriacus Legend* further strengthens this Jerusalem focus. Not only is the king of the Greek's victory ensured by the cross's nails initially found on Golgotha, but the reference to an unridden horse also provides a scriptural echo of Jesus's entry into Jerusalem. For Syriac Christians, this apocalyptic appropriation of sacred space would have been especially poignant during a time when 'Abd al-Malik was establishing Jerusalem as an Islamic center and began to regulate Christian displays of the cross.

The final anti-Arab apocalypse written during the reign of 'Abd al-Malik is known as the *Apocalypse of John the Little* and appears as the last section of a Miaphysite text titled the *Gospel of the Twelve Apostles*.[62] Unlike *Pseudo-Methodius*, this slightly later apocalypse portrays the Arabs as the last of Daniel's four kingdoms. Once the previous kingdoms of the Romans, Persians, and Medes have become corrupt, God fulfills Daniel's prophecy that "the king of the South will be strong."[63] The Lord calls forth from the descendants of Ishmael a "people of a deformed aspect," led by a warrior whom they claim is a prophet. These people of the South conquer the people of the North, causing them to suffer greatly, especially under constant demands for tribute. Because they "hate the Lord's name," during the final ten and a half years of their rule, the people of the South persecute Christians. In response, God's angel causes a civil war, dividing them into two parties, each claiming a different king. A bloody conflict follows at the "fountain of the water," an allusion to the fountain of Zamzam in Mecca, where in 692, 'Abd al-Malik defeated Ibn al-Zybayr.[64] At this point, "a man from the North" will rise up and begin to destroy the Arab forces. This figure is very different from *Pseudo-Methodius*'s and the *Edessene Apocalypse*'s king of the Greeks. The man from the North proclaims that his victories come not from his own power, and the text reminds its reader that it is the Lord who forces the people of the South back to lands from which they came. The man from the North neither pursues them nor ultimately defeats them. Rather, God reduces them "without a battle" to the point where they will never again take up arms.[65]

Most likely written toward the end of 'Abd al-Malik's reign,[66] the *Apocalypse of John the Little* gives the Byzantine emperor a much smaller role in the Arabs' downfall. It provides little discussion of why the Islamic conquests occurred in the first place, there is no reconquest of Jerusalem, and the apocalypse does not conclude with the world's end. Its anti-Arab message is also framed by the anti-Chalcedonian and anti-Jewish polemics in the documents that immediately precede it in the manuscript. It thus "marks a transition between a period of apocalyptic hope and a more stable though more negative situation in which the various Christian churches, the Jews and the Muslims had to deal with each other and find their identities and boundaries."[67]

Preparing for the Long Haul: Conquest Accounts in the First Half of the Eighth Century

As the Umayyad dynasty solidified under 'Abd al-Malik and his successors, Christian hopes for a quick end to Arab rule began to fizzle; after the *Apocalypse of John the Little*, there are no other extant Syriac apocalypses for more than two centuries.

Discussion of the conquests in other genres, however, continued to proliferate. These conquest accounts from the first half of the eighth century do not describe specific battles or predict an impending eschaton. Instead, they situate the conquests within a broader context of scriptural exegesis, king lists, and apologetics. In contradistinction to the late-seventh-century apocalypses, these slightly later texts downplay the historical and theological significance of the conquests. They suggest that although the Arabs have established a long-lasting kingdom, this kingdom's rise and persistence should present little challenge to Christianity.

Just as the late-seventh-century apocalypses tried to combat the increasingly obvious longevity of Arab rule by proclaiming its imminent end, so, too, did attempts to minimize the conquests' significance come at a time when their results further threatened Syriac communities. 'Abd al-Malik's successors expanded his policies of Islamization. Muslim officials more readily intervened in church affairs.[68] We begin to find more explicitly anti-Christian measures such as 'Umar II (r. 717–720) forbidding non-Muslims to give legal testimony against Muslims.[69] The early eighth century also witnessed greater pressures for conversion, especially after 'Umar II legislated that converts to Islam would now be exempt from the poll tax.[70] Syriac literature of the early eighth century also reflects a growing awareness of the theological challenges put forth by Islam, with the first disputation texts appearing in the early 700s.[71] In such a context, it is not surprising that Syriac Christians would also reevaluate their interpretations of the Islamic conquests.

The Miaphysite bishop Jacob of Edessa provides a useful illustration for the conquests' changing role around the turn of the eighth century. Although Jacob makes dozens of references to Muslims in his writings, there appears only one mention of the conquests in Jacob's extant works.[72] It occurs among a collection of Jacob's brief scriptural commentaries, or *Scholia*, and it is unclear when in Jacob's lifetime it was written. The comment is on the biblical passage 1 Kings 14:21–28, which attributes the Egyptian pharaoh Shishak's successful invasion of Jerusalem to the Israelites' sins. After explaining how the ancient Israelites are a type for Christians, Jacob writes:

> Therefore, on account of the evil of Rehoboam and Judah, God brought on them Shishak, the king of Egypt. And, as holy scripture relates, he took them captive and scattered them and overthrew their cities because of their sins and their provocation. And thus also us: Christ has handed us over because of our sins and many iniquities. And He has subjected us to the Arab's hard yoke. . . . Because we did not notice all this grace and freedom that was given to us and we were ungrateful and deniers of grace, we were handed over to servitude and slavery, just as ancient Judah [was]—for prey and captivity.[73]

On one level, Jacob is doing nothing new here. Like his predecessors, Jacob suggests that the conquests and Eastern Christianity's subjugation to Islamic rule were the result of divine retribution for Christian sinfulness. But Jacob is the first Syriac Christian to develop fully an exegetical strategy that will soon dominate writings about the conquests: he explicitly relates the losers of one holy war to those of another. Just as the sins of God's people in the tenth century B.C.E. allowed a foreign king to take control of Jerusalem and enslave God's chosen, the same happened in the seventh century C.E. The result is just the opposite of what we find in the earlier apocalypses. Now the conquests are no longer extraordinary events so unprecedented that they signal the end of the world. Instead, the conquests are a repeat of biblical history.

Although at first it might seem counterproductive to align oneself with the losers of history, such an analogy has some very concrete payoffs. Not only does the appeal to Christian sin offer a tidy reason for the Arabs' initial military success, but it also points toward the Arabs' eventual, albeit no longer imminent, demise. Even though the Israelites' captivity under foreign invaders lasted for decades or even centuries, their repentance eventually motivated God to destroy their conquerors and free his people. When viewed through the lens of the Hebrew scripture, being God's warrior in a holy war is not always a sign of divine favor.

A different strategy for minimizing the conquests' significance appears in two early-eighth-century texts that speak about Muslim rulers. The first, the *Chronicle ad 705*, is a brief list of caliphs written between 705 and 715.[74] The list begins, "Muhammad entered the land [in] the year 932 of Alexander, son of Philip, the Macedonian. And he reigned seven years. And after him Abu Bakr reigned two years. And after him . . ." The record continues to the beginning of al-Walid I's reign in 705.[75] Although it is filled with several chronological errors and omissions, what makes this inventory particularly striking is its nonchalant presentation. The Prophet Muhammad is just like any other king, there is no need to explain the conquests, and one king follows the other just as in any other kingdom.

Written just a few years later is the aptly named *Chronicle of Disasters*, which explains how a long list of catastrophes "happened according to the just, incomprehensible, and wondrous judgments of God."[76] This inventory of calamities begins with a comet's appearance "when the kingdom of the Sons of Ishmael held power and its control stretched over the entire land, in the days of Walid son of Abd al-Malik, son of Marwan, who reigned at that time."[77] One has to make it through a plague, a drought, a locust infestation, a hurricane, a hailstorm, and several earthquakes before encountering the second reference to Arab rule, when Walid dies and is succeeded by his brother Sulayman, who gathers up all of the Saracens' wealth into a single treasury in Jerusalem. The list ends fairly anticlimactically with a hailstorm killing a number of birds. More interesting than these fowls' unfortunate fate, however, is the way the author interweaves these natural catastrophes with the two references to Umayyad caliphs. Although the text does not explicitly link the kingdom of Ishmael with other listed items, the intercalation of these two rulers in the midst of more conventional misfortunes certainly suggests that these caliphs and their rule may also be part of God's chastisement of Christian sinners.

Both the *Chronicle ad 705* and the *Chronicle of Disasters* are dull reading, and that is part of the point. Reducing the rise of Islam to simply a list of kings or sandwiching the notice of a new Muslim ruler between one hailstorm that damages vineyards and another that destroys birds domesticates the conquests. The last Umayyad-era conquest account, however, shows just how much was at stake in these seemingly innocuous discussions of events. In the 720s, an East Syrian writer claimed to have recorded a conversation between an unnamed monk from the monastery of Beth Hale and an unspecified Arab official who was visiting the monastery. The resulting *Disputation between a Monk of Beth Hale and an Arab Notable* contains an eight-folio discussion between these interlocutors concerning topics such as trinitarian theology, Christian veneration of relics, and the origins of the Qur'an.[78] This supposed transcript ends with the Arab declaring that if it were not for the fear of repercussions, many Arabs would convert to Christianity.[79]

In the *Disputation*, discussions of the conquests play such a central role that its most recent interpreter proclaims, "The relation between political power and right religion is the main problem in the *Disputation*."[80] The Arab notable first raises this issue when he uses Arab military success as proof for Islam's doctrinal correctness: "This is the sign that God loves us and agrees with our confession: that He gave to us authority over all religions and over all nations. See—they are slaves subject to us."[81] Although here written by a Christian author, the argument is identical to that found in a number of early Islamic sources. Passages in Christian works such as the *Book of Main Points* and *Pseudo-Methodius* tried to preempt this line of reasoning, but the *Disputation* is the first Syriac text to have a Muslim character explicitly articulate this challenge.

The monk initially raises two objections. First, similar to what Jacob of Edessa implied in his appeal to biblical history, the monk notes that the world has seen the rise and fall of many kingdoms and that those who first seemed to be military victors later suffered defeat, especially those kingdoms that God used to chastise the Israelites. Then, unlike previous conquest accounts, which often emphasize how the Arabs took control of most of the known world, the monk notes that "You, sons of Ishmael, you hold a small part of the earth, and the whole creation is not subject to your authority."[82] In support, the monk presents a long list of lands and peoples not yet conquered. After having minimized the conquests' chronological and geographical significance, the monk turns to defending specific Christian beliefs and practices.

The two interlocutors return to the conquests at the very end of the *Disputation*, when the Arab asks a question that has undoubtedly been puzzling many eighth-century Christians: "What is the reason why God has handed you over into our hands, and you are driven by us like sheep to slaughter; and your bishops and priests are killed, and the rest are subjugated and enslaved, night and day, to the king's burdens, more bitter than death."[83] At first glance, the

Disputation's responses are almost identical to *Pseudo-Methodius*, on which they clearly depend.[84] There remain, however, two important differences between the *Disputation* and its predecessors. First, by using the format of a dialogue and combining points found scattered throughout works such as *Pseudo-Methodius* into a single paragraph, the *Disputation* provides an easily accessible and potentially reassuring list of why the historically, geographically, and scripturally informed Christian should not see the conquests as a sign of Christianity's inferiority to Islam. Second, the *Disputation* takes what was previously a defensive argument—that despite Arab military success, Christians remain God's chosen—and transforms it into a seemingly counterintuitive claim: the Arabs' victory in the conquests actually proves God's disdain for Muslims. This line of reasoning begins when, unlike in *Pseudo-Methodius*, the *Disputation* quotes Hebrews 12:8 in the second person. "The Lord chastises whomsoever He loves. And if *you* are without chastisement, *you* are strangers and not sons." The implication emerges that *your* lack of suffering is not a sign of divine favor but stems from *you* not being one of God's sons; since the Sons of Ishmael are not part of God's family, God does not even bother to use adversity to correct their behavior. The *Disputation* then combines this motif of kinship with that of inheritance. In the last lines of the manuscript, we learn that God punishes Christians in the temporal world so that they can inherit heaven. Similarly, although a righteous Son of Hagar will not abide in eternal torment, in God's kingdom he still will be considered "as a hired man and not as a son."[85] The *Disputation* thus ends with a sort of divine irony. Through the Islamic conquests, God gave the Arabs territory in this world as a sign that they would not be God's true heirs in the world to come.

Conclusion

Less than a century separated the *Disputation between a Monk of Beth Hale and an Arab Notable* from the *Account of 637*. Nevertheless, the vast differences between the former, a carefully constructed, eight-folio disputation, and the latter, containing brief scribblings on a Gospel fly-leaf, show how much had changed in the intervening hundred years. We need to remember that most later Syriac writers knew less, not more, about the Islamic conquests than their predecessors. The expansion and proliferation of Syriac conquest accounts did not stem from increased knowledge about seventh-century history but, rather, was a form of cultural memory work in which Syriac Christians retold and reinterpreted the Islamic conquests as a tool for addressing contemporary challenges that they and their communities faced. Although genre, theological affiliation, and authorial agenda made each account unique, there remained a strong correlation between their depictions of the Islamic conquests and the historical situation of their authors. The earliest accounts' focus on specific battles and the brevity of their discussions reflected a mid-seventh-century impression of the conquests as just one in a long, ongoing series of military invasions of northern Mesopotamia. The second Arab civil war and 'Abd al-Malik's policies of Islamization caused Syriac authors of the late seventh and early eighth centuries to invest the conquests with much greater significance. Partially in response to the building of the Dome of the Rock, these apocalyptic writings more directly referred to holy war, the reconquest of Jerusalem, and an imminent eschaton. As the second Arab civil war became an increasingly distant memory and Syriac Christians began to face increased pressure for assimilation and conversion, apocalyptic expectations were replaced with more apologetic concerns. Eighth-century authors often downplayed the extent and importance of the conquests, either treating them as a fairly mundane transfer of kingship from one power to another or drawing on biblical parallels to depict the conquests as only a temporary chastisement for Christian sins.

Despite these chronological developments, throughout the first century of Islamic rule, Syriac conquest accounts were constantly driven by the issue of theodicy. Drawing on a long-standing view of God guiding history, Syriac accounts always saw the conquests as divinely inspired. This led to a debate about why God had declared a holy war on Christianity and what would happen to the new warriors he deployed against Christians. Such questions only intensified as Arab rule continued, as Islam became a more visible presence, and as Syriac Christians came under increased pressure to defend their beliefs and practices. Neither Syriac conquest accounts from the first hundred years of Muslim rule nor those from subsequent centuries ever reached a consensus regarding these issues. The very diversity of their opinions challenges any portrayal of a unified Christian reaction to the Arab defeat of Byzantine and Persian forces. Thus, we may conclude that many of the reductionist modern depictions of the Islamic conquests are based more on contemporary concerns and prejudices than they are on the accounts written by the first generations of Christians to encounter Islam.

Notes

1. See, for example, Paul Fregosi, *Jihad in the West: Muslim Conquests from the 7th to the 21st Centuries* (Amherst, N.Y.: Prometheus, 1998); Christopher Catherwood, *Christians, Muslims, and Islamic Rage: What Is Going On and Why It Happened* (Grand Rapids, Mich.: Zondervan, 2003); Robert Spencer, *The Myth of Islamic Tolerance: How Islamic Law Treats Non-Muslims* (Amherst, N.Y.: Prometheus, 2005).
2. For this chapter, I examine only those Syriac works that specifically discuss the Islamic conquests. This is only a fraction of the much larger corpus of early Syriac writings on Islam. For a listing and bibliography of most seventh- through ninth-century Syriac texts that speak of Muslims, see Michael Penn, "Syriac Sources for Early Christian/Muslim Relations," *Islamochristiana* 29 (2003): 59–78; and Robert G. Hoyland, *Seeing Islam as Others Saw It: A Survey and Evaluation of Christian, Jewish and Zoroastrian Writings on Early Islam* (Princeton, N.J.: Darwin, 1997).

3. These Christians supported the decisions of the Council of Chalcedon in 451. Because of their agreement with Byzantine Christology, their opponents often called them Melkites, from the Syriac word for "king."

4. This group is also often called Monophysites or, especially among their opponents, Jacobites after the name of one of their early bishops, Jacob Baradeaus. They also are known as Syrian Orthodox, which also designates many modern Christians who trace their lineage back to the early Miaphysites.

5. Their opponents often call this group Nestorians after the fifth-century bishop of Constantinople condemned by the Council of Ephesus in 431. The Assyrian Church of the East and the Ancient Church of the East are the most well-known heirs to this tradition.

6. The original manuscript is described in William Wright, *Catalogue of the Syriac Manuscripts in the British Museum*, 3 vols. (London: Trustees of the British Museum, 1870–73), 1:65–66. On the basis of paleography, Wright dates this copy of Mark and Matthew to the sixth century. Syriac edition in Theodor Nöldeke, "Zur Geschichte der Araber im 1. Jahrh. d.h. aus Syrischen Quellen," *Zeitschrift der Deutschen Morgenländischen Gesellschaft* 29 (1876): 77–79; and E. W. Brooks, *Corpus Scriptorum Christianorum Orientalium* (CSCO), 3:75. English translations appear in Hoyland, *Seeing Islam*, 117; and Andrew Palmer, *The Seventh Century in the West-Syrian Chronicles* (Liverpool: Liverpool University Press, 1993), 2–4.

7. Syriac edition in Brooks, CSCO 3: 77–155. English translations of selected entries in Palmer, *The Seventh Century*, 13–23.

8. Brooks, CSCO, 3:147–48.

9. Ibid., 148.

10. Isho'yahb III, Letter 14C (Duval, CSCO, 11:251.). English translation of excerpts from Letter 14C in Hoyland, *Seeing Islam*, 179.

11. Syriac edition in CSCO, 1:15–39. German translation in Theodor Nöldeke, "Die von Guidi Herausgegebene Syrische Chronik übersetzt und commentiert," in *Sitzungeberichte der Kaiserlichen Akademie der Wissenschaften Philosophisch-Historische Klasse* 128 (Vienna, 1893): 5–48.

12. CSCO, 2:30, 38.

13. Syriac edition in CSCO, 139:60–71. German translations in Harald Suermann, *Die Geschichtstheologische Reaktion auf die Einfallenden Muslime in der Edessenischen Apokalyptik des 7. Jahrhunderts*, vol. 256: *Europäische Hochschulschriften* (Frankfurt am Main: Peter Lang, 1985), 12–32; and CSCO, 321:79–94. The date of this text's composition remains somewhat uncertain. For recent discussions concerning when to date this text, see Gerrit J. Reinink, "Pseudo-Ephraems 'Rede über das Ende' und die Syrische eschatologische Literatur des Siebenten Jahrhunderts," *ARAM Periodical* 5 (1993): 437–63; and Hoyland, *Seeing Islam*, 262–63.

14. CSCO, 320:61.

15. CSCO, 320:62.

16. Syriac edition in Sebastian Brock, "An Early Syriac Life of Maximus the Confessor," *Analecta Bollandiana* 91 (1973): 302–13; English translation 314–19. Uncertainty remains regarding the *Life*'s authorship and date of composition. See Brock, "An Early Syriac Life," 336; and Hoyland, *Seeing Islam*, 139, for discussions of the work's authorship and date of composition.

17. *Life of Maximus the Confessor* (Brock, "An Early Syriac Life," 302).

18. *Life of Maximus the Confessor* (Brock, "An Early Syriac Life," 309–13).

19. Victoria L. Erhart, "The Church of the East during the Period of the Four Rightly-Guided Caliphs," *Bulletin of the John Rylands Library of Manchester* 78 (1996): 61–63. Among Muslim sources, the Byzantine-Persian wars appear in Qu'ran 30:2–6 and in later hadiths.

20. Gerrit J. Reinink, "Following the Doctrine of the Demons: Early Christian Fear of Conversion to Islam," in Wout J. van Bekkum, Jan N. Bremmer, and Arie L. Molendijk, eds., *Cultures of Conversions* (Leuven: Peeters, 2006), 129; Robert Hoyland, "Introduction: Muslims and Others," in Robert Hoyland, ed., *Muslims and Others in Early Islamic Society* (Aldershot, U.K.: Ashgate, 2004), xxii–xxv; Michael G. Morony, "The Age of Conversions: A Reassessment," in

Michael Gervers and Ramzi Jibran Bikhazi, eds., *Conversion and Continuity: Indigenous Christian Communities in Islamic Lands, Eighth to Eighteen Centuries* (Toronto: Pontifical Institute
for Mediaeval Studies, 1990), 135–37.

21. John L. Boojamra, "Christianity in Greater Syria after Islam," *St. Vladimir's Theological
Quarterly* 35, no. 1 (1991): 229; Hugh Kennedy, *The Prophet and the Age of the Caliphates: The
Islamic Near East from the Sixth to the Eleventh Century* (New York: Longman, 1986), 87–88;
Michael G. Morony, *Iraq after the Muslim Conquest* (Princeton, N.J.: Princeton University
Press, 1984), 97–98.

22. Chase F. Robinson, *Empire and Elites after the Muslim Conquest: The Transformation of Northern Mesopotamia* (Cambridge, U.K.: Cambridge University Press, 2000), 44–50; Erhart, "The
Church of the East," 60–61.

23. There is not yet a published edition of the entire *Book of Main Points*. Alphonse Mingana,
Sources Syriaques I (Leipzig: Dominican, 1907), includes an edition of Books 10–15 based on
a single manuscript. A French translation of Book 15 is in Mingana, *Sources Syriaques*,
I:172–97. An English translation of the end of Book 14 and most of Book 15 is in Sebastian
Brock, "North Mesopotamia in the Late Seventh Century: Book XV of John Bar Penkaye's
Ris Melle," *Jerusalem Studies in Arabic and Islam* 9 (1987): 57–73.

24. For discussion of when John most likely wrote the *Book of Main Points*, see Hoyland, *Seeing
Islam*, 199–200; and Brock, "North Mesopotamia," 52.

25. For discussion of this rebellion, see Gerrit J. Reinink, "East Syrian Historiography in
Response to the Rise of Islam: The Case of John Bar Penkaye's Ktaba D-Res Melle," in H. L.
Murre-Van den Berg, J. J. Van Ginkel, and T. M. Van Lint, eds., *Redefining Christian Identity:
Cultural Interaction in the Middle East since the Rise of Islam* (Leuven: Peeters, 2005), 79, 81;
Gerrit J. Reinink, "Paideia: God's Design in World History according to the East Syrian
Monk John Bar Penkaye," in Erik Kooper, ed., *The Medieval Chronicle II: Proceedings of the 2nd
International Conference on the Medieval Chronicle, Driebergen/Utrecht July 16–21, 1999*
(Amsterdam: Rodopi, 2002), 191; Hoyland, *Seeing Islam*, 197–98; Harald Suermann, "Das
arabische Reich in der Weltgeschichte des Johannan bar Penkaje," in Piotr O. Scholz and
Reinhard Stempel, eds., *Nubia et Oriens Christianus: Festschrift für C. D. G. Müller zum 60.
Geburtstag* (Köln: J. Dinter, 1987), 65–66.

26. John bar Penkaye, *Book of Main Points*, 14 (Mingana, *Sources Syriaques*, I:141–42).

27. Ibid.

28. See Reinink, "Paideia," 191–94, for how "God's *paideia* is the guiding principle of John's
concept of history."

29. John bar Penkaye, *Book of Main Points* 14, 15 (Mingana, *Sources Syriaques*, I:142, 145).

30. Ibid., 15 (I:145).

31. Ibid., 15 (I:147, 154).

32. Ibid., 15 (I:160–65.).

33. For a discussion of God removing his care (*btiluta*) from the world, see Reinink, "East Syrian
Historiography," 85–87.

34. John bar Penkaye, *Book of Main Points* 15 (Mingana, *Sources Syriaques*, I:167).

35. Ibid.,15 (I:165.).

36. Reinink, "East Syrian Historiography," 79.

37. Or, as Reinink writes, "He explains the present by giving an account of the past from the
very beginning of the world"; "East Syrian Historiography," 83.

38. Han J. W. Drijvers, "Christians, Jews and Muslims in Northern Mesopotamia in Early
Islamic Times: The Gospel of the Twelve Apostles and Related Texts," in Pierre Canivet and
Jean-Paul Rey-Coquais, eds., *La Syrie de Byzance à l'Islam, VIIe–VIIIe Siècles* (Damascus: Insti-
tut Français de Damas, 1992), 68; Gerrit J. Reinink, "Ps.-Methodius: A Concept of History in
Response to the Rise of Islam," in Averil Cameron and Lawrence I. Conrad, eds., *The Byzan-
tine and Early Islamic East*, vol. 1: *Problems in the Literary Source Material* (Princeton, N.J.:
Darwin, 1992), 186. For a discussion of ambitious building projects, see Oleg Grabar, *The
Dome of the Rock* (Cambridge, Mass.: Harvard University Press, 2006), 59–119; Chase F. Robinson, *'Abd al-Malik*, in Patricia Crone, ed., *Makers of the Muslim World* (Oxford: Oneworld,

2005), 71–75; Oleg Grabar, *The Shape of the Holy: Early Islamic Jerusalem* (Princeton, N.J.: Princeton University Press, 1996), 52–116. For more detailed discussion of 'Abd al-Malik's coins, see Robinson, *'Abd al-Malik*, 71–75. For a discussion of his census and tax increase, see Drijvers, "Christians, Jews and Muslims," 67; Sidney H. Griffith, "Images, Islam and Christian Icons," in Canivet and Rey-Coquais, *La Syrie de Byzance à l'Islam*, 126; Reinink, "Ps.-Methodius," 180.

39. Hoyland, *Seeing Islam*, 48.

40. Ibid., 700; Griffith, "Images," 125.

41. Although at first Arab coins resemble earlier coin types, they replaced Byzantine and Sassanian motifs with specifically Islamic ones, especially in the 690s. For discussions of the significance of these coin changes, see Gerrit J. Reinink, "Political Power and Right Religion in the East Syrian Disputation between a Monk of Bet Hale and an Arab Notable," in Emmanouela Grypeou, Mark N. Swanson, and David Thomas, eds., *The Encounter of Eastern Christianity with Early Islam* (Leiden: Brill, 2006), 153; Hoyland, *Seeing Islam*, 16; Sheila S. Blair, "What Is the Date of the Dome of the Rock?" in Julian Raby and Jeremy Johns, eds., *Bayt al-Maqdis: 'Abd al-Malik's Jerusalem* (Oxford: Oxford University Press, 1992), 64, 67.

42. For English translations of the Dome of the Rock inscriptions see Hoyland, *Seeing Islam*, 696–99; and Blair, "What Is the Date?" 86–87.

43. Sidney H. Griffith, *The Church in the Shadow of the Mosque: Christians and Muslims in the World of Islam* (Princeton, N.J.: Princeton University Press, 2008), 32–33; Reinink, "Political Power," 153; Gerrit J. Reinink, "Early Christian Reactions to the Building of the Dome of the Rock in Jerusalem," *Xristianskij Vostok* 2 (2002): 228–30. For a discussion of the Dome of the Rock as a Muslim appropriation of Jerusalem and a challenge to the Church of the Holy Sepulchre, see Josef van Ess, "'Abd al-Malik and the Dome of the Rock: An Analysis of Some Texts," in Raby and Johns, *Bayt al-Maqdis*, 90, 101. For a discussion of its inscriptions, see Grabar, *The Shape of the Holy*, 56–71.

44. Griffith, *The Church in the Shadow*, 14; Griffith, "Images," 126–29.

45. Syriac edition in CSCO, 540. German translation in CSCO, 541. English translation of selected sections by Sebastian Brock in Palmer, *The Seventh Century*, 230–42.

46. *Apocalypse of Pseudo-Methodius*, Introduction (CSCO, 540:1).

47. For a discussion of when to date *Pseudo-Methodius*'s composition, see Hoyland, *Seeing Islam*, 264; CSCO, 541:xii–xxix; Gerrit J. Reinink, "The Romance of Julian the Apostate as a Source for Seventh-Century Syriac Apocalypses," in Canivet and Rey-Coquais, *La Syrie de Byzance à l'Islam*, 81, 85; Reinink, "Ps.-Methodius," 186.

48. For a discussion of 'Abd al-Malik's tax reform and the resulting tax increases, see Reinink, "Ps.-Methodius," 180.

49. For a discussion of *Pseudo-Methodius* having been written as a response to rumors concerning the construction of the Dome of the Rock, see Reinink, "Early Christian Reactions," 233–34; Reinink, "The Romance of Julian the Apostate," 79; Reinink, "Ps.-Methodius," 182–83.

50. *Apocalypse of Pseudo-Methodius*, XI:5 (CSCO, 540:25).

51. Ibid., X:6 (540:23). Reinink, "Ps.-Methodius," 150, n. 2, argues that *Pseudo-Methodius* sees 622, the traditional date for the Hijra, as the starting point for the seventy years of Arab rule. The author thus initially anticipated the Sons of Ishmael's end within a year or two.

52. *Apocalypse of Pseudo-Methodius*, XIII:6 (CSCO, 540:34).

53. Ibid., XIII:11–XIV:14 (540:38–48).

54. There has been considerable discussion concerning the theological affiliation of *Pseudo-Methodius*, although in recent years, there has been a growing consensus that the original author was Miaphysite. In particular, see Reinink, "Ps.-Methodius," 159–64; Paul J. Alexander, *The Byzantine Apocalyptic Tradition* (Berkeley: University of California Press, 1985), 28–29.

55. Bernard McGinn, "Apocalypticism and Violence: Aspects of their Relation in Antiquity and the Middle Ages," in Thomas J. Heffernan and Thomas E. Burman, eds., *Scripture and Pluralism: Reading the Bible in the Religiously Plural Worlds of the Middle Ages and Renaissance* (Leiden: Brill, 2005), 221.

56. Ibid., 221.

57. Syriac edition in François Nau, "Révélations et légendes: Méthodius-Clément-Andronicus," *Journal Asiatique* 9 (1917): 425–34. English translation in Palmer, *The Seventh Century*, 244–50.

58. Because the two extant manuscript witnesses to this text are both fragmentary and do not include the beginning of the apocalypse, some scholars refer to the work as the *Edessene Fragment*.

59. For a discussion of how the author of the *Edessene Apocalypse* appropriates the *Judas Cyriacus Legend*, see Reinink, "Early Christian Reactions," 237–39; Reinink, "The Romance of Julian the Apostate," 82–85. For a Syriac edition, an English translation, and discussion of extant witnesses to the *Judas Cyriacus Legend*, see CSCO, 565.

60. The *Edessene Apocalypse* refers to the year 694, which most likely reflects the Edessene calendar and thus corresponds to 692 C.E. See Palmer, *The Seventh Century*, 243; Reinink, "The Romance of Julian the Apostate," 81; Gerrit J. Reinink, "Der Edessenische 'Pseudo-Methodius,'" *Byzantinische Zeitschrift* 83 (1990): 36–38.

61. *Edessene Apocalypse* (Nau, "Révélationes et légendes," 425–34).

62. Syriac edition in J. Rendel Harris, *The Gospel of the Twelve Apostles Together with the Apocalypses of Each One of Them* (Cambridge, U.K.: Cambridge University Press, 1900), 15–21. English translation, 34–37.

63. Daniel 11:5.

64. Drijvers, "Christians, Jews and Muslims," 73; Han J. W. Drijvers, "The Gospel of the Twelve Apostles: A Syriac Apocalypse from the Early Islamic Period," in Cameron and Conrad, *The Byzantine and Early Islamic East*, 207.

65. *Apocalypse of John the Little* (Harris, *The Gospel of the Twelve Apostles*, 15–21).

66. Drijvers, "The Gospel of the Twelve Apostles," 208.

67. Drijvers, "Christians, Jews and Muslims," 74.

68. Michael G. Morony, "Religious Communities in Late Sasanian and Early Muslim Iraq," in Hoyland, *Muslims and Others*, 129.

69. Hoyland, *Seeing Islam*, 596.

70. Previously, conversion to Islam did not necessarily exempt one from paying the poll tax (*jizya*). See Hoyland, *Muslims and Others*, xxvi; Hoyland, *Seeing Islam*, 596; Kennedy, *The Prophet*, 107.

71. For example, the *Disputation of John and the Emir*, Syriac edition and English translation in Michael Philip Penn, "John and the Emir: A New Introduction, Edition and Translation," *Le Muséon* 121 (2008): 83–109; and the *Disputation between a Monk of Beth Hale and a Muslim Notable*.

72. Unfortunately, Jacob's *Chronicle* is only incompletely preserved, and the surviving manuscript breaks off after the entry for the year 631, so we most likely are missing the majority of what Jacob wrote about the conquests. The extant sections of the *Chronicle* do, however, speak of the beginning of the kingdom of the Arabs, which Jacob dates to 620/21, and contains brief references to Muhammad and to Arab raids in Palestine.

73. George Phillips, *Scholia on Passages of the Old Testament* (London: Williams and Norgate, 1864), 27.

74. Syriac edition in J. P. N. Land, *Anecdota Syriaca* (Leiden: Lugnuni Batavorum, 1862), 11. English translations in Hoyland, *Seeing Islam*, 394; and Palmer, *The Seventh Century*, 43.

75. *Chronicle ad 705* (Land, *Anecdota Syriaca*, 1:11).

76. Syriac edition in François Nau, "Un colloque du Patriarche Jean avec l'émir des Agaréens et faits divers des années 712 à 716," *Journal Asiatique* 11, no. 5 (1915): 253–56. English translation in Palmer, *The Seventh Century*, 45–47.

77. *Chronicle of Disasters* (Nau, "Un colloque du Patriarche Jean," 253–56).

78. Unfortunately, there is no published edition or translation of the *Disputation*, and only sections of it appear in passages translated by Griffith, Hoyland, and Reinink, who have seen a copy of the *Diyarbakir Syriac 95*. For arguments regarding when the *Disputation* was written, see Gerrit J. Reinink, "The Lamb on the Tree: Syriac Exegesis and Anti-Islamic Apologetics,"

in Ed Noort and Eibert Tigchelaar, eds., *The Sacrifice of Isaac: The Aqedah (Genesis 22) and Its Interpretations* (Leiden: Brill, 2002), 111–13; Sidney H. Griffith, "Disputing with Islam in Syriac: The Case of the Monk of Bet Hale and a Muslim Emir," *Hugoye: Journal of Syriac Studies* 3, no. 1 (2000); Hoyland, *Seeing Islam*, 469.

79. Quoted in Griffith, "The Case of the Monk."
80. Reinink, "Political Power," 169.
81. Quoted in ibid., 160–61.
82. Quoted in ibid., 169.
83. Quoted in ibid.
84. For the *Disputation*'s dependence on *Pseudo-Methodius*, see ibid.
85. Quoted in Griffith, "The Case of the Monk."

PART TWO

THE CRUSADES

Throughout the Middle Ages, Muslim and Christian rulers fought one another all along the Mediterranean littoral. The Reconquista, the reconquest of Sicily, and the Crusades brought large numbers of Christian and Muslim warriors into close contact with one another, not just as foes but often as allies. The changing fortunes of war meant that Christian, Jewish, and Muslim populations changed masters repeatedly.

The beginning of the era of the Crusades is conventionally set at the Council of Clermont in 1095 and the summons to what we now call the First Crusade. But since Gratian's *Decretum* appeared half a century later, the discussions surrounding this council and this call took place without any coherent idea of just war in existence. In this period, jihad doctrine was by far more fully developed than just war doctrine. Islam's classical age, after all, coincided with Europe's "dark ages."

It is quite commonplace to find bold assertions about the "transmission of ideas" between Christians and Muslims during the era of the Crusades, with Jews often placed in the role of intermediaries. The boldest of all is the claim that the crusading idea itself was born out of Christian assimilation of jihad into the still-inchoate ideas of just war and holy war. As Jacques Ellul famously averred in *The Subversion of Christianity*, the Islamic jihad introduced into Christianity both holy war and just war:

> One fact, however, is a radical one, namely, that the Crusade is an imitation of the *jihad*. . . . [W]ith the Muslim idea of a holy war is born the idea that a war may be good even if it is not motivated by religious intentions so long as it is waged by a legitimate king. Gradually the view is accepted that political power has to engage in war, and if this power is Christian, then a ruler has to obey certain precepts, orientations, and criteria if he is to act as a Christian ruler and to wage a just war. We thus embark on an endless debate as to the conditions of a just war, from Gratian's decree to St. Thomas. All this derives from the first impulse toward a holy war, and it was the Muslim example that finally inspired this dreadful denial of which all Christendom becomes guilty.[1]

Other writers are more circumspect and less tendentious. Some suggest a significant role for the Benedictine order of Cluny in galvanizing the Reconquista as a Christian holy war.[2] In 1088, the city of Toledo became the principal see of the Spanish church at the direction of Pope Urban II, a Cluniac, who would launch the First Crusade seven years later. Toledo had been taken from the Moors by Alfonso VI of León-Castile just three years earlier, and with its Arab and Jewish population largely intact, it had become the center of translation of Muslim and Jewish works into Latin.[3] Could Toledo have provided the conduit for ideas between Muslims and Christians?

Given the absence of any direct evidence, most scholars of the Crusades are unwilling to make any speculations on possible Muslim influences on crusading ideology. Ellul's claims notwithstanding, there was certainly enough material from within the scriptures and Greco-Roman natural law thinking to justify the crusade.[4]

Some of the most astute Muslim observers of the Crusades understood them as a different type of conflict from previous wars with Christians. They assimilated them into an Islamic frame of reference. Al-Sulami and Ibn al-Athir described the Franks as engaged in a Christian jihad to help their coreligionists under Muslim rule and to conquer Jerusalem. Both blamed the Muslim defeats on the political and moral decay within Islam, one manifestation of which was the abandonment of jihad.[5] The Counter-Crusades were thus spurred by a revival of jihad thinking, which brought to the fore issues related to defensive jihad and the sanctity of Jerusalem in Muslim piety.[6]

Notes

1. Jacques Ellul, *The Subversion of Christianity*, trans. Geoffrey W. Bromiley (Grand Rapids, Mich.: Eerdmans, 1986), 103–4.

2. Vicente Cantarino, "The Spanish Reconquest: A Cluniac Holy War against Islam?" in Khalil I. Semaan, ed., *Islam and the Medieval West: Aspects of Intercultural Relations* (Albany: State University of New York Press, 1980), 82–109.

3. Anwar Chejne, "The Role of al-Andalus in the Movement of Ideas between Islam and the West," in Semaan, *Islam and the Medieval West*, 115–20.

4. H. E. J. Cowdrey, "The Genesis of the Crusades: The Springs of Western Ideas of Holy War," in Thomas Patrick Murphy, ed., *The Holy War* (Columbus: Ohio State University Press, 1976), 9–32; Jonathan Riley-Smith, *The Crusades, Christianity, and Islam* (New York: Columbia University Press, 2008), chap. 1; Thomas Asbridge, *The First Crusade: A New History* (Oxford: Oxford University Press, 2004), 21–31.

5. W. Montgomery Watt, *Muslim-Christian Encounters: Perceptions and Misperceptions* (London: Routledge, 1991), 82; Robert Irwin, "Islam and the Crusades," in Jonathan Riley-Smith, ed., *The Oxford Illustrated History of the Crusades* (Oxford: Oxford University Press, 1995), 225–26.

6. See S. D. Goitein, "The Sanctity of Jerusalem and Palestine in Early Islam," *Studies in Islamic History and Institutions* (Leiden: Brill, 1966), 140–48; Emmanuel Sivan, "Le caractère sacré de Jérusalem dans l'Islam aux XIIe–XIIIe siècles," *Studia Islamica* 27 (1967): 149–82.

4

Imagining the Enemy

Southern Italian Perceptions of Islam at the Time of the First Crusade

JOSHUA C. BIRK

The exploits of the southern Italian leaders Bohemond and Tancred during the First Crusade are the stuff of legend. They have also drawn considerable scholarly attention. Very little scholarship has been directed, however, to the broader topic of southern Italian interactions with Muslims during the latter half of the eleventh century and how those interactions shaped their encounters with Muslims during the First Crusade. When scholars do refer to southern Italian encounters with Islam, they tend to focus on conflicts with Muslim emirates in Sicily or on battles against Muslim mercenaries serving the Byzantine empire during Bohemond's expedition into eastern Europe in the 1080s.[1] Even when acknowledging contact, historians have not discussed how those experiences shaped the perceptions and actions of southern Italians during the First Crusade.

An examination of the reality of Muslim-Christian contacts in eleventh-century southern Italy reveals a complex picture. Muslims had ruled parts or all of Sicily for more than two centuries, beginning with the Arab invasion from North Africa in 827. When the First Crusade began, Muslim rule on the island had only recently been extinguished with the Norman capture of the last Muslim strongholds on the island in 1091. The history of Muslim-Christian relations throughout this period was one of both military cooperation and conflict. The southern Italian crusader was accustomed to fighting *alongside* Muslims, not simply against them. By 1095, southern Italian leaders had made extensive use of Muslim soldiers for more than two decades. Muslim soldiers, under the command of Christian warlords, were a constant presence in southern Italian campaigns in the 1090s.

This background both challenges assumptions about the ways in which crusaders perceived their adversaries and helps to explain the behavior of southern Italian commanders during the First Crusade. It also sheds light on why the *Gesta*

Francorum, one of the few accounts of the First Crusade written by an author from southern Italy, departs from the pattern of its contemporaries. The overwhelming majority of the histories of the First Crusade were composed by northern French authors, all of whom were clerics.[2] Unlike his northern European contemporaries, the author of the *Gesta Francorum* rarely uses the language of holy war, and theological justifications for the First Crusade are prominently absent. In this chapter, I explore how and why the depiction of Muslims in the *Gesta Francorum* differs from those of northern French writers. Comparing the representation of Muslims in the *Gesta Francorum* with those in the history of Geoffrey of Malaterra, a contemporary southern Italian monk who composed a chronicle of the Norman conquest of Sicily and southern Italy, highlights the importance of regional differences in the depiction of Muslims in histories of the First Crusade.

Muslims in the Medieval Mind

Latin accounts of the First Crusade written in the early twelfth century never mention the word "Muslim" or any comparable designation. Instead, the chroniclers describe their adversaries as "enemies of God," "infidels," and, most frequently, "pagans." John Tolan argues that clerical authors had a limited set of intellectual categories for conceiving of non-Christians.[3] In the medieval imagination, all non-Christians were either heretics, Jews, or pagans. When confronting Islam, Latin Christian authors had no intellectual space for a new religion and needed to place Muslims within an existing framework of categories. Some of these early-twelfth-century authors mention "Machomet," that is, the Prophet Muhammad, but his followers revere him as a god, not as a prophet. These pagans also worship other gods, including Mars and Apollo, and their temples abound with idols to these and other deities.[4]

Not only did these authors imagine Muslims as worshipping the deities of classical Rome, but they also saw Muslims as continuing the pagan Roman persecution of Christians. The violent assaults and abuses that Christians allegedly suffered at the hands of pagan attackers justified the military response of the crusade. Tolan argues that these writers cast the crusaders in the role of apostles, combating Muslim forces who are modeled on bands of ancient pagan persecutors. The crusade itself is seen as the culmination of a struggle between paganism and Christianity, which has played out since the death of Christ.[5] Raymond d'Aguilers, for example, describes the crusade as vengeance for the crucifixion of Christ.[6]

Some accounts go even further in depicting the Muslims' persecution of early Christians. They create an image of pagans celebrating an antisacrament—ceremonies that serve as a dark mirror to Christian counterparts—in which the holy places of Jerusalem are subjected to ritual defilement and Christians suffer hideous tortures. Robert the Monk writes that the Persians[7] "overturn the altars, having defiled them with their own filth, they circumcise Christians, and take the resulting blood and gore and either pour it upon the altars or submerge it into baptismal vessels."[8] Raymond d'Aguilers describes rituals in which pagans reenact the torment and crucifixion, assaulting Christ in effigy, a timeless perpetuation of their earlier crime.[9] Peter Todebode describes a Muslim procession in which pagans answer the crucifix displayed during Christian processions with an idol of Muhammad mounted atop a lance.[10]

Among the early historians of the First Crusade, only Guibert of Nogent imagines Muslims as monotheists. He asserts that the perception of Muslims as pagans who worship Muhammad is a popular error. He recognizes that Muslims view Muhammad as a prophet and declares that Muhammad was not a pagan but a Christian heretic. Taught by a disgruntled priest, whom Guibert compares to Arius of Alexandria, the father of Arianism, Guibert sees Muhammad as using chicanery and deceit to stage a variety of false miracles in an effort to win converts. Islam, for Guibert, is essentially a continuation of ancient heresy.[11]

Several authors framed the crusade in specifically eschatological terms. For Guibert of Nogent, vanquishing the Muslims and establishing a Christian state in Jerusalem was a precondition for the emergence of the Antichrist and the Second Coming of Jesus.[12] Ralph of Caen viewed "Machomet" himself as the first Antichrist, aligning his worshippers with demonic forces.[13] Peter Todebode associated the pagans with Babylon and Khurasan, typically thought to be places of origin for the Antichrist.[14]

In brief, the northern French writers who composed the early-twelfth-century accounts of the First Crusade described the belligerents in binary terms. Their enemies were the evil mirrors of Christians, carrying out bloody defilement of sacred space. They were enemies of God and stood in opposition to all things holy. These adversaries could only be understood and described in entirely negative terms.

Clerics wrote these early accounts in what Richard Southern describes as an age of ignorance in Latin European knowledge of Islam.[15] Benjamin Kedar, however, argues that a great deal of information about Islam was available during this period, but there was no interest in organizing and disseminating that knowledge before the First Crusade.[16] Only after the First Crusade did a broad-ranging interest in Islam and Muslims emerge among the intellectual elites of Latin Europe. Although the histories of the First Crusade contain a wealth of misinformation, they paved the way for an expanding interest in and knowledge of Islam in the following centuries. As Bernard Hamilton argues, the crusaders' experience of Islam was not entirely negative, and they returned with a wealth of information and greater interest in Islam that would lead to a more systematic examination by Europeans in the twelfth and thirteenth centuries.[17] Despite that knowledge, as Suzanne Akbari shows, the trope of the pagan Muslim and his antisacramental violence persisted long after the intellectual elite developed a clearer understanding of the Islamic faith.[18] Margaret Jubb argues that even with a growing awareness of the realities of

Islam, authors continued to deploy time-worn anti-Muslim stereotypes in the twelfth and thirteenth centuries for a variety of rhetorical and polemical purposes.[19]

The ignorance or deliberate misinformation that Latin Europe persisted in promoting does not reflect the real experiences of those in close contact with Muslims. Contrary to the inimical representations of Islam in the clerical accounts of the First Crusade, soldiers participating in the expedition showed a willingness to work across religious boundaries. Thomas Asbridge argues that the First Crusaders rejected a monochromatic approach to Islam and embraced a realpolitik in their dealings with Muslims.[20] Crusaders did not perceive Muslims with an inflexible hatred, and they were willing to negotiate with Muslims just as they would with a hostile Christian enemy.[21]

Muslims and Christians in Southern Italy

Geoffrey of Malaterra composed his *De rebus gestis Rogerii Calabriae et Siciliae Comitis et Roberti Guiscardi Ducis fratris eius* (The Deeds of Count Roger of Calabria and Sicily and of Duke Robert Guiscard, His Brother)[22] roughly contemporaneously with the *Gesta Francorum*, offering us an opportunity to contextualize southern Italian depictions of Muslims in written texts. Malaterra's work offers a wealth of detail on the Sicilian campaigns of the late eleventh century and consequently on the involvement of Muslims in Norman armies. Geoffrey was a monk who had traveled to Sicily from north of the Alps,[23] eventually settling in the Latin monastery of Saint Agatha in Catania, which Roger I founded in 1091. This chronicle covers the events of 1098 and mentions the departure of Bohemond on crusade but not the successful conquest of Jerusalem in 1099, indicating that it was probably completed in the interim. Malaterra wrote his history at the request of Roger himself, and the text was intended to record his patron's accomplishments in Sicily and southern Italy. Although the action in the texts occasionally digresses to cover the exploits of Roger's brother, Robert Guiscard, the bulk of the narrative focuses on Roger himself, making it the only source for many events of the campaigns across Sicily.

Like the authors of the chronicles of the First Crusade, Malaterra employs no consistent term for Muslims. He frequently refers to Muslims from Sicily as "Sicilians," while using "Arab and African" to describe Muslims from elsewhere in the Mediterranean.[24] In more general terms, he describes Muslims collectively as "Saracens," although he occasionally uses explicitly religious terms such as "pagan" or "infidel."

Malaterra makes no effort to understand or explain Muslim religious practice, except for the rare mention of the practice of idolatry.[25] He is clear that the Muslims have their own system of religious laws[26] and describes instances when they swear oaths upon their religion's texts to enter into the service of Christian rulers.[27] Because his Norman patrons used Islamic legal and religious practices to secure the loyalty of subject populations, Malaterra cannot exhibit the kind of blanket hostility toward Muslims that pervades many of the crusader sources. Imagining Islamic religious ritual as antisacramental becomes unthinkable because of the way in which southern Italian commanders integrate Muslim populations into their own political systems.

He offers many accounts of honorable and valiant Muslim soldiers[28] and is capable of portraying Muslims in what he sees as a sympathetic light. For example, he offers an account of a Saracen forced to flee from the city of Messina when it falls to the Norman invaders. He pleads with his sister to accompany him, but she is afraid to depart. Malaterra stresses that this young man is so committed to the laws of his people that he is obligated to kill his own sister to prevent her from being violated at the hands of Christians: "He preferred to become the murderer of his sister and to weep for her, rather than that his sister become a violator of their law and have illicit sex with someone who did not follow it."[29] Malaterra offers a more positive view of Muslims than of Greek Christians, whom he describes in blanket terms as "always a most deceitful race."[30]

Malaterra deploys the language of holy war in his text, depicting Muslims as enemies of God and crediting divine favor in strengthening the Norman cause.[31] However, as Kenneth Baxter Wolf argues in the introduction to his English translation of the text, Malaterra subordinates the religious elements of the text in favor of praising the Norman *aviditas dominationis*, or "desire for domination." Roger and the other southern Italian soldiers are holy warriors only by happenstance. They fight against all opponents in efforts to extend their dominion. But when they happen to fight against Muslims, Malaterra deploys the language of holy war, because in this case, they are expanding the boundaries of Christendom.[32]

Malaterra and the *Gesta Francorum* overlap briefly in their depiction of the southern Italian contingent hearing of Pope Urban's pleas and agreeing to join the First Crusade. The *Gesta's* account paints an iconic picture.[33] In 1096, as various southern Italian magnates laid siege to the city of Amalfi, warriors bearing the sign of the cross, a signal that they had pledged to make the armed pilgrimage to Jerusalem, began to travel through the region. Bohemond of Taranto, upon hearing of the mission, pledged to join the cause and cut up his own cloak—probably an Islamic textile[34]—to make crosses for himself and his followers, which they would sew onto their garments to display their commitment to the crusade. Were these Christian warriors, when they first heard of the crusade, in the company of Muslim soldiers? At first glance, the question seems ludicrous. None of the chroniclers mentions the presence of Saracens while the crusade was preached. Malaterra similarly makes no mention of the presence of Muslims at the 1096 siege of Amalfi. Yet the broader pattern of military activity in southern Italy at the end of the eleventh century makes the presence of Muslims quite plausible.

Southern Italian military cooperation with Muslims began during the course of the Norman conquest of Sicily. The conquest of Sicily seems to have been a religious conflict, perhaps prefiguring the Crusades. In 1059, Robert Guiscard had sworn an oath of vassalage to the papacy as "Robert, by the Grace of God and St. Peter, Duke of Apulia and Calabria, and, in the future, with the help of both of them, Duke of Sicily."[35] However, the Norman invasion of Sicily began not in opposition to Muslim power but in partnership with it. In 1061, a disaffected Muslim amir, Ibn al-Thumna, fled Sicily, crossed over to Reggio on the southern Italian mainland, and enlisted the aid of Roger and his brother Robert Guiscard to reestablish his position in Sicily.[36] Malaterra stresses the honorable accord that Ibn al-Thumna (whom he calls Betumen) and Roger reached. Ibn al-Thumna's men served as scouts and guides for southern Italian war bands during the initial invasions of the island. When circumstances forced Roger to return to the mainland, Malaterra records that he left Ibn al-Thumna in command of his soldiers during his absence.[37]

Ibn al-Thumna's assassination by fellow Muslims in the spring of 1062 put an end to this cooperation, but Norman war leaders began to integrate Muslim soldiers into their military units over the course of the thirty-year conquest of Sicily. They seem to have been reluctant to deploy Muslim soldiers against other Muslims, in all likelihood because of concerns about their loyalty in such conflicts, but instead preferred to use them against Christian opponents. The first explicit reference to large bodies of Muslim troops fighting alongside southern Italians is in records of the siege of Salerno in 1076.[38] Muslim troops also made up a portion of the army that Robert Guiscard used to invade Rome and free Pope Gregory VII from the control of the German king Henry IV in 1084.[39]

The last Muslim strongholds in Sicily fell in 1091. With the whole island under his control, Count Roger of Sicily began to use his military might to become the dominant Norman figure in southern Italian conflicts. Throughout the 1090s, Roger increasingly used his Muslim soldiers to project his own power. The count launched four military incursions into the peninsula over the decade: against Cosenze in 1091,[40] battling William of Grandmesnil in 1094,[41] laying siege to Amalfi in 1096,[42] and attacking a rebellious Capua in 1098.[43] Geoffrey of Malaterra describes "thousands of Saracens" among Roger's forces in the 1091 and 1094 campaigns and claims that "the Saracens formed the largest part of the army" in 1098. Edomer, a biographer of Saint Anselm, confirms the presence of thousands of Muslim soldiers at Capua and laments that Roger prevented Anselm from converting these soldiers to Christianity.[44]

In 1096, Count Roger's nephew, Roger Borsa, faced a rebellion from the city of Amalfi. Desperate to regain the city, Borsa promised his uncle half of Amalfi if he helped him retake it. In light of the pattern of military activity over the rest of the decade, it would be unusual if Roger did not muster Muslim soldiers to retake this valuable city. The fact that these Muslim soldiers specialized in siege warfare[45] makes the possibility of their absence from such an operation even less likely. Malaterra gives no description of the forces that Count Roger deployed against Amalfi. The lack of any explicit reference to Muslim soldiers may indicate that Malaterra was reluctant to call attention to the Saracen presence in Christian-led armies at the beginning of southern Italian participation in the crusade.

Such silence has precedence in Malaterra's previous work. When Robert Guiscard marched on Rome to rescue Pope Gregory VII from forces loyal to Emperor Henry IV, he mobilized an army that included his brother's Muslim soldiers.[46] Neither Malaterra[47] nor William of Apulia,[48] the other prominent southern Italian chronicler who describes these events, mentions the presence of Muslim soldiers among the forces who rescued the pope and, in the process, sacked the Holy City. Only northern European chronicles hostile to the pope, composed by those who did not share Malaterra's or William's reticence, mention the presence of these "Saracen" soldiers. Unless Count Roger departed radically from the military behavior that he exhibited through the rest of the 1090s, the absence of Muslim soldiers from the accounts of the siege of Amalfi reflects a similar reticence. The southern Italian soldiers at Amalfi had a long history of fighting alongside Muslim allies and were in all likelihood camped next to Muslims when they heard word of the First Crusade. How did the experience of working with Muslims shape the way in which they understood and interacted with the "Saracens" they encountered during the course of the expedition?

Muslims in the *Gesta Francorum*

The *Gesta Francorum et aliorum Hierosolimitanorum* (The Deeds of the Franks and the Other Pilgrims to Jerusalem) is one of the earliest written accounts of the First Crusade and conveys vivid, eyewitness observations of the expedition. The text was composed either in segments over the course of the campaign or shortly after its end.[49] The *Gesta Francorum* proved quite popular and was used extensively in the composition of subsequent history. In 1105, Robert of Reims, Baudri of Borgueil, and Guibert of Nogent all rewrote versions of the *Gesta* account, attempting to elevate it to a more formal style. Peter Tudebode's *Historia de Hierosolymitano itinere* and the *Historia belli sacri* both borrow heavily from the *Gesta Francorum*.[50] Despite the impact of the text, we have few details about its anonymous author. The author was from southern Italy, most probably Apulia, and served in the retinue of Bohemond.[51] The author traveled with Bohemond until the conclusion of the siege of Antioch, after which point Bohemond abandoned the crusade, leaving the author to join the contingent of Raymond of Toulouse.

Much of the recent scholarly debate about the *Gesta* has centered on the probable profession of the author. In her edition of the text, Rosalind Hill concludes that the author was a knight, playing an active role in several military engagements.[52] Colin Morris disputes this assessment, asserting that historians have underappreciated the Latin style of the *Gesta*, which suggests a clerical author for the text.[53] Both Emily Albu and Conor Kostick have recently attempted to find intermediate positions, arguing that the distinction between clerics and laymen was not a clear one and that the author was an active participant in combat with some clerical training.[54] In a number of ways, particularly in its depiction of the

Muslim adversaries of the crusaders, the *Gesta* departs from the other early-twelfth-century accounts of the First Crusade, all of which were composed by churchmen. The possibility that the text represents the views of a soldier helps to explain why the *Gesta* differs from other accounts. However, in focusing the debate on the question of the professional background of the author, historians may have overlooked the influence of regional differences on chronicles of the First Crusade.

Before outlining the ways in which the depiction of Muslims in the *Gesta Francorum* departs from those of other Latin accounts of the First Crusade, one must acknowledge the limits of the author's knowledge. Much like Malaterra, the southern Italian contingent of crusaders shared the assessment that Muslims were polytheists. The *Gesta* frequently uses the term *paganus*, or "pagan," to describe the Muslim adversary.[55] It describes the Muslim leader Kerbogha as praying to "Machomet" and a number of other gods.[56] The author of the *Gesta* shows an awareness that Muslims possess their own religious texts and their own system of religious law,[57] as had Malaterra. However, he shows no understanding of the specifics of the religious texts. While Malaterra describes instances of Muslims swearing allegiance in service to Christians in accordance with their own law,[58] the author of the *Gesta Francorum* does not mention instances in which Muslim laws were used to cement alliances between Muslims and Christians. He imagines that the pagans have a religious structure mirroring that of Christianity. For example, in one conversation, Kerbogha, the commander of the Muslim army that comes to relieve Antioch, dictates a letter addressed to "the caliph, our pope."[59]

The author never discusses who these "pagans" are, what they believe, or why warfare against them is justified. Unlike northern French accounts, the *Gesta* author refrains from presenting theological justifications for the crusade and never articulates a theory of holy or just war.[60] Like Malaterra, the author of the text refers to Muslims as "enemies of God and Christendom"[61] and explains crusader victories as manifestations of divine favor. As a general rule, the author of the *Gesta* avoids attempts to demonize his enemies. Only in a single passage does he dehumanize his adversaries and suggest that they are aligned with the devil: the Muslim soldiers advance "uttering diabolical noise" and "shrieking and shouting like demons."[62]

Throughout the *Gesta Francorum*, the author makes reference to different groups among the enemy. He identifies them as Arabs, Turks, Saracens, Kurds, Persians, and a variety of other groups. At first glance, this would seem to indicate the author's awareness of the ethnic diversity among Muslims. Yet he also dubs his adversaries collectively as unsophisticated barbarians.[63] Closer examination reveals that the author relies on a host of archaic stereotypes that he superimposes on a medieval reality.[64] He conflates ethnic groups of Muslims with heretical Christian sects, lumping among the enemy Azymites and Paulicians.[65] The *Gesta Francorum* does not maintain any firm distinction between what we would consider ethnic and religious categories. During the siege of Antioch, Kerbogha is depicted as extending an offer to the crusaders to renounce their god and become Turks. If they do so, they will be given wealth, land, and elevated status.[66] This offer parallels the offer that Bohemond extends to his Muslim enemies, and the author clearly envisions "Turk" as a religious identity and the act of becoming a "Turk" as the inverse of converting to Christianity.

However, the author never adopts the antihagiographical or antisacramental descriptions common in other crusader texts. As previously discussed, other authors first introduce these tropes in their account of Urban's speech at the Council of Clermont using the sacrilegious behavior of pagan Saracens as justification for the crusade. The *Gesta Francorum* gives only a brief summary of the speech, and the author emphasizes the redemptive nature of the expedition along with the humility and suffering in Christ's name, without reference to Saracen atrocities: "Brothers, you must suffer for many things for the name of Christ, wretchedness, poverty, nakedness, persecution, need, sickness, hunger, thirst and other such troubles, for the Lord says to his disciples, 'You must suffer many things for my name.'"[67]

Without a detailed reconstruction of the pope's speech, the chronicle does not engage in the anti-Islamic invectives that frame other Latin narratives of the First Crusade. Notions of holy war and just war that permeate northern French chronicles are not developed in the *Gesta*. This absence suggests the probable attitudes of the southern Italian contingent on the expedition to Jerusalem. Muslims were most certainly pagans, and the war against them offered the opportunity for repentance. However, the southern Italians may very well have been skeptical of the charges brought against Muslims by the intellectual elites of northern Europe. Even while fighting against Muslims, they would have struggled to accept the Manichaean depiction of the conflict between Muslims and Christians. They were keenly aware of the possibilities for cooperation—albeit cooperation under Christian dominance—in a way that separated them from their fellow crusaders.

Historians frequently note that the author of the *Gesta* allows for a more positive view of Muslims than other contemporary writers, citing his depiction of Turkish knights: "[The Turks] say that they are of common stock with the Franks, and that no men ought to be knights by nature except the Franks and themselves. . . . Certainly if they [the Turks] were steadfast in the faith of Christ . . . no one would be able to find men stronger or more courageous or more naturally suited to war. Nevertheless, by God's grace they were defeated by our men."[68] Margaret Jubb argues that the *Gesta*'s author needs to elevate the stature of his opponents in order to magnify the victory of the crusaders.[69] Yet other historians of the First Crusade, writing with the same intention of glorifying the crusaders, refrain from similar elevation of their enemies. This discrepancy can be seen in Robert the Monk's *Historia Iherosolitana*. Robert, who based his text on the *Gesta Francorum*, largely replicated its story line but improved its style and departed from his source text when he felt a need to change the "attitude and ethos of the text."[70] Robert's text notably departs from the *Gesta*'s laudatory description of its adversaries. It shows none of the same admiration for Turkish military prowess; instead, the Turks are depicted as cowardly braggarts easily overcome by the crusaders.[71]

The *Gesta*'s author shows no indication that he understands the concept of jihad or that he has a firm grasp on how his opponents construct ideas about just war. Colin Morris has argued that the *Gesta Francorum* shares many characteristics with the genre of *chanson de geste*, vernacular narrative songs popular in Europe at the time.[72] Rather than showing an awareness of specifically Muslim understandings of war, the author imagines his enemies, particularly the fierce Turks, as the adversaries typical in these popular romances. Their behavior mirrors what we would expect to see from rapacious Frankish knights.

After the crusaders conquered the city of Antioch and killed Yaghi Siyan, the city's governor, Shams al-Dawla, the governor's son, appealed to Kerbogha to avenge his father's death. According to the *Gesta*, he promised *hominium*, or homage, to Kerbogha and to hold the citadel of Antioch *in tua fidelitate*, in fealty to Kerbogha, if the commander could kill the Franks.[73] Kerbogha and his fellow Turks use the vocabulary of feudal lordship to describe their relationship with one another. In this case, Kerbogha refuses Shams al-Dawla's request, responding that he will take control of the citadel himself and then turn it over to one of his trusted lieutenants. The entire scene in the *Gesta*, in which a distraught son seeks aid to slay the men who killed his father and an abusive lord takes advantage of tragedy to strip the son of his patrimony, could have come directly out of the *chansons de geste*[74] and suggests that the *Gesta*'s author envisions the Turkish warrior elite in ways that would have seemed familiar to his contemporary European audience.

The author of the *Gesta* extends his praise not just to the military prowess of the Turks but also to their moral character. The author has special praise for the Muslim soldiers who held Aregh, a castle east of Antioch, identifying them as particularly brave and steadfast.[75] Indirectly also, the *Gesta* paints favorable portraits of individual Muslims. For example, in a conversation between Kerbogha and one of his commanders, the Muslim leader praises his subordinate as "truthful, kindly and peaceable" and addresses him as "an honorable man."[76]

Hill argues that the *Gesta*'s presentation of Muslims differs from that of other texts because of the author's military experience. The favorable passages show a mutual respect among elite warriors despite religious difference.[77] Similarly, Albu asserts that these passages reflect years of experience on the crusade, which taught the author that a Turkish prince could behave virtuously.[78] But dwelling on the question of whether the author was a soldier or a cleric obfuscates equally relevant parts of his background. As a writer accustomed to the notion of Muslims fighting alongside Christian allies, the author of the *Gesta* is predisposed to see them as potentially useful, skilled, and valorous. Malaterra offers similar praise for Muslim soldiers at various points in his text. The historiographical debates about the profession and class of the author may offer insight into why his depictions of Muslims differ from those of other accounts of the First Crusade, but an exploration of the use of Muslim soldiers in southern Italian wars and the way in which southern Italian accounts depict those soldiers is equally relevant to an understanding of the *Gesta Francorum*.

When the crusade stalled at Antioch, Bohemond entered into secret negotiations with the garrison commander of one of the city's towers. Most accounts of the siege describe this commander as an Armenian armor maker who had once been Christian but had converted to Islam.[79] This commander had been abused by the leaders of Antioch, and Bohemond was able to exploit his dissatisfaction and coax him into handing over the tower.[80] The *Gesta*, along with other sources dependent on it, depicts the commander not as a dissatisfied Armenian convert but as "an Amir of the Turkish race whose name was Pirus, who formed an intense friendship with Bohemond."[81] According to the *Gesta*, in return for the surrender of the tower, Bohemond promised Pirus that he would receive baptism, wealth, and title.[82] The night before the capture of Antioch, Pirus sent his son to Bohemond as a guarantee of his acceptance of Bohemond's offer. The garrison commander gave Bohemond's forces entry into the city, allowing the crusaders to circumvent Antioch's formidable defenses and avert a potentially disastrous end to the crusade. Historians have generally held that the commander's identity in the *Gesta* is incorrect. Hill suggests that the narrative of the tower's surrender becomes comprehensible only if the garrison commander was a converted Christian.[83]

The fall of Antioch through the betrayal of one of its defenders had antecedents in recent southern Italian military experience. Bohemond's willingness to enter into secret negotiations across religious boundaries reflects strategies that his family had previously used when fighting against entrenched Muslim fortifications in Sicily. Bohemond's uncle, Roger, seized the Sicilian city of Castronovo from Muslim forces in 1078 in a similar fashion. A local miller who had suffered abuse at the hands of the city's commander seized control of a fortified tower within the city. Roger negotiated with the dissatisfied miller, gaining access to the tower and finally the city itself. Malaterra never mentions the religious affiliation of the miller, but he was most likely a Greek Christian or a Muslim.[84]

A similar series of events occurred in Roger's conquest of Castrogiovanni in 1087. Roger entered into secret negotiations with Hammud, the Sicilian amir of Castrogiovanni, to gain the surrender of that fortified city. He held Hammud's wife and children hostage and was able to use them to negotiate the surrender. In exchange for the surrender of his city and his conversion to Christianity, Roger granted Hammud land holdings in Calabria. Although different in certain important respects from events in Antioch, this case offers another example of a Norman lord dealing secretly with a Muslim military commander, using family members as hostages, and promising wealth and position in exchange for conversion and the surrender of a fortified area.[85]

The author of the *Gesta Francorum* probably erred in imagining the turncoat garrison commander of Antioch to be a Turkish amir. But this error highlights again how the southern Italian experience colors the author's perception of the crusade. The *Gesta*'s author makes the mistake of assuming the replication of patterns of conquest from Sicily. The error is the result not of incomprehensible confusions but of incorrect assumptions about religious fluidity that seem perfectly understandable in the context of recent military ventures in southern Italy and Sicily. In Antioch, as it had been in Castronovo and Castrogiovanni, the background of the southern Italian crusaders proved particularly amenable to the stratagem of turning an enemy to betray the city's defenses. They had first-hand experience of the enemy, and some could speak Greek and Arabic, which allowed them to enter such negotiations where other leaders of the crusade could not.

The capture of Jerusalem in 1099 also illustrates how the actions of southern Italian leaders and how a southern Italian author described them differed from those of their coreligionists. During the sack of Jerusalem, the *Gesta*'s author reports, the Muslim population sought refuge on the roof of the al-Aqsa Mosque, which he identifies as the Temple of Solomon. Tancred, along with Gaston of Béarn, gave his banner to these Muslims, placing them under his protection, presumably so that he could ransom them after the battle.[86] While Tancred saw these Muslims as potentially valuable assets that he could exploit, other crusaders understood them as infidels who should be put to the sword. The *Gesta* reports that other soldiers ignored Tancred's banner, climbed to the roof, and executed the prisoners, much to Tancred's displeasure.

Other eyewitness accounts of the sack of the city either ignore this incident entirely or paint a radically different picture of these events.[87] Peter Tudebode, a Poitevin cleric who used the *Gesta* as a source for his own writings, repeats the *Gesta* account almost word for word, mirroring the *Gesta* in claiming that Tancred gave banners to these Muslims to protect them on July 15, 1099.[88] But Tudebode breaks from the *Gesta* in describing the cause of the massacre. He inserts an additional sentence in which "Tancred sent the command that the Christians should go to the Temple and kill the Saracens." Tudebode offers no explanation for this reversal, but for the cleric from west-central France, one who wanted to assert a strong theological message about the sanctity of the idea of crusade, the notion that a hero of the capture of Jerusalem would tolerate the polluting infidels within the holy site seemed nonsensical. Rather than allow the enemies of God to continue defiling the sacred spaces of Christianity, Tudebode, in his mind, "corrects" the account and inserts the detail that Tancred must have ordered the slaughter. For the southern Italian author of the *Gesta Francorum*, one accustomed to working with Muslims, Tancred's desire to keep valuable prisoners alive and defend them from general slaughter seemed sensible and in custom with patterns of conflict between Muslims and Christians in Sicily.

Conclusion

Although scholars have recognized that the depictions of Muslims in the *Gesta Francorum* differ markedly from those of other accounts of the First Crusade, they rarely acknowledge the importance of regional background in shaping the attitudes of the author. The recent military experience of southern Italians had demonstrated the potential benefits of having Muslim troops within Christian military forces. Almost all of the southern Italian soldiers would have campaigned at some point in the decade before the crusade alongside Muslim forces. That experience shaped the way in which southern Italian authors depicted Muslims, even Muslims fighting against them. Like their northern European counterparts, these authors indicate no detailed understanding of Islam. But unlike their counterparts, they did not imagine Muslims as anti-Christian infidels, nor did they invoke holy war or engage in polemical attacks that would close possibilities of pragmatic cooperation. To the contrary, they were far more likely to ascribe positive traits to their opponents, both as individuals and as a group.

Notes

1. Tom Asbridge, "Knowing the Enemy: Latin Relations with Islam at the Time of the First Crusade," in Norman Housley, ed., *Knighthoods of Christ* (Aldershot, U.K.: Ashgate, 2007), 18–19. Asbridge acknowledges southern Italian "contact with Muslims in southern Italy and the Balkans" but never discusses the influence that this familiarity had on the experiences of crusaders.
2. This chapter focuses on Robert the Monk, *Historia Iherosolimitana*, in *Recueil des historiens des Croisades: Historiens occidentaux*, 5 vols. in 7 (Paris: Académie des Inscriptions et Belles-Lettres, 1844–1895), 3:717–828; Ralph of Caen, *Gesta Tancredi in expeditione Hierosolymitana*, in *Recueil des historiens*, 3:587–716; Raymond d'Aguilers, *Le "Liber" de Raymond d'Aguilers*, ed. J. Hill and L. Hill (Paris: Librairie Orientaliste Paul Geuthner, 1969); Peter Tudebode, *Historia de Hierosolymitano itinere*, ed. J. Hill and L. Hill (Paris: Librairie Orientaliste Paul Geuthner, 1977); Guibert of Nogent, *Dei gesta per Francos*, ed. R. B. C. Huygens, Corpus Christianorum Continuatio Mediaevalis 127A (Turnhout: Brepols, 1996).
3. John Tolan, *Saracens: Islam in the Medieval European Imagination* (New York: Columbia University Press), 12–20, 69–104.
4. Ralph of Caen, *Gesta Tancredi*, 695–96.
5. Tolan, *Saracens*, 116.
6. Raymond d'Aguilers, *Le "Liber,"* 150–51.
7. Robert the Monk, like many authors of the early accounts of the First Crusade, sees his opponents as a vast confederation of various barbarous peoples. While he identifies Turks, Arabs, Persians, Syrians, Saracens, Publicani, and others, he provides no firm definitions of the distinctions that exist among these groups. In his opening chapter, he identifies the Persians as the race responsible for atrocities committed against Christians and attacks on Constantinople but uses the term infrequently throughout the rest of the text and generally pairs it with "Arab."
8. Robert the Monk, *Historia Iherosolimitana*, 727–28.
9. Raymond d'Aguilers, *Le "Liber,"* 145.
10. Peter Tudebode, *Historia*, 137.

11. Guibert of Nogent, *Dei gesta*, 94–101.

12. Ibid., 113–17.

13. Ralph of Caen, *Gesta Tancredi*, 695.

14. Tolan, *Saracens*, 314, n. 35.

15. Richard Southern, *Western Views of Islam in the Middle Ages* (Cambridge, Mass.: Harvard University Press, 1962), 1–33.

16. B. Z. Kedar, *Crusade and Mission: European Approaches towards the Muslims* (Princeton, N.J.: Princeton University Press, 1984), 3–41.

17. Bernard Hamilton, *Crusaders, Cathars and the Holy Places* (London: Variorum, 1999), 317.

18. Suzanne Akbari, *Idols in the East: European Representations of Islam and the Orient, 1100–1450* (Ithaca, N.Y.: Cornell university Press, 2009), 245–47.

19. Margaret Jubb, "The Crusaders' Perception of Their Opponents," in Helen Nicholson, ed., *Palgrave Advances in the Crusades* (Basingstoke, U.K.: Palgrave Macmillan, 2005), 225–44.

20. Asbridge, "Knowing the Enemy," 19.

21. Ibid., 25.

22. Geoffrey Malaterra, *De rebus gestis Rogerii Calabriae et Siciliae comitis et Roberti Guiscardi ducis fratris eius*, ed. Ernesto Pontieri, Rerum Italicarum Scriptores, 2nd ed., vol. 5, pt. 1 (Bologna: B. Zanichelli, 1927–28).

23. Ernesto Pontieri, in Malaterra, *De rebus gestis Rogerii*, iv, claims that Geoffrey came from Normandy, but Kenneth Baxter Wolf casts doubt on this claim in his *Making Histories: The Normans and Their Historians in Eleventh-Century Italy* (Philadelphia: University of Pennsylvania Press, 1995), 144.

24. Malaterra, *De rebus gestis Rogerii*, 41–42.

25. Ibid., 29–30.

26. Ibid., 53.

27. Ibid., 33.

28. Ibid., 30–31, 41–42.

29. Ibid., 32–33.

30. Ibid., 40.

31. Ibid., 42–45.

32. Kenneth Baxter Wolf, introduction to Geoffrey Malaterra, *The Deeds of Count Roger of Calabria and Sicily and of His Brother Duke Robert Guiscard*, trans. Kenneth Baxter Wolf (Ann Arbor: University of Michigan Press, 2005), 17–33.

33. Rosaline Hill, ed., *Gesta Francorum et aliorum Hierosolimitanorum* (London: T. Nelson, 1962), 7.

34. Janet Snyder, "Cloth from the Promised Land: Appropriated Islamic *Tiraz* in Twelfth-Century French Sculpture," in Jane Burns, ed., *Medieval Fabrications: Dress, Textiles, Clothwork and Other Cultural Imaginings* (New York: Palgrave Macmillan, 2004), 148–49.

35. Paul Fabre and L. Duchesne, eds., *Le Liber censuum de l'Église romaine*, 3 vols. (Paris: Fontemoing, 1889–1952), 1:422; Graham Loud, *The Age of Robert Guiscard: Southern Italy and the Norman Conquest* (New York: Longman, 2000), 188–89; Alex Metcalf, *The Muslims of Medieval Italy* (Edinburgh: Edinburgh University Press, 2009), 91.

36. Jeremy Johns, *Arabic Administration in Norman Sicily: The Royal Diwan* (New York: Cambridge University Press, 2002), 31–33. Johns asserts that the Normans initially came to Sicily as Ibn al-Thumna's mercenaries but offers no clear evidence, other than cooperation between the two parties, to support this claim.

37. Malaterra, *De rebus gestis Rogerii*, 35.

38. Ibid., 40–42. Malaterra is not entirely consistent in his usage of terms to identify Muslims. Occasionally, he uses "Arab" to refer to Muslims from Sicily.

39. Landulf the Senior, *Historiae mediolanensis*, Rerum Italicarum Scriptores, 2nd ed., vol. 4, pt. 2 (Bologna: N. Zanichelli, 1942), 127–28.

40. Malaterra, *De rebus gestis Rogerii*, 96.

41. Ibid., 100.

42. Ibid., 102.

43. Ibid., 104–6.

44. Eadmer, *The Life of St. Anselm, Archbishop of Canterbury*, ed. Richard Southern (London: T. Nelson, 1962), 110–12.

45. Randall Rogers, *Latin Siege Warfare in the Twelfth Century* (Oxford: Clarendon , 1992), 100–113.

46. Loud, *The Age of Robert Guiscard*, 211; Louis Hamilton, "Memory, Symbol and Arson: Was Rome 'Sacked' in 1084?" *Speculum* 78, no. 2 (2003): 278–399.

47. Malaterra, *De rebus gestis Rogerii*, 79–81.

48. William of Apulia, *Gesta Roberti Wiscardi*, ed. and trans. Marguerite Mathieu, *La Gesta de Robert Guiscard* (Palermo: Istituto Siciliano di Studi Bizantini e Neoellenici, Testi e Monumenti, 1961), 234.

49. Colin Morris, "The Gesta Francorum as Narrative History," *Readings in Medieval Studies* 19 (1993): 56.

50. For an account of the textual influence of the *Gesta Francorum*, see John France, "The Anonymous *Gesta Francorum* and the *Historia Francorum qui Ceperunt Iherusalem* of Raymond Aguilers and the *Historia de Hierosolymitano Itinere* of Peter Tudebode: An Analysis of the Textual Relationship between Primary Sources of the First Crusade," in John France and William G. Zajac, eds., *The Crusades and Their Sources: Essays Presented to Bernard Hamilton* (Aldershot, U.K.: Ashgate, 1998), 39–70.

51. Conor Kostick, *The Social Structure of the First Crusade* (Leiden: Brill, 2008), 8–9. For a full account of the numerous questions surrounding the *Gesta*, see Jay Rubenstein, "What Is the *Gesta Francorum* and Who Was Peter Tudebode?" *Revue Mabillon* 16 (2005): 179–204.

52. Hill, introduction to *Gesta Francorum*, xiii.

53. Morris, "The Gesta Francorum," 67.

54. Emily Albu, "Probing the Passions of a Norman Crusader: *The Gesta Francorum et aliorum Hierosolimitanorum*," in John Gillingham, ed., *Anglo-Norman Studies 27: Proceedings of the Battle Conference 2004* (Woodbridge, U.K.: Boydell, 2005), 2; Kostick, *The Social Structure*, 15.

55. *Gesta Francorum*, 20.

56. Ibid., 52.

57. Ibid., 55, 82. In each case, Hill generously translates these vague words as "the Koran."

58. Malaterra, *De rebus gestis Rogerii*, 53.

59. *Gesta Francorum*, 52.

60. Tolan, *Saracens*, 110.

61. *Gesta Francorum*, 22. Again as "enemies of God," 40.

62. Ibid., 18.

63. Ibid., 20.

64. Svetlana Luchitskaja, "Barbarae nations: Les peuples musulmans dans les chroniques de la première croisade," in Michel Balard, ed., *Autour de la Première Croisade: Actes du Colloque de la Society for the Study of the Crusades and the Latin East, Clermont-Ferrand, 22–25 Juin, 1995* (Paris: Sorbonne, 1996), 99–107.

65. *Gesta Francorum*, 49.

66. Ibid., 67.

67. Ibid., 1–2.

68. Ibid., 21.

69. Jubb, "The Crusaders' Perception," 233–34.

70. Carol Sweetenham, introduction to *Robert the Monk's History of the First Crusade: Historia Iherosolimitana* (Aldershot, U.K.: Ashgate, 2005), 16.

71. Robert the Monk, *Historia Iherosolimitana*, 787.

72. Morris, "The Gesta Francorum," 61–62.

73. *Gesta Francorum*, 50.

74. Rubenstein, "What Is the *Gesta Francorum*?" 198–99.

75. *Gesta Francorum*, 23.

76. Ibid., 51.

77. Rosalind Hill, "The Christian View of the Muslims at the Time of the First Crusade," in P. M. Holt, ed., *The Eastern Mediterranean Lands in the Period of the Crusades* (Warminster, U.K.: Aris and Phillips, 1977), 2.

78. Albu, "Probing the Passions," 13.

79. Ibn al-Athir, *The Chronicle of Ibn al-Athir for the Crusading Period from* al-Kamil fi'l-ta'rikh, vol. 1, trans. D. S. Richards (Burlington, U.K.: Ashgate, 2006), 14–15; Raymond d'Aguilers, *Le "Liber,"* 64; Ralph of Caen, *Gesta Tancredi*, 651–52.

80. For a full account of this episode, see Joshua Birk, "The Betrayal of Antioch: Narratives of Conversion and Conquest during the First Crusade," *Journal of Medieval and Early Modern Studies* 41, no. 3 (2011): 463–85.

81. *Gesta Francorum*, 44; "Admiraldus," in Robert the Monk, *Historia Iherosolimitana*, 796. The *Gesta Francorum*, 46, identifies him as a Turk despite the fact that he is presented as speaking Greek.

82. Literally, "many honors"; *Gesta Francorum*, 44.

83. Ibid., 44, n. 1.

84. Malaterra, *De rebus gestis Rogerii*, 63–64. A significant Greek Christian population continued in Sicily during Muslim rule. While Malaterra is clear that the miller is not a Latin Christian, he never positively identifies this man's religion.

85. Ibid., 87–88.

86. *Gesta Francorum*, 91–92.

87. For a full account of the variances in the narratives of the capture of the city, see Benjamin Kedar, "The Jerusalem Massacre of July 1099 in the Historiography of the Crusades," in Benjamin Kedar, Jonathan Riley-Smith, and Helen Nicholson, eds., *The Crusades*, vol. 3 (Aldershot, U.K.: Ashgate, 2004), 15–75.

88. Peter Tudebode, *Historia*, 143, 150. Concerning the relationship between the two texts, France ("The Anonymous *Gesta Francorum*") argues that Tudebode uses the *Gesta* as his source, while Rubenstein ("What Is the *Gesta Francorum*?") argues that both texts are derived from a now lost common source.

5

Ibn 'Asakir and the Intensification and Reorientation of Sunni Jihad Ideology in Crusader-Era Syria

SULEIMAN A. MOURAD AND JAMES E. LINDSAY

The prominent jurist and theologian Ibn Taymiyya (d. 1328) was once asked his opinion about the legality of confiscating Christian churches in Cairo and elsewhere. In his response, which is preserved in his *Kitab al-jihad* (Book of Jihad; part of the massive collection of his legal opinions), Ibn Taymiyya digressed into a vituperative discussion of several Shi'i sects in which he declared that

> they are not Muslims [*kharijin 'an shari'at al-Islam*] in the judgment of all the sects of Islam; that is, in the opinion of the scholars, the rulers, and the public of the Hanafis, Malikis, Shafi'is, Hanbalis, and others. Fighting them is therefore lawful. . . . Those of them—the Nizari Isma'ilis, the Nusayris, the Druzes, and others like them—who live in Muslim lands have aided the Mongols in their war against the Muslims. Indeed, Hulegu's vizier, al-Nusayr [Nasir al-Din] al-Tusi, was one of their imams. They are the most notorious enemies of the Muslims and Muslim rulers. Next are the Rafidis [Fatimids and Twelvers], for they ally themselves with whoever fights the Sunnis.[1] They allied with the Mongols and with the Christians. Indeed, there was a truce between the Rafidis and the crusaders [*al-Faranj*] in the coastal areas. The Rafidis would ship to Cyprus the Muslims' horses and armor, the sultan's captive soldiers as well as other fighters and young warriors. When the Muslims defeat the Mongols, they mourn and are saddened, but when the Mongols defeat the Muslims, they celebrate and rejoice. They are the ones who advised the Mongols to kill the [Abbasid] caliph and massacre the people of Baghdad [in 1258]. . . . Those knowledgeable about Islam know that the Rafidis favor the enemies of religion. . . . They are hypocrites [*munafiqun*]. . . . The Rafidis are the most evil

among those who follow the direction of prayer [*sharr al-tawa'if al-munta-sibin ila al-qibla*].²

When Ibn Taymiyya refers to Muslims here, he means Sunnis—those who, in his opinion, follow the true and proper Islam. The Shi'i groups he mentions earned his condemnation not only for their heretical beliefs but also for their traitorous aiding of the crusaders and Mongols in wars against the Muslims. Ibn Taymiyya states unambiguously in his *Qital ahl al-baghi* (Fighting the People of Falsehood): "There is no doubt that waging jihad against these people and imposing on them the legal punishments are the utmost forms of obedience and fulfillment of religious obligation."³ That he concludes his comments about the Rafidis by referring to them as "the most evil among those who follow the direction of prayer" seems to indicate that he did, in fact, tolerate their claim to be Muslims but only as Muslims of the worst sort.

Ibn Taymiyya concedes that Sunni Muslim jurists before him rarely justified killing or waging jihad against fellow Muslims on the basis of dogmatic or political difference; he argues simply that they were wrong not to do so.⁴ Was Ibn Taymiyya's call to jihad against errant Muslims unprecedented in Sunni scholarship? Does his argument represent a radical new development in jihad doctrine? The short answer to both questions is no. In fact, Ibn Taymiyya bears no responsibility for *initiating* this development, for the intensification and reorientation of Sunni jihad ideology was well under way by the time he arrived on the scene. As we demonstrate in this chapter, members of the mainstream Sunni political and religious establishment in Syria, most notably Ibn 'Asakir of Damascus (d. 1176), had advocated the reinvigoration of jihad ideology in the wake of the First Crusade (nearly two centuries before Ibn Taymiyya embarked on his scholarly career) in order to unify the Sunni Muslims of Syria and to fight the external and internal enemies of God and Islam—the infidel Christian invaders and the heretical Shi'is, respectively.

We are not arguing that Ibn Taymiyya did not contribute significantly to the intensification of Sunni jihad ideology. Rather, we emphasize that since Ibn Taymiyya was born in the mid-thirteenth century, he was raised in a political and religious milieu that was already deeply saturated with a reanimated jihad doctrine and extensive jihad propaganda. That is, Ibn Taymiyya's arguments and rhetoric echo—very aggressively, to be sure—normative beliefs in his day that reflected what many among the Sunni religious establishment believed to be the true teachings of God in his revelation (the Qur'an) and those of his Prophet Muhammad. Ibn Taymiyya's passionate advocacy of jihad doctrine simply reinforced the long-standing view that the enemies of Islam included the crusaders (the enemy without) in addition to Shi'is, the recently and insufficiently Islamized Mongol Il-Khans, and other errant Muslims (the enemy within).

The "Enemy Within" before the Crusades

As is well known, clashes within Islam started as soon as its founder, Muhammad, died. His followers were divided over a range of questions about what the new *umma* should be, who should belong to it, who should lead it, what were the qualifications for leadership, and so forth. The various factions and tendencies are far too numerous to mention here. For our purposes, we will focus on two broad camps: one group, arguing on the basis of close kinship, advocated for Muhammad's son-in-law and paternal cousin 'Ali to succeed him; the other group advocated the view that the leaders among the Muslims ought to decide the issue of succession. Several rebellions and suppressions during the course of the seventh and eighth centuries ensured that the rift between the two broad camps would never heal. Out of this politicoreligious split, what came to be known as the Shi'is and the Sunnis emerged in the ninth century as two distinct religious sects in Islam, each with its own theology, schools of law, and political ideologies. The mid-tenth century ushered in what is commonly known as the "Shi'i century," where most of the central Islamic lands were ruled by Shi'i dynasties: Iran, Iraq, and central Mesopotamia were ruled by a Zaydi Shi'i dynasty, the Buyids (945–1055), who also patronized Twelver Shi'ism; northern Syria and western Mesopotamia were ruled by a Twelver Shi'i dynasty, the Hamdanids (945–1004); and southern Syria, Egypt, and parts of the Hijaz were ruled by the Isma'ili Shi'i Fatimid caliphs (969–1171).[5]

The concept of the "enemy within" and the urge to wage jihad against them had been known before the Crusades. However, those who employed the rhetoric of jihad against fellow Muslims generally were not viewed as representative of mainstream Islamic thought or practice. In fact, while jihad was always understood as the duty to fight by various means the enemies of God and Islam, the articulation of the doctrine of jihad with respect to fellow Muslims in the precrusader period was somewhat hesitant and ambiguous in that the tendency was to constrain it with a sophisticated legal jargon in order to ensure that its improper internal application against fellow Muslims—however rebellious they may have been—did not lead to chaos or *fitna*.[6] This policy was, in part, a response by the jurists to the most dramatic example of *fitna* in early Islam: the beliefs and bloody campaigns of the Khawarij, a third camp apart from Sunnis and Shi'is who believed that it was the duty of "good" Muslims to wage jihad against "bad" Muslims. Such views were deemed to be well beyond the mainstream by nearly all parties.[7]

Consequently, early Islamic scholarship shows some restraint in its interpretation of the Qur'anic command to "fight [*jihad*] the hypocrites and the infidels" found in verse 9:73 (at least with respect to the hypocrites). According to the celebrated Qur'an exegete and jurist al-Tabari (d. 923), the overwhelming majority of early Muslim jurists and exegetes argued that while the unbelievers or infidels were to be fought by every possible means, and above all by the sword, the hypocrites were to be fought either by means of argumentation (*al-lisan* or *al-kalam*) or by the strict application of God's laws (*iqamat al-hudud*). Al-Tabari appeals to Islamic tradition and past practice to explain why one should be lenient toward the hypocrites, especially if they openly affirm Islam. He argues that the teachings of Islam emphasize that when a hypocrite declares himself a Muslim, even if he secretly believes otherwise, his life and property are not to be compromised (*yuhqan damuhu wa maluhu*), since God prohibited the Muslims from speculating about what people secretly uphold.[8] This view echoes an earlier statement by the influential jurist al-Shafi'i (d. 820), who argues that Muslim rulers must heed the example of Muhammad in dealing with hypocrites, namely that they should be judged by what they publicly profess, not by what they harbor in their hearts, irrespective of what God says about them, for God only speaks about their eternal fate in the hereafter and not about how they are to be treated in this world.[9]

In the formative period of Islam, most Muslim scholars, especially those representing the mainstream, were uncomfortable with applying the ideology of jihad against their fellow Muslims. Jihad in the first three centuries of Islamic history was understood as a duty to fight by various means the enemies of God and Islam, and given the demographic and political realities of the early centuries, the enemies of God and Islam were abundant. They were largely perceived to be pagan and polytheist Arabs during the early Rashidun period and subsequently Byzantines, Persians, Hindus, and other peoples and states beyond the frontiers of the rapidly expanding Islamic empire, not internal Muslim dissidents.

All of this started to change in the late eleventh century, when we begin to see the emergence of a Sunni revivalism and assertiveness in response to a number of factors. We will focus our attention on two that directly affected the intensification of jihad ideology in Syria. The internal factor is the Shi'i century noted above, during which the core territories of Islam were ruled by Shi'i regimes. The external factor is a broad range of Christian counterattacks—the beginnings of the Reconquista in Spain, the Norman conquest of Sicily and southern Italy, and, most important for our purposes, the crusader conquests in northern Mesopotamia and Syria because of the challenge they posed to the Islamic heartland.[10]

We see this Sunni revivalist impulse in the context of the Fatimid presence in Syria and the threat that it (and that of their fellow travelers) posed to Seljuk designs in the region even before the arrival of the crusaders. The Seljuk vizier, Nizam al-Mulk (d. 1092), has much to say about the threat to good order posed by Shi'is in his own day. To provide but one example, he includes in his *Book of Government* a hadith that advocates waging jihad against Rafidis (his term for Isma'ilis—both Fatimids and Nizaris). According to the hadith, 'Ali (Muhammad's cousin and son-in-law and, according to Shi'is, his legitimate successor) and Fatima (Muhammad's daughter and 'Ali's wife, from whom the Fatimid dynasty derived its name) came to see Muhammad one day.

The Prophet (upon him be prayers and peace) raised his head and said, "O 'Ali, greetings to you, for you and your kinsmen will be in paradise. But after you a people will rise up professing to love you, pronouncing the creed and reciting the Qur'an; and they will be called Rafidis. If you find them wage holy war against them for they are polytheists, that is, unbelievers."[11]

That Nizam al-Mulk had good reason to be suspicious of Rafidi intentions was borne out in 1092, when he was murdered by a Nizari assassin.[12]

It is against this background that the transformation and intensification of jihad ideology in mainstream Sunni thought occurred in response to the events of the Shi'i century and the crusader invasions. In the wake of the crusader invasions, the impulse to revive Sunnism and to restore Sunni supremacy in Syria became increasingly potent. Consequently, the intended enemies against whom this reinvigorated jihad was preached were both Islam's external enemies, the Christian crusaders, and Sunnism's internal enemies, specifically the Shi'i Fatimid regime in Egypt and its sympathizers in Syria. An agenda emphasizing jihad against Christian forces was to be expected of any Muslim ruler in Syria ever since the initial conquests of Byzantine lands in the seventh century. But the use of jihad ideology against "errant" or "deviant" Muslims beginning in the eleventh and twelfth centuries represents a significant departure from the traditional scholarly aversion in Sunni Islam to identifying intra-Muslim conflicts as jihads. Moreover, the advocacy of jihad exclusively centered around selected Qur'anic verses and prophetic hadith that we see in the work of Ibn 'Asakir and other scholars of the crusader period also represents a methodological reorientation designed to motivate as broad an audience as possible—scholars, soldiers, merchants, commoners, and others—precisely because such an approach goes against the meticulous attention to legal requirements and nuances that much of the earlier scholarly tradition emphasized.

The Preaching of Jihad in the Early Crusader Period

In 1105, a scholar of Arabic grammar named al-Sulami (d. 1106) took to the pulpit in the mosque of Bayt Lihya, a village on the eastern outskirts of Damascus, to preach his recently completed *Kitab al-jihad* to a small number of young apprentices and to denounce his fellow Muslims for their weakness and divisiveness, which had allowed the crusader enemies to attack them and seize their lands. Al-Sulami's work is modeled on earlier jihad treatises in that it is made up of chapters that present the duty of jihad as laid out in the Qur'an and hadith, along with discussions of Islamic legal theory and application (e.g., who may wage jihad, how to treat the enemy, how to divide the booty, etc.). In this respect, al-Sulami's text replicates earlier styles of jihad preaching that were promulgated for the most part against the Byzantines.[13]

Al-Sulami is noteworthy for two new insights that had an impact on the intensification of jihad ideology in the twelfth century. First, al-Sulami blames the miserable situation in Syria on the Muslims' weak spiritual condition. Hence, in his opinion, a religious purification—what he calls the "greater" or spiritual jihad—is required before they could successfully embark on the "lesser" or military jihad to defeat the invaders. It is important to note that al-Sulami does not say that greater jihad supersedes lesser jihad or that Muslims must abandon the lesser military jihad for the greater spiritual jihad. Moreover, he was the first to depict the Crusades as part of a larger Christian campaign to seize the lands of Islam, which had started in Spain (al-Andalus) and Sicily and had now reached greater Syria.[14] The notable thirteenth-century historian Ibn al-Athir (d. 1233) viewed the Crusades in a similar vein.[15]

Al-Sulami was not the only scholar in Damascus to preach jihad in reaction to the crusader invasion of Muslim lands and their capture of the holy city of Jerusalem in 1099. Although we know of only one instance when his book was used after his death to preach jihad (a public reading at the Umayyad Mosque in Damascus in 1113), it must have contributed to the popularization of jihad preaching and propaganda in Damascus, sometimes at the instigation of the political rulers but often as an angry reaction on the part of religious scholars to the ruler's and the public's lack of motivation and their unwillingness to stand up and fight the invading crusaders.

The most explicit example of documented jihad propaganda and indoctrination in Syria comes from the reign of the Seljuk amir Nur al-Din (d. 1174), who rose to power following the murder of his father, Zangi, in 1146. He ruled from Aleppo (the former capital of the Twelver Shi'i Hamdanids) until he captured Damascus in 1154. Nur al-Din spent most of his career fighting other Muslim rulers in northern Syria and to a lesser extent crusaders, in an effort to unify Muslim Syria. He also had a keen interest in conquering Egypt, which was under Fatimid rule, and incorporating it into his domain. Consequently, Nur al-Din made jihad the central ideology of his regime and rallied the population by employing a host of religious scholars and preachers to promote it. There is no doubt that he acted out of self-interest, seeking to stabilize his realm and overcome his opponents. But it is the effectiveness of his jihad propaganda that contributed significantly to the reinvigoration of jihad ideology in the minds of Syria's mainstream Sunni religious establishment and public.

As noted above, most mainstream Sunni jurists before the Crusades had been cautious in their treatment of jihad as a problematic religious duty, one that had to be kept well guarded and controlled by jurists lest it lead to internal chaos or *fitna*. They also consistently asserted that it was the caliph alone who possessed the right and prerogative to call for jihad and that the people were under no personal obligation to wage jihad until the caliph summoned them to it. Certainly, there were exceptions to the rule, such as 'Abdallah ibn al-Mubarak (d. 797) and the movement he represents, a group of jurists and hadith scholars who took to asceticism and were angered by the reluctance of late Umayyad and early Abbasid caliphs to wage jihad against the Byzantines, the preferred infidel enemy since the early Islamic conquests.[16] Taking matters into their own hands, Ibn al-Mubarak and his disciples began to promote jihad against these external enemies of Islam as an obligation that is incumbent on each Muslim individual who is able to contribute to the cause of jihad in some fashion.[17] When the celebrated jurist al-Shafi'i articulated his concept of jihad as both a personal obligation (*fard 'ayn*) and a communal obligation (*fard kifaya*), he was very much influenced by the views of this movement.[18]

The effectiveness of Nur al-Din's propaganda can be judged by its success. Nur al-Din was indeed able to unite Syria along with southeastern Anatolia and northern Mesopotamia under his rule, and in 1171, his general, Saladin, succeeded in toppling the last Fatimid caliph in Cairo. But an important factor in the success of Nur al-Din's jihad propaganda was that the local population was already quite familiar with it, for jihad had been preached in Damascus by a number of religious scholars in addition to al-Sulami since the early twelfth century, most likely on their own initiative and with little support from the Burid rulers of the city. Nur al-Din was therefore skillfully exploiting the earlier efforts of a militant group of scholars and their very receptive audience.

Some of these hadith scholars who preached jihad in Damascus had been displaced from their hometowns, such as Jerusalem, Nablus, and Tyre, as a result of crusader occupation or threat, and they sought refuge in and around Damascus. In his *Mu'jam al-shuyukh* (Compendium of Teachers), the notable hadith scholar Ibn 'Asakir provides a rare glimpse of the fundamental role these displaced scholars played in the dissemination of jihad ideology in Syria in the period between the First and Second Crusades.[19] These displaced scholars, whom Ibn 'Asakir describes as zealots in their defense and promotion of Sunnism, were actively involved in the transmission of hadith on jihad and were instrumental in the propagation of jihad ideology in Damascus.[20] Their efforts were ineffective at first, as they had little, if any, support from the local political establishment. In fact, for much of the first half of the twelfth century, the Burid rulers of Damascus had allied themselves with the kingdom of Jerusalem; they were justifiably worried and fearful of the intentions of Zangi and Nur al-Din in Syria, especially after Zangi managed to capture the city of Edessa in 1144, ending the crusader rule that had lasted there since Baldwin captured it during the First Crusade in 1098.[21]

The fall of Edessa to Zangi was the pretext for the Second Crusade, but instead of moving against Edessa, the leaders of the Second Crusade decided to attack Damascus.[22] Their failure to capture the city in 1148 proved to be a turning point in the history of the Muslim "Counter-Crusade": the popular mood in Damascus firmly shifted from perceiving the crusaders as possible allies against Zangi and his son Nur al-Din to considering Nur al-Din as their savior from the threat of crusader conquest.[23] It is thus not surprising that the local Damascene rulers soon lost the support of the local population and had to turn the city over to Nur al-Din in 1154.

Nur al-Din's jihad ideology was intended to achieve two broad religious and political goals. First, the jihad rhetoric stressed that there was a need for one ruler to unify the divided Syrian Muslims under the banner of Sunni Islam and to put an end to all internal political and sectarian divisions, specifically those posed by the Fatimid regime in Egypt and its sympathizers in Syria. Second, it called on the Muslims to employ the strength of that unity to defeat the crusaders. These were not easy goals to achieve given the political and religious divisions among the Muslims in Syria and the strength of the crusader states in Jerusalem and coastal Syria. But they were the very goals that al-Sulami and the displaced scholars in Damascus had long advocated. Hence many Damascene Sunni religious scholars were eager to serve a capable ruler such as Nur al-Din, who would take up such a formidable and righteous task. One such scholar was the venerable Ibn 'Asakir, who quickly became a close adviser of Nur al-Din and was very much involved in devising and disseminating the sultan's jihad ideology.

Ibn 'Asakir and the Second Crusade

Ibn 'Asakir belonged to a notable family of jurists and religious scholars who played leading roles for more than two centuries in medieval Damascus. He achieved a high reputation as one of the city's and Syria's leading Sunni scholars as a result of his extensive travels in the Muslim world to study religious sciences, especially hadith. One particular group of teachers—the displaced scholars from Jerusalem, Nablus, and Tyre noted above—had a direct impact on shaping the young scholar's religious views, especially with respect to jihad ideology.

Ibn 'Asakir witnessed firsthand the attack of the Second Crusade against his hometown and preserved rare testimonies concerning the popular reaction to the attack and the defense of the city. The reaction of one particular scholar, a jurist of the Maliki school of Sunni law and teacher of Ibn 'Asakir named Yusuf ibn Dunas al-Findalawi, is worth mentioning. Al-Findalawi was from North Africa and came to reside in Damascus following his pilgrimage to Mecca. When the army of the Second Crusade attacked Damascus, he went out to fight against them. He was killed on Saturday, July 25, 1148, in the village of Nayrab, in the foothills of Mount Qasyun, which overlooks Damascus from the northwest. According to Ibn 'Asakir, the Damascene army chief tried to deter al-Findalawi, who replied that he had sold his soul to God and that God had accepted the sale—a reference to Qur'an 9:111: "God has purchased from the believers their souls and wealth in return for paradise. They fight in his path, and kill or get killed. It is a binding promise."[24]

The sense of urgency that led notable religious scholars to involve themselves directly in combat marks a significant change in the mood among the Sunnis of Damascus. The Second Crusade's attack on the city marks the moment when members of the Sunni religious establishment began to take matters into their own hands. Not only had they lost confidence in the ability of the military leadership to defend Damascus, but they also were anxious that the city might never be safe unless the whole of Syria was united by a powerful Sunni ruler and Sunnism was restored to its rightful place of dominance. In addition, there is clear evidence that Nur al-Din played a direct role in luring the Sunni religious establishment to his camp.

The Second Crusade seems to have convinced Ibn 'Asakir that he should become directly involved in the dissemination of jihad ideology. In contrast to his somewhat passive involvement of studying hadith on jihad noted above, he now became actively engaged in writing about and teaching the subject. For example, in his *Ta'rikh madinat Dimashq* (History of Damascus), Ibn 'Asakir informs his readers that he taught a seminar on Ibn al-Mubarak's *Kitab al-jihad* to a group of students that included 'Izz al-Dawla, the older brother of the celebrated amir and poet Usama ibn Munqidh (d. 1188).[25] After the seminar ended, 'Izz al-Dawla went straightway to fight the crusaders in Ascalon (where they had turned their attention following the failure at Damascus)[26] and achieved martyrdom there in the summer of 1151.[27] The degree to which Ibn 'Asakir influenced any of his students' convictions or actions cannot be established with certainty. But the apparent correlation between the failed attack of the Second Crusade against Damascus in 1148 and Ibn 'Asakir actively joining the band of jihad propagandists shortly thereafter is clear enough.

Ibn 'Asakir and Nur al-Din

Six years after the failed Frankish siege of Damascus, the city fell to Nur al-Din in 1154. The city's Sunni scholars, including Ibn 'Asakir, welcomed Nur al-Din as a hero and placed themselves in his service.[28] They saw the sultan as the ideal candidate to liberate Syria from the crusader menace and reunite it after centuries of intra-Muslim division and hostility. Owing to Nur al-Din's efforts, the alliance between Sunni politicians and religious scholars was firmly joined to the ideology of jihad and the revival of Sunni Islam.[29] Nur al-Din employed in his army a host of religious scholars and preachers whose sole function was to indoctrinate and stimulate the troops and the public.[30] Moreover, he ordered that an extensive network of religious and secular institutions and monuments (mosques, minarets, schools, hospitals, city walls, fortifications, etc.) be built throughout his realm. The intention of these buildings and monuments was to further enhance the sultan's religious and public image. The structures are also testimony to his use of propaganda to advance his political and religious ambitions, as most of the dedicatory inscriptions on the buildings and monuments celebrate him as the great jihad warrior.[31] His building campaigns succeeded in gaining tremendous support from the scholars and the Sunni masses and undoubtedly contributed to the revival of Sunnism in Syria.[32]

Nur al-Din found in Ibn 'Asakir a particularly ardent defender of Sunni Islam and ordered that a school for the study of hadith (known as Dar al-Hadith al-Nuriyya or Dar al-Sunna) be built for his scholarly ally.[33] Ibn 'Asakir shaped the school into the intellectual epicenter of Nur al-Din's jihad propaganda. Its output was deployed against the internal and external enemies of Sunni Islam throughout Nur al-Din's realm, continuing long after its founder's death.[34]

In a biography of Nur al-Din included in his *History of Damascus*, Ibn 'Asakir provides little information about the career of his patron except that it was mostly spent fighting the crusaders and ending heresies. Nevertheless, his words leave no doubt that he considered the triumph of Sunnism in Syria and Egypt (a consequence of Nur al-Din's many wars against other Muslims) to be Nur al-Din's most important achievement, the highlight of his reign. Ibn 'Asakir memorializes the significance of Nur al-Din's capture of the city of Aleppo as follows: "He reintroduced Sunnism and reestablished true religion, corrected the heresy that they used to follow in the call for prayer, crushed the heretical Shi'is, and revivified the four Sunni schools of jurisprudence."[35] Similarly, Ibn 'Asakir celebrates Nur al-Din's ending two centuries of Shi'i Fatimid rule in Egypt: "Finally, Sunnism became triumphant in Egypt and the sermons were read in the name of the Abbasid caliph after almost complete despair. God had relieved the Egyptians from disaster and ended their suffering. Therefore, God is deserving of thanks for His graces and for the success of conquests."[36]

These testimonies were written when Nur al-Din was still alive, so presumably, Ibn 'Asakir was expressing not only his sentiments toward the sultan but also his allegiance to him. Yet one should not underestimate the new sense of empowerment that the Sunni religious establishment enjoyed during Nur al-Din's reign as a result of the sultan's exceptional generosity and sponsorship.[37] Given the sultan's success in unifying the various parts of Syria and Egypt under his rule, along with his plan for the revivification of Sunnism, the Sunni religious establishment's expectations of him had been realized beyond their wildest dreams. Hence their words of praise reflect a deep and sincere veneration of him for accomplishing what they once may have thought was unattainable in their lifetimes.

Ibn 'Asakir's *Forty Hadiths for Inciting Jihad* and the Intensification of Sunni Jihad Ideology

Sometime in the 1160s, Nur al-Din asked Ibn 'Asakir to compose a short book of forty hadiths on the virtues of waging jihad. The sultan's objective was to employ this book in religious propaganda. He could not think of a better authority to speak to the binding duty of jihad than the prophet of Islam himself or a better scholar for achieving the task than Ibn 'Asakir, the greatest authority on hadith in Syria at the time. The scholar enthusiastically took up the challenge, and rather than producing a legal treatise on jihad which would have required that he address all sorts of legal questions and exceptions, he produced an easily accessible collection of prophetic traditions titled *al-Arbaʿun hadithan fi al-hathth ʿala al-jihad* (The Forty Hadiths for Inciting Jihad).[38] By producing a manual that only included hadiths some of which cite or allude to Qurʾanic verses that stress the duty of jihad, Ibn ʿAsakir was able to strip the Sunni jihad doctrine of its legal and juristic edifice and recenter it on an unambiguous and firm foundation of divine and prophetic instruction. Of the thousands of hadiths that Ibn ʿAsakir could have included on the subject, he intentionally chose forty that enabled him to transform Muhammad into a jihad advocate and cast Islam as a religion that emphasizes the duty to wage jihad above all others. That Nur al-Din and Ibn ʿAsakir were so successful in this endeavor demonstrates that the Sunnis in Damascus and greater Syria were already predisposed to these kinds of works and that they were amenable to being exploited by them.

The introduction to the *Forty Hadiths* provides us with invaluable information about religious propaganda and the interconnectedness of political opportunism and religious discourse under Nur al-Din. Ibn ʿAsakir writes that Sultan Nur al-Din

> expressed his desire that I collect for him forty hadiths relating to jihad that have clear texts and uninterrupted sound chains of transmission so that they could stimulate the valiant jihad fighters . . . and stir them up to truly perform when they meet the enemy in battle, as well as incite them to uproot the unbelievers and tyrants who, because of their unbelief, have terrorized the land and proliferated oppression and corruption—may God pour on them all types of torture, for He is all-watching. So I hastened to fulfill his desire and collected for him what is suitable for the people of learning and inquiry. I especially exerted a tremendous effort in collecting them in the hope that I should receive the reward [from God] for enlightening and guidance.[39]

There is no doubt that when Ibn ʿAsakir refers to those who have "terrorized the land and proliferated oppression and corruption," he means the crusaders and the Muslim military leaders, both Sunnis and Shiʿis, who were responsible for the disunity, turmoil, and weakness of Muslim Syria. Since Ibn ʿAsakir did not identify these people by name, his patron and his hearers could employ such jihad rhetoric against any they deemed to have "terrorized the land and proliferated oppression and corruption," crusaders and Muslims alike.

Yet what is more interesting for our purposes is that such a work was even needed for propaganda—that is, to be read to the troops and the public in order to stimulate them to fulfill properly a highly prized religious duty, the obligation to wage jihad against God's enemies. It is not surprising, then, that the sultan sought hadiths that were clear, straightforward, and comprehensible to all audiences. That Ibn ʿAsakir's *Forty Hadiths* became very popular among the Sunni religious establishment in Damascus is confirmed by the many teaching sessions of the book organized by important religious scholars and held in prestigious religious centers in Damascus, such as Nur al-Din's Dar al-Hadith and the Umayyad Mosque, between 1170 and 1230.[40] Ibn 'Asakir obviously expected a reward from his patron for authoring the *Forty Hadiths* but he was more keen on receiving the eternal rewards bestowed by God on those who took on the responsibility of properly guiding and enlightening the Muslim public.

Four major themes characterize the forty hadiths gathered by Ibn 'Asakir: the importance of the religious duty of waging jihad, the punishments for neglecting its fulfillment, the rewards for jihad fighters, and the prerequisites they are to fulfill. These four themes were meant to encapsulate, in Ibn 'Asakir's opinion, the most important aspects of the ideology of jihad in a very precise and clear manner. The following excerpts illustrate each of the four themes:[41]

(Hadith 1) The Messenger of God was asked: "Which aspect of belief is the best?" He replied: "The belief in God—glory and greatness belong to Him." He was then asked: "And what comes next?" He replied: "Next is jihad in the path of God—glory and greatness belong to Him." He was asked again: "And what comes next?" He replied: "An accepted pilgrimage."

(Hadith 13) The Messenger of God said: "Lining up for a battle in the path of God is worthier than sixty years of worship."

(Hadith 16) The Messenger of God said: ". . . At the end of days, there will appear a group of people who do not believe in jihad. God took an oath upon Himself that everyone who says that will be tortured like no other sinful human being."

(Hadith 21) The Messenger of God said: "The deeds of the dead person are sealed, except those of the garrisoned warrior in the path of God whose deeds accumulate rewards until the Day of Resurrection and who will also be saved from the torment of the grave."

(Hadith 29) The Messenger of God was heard saying: "God will admit into paradise three men for every arrow: the one who makes it and hopes it is used for something good, the one who donates it to be used in the path of God, and the person who shoots it in the path of God. . . ."

(Hadith 40) The Messenger of God said: "The slain-dead are of three types. One is a believer who exerts his life and wealth waging jihad in the path of God—glory and greatness belong to Him—and when he meets the enemy in battle he fights them until he is killed. He is a tested martyr whose abode will be the Tent of God, underneath His Throne; nothing separates him from prophets except their rank of prophethood. Another is a believer, having already committed transgressions and sins, who exerts his life and wealth waging jihad in the path of God, and when he meets the enemy in battle he fights them until he is killed. His transgressions and sins are cleansed, for the sword purifies from sins. He will also be admitted to paradise from whichever gate he chooses, for paradise has eight gates, and Hell has seven gates with some deeper than others. And a third is a hypocrite [*munafiq*] who exerts his life and wealth waging jihad in the path of God—glory and greatness belong to Him—and when he meets the enemy in battle he fights them until he is killed. He is in Hell, because the sword does not wipe out hypocrisy [*nifaq*]."

There is no doubt that Ibn 'Asakir considered these hadiths to have been applicable in Muhammad's day, but he chose them for inclusion in his collection because he believed that they were also relevant to his own day and, according to Hadith 16, would continue to be so until the end of days. Not only does Ibn 'Asakir use them to argue against Muslims who were reluctant to participate in jihad, but he also employs them to highlight the indirect ways in which one can participate in jihad, by sponsoring or manufacturing what jihad fighters need in order to wage jihad effectively and successfully. And like al-Sulami before him, he uses them to emphasize that jihad requires each person to correct his beliefs and practices in order to be worthy of jihad's eternal rewards. As Hadith 40 states, a jihad fighter must also be an authentic Muslim; he cannot be a hypocrite or a heretic such as a Shi'i Fatimid caliph in Egypt or one of his followers.

Conclusion

The examples we have discussed here demonstrate that an intensification and reorientation of jihad ideology began to take root in mainstream Sunni religious discourse as a direct response to the crusader invasion and in reaction to the Shi'i century. Because al-Sulami, Ibn 'Asakir, and other Sunni scholars in Syria believed that the Crusades and other Christian attacks of the eleventh century were only successful because of the *internal* political divisions and religious weaknesses in the Muslim lands, they advocated jihad against the enemies within, who were responsible for this deplorable state.[42] In this respect, Ibn 'Asakir and his contemporaries departed from the earlier mainstream Sunni discourse on jihad, which did not tolerate its use against fellow Muslims and which was more focused on legal nuances than on literal application of selected Qur'anic verses and prophetic hadith.

While al-Sulami was concerned primarily with the enemy without, his *Kitab al-jihad* signals the first stage in this transformation and intensification of jihad ideology. He argues that spiritual purity, in the sense of cultivating sound religious beliefs and practices, is necessary for the jihad of the battlefield to be successful in this life and to yield eternal rewards in the next. His *Kitab al-jihad* ushers in the age in which an increasing number of Sunni scholars began to tie the ideology of jihad specifically to the classification of Muslims as good and bad.

Sunni jihad propagandists in later decades and centuries, partly on their own initiative but also at the instigation of the political leadership, cemented this intensification by expanding the ideology of jihad to include direct and indirect attacks on other Muslim groups, especially Shi'is. Their powerful jihad preaching incorporated the more restrictive religious view that a proper Sunnism must reign supreme in the lands of Islam in order to defeat the Christian invaders—whether Christian princes in Spain, Normans in Sicily, or crusaders in Syria. Therefore, any Muslim group that fell outside the boundaries of this proper Sunnism were considered enemies within and had to be fought under the same righteous banner of jihad that was to be directed against the enemies without, the Christian invaders.

The discussion above helps us better understand the intensification and reorientation of Sunni jihad ideology during the crusader period, but it does not explain how or why this ideology remained normative in Sunni religious discourse long after the last crusader outpost in Syria fell in 1291. The explanation, we contend, lies in the Sunni consensus that developed in this period that only through religious renewal and reform could the Muslims turn the tide of Christian military successes. Since Sunnism was built on the foundation of the Qur'anic admonition to "obey God and his messenger" (8:20, 46; 9:71), it was logical for Sunni scholars to blame their misfortunes on the Muslims' failure to heed God's commands and the example of his messenger. Consequently, as religious scholars turned to the Qur'an and the life of Muhammad for guidance on how to respond effectively to the crisis created by the crusader invasions, they gravitated to the militant Qur'anic passages from the Medinan phase of Muhammad's career and hadith that advocated militant jihad against unbelievers. As this material was preached to receptive audiences in Syria and elsewhere, many became convinced that their own salvation depended on their embracing Islam's militant message as they discerned it in God's word, the Qur'an, and Muhammad's example, the *sunna*.

This intensified and reoriented jihad ideology, which was effectively promoted and disseminated by Nur al-Din and his "minister of propaganda," Ibn 'Asakir, and by other Sunni scholars in Syria, demonstrates that the crusader challenge precipitated a paradigm shift within mainstream Sunni Islam that also affected perceptions of identity. Many mainstream Sunni scholars became less cautious and more assertive in judging who was inside and who was outside the Muslim fold, thus bestowing a lasting legitimacy on the duty of jihad against enemies both within and without. In short, the prevalent conditions contributed to this particular jihad rhetoric becoming normative in Sunni religious thought and to some extent definitional of the Islamic persona. Its lasting impact on Islamic identity is that the duty of fighting jihad against God's enemies—however defined—became an essential component in mainstream Sunni religious discourse and thus was easily invoked in any circumstances that could be depicted as approximating—however tendentiously—the types of challenges that Muhammad had faced in Medina, that the early community faced during the Rashidun period, or that the Muslims faced during the Crusades.

In short, the intensification and reorientation of jihad ideology became normative in Sunni religious thought as mainstream Sunni scholars started to adopt it and promote it as part of their strategy to combat threats to the revivification of Sunnism and the restoration of Sunni supremacy after the periodic domination of the Islamic heartlands—Syria, Egypt, and Iraq—by various Shi'i, crusader, and/or Mongol Il-Khan regimes during the eleventh, twelfth, and thirteenth centuries. The words of Ibn Taymiyya cited at the beginning of this chapter are a case in point. It is no surprise that Ibn Taymiyya's fatwas offered religious legitimacy for the many military campaigns conducted as jihads in Syria against Nizari Isma'ilis, Nusayris, and Druzes by Mamluk and Ottoman sultans.[43]

Modern Sunni radical thought owes a great deal to this medieval intensification and reorientation of jihad ideology, too, as even a cursory survey of the jihadist literature demonstrates.[44] However, unlike their medieval and Ottoman predecessors, who primarily targeted Shi'is as Sunnism's internal enemies, some modern Sunni radicals are quite eager to cast their net far wider and to include also a great number of their fellow Sunnis. Although many modern Muslim scholars have criticized the arguments of contemporary jihad propagandists as a uniquely modern radicalization of jihad ideology, their criticism fails to acknowledge the medieval origins of this discourse or the fact that such influential figures as Hasan al-Banna, Sayyid Qutb, and 'Abdallah 'Azzam, along with their disciples, are quite cognizant of their ideology's medieval roots.[45] They enthusiastically appeal to many of the hadiths included in Ibn 'Asakir's *Forty Hadiths*; they frequently refer to Ibn Taymiyya's fatwas on combating errant or hypocritical Muslims. Modern jihadists embrace the same methodology of jihad advocacy that Ibn 'Asakir helped set up and actively disseminate and that Ibn Taymiyya did much to solidify. Moreover, like their medieval and early-modern predecessors, modern Sunni jihadists are quite certain that it is they who are the authentic Muslims, for it is they and they alone who simply and dutifully "obey God and his messenger."

Acknowledgments

This chapter draws on Suleiman A. Mourad and James E. Lindsay, *The Intensification and Reorientation of Sunni Jihad Ideology in the Crusader Period: Ibn 'Asakir (1105–1176) and His Age, with a translation of Ibn 'Asakir's Forty Hadiths for Inciting Jihad* (Leiden: Brill, forthcoming).

Notes

1. In this section of his fatwa, Ibn Taymiyya uses the term *al-rafida*, meaning "turncoats" or "traitors," as a standard epithet to describe Shi'is in general; later in his fatwa, he uses it specifically to refer to the Fatimids in a scathing rebuke of their beliefs and policies. For a complete translation and detailed analysis of this fatwa, see Mourad and Lindsay, *The Intensification*, chap. 7.
2. Ibn Taymiyya, *Majmu' al-fatawa*, ed. Mustafa 'Ata (Beirut: Dar al-Kutub al-'Ilmiyya, 2000), 16 (pt. 28): 279–80.

3. Ibn Taymiyya, *Majmu' al-fatawa*, 19 (pt. 35): 77. The chapter on Ibn Taymiyya and jihad in Rudolph Peters, *Jihad in Classical and Modern Islam* (Princeton, N.J.: Markus Wiener, 1996), 43–54, does not seriously engage Ibn Taymiyya's call for jihad against errant Muslims, nor does it specify what Ibn Taymiyya means by "Muslims."

4. Ibn Taymiyya, *Majmu' al-fatawa*, 16 (pt. 28): 217.

5. On the various strains of Shi'ism, see Moojan Momen, *An Introduction to Shi'i Islam* (New Haven, Conn.: Yale University Press, 1985); and Farhad Daftari, *The Ismailis: Their History and Doctrines* (New York: Cambridge University Press, 1990).

6. On jihad preaching in Islam, see Nial Christie and Deborah Gerish, "Parallel Preaching: Urban II and al-Sulami," *Al-Masaq: Islam and the Medieval Mediterranean* 15, no. 2 (2003): 139–48; Nial Christie and Deborah Gerish, *Preaching Holy War: Jihad and Crusade, 1095-1105* (Aldershot, U.K.: Ashgate, 2009); Christopher van der Krogt, "Jihad without Apologetics," *Islam and Christian-Muslim Relations* 21, no. 2 (2010): 127-47; Reuven Firestone, *Jihad: The Origin of Holy War in Islam* (New York: Oxford University Press, 1999); Michael Bonner, *Jihad in Islamic History: Doctrines and Practice* (Princeton, N.J.: Princeton University Press, 2006); David Cook, *Understanding Jihad* (Berkeley: University of California Press, 2005); Peters, *Jihad*; and Emmanuel Sivan, *Radical Islam: Medieval Theology and Modern Politics* (New Haven, Conn.: Yale University Press, 1985). On jihad ideology before the Crusades, see Roy P. Mottahedeh and Ridwan al-Sayyid, "The Idea of the Jihad in Islam before the Crusades," in Angeliki E. Laiou and Roy P. Mottahedeh, eds., *The Crusades from the Perspective of Byzantium and the Muslim World* (Washington, D.C.: Dumbarton Oaks, 2001), 23–29.

7. Paul L. Heck, "Eschatological Scripturalism and the End of Community: The Case of Early Kharijism," *Archiv für Religiouswissenschaft* 7 (2005): 137-52.

8. Al-Tabari, *Jami' al-bayan fi ta'wil al-Qur'an* (Beirut: Dar al-Kutub al-'Ilmiyya, 1999), 6:419–20.

9. Al-Shafi'i, *Kitab al-umm* (Cairo: al-Matba'a al-Kubra al-Amiriyya, 1903–7), 5:111.

10. A third factor not discussed in this chapter is the renewed conquests of India under Mahmud of Ghazna (d. 1030) and his successors that were explicitly depicted as jihad campaigns against the infidel Hindus. On the Ghaznavids and the conquest of India, see C. E. Bosworth, *The Ghaznavids: Their Empire in Afghanistan and Eastern Iran, 994–1040* (Edinburgh: Edinburgh University Press, 1963); and Mohammad Habib, *The Political Theory of the Delhi Sultanate* (Allahabad: Kitab Mahal, 1961), 46–47.

11. Nizam al-Mulk, *The Book of Government or Rules for Kings: The Siyar al-Muluk or Siyasat-Nama of Nizam al-Mulk*, trans. Hubert Darke (Richmond, U.K.: Curzon, 2002), 163.

12. The Nizaris were famously known at that time as *al-Hashshashin*, from which the European name "Assassins" is derived.

13. On Muslim attitudes toward the Byzantines, see Michael Bonner, *Aristocratic Violence and Holy War: Studies in the Jihad and the Arab-Byzantine Frontier* (New Haven, Conn.: American Oriental Society, 1996); and Nadia Maria El-Cheikh, *Byzantium Viewed by the Arabs* (Cambridge, Mass.: Harvard University Press, 2004).

14. On al-Sulami and his *Book of Jihad*, see Niall Christie, "Motivating Listeners in the *Kitab al-Jihad* of 'Ali ibn Tahir al-Sulami (d. 1106)," *Crusades* 6 (2007): 1–14; and Paul E. Chevedden, "The View of the Crusades from Rome and Damascus: The Geo-Politics and Historical Perspectives of Pope Urban II and 'Ali ibn Tahir al-Sulami," *Oriens* 39 (2011): 257–329. Christie is preparing a new edition and translation of al-Sulami's text, which will be published by Ashgate.

15. Ibn al-Athir, *Al-Kamil fi al-ta'rikh*, ed. C. J. Tornberg (Beirut: Dar Sadir, 1966), 10:272–73.

16. On jihad as a manifestation of ascetic practice, see Thomas Sizgorich, *Violence and Belief in Late Antiquity: Militant Devotion in Christianity and Islam* (Philadelphia: University of Pennsylvania Press, 2009), 168–95.

17. On this movement, see Bonner, *Aristocratic Violence*; and Deborah Tor, "Privatized Jihad and Public Order in the Pre-Seljuq Period: The Role of the *Mutatawwi'a*," *Iranian Studies* 38, no. 4 (2005): 555–73.

18. Al-Shafi'i, *Al-Risala*, ed. A. Muhammad Shakir (Beirut: Dar al-Fikr, 1979), 363–64 (sect. 980); cf. Majid Khadduri, trans., *Islamic Jurisprudence: Shafi'i's Risala* (Baltimore, Md.: Johns Hopkins University Press, 1961), 84.

19. Ibn 'Asakir, *Mu'jam al-shuyukh*, 3 vols., ed. Wafa' Taqiy al-Din (Damascus: Dar al-Basha'ir, 2000), contains descriptions of more than 1,621 male teachers whom the author had met and studied with over the course of his illustrious scholarly career. Ibn 'Asakir also composed a similar though smaller *Mu'jam* for approximately eighty of his female teachers.

20. See Mourad and Lindsay, *The Intensification*, chap. 3.

21. On the career of Zangi, see Carole Hillenbrand, "'Abominable Acts': The Career of Zengi," in Jonathan Phillips and Martin Hoch, eds., *The Second Crusade: Scope and Consequences* (Manchester, U.K.: Manchester University Press, 2001), 111–32.

22. On the issues relating to the Second Crusade, see Giles Constable, "The Second Crusade as Seen by Contemporaries," *Traditio* 9 (1953): 213–79; Alan J. Forey, "The Second Crusade: Scope and Objectives," *Durham University Journal* 55 (1994): 165–75; and Martin Hoch, "The Choice of Damascus as the Objective of the Second Crusade: A Re-evaluation," in Michel Balard, ed., *Autour de la Première Croisade: Actes du Colloque de la Society for the Study of the Crusades and the Latin East—Clermont-Ferrand, 22–25 Juin 1995* (Paris: Sorbonne, 1996), 359–69.

23. See Yaacov Lev, "The Jihad of Sultan Nur al-Din of Syria (1146–1174): History and Discourse," *Jerusalem Studies in Arabic and Islam* 35 (2008): 227–84.

24. See Ibn 'Asakir, *Ta'rikh madinat Dimashq*, ed. 'Umar al-'Amrawi and 'Ali Shiri (Beirut: Dar al-Fikr, 1995–2001), 74:235. See also Jean-Michel Mouton, "Yusuf al-Fandalawi, cheikh des malékites de Damas sous les bourides," *Revue des Études Islamiques* 51 (1983): 63–75.

25. For the valuable memoirs of Usama ibn Munqidh, see *Kitab al-i'tibar* (Baghdad: Maktabat al-Muthanna, 1964). An English translation is found in *The Book of Contemplation: Islam and the Crusades*, trans. Paul M. Cobb (London: Penguin, 2008). For biographical details, see Paul M. Cobb, *Usama ibn Munqidh: Warrior-Poet in the Age of the Crusades* (Oxford: Oneworld, 2006).

26. On the Second Crusade's plan to attack Ascalon, see Martin Hoch, "The Crusaders' Strategy against Fatimid Ascalon and the 'Ascalon Project' of the Second Crusade," in Michael Gervers, ed., *The Second Crusade and the Cistercians* (New York: St. Martin's, 1992), 119–28.

27. Ibn 'Asakir, *Ta'rikh Dimashq*, 43:239. The Banu Munqidh family was in control of the Shayzar castle, on the Orontes River to the west of the city of Hama, and were particularly involved with Nur al-Din's Counter-Crusade.

28. Nikita Elisséeff, *La description de Damas d'Ibn 'Asakir* (Damascus: Institut Français de Damas, 1959), xxii. At the time, Damascus had a sizable Shi'i population, made up of Twelvers and Isma'ili Fatimids.

29. On the career of Nur al-Din, see Nikita Elisséeff, *Nur ad-Din: Un grand prince musulman de Syrie au temps des croisades (511–69 H./1118–1174)* (Damascus: Institut Français de Damas, 1967); and Carole Hillenbrand, *The Crusades: Islamic Perspectives* (Edinburgh: Edinburgh University Press, 1999), 117–70.

30. See Elisséeff, *Nur ad-Din*, 3:735; and Hillenbrand, *The Crusades*, 119–22.

31. See Yasser Tabbaa, "Monuments with a Message: Propagation of Jihad under Nur al-Din," in Vladimir P. Goss, ed., *The Meeting of Two Worlds: Cultural Exchange between East and West during the Period of the Crusades* (Kalamazoo, Mich.: Medieval Institute, 1986), 223–40.

32. On the function of these buildings and monuments, see Hillenbrand, *The Crusades*, 122–31; and Yasser Tabbaa, *The Transformation of Islamic Art during the Sunni Revival* (Seattle: University of Washington Press, 2001).

33. Only a few traces of the building (notably the niche of the prayer hall) remain in old Damascus in what is known as the 'Asruniyya market area; see Qutayba al-Shihabi, *Mu'jam Dimashq al-tarikhi* (Damascus: Wizarat al-Thaqafa, 1999), 1:274.

34. Elisséeff, *La description*, xxii–xxiii; and Hillenbrand, *The Crusades*, 127.

35. See Ibn 'Asakir, *Ta'rikh Dimashq*, 57:120.

36. See ibid., 57:123. Invoking the Abbasid caliph here underscores his symbolic importance as spiritual head of Sunnism.

37. On the career of Nur al-Din and his support and sponsorship of the Sunni religious establishment in Syria, see Elisséeff, *Nur ad-Din*, 3:750–79.

38. This work is also known as *al-Arba'un fi al-ijtihad fi iqamat al-jihad* (The Forty Hadith on the Obligation to Wage Jihad). In addition to our edition and translation in *The Intensification*, two previous editions of Ibn 'Asakir's *Forty Hadith* exist, the first by 'Abd Allah ibn Yusuf (Kuwait: Dar al-Khulafa' li al-Kitab al-Islami, 1984) and the second by Ahmad 'A. Halwani in his *Ibn 'Asakir wa dawruhu fi al-jihad didd al-Salibiyyin fi 'ahd al-dawlatayn al-Nuriyya wa al-Ayyubiyya* (Damascus: Dar al-Fida', 1991), 101–49.

39. Mourad and Lindsay, *The Intensification*, pt. 2.

40. On the many teaching sessions of Ibn 'Asakir's *Forty Hadith*, see ibid., chap. 6. It is noteworthy that the colophons and dates of teaching sessions 3 and 4–9, held in 1221 and 1227–30 at different locations in Damascus, coincide with the Fifth Crusade and the Crusade of Frederick II, respectively. The best-attended teaching session, number 8, took place over two days in April 1229, one month after Frederick II had entered Jerusalem.

41. For a complete examination of Ibn 'Asakir's *Forty Hadith*, see ibid., chap. 5. The hadith quoted below are taken from ibid., pt. 2.

42. For examples of other Sunni scholars who promoted the radicalization of jihad after Ibn 'Asakir, see Mourad and Lindsay, *The Intensification*, chaps. 4, 6, 7; and Devin J. Stewart, "The *Maqamat* of Ahmad b. Abi Bakr b. Ahmad al-Razi al-Hanafi and the Ideology of the Counter-Crusade in Twelfth-Century Syria," *Middle Eastern Literatures* 11, no. 2 (2008): 211–32.

43. For an examination of many major Ottoman jurists who invoked Ibn Taymiyya's fatwa, see Mourad and Lindsay, *The Intensification*, chap. 7.

44. For examples of the theological and juridical reasoning of modern Sunni jihadists that draw on the Qur'an, hadith on jihad, and the thought of Ibn Taymiyya and other classical scholars, see Sayyid Qutb, "Jihad in the Cause of God," in A. B. al-Mehri, ed., *Milestones: Ma'alim fi al-tariq* (Birmingham, U.K.: Maktabah, 2006), 63–86; Hasan al-Banna, "Kitab al-Jihad," in al-Mehri, *Milestones*, 217–40; 'Abdallah 'Azzam, *Join the Caravan* (London: Azzam, 2001); Osama bin Laden, *Messages to the World: The Statements of Osama bin Laden*, ed. Bruce Lawrence, trans. James Howarth (London: Verso, 2005); Shmuel Bar, *Warrant for Terror: Fatwas of Radical Islam and the Duty of Jihad* (Lanham, Md.: Rowman & Littlefield, 2006); Raymond Ibrahim, trans. and ed., *The Al Qaeda Reader* (New York: Doubleday, 2007); Gilles Kepel and Jean-Pierre Milelli, eds., *Al Qaeda in Its Own Words*, trans. Pascale Ghazaleh (Cambridge, Mass.: Harvard University Press, 2008).

45. See, for example, Mahmud Muhammad Taha, *The Second Message of Islam*, ed. and trans. Abdullahi Ahmed an-Na'im (Syracuse, N.Y.: Syracuse University Press, 1987); Abdullahi Ahmed an-Na'im, *Toward an Islamic Reformation* (Syracuse, N.Y.: Syracuse University Press, 1990); Abdulaziz Sachedina, *The Islamic Roots of Democratic Pluralism* (New York: Oxford University Press, 2001); Khaled Abou el-Fadl, *Rebellion and Violence in Islamic Law* (Cambridge, U.K.: Cambridge University Press, 2001); and Khaled Abou el-Fadl, *The Great Theft: Wrestling Islam from the Extremists* (New York: HarperSanFrancisco, 2005). In his *Arguing the Just War in Islam* (Cambridge, Mass.: Harvard University Press, 2007), John Kelsay advocates the approach of scholars such as Taha, an-Na'im, Sachedina, and Abou el-Fadl; but see Ella Landau-Tasseron's critique of Kelsay's approach in "Is *Jihad* Comparable to Just War? A Review Article," *Jerusalem Studies in Arabic and Islam* 34 (2008): 535–50.

6

Angles of Influence

Jihad and Just War in Early Modern Spain

G. SCOTT DAVIS

In the first half of the sixteenth century, a group of Spanish Dominicans—most notably Francisco de Vitoria, Domingo de Soto, and Melchor Cano—developed the moral theology of Aquinas to criticize slavery, the conquest of the Americas, and the emerging doctrine of blood purity.[1] This "Second Scholastic," or "School of Salamanca," is frequently credited with laying the foundations for international law and the modern just war tradition.[2] In addition, Vitoria and Soto stand firmly against both the "national messianism" and "sectarian apocalypticism" that Norman Housley discerns in fifteenth- and sixteenth-century Spain.[3] Given the frequently encountered notion of *convivencia* applied to relations among Christians, Jews, and Muslims of medieval Iberia, it is not unreasonable to wonder whether there might be some influence running from the thinkers of al-Andalus either to the Spanish Dominicans directly or from the Islamic thinkers of the earlier Middle Ages through Thomas Aquinas to his followers in sixteenth-century Spain.[4] In what follows, I will argue that the more rigorous we make our standards for attributing influences, the less credible these claims become. Even properly chastened, however, I conclude that there are some possible angles of influence that, while so far unproven, show promise for drawing some connections between the medieval Christian encounter with Islam and early modern just war thinking.

A Promising Dead End: Aristotle, Ibn Rushd, and Aquinas

It would be both simple and satisfying if we could draw a line of influence through the great twelfth-century commentator, Ibn Rushd (Averroës). Ibn Rushd followed his grandfather, also named Ibn Rushd, as one of the most important legal scholars of al-Andalus.[5] He was also one of the greatest commentators on the works of Aristotle. Furthermore, it is well known that the grandson's commentaries were both widely available and highly controversial in thirteenth-century Paris.[6] Thomas himself cites Ibn Rushd in many places, from the commentary on the *Sentences* through the commentaries on Aristotle to the *Summa Theologiae*. If we could reconstruct Ibn Rushd's account of just war, it would be possible, at least in principle, to consider its impact on Saint Thomas.

Unfortunately, this is not as easy as we would like. Charles Butterworth remarks that unlike al-Farabi, Ibn Rushd "discussed just war only indirectly and even then in no more than one or two of [his] writings."[7] Nonetheless, it is possible to reconstruct several components of Ibn Rushd's understanding of war. Like Plato, and indeed like almost all thinkers before the modern period, Ibn Rushd takes war to be a normal part of social life and preparation for it to be among the "useful civic matters."[8] This follows from the need for "the coercion of difficult nations," due either to the "primary intention of removing from other cities that which they detest . . . or to a secondary intention in relation to guarding against what might possibly harm the city from without."[9] Ibn Rushd identifies this with "just war."

In the discussion of jihad in his *Bidayat al-mujtahid* (The Jurist's Primer), a discussion of conflicting interpretations among the schools of Islamic law, Ibn Rushd expands on the relation of justice to jihad, with explicit reference to the virtuous action enjoined on the community of Muslims. The *Bidayat*, however, is primarily interested in the nature and origins of conflicting legal judgments, and it is often unclear which interpretation Ibn Rushd intends to follow. Thus, he notes that "scholars agree that all polytheists should be fought," while acknowledging that Malik, whose school dominated al-Andalus, maintains "that it would not be allowed to attack the Ethiopians and the Turks on the strength of the Tradition of the Prophet: 'Leave the Ethiopians in peace as long as they leave you in peace.'"[10] Presumably, the tradition applies to the Turks on the principle of analogy and the operative phrase "as long as they leave you in peace." Ibn Rushd adds that Malik questioned the authenticity of the tradition "but said: 'People still avoid attacking them.'"[11] To the extent that Ibn Rushd, as an adherent of Maliki jurisprudence, is committed to following the founder's precedent, this may suggest that restraint is preferable in terms of the best interests of the community.

After considering various controversies and their sources in divergent traditions, Ibn Rushd finally pronounces:

> Basically, however, the source of their controversy is to be found in their divergent views concerning the motive why the enemy may be slain. Those who think that this is because they are unbelieving do not make exceptions for any polytheist. Others, who are of the opinion that this motive consists in their capacity for fighting, in view of the prohibition to slay female unbelievers, do make an exception for those who are unable to fight or who are not as a rule inclined to fight, such as peasants and serfs.[12]

Presumably, given that Malik cites multiple versions of the prohibition on killing women, Ibn Rushd follows the second opinion, but it is not clear whether he takes this to be the best argument.

Noah Feldman, however, notes a distinctively Aristotelian twist in Ibn Rushd's middle commentary on the *Ethics*, which may clarify his position. He is explicating the discussion of *Ethics* V, chapter 7, where Aristotle argues that "when the law speaks generally but a case arises that is not covered by the general statement, it serves the virtue of equity to correct the omission and to rectify the law."[13] Ibn Rushd notes that for Muslim law, "the command in it regarding war is general, until they uproot and destroy entirely whoever disagrees with them."[14] But virtue dictates that

> there are times when peace is more choiceworthy than war. And as for the fact that the Muslim public requires this generality, despite the impossibility of destroying and uprooting their enemies entirely . . . is ignorance on their part of the intention of the legislator, may God watch over him. Therefore it is appropriate to say that peace is preferable to war sometimes.[15]

Feldman goes on to draw the conclusion that "the duty of holy war has not been lifted, but it has been rationalized by an interpretation that avoids requiring self-destructive behavior from the Muslim community."[16]

This may be too cautious. In his *Decisive Treatise*, Ibn Rushd argues that those capable of understanding them are obliged to study "the books of the Ancients."[17] These intellectuals are the very same individuals who are charged with interpreting shari'a, Islamic law. In 1125, Ibn Rushd the grandfather distinguished three groups within the community of jurists: those who memorize Malik's positions without understanding, those who understand the coherence of Malik's reasoning without being able to reach conclusions on their own, and those who can reason from revelation and principle to positive conclusions. This last group has

> the freedom to exercise *ijtihad* [independent judgment] since they have perfected the tools of original legal reasoning on the basis of the revealed texts. The qualifications permitting them to practice *ijtihad* are not a matter of quantitative memorization of legal doctrines; rather, they are the refined qualities of legal reasoning and an intimate knowledge of the Quran, the Sunna, and consensus.[18]

The grandfather illustrates here the continuing independence of Andalusian Maliki shari'a, which had initially focused more on Malik's principles of judicial reasoning, his *ra'y*, than on the specific traditions he transmitted.[19] What counts is not mastery of traditions but refined legal intellect. Ibn Rushd the grandson follows his grandfather and implies that this highest level of jurist should understand his activity in terms of the wisdom of the ancient philosophers. It is crucial that jurists think for themselves because difference of opinion is inevitable, if only because "the situations that may arise between people are infinite in number, whereas the texts, actions and tacit approvals of the Prophet are finite in number."[20]

Brought together, the components of the grandson's thinking suggest that war will be a necessity for any community, including that which attempts to subordinate itself to God's will. Justice requires the implementation of shari'a by authorities informed by philosophical thought. To the extent that Ibn Rushd the grandson follows the lead of Malik, he is committed to protecting noncombatants and to a comparatively restrained policy with regard to combatants. In matters of community uprightness, dealing justly trumps everything. Malik writes, for example, "as for the people with a treaty . . . their property and lives are protected by the treaty they made. Only the terms of the treaty are demanded of them."[21] In this matter, as in that of safe conduct, the Muslims are bound by their word or by gestures that can be interpreted as words. To do otherwise is to fail to practice jihad in the way of Allah.

Right authority, just cause, reasonable proportion, and discrimination in battle—all of this suggests a close precursor to Thomas Aquinas's account of justice in war, with at least a hint of Aristotelian moral theory in the background. Unfortunately, Thomas does not know Ibn Rushd's *Bidayat*. Nor does he seem to know the remark from Ibn Rushd's commentary isolated by Feldman. Robert Busa's *Index Thomisticum*, which allows electronic searches of the best available editions, returns 142 references to Ibn Rushd in Thomas's works, but none of them seems to be to the commentaries on the *Ethics*.[22] Ibn Rushd does not appear in Thomas's commentary on the *Ethics*, nor does he show up in the relevant discussions of *Summa Theologiae* 2a2ae. If there is an important Islamic contribution to this strand of just war thinking, it will have to be approached indirectly.

Ideas in the Air: Marcel Boisard on the Influence of Islam

One of the most widely cited attempts to trace the influence of Islam on Western political thought is Marcel Boisard's "On the Probable Influence of Islam on Western Public and International Law." Boisard, a distinguished diplomat long connected to the International Committee of the Red Cross, acknowledges:

> To analyse the influences in the field of law is a difficult task. Identical ideas may be generated spontaneously without showing any imprint whatsoever. What is more, the time lag, generally fairly long, that spans the time between the impact of a symbol and its concrete acceptance is a further source of difficulty.[23]

But having issued this note of caution, Boisard ranges across time and place with breathtaking abandon and little detailed documentation. Consider the following passages from a single page:

> If concrete influences are difficult to determine . . . it is nonetheless certain that they deeply affected the popular mind. . . . The direct victims of combat . . . in all probability also contributed to a transmission of certain conceptions and ideas that had been encountered in the Orient. The author of *Don Quixote* was imprisoned in Algiers. . . . Certain members of European noble families were taken hostage and sent to Muslim courts. Treated as guests, they probably cannot but have been impressed by Muslim culture of which they were the direct propagators upon their return home.[24]

Invoking probabilities and undocumented "certainties" is unavoidable in a certain kind of popular writing, but it is worrisome in any attempt to trace the specific influence of one set of ideas on another. This is even more the case when popular assertion flies in the face of scholarly consensus.

A troubling example of this occurs in Boisard's discussion of the *Siete Partidas*. The *Siete Partidas* are the most important product of the ambitious project to codify the laws of Castile drawn up under the aegis of Alfonso X.[25] Boisard reads the *Siete Partidas* "both in form and content as a direct adaptation of Muslim law."[26] This does not square with the scholarly consensus, which sees the motivation primarily in the rise of the study of both canon and Roman law in the preceding century. As Robert MacDonald puts it:

> The glossators and other university scholars were primarily responsible for the reception of common law into Castile. Common law refers to the juridical system, arising in Italy, that resulted from the contact (but not the fusing) of Justinian Roman law, canon law, and feudal law, and it also takes in maritime law.[27]

What may have misled Boisard is the status of customary law. The *fueros* of medieval Spain were charters, issued particularly to recaptured frontier towns, that codified relations between citizens and their ostensible rulers. They "could also include modifications of existing law and special legal regulations that then became part of the privileges of the citizenry."[28] They often reconfirmed preexisting practices and in that sense were likely to incorporate the sorts of concessions made to the towns in earlier days by their Muslim overlords.[29] In any case, the *Siete Partidas* shows no self-conscious attempt to adapt models drawn from Islamic law.[30]

How do Muslims themselves figure in the *Siete Partidas*? The discussion of Muslims comes between those of Jews and heresy. The ten statutes begin with a description of the Muslims as "a people who believe that Mohammed was the Prophet and Messenger of God."[31] Although their belief is false, "so long as they live among Christians with their assurance of security, their property shall not be stolen from them or taken by force; and we order that whoever violates this law shall pay a sum equal to double the value of what he took."[32] Christians are enjoined to attempt conversion by "kind words," never with violence. While the penalty for Christian apostasy is infamy, a crippling legal status, if the apostate renders great service to the community and subsequently repents and seeks to return to the faith, "we consider it proper that he also be released from the penalty of being considered infamous, that he shall not lose his property; and that no one thereafter shall dare to reproach him or his conduct . . . just as if he had never renounced the Catholic faith."[33]

Sex with a Christian virgin leads to stoning for the Muslim, but this illustrates no particular antagonism between the religions, since a Christian "man who is accused and convicted of having committed adultery must be put to death."[34] Furthermore, "if Christians who commit adultery with married women deserve death on that account, much more do Jews who have sexual intercourse with Christian women."[35] In fact, Muslims seem to get a slight break here, for "if a Moor has intercourse with a common woman who abandons herself to everyone, for the first offence, they shall be scourged together through the town, and for the second, they shall be put to death."[36] These titles seem to reflect nothing more than the fact, as James Brundage puts it, that during the thirteenth century, "nonmarital sex became a problem of growing interest to the Church's lawyers, as did the evidence and procedures in sex cases."[37] Given his desire to be comprehensive in legislating for his realm, if it was a problem for the canon lawyers, it was a problem for Alfonso.

Fallacy and Influence

Nothing I have said above makes it impossible for influence to have flowed in the ways that Boisard imagines, but nothing Boisard has argued shows that it did. What's maddening about Boisard is the casual willingness to ignore the fallacy of *post hoc ergo propter*. To think that because something happened after something else, it happened because of that something is a powerful temptation. Sometimes it's true, but sometimes it isn't. Consider: "I first met Mark's wife at their wedding. Nine months later, she had her first child." If I can truthfully say that I had no inappropriate interactions with Mark's wife, then the fact that the first event took place has no connection to the second. For all we know, the child would have been born had I been stranded at the Dallas airport the weekend of the wedding.

Sometimes it's just very hard to know. For instance, Sharon LaFraniere, reporting for the *New York Times*, writes on February 6, 2009:

Nearly nine months after a devastating earthquake in Sichuan Province, China, left 80,000 people dead or missing, a growing number of American and Chinese scientists are suggesting that the calamity was triggered by a four-year-old reservoir built close to the earthquake's geological fault line.[38]

Did building the dam so close to the fault line trigger the quake? It might have, but earthquakes are hard to predict in the short run. Over time, it is highly probable that a quake would have occurred regardless. The seismologists, not to mention the lawyers, would like to know whether the building of the dam *caused* the earthquake.

Unfortunately, the very notion of causality is contested. At least since Hume, it has been a subject of intense philosophical debate.[39] Putting aside a great number of ontological and methodological issues, however, a minimal condition for claims of causation is that there be sufficient evidence to satisfy certain counterfactual propositions of the form:

If X had not happened, then Y would not have happened.

The attempt here is to capture the idea that Y didn't simply happen after X but that the occurrence of Y in some sense depended on X. *Post hoc ergo*, in other words, is a fallacy because it assumes precisely what needs to be demonstrated.

If we take "influence" to be a comparatively weak causal connection, then arguments for influence can be arranged along a graded rule of argument forms, from weakest to strongest. Since:

A produced X at time t; B produced Y at time t + d

would be guilty of *post hoc ergo*, the weakest form would be something like:

A did X, then B did Y.

Here we could imagine something like a report of a tennis match, where the reporter can take for granted that his audience understands the context of the game and the importance of each volley to the outcome. An argument for it has a low burden of proof, but it has almost no interest. Presumably, had the audience members actually been there, they could have forgone the report altogether.

The strongest argument would be the counterfactual:

B would not have produced Y at t if A had not produced X at t - d.

This seems to capture the fullest form of influence.[40] Such claims will frequently be of great interest but will have a very high burden of proof, since they assert not simply person-to-person influence but artifact-to-artifact influence. Since artifacts are themselves the products of human ingenuity, the argument will have to show not simply that A influenced B but that the particular product of A's action at a particular time influenced the different product created by B at a given time. If we take into account the human tendencies to excess on the one hand and pride on the other, even the existence of authenticated first-person statements such as "I could not have written my poem had I not read yours" or "I never read that author; how surprising that he should have anticipated me so closely" offer only partial evidence. For all we know, Wally might have written substantially the same poem if he had never run across Bill's. He might simply be excessive in his admiration.[41]

Somewhere in the middle will be the various versions of the argument:

> B produced Y at t because A wrote X at t - d.

I say "versions" because A's connection to B can be more or less proximate and still have the claim turn out to be true. Thus, the "because" here can be represented by any number of possible counterfactuals, any of which might give a different slant on the sort of influence and the evidence for it. There might, for example, be counterfactuals of commission, of rivalry, of respect or disdain. In short, the types of influence in matters human are both unlimited and unpredictable, and the arguments for influence should mirror those realities. These arguments will typically need to balance interest and burden of proof, with the one being in direct proportion to the other.

Art history cases such as the following abound:

1. Picasso would not have painted *Les demoiselles d'Avignon* if Courbet had not painted *L'atelier du peintre*.
2. Picasso would not have painted *Les demoiselles d'Avignon* if Cézanne had not painted *Les grandes baigneuses*.

Either or both of these claims might be true. I don't, off the top of my head, know how interesting or controversial they are. I imagine that it would be hard to meet the burden of proof for the strong counterfactual, where no other painting can be substituted in any clause, and the art historian may be left with the much weaker:

3. Because Courbet and Cézanne painted *L'atelier* and *Les grandes baigneuses*, Picasso was in a position to imagine and paint *Les demoiselles*.

Depending on the current interpretive climate, this might be interesting enough to argue, but it might not.[42] Even where the interpretive stakes are high enough to be interesting, it will be important to remember, as Michael Baxandall puts it, that Y is rarely if ever the passive recipient of influence. "Picasso," as Baxandall writes, "acted on Cézanne quite sharply. For one thing, he rewrote art history by making Cézanne that much larger and more central a historical fact in 1910 than he had been in 1906."[43]

Interpreting *Jus in Bello*: A Case Study in Influence

The dual measures of interest and burden of proof will themselves vary with the scholarly milieu. It may be worthwhile, to get a sense of how the proposed analysis is supposed to work, to sketch a conflict between two interpretations and then to imagine how an advocate of Boisard's position might introduce yet a third competitor as candidate for the best explanation. The case I propose is that of the law of war concerning those groups that are immune from attack.[44] In general, James Turner Johnson and I agree about the contours of medieval just war thinking. But we disagree on a crucial point. I am inclined to argue that the Aristotelian tradition, as modified by Thomas Aquinas in the light of Church teaching, contains all of the resources necessary to generate a fully realized account of justice in the prosecution of war. Johnson, however, maintains that *jus in bello* is only implicit in the theological tradition and requires not just the revival of Roman law but, "second, the somewhat inchoate but widely influential code of conduct for the knightly class, the chivalric code."[45] Johnson worries over the failure of the canonists and theologians to specify who is immune from direct attack. "The canonical effort to protect noncombatants in wartime," he writes,

> began slowly and with a marked degree of insularity in its expression. Gratian's statement . . . denied to certain classes of ecclesiastic the right to participate in war and accordingly extended to them the right of protection in wartime. In the following century Gregory IX's *De Treuga et Pace* extended this earlier canonical list of noncombatants . . . to include clerics, monks, friars, other religious, pilgrims, travelers, and peasants cultivating the soil.[46]

Honoré Bonet, however, extends this list to "bishops, abbots, monks, doctors of medicine, pilgrims, women, blind persons, all other men of the Church not named earlier, the deaf, the dumb, woodmen, and farmers," all of whom should be spared, apparently, because "they do nothing to favor one side or another in a war, but rather work, as he says explicitly of the farmer, 'for all men.'"[47] Bonet, on Johnson's reading, represents an amalgam of "the churchly tradition alongside the chivalric."[48] The chivalric code, here, is dependent on "the knight's sense of distinctness as a member of a special class." Johnson goes on to characterize this as having

> both a positive and a negative side: positively, it encouraged the knights out of a sense of *noblesse oblige* to protect the weak and innocent; negatively, it

led to prejudice and harsh treatment against anyone not of the knightly class who became involved in military combat. But in both its aspects this self-conception as a unique class, with unique responsibilities as well as privileges, came from the tradition of chivalry itself; it was not an ideal grafted on by the Church.[49]

Here is a nice, strong claim for influence. The implication is that had there been no chivalric code, noncombatant immunity would not have developed as it did. How do we test it? On my analysis, we might formulate the counterfactual of influence as:

> Had it not been for the tradition of chivalry, the history of noncombatant immunity in the law of war would not have developed as it did.

This, of course, may well be true, but I am interested in a narrower claim, focused on the concept of noncombatant immunity found in the work of the Second Scholastic, specifically in Francisco de Vitoria, who writes, "first, *it is never lawful in itself intentionally to kill innocent persons,*" and goes on to expand:

> It follows that even in wars against the Turks we may not kill children, who are obviously innocent, nor women, who are presumed innocent at least as far as the war is concerned (unless, that is, it can be proved of a particular woman that she was implicated in guilt). It follows also that one may not lawfully kill travellers or visitors who happen to be in the enemy's territory, who are presumed innocent. And the same is true of clergy and monks, unless there is evidence to the contrary or they are found actually fighting in the war. I think there can be no doubt about this.[50]

Here and in the parallel discussions *On Homicide* and in the commentary on Thomas's *Summa Theologiae*, 2a2ae, 64, Vitoria cites scripture, canon law, and Thomas himself, equating innocence with regard to war explicitly with not fighting in the war.

My counterclaim, then, would not be that Johnson's counterfactual is incorrect, broadly construed, but that

> Had the chivalric tradition never existed, the law of war as understood by the Second Scholastic would have developed unchanged, based on the teachings of Thomas Aquinas and the official documents of the Church alone.

This would, if sustained, yield me the claim that the chivalric tradition was irrelevant to Thomist teaching on just war, from which I could then go on to maintain that insofar as the distinctive Church teachings merely elaborate, as opposed to furnishing, the central arguments, Thomas and his followers may rightly be seen as thinkers in a distinctly Aristotelian account of ethics in war.[51] Johnson, of course, has a number of potential responses, to which I would then be obligated to provide rejoinders. Even if this debate were never resolved, it would still illustrate how counterfactuals of influence may be formulated and evidence offered for and against.

Suppose, now, that Boisard or someone influenced by him was still convinced of the impact of Islam on medieval and early modern just war thinking. He might return to the claim that despite its stated reliance on "the sayings of the Saints and of wise men of Antiquity," the discussion of "armed conflict" in Alfonso's *Siete Partidas* was

> preceded in Muslim Spain around 1280 by the *Villayet*, a text that enumerates the centuries-old Muslim laws of war. Mentioned were the protection of children, old people, women, invalids, and the mentally ill, the safeguard of political representatives and those in need of safe conduct, as well as injunctions against bad faith, and perfidious and disloyal actions.[52]

To sustain this third rival analysis, Boisard or his representative would first need to identify the provenance and influence of the *Villayet*, for the reference is unclear, and Boisard provides no bibliographical help. Furthermore, they would have to explain an important chronological discrepancy. The consensus among students of the *Partidas* is that they were "completed between 1256 and 1265."[53] They were preceded, according to some scholars as early as 1253, by another of Alfonso's legal compilations, *el-Espéculo*.[54] If these dates are accurate, then the *Villayet* can hardly have been an influence, even if Alfonso's compilers were using Arabic sources, a point that is also treated skeptically in the literature.[55]

Aside from difficulties in chronology, Boisard and his supporters would have to sustain the claim:

> Had it not been for the impact of the *Villayet* (or closely similar documents) on the intellectual community of medieval Spain, the law of war as understood by the Second Scholastic would not have developed as it did.

This is, of course, much stronger than the likelihood that a given document preceded another. But claims for influence *should* be held to that heavier burden of proof. When the *Siete Partidas* introduces the discussion by distinguishing wars as *justa, injusta, civilis,* and *plusquam civilis,* it would seem to rely on exactly the sort of legal text that students of the document generally assume. Thus, part of the burden of proof will include explaining why what looks like reliance on one sort of text should really be seen as reliance on a different sort. Until the followers of Boisard meet this burden, they will not advance beyond the questionable claims of *post hoc ergo*.

Islam, Aquinas, and the School of Salamanca

Instead of attempting to argue my interpretation, over and against that of either Johnson or Boisard, I will end by suggesting three potential approaches to seeking an Islamic influence on the just war thinking of the Second Scholastic. One approach would turn on the claim:

> Had it not been for the distinctively Maliki approach to jihad in al-Andalus, just war thinking would not have developed as it did.

The Maliki school of shari'a, at least in early medieval al-Andalus, was inclined to restrict "forbidding wrong and commanding right" to the secular authorities, thus limiting the individual impetus to follow this command. Ibn Rushd the grandfather writes that "only the authorities are able to deal with offences of the kind in question across the board."[56] Believers should follow the injunction of Qur'an 5:105 to "look to their own souls and ignore the misdeeds of others."[57] Dominique Urvoy, tracing the Andalusian development of jihad, sees a move from religious motivation, to the official protection of Islamic lands, to what a contemporary critic sees as "repugnance for military expeditions and . . . aversion for holy war."[58] That some scholars volunteered for jihad armies in twelfth-century al-Andalus, as Michael Bonner reports, does not necessarily contradict Urvoy's account of the status of jihad, particularly in al-Andalus's urban centers.[59] The project, then, would be to determine whether there is any evidence to suggest that the distinctively Andalusian attitude toward jihad in the eleventh and twelfth centuries had any impact on thinkers who might have transmitted it to the West.[60]

A second line of research might focus on the Order of Preachers, which got its start in Old Castile. Is there a strand of influence in the early Dominican tradition that might have disposed it to a form of just war thinking that restricted conflict with nonbelievers? The story of Dominic's early religious life in Castile and his subsequent mission to the heretics is well enough known. Jacob de Voragine's life of Dominic in the *Golden Legend* tells of his compassion for a woman whose brother was held by the Muslims and his offer to sell himself in exchange but notes that "God did not allow this, foreseeing that the saint would be needed for the spiritual redemption of many captives."[61] The rules for exchange were well known on both sides and formalized in various *fueros* from at least 1131.[62] In the thirteenth century, a religious order emerged along the frontier to facilitate ransoming, although there seems to be little evidence for the sort of substitution that Dominic offers.[63] In Jean de Mailly's life of Dominic, there is a curious detail that may hint at the active choice not to address his work to Muslim-Christian relations. Reginald, dean of an Orléans church, "arrived in Rome, intending to cross the sea with the bishop of Orléans."[64] A cardinal mentions the newly formed Order of Preachers, and, with a bit of help from the blessed Virgin, Reginald is diverted from the Holy Land and brought into the order. It might be that Dominic persuaded Reginald that preaching to heretics was more valuable than preaching to Muslims, but the text leaves us unsure.

Finally, there is the possibility that Thomas's work in the second part of the *Summa Theologiae* was influenced by a developing argument within the Dominican order, namely a debate about the wisdom of crusading, not in Spain but in the East. In a recent essay, Thomas O'Meara cites Peter Engels's judgment that "while the first Crusaders appeared full of prejudices about an idolatrous religion, the next generation more and more changed their viewpoint."[65] In particular, William of Tripoli, a Dominican of Acre and exact contemporary of Thomas Aquinas, stands out as a critic of the crusading enterprise as a whole. William displays a detailed understanding of Islam and recommends eschewing military force in favor of "love and true friendship with God and neighbor."[66]

In this, William stands in marked contrast to Humbert of Romans, sometime master-general of the order, who composed his *Treatise on Preaching the Cross against the Pagan Saracen Infidels* not long after 1266. Penny Cole describes the *Treatise* as "an omnibus, a reference collection of ideas and information about crusading up to his own day."[67] Humbert's goal here, and in the subsequent *Opus Tripartitum*, is to rally the men of Europe to a new crusade. In both, Humbert is clearly animated not only by concern for the Eastern Church but, as Cole puts it vis-à-vis *On Preaching the Cross*, a "single-minded intractable hostility." He writes of Muhammad that "the man, and after his death his image should be pelted with excrement."[68] Edward Brett, writing of the *Opusculum Tripartitum*, describes the argument as "sophism *par excellence*," going on to admit that it is "a weak argument, which had no possibility of converting those who postulated the above objection," namely that of William. Brett concludes that "this is especially apparent when one remembers that those who favored peaceful missionary work bore the mark of respectability, for they included many notable churchmen, even some friars."[69]

Brett takes William to be one of those notables, and there is a good possibility that Thomas was familiar, if not with William, then with his views. O'Meara notes that William appears in three bulls issued by Urban IV from Orvieto in 1264, while Thomas Aquinas was in residence at the priory there.[70] It was at this time that Thomas completed the *Summa contra Gentiles*, along with two short works, *Against the Errors of the Greeks* and *On Arguments for the Faith, for the Cantor of Antioch*. This latter piece, in ten brief chapters, is a response to worries about Saracens, "mockers of the faith," who deride the fact that "we say that Christ is the son of God, since God does not have a wife; and call us insane since we maintain that God is three persons, thinking by this that we mean there are three gods." Thomas goes on to note that "in asserting their errors, they illustrate what the lord says in the Gospel: 'There are many mansions in my father's house.'"[71] Although he is willing to help the cantor, Thomas insists that "in these matters deploy moral and philosophical arguments, which the Saracens acknowledge. It is pointless to introduce authorities against them that they do not acknowledge."[72] In short, as Torrell puts it, "the Christian arguer cannot aim at proving the faith, but only at defending it and showing that it is not false."[73] From the references to the *Summa contra Gentiles*, he concludes that *On Arguments* was written shortly after that work, probably in 1265. O'Meara follows Torrell in judging the piece "an apologetic of a high quality"[74] and speculates that Thomas may have been influenced by either the writings of William or some report from Dominicans living in the East.

Unfortunately, Thomas does not appear to mention William, and his references to Muslims generally are few.[75] What is certain is that almost a decade later, Thomas was summoned by Gregory X to the Council of Lyons, where, among other things, the prospects for a new crusade were to be discussed. "Before the council convened in May 1274," writes Christopher Tyerman, "Gregory sought advice from politicians and churchmen professionally involved. A number of treatises were submitted containing advice that varied from a catalogue of ecclesiastical, including crusading, shortcomings by a Franciscan to a plea by an Acre Dominican, William of Tripoli, for the conversion, not destruction, of the Muslims."[76] The council was also the occasion for Humbert's *Opus Tripartitum*. In the end, Humbert's view carried the day, but the project was abandoned after Gregory's death at the beginning of 1276.[77]

Aquinas himself never made it; he died en route, at the beginning of March 1274. While it is almost certain that he was aware of the dispute among his brothers, we do not know what Thomas might have said in the debate between Humbert and William. It is frequently assumed that he was a proponent of crusading, but the grounds for this are uncertain. All of his references to *crucesignatus* come in *Quodlibet II*, the majority of them in question 8, which deals with the remission of sin and the satisfaction of crusading vows. Tyerman cites *Summa Theologiae* 2a2ae, 188, as the point where "Thomas Aquinas needed to spell out the meritorious connection between fighting God's war and a penitential vocation."[78] It would indeed be helpful to know what Thomas thought of the crusading tradition, but we don't. What we do know is that his family was deeply implicated in the conflicts between the papacy and Frederick II and that criticism of the papal use of the crusade against Christians was widely abroad in the thirteenth century.[79] Landolfo, Thomas's father, was "one of Frederick's barons. . . . At least two and probably more of Thomas' brothers served at different times in the imperial army."[80] Torrell writes:

> Rinaldo, the second son, was at first a partisan of Frederick II, but joined the pope when Innocent IV deposed the emperor in 1245. The emperor, however, put him to death in 1246 for conspiring against him. The family

considered him a martyr for the cause of the Church. Thomas, too, seems to have believed the same, since in a dream vision his sister Marotta, recently deceased, informed him of the eternal destiny of his two brothers: Rinaldo was in heaven, while Landolfo was in purgatory, the only thing we know about the latter.[81]

Assuming that Landolfo had maintained the family connection with Frederick, it seems that partisans for either side can, at least eventually, make their way to heaven.

Conclusion

I have argued, not with any particular originality, that influence is difficult to document. If we view it as a comparatively weak form of causality, then the best way to interpret claims for influence will be in terms of their ability to license certain counterfactuals. This ability, in turn, will rest on the comparative balance of the evidence for two or more competing counterfactuals. This evidence will itself be of the usual historical sort, turning on documents and artifacts gleaned from the various sources available. Judgments about the influence of one or the other piece of evidence will themselves turn on similar counterfactual claims. All of this will be subject to the shifting norms of historical judgment and the changing base of evidence in a given field. In the case of Cézanne's influence on Mondrian, for instance, there are catalogues documenting which works were in which exhibits, Mondrian's own remarks about his ongoing work, the writings and recollections of other contemporaries, and so on. In the case of Thomas Aquinas and the School of Salamanca, there is not as much to work with. Almost all of the claims for influence linking the thirteenth-century saint with the sixteenth-century Spanish theologians will be subject to a greater sense of uncertainty than the art historian's claims about Cézanne. So far, I have argued, the claims for Islamic influence on just war thinking in medieval and early modern Spain are even more uncertain. That doesn't mean that the case cannot be made. But at least insistence on basing such claims on the available evidence relevant to the specific counterfactuals will keep our attributions grounded in the data.

Notes

1. For Vitoria and Soto, see G. Scott Davis, "Conquest and Conscience: Francisco de Vitoria on Justice in the New World," *Modern Theology* 13, no. 4 (1997): 475–500; and G. Scott Davis, "Humanist Ethics and Political Justice: Soto, Sepulveda, and the 'Affair of the Indies,'" *Annual of the Society of Christian Ethics* 19 (1999): 193–212. For Cano on *limpieza de sangre*, see Henry Kamen, *The Spanish Inquisition: A Historical Revision* (New Haven, Conn.: Yale University Press, 1997), 247. Surprisingly, there seems to be no extended general history of

the School of Salamanca in English. Juan Belda Plans, whose introduction to Melchor Cano, *De locis theologicis*, ed. and trans. Juan Belda Plans (Madrid: Biblioteca de Autores Christianos, 2006), is the most extensive recent discussion of that author and his context, has produced what appears to be the most recent account of the school, *La Escuela de Salamanca y la renovación de la teología en el siglo XVI* (Madrid: Biblioteca de Autores Cristianos, 2000), but I have not been able to consult it. There is a volume by Jaime Brufau Prats, *La Escuela de Salamanca ante el Descubrimiento del Nuevo Mundo* (Salamanca: Editorial San Esteban, 1989), but this is a collection of older essays, only one of which (chap. 8) goes substantially beyond Vitoria and Soto.

2. The classic statement of this position is James Brown Scott, *The Spanish Origin of International Law* (Oxford: Oxford University Press, 1934). Within this tradition of interpretation, the later-sixteenth-century Jesuit Francisco Suárez (1548–1617) is invariably coupled with Vitoria. James Turner Johnson affirms the importance of Vitoria and Suárez but argues for the importance of "taking into account representatives from the Netherlands and England as well." See Johnson, *Ideology, Reason, and the Limitation of War: Religious and Secular Concepts, 1200–1740* (Princeton, N.J.: Princeton University Press, 1975), 153. Richard Tuck, *The Rights of War and Peace: Political Thought and the International Order from Grotius to Kant* (Oxford: Oxford University Press, 1999), acknowledges the importance of the School of Salamanca—he is generally more aware of the importance of Soto than other commentators—but he misreads Vitoria as justifying conquest. Tuck draws, correctly, a distinction between the scholastic tradition of Vitoria and Soto and the humanist tradition of Grotius but seems, to my mind, to draw the wrong conclusion about how we should think of international ethics. My view, for which I argue in work forthcoming, is that where Suárez is right, he is almost wholly derivative from Vitoria, and where he is most original—in his interpretation of the law of nations—he runs contrary to the best impulses of the Thomist tradition. I am thankful that the argument of this chapter does not require my making good on that argument here.

3. See Norman Housley's summary to *Religious Warfare in Europe, 1400–1536* (Oxford: Oxford University Press, 2002), 190–205. Although Housley notes Vitoria as a critic of religious war and cites James Turner Johnson's *Holy War Idea in Western and Islamic Traditions* (University Park: Pennsylvania State University Press, 1997) to that conclusion, his one extended remark on Vitoria distorts his position severely. See Housley, *Religious Warfare*, 15.

4. *Convivencia* is more popular with literary and cultural historians than with social historians of medieval Iberia, who are inclined to see mostly indifference of the communities to each other. The notion has taken on a political hue in the light of the attacks of September 11, 2001. Shortly after the attacks, for instance, Maria Rosa Menocal added a postscript to her recently completed volume on the culture of medieval Spain. The book, she remarks, is "an account of and tribute to the culture of tolerance brought to Europe by the Umayyads. But the book is also necessarily an account of the forces of intolerance that were always present and that ultimately triumphed." See Maria Rosa Menocal, *Ornament of the World: How Muslims, Jews, and Christians Created a Culture of Tolerance in Medieval Spain* (New York: Little, Brown, 2002), 282. A more cautious view is expressed by Thomas Glick in *Islamic and Christian Spain in the Early Middle Ages* (Princeton, N.J.: Princeton University Press, 1979), particularly the introduction, on controversies in Spanish historiography, and chap. 5, on ethnic relations. Glick also adds a helpful introduction to *Convivencia: Jews, Muslims, and Christians in Medieval Spain* (New York: George Braziller, 1992), which he edited with Vivian Mann and Jerrilynn Dodds, in conjunction with an exhibition at the Jewish Museum. Most recently, Kenneth Wolf's "Convivencia in Medieval Spain: A Brief History of an Idea," *Religion Compass* 3, no. 1 (2009): 72–85, provides a critical introduction with bibliography. The starting point for introductions to the full spectrum of life in al-Andalus and its impact on the rest of the world is Salma Khadra Jayyusi, ed., *The Legacy of Muslim Spain* (Leiden: E. J. Brill, 1992).

5. The grandson is the philosopher and commentator known in the West as Averroës. To avoid confusion, I intend to use the convention found in scholars of Islam and distinguish "Ibn

Rushd the grandfather" from "Ibn Rushd the grandson" where necessary. Dominique Urvoy, "The *'Ulama'* of al-Andalus," in Jayyusi, *The Legacy*, 849–77, gives a broad introduction to the legal history. Miguel Cruz Hernández, "Islamic Thought in the Iberian Peninsula," in Jayyusi, *The Legacy*, 779–803, locates Ibn Rushd the grandson in the general sweep of Andalusian thought, while Jamal al-Din al-Alawi's "The Philosophy of Ibn Rushd," in Jayyusi, *The Legacy*, 804–29, provides an introduction to that thinker.

6. The consensus is that the works of Ibn Rushd the grandson were known no later than 1225 and that through the 1250s, "theses from Arabic philosophy passed into use in the schools and would be so highly assimilated that their Averroist origin would be lost (which explains, among other things, how it is that Thomas frequently uses Averroës without quoting him." Jean-Pierre Torrell, *Saint Thomas Aquinas*, vol. 1: *The Person and His Work* (Washington, D.C.: Catholic University of America Press, 1996), 192. Torrell's notes include references to the most important recent bibliography, in particular the work of the great scholar of Aristotle's ethics and its impact on Aquinas, René Antoine Gauthier.

7. Charles Butterworth, "Al-Farabi's Statecraft: War and the Well-Ordered Regime," in James Turner Johnson and John Kelsay, eds., *Cross, Crescent, and Sword: The Justification and Limitation of War in Western and Islamic Tradition* (Westport, Conn.: Greenwood, 1990), 80.

8. *Averroës on Plato's "Republic,"* trans. Ralph Lerner (Ithaca, N.Y.: Cornell University Press, 1974), 93. I follow Lerner in giving the pages of Rosenthal's Hebrew edition when citing Ibn Rushd's text; otherwise, I cite Lerner's page numbers. The translator identifies Plato's *Republic* as "the beginning of the second part of political science" (Lerner, 153), the first part of which is covered by Aristotle's *Nicomachean Ethics* and Ibn Rushd's commentary on it. Ibn Rushd himself notes that the second part is laid out in Aristotle's *Politics* and that he has undertaken the commentary on Plato because "Aristotle's book on governance has not yet fallen into our hands" (22).

9. Ibid., 26–27.

10. "The Chapter on Jihad from Averroes' Legal Handbook *al-Bidaya*," in Rudolph Peters, *Jihad in Classical and Modern Islam* (Princeton, N.J.: Markus Weiner, 1996), 30.

11. Ibid.

12. Ibid., 35.

13. Noah Feldman, "War and Reason in Maimonides and Averroes," in Richard Sorabji and David Rodin, eds., *The Ethics of War: Shared Problems in Different Traditions* (Aldershot, U.K.: Ashgate, 2006), 102. Lerner, *Averroës*, also calls attention to this passage in his note to 60.4, but he doesn't draw the connection to the discussion of equity. Lacking both the Hebrew and the Arabic, not to mention a copy of the dissertation, I can't tell if Feldman or Ibn Rushd keys this discussion to *EN* V.7. The relevant text is more properly 1137b–1138a, where Aristotle introduces the technical sense of *epieikeia*, which is frequently translated as "equity."

14. Feldman, "War and Reason," 103.

15. Ibid.

16. Ibid., 104

17. *The Decisive Treatise and Epistle Dedicatory*, trans. Charles Butterworth (Provo, Utah: Brigham Young University Press, 2001), 6.

18. Wael B. Hallaq, *Authority, Continuity and Change in Islamic Law* (Cambridge, U.K.: Cambridge University Press, 2001), 4.

19. See Alfonso Carmona, "The Introduction of Malik's Teaching in al-Andalus," in Peri Bearman, Rudolph Peters, and Frank Vogel, eds., *The Islamic School of Law: Evolution, Devolution, and Progress* (Cambridge, Mass.: Harvard University Press, 2005), 41–56; and Maribel Fierro, "Proto-Malikis, Malikis, and Reformed Malikis in al-Andalus," in Bearman, Peters, and Vogel, *The Islamic School*, 57–76.

20. Yasin Dutton, "The Introduction to Ibn Rushd's *Bidayat al-Mujtahid*," *Islamic Law and Society* 1, no. 2 (1994): 197. For an introduction to Maliki jurisprudence, see Yasin Dutton, *The Origins of Islamic Law: The Qur'an, the Muwatta and Madinan Amal* (London: Routledge, 1994). Some important caveats are issued by Christopher Melchert in his review, "*Origins of Islamic Law*," *Journal of the American Oriental Society* 121, no. 4 (2001): 713–15.

21. Malik ibn-Anas, *Al-Muwatta of Imam Malik Ibn Anas: The First Formulation of Islamic Law*, trans. A. A. Bewley (London: Routledge, 1989), 183.

22. This is available at www.corpusthomisticum.org. The Web edition is edited by Eduardo Bernot and Enrique Alarcón. The site as a whole is maintained by Alarcón.

23. Marcel Boisard, "On the Probable Influence of Islam on Western Public and International Law," *International Journal of Middle East Studies* 11, no. 4 (1980): 429.

24. Ibid., 431.

25. See Joseph O'Callaghan, "Alfonso X and the *Partidas*," his introduction to the *Las Siete Partidas*, 5 vols., ed. Robert I. Burns, trans. Samuel P. Scott (Philadelphia: University of Pennsylvania Press, 2001), 1:xxx–xl, which provides the basic background, with substantial bibliography. Note that the text of the *Partidas* is paginated continuously through the five volumes, while each volume has individually paginated frontmatter. Further background, including substantial philological analysis, is provided in Robert MacDonald, *Libro de las Tahuerías: A Special Code of Law, concerning Gambling, Drawn up by Maestro Roldán at the Command of Alfonso X of Castile* (Madison, Wis.: Hispanic Seminary of Medieval Studies, 1995), and, in even greater detail, albeit in Spanish, in Robert MacDonald, *Espéculo: Texto Juridico atribuido al Rey de Castile Don Alfonso X, el Sabio* (Madison, Wis.: Hispanic Seminary of Medieval Studies, 1990). Innocent readers should not be misled by Boisard's misidentification of the king as Alfonso IX.

26. Boisard, "On the Probable Influence," 435

27. Robert MacDonald, "Law and Politics: Alfonso's Program of Political Reform," in Robert I. Burns, ed., *The Worlds of Alfonso the Learned and James the Conqueror: Intellect and Force in the Middle Ages* (Princeton, N.J.: Princeton University Press, 1985), 171–72.

28. Roger Collins, *Early Medieval Spain: Unity in Diversity, 400–1000* (New York: St. Martin's, 1983), 248.

29. Many of the complexities of the interaction between Muslim and Christian in the early Middle Ages can be gleaned from Thomas Glick, *Islamic and Christian Spain*.

30. This is not to say that the *Siete Partidas* does not employ vocabulary drawn from Arabic. But these terms had long been part of the Castilian vocabulary. On these matters, see Glick, *Islamic and Christian Spain*, esp. 297–99 and the index entries under "Arabisms."

31. *Las Siete Partidas*, 1438.

32. Ibid.

33. Ibid., 1441.

34. Ibid., 1418.

35. Ibid., 1436.

36. Ibid., 1442.

37. James Brundage, *Law, Sex, and Christian Society in Medieval Europe* (Chicago: University of Chicago Press, 1987), 578.

38. Sharon LaFraniere, "Scientists Point to Possible Link between Dam and China Quake," *New York Times*, February 6, 2009, p. 1.

39. To give merely the basic outline of the story would be a major undertaking. A valuable introduction to the issues may be found in J. L. Mackie, *The Cement of the Universe: A Study in Causation* (Oxford: Oxford University Press, 1974). A very interesting approach, which begins where Mackie leaves off, has been developed by Nancy Cartwright in *Nature's Capacities and Their Measurement* (Oxford: Oxford University Press, 1989). Cartwright deploys notions drawn from economics, which speak to her interest in measurability. The approach to influence through counterfactuals, which I plan to develop here, goes back at least to the 1940s, and a number of important essays are brought together in Ernest Sosa, ed., *Causation and Conditionals* (Oxford: Oxford University Press, 1975). David Lewis's influential essays on causation, including an expanded version of the one in Sosa, are collected in *Philosophical Papers*, vol. 2 (Oxford: Oxford University Press, 1986). His last word on the subject is "Causation as Influence," *Journal of Philosophy* 97, no. 4 (2000): 182–97.

40. In "Causation as Influence," Lewis addresses a number of issues having to do with "redundant" causation, as when, for example, one rock hits a bottle a split second before another

rock would have. These discussions also help in getting clearer about what sort of constraints there might be on interpreting human interactions and the ascription of influence, but I will not develop them here.

41. Perhaps the most famous philosophical example is Descartes's (feigned?) surprise that Augustine anticipated the *cogito*, as in his letter to Colvius of November 14, 1640: "I am obliged to you for drawing my attention to the passage of St. Augustine relevant to my *I am thinking, therefore I exist*. I went today to the library of this town to read it, and I find that he does really use it to prove the certainty of our existence." Descartes, *Philosophical Letters*, trans. and ed. Anthony Kenny (Oxford: Oxford University Press, 1970), 83–84.

42. These last paragraphs were written in October 2008, well before I heard of the major exhibition "Cézanne and Beyond" held at the Philadelphia Museum of Art from February 26 to May 17, 2009. That exhibition, juxtaposing as it did the work of Cézanne with a disparate group of subsequent artists, illustrates the complexity of the various forms of influence. If we take just the case of Mondrian, it seems fairly clear that had the Dutch artist not encountered Cézanne's *Gingerpot with Pomegranate and Pears*, he would not have produced his own *Still Life with Gingerpot I* of 1911. This is clearly the precursor of *Still Life with Gingerpot II* of 1912, which in turn gives rise to *Composition No. II* of 1913. From here, there seems to be a clear line of progression to the well-known abstractions of which *Broadway Boogie-Woogie* is probably the most famous. How and at which points any of this may be related to Mondrian's membership in the Theosophical Society, beginning in 1909, goes beyond my art history knowledge. See Joop Joosten, "Cézanne and Mondrian: 'A New Way to Express the Beauty of Nature,'" in Joseph Rishel and Katherine Sachs, eds., *Cezanne and Beyond* (Philadelphia: Philadelphia Museum of Art, 2009), 137–57. The more important point is that whatever lines of influence Cézanne may have had on Mondrian may well have been markedly different from those exercised on Picasso or Jasper Johns. Thus, even the influence of a single figure on subsequent generations may be extremely resistant to generalization. Michael Baxandall's *Patterns of Intention: On the Historical Explanation of Pictures* (New Haven, Conn.: Yale University Press, 1985) has been particularly influential in my thinking on these matters.

43. Baxandall, *Patterns of Intention*, 61. Baxandall's strictures on the attribution of "influence" here seem to me very important, and I hope that nothing I say appears contrary to them.

44. I propose this as a hypothetical debate, and, with regard to the details, so it is. But I have benefited from extended discussions with Johnson on the matter and am convinced that the disagreement is both real and important. In any case, I am greatly in Johnson's debt.

45. James Turner Johnson, *Just War Tradition and the Restraint of War: A Moral and Historical Inquiry* (Princeton, N.J.: Princeton University Press, 1981), 122.

46. Ibid., 132.

47. Ibid., 141.

48. Ibid.

49. Ibid., 140.

50. Francisco de Vitoria, *On the Law of War*, 3.1, in *Political Writings*, ed. Anthony Pagden and Jeremy Lawrence (Cambridge, U.K.: Cambridge University Press, 1991), 314–15; italics in original. The editors go on to note that the early printed editions "amplify the list of innocent non-combatants in this sentence as follows: 'In wars against fellow-Christians, the same argument holds true of harmless farming folk, and other peaceful civilians (*gens togata*).'"

51. This is, as it happens, the position I have argued in G. Scott Davis, *Warcraft and the Fragility of Virtue: An Essay in Aristotelian Ethics* (Moscow: University of Idaho Press, 1992).

52. Boisard, "On the Probable Influence," 435.

53. O'Callaghan, "Alfonso X," xxxix.

54. MacDonald, *Espéculo*, xxxi.

55. A lively and up-to-date account of Alfonso X's legislative program and its place in the history of his reign can now be found in Peter Linehan, *Spain, 1157–1300: A Partible Inheritance* (Oxford: Blackwell, 2008), esp. 121–32, 204–9.

56. Michael Cook, *Commanding Right and Forbidding Wrong in Islamic Thought* (Cambridge, U.K.: Cambridge University Press, 2000), 364.

57. Ibid.

58. Dominique Urvoy, "Sur l'evolution de la notion de Gihad dans l'Espagne musulmane," *Mélange de la Casa de Velázquez* 9 (1973): 337–38, 352. The disdain for Andalusian laxness emerges with even greater force in Maribel Fierro's discussion of "spiritual alienation and political activism" in twelfth-century Andalusia. According to the received interpretation of the *hadith*, "Islam began as a stranger and shall return to being a stranger just as it began," abandoning jihad was a sign of the "two intoxifications" that presage the period of evil in which "the true believer will be considered a liar and will be punished for obeying God." Maribel Fierro, "Spiritual Alienation and Political Activism: The Guruba in al-Andalus during the Sixth/Twelfth Century," *Arabica* 47, no. 2 (2000): 234.

59. See Michael Bonner, *Jihad in Islamic History: Doctrines and Practice* (Princeton, N.J.: Princeton University Press, 2006), 111–12.

60. One suggestion, which might be of interest to scholars more sympathetic to chivalry, would be to wonder whether the work of the translation "school" at Toledo, which clearly influenced Peter the Venerable (see James Kritzek, *Peter the Venerable and Islam* [Princeton, N.J.: Princeton University Press, 1964]), also had an impact on the work of the Majorcan polymath and would-be apostle to the Muslims, Ramon Llull, particularly his *Book of the Order of Chivalry*. The situation, however, is made even more complicated by the fact that Llull draws on *Partida* II, title XXI, "Concerning Knights," thus reproducing the conflict among Boisard, Johnson, and myself. See Anthony Bonner, ed., *Doctor Illuminatus: A Ramon Llull Reader* (Princeton, N.J.: Princeton University Press, 1985), for an introduction to the world of Llull studies.

61. Jacobus de Voragine, *The Golden Legend*, 2 vols., trans. W. G. Ryan (Princeton, N.J.: Princeton University Press, 1993), 2:46. The intellectual background to the emergence of the fraternal orders is brilliantly articulated in M.-D. Chenu, *Nature, Man, and Society in the Twelfth Century*, ed. and trans. Jerome Taylor and Lester Little (Chicago: University of Chicago Press, 1968), chaps. 6–7. Simon Tugwell, *Early Dominicans: Selected Writings* (Mahwah, N.J.: Paulist, 1982), is a valuable collection of primary texts in translation, with an authoritative historical discussion. The offer to stand ransom is not simply a pious gesture, although Dominic does seem to have offered himself more than once for various good works. Dominic's offer should be seen as part of another ongoing arena in which Christians and Muslims interacted with the expectation of fair exchange, namely the practice of ransoming captives from one community back to the other. For most of the medieval period, to venture into the frontier put an individual at risk from raiding parties. "The most practical means for a captive to gain freedom," writes James Brodman, "was redemption, i.e., through the payment of a ransom in money or in kind, or through the exchange of a suitable captive held by the other side." James William Brodman, *Ransoming Captives in Crusader Spain: The Order of Merced on the Christian-Islamic Frontier* (Philadelphia: University of Pennsylvania Press, 1986), 6.

62. Brodman, *Ransoming Captives*, 7.

63. Ibid., 113.

64. Tugwell, *Early Dominicans*, 56.

65. Thomas F. O'Meara, "The Theology and Times of William of Tripoli, O.P.: A Different View of Islam," *Theological Studies* 69 (2008): 81–82.

66. Ibid., 95. William plays a prominent role in Palmer Throop, *Criticism of the Crusade: A Study of Public Opinion and Crusade Propaganda* (Amsterdam: Swets and Zeitlinger, 1940), which translates notable sections of *De Statu Saracenorum*. A critical edition of that work, and of the *Notitia de Machometo*, has now been produced, but I have not been able to consult it. O'Meara, "The Theology and Times," provides the relevant references. Elizabeth Siberry downplays the importance of William in *Criticism of Crusading, 1095–1274* (Oxford: Oxford University Press, 1985), but she cannot dismiss the reality of a debate within the Dominican community about the time when Aquinas was finishing the *Secunda Secundae*, which is

central to my argument below. Discussing Siberry, Hans Eberhard Mayer writes that the book "is useful as a rich collection of material and for its study of twelfth-century crusading criticism, but it is a curiously one-sided piece of work. While the defenders of the papacy with regard to the crusades against heretics and the Hohenstaufen are taken at face value, the critics are throughout dismissed." Hans Eberhard Mayer, *The Crusades*, 2nd ed., trans. John Gillingham (Oxford: Oxford University Press, 1988), 320.

67. Penny Cole, "Humbert of Romans and Crusade," in Marcus Bull and Norman Housley, ed., *The Experience of Crusading*, vol. 1 (Cambridge, U.K.: Cambridge University Press, 2003), 164. Humbert of Romans is not as well studied as might be expected of such an important figure. Edward T. Brett, *Humbert of Romans: His Life and Views of Thirteenth-Century Society* (Toronto: Pontifical Institute of Medieval Studies, 1984), is the most detailed discussion in English. Tugwell, *Early Dominicans*, 31–35, has a very valuable discussion. Humbert figures prominently in Penny Cole, *The Preaching of the Crusades to the Holy Land, 1095–1270* (Cambridge, Mass.: Medieval Society of America, 1991). Cole notes that she is at work on a critical edition of *On Preaching the Crusade*, but as of this writing, it has not appeared.

68. Cole, "Humbert of Romans," 167.

69. Brett, *Humbert of Romans*, 179.

70. O'Meara, "The Theology and Times," 86–87.

71. Thomas Aquinas, *De rationibus fidei ad Cantorem Antiochem*, in *Corpus Thomisticum*, ed. Robert Busa, online edition of the Leonine text of 1968, cap. 1, at www.corpusthomisticum.org.

72. Ibid.

73. Torrell, *Saint Thomas Aquinas*, 352.

74. O'Meara, "The Theology and Times," 88.

75. The *Index Thomisticus* notes thirty-two instances of "Saracen" and its cognates in twenty-six works. "Muhammad," in variations of "Mahumetus," occurs in six works. *Summa Theologiae* 2a2ae, 10, on unbelief generally, distinguishes the unbelief of the Jews and the heretics from "infidelitas gentilium sive Paganorum" (the disbelief of the gentiles or pagans), but it is not clear how broad a scope is intended. The one occurrence of "Saracen" in this question—"Christiani possunt habere servos infideles, vel Iudaeos vel etiam Paganos sive Saracenos" (Christians may have servants who are unbelievers, whether Jews or even pagans or Saracens; a. 9, arg. 3)—leaves it unclear whether "Saracenos" are identical to "Paganos" or merely a subset of them.

76. Christopher Tyerman, *God's War: A New History of the Crusades* (Cambridge, Mass.: Harvard University Press, 2006), 815.

77. See ibid., 815–16.

78. Ibid., 256.

79. Housley seems inclined to follow Siberry in discounting much of this criticism, writing of Throop's remark on "the decaying prestige of a papacy too inclined to use spiritual weapons for apparently secular aims" that "this argument is valid only if it can be shown that public opinion was uniformly or at least overwhelmingly hostile to the use of the crusade against Christian lay powers. Joseph Strayer was doubtful if this could be proved." Norman Housley, *The Italian Crusades: The Papal-Angevin Alliance and the Crusades against Christian Lay Powers, 1254–1343* (Oxford: Oxford University Press, 1982), 6–7. While this would be true of popular opinion generally, it is hard to imagine that such criticisms would not have been common in the household of "one of Frederick's barons." To imagine that Thomas, as a religious, would have been an unquestioning supporter of the pope is an anachronistic projection of contemporary wishes onto medieval realities. Still, this remains speculative.

80. Simon Tugwell, ed., *Albert and Thomas: Selected Writings* (Mahwah, N.J.: Paulist, 1988), 201.

81. Torrell, *Saint Thomas Aquinas*, 3.

7

Religious War in the Works of Maimonides

An Idea and Its Transit across the Medieval Mediterranean

GEORGE R. WILKES

One of the most preeminent medieval Jewish legal authorities, Moses ben Maimon (c. 1137–1204, commonly referred to as Maimonides in Western literature) developed a notion of religious war that was revolutionary in relation to the rabbinic tradition and without which it is difficult to understand modern religious Jewish discourse about the laws of war. Much of his account of the nature of a "war for religion" was rejected or ignored by many of his most ardent followers. Nevertheless, today his treatment of the laws of war is widely credited by Jewish scholars, in universities and *yeshivot* (rabbinical schools) alike, as both authoritative and representative of the normative rabbinic tradition. Consequently, it is sometimes presented as a sufficient basis in itself for subsequent legal reasoning about wars, without recourse to further texts.

This conundrum derives first and foremost from Maimonides's remarkable command both of Jewish sources and of Greek and Islamic philosophical and juridical thought. Much of his continuing status as a legal authority derives from the audacious brilliance with which he identified eternal laws from the whole range of Jewish texts, from the scriptures to the two Talmuds and post-Talmudic literature. Furthermore, in some areas of biblical law, most notably in relation to war, Maimonides was the only medieval commentator who sought to systematize the halakha, or law, a halakha that only appeared in more fragmented fashion in earlier Jewish sources. For these reasons, Maimonides's presentation of eternally valid biblical laws of war remains a natural first resort for those Jewish scholars who seek to understand how biblical law relates to contemporary challenges.

Not uncommonly, Maimonides's great legal code, the *Mishneh Torah* (Repetition of the Torah), arrives at a judgment that is far from immediately obvious on the basis of the main sources of the textual tradition. It is difficult to know if his interpretation is taken from a little-known rabbinic source, since as a rule, he did not give references to the sources he relied on. That he understood the halakha in the light of a fairly distinctive philosophy is very evident in the text of the *Mishneh Torah*. The final section of the *Mishneh Torah*, titled "Kings and Their Wars," resembles in a number of respects the philosophy of Muslim thinkers whom Maimonides respected, although he, seeking an authoritative statement of Jewish law, does not make this explicit. As a result, whereas many Orthodox Jewish thinkers treat the text as definitive of biblical law, others see it as overly influenced by Aristotelian or Platonic philosophy, a factor that might explain the transformation of a quietist, reactive rabbinic tradition into a philosophy commanding activist solutions to social problems, including warfare. A later, more mystical Neoplatonic understanding, which many thinkers of his generation associated with Aristotle and Plato, might help to explain the unusual centrality of religious objectives and qualities in Maimonides's war of religion. In keeping with the Islamic environment in which he lived, Maimonides did not distinguish between "religion" and "law," the two being semantically equivalent in both the Hebrew and the Arabic of his day. The notion of a war of religion nevertheless receives distinctive treatment in the Islamic jurisprudence of his day, and we shall see that more metaphorical, spiritual, or mystical interpretive approaches to warfare, or jihad, complicated contemporary Jewish attempts to grapple with the topic, much as they did in Islam.

This chapter describes some distinctive features of Maimonides's approach to war, before describing the extent to which he was influenced by his Islamic sources and environment. This Islamic background emerges through veiled references in "Kings and Their Wars" to well-understood approaches to jihad in his day and also influenced his selection of genre and of biblical and rabbinic sources, both of which indicate the political and philosophical agendas underlying his treatment of war. This chapter, therefore, begins with an outline of "Kings and Their Wars" and then moves to a discussion of the Islamic contexts in which Maimonides wrote. It ends with observations on Maimonides's use of biblical and rabbinic material in his identification of an eternal law of war, which applied to all biblical kings and which he believed would apply again with the coming of the messiah.

Born in Córdoba, at the heart of Islamic Spain, Maimonides was raised in an environment in which Greek and Arab philosophy were integrated with classical Jewish teaching from the earliest years of schooling. Religious violence troubled the rest of his life, presenting a series of occasions for reflection on the relationship between religion and war. The Almohad (al-Muwahhidun) invasion of 1148 demolished Cordoban society and its relatively tolerant culture, leaving the Jews living there with the choice of flight or conversion to Islam. This resulted in a large population of Jews who became nominally Muslim and were tolerated as such by the Almohads, even when their conversions were doubted, because some Almohad scholars argued that a forced conversion was not legally binding. Maimonides and his family fled, making their way, ironically, to the Almohad capital in Morocco,

Fez, where Maimonides appears to have lived, at least outwardly, as a Muslim.[1] Some five years later, Maimonides traveled to the Holy Land, and from there to Fatimid Egypt, where he became a physician to the courts of the Fatimids and their Ayyubid successors, a leading figure in the Egyptian Jewish community, and a religious authority whose judgments were sought by Jews from the whole region surrounding the Mediterranean and Arabian seas. Maimonides's rise to prominence was accelerated by his role in negotiating the release of Jews captured by the crusaders.[2] As a protected minority (*dhimmi*) within the Islamic realm, Jews were not allowed to bear arms, although in the recent past, both Muslim and Christian antagonists in Spain had welcomed Jewish warriors and military leadership.[3] Reflecting the constraints on life as a *dhimmi*, Maimonides's legal rulings do not include discussion of cases involving the use of armed force except in two instances: two of his most renowned letters treat the choices that Jews faced when a hostile government forced them, on pain of death, to convert to Islam.[4]

As soon as Maimonides's students began to spread among Jewish communities under Christian rule, his teachings on war appeared unusual. The final part of this chapter focuses on discussion of war among Maimonides's readers from Spain and Provence. Increasingly alienated from Arab thought in the course of the thirteenth and fourteenth centuries, they often grappled eagerly with Maimonides's intellectual strategies for withstanding the pressures of life as a religious minority but departed from them where the intellectual climate differed from that on the other side of the Mediterranean. The nature of religious war was one area in which this was true.

War in the Work of Maimonides

The *Mishneh Torah*, Maimonides's restatement of the law given by God to Moses at Mount Sinai, was completed in 1178 or shortly thereafter. It was the first and last of his works to treat war at any length, and the picture of religious war that he presents is not matched in his other works. In his earlier *Commentary on the Mishnah* (*Kitab al-siraj*, later translated into Hebrew as *Perush ha-Mishnah* or *Perush ha-Mishnayot*, c. 1168), the topic only arises in a fragmented fashion, the teachings of the Mishnaic sages about the virtues of peace being at least as prominent as the few short passages relating teachings about war.[5] The last of his three major works, the *Guide for the Perplexed* (*Dalalat al-ha'irin*, later translated into Hebrew as *Moreh ha-nebukhim*), finished in 1190, touches only tangentially on permission to kill in a series of repeated assertions that a man who has not "actualized his intellect" is like a beast, by consequence of which he may be killed with no more guilt than accrues from the killing of an animal.[6] No passage makes clearer the distance Maimonides has traveled from earlier rabbinic discourse about war, which never approached the subject with such a philosophical, or medical, detachment.

The dramatic shift in focus from one work to the next may be deemed a function of their distinctive purposes.[7] The *Commentary on the Mishnah* attempts to make the teachings of the *Mishnah* accessible to those readers of Judeo-Arabic (Arabic written in Hebrew characters, with a range of vocabulary taken from Hebrew) for whom the *Mishnah* was intellectually foreign. In this context, the *Mishnah*'s praise for peace is given a philosophical twist, representing less the physical absence of combat than the conditions in which the religious intellectual may live the good life and work on his relationship with the Divine.[8] The *Guide for the Perplexed* performs a similar task in relation to those aspects of the Bible that philosophically educated, Arabic-speaking Jews would find exposed to derision in their encounters with advocates of other religious traditions or with philosophically trained skeptics. Maimonides does not present the biblical accounts of mass slaughter as a challenge to the educated mind, remarking on the inhumanity of a person who will only use his bestial faculties when it serves to highlight the centrality of reason for the life that God intends humans to lead. By contrast, the *Mishneh Torah* is literally a restatement or repetition of the law, including those areas of the law that Jews were not able to practice without sovereignty and without a Temple, areas that students of halakha had not needed to give systematic attention since the Jerusalem and Babylonian editions of the Talmud were edited (400–650 C.E.). The work bears the marks of Maimonides's broader philosophical project, characteristically Aristotelian—which helps to explain why all areas of human activity, including war and Temple service, are deemed by Maimonides to be more important than his predecessors had indicated—while being written in a deliberately simple Hebrew for the sake of unpretentious Jewish readers in communities across the world. The final, eighty-third book of the work, on "Kings and Their Wars," is presented as an elaboration of the list of commandments related to war taken from the enumeration of the entire list of 613 commandments that Maimonides had already compiled, in Judeo-Arabic, *Kitab al-fara'id* (Book of the Commandments, or *Sefer ha-mitzvot* in its Hebrew translation).

Some coherence between the divergence of spirit in which war and peace are treated in the *Commentary on the Mishnah* and the *Mishneh Torah* may be sought in Maimonides's understanding of religious war, outlined in chapters 5 and 6 of "Kings and Their Wars." Here Maimonides describes a war fought on behalf of religion, which is fought on behalf of the peace brought by religion and consequently against the enemies of religion, idolaters. This *milhemet mitzvah* (literally, "commanded war") groups together the wars that God commanded the biblical Israelites to undertake against the Canaanites and the Amalekites with wars of self-defense, treating them all as wars fought for a religious purpose. According to Maimonides, the first war a king embarks on must be "for a 'religious cause'" (5:1). "Kings and Their Wars" asserts that the king's wars play a central part in the elimination of idolatry and the achievement of peace in the messianic time (12:2), although it does not explicitly state that the elimination of idolatry is sufficient cause for a *milhemet mitzvah*. The book instead frames war as a prerequisite to governance, just as the biblical kingdom could only be established after the Israelites had joined battle against their inimical enemies, the Amalekites (1:1, 2, 8). In the course of a war that had been launched, cities or individuals who were captured or surrendered or otherwise made treaty with the Israelites had to accept the worship of God and the rejection of idolatry, along with the other commandments given by God to Noah, and subjection to the Israelite kingdom (6:1, 3; 8:9). The importance of this religious purpose was to guide every aspect of the king's conduct, as is made clear in chapter 4: "All he did should be in the name of heaven, and his aim and purpose should be to increase knowledge of true religion and fill the world with righteousness and to break the arm of the wicked fighting the wars of the Lord" (4:10).

In contrast with the "religious war," a second category of justifiable combat, the *milhemet reshut* (authorized or permitted war), covers offensive engagements fought "to extend the frontier of Israel or to increase its prestige" (5:1). This distinction between commanded and merely permitted wars, or between defensive and offensive, has three consequences. A *milhemet reshut* could only be waged with the consent of the court, the *Bet Din* (House of Judgment), which elsewhere Maimonides equates with a Sanhedrin. In such a war, children and women might not be killed. Finally, in this category of war alone would the full range of biblical exemptions from combat apply (chapter 7). Maimonides's account of the two types of war does not imply that the *milhemet reshut* is a less legitimate form of combat than the *milhemet mitzvah*, merely a different type of engagement. The soldier who fights in a *milhemet reshut* may still "be worthy of life in the world to come" if his "intention was to sanctify the Holy Name [of God]" (7:15). The army that fought to expand the boundaries of Israel still had to ensure that its camp would be "consecrated," again indicating the sanctity of a *milhemet reshut*. The consecration of the army extended to the provision that soldiers were commanded to dig a hole to relieve themselves and then to cover it outside the camp if they were encamped and wherever they were in the field (6:14, 15).

The primary interest of the book lies in the institution and strength of a king, and this informs much of Maimonides's approach to legitimate warfare. The book focuses first on the qualifications, duties, and general purpose of kingship, and war then arises as a topic in its own right but still in the context of the duties and prerogatives of the monarch. Early on, it is established that the king's authority is granted to him and his successors forever (1:7, 9), and the laws described are eternally applicable, as is emphasized by the chapters on the wars of the messiah that close the book (11, 12). It could credibly be argued that the book presents a somewhat utopian picture of a pious messiah figure of a king and that the laws applying to the king's wars can only apply at times when God intervenes in history. Maimonides refers to kings from throughout the Bible and also to Bar Kochba, the messianic pretender of the second century, and to the future messiah. However, the book might equally reflect on the legal position that applies wherever men will get themselves together to defend themselves and their religion through armed force, a duty that is not bound to a particular period of history. An activist perspective also focuses the book on what a king and his soldiers should and could do in making war, although the book does not minimize the biblical prohibitions on unlawful killing or destruction (3:10, 6:9) or the command to leave an escape route for a besieged population to flee unharmed (6:7). Maimonides's monarchist perspective, moreover, allows for less difference between the *milhemet mitzvah* and the *milhemet reshut* than appears from accounts that explain the difference between the two in terms of scriptural authority or with a greater focus on situational ethics. Finally, Maimonides's concern for the king's ability to instill fear and respect into the population (chapter 2) justifies the suppression of rebellion (3:8) and may even justify a *milhemet reshut*, an offensive campaign fought to increase Israel's "prestige" (5:1).

The Influence of Maimonides's Islamic Environment

"Kings and Their Wars" was completed shortly after the crusader invasion of Egypt in 1168 and the subsequent fall of the Isma'ili Fatimid caliphate at the hands of its Sunni antagonists, the Ayyubids Nur al-Din and Saladin. Its dissemination, even in Hebrew, carried all the more risk once the Ayyubids began to root out Fatimid loyalists and officials from the religious minorities. If pressed, Maimonides could have argued that the work was not a practical guide. He might also, with some justice, claim that its general approach to monarchy and war was far closer to Saladin's ideology than to that of his predecessors.

Nothing in Maimonides's account of halakha suggests that he had a particular Islamic model or text to which he was working. On the contrary, the text bears comparison with a range of sources that Maimonides had read or otherwise been exposed to. Thus, because of his broad philosophical education in Spain, the thought of al-Farabi had a particularly weighty impact on his approach to politics, as much as it had on fellow Cordoban Ibn Rushd, with whose work "Kings and Their Wars" has also been compared.[9] Maimonides's text also reflects his experience of a series of political regimes inspired by quite different legal schools, at first Shi'a and later Sunni, in Spain, Morocco, and Egypt. His writings do not suggest that he was using the works of the Muslim jurists, although he had a broad knowledge of Islamic jurisprudence,[10] and "Kings and Their Wars" would fit comfortably alongside a genre of legal commentaries that seek to explain the application of the law to a broad audience, al-Ghazali's *Book of Counsel for Kings* (*Nasihat al-muluk*) being comparable in that sense. If Maimonides did not read such works, the social reality influencing the authors and partly influenced by their works nevertheless shapes his notion of the nature of war, the role of the king, and the expectations of soldiers and civilians in wartime. Whereas the exact, direct influence of Islam on his work may be contestable, it would be difficult to understand his approach to war without reference to his Islamic context.

A war of religion: Fighting the Lord's war, breaking the arm of the wicked

By contrast with Talmudic literature,[11] "Kings and Their Wars" suggests the continuing force of the mandate for a form of offensive war (5:1), fought in the name of God (4:10) or for the principle of the unity of God (7:15) and to "break the arm of the wicked" (4:10). Classical juridical literature on jihad, created under the Abbasids in the eighth and ninth centuries, was in line with each aspect of this description of justified war, and while Maimonides was composing the *Mishneh Torah*, Saladin was seeking support from jurists interested in the revival of a form of jihad on these very lines.[12]

The conjunction of the Qur'anic "struggle in the path of God" (*jihad fi sabil Allah*) with the judicious use of military force led some of the earlier and most authoritative Islamic commentators, such as al-Bukhari, to define a military jihad as war fought in the path or cause of Allah.[13] Warring for the principle of the unity of God's name was also of widespread usage, such that Maimonides's adoption of this slogan could (but need not) reflect either his exposure to the Almohads ("al-Muwahhidun" literally means "those who uphold the unity of God," understood as those who battle against *shirk*, or polytheism) in Córdoba and Fez, or the growing pressure to drive the crusaders from Egypt and the Holy Land across the twelfth century, also commonly associated with the defense of monotheism against *shirk*.[14]

The focus that was evident throughout the body of Islamic literature on the use of force with the goal of bringing unbelievers within the borders of a just, Muslim polity was an unavoidable feature of his Cordoban youth under the Almoravids, too. After establishing a large empire through jihad in northwest Africa, Almoravid (al-Murabitun) forces crossed into Iberia in the late eleventh century, invited by the Ta'ifa rulers to stem and reverse the advance of Christian forces into *dar al-Islam*. The Almoravid movement infused a revived zeal for jihad in Andalusia. Maimonides's reference to making war to expand the borders of the kingdom (5:1) is all the more striking because it presents a justification for war not mentioned in the Talmud. Nevertheless, whereas in contemporary Islamic jurisprudence this was a fundamental feature of a legitimate jihad, Maimonides includes this not in the *milhemet mitzvah*, the category that most naturally translates into the jihad of classical Islamic jurisprudence, but in the more circumscribed category of *milhemet reshut*, warfare that was not obligatory but was within the authority of the king to initiate.

The problem diminishes if both types of warfare are considered, in differing degrees, religious in their aim. Maimonides may not have engaged consciously with the early Islamic scholarship that presented the offensive jihad as opening the world to the influence of natural religion,[15] but he was fulsomely appreciative of al-Farabi's conviction that the virtuous must bring governance to the uneducated, where necessary through the use of force, both within and beyond the state.[16] It is possible that, like al-Farabi and Ibn Rushd, Maimonides envisioned a world ultimately governed by a single virtuous state.[17] The messianic chapters at the end of "Kings and Their Wars" (11, 12) do not make this explicit, and the text could as easily fit a more elitist eschatology whereby war is only made to secure a peace that will enable the righteous to turn their attention to the true purpose of life, a trope from al-Farabi's work that concludes Maimonides's treatise (12:4).

Maimonides's war of religion rests more explicitly on a second factor that justifies the extension of the frontiers of the kingdom: that the virtuous are in an ongoing state of war with the wicked. Amalek, the perennial enemy to the Jews, represents this force at the outset of the book (1:1–2), at the end of which stands "the wicked heathen who are called wolves and leopards" (12:1). In the face of the Crusades, jurists across the Islamic world justified a vigorous frontier warfare in similar defensive terms, some also, like Maimonides, viewing expansionist initiatives as optional rather than obligatory.[18] Maimonides preferred the argument that an offensive war that punished wrongdoers was sanctioned,[19] a point that was also a feature of Islamic jurisprudence and political philosophy alike—and absent from the rabbinic tradition. Like al-Farabi's just ruler, the king in Maimonides's text was empowered to "break the arm of the wicked" (4:10), a phrase from the Psalms (10:15) that in its biblical context referred to God's action, not that of a human.

Appointing a King because Warfare Is Necessary

There are respects in which Maimonides shared the premises of the elitist position held by al-Farabi and other proponents of a politics centered on a strong and virtuous imam, notably within Almohad, Isma'ili, and other Shi'i circles.[20] Nevertheless, the constraints imposed on his king bear closer comparison with the works of contemporary Islamic philosophers and jurists outside these movements.

The essential purpose of the imam of al-Farabi, like that of the king of Maimonides, is to inspire fear in his population and among his enemies, without which virtue will be trampled by the wicked.[21] For this reason, neither Maimonides nor al-Farabi focuses unduly on limitations to the royal prerogative in making war.[22] "Kings and Their Wars" does not suggest a program for instilling virtue into the multitude, and, like Ibn Bajja, a fellow Spaniard whose work he respected, Maimonides appears to depart from the notion that the king must strive for a virtuous city. Although Maimonides elsewhere links spiritual and martial virtue with the fundamental fortunes of the ancient Jewish state,[23] the king does not have to engage with the populace beyond hearing grievances and judging disputes (2:6). The king is not a divinely inspired legislator or spiritual guide, a role that was basic to the political thought of his earlier Islamic influences and that Maimonides reserved for Moses in his *Guide for the Perplexed*.[24] In common with a more classically Sunni jurisprudence, the king of the *Mishneh Torah* is bound to respect the scholars of the law (2:5) and is also to seek their approval in making optional wars (5:1).[25] The king is arbiter in cases of rebellion (3:8) but might be disobeyed in order to fulfill a biblical commandment, and "no one should listen to him" should he issue orders to break a commandment (3:9). Wise, God-fearing, and duty-bound to obey the law (1:7), the king—following al-Farabi's model—was to avoid tyranny, which derives from placing the pursuit of power above the pursuit of virtue or happiness: al-Farabi states the principles,[26] and Maimonides gives examples. In principle, a king who displayed a love of power or riches for their own sake should be flogged (3:3–4), although Maimonides notes that the biblical model was circumscribed by "the wise men" (of the pre-Mishnaic period), who decided that kings should not be subject to judgment (3:7). Maimonides's sages thus played a role not dissimilar to that of the wise advisers of Shi'i literature or the jurists of classical Sunni jurisprudence. However, the king's limited legislative sway placed him wholly out of step with the imam of Maimonides's earlier Islamic models and in line with the firm but just ruler of contemporary orthodox Sunni scholars associated with the revival of jihad under Nur al-Din and Saladin.[27]

The Reward of the Soldier and the Fate of Those He Conquers

The absence of clear rabbinic precedent for the assertion that the soldier who fights with courage and faith would inherit the world to come (7:15) has prompted a number of scholars to suggest an Islamic source.[28] The theme appears in the Qur'an (3:169; 9:21), was a basic feature of the canonical legal commentaries[29] and of contemporary twelfth-century preaching in support of jihad,[30] and appears in a wide range of commentaries that Maimonides could have read or been told of: Maliki texts on jihad, such as those attributed to Malik himself or to Ibn Tumart, whose supporters held sway in Almohad circles. In keeping with classical Islamic legal scholarship, Maimonides does not limit the reward for martyrdom to the war of religion in its most narrow definition, the *milhemet mitzvah*.[31] Maimonides's martyr does not, however, erase his sins through death in battle—a departure from Islamic teaching—and there is no reference to war in the section of the *Mishneh Torah* dedicated to repentance.

Nevertheless, Maimonides's war of religion parallels Islamic jurisprudence in other respects. While Maimonides briefly notes the prohibition of unlawful killing, he also preserves without qualification the biblical injunction to eliminate Amalekites and Canaanites, women and children included, as a law that applies for all generations. The Mishnaic and Talmudic sages had sought to minimize the enormity of this form of commanded warfare, limiting it to the wars directly commanded by God in the first period of biblical history and also explaining that even these wars were preceded by attempts to seek peace.[32] Maimonides affirms the second point (6:1)[33] without suggesting that there was a need to explain or defend the slaughter of the enemy. In the Islamic philosophical and legal texts of his day, the status of the citizens of a conquered city or territory and the extent of the duty to eliminate idolators were the subject of a wide diversity of opinion. Mainstream Islamic jurisprudence prohibited the killing of women and children,[34] although there were some earlier precedents for inferring their hostility to Islam and on that basis judging that their deaths incurred no guilt.[35] Maimonides was far from the only Aristotelian to reflect that killing people who would not raise themselves from the level of the beasts was a trivial matter, although this is made explicit only in the more philosophical *Guide for the Perplexed*, not in his legal code.[36] In the *Mishneh Torah*, this absolute bar on compromise with polytheists is implied in the rules for subjugation of conquered populations. These parallel the stricter rulings on the status of polytheists after a successful jihad,[37] although in relation to the rules he suggested for conquered monotheists, Maimonides's text compares with the more moderate Islamic regulations such as had applied in Córdoba under the Almoravids and in Cairo under the Fatimids: they were to acknowledge a basic code of monotheistic belief and law, to pay tribute and acknowledge their subjugation to Israel.[38] By contrast, the demand that these "descendants of Noah" not hold offices and be suitably humbled "so that they would not dominate" (6:1) echoed the stricter regime for non-Muslims under Saladin.[39] In common with mainstream Islamic jurisprudence, Maimonides states explicitly that there was to be no forced conversion: "Those who did not wish this were not coerced to accept the Torah" (8:10).

Jewish Sources in "Kings and Their Wars"

Above and beyond the influence of extra-halakhic, non-Jewish influences on the approach taken to war in the *Mishneh Torah*, Maimonides creates a unique picture of the Jewish laws of war through the judicious framing of impeccably canonical sources.

The monarchic perspective on war derives partly from the wholly natural selection of the Deuteronomic description of the laws relating to kings and their wars (Deuteronomy 17–24), a single unit in terms of traditional rabbinic exegesis. The primary Mishnaic discussion of war (*Sotah* 8) similarly focuses on Deuteronomy 20, albeit giving the bulk of its attention to the language of the speeches at the initiation of a battle and the reasons and conditions for military exemptions. Maimonides proceeds in a very rough fashion through the biblical laws relating to the king, although his arrangement of the subject entails jumping backward and forward in order first to encompass laws of fundamental importance to his focus on the king and his enemies, before turning to the issues with which Deuteronomy 20 begins, in which the king does not feature and the character of the enemy is deemed unimportant. "Kings and Their Wars" provides more than an enumeration of laws laid down in the Pentateuch. It casts those laws in the context of quotations from a broader biblical ideology in which the "wars of the Lord" (Numbers 21:14–15) are fought against Amalek and against idolatry (Deuteronomy 7,

Exodus 23:32–33). This ideological framework, while firmly rooted in the Bible, departs from the Talmudic precedents for the discussion of the laws of war.[40]

Maimonides's presentation of the laws of war is also affected by the notion that the Bible reveals commandments that are eternally valid, a law that has not been superseded and that embraced as wide a range of subjects as shariʿa did. The assertion is reflected in one of the *Mishneh Torah*'s most fundamental purposes, to combat the polemics of Karaites and other skeptics according to whom Jewish law is not firmly based on the Mosaic revelation. In "Kings and Their Wars," a first consequence of this is the depiction of an unchanging legal basis for war set out clearly in the Pentateuch but also evidenced throughout the prophetic books of the Bible and subsequent writings. The monarchy of the *Mishneh Torah* is primarily that which is described in the books following the Pentateuch, and David and Samuel (and, earlier in the work, Solomon) are held up as models for this legal arrangement. Their wars are presented as a part of the same war against idolatry that began with Abraham in Genesis 14. While the special position of Moses is emphasized in the *Guide for the Perplexed*, here it is overlooked. Maimonides looks for eternal laws, and for the motivation for these laws, outside the Pentateuch, a bold departure from his own claim to base these laws on the Pentateuch. First, the spoils of war are to be divided among the warriors and the guards of the camp, the arrangement noted in 1 Samuel 30:24 but not the wording of the Pentateuch, where warriors and priests divided the spoil in battle (Numbers 31:41–42, 53). Second, whereas the Mishnah and the Talmud present the conquest of Canaan under Joshua and the battle against Amalek as exceptional responses to divine command, Maimonides places them in continuity with the commanded wars of later kings, a radical step given the Talmudic judgment that many, if not most, of these later wars were merely permitted and not commanded.[41] Finally, the later books of the scriptures supply the terminology for the war against the wicked. Maimonides cites or adapts a range of phrases from these books dealing with God's destruction of the "arm" or the "hand of the wicked" (e.g., Psalms 10:15, 37:40, 74:1, 82:4, and 97:10). Here the king becomes the instrument of God's wrath, for it is the king who is to "fill the world with righteousness and to break the arm of the wicked fighting the wars of the Lord" (4:10).

This is a far cry from the design of the editors of the Mishnah and the Babylonian Talmud to establish rules restraining war by discounting as precedents the conquest of Canaan and the fight against Amalek. However, Maimonides's biblical war with idolatry has well-known echoes in rabbinic liturgy. Moreover, the monarchic perspective and the focus on the continuing battle against Amalek could be said to rest more firmly on extra-Talmudic commentaries than on the normative texts in the Talmud.[42] The master of a wide range of texts, scornful of some of his predecessors' work for not showing the same breadth of knowledge, Maimonides nevertheless gives no sources more specific than occasional references to "the sages" and "the tradition." For that reason in particular, the *Mishneh Torah* was viewed by many contemporaries as an unreliable basis for halakhic reasoning.

The novel approach taken in the *Mishneh Torah* contrasts strikingly with the works of earlier Jewish philosophers from Islamic areas, for whom war was far more likely to be presented within the context of the individual's struggle with his own evil urges, a challenge and a blight on civilization that should be avoided at all costs.[43] Fellow Spaniard Abraham ibn Da'ud (1110–1180), whose work parallels and may have influenced Maimonides's understanding of religious law, epitomizes the apparent consensus with which the *Mishneh Torah* broke. For Ibn Da'ud, the lesson of the revolt of the second-century messianic pretender Bar Kochba was never to pursue messianic ends through military means.[44]

Given the liberties taken in "Kings and Their Wars," there will be no surprises in the uneven reception that Maimonides's Jewish laws of war received, as outlined in the next section of this chapter. Indeed, the extent to which the book has proven influential might be considered more surprising. Maimonides's evidently serious interest in warfare was combined with a package of religious and philosophical agendas, some of which have been more influential, some less so. Given the lack of practical application for these laws at the time, the purpose of the text may well be better located in terms of Maimonides's interest in creating a text that allowed readers a greater understanding of the principles underlying the halakha, rather than a practical tool kit for making war. An indication of Maimonides's priorities appears from the statement that the king cannot be obeyed if he says that someone should disobey a divine commandment (3:9), overlooking the Talmudic provision, included earlier in the *Mishneh Torah*, for overriding these biblical *mitzvoth* in emergency situations.[45] "Kings and Their Wars" is not a practical manual on the pattern of the "mirrors for princes" literature.

Maimonides's Successors and the Laws of War

"Kings and Their Wars" has made a significant impact on Jewish thought, never more so than in the period from the 1930s, when it was deemed to have practical relevance in the Land of Israel. Its impact on the generations that followed Maimonides, a subject that has received very little academic attention, was more uneven. A shift in religious philosophy toward Neoplatonism was clearly accompanied by a reversal of the values and religious doctrines reflected in Maimonides's commentary. Moreover, the growing intellectual independence of Jewish communities under Christian rule distanced even his most ardent followers from the context in which the *Mishneh Torah* was written.

Nothing suggests the magnitude of this shift more clearly than the growing numbers of polemical essays written in defense of Judaism, or of a particular philosophical understanding of Judaism, by Jews under Christian rule in Spain and Provence. A number of these works were titled *Milhamot HaShem* (Wars of the Lord), understood as wars of words fought between the protagonists of one religion, or one approach to religion, against those of another.[46] The decades after Maimonides's death witnessed the intensification of polemics over his work within the Jewish communities under Christian and Muslim rule, and after the first book of the *Mishneh Torah* and the *Guide for the Perplexed* were burned in Montpellier in 1232, Maimonides's son Abraham penned his own *Milhamot HaShem*, with no discussion of the military wars that feature in the *Mishneh Torah*.[47]

On both sides of the Mediterranean, the growing influence of Neoplatonic and mystical interpretations affected the avowed followers of Maimonidean philosophy and their antirationalist antagonists. In this context, the qualities of prophetic and godly kings pressed themselves more insistently on political philosophy, making Maimonides's normalization of secular kingly authority and of their optional wars more problematic. *Sefer ha-mebaqqesh* (The Book of the Seeker) by Shem Tob ibn Falaquera (c. 1225–1295), probably written in Christian Spain, demonstrates the reordering of values through a dialogue between a Warrior, whose "bestial" form of courage is ultimately derided, and a Seeker, who concludes that "there is none so brave as the man who rules his spirit."[48] This is in some respects a reassertion of the normative order in which Jewish commentaries had perceived the religious form of war before "Kings and Their Wars," a discourse also familiar to Jews in the Muslim world through the influence of Sufi thought on Jewish ethical tracts. Ibn Falaquera's Warrior represents a range of arguments for a military war based on biblical sources, arguments that parallel the use of biblical sources in the *Mishneh Torah*. The Seeker rejects them, affirming a biblical reading that focuses on spiritual struggle and self-conquest.

Ibn Falaquera and his contemporaries were far less likely to have problems with the notion that the war of religion was occasioned by the challenge of idolatry or that a man who had not actualized his intellectual potential—a feature of man's relationship with God—was, in Ibn Falaquera's phrase, "not better than cattle."[49] The implacable enmity between Israel and idolators, however, was rarely presented in as absolute a form as Maimonides cast it. The Provençal rabbi Abraham ben David of Posquières (c. 1125–1198), for instance, singled out this issue in his commentary on the *Mishneh Torah*, one of the earliest and most critical commentaries on Maimonides's work. According to Abraham ben David, Maimonides was wrong to suggest that the aim of the command to wipe out the Canaanites could be extended to idolators in general; similarly, the absolute ban on even temporary passage for idolators in a Jewish state was not of Talmudic origin.[50] Although Abraham ben David, Ibn Falaquera, and many of their contemporaries understood the war with idolatry as more than a metaphor, they fairly consistently suggested the need for a more qualified understanding of the nature of the enemy and of the permitted forms of combat and relationship across the lines.

The relatively permissive approach taken to the war-making prerogative of the king in "Kings and Their Wars" was one of the areas in which qualification was commonly sought. As Reuven Kimelman notes, Maimonides's judgment that there was a biblical commandment to appoint a king was widely accepted among subsequent generations, more so than had been the case in earlier works on the subject.[51] But the powers granted to the king were nevertheless of increased concern for those growing numbers of Neoplatonists, some of whom identified the king as both prophet-legislator and philosopher-king and others for whom the burden of a greater degree of moral perfection fell on the people as a whole. The notion that some classes of polytheists or of otherwise barbaric peoples might be killed without qualms also disappeared from the commentaries written in Provence, although Abraham ben Maimon, by contrast, continued to affirm this in the context of his ethical tract *The High Ways to Perfection*.[52] Thus, in Ibn Falaquera's philosophical commentaries *Reshit hokhmah* (The Beginning of Wisdom) and *Moreh ha-moreh* (Guide to the Guide), statesmanship, based on a model of the leader as prophet-legislator and philosopher-king that derived from Ibn Rushd, al-Farabi, and Ibn Qutayba, is wholly divorced from military affairs, and a man who does kill must weigh his own responsibility for that act even if he kills for fear of his own life.[53] In his commentaries on the Torah and on Maimonides's *Book of Commandments*, Moses ben Nahman (Nahmanides, 1194-c. 1270), a Catalan and one of the preeminent commentators of the thirteenth century, insisted that the laws of war be conceived more consistently with religious checks on the king in mind. Thus, the king was to follow the directions both of the scholars sitting in the Sanhedrin and of the priests charged with the oracular *Urim* and *Tumim*, not only in an optional war (*milhemet reshut*), as Maimonides asserted, but also in a commanded war of religion.[54] To Nahmanides, it mattered little whether the war was undertaken by a king or another figure with jurisdiction over the people. What did matter was that the war they waged conformed scrupulously to the will of God, on whose providential intervention victory and defeat depended. By contrast with Maimonides's rationalist, political explanations of biblical events, such as the killing of the sons of Shechem (Genesis 35:25), for Nahmanides, the cause and fate of biblical protagonists rested on their intentions and relationship to God. A separate, spiritualizing agenda characterized some of the more extreme Maimonidean commentaries written in Provence, for whom the parties to biblical wars represented intellectual and moral qualities or their absence. Amalek, for instance, represented the bestiality that lies within human beings, rather than the most hostile aggressor against whom Israel must physically defend its borders.[55]

Maimonides's judgment that for the righteous, death in battle would not go unrewarded in the afterlife touched on a broader debate particularly alive among Spanish and Provençal Jewry, one about martyrdom, as Bernard Septimus indicates in his article on Moshe Narboni (c. 1300–1362) and Shem Tob ben Joseph ibn Shem Tob (fl. 1442–1455).[56] In relation to the wars that Israel had fought and that under the messiah they would fight in the future, Nahmanides implicitly gave the notion of martyrdom somewhat shorter shrift, holding that if the soldiers of Israel were righteous, they would not die in battle.[57] This extensive intrusion of God into history was unsatisfying to Maimonidean naturalists such as Shmuel ibn Tibbon (c. 1150–1230), for whom battles were not controlled by providence and according to whom it made no sense to exempt those who feared death in battle if there was a guarantee that they would not die.[58]

The extent to which the distinctive assertions made in "Kings and Their Wars" were forgotten or rejected in the biblical, ethical, and philosophical commentaries of subsequent generations undoubtedly reflected the unique purpose of the work. In a Christian context, and particularly in the face of growing missionary efforts in the thirteenth and early fourteenth centuries, the exegetical agenda underpinning the *Mishneh Torah* here was replaced in the works of avowed Maimonideans by different polemical needs and by different cultural understandings about revelation and about the biblical prophets and kings. The agendas of the rabbinic commentators who did treat Maimonides's work in a legal context also shifted, such that few commentators before the fifteenth century took "Kings and Their Wars" as a subject for sustained practical and political analysis. Medieval commentaries on this section of the *Mishneh Torah* were selective in their focus. Like Abraham ben David's *Hassagot*, they often focused on points of contention and often focused on religious topics of minor significance to the political core of the treatise. No critic of the *Mishneh Torah* asserted that Maimonides was mistaken in encompassing political subjects in a work on the halakha, although his influence ultimately did not make an impact on the mainstream halakhic codification process, which developed on the basis of a framework that marginalized subjects without a practical, contemporary application for Jewish communities. Furthermore, Maimonides's perspective on the wars of kings was clearly not shared by a number of commentaries on the Mishnah or the Talmud that did treat war and kingship but did so in much the same fragmented fashion as emerges from Maimonides's *Commentary on the Mishnah* and with a correspondingly greater emphasis on the relevance of the biblical teachings on war for broader moral and religious inquiry.[59]

Conclusion

In the centuries that followed Maimonides's death, in spite of the widespread acknowledgment of the magnitude of his achievement as a scholar, Maimonides's notion of religious war—a war on behalf of religion, a war against hostile idolators, a war in which the distinctions between defensive and offensive engagements were drawn far less clearly than had hitherto been the case—remained idiosyncratic. Today, in spite of this, his concise overview of the laws of war is often treated, by Jewish scholars in universities and *yeshivot* (rabbinical schools) alike, as a first port of call in describing a Jewish understanding of the application of law to war.

Read at face value, "Kings and Their Wars" reflects political and religious agendas that were very current in Ayyubid Cairo at the time of its composition— more current than the political philosophy of al-Farabi and Ibn Rushd, focused on the duties of the ruler (imam) that colored some of his other works. The plain reading of the text suggests approbation for an unusually vigorous military policy. A close reading of some parts of the text could allow a more circumscribed view of the use of force, particularly by secular rulers, although this is not absolutely clear. If this was accepted, an argument that Maimonides was in part dissembling in order to present guidance that suited his environment and exegetical agenda might carry some weight. The *Commentary on the Mishnah* suggests a starkly contrasting perspective to the *Mishneh Torah*, far closer to the balance of traditional rabbinic commentary on the subject and more focused on the relationship of war to broader ethical imperatives. Even the *Book of the Commandments*, the skeleton on which the *Mishneh Torah* was then hung, suggests a less radical embrace of the war for religion. "Kings and Their Wars" is clearly intended not as a practical guide to the making of war but, rather, as a framework for the understanding of biblical text and rabbinic tradition as enduring guides at a time when they were believed to clash with rational, effective politics.

The commentators who followed Maimonides left no evidence that they believed that he was dissembling, and for a long time, they treated his legal judgment as one opinion among many, and one of no compelling force. As Maimonides's readers spread across Jewish communities under Christian rule, they were distanced from the context in which "Kings and Their Wars" had been conceived. Rapidly, Aristotelian naturalism was either replaced by Neoplatonic philosophies or was mixed with Neoplatonism in an enhanced naturalism that accommodated more mystical notions of reason and the intellect. In this context, the development of the ethical personality and the relationship with the divine became more central than was made explicit in "Kings and Their Wars." Since even more ardent Aristotelians, with Ibn Falaquera, followed this trend, "Kings and Their Wars" had only a small natural constituency among philosophers. Its reception amongst halakhists in this period is harder to judge, because of the paucity of commentaries on the text. The history of the post-Maimonidean halakha of war is still largely an unwritten chapter. The commentators (such as Nahmanides) whose views contrasted most with Maimonides have naturally drawn most attention in the literature. This is perhaps a backhanded tribute to the impact he made. Be that as it may, his contemporaries and succeeding generations appear not to have been ready to base a halakha of war on an essay that broke so radically with the normative tradition, both in its format and in its content.

Notes

1. Joel L. Kraemer, *Maimonides: The Life and World of One of Civilization's Greatest Minds* (New York: Doubleday, 2008), 116–24.
2. See Andrew S. Ehrenkreutz, "Saladin's Egypt and Maimonides," in Joel L. Kraemer, ed., *Perspectives on Maimonides: Philosophical and Historical Studies* (Oxford: Littman/Oxford University Press, 1991), 303–8; and for further background, Kraemer, *Maimonides*, 216–32, 272–73.

3. On Jewish soldiers in Spain, see Norman Roth, *Medieval Jewish Civilization* (London: Routledge, 2003), 35–37; and Norman Solomon, "The Ethics of War: Judaism," in Richard Sorabji
   and David Rodin, eds., *The Ethics of War: Shared Problems in Different Traditions* (Aldershot,
   U.K.: Ashgate, 2006), 114–15.

4. Avraham Y. Finkel, *Rambam: Selected Letters of Maimonides: Letter to Yemen and Discourse on
   Martyrdom* (Scranton, Pa.: Yeshivath Beth Moshe, 1994).

5. The commentary on *Sotah* 8:7, for instance, briefly discusses two of the three types of Mishnaic war, in the context of a discussion of military exemptions, and a passage on *Sanhedrin*
   1:5 describes warfare against "the Ishmaelites" as an optional war.

6. Maimonides, *Guide for the Perplexed*, book 3, chaps. 18, 33, 41.

7. Thus, Raymond L. Weiss, *Maimonides' Ethics: The Encounter of Philosophic and Religious Morality* (Chicago: University of Chicago Press, 1991), 25, on the difference between the *Commentary on the Mishnah* and "Kings and Their Wars."

8. The commentary on *Avot* 4:1, for instance, describes the *gibbor* (strong man or warrior) as
   the person who conquers his evil impulses.

9. Noah Feldman, "War and Reason in Maimonides and Averroes," in Sorabji and Rodin, *The
   Ethics of War*, 92–107.

10. Gideon Libson, "Maimonides' Halakhic Writing against the Background of Muslim Law and
    Jurisprudence of the Period" (in Hebrew), in Aviezer Ravitsky, ed., *Maimonides: Conserva-
    tism, Originality, Revolution* (Jerusalem: Zalman Shazar Center, 2008), chap. 12.

11. As has been noted by a number of scholars, e.g., Solomon, "The Ethics of War," 108–37.

12. See, e.g., Carole Hillenbrand, *The Crusades: Islamic Perspectives* (Edinburgh: Edinburgh Uni-
    versity Press, 1999), 108; Hadia Dajani-Shakeel, "A Reassessment of Some Medieval and
    Modern Perceptions of the Counter-Crusade," in Hadia Dajani-Shakeel and Ronald A.
    Messier, eds., *The Jihad and Its Times: Dedicated to Andrew Stefan Ehrenkreutz* (Ann Arbor:
    University of Michigan Press, 1991), 41–70.

13. *Sahih al-Bukhari*, vol. 4, books 52–53, 56.

14. Dajani-Shakeel, "A Reassessment," 63.

15. See, e.g., Yasir S. Ibrahim, ed., *Al-Tabari's Book of Jihad: A Translation from the Original Arabic*
    (Lewiston, N.Y.: Edwin Mellen, 2007), 57–60, sects. 1, 1.1.

16. Al-Farabi, *Tahsil* 31:17. See Muhsin Mahdi, *Alfarabi and the Foundation of Islamic Political
    Philosophy* (Chicago: University of Chicago Press, 2001), 139–40; Charles Butterworth: "Al-
    Farabi's Statecraft: War and the Well-Ordered Regime," in James T. Johnson and John Kel-
    say, eds., *Cross, Crescent and Sword: The Justification and Limitation of War in the Western and
    Islamic Traditions* (New York: Greenwood, 1990), 79–100; and Joel L. Kraemer, "The *Jihad* of
    the *Falasifa*," *Jerusalem Studies in Arabic and Islam* 10 (1987): 372–90. The comparison
    among the perspectives of Maimonides, Ibn Rushd, and al-Farabi is noted in Joel L. Krae-
    mer, "Maimonides' Messianic Posture," in Isadore Twersky, ed., *Studies in Medieval Jewish
    History and Literature*, vol. 2 (Cambridge, Mass.: Harvard University Press, 1984), 140–41.

17. Kraemer, "Maimonides' Messianic Posture."

18. See Suleiman Mourad and James Lindsay, chapter 5 in this volume.

19. *Mishneh Torah*, Sanhedrin 2:7.

20. This perspective on war and on politics as a whole was also advanced by other contemporary
    Spanish philosophers, such as Ibn Bajja, for whom Maimonides expressed admiration.

21. Mahdi, *Alfarabi*, 140.

22. A similar point is made by David Cook in reviewing the works of early jurists such as al-
    Shafi'i, in *Understanding Jihad* (Berkeley: University of California Press, 2005), 29–30. The
    absence of attention to such proscriptions in the work of Maimonides and al-Farabi is still
    more pronounced.

23. In a letter to the rabbis of Provence, Maimonides argued that the fall of the Temple and the
    exile were caused by a distracting passion for astrology, which led them to fail to train for
    war; trans. Ralph Lerner, in Ralph Lerner and Muhsin Mahdi, eds., *Medieval Political Philos-
    ophy: A Sourcebook* (Ithaca, N.Y.: Cornell University Press, 1963), 229; cited by Kraemer,
    "Maimonides' Messianic Posture," 133.

24. *Guide for the Perplexed*, book 2, 35. Moses therefore approximates Plato's ideal ruler, just as Muhammad did for al-Farabi.

25. The king's duty to honor the scholars is also stated earlier in the *Mishneh Torah*, Sanhedrin 2:11. Here the qualifications of members of the court are set down. Knowledge of military affairs is conspicuously not mentioned.

26. Mahdi, *Alfarabi*, 141, 143.

27. Hillenbrand, *The Crusades*, 119, 131. While Lenn Goodman goes further to suggest that Maimonides's king is effectively a constitutional monarch or magistrate, the king is not subject to effective checks on his acquisition or exercise of power, since these would reduce the citizens' fear of him. Lenn Goodman, *Judaism, Human Rights, and Human Values* (Oxford: Oxford University Press, 1998), 72–78.

28. Gerald J. Blidstein, '*Ekronot mediniyim be-mishnat ha-Rambam* [Political Concepts in Maimonidean Halakha] (Jerusalem: Bar Ilan, 1983), 234–42; Kraemer, "Maimonides' Messianic Posture," 132; Solomon, "The Ethics of War," 116.

29. Cook, *Understanding Jihad*, 24.

30. Hillenbrand, *The Crusades*, 102.

31. On the expansion of the category of martyrdom in Islamic legal scholarship, see David Cook, *Martyrdom in Islam* (Cambridge, U.K.: Cambridge University Press, 2007), 32.

32. See, among many works on this topic, Solomon, "The Ethics of War," 108.

33. Although in his earlier listing of commandments, the duty to seek peace appeared to be confined to the optional *milhemet reshut* (*Sefer ha-mitzvot*, 602), the language used in the *Mishneh Torah* approximates still further the Islamic precedent: "No war was declared against any people before peace had been offered to them." A number of rabbinic texts suggest that the way to war was only opened after the offer of possible peace terms; see Sifre on Deuteronomy 20:19 and Deuteronomy Rabbah, 5:14.

34. See, for example, Imam Malik, *Al-Muwatta*, Book of Jihad, 21.3, trans. A'isha 'Abdarahman at-Tarjumana and Ya-qub Johnson (Norwich, U.K.: Diwan, 1982), 198–99.

35. Al-Tabari, *Ta'rikh al-rusul wa al-muluk*, 5 vols. (Beirut: Dar al-Kutub al-'Ilmiyya, n.d.), 2:189; cf. al-Tabari, *The Last Years of the Prophet*, trans. Ismail K. Poonawala (Albany: State University of New York Press, 1990), 69; Ibn Ishaq, *Sirat Rasul Allah (The Life of Muhammad)* (New York: Oxford University Press, 1980), 676. By the time Maimonides wrote, Qur'an 9:5, the so-called verse of the sword—like the Deuteronomic command to eliminate idolators from the territory of Canaan—was widely interpreted as having lapsed, in this case with the elimination of polytheism from Arabia.

36. On Ibn Rushd's parallel treatment of this subject, see Feldman, "War and Reason," 92–107.

37. Maimonides prohibited treaties with idolators, asserted that captured women should be killed if after one year they would not reject idolatry (both innovations in terms of rabbinic law), and rejected the provision of safe passage to polytheists, which recent generations of Islamic scholars had adopted in order to facilitate trade and contacts with the crusaders. See further discussion of the rejection of safe passage in Blidstein, '*Ekronot*, 216. As Blidstein notes (pp. 219–20), the demand that conquered populations accept a limited code of Noahide law was not included in Maimonides's earlier list of commandments, the *Sefer ha-mitzvot*.

38. For further discussion, see Feldman, "War and Reason." The general principle that a conquered population should pay tribute and serve Israel is already laid down in Deuteronomy 20:11.

39. Yaacov Lev, *Saladin in Egypt* (Leiden: Brill, 1999), 185.

40. Blidstein, who calls this "ideological war," suggests that it relates more closely to contemporary Islamic influences. Gerald J. Blidstein, "Holy War in Maimonidean Law," in Joel L. Kraemer, ed., *Perspectives on Maimonides: Philosophical and Historical Studies* (Oxford: Littman/Oxford University Press, 1991), 209–20.

41. The statement attributed to Rava in the Babylonian Talmud, Sotah 44b, makes this point most forcefully.

42. This aspect of Maimonides's relationship to Jewish sources is touched on in Gerald J. Blidstein, "The Monarchic Imperative in Rabbinic Perspective," *AJS Review* 7–8 (1982–83): 24.

The change in perspective may also be related to the impact of the Jerusalem Talmud, which Maimonides sought to reintegrate within Jewish legal studies, with some success.

43. See, for example, Menahem Mansoor et al., eds., *The Book of Direction to the Duties of the Heart from the Original Arabic Version of Bahya ben Joseph ibn Paquda's al-Hidaya ila Fara'id al-Qulub* (London: Routledge and Kegan Paul, 1973), 171–72, 277.

44. Richard G. Marks, *The Image of Bar Kokhba in Traditional Jewish Literature: False Messiah and National Hero* (University Park: Pennsylvania State University Press, 1993), 57–80.

45. *Mishneh Torah, Hilkhot mamrim* 2:4.

46. See, for example, Jacob ben Reuven's *Milhamot ha-Shem*, written in twelfth-century Castile; the work of the same title by Moses ben Nahman (Nahmanides), composed in thirteenth-century Catalonia; and the eponymous work by Gershon ben Levi (Gersonides), written in Provence in the early fourteenth century.

47. Fred Rosner, ed., *The Wars of the Lord by Abraham Maimonides in Defence of His Father Moses Maimonides* (Haifa: Maimonides Research Institute, 2000).

48. M. Herschel Levine, *Falaquera's Book of the Seeker (Sefer Ha-Mebaqqesh)* (New York: Yeshiva University Press, 1976), esp. 28–31.

49. Ibid, 10.

50. Rabad's *Hassagot* on "Kings and Their Wars," published in most editions of the *Mishneh Torah*. Blidstein, *'Ekronot*, 216.

51. Reuven Kimelman, "Abravanel and the Jewish Republican Ethos," in Daniel H. Frank, ed., *Commandment and Community: New Essays in Jewish Legal and Political Philosophy* (Albany: SUNY Press, 1995), 199–200.

52. Samuel Rosenblatt, ed., *The High Ways to Perfection* (New York: Columbia University Press, 1927), 154–55.

53. Levine, *Falaquera's Book of the Seeker*, xxxv; and Raphael Jospe, *Torah and Sophia: The Life and Thought of Shem Tov Ibn Falaquera* (Cincinnati: Hebrew Union College Press, 1988), 111–13, 127.

54. Nahmanides, commentary on the seventeenth negative commandment in the *Sefer ha-mitzvot*.

55. See discussion in Elliott S. Horowitz, *Reckless Rites: Purim and the Legacy of Jewish Violence* (Princeton, N.J.: Princeton University Press, 2006), 134–35.

56. Bernard Septimus, "Narboni and Shem Tov on Martyrdom," in Twersky, *Studies in Medieval Jewish History and Literature*, 447–55.

57. Nahmanides, *Commentary on the Torah*, Deuteronomy 20:1.

58. James T. Robinson, *Samuel ibn Tibbon's Commentary on Ecclesiastes* (Tübingen: Mohr Siebeck, 2007), 344–45.

59. See, for example, Menahem ha-Meiri, *Bet ha-behirah* (Halberstadt/Tel Aviv: Lito-ofset Lion, 1860/1960), commentary on Mishnah Sotah 8:141–43.

PART THREE

GUNPOWDER EMPIRES, CHRISTIAN AND MUSLIM

The years 1450 to 1800 witnessed the consolidation of many of the modern "nation-states" of western Europe and the creation by some of them of vast overseas empires. This period also saw the nearly simultaneous rise of the three great modern Muslim empires, Ottoman, Safavid, and Mughal. On either side of the Mediterranean, Muslims and Christians exchanged territory, so to speak. The Ottomans finally captured Constantinople in 1453, and the Reconquista finally ended in 1492 with the capture of Granada, the last Muslim stronghold in Spain. The confrontation between Christendom and Islam in the coming centuries would be focused on the weakest part of Europe, its southeastern regions. After a period of expansion in the fifteenth and early sixteenth centuries, Ottoman power would gradually but steadily recede. Rapid advances in military technology gave decisive and long-lasting advantage to European states.

The era of the gunpowder empires saw the diminishing of holy war rhetoric between Muslims and Christians, at least officially and against each other. From the sixteenth century onward, the just war tradition witnessed continuous and rapid development, fueled first by Catholic theologians such as Vitoria and Suárez and later by the founders of international law, Gentili, Grotius, Pufendorf, and Vattel, among others. The cumulative effect of these men's work was to secularize just war thinking. Holy war rhetoric, when it did appear, was directed as much against Christian "heretics" and dissenters as it was against Muslims and other infidels.

While appeals to jihad and the *ghazi* (warrior for the faith) tradition of early centuries continued to be heard in the Ottoman empire, a pragmatic *raison d'état* increasingly animated statecraft. Holy war rhetoric was mobilized as much against the Shi'i Safavid state as it was against any Christian power. The classical jihad doctrine was never formally renounced in the Ottoman empire or any other state, but it was clearly in abeyance. The Islamic theory of world order was making way for norms and practices fashioned by Europe.

8

Martyrdom and Modernity

The Discourse of Holy War in the Works of
John Foxe and Francis Bacon

BRINDA CHARRY

Early modern England, with the rest of Europe, witnessed immense changes in the ways in which war was conceptualized and practiced. Advances in warfare resulting from developments in fortification, the widespread manufacture and use of gunpowder, the gradually increasing reliance on standing armies made up of professional soldiers, along with other sociopolitical developments, including the rise of the nation-state, the Reformation, sustained encounters with foreign peoples, the emergence of something akin to modern diplomacy and international law, and the protocapitalism of the period, made it inevitable that war was conceived of and carried out differently. The age also saw a dramatic rise in the number of texts discussing warfare—its ethical aspects, military strategy, and political repercussions. Many of these texts were produced on the Continent, but printing technology and translations made them more accessible to an English audience than ever before. Humanist thinkers deliberated on the nature and meaning of war, and they reached vastly different conclusions. For Erasmus, writing in 1511, "war is so monstrous a thing that it befits beasts and not men, so violently insane that poets represent it as an evil visitation of the furies, so pestilential that it causes a general corruption of character, so criminal that it is best waged by the worst men, and so impious that it has no relation to Christ."[1]

The pacifist or quasi-pacifist approach of Erasmus's generation was, however, short-lived (if it had ever been popular), as exemplified by Machiavelli, whose book *L'arte della guerra*, first translated into English as *The Arte of Warre* in 1560, makes clear. While Machiavelli is certainly no warmonger, he considered war a political inevitability, often necessary for the sustenance of the monarch and the state. *The Arte of Warre*, though more concerned with military strategy than with the philosophical/ethical questions surrounding warfare, does ponder the political merits of peace and war and concludes that a king who "is wise and wants to govern prudently" will remember "if he has around him either too great lovers of peace or too great lovers of war they will make him err."[2] This acceptance of war is reflected in the works of international law by Francisco de Vitoria and Hugh Grotius, both of whose "impact on the conceptualization of just war ideas is of the greatest importance," as James Turner Johnson explains.[3] Vitoria and Grotius attempted to limit the scope of war and work out principles of negotiation, and their work subsequently laid the ground for modern international law governing warfare between nations. As J. R. Hale puts it, the "eclectic pragmatism" of these jurists was "more appealing and influential" even to their contemporaries than plain pacifism.[4]

While Vitoria's and Grotius's works on international law are undoubtedly of great historical and legal significance, I wish to examine how just war and holy war were discussed in a far more unsystematic, uneven, confusing manner by other writers, with the contention that this unevenness is itself significant. As a student of language and literature, I am particularly interested in the rhetorical and discursive strategies deployed by early modern English writers in their writings on holy war and what paying attention to these strategies will tell us about how the general reader's attitudes toward holy war were shaped. If one acknowledges that culture and cultural production are key categories to understanding any social formation, it is also important to distinguish one cultural site from another. I therefore juxtapose two texts that belong to very different genres: an account of the stories of Christian martyrs, *Acts and Monuments*, first published in 1563 by the English Protestant cleric John Foxe, and a fictional dialogue on holy war in the scholarly humanist tradition, *An Advertisement Touching a Holy War*, written in 1622 or 1623 by the English statesman and philosopher Francis Bacon. Both works address the issue of holy war against the Ottoman Turks, but they are motivated by vastly different impulses and belong to very different discursive traditions, and they consequently vary in their circulation and social effects. As documents fully involved in and emerging from a particular historical moment, they are reminders of what Edward Said calls the "worldliness" of texts, not simply reflecting but participating in and occasionally interrogating other conversations on both holy war and intercultural engagement.[5] They are clearly sites of ideological struggle, examples of what literary scholar Jean Howard describes as "differences within the sense-making apparatus of a culture."[6] Studying the "representative" and "discursive" function of these cultural documents is meant not to elide the very material reality of war, holy or otherwise, but to draw attention to the fact that all ideology, including the ideology of holy war, is constructed and "re-presented" as the "real."

"Precious and Godly Work": Holy War in the Reformation Era

Any discussion of Foxe's and Bacon's texts has to be situated in the context of holy war discourse in the Reformation. Machiavelli's writings, along with a number of other war manuals, tended to treat war as human activity motivated by careful political judgment and ruled by reason and intellect rather than passion or religious sentiment. At the same time, it was not uncommon to view military activity as religious work. Even Machiavelli believed that religious belief could produce disciplined and resilient soldiers.[7] Holy war discourse was apparent in the post-Reformation conflicts over religious difference right through the Puritan revolution. Martin Luther explains, "When I think of the office of soldier, how it punishes the wicked, slays the unjust, it seems an unchristian work and entirely contrary to Christian love; but if I think how it protects the good . . . then it appears how precious and godly this work is."[8] Similarly, as an Englishman named Thomas Trusell writing in 1619 puts it, "the Lord our God useth no occupation of men in his work and proceedings as he doth military men: for by them hee doth execute his wrathe upon the rebellious and faithless, and also by the same meanes it pleaseth Him to deliver his righteous from oppression."[9] James Turner Johnson cites notable theologians such as the Swiss reformer Heinrich Bullinger, the English Catholic cleric William Cardinal Allen, and the Puritan cleric William Gouge to argue that many in the period subscribed to the view that "wars based in difference of religion are the most just of wars, far more than those fought for nonreligious reasons."[10]

The third corner to the Renaissance religious triangle was Muslims. Both Catholic and Protestant powers were anxious to promote ties with Ottoman Turkey, Moorish North Africa, and, particularly in the case of the English and the French, Mughal India. These Islamic polities were viewed as prestigious and powerful; historian Richard Knolles, who composed the first English history of Ottoman Turkey, described the Ottomans as the "present terrour of the world."[11] It was generally recognized that Muslim powers, especially the Ottoman empire, were part of the European geopolitical scene and had to be wooed as trading partners and political allies. While it is true that the Western reaction to the capture of Constantinople in 1453 by the Ottomans was a call for crusade, no organized crusade had been launched. Various European powers had clashed with Ottoman forces over Rhodes (1522–23), Hungary (1526), Belgrade (1526), Buda (1529), Vienna (1529), and Cyprus (1571), with Ottoman control over southeastern Europe resulting in long and inconclusive wars between 1593 and 1606. Yet the Reformation had irrevocably altered the idea and unity of "Christendom." Christopher Tyerman, in his work on English involvement in the Crusades, argues that the Reformation, along with the fact that crusade was a canonical institution and a part of the Catholic church's penitential system subjected to the reformers' assault, inevitably led to the decline of the crusade ideology in early modern Europe. The "international crusading" of the Middle Ages "had to compete with national wars as alternative fields for noble deeds and martial endeavor." However, Tyerman also acknowledges that "elements of the [crusade] ideal persisted, even while the formal apparatus had been abandoned in Tudor England."[12]

The complexity and contradiction that inform Elizabethan and Jacobean attitudes toward "holy war" against Muslims have to be confronted in any examination of the period and are almost impossible to resolve. Queen Elizabeth I was hard put to decide who was the greater threat, King Philip II of Spain or the Turkish sultan. Excommunicated by Rome, she persisted in working toward trade agreements with Ottoman and Moorish rulers and even expressed interest in an Anglo-Ottoman and possibly an Anglo-Moorish alliance against Spain. In his eagerness to push for this alliance, her ambassador Edmund Hogan foregrounds similarities between England and Morocco and downplays the differences in theology and religious practice that preachers back in England obsessively dwelled on in their attacks on Islam. The Moorish ruler, he claims, "beareth a greate affection to our nation than to others because of our religion, which forbiddeth the worship of idols."[13] The anti-idolatry of both Protestants and Muslims was something that Elizabeth emphasized in her correspondence with the Turkish sultan. The Ottomans and her people, she writes, had at least one thing in common: they each followed a religion "which forbiddeth the worship of idols."[14] Yet in 1571, news of the Christian victory at Lepanto was received in England with great rejoicing, and a sermon of thanksgiving was preached at Saint Paul's "to give thanks to almightie God for the victorie, which of his merciful clemence it had pleased him to grant to the Christians in the levant seas, against the common enemies of our faith."[15]

Given this contradictory evidence, modern-day historians differ on whether there was really something approximating crusade in early modern Europe and whether England participated in it. For Alberto Tenenti, the sea battles between English and Turkish or Moorish pirates on the Mediterranean "transcended religious barriers" and were "only nominally a crusade: the point of it was not to inflict strategic defeats on one's adversary so much as to plunder, sack and get rich at his expense."[16] On the other hand, Nabil Matar states that while fine distinctions among "holy war," "just war," and "crusade" were of little or no interest to most English writers of the period, "holy war" ideology was alive and well: "For English writers, any war with Muslims was a 'holy warre' simply because the Muslims were seen to oppose the Christian God and to have usurped the Christian land of Palestine." Matar further insists that all Europeans, the English included, "transported their anti-Muslim ideology of religious war across the Atlantic and applied it to the American Indians."[17]

It is impossible, and to a large extent futile, to argue for or against the prevalence of crusade ideology in early modern England. In what follows, I focus instead on how both John Foxe and Francis Bacon are informed by and engage with issues and concerns that characterized and shaped early English modernity. If, as twentieth- and twenty-first-century scholars are anxious to emphasize, the sixteenth and seventeenth centuries should be conceived of as the "early modern" period, implying a continuity with our own "modern" present, how do texts on holy war engage with other social developments that characterize the time period, most important, the emergence of the nation-state, the Reformation, and the difficult and complex transition to "modernity"?

John Foxe's *Acts and Monuments*

John Foxe (1517–1587) is the author and martyrologist whose multivolume work *Acts and Monuments* is central to the canon of English Protestant literature. Foxe was an Oxford-educated Protestant cleric who was exiled from England during the reign of the Catholic Mary Tudor and returned to his home country when the Protestant Elizabeth's reign began. *Acts and Monuments* was written in response to the persecution of English Protestants during the reign of Mary Tudor and celebrates English resilience in the face of religious persecution. However, Foxe claims, this persecution (and the heroic response to it) has a long-standing history. He begins with the history of the early English church, presents the reader with an account of medieval English kings fighting against foreign powers, continues with an account of the contributions of John Wycliffe to the Reformed church, goes on to describe English martyrs—peasants, merchants, aristocrats, and clergymen—who stood up to and were killed by Catholic persecution, and closes finally with a celebratory account of the life and accession of England's "Protestant Queen," Elizabeth I.

The 1570, 1576, and 1583 editions of Foxe's text interrupt the English story with a fairly long narrative on the Ottoman Turks. This narrative finds a place in the section relating the history of the church since the days of Wycliffe. These days have been both turbulent and marvelous, in Foxe's estimation, for "in the compasse of the sayd last 300 yeares are contained great troubles and perturbations of the Church, with the meruailous reformation of the same through the wonderous operation of the almighty."[18] It is in the context of the tumultuous events of the last few centuries that Foxe narrates the history and place of the Ottomans. Although he is reluctant "to overlay this our volume with heapes of forreigne historyes, which have professed chiefly to entreat of Actes and Monuments here done at home," he maintains that it is crucial for a Christian audience to know the Turks' "order and doinges, and of theyr wicked proceedings, theyr cruell tyranny, and bloudy victories."[19]

There is little doubt that Foxe has any hesitation in responding to this "cruell tyranny" with war. Devout Christian though he might be, he (like other reformers) saw no reason not to respond to violence with violence. Besides, war against those who are responsible for the "great annoyance and peril of Christendome" is inevitably "holy."[20] Foxe's Turkish narrative is embedded in a martyrology, a genre in which descriptions of death are deliberately presented in violent and gruesome detail but where death for a "good cause," namely the cause of the Reformed church in this case, is also rendered sublime and transcendental. Every Christian soldier is a martyr, and every martyr for the religious cause is a righteous soldier. It is then perhaps inevitable that the battle against Muslims be represented as "holy."

James Turner Johnson writes that in Christian and Muslim religious traditions, "the idea of holy war is closely linked to a religiously defined separation between two worlds, one ordered toward God and the other not."[21] This is apparent in Foxe. On the one hand, he acknowledges the Ottomans' place in history by giving us a long, fairly detailed account of their rise to power, the military exploits and conquests of the sultans from the early centuries to the present, and internal divisions and factions within the empire. In presenting this piece of historical scholarship, Foxe is not unlike other European commentators who were beginning to acknowledge, albeit reluctantly, that the Ottomans indeed had a history that needed to be recounted. However, Foxe also sees the struggle with these infidel powers as a cosmic struggle, ahistorical and divorced from context. In this mythical battle, the real players are God and the devil: "The whole power of satan, the prince of this world, goeth wyth the Turkes. Which to resiste, no strength of mans arme is sufficient, but onely the name spirit, and power of our Lord Jesus the sonne of God, goyng with us in our battyles."[22] The war with the Turk becomes a battle of good against evil, the righteous taking on the damned. The Turks are then represented not as modern-day antagonists fighting for political ends but as incarnations of the Beast of the Apocalypse, "degenerating from the nature of men to devils, neither by reason will be ruled, nor by any bloud of slaughter satisfied," stirred up by "Satan the olde dragon for the great hatred he beareth Christ."[23] They are equated with the Antichrist and the ancient heathen persecutors of the Christians. This consequently denies or negates their valid place in the real and the contemporary.

In spite of his painstaking account of Turkish history, when Foxe urges his readers to war, he clearly considers his rhetoric more persuasive if it ignores the geopolitical realities of Europe. The complexity of this reality is overshadowed by the passion of his religious conviction that "faith getteth victory. The sword of the Christians, with the strength of Christ, shall soone vanquishe the Turkes pryde and fury."[24] Again, the genre of martyrology—a blend of history, myth, sermon, and prophecy—provides Foxe with the ideal vehicle to propound the notion that war with the Muslim infidel is real and immediate yet transcendental and holy.

However, Foxe's call for holy war does not entirely recall the medieval discourse of holy war. Protestant Reformers all over Europe turned to the language of crusade to describe the rift within Christendom, and the English were no exception. Writing in a letter in 1512, Henry VIII had described the French as "Turks, heretics and infidels," and in Foxe's own time, the Anglo-Spanish conflicts were often interpreted as a crusade.[25] While "there was no officially formulated Protestant doctrine of crusade," for the reformers, "the language, emotions, and some of the theoretical justifications for violence against religious and political foes of the True Religion bear the unmistakable imprint of crusade theories."[26] Foxe's "Turkish narrative" is obviously a post-Reformation piece in that Foxe condemns the Roman Catholics as vehemently as he does the Muslims. He accuses the "Bishop of Rome" of "impure idolatry, and prophanations"[27] and is hard put to decide who is the greater foe, the Turk or the Catholic:

Now in comparing the Turke with the pope, if a question be asked whether of them is the truer or greater Antichrist, it were easy to see and judge, that the Turke is the more open and manifest enemye agaynst Christe and hys Church. But if it be asked, whether of them two hath bene the more bloudy and pernitious aduersary to Christe and his members: or whether of them hath consumed and spilt more Christian bloud, he with sword, or this with fire and sword together, neither is it a light matter to discerne, neither is it my part here to discusse, which do onely write the history, and the Acts of them both.[28]

Although Foxe is inclined to represent the struggle with the Turks as mythical, ahistorical, and eternal, the fragmentation of Christendom is an event that he can neither forget nor ignore. This, in turn, contributes to a modern turn that his narrative takes: the movement from providential to modern notions of time and history. While Foxe's account is by no means "secular" in the modern sense, it is characterized by a change that, as Phyllis Rackin argues, marks the transition from medieval to early modern historiography. Medieval chronicles assumed that the first cause of all things was the will of God, "the alpha and omega who contained past, present, and future in one eternal, unchanging presence," and gave less importance to "the material, human causes of secular historical change." Early modern historical narratives were marked by "the movement from a vision centered on the timeless province of God to the humanistic consciousness that assigned new importance to the transitory material life of this world."[29] A dialectic tension between the two modes of thought is discernible in Foxe's text. One the one hand, the ascendancy of the Turks is clearly a manifestation of the workings of providence, part of a divine plan: "These grievous afflictions and troubles of the Church, though they be sharpe and heavy unto us, yet they come not by chance or mans working onely, but even as the Lord himself hath appointed it, and doth permit the same." This point is reiterated throughout Foxe's text. The "terrour . . . moved and gendred by these Turkes" is caused by God's will "for such endes as his devine wisdome doth best know."[30] A singular force that causes change but is itself unchanging determines the workings of history. The insertion of this element in any account of history, writes Thomas Betteridge, introduces "an inherently ahistorical, if not anti-historical, truth into its midst. In other words, once an event becomes apocalyptic it implicitly becomes not of history, and, in a sense, drops out of historical discourse; it becomes scriptural."[31] Foxe never really abandons this providentialist view of history. He tries, however, to decipher God's "endes" and concludes that the Turks are "the scourge of God for our sinnes and corrupte doctrine which in the sequele hereof, more evidently may appear to our eyes, for our better admonition."[32] Therefore, while God is still at the hub of the wheel of history and is the ultimate determining force behind all things, human action does contribute to determining the course of things. Not surprisingly, Foxe lays much of the blame at the door of the pope and corrupt Roman Catholic practices and doctrines. He takes it upon himself to define a truly holy war by saying that a Catholic battle against the Turks with weapons such as "workes, Masses, traditions and ceremonies" is bound to fail. What is needed is to take up arms against the Turk "with Christ and with the power of his glory, whith if we did, the field were wonne."[33] Foxe has an answer for those who wonder why Christians, the favored of God, have not been successful so far in their military ventures against the Turks:

> This is certain, that there hath lacked no care or diligence in the B[ishop] of Rome, to stirre men vp to that business [of destroying the Turks]: so on the [Catholic] Princes behalfe there hath lacked no courage nor strength of men, no contribution of expenses, no supportation of charges, no furniture or abilement of warre: onely the blessybge [sic] of God semeth to have lacked.

This divine support is missing because "the sincere doctrine of christen faith delivered and left unto us in the word of God, had not ben so corrupted as in the Churche of Rome."[34]

In Foxe's view, the Turks have disturbed religious and social order, they indulge in "most deadly, cruell, and perpetuall warre, to worke all mischief, destruction and desolation," so it is a matter of urgency that the chaotic, unruly, untamed powers they have unleashed be countered through reciprocal acts of violence.[35] The logic of reciprocating violence with violence is appealing in its orderliness. Since violence is, however, inherently unappealing in that it is chaotic and destructive, it is depicted as orderly in that it is being licensed by God and as having a place in a larger, providential scheme. Foxe's appeal to God to aid the Christian forces in their attempts to destroy the Turks is, oddly enough, couched in the language of healing: "All the partes and bones of the body be shaken out of place. Wherfore we beseech thee (O Lord) put to thy holy hande, and set them in the right ioynt agayne."[36] But the rhetoric is motivated by the same attempt to see divinely sanctioned and supported violence as restoring universal harmony and organic, fundamental order.

In the face of overwhelming Turkish power, which is a consequence of God's disappointment at Christian wrongdoing and folly, even the Protestant-Catholic conflict, which dominated Foxe's life and which is certainly central to his work as a whole, is sidelined. Foxe does not alter his anti-Catholic stance; he is vehement in his criticism of Rome in the "Turkish section" of his narrative. However, he strategically describes the conflict with Catholics merely as "domesticall wars."[37] While divine support clearly continues to be crucial to victory in the Christian-Turkish war, human beings need to take responsibility for their actions. The Turkish enemy should provoke Christians to unite and reflect on their own folly. "We fight agaynst a persecutour, being no lesse persecutours our selues. We wrastle against a bloudy tyraunt, and our handes be as full of bloud as his. He killeth

Christes people with the sword: and we burne them with fire."[38] The use of the plural "we" in this statement seems to imply that Foxe sees himself in communion with the Catholics and in a rare moment is willing to accept that all Christians—the reformers included—are to blame for the suffering of Christ's followers at the hands of the Turks. Much-needed introspection and reform in the Christian church could possibly result in "brotherly concord and agreement."[39]

To what extent does the modern fraternity of the "nation" make its way into Foxe's call for crusade? Some historians, notably Liah Greenfeld in *Nationalism: Five Roads to Modernity*, assert that the nation and nationalism are quintessentially modern phenomena and that early modern England is the first nation in the world.[40] While it is true that Tudor and Stuart attempts to centralize political power, the growing prestige of the English language and literature, and a national church and English Bible all contributed to the imaginings of the English nation, the specific "modernity" of the English nation is clearly debatable. As far as *Acts and Monuments* is concerned, for scholars such as William Haller, Foxe's work deliberately and self-consciously propounds the nation of the English as the chosen people of God.[41] Haller's "elect nation thesis" has been countered by later scholars such as Patrick Collinson and Richard Helgerson (among others), who claim that Foxe's work did attempt to create, to an extent, a national consciousness but was more invested in creating a supranational one. Foxe's subject "was not so much England as the church, to which he attributed a universal and mystical identity, the whole body of the elect scattered over the face of the earth,"[42] and it is this spiritual community of Reformed Christians, a community that surpasses the nation, "to which Foxe's sympathetic readers are instructed to pay their primary allegiance."[43]

Foxe's Turkish narrative affects his view of the significance of the English nation in interesting ways. If the relatively recent and rapid rise of the Ottomans that Foxe outlines for his reader in his painstaking (though not unbiased) account makes them brash upstarts on the world scene, how is the young, Reformed nation of England any different? This is a question that Foxe's Turkish narrative inevitably raises but that he chooses to ignore. Although he concedes national boundaries, for example, by stating that the purpose of the Turkish section of his narrative is "to geue this our nation also somethyng to vnderstand, what hath bene done in other nations by these cruell Turkes," he chooses to merge the English cause with a larger cause.[44] He actually reprimands the English for their complacency and indifference to the threat posed by the Turks: "We goyng no further then our own countrey, and onely feelyng our owne crosse, do not compare that which wee feele, with the great crosses, whereunto the Churches of Christ comonly in other places abroad, are subiecte."[45]

Foxe's call for holy war is then clearly distinguished by the fact that it stands at a temporal crossroads. The categorical call for war against the Turks and the unshaken belief that the Christian forces are supported by God make his text somewhat premodern in its dismissal of the complex geopolitical realities of the time that encompassed trade, diplomatic ties, and political alliances with the Otto-mans. Similarly, Foxe invokes the nation and simultaneously renders it less important; he calls for a larger community that might seem reminiscent of Chris-tendom but whose creation is based on a strategically and deliberately wrought unity rather than any clearly delineated spiritual communion. If a more exalted Christian fellowship against the Turks is possible at all, it must, Foxe insists, be based on a Reformed church.[46] Such a fraternity will then be simultaneously "modern" in that it is built on reform but also ancient and venerable in that it would be a recovery of the original Christian church. By resorting to providential explanations, even as he emphasizes human agency, by adopting and moving among multiple discursive modes—prophetical, political, eschatological, and earthly—Foxe's call for crusade exemplifies the complexities and the contradic-tions of early modernity.

Francis Bacon's *An Advertisement Touching a Holy War*

Francis Bacon (1561–1626), often described as the pioneer of a scientific method based on empiricism and rationality, is—unlike Foxe—no zealous man of reli-gion. He is best known for his project for a new science that is based on method-ical research and whose purpose is the conquest of nature and the betterment of humankind. His authorship of *An Advertisement Touching a Holy War* appears to be a curious anomaly in his body of work. Composed some sixty years after Foxe's work and some eighteen years after Bacon's famous *Advancement of Learning*, the *Advertisement* is in the form of a dialogue among five men that takes place in Paris in the house of one Eupolis. Dialogue was a fairly popular early modern genre, and as Benedict Robinson and Zachary Lesser put it, "conversations were meant as preparation for an active political and civil life. . . . Education enabled the courtier to offer political counsel; humanist writing presented itself as advice to princes."[47] There are five participants in Bacon's dialogue: a "Protestant Zelant," a "Roman Catholic Zelant," a "Militar Man," a "Politique," and a "moderate Divine," although the last two men do not speak.[48]

The first recorded instance of Bacon's use of the rhetoric of holy war is in 1617, when he urged King James I to take naval action against Algerian pirates who were attacking English ships plying the Mediterranean. When a royal Anglo-Spanish marriage alliance was being considered that same year, Bacon hoped that any political alliance that might follow would "make the difference in religion as laid aside and forgotten" and "be a beginning and seed . . . of a holy war against the Turks whereunto it seems the events of time doth invite christian kings."[49] James did order an attack on Algiers, which failed. The campaign was not dis-cussed as a "holy war" in government records. As Matar points out, "the accounts in the minutes of the Privy Council reveal no religious language and speak only of security needs."[50]

Bacon invokes holy war again about six years later in *Advertisement*. The text was composed a few months after he was convicted for corruption by the House of Lords, and the composition of the text at that particular time possibly had something to do with the need to redeem himself in the eyes of his monarch. In his letter of dedication to the Anglican bishop Launcelot Andrews, who was well known for his moderate religious views but who, Matar reminds us, had also preached a sermon in 1599 on the justness of Christian war, Bacon states that his earlier writings on natural philosophy and history either focused on "the general good of men in their very being and the dowries of nature" or were prompted by the "duty I owed somewhat unto mine country, which I ever loved." However, these previous writings were secular: "methougt they went all into the city, and none into the temple; where, because I have found so great consolation, I desire likewise to make some poor oblation." In composing *Advertisement*, "therefore I have chosen an argument mixt of religious and civil considerations; and likewise contemplative and active."[51]

Scholarly readings of *Advertisement* are few and have differed widely. For James Spedding, the nineteenth-century editor of Bacon's *Complete Works*, the text is interesting largely because it demonstrates Bacon's ability to write in the dialogue form. But Spedding was of the opinion that the content of *Advertisement* was irrelevant to a Victorian readership "except as indicating a stage in the history of opinion."[52] J. Max Patrick argues that it was prompted by Bacon's recognition that a popular external war was a "time-tested practical cure for internal dissensions."[53] More recent scholarship has been preoccupied with the question of whether the text ultimately advocates holy war. For Nabil Matar, *Advertisement* is clearly "a vindication of the unsuccessful attack on Algiers," and Bacon urges "the Protestants to wage a holy war against the Muslims in which they would either destroy the Muslims or convert them."[54] Laurence Lampert is of the view that Bacon was known for his moderate religious views, as evident in writings such as the *New Atlantis*, in which he visualized a society grown so civil that it rejects all war. Therefore, *Advertisement* is really a statement against religious zealotry and was written "with the conscious intention of curbing the religious fanaticism that had gripped Europe for a century and threatened another dark age."[55] Robert Faulkner, too, is of the view that Bacon's text makes clear that "the true holy war will be an enlightened war against religion and against nature on behalf of liberty and the real progress of humanity."[56] Bacon strongly feels, argues Faulkner, that wars for religion can only impede real progress and that the most worthy wars are those fought by humanity to free itself of the stranglehold of religion.

Some of Bacon's other writings indicate that he was no opponent of war as such. Drawing on the popular trope of the body politic in his *Essays*, he argues that a civil war is undesirable and unhealthy because it "is like the heat of a fever," while "a foreign war is like the heat of exercise, and serveth to keep the body in health."[57] Furthermore, he writes that war for conversion is unjustified: "We may not take up the third sword, which is Mahomet's sword, or like unto it—that is, to propagate religion by wars, or by sanguinary persecution to force consciences";[58] but he disagrees with "some of the Schoolmen" (probably referring to medieval philosophers, Thomas Aquinas in particular) that wars have to be provoked in order to be considered "just." Even reasonable and justifiable fear of imminent attack from an alien power, he writes, "is a lawful cause of a war."[59] In a piece titled "Considerations Touching a War with Spain," written in 1624 (probably shortly after *Advertisement*), Bacon reiterates this point. England has cause to fear Spanish imperial ambition, and "a just fear is a just cause of war; and that a preventive war is a true defensive." In "Considerations," Bacon situates just war in the context of post-Reformation politics: Spain, albeit a Christian state, is to be feared, perhaps more so than the Ottomans. Besides its political ambitions, Spain poses a religious threat, and the English are therefore fully justified in feeling "a just fear of the subversion of our Church and religion." It is debatable, Bacon writes, whether an offensive war can be a just one, but a war against Spain to defend English religious institutions is clearly a just one: "No man will doubt, that a defensive war against a foreigner for religion is lawful."[60]

Advertisement, too, gives no indication of being an antiwar text. However, the fact that it is incomplete and structured as a dialogue makes it impossible to reach any decisive conclusion regarding Bacon's personal stance on just or holy war. One of the characters, Pollio (the "Protestant Zelant"), argues that a holy war is an impossibility: "I am of the opinion that except that you could bray Christendom in a mortar and mould it in a new paste, there is no possibility of holy war."[61] Pollio also constantly interrupts the proponents of holy war with reminders of the Protestant-Catholic schism and other instances of Christian-on-Christian violence and of historical instances of civil moderation (as opposed to religious zeal). Other characters raise more questions than they answer, questions that occupied theologians and jurists of the period: Is a war for the propagation of religion justified? Can a war to reconquer Christian lands that have been desecrated be considered "holy"? What are the limits of war? *Advertisement* is admittedly an uneven, confused text, polyvocal and dialogic, simultaneously proposing and undermining perceptions of war and its justness. In what follows, I do not attempt to determine the text's stand on holy war, nor do I claim that the text is a well-structured, systematic treatise on justified war, like the works composed by jurists of the period. I discuss the speeches of two of the characters, Martius (described as "a Militar Man") and Zebedaeus (a "Catholic Zelant"), who both appear to be advocates of holy war in opposition to Pollio. My aim is to probe the ways in which the discourse of holy war in Bacon's text and the criteria that participants in the dialogue enumerate as they justify why war against the Ottomans should be seen as "holy" intersect with other questions and issues central to a society's progress toward modernity as Bacon viewed it.

Martius, described by another character as "a divine in armor," is the first proponent of holy war to speak at length in the text. He states that "a war upon the turk is more worthy than upon other gentiles, infidels, or savages, that either have been or now are, both in point of religion and in point of honor."[62] For Martius, the martial enterprises of the modern age lack the grandeur, nobility, and honor associated with wars of old: "By the space now of half a century of years there had been . . . a kind of meaness in the designs and enterprises of Christendom." This "meaness" of modern wars is attributed to the fact that they are fought for secular interests, for "some petty acquests of a town, or a spot of territory."[63] While Martius seems to call for the recovery of medieval crusade ideology (as it was popularly conceived in the early modern period), he also, however indirectly, strives to redefine "honor" in more contemporary terms. He feels that the conquest of the New World is not necessarily a religious mission, because the primary aim of the enterprise is wealth and "temporal profit and glory" rather than the propagation of the Christian faith, "so that what was first in God's providence was but second in man's appetite and intention."[64] However, Martius does recognize that the wealth and honor accruing from the conquest of the Americas does contribute to the glory of Christian nations. His attitude toward war for empire is therefore a blend of admiration and disapproval. The best kind of holy war, he concedes, can never divorce itself from worldly gain; it is one in which "both the spiritual and temporal honor and good have been in one pursuit and purchase conjoined."[65]

Similarly, the ends of international commerce are too worldly to match up to the lofty spiritual mission of the crusaders, but mercantilism is a crucial element of modernity and foundational to a modern nation-state. Bacon emphasizes this point when he writes in his *Essays* that if merchants "flourish not, a kingdom may have good limbs, but will have empty veins, and nourish little."[66] Indeed, Martius describes the merchants who venture out to sea as examples to be emulated. They are the modern heroes who "have made a great path in the seas unto the ends of the world . . . and all this for pearl, or stone, or spices." While Martius regrets that "for the pearl of the kingdom of heaven . . . not a mast hath been set up," he also implies that war cannot replace mercantilism. Those who facilitate global trade contribute to a nation's economic well-being. Further, Bacon recognizes that trade is not always peaceful activity characterized by partnership between states. When he writes that merchants have "set forth ships and forces of Spanish, English and Dutch, enough to make China tremble," he appears to imply that trade necessarily involves aggression and dominance and can lead to consequential shifts in the balance of power.[67] Consequently, war is not distinct from mercantilism; it should, rather, be inspired by it and complement it, even while aspiring to a certain "holiness" of purpose.

Zebedaeus, who has the longest speech in the dialogue, categorically states that "a war to suppress that [Ottoman] empire, though we set aside the cause of religion, were a just war." In his argument, Zebedaeus, too, moves between and even conflates divine and secular reasons for this: "A war against the turk is lawful,

both by the laws of nature and nations, and by the law divine which is the perfection of the other two."[68] Zebedaeus turns to Aristotelian thought to explain "laws
of nature." In his *Politics*, Aristotle discusses master-slave relations and argues
that just as "it is natural and expedient" that the soul rules the body, the intellect
the appetite, and that man is superior to animals, "the same must also necessarily
apply in the case of mankind as a whole; therefore all men that differ as widely as
the soul does from the body and the human being from the lower animal . . . these
are by nature slaves, for whom to be governed by this kind of authority is advan-
tageous."[69] This "natural" hierarchy, Bacon consistently argues in much of his
writing, is apparent in governments. In a letter to King James, he writes that
"There is a great affinity and consent between the rules of nature, and the true
rules of policy: the one being nothing else but an order of government and the
other an order in the government of an estate."[70] Nature is organized along discernible hierarchical principles, and so should the human world be. This correspondence between nature and government makes it necessary to study both. In
Advertisement, too, Bacon has Zebedaeus assert that the natural capacity to govern "hath a being both in particular men and nations." But he qualifies the statement by indicating that that "capability" is not measured by intellect alone, for
"there is no less required for government, courage to protect . . . honesty and pro-
bity of the will, to abstain from injury."[71] While he avers that "men will never agree
upon it, who is more worthy . . . fitness to govern is a perplexed question," and
that worthiness cannot be easily measured, what is clear is that there are "a heap
of people (though we term it a kingdom or state)" who are clearly unworthy, "altogether unable or indign to govern." In these cases, "it is a just cause of war for
another nation, that is civil or policed, to subdue them."[72]

The rest of Zebedaeus's speech goes on to define "fitness" or "worthiness" to
rule. A fit government is one that rules by the laws of nature and nations. He
determines that natural law is divine in origin and that a state that organizes
itself around just law is founded "in the image of God." Consequently, in order to
be considered a civil society or a nation rather than "multitudes only and swarms
of people . . . the constitution of the state and the fundamental customs" ought to
be dictated by these laws, "for like as there are particular persons outlawed and
proscribed by civil laws of several countries; so are there nations that are outlawed
and proscribed by the law of nature and nations, or by the immediate commandment of God."[73] A war upon these states, Zebedaeus declares, is just and lawful. He
gives a series of examples of "unlawful nations." Some of these are so categorized
because they engage in acts of organized or semiorganized violence and spread
terror and fear. Hence the Moorish pirates of Algiers are enemies of the whole of
humankind. Against such enemies, Zebedaeus argues, one can dispense of many
of the formalities and regularities that govern, or ought to govern, war. "There is
a natural and tacit confederation amongst all men against the common enemy of
society," and "there needs no request from the nation grieved, but all these formalities the law of nature supplies in the case of pirates."[74]

Under "common enemies of society," Zebedaeus lumps together a number of groups in a rather arbitrary manner. He includes the Assassins, drawing upon myths of the violence and fanaticism of the Nizari Isma'ili sect that had circulated in Europe since the Crusades. Interestingly, he does not restrict membership to this club of undesirables to non-Christian groups. The radical Protestant sect of the Anabaptists, who established a theocracy in Munster in 1534–35 until they were destroyed by Catholic and Lutheran forces, is also included. Bacon's reasoning behind pairing the Assassins and the Anabaptists is clarified to an extent if one turns to his essay "Of Unity in Religion." There Bacon condemns those who propagate religion by war (he cites the followers of "Mahomet" as examples) and those who not only draw the "temporal sword" in the name of religion but also put the sword "into the hands of the common man" (he cites the Anabaptists as examples of this).[75] Thus, Bacon advocates holy war against those groups that espouse holy war. Both in "Of Unity in Religion" and in *Advertisement* (at least as voiced by Zebedaeus), Bacon is anxious to distinguish his holy war from those of the groups he condemns. His own version of holy war is different—it is not offensive war fought to propagate religion but is war fought to restore social order.

However, such lawless, violent groups as the Assassins and the Anabaptists are not the only ones that flout natural law. The text invokes other kinds of "unnatural" government and in the process of doing so engages with discourses of order and disorder and their relationship to violence. As culture critic Terry Eagleton has recently argued, violence is closely connected to discourses of orderliness. Behind the intent to wreak havoc and create disorder is a contradictory impulse, a need, some would argue, that verges on the pathological for perfect social order.[76] Zebedaeus gives the Amazons as an example of a disorderly, unnatural society against which holy war can be lawfully declared. He is, of course, referring to the mythical tribes of South America ruled by women. Such a government is "preposterous," as "it is against the first law order of nature, for women to rule over men."[77] Female leadership had been a fact of English politics for more than half a century until James I ascended to the throne in 1603. While female sovereigns did create some trepidation, as evident in diatribes such as John Knox's *First Blast of the Trumpet against the Monstrous Regiment of Women*,[78] Bacon cannot, even under the guise of Zebedaeus, offend Queen Elizabeth I's recent memory. Therefore, Zebedaeus hastily adds that while individual women can be rulers as they are supported by "counsel and subordinate magistrates masculine," the absolute control of the family and structures of state by women is an "error in nature." Similarly, the Mamluks, a case of slaves assuming power over masters, are an abomination of nature. Zebedaeus's discourse on the necessity of holy war therefore gives expression to a number of social anxieties that are characteristic of the early modern period. In an age that witnessed female leadership, along with growing social mobility, the fear of gender and class reversal surfaced repeatedly. War and the violence it involves are disorderly, but there are more grave disruptions of social and moral order to which war serves as a corrective. Indeed, *Advertisement* indicates that it is the human, universal need for order that leads to the "necessary" violence of war; disorder and order are in opposing but dependent relationships. Violence counters social disorder, and conversely, it is the need for order that provokes the disorderliness of violence. As Eagleton succinctly puts it, "the urge to order is itself latently anarchic."[79]

Bacon introduces, through the character Pollio, another understanding of "civil" and "uncivil" peoples. Unlike Zebedaeus's definition of civility, Pollio's is based not on political orderliness and recognizable political structures and institutions (as in the case of the pirates and the Assassins) or on "natural" versus "unnatural" ways of being (as in the case of the Amazons) but rather on religious belief and practice. Christian peoples are the most civil, while polytheistic, idol-worshipping peoples are the least so, in that their religious practices have no semblance to Christianity. By this account, the Turks are not an entirely uncivil people (unlike the people of the Americas, who are *ferae naturae*, or of a "wild nature"). On the other hand, they have all the marks of civility, in that they are not idolators and "do acknowledge God the Father, creator of heaven and earth, being the first person in the Trinity, though they deny the rest."[80]

Many early modern thinkers, most notably Montaigne, had challenged the classification of the natives of America as uncivilized, and Bacon's Martius also does so.[81] In opposition to Pollio's contention, Martius chooses to define civility in terms of sophistication of government rather than affinity to Christianity and finds the Peruvians and the Mexicans, with their sophisticated systems of justice and elective monarchy, to be civil. The people of India are also considered civil by him for no clear reason; they are described as "a fine and dainty people, frugal and yet elegant, though not military." Martius then proclaims that the empire of the Turks may be truly affirmed to be more barbarous than these. Violent dynastic politics ("a cruel tyranny, bathed in the blood of their emperors upon every succession"), the absence of a distinct class system ("no nobles, no gentlemen, no freemen, no inheritance of land"), the ill treatment of women ("a people . . . that regardeth not the desires of women") all contribute to the categorizing of the Ottomans as an uncivil people.[82] Martius, like Zebedaeus, understands civility less in terms of religion or even morality; it is instead measured by a yardstick provided by political and social systems and ideologies recognized as "acceptable."

The notion of civility expounded by Martius in the *Advertisement* has affinities with Bacon's major intellectual project, the "advancement" of human learning, a project integral to his vision of the "modern." While "progress," particularly "scientific progress," is usually seen as a feature of nineteenth-century European thinking, the beliefs and ideals associated with it are discernible in the early modern period. Richard Eden is one of the many early modern Englishmen who celebrates the advancement and modernity of his age when he writes that "our age may seeme not only to contend with the ancients but also in many goodly inventions of Art and wit to far exceed them."[83] Bacon, too, is very clear about the human role in the making of history, and he envisions a world in which human beings are involved in the steady, orderly progress of mankind, a program best achieved through the methodical, systematic study of nature and what it can yield for human use. In *Advertisement*, the Turks are described by Martius as an uncivil people also because they are "without letters, arts or sciences; they can scarce measure an acre of land, or an hour of the day: base and sluttish in buildings, diets and the like; and in a word, a very reproach to human society."[84] The same "letters, arts and sciences" are an important measure of human civility and progress in Bacon's *The Advancement of Learning* (1605), perhaps the best-known manifesto for scientific progress in its time. In this work, Bacon states that "Learning taketh away the wildness and barbarism and fierceness of men's minds," and it is "by learning man excelleth in that wherein man excelleth beasts." While "buildings, foundations and monuments" might be considered marks of civility and civilization, "the monuments of wit and learning are more durable than any of these." Still, a society that does possess "letters" does not distance itself from war. Rather, "both in persons and times there hath been a meeting and concurrence in learning and arms, flourishing and excelling in the same men and same ages . . . in states, arms and learning, whereof the one correspondeth to the body, the other to the soul of man, have a concurrence or near sequence in time."[85] Therefore, in *Advertisement*, Martius implies that truly civil societies excel in both letters and arms, and consequently these have the right and ability to attack those less civil societies that are perceived as lacking in culture and science. While Martius's argument for the "uncivility" of the Turks is immediately countered by Pollio and subsequently supported by Zebedaeus, what is of interest here is that *Advertisement* invokes a category of analysis less commonly addressed by other early modern thinkers. For Bacon, the philosopher and proponent of science, the collective human mission is toward progress and the betterment of human life and society by understanding nature with a view to conquering it. A society that fails to subscribe to this notion of progress (and Martius sees the Turks as one such) is an impediment to the collective human mission and is equated not with the "human" but with the "natural." Consequently, such a society needs to be conquered and tamed.

Charles Whitney argues that Bacon's social and intellectual program of learning is a modern one if one sees "modernity as historical self-consciousness . . . that is . . . a preoccupation with asserting or discovering temporal discontinuity between the present and past, innovation and tradition . . . the making of special 'nows'— deliberately locating oneself in the now and looking for significant differences between now and the past." It was in the early modern period that a discernible discontinuity between past and present was established. Whitney further argues that "Bacon's program would thus appear to be absolutely modern: Bacon expresses his historical self-consciousness by insisting on his own and his age's independence from the past, and by calling for the invention of novelties that will further distinguish present from past and future from both."[86]

If one accepts Whitney's proposition that modernity involves locating differences between "then" and "now," in a text such as *Advertisement* which engages with questions of cultural and social difference, it also involves identifying and insisting on differences between "us" and "them." As anthropologist Johannes Fabian argues, cultural separation and distancing are characteristic of modern notions of progress. Time in modern narratives is what Fabian terms "typological": a measure of sociocultural significance that describes a "quality of states": the European self is "forward-looking," "modern," and therefore by implication "better," while the Other is "degenerate" and "primitive." Quite simply, all living societies are "irrevocably placed on a temporal slope, some upstream, and others downstream." The Other is not simply *perceived* as either "primitive" or "degenerate," he is *constituted* by the denial of "coevalness or co-temporaneity."[87] In *Advertisement*, Martius seems to imply that the Other is not "evil" in some simple, moralistic sense; the problem is that the Christian West and the Islamic world are on two entirely different trajectories and temporalities, as represented by the perceived lack of intellectual curiosity and "progress" in the Ottoman empire and the Muslim world generally. It is widely acknowledged today that Muslim scholars contributed significantly to the advancement of science, and Arabic translations of classical Greek texts played an essential role in bringing about the European Renaissance. Yet in *Advancement of Learning*, Bacon denies the contribution of *all* past learning to progress-driven "modern" science. He consistently asserts that truth about nature is best discovered by studying nature and should not be simply received from past scholars. The Arab philosophers are, of course, part of this past. Bacon writes: "So in natural history, we see there hath not been that choice and judgment used as ought to have been; as may appear in the writings of Plinus, Cardanus, Albertus and divers of the Arabians, being fraught with much matter, a great part not only untried; but notoriously untrue."[88] However, even when he does concede his European predecessors a place in the history of scientific learning, he neglects to mention Arab learning. "Three periods only can be counted," Bacon writes, "when the wheel of knowledge really turned: one among the Greeks, the second with the Romans, the last among the nations of Western Europe."[89] So, if the past has contributed to the study of "natural philosophy" at all, the contributions have come wholly from Europe. Bacon also argues in *Advancement of Learning* that true religion is based on reason, and of all faiths, Christianity is the one most based on rational thinking:

> But most especially the Christian faith, as in all things, so in this deserveth to be highly magnified; holding and preserving the golden mediocrity in this point between the law of the heathen and the law of Mahomet, which have embraced the two extremes. For the religion of the heathen had no constant belief or confession, but left all to the liberty of argument; and the religion of Mahomet, on the other side, interdicteth argument altogether: the one having the very face of error,

and the other of imposture: whereas the Faith doth both admit and reject disputation with difference.[90]

Islam is therefore seen as discouraging intellectual growth and rational scientific thinking. Consequently, in his dialogue on holy war, this is seen as a mark of the "uncivility" of the Turks. They are a primitive force that resists progress and modernity, and what is more, they are responsible for the degeneration of the world. They have, Martius states, "made the garden of the world a wilderness," a thought echoed by other early modern travelers and writers.[91] George Sandys, for example, is one among many European commentators who points out that the Egyptians "had first invented Arithmetick, Musick and Geometry," but the "Mahometans . . . subverted all excellence with their barbarousness." When Islam "is planted," he writes, it "roots out all virtue, all wisedome and science . . . laying the earth to waste, dispeopled and uninhabited."[92] Samuel Purchas, too, writes that the Turks have turned "the heart of the habitable world, [the] academie of learning," into a wasteland of "miserie and mischief."[93] The Turks are not only a primitive people in all of these early modern English texts, but they are also a force that attempts to reverse scientific and intellectual progress. In *Advertisement*, this makes any war against them justifiable. This justification differs from the more prevalent one that allowed war against the Turks not because they were an uncivilized enemy but because such conflict was viewed, in the words of George Clark, as "outside the usages which countries of western and central Europe had built up in terms of chivalry and law."[94] Again, while I think that it is not possible to determine conclusively Bacon's own views through the *Advertisement*, it is significant that the thinker who dedicated much of his intellectual life and writing career to arguing for a science that would subdue nature, devotes a fairly lengthy section of his text on holy war to argue (through his character Martius) that the Ottomans are an "uncivilized" people. A more civilized, "modern" society is justified in subduing and overcoming that which is defined as its opposite, an uncivil society that is averse to the movement toward modernity but is also "unnatural" in its defiance of moral and social order. The most worthy struggle is the one for order, progress, and modernity.

Conclusion

John Foxe's *Acts and Monuments* and Francis Bacon's *An Advertisement Touching a Holy War* both serve as reminders of how discourses of "holy war" appeared in unexpected forums in early modern England. The fact that both a cleric and theologian (Foxe) and a statesman and philosopher (Bacon) deployed the rhetoric of holy war gives us a sense of just how pervasive and powerful that rhetoric was. Neither author sought to present a coherent, systematic understanding of holy war or just war; instead, they used these concepts to convey important political messages to their intended audiences.

Foxe and Bacon approach their subjects from quite different perspectives and evoke very distinct notions of sociopolitical and cultural difference. Their work indicates the impossibility of generalizing about either discourses of holy war or constructions of alterity in early modern England. Foxe's complicated treatise alternates between past and present, transcending historical time. By invoking religious difference to justify righteous war, he seems rooted in the past, in the era of the Crusades. But it is clear that his discourse on Turks and Moors is based on current political fears and antagonisms among the rival kingdoms of sixteenth-century Europe. He talks of war as willed and destined by God, but he clearly sees human agency in the prosecution of righteous war.

In Bacon's *Advertisement*, religion and religious difference as grounds for war operate in even more subtle and complex ways. The single advocate for fighting on behalf of religion and honor attempts to situate war in the new era of nationalism and the equally modern economy of mercantile capitalism. The bulk of Bacon's text, however, focuses not on religion at all but instead on notions of civility and social order. Unlike Foxe, Bacon looks decisively forward to an unfolding future. As a thinker preoccupied with the idea of human "advancement" and progress, Bacon sees the Turks as an uncivil people who are not only remnants of a dying past but who also actively hinder the inevitable, necessary, and exciting movement toward the future. Bacon's vision of the future sees a marriage of Christianity and modernity, religion and progress.

In the end, we have two authors who are very much the product of their complicated, turbulent, and fascinating times. Their works are similar in that their engagement with the question of "holy war" is marked by the early modern period's struggle for self-definition—a struggle affected by ideas of the Other, imagined and represented as stationed on the other side of cultural, social, and real battle lines.

Notes

1. Desiderius Erasmus, *The Praise of Folly*, trans. Leonard Dean (Chicago: University of Chicago Press, 1946), 112–13.
2. Niccolò Machiavelli, *The Art of War*, trans. Christopher Lynch. (Chicago: University of Chicago Press, 2003), 1:190.
3. James Turner Johnson, *The Holy War Idea in Western and Islamic Traditions* (University Park: Pennsylvania State University Press, 1997), 175.
4. J. R. Hale, *War and Society in Renaissance Europe: 1450–1620* (Montreal: McGill-Queen's University Press, 1998), 41.
5. Edward Said, *The World, the Text, and the Critic* (Cambridge, Mass.: Harvard University Press, 1983), 21.
6. Jean Howard, *The Stage and Social Struggle in Early Modern England* (New York: Routledge, 1993), 7.
7. Machiavelli, *The Art of War*, 4:135.
8. Martin Luther, "Tract Whether Soldiers Can Be Saved," *Works of Martin Luther*, 6 vols. (Philadelphia: A. J. Holman, 1915–32), 5:35–36.

9. Thomas Trusell, *The Soldier Pleading His Own Cause* (London, 1619), page signature C8.

10. James Turner Johnson, *The Holy War Idea*, 58. Johnson adds that this "sets in context Victoria's argument to the contrary, 'Difference of religion is not a cause of just war.'"

11. Richard Knolles, *The Generall Historie of the Turkes* (London, 1603), 1.

12. Christopher Tyerman, *England and the Crusades, 1095–1588* (Chicago: University of Chicago Press, 1996), 324, 345.

13. Richard Hakluyt, *The Principal Navigations, Voyages, Traffiques and Discoveries of the English Nation*, 10 vols. (London: J. M. Dent, 1927), 4:159.

14. Ibid., 6:289.

15. Quoted in Tyerman, *England and the Crusades*, 349.

16. Alberto Tenenti, *Piracy and the Decline of Venice* (London: Longman's, 1967), 86, 64.

17. Nabil Matar, *Turks, Moors, and Englishmen in the Age of Discovery* (New York: Columbia University Press, 1999), 139, 130.

18. John Foxe, *Acts and Monuments*, 6:625. All quotations from John Foxe, *Acts and Monuments* [. . .] (1576 ed.), available online at http://www.johnfoxe.org.

19. Ibid., 6:700.

20. Ibid.

21. Johnson, *The Holy War Idea*, 48.

22. Foxe, *Acts*, 6:700.

23. Ibid., 6:723.

24. Ibid., 6:701.

25. "Venice: May 1512," *Calendar of State Papers Relating to English Affairs in the Archives of Venice*, vol. 2, 1509–19 (London: Longman, Green, Longman, Roberts, and Green, 1867), 58–64, entry 169.

26. Tyerman, *England and the Crusades*, 368.

27. Foxe, *Acts*, 6:738.

28. Ibid., 6:739.

29. Phyllis Rackin, *Stages of History: Shakespeare's English Chronicles* (Ithaca, N.Y.: Cornell University Press, 1990), 6, 8–9.

30. Foxe, *Acts*, 6:728.

31. Thomas Betteridge, *Tudor Histories of the English Reformation, 1530–83* (Aldershot, U.K.: Ashgate, 1999), 16.

32. Foxe, *Acts*, 6:700

33. Ibid., 6:701.

34. Ibid., 6:738.

35. Ibid., 6:702.

36. Ibid., 6:739.

37. Ibid., 6:700.

38. Ibid., 6:701.

39. Ibid., 6:721.

40. Liah Greenfeld, *Nationalism: Five Roads to Modernity* (Cambridge, Mass.: Harvard University Press, 1992).

41. William Haller, *Foxe's First Book of Martyrs and the Elect Nation* (London: Jonathan Cape, 1963).

42. Patrick Collinson, *The Birthpangs of Protestant England* (New York: St. Martin's, 1988), 14.

43. Richard Helgerson, *Forms of Nationhood: The Elizabethan Writing of England* (Chicago: University of Chicago Press, 1992), 103.

44. Foxe, *Acts*, 6:701.

45. Ibid., 6:725.

46. "For what man beholdyng the lyfe of vs Christians, will greatly meruell, why the Lord goeth not with our armye to fight agaynst the Turkes? And if my verdite might here haue place, for me to adde my censure, there appeareth to me an other cause in this matter yet greater then this aforesayd: whiche to make playne and euident in ful discourse of wordes, laysure nowe doth not permit. Briefly to touch what I conceaue, my opinion is this: that if the syncere

doctrine of Christen fayth deliuered and left vnto vs in the word of God, had not ben so corrupted in the Churche of Rome, God offended wyth idolatry and wrong fayth of the Christians, or if the Byshop of Rome would yet reclame his impure idolatrie, and prophanatious and admitte Christe the lambe of God to stand alone, without our vnpure additions, to be our onely iustification, accordyng to the free promise of Gods grace: I nothing doubt but the power of this fayth groundyng onely vppon Christ the sonne of God, had both framed our lyues into a better disposition: and also soone would, or yet will bryng downe the pride of that proude Holofernes." Ibid., 6:738. See also "A Prayer Agaynst the Turkes," ibid., 6:739.

47. Benedict Robinson and Zachary Lesser, eds., *Textual Conversations in the Renaissance: Ethics, Authors, Technologies* (Aldershot, U.K.: Ashgate, 2006), 2.

48. Francis Bacon, *An Advertisement Touching a Holy War*, ed. Laurence Lampert (Prospect Heights, Ill.: Waveland, 2000), 17.

49. Francis Bacon, *The Works of Francis Bacon*, ed. James Spedding, Robert Ellis, and Douglas Heath, 14 vols. (London, 1858–74), 14:158.

50. Matar, *Turks, Moors, and Englishmen*, 151.

51. Bacon, *An Advertisement*, 15.

52. Spedding, *The Works*, 7:5–6.

53. J. Max Patrick, "Hawk vs. Dove: Francis Bacon's Advocacy of Holy War," *Studies in the Literary Imagination* 4, no. 1 (April 1971): 168.

54. Matar, *Turks, Moors, and Englishmen*, 152, 153.

55. Laurence Lampert, "Interpretive Essay," in Bacon, *An Advertisement*, 42.

56. Robert K. Faulkner, *Francis Bacon and the Project of Progress* (Lanham, Md.: Rowman & Littlefield, 1993), 226.

57. Francis Bacon, "Of the True Greatness of Kingdoms and Estates," *The Essays*, ed. John Pitcher (London: Penguin, 1985), 153.

58. Bacon, "Of Unity in Religion," *The Essays*, 70.

59. Bacon, "Of Empire," *The Essays*, 117.

60. Bacon, "Considerations Touching a War with Spain," *The Complete Works of Francis Bacon*, 3 vols., ed. Basil Montagu (Philadelphia, 1841), 2:207, 208, 212.

61. Bacon, *An Advertisement*, 26.

62. Ibid., 24.

63. Ibid., 19.

64. Ibid., 22.

65. Ibid.

66. Bacon, "Of Empire," 119.

67. Bacon, *An Advertisement*, 19–20.

68. Ibid., 30.

69. Aristotle, *Politics*, ed. Gregory R. Crane, Perseus Digital Library Project, online at http://www.perseus.tufts.edu (accessed August 26, 2008).

70. Bacon, *The Letters and the Life of Francis Bacon*, 5 vols., ed. James Spedding (London, 1892) 3:90–91.

71. Bacon, *An Advertisement*, 31.

72. Ibid., 32.

73. Ibid., 33, 34.

74. Ibid., 35.

75. Bacon, "Of Unity in Religion," 70.

76. Terry Eagleton, *Holy Terror* (New York: Oxford University Press, 2005).

77. Bacon, *An Advertisement*, 36.

78. John Knox, *First Blast of the Trumpet against the Monstrous Regiment of Women* (London, 1558). Knox directed his attack against the Catholic queens Mary Queen of Scots and Mary Tudor, but his general diatribe against female rulers turned the Protestant Elizabeth I against him.

79. Eagleton, *Holy Terror*, 12.

80. Bacon, *An Advertisement*, 24.

81. Michel de Montaigne, "On the Cannibals," *The Complete Essays*, ed. and trans. M. A. Screech (New York: Penguin, 1993), 228–41.

82. Bacon, *An Advertisement*, 23, 24.

83. Richard Eden and Joannes Taisnier, "Dedication," *A Very Necessarie and Profitable Booke concerning Navigation* (London, 1579).

84. Bacon, *An Advertisement*, 24.

85. Bacon, *The Advancement of Learning* (London: Oxford University Press, 1966), Book 1, VII.1, 65; VIII.6, 70; II.2, 13.

86. Charles Whitney, *Francis Bacon and Modernity* (New Haven, Conn.: Yale University Press, 1986), 9, 11.

87. Johannes Fabian, *Time and the Other* (New York: Columbia University Press, 1983), 23, 17, 31.

88. Bacon, *The Advancement of Learning*, IV.35.

89. Bacon, "Thoughts and Conclusions," *The Philosophy of Francis Bacon*, ed. and trans. Benjamin Farrington (Chicago: University of Chicago Press, 1966), 95.

90. Bacon, *The Advancement of Learning*, XXV.4, 241.

91. Bacon, *An Advertisement*, 24.

92. George Sandys, *A Relation of a Journey Begun An Dom 1610: Four Books Containing a Description of the Turkish Empire, of Egypt, of the Holy Land, of the Remote Parts of Italy and the Islands Adjoining* (London, 1627), 104, 114, 115.

93. Samuel Purchas, *Purchas His Pilgrimes* (London, 1614), III.13, 315.

94. George Clark, *War and Society in the Seventeenth Century* (Cambridge, U.K.: Cambridge University Press, 1958), 19.

9

Ottoman Conceptions of War and Peace in the Classical Period

A. NURI YURDUSEV

This chapter examines Ottoman conceptions of war and peace from the fourteenth to the eighteenth centuries, the classical period of the empire. The argument presented here is that the Ottoman conception of war and peace developed not just out of the precepts of classical Islamic teaching but also from the evaluation of the realities of the period. The evolution of Ottoman conceptions during this era may accordingly be categorized into two periods: the early or foundational period from the beginning of the fourteenth century to the mid-fifteenth century, when traditional notions of *ghaza* (religiously motivated warfare) were dominant; and the period of growth from the mid-fifteenth century to the late seventeenth century, when *raison d'état* and European ideas of statecraft found their way in, although rhetorical lip service to the *ghaza* continued.

To begin with, I take issue with the conventional account by the diplomatic historians. Among them is a prevalent view that the Ottoman empire, being faithful to Islamic precepts, carried out its relations with the non-Muslim world, and thus with Europeans, on the basis of a conception of a permanent (actual or potential) state of war. This conception held that Islam required the empire to conduct its external relations within the framework of the dichotomy of *dar al-Islam* (the "abode of Islam," where Islamic law is enforced) versus *dar al-harb* (the "abode of war," where the infidels live outside the law of Islam and with which the Muslims are at war). This dichotomy thus envisioned a permanent state of war between the two spheres. The assumption underlying the conventional account is that the Ottomans in their foreign relations adopted an "orthodox" version of Islam. Therefore, one cannot expect the Ottomans to accept as possible normal, peaceful relations between Ottomans/Muslims and Europeans/non-Muslims.

Here are some examples. According to J. C. Hurewitz, "as a universal religion Islam [and thus the Ottoman empire] remained theoretically at war with the infidel world."[1] It was the combination of Ottoman military might and traditional

Islamic learning, argues Bernard Lewis, that led the Ottomans "to despise the barbarous Western infidel from an attitude of correct doctrine." The concept of jihad divided the world into "two great zones, the house of Islam and the house of war, with a perpetual state of war, or at best truce, between them."[2] The reason the Ottoman empire did not enjoy peaceful diplomatic relations with Europe, declares M. S. Anderson, resulted from a deep-seated view of the world that drew "a clear dividing-line, one impossible to cross, between the 'abode of Islam' and the outside non-Muslim world, the 'abode of war.' Between these different worlds relations must always be those of actual or at least potential hostility."[3] In their external relations, the Ottomans, in Thomas Naff's account, assumed the Islamic worldview according to which the Muslims were under the obligation of jihad to wage holy war against the abode of war until the ideal of a single, universal Muslim community under a single law was realized.[4] To be fair, Naff is more cautious than others. He acknowledges that the boundaries between the so-called Ottoman *dar al-Islam* and the European *dar al-harb* were not altogether impenetrable.[5] Ercüment Kuran writes that the Ottoman empire, following the law of Islam, did not sign peace treaties with the European infidels.[6]

On these accounts, the Ottoman empire is regarded not as a polity established by Muslims but as one strictly based on the orthodox rules of Islam. Both its internal and external governmental or administrative affairs were determined in the light of the law of Islam, namely the shari'a. Consequently, it is held, the Ottoman empire continued its policy of permanent holy war with the infidels until the empire clearly lost its superiority over the Europeans in the eighteenth century. Against this view, we need to begin by asking how "Islamic" the Ottoman empire was.

In Ottoman historiography, there are four different theses regarding the origins and the nature of the empire. The first one, proposed by Herbert Gibbons, argues that the Ottoman empire was a direct/indirect continuation of the Byzantine empire and that the Ottoman system was derived from Byzantine institutions.[7] The second argument was put forward by Mehmed Fuat Köprülü in his lectures given at the Sorbonne in 1934. In response to Gibbons, he argued that the origins of the Ottoman empire and its character could be considered as part of the movements of migrating Turkish tribes and thus within the Turkic tradition.[8] Third, according to Paul Wittek, the Ottoman empire was a *ghazi* state established by the *ghazis* who strived for *ghaza*/jihad and conquest.[9] Finally, it is also common to treat the Ottoman empire as an example of nomadic empires generally, springing from tribal institutions.[10]

Of all of these theses, the *ghazi* thesis has been the one most widely supported. Ever since Wittek, many scholars, as seen in the writings of the historians quoted above, have argued that the Ottoman empire was an Islamic empire, founded by warriors devoted to the spread of Islam in infidel lands. Accordingly, the empire was organized on the principles of Islam, and its law, government, and external affairs were directed by the shari'a. As an Islamic state based on the policy of *ghaza*, "perpetual warfare carried on against unbelievers," the Ottoman empire from its very beginning was "geared for conquest. It constantly had to expand, gain new territory, and provide new outlets for the energies of the ghazis."[11]

It is undoubtedly true that the Ottoman government officially claimed to be an Islamic system. Ottoman rulers always promoted themselves as defending the cause of Islam. Ottoman rulers repeatedly made it known that they would go to war when they were attacked and Islam was insulted. They considered themselves to be the servants and protectors of Islam. The principal Ottoman institutions were referred to as being "of Islam." Ottoman territories were referred to as "the land of Islam," its sovereign as "the padishah of Islam," its army as "the soldiers of Islam," and the head of its religious bureaucracy as "the shaykh of Islam." Further-more, the state itself was described as "Devlet-i Aliyye'yi Muhammediyye" (the Sublime State of Muhammad) when it was referred to in its official texts. The state supposedly tried always to observe Islamic rules by means of fatwas sought from the shaykh al-Islam. This was how the Ottoman empire appeared in theory and in official texts. But to what extent did the practice match the theory?

In fact, when the actual historical record is taken into account, it is clear that the Ottoman empire was not an "orthodox" Islamic state. Its governmental and ad-ministrative affairs were not directed under the strict observance of Islamic law. It is widely agreed that the Ottoman empire was heavily influenced by customary law and was respectful of local customs. According to Halil İnalcık, in line with the Turkish state tradition, which entrusted the ruler with the authority to promulgate rules for the regulation of state affairs, the Ottoman sultans themselves issued the *qanun-names*, or "books of law," the most famous of them initiated by Mehmed II (r. 1444–1446, 1451–1481).[12] In other words, the administration was based not only or primarily on Islamic law but also on the state law or law of the ruler.

Furthermore, both in terms of texts and in terms of the actual historical prac-tice, it is hardly possible to argue for a monolithic worldview based on the duality of *dar al-Islam* versus *dar al-harb*. In the history of Islamic societies, we see various practices. In terms of theory alone, it is not possible to justify a perpetual war between Muslims and non-Muslims if the entirety of the Qur'an is taken into ac-count. The Qur'an expressly states, for example, that if the non-Muslims incline toward peace, then the Muslims are advised to make peace (Q. 8:61). Of course, one may find textual support for the contrary view. Yet it is debatable if jihad means the obligation to make constant war against non-Muslims.[13] Even within the classical Islamic theory, alongside the concepts of *dar al-Islam* and *dar al-harb*, some jurists outlined a third concept, *dar al-sulh* (the "abode of truce," where Mus-lims and non-Muslims live according to terms of peace).

Regardless of what is found in the texts and however these texts may be inter-preted, what is significant to historians is the actual historical record. In Muslim as in Christian societies, texts were historically understood and applied in var-ious ways.

The Ottoman practice was rather pragmatic. The Ottomans pragmatically inter-preted the precepts of Islam, especially with regard to external affairs. They made use of the *aman* system (granting safe conduct within their territory) and the *ahd-name* (charters of security or political autonomy) both with respect to their subject non-Muslim populations and in their external relations with foreign powers and individuals. They did not actually follow a policy of permanent war and routinely based their statecraft on "existing customs" and "agreements." When Mehmed II granted capitulations to the Venetians in 1454, it was stated that the decision was taken according to the existing custom, by which was meant the previous capitulatory agreement between the Byzantine empire and the Venetians.[14] The respect for existing customs on the principle that agreements made should be honored can be seen in the practice and implementation of the *aman* system. After the fall of Constantinople in 1453, Mehmed II granted the Greeks, Genoese, and Latins *aman*. When Selim I (r. 1512–1520) later wanted to get rid of some Byzantine notables in Istanbul because of their suspected efforts to reestablish the Byzantine empire, the sultan was reminded of the *aman* given by Mehmed II, and he retreated from his compulsory conversion or expulsion policy. Similarly, Suleiman the Magnificent (r. 1520–1566), in his *firmans* (edicts) of 1558–1560 to the *beys* (governors) of Bosnia and Buda, stressed that they must observe the *ahd-u aman* (the treaty of security to the non-Muslim peoples) of the sultan.[15]

Islamic doctrine did not prevent the Ottomans from reaching out or making agreements with non-Muslims. It is true that such agreements in the early classical period were considered to be unilateral truces rather than bilateral treaties. Yet they signed truces for long periods, and they were more or less automatically renewed, so that in practice, there was a permanent state of peace with a considerable number of states. While Dorothy Vaughan speaks of a "pattern of alliance" between the Turks and Europe, Daniel Goffman makes the point that the Ottomans were an indispensable part of, and fully integrated into, the European diplomatic system.[16] One can find many other examples demonstrating that the Ottomans did not strictly abide by a policy that the *ghaza* or jihad thesis would have us believe they did. What we know is that the Ottomans generally observed the rules of expediency or the requirements of realpolitik. The Ottoman empire was not an orthodox Islamic polity, if by "orthodox" we mean a state operating according to the classical Muslim jurists' notions of world order. Based on this general framework, we can hardly surmise that the Ottoman conception of *ghaza* and war could be reduced to the idea of "holy war." What, then, was their conception and practice of war?

Ghaza and the Ottoman Conception of War

In the Ottoman chronicles, the words *ghaza*, *jihad*, and *harb* were often used interchangeably to mean "war." These terms were not exactly identical, having their own nuances and legal provisions, and they were never used with consistent meanings. Still, we find all three used in the Ottoman chronicles and legal texts when the subject is war. Bearing this in mind, I shall mostly use the term *ghaza* in my examination of the Ottoman conception of war. I will deal first with the issue of whether the *ghaza* existed as a notion and practice from the beginning of Ottoman rule or was a later, fifteenth-century construction.

Some scholars have suggested that the notion of *ghaza* did not exist before the fifteenth century. The idea emerged as the Ottomans became an increasingly settled society. In order to exalt their forefathers and justify their raids and plunders, the idea of *ghaza* was developed and retrospectively applied by fifteenth-century Ottomans. Moreover, the words *ghaza* and *ghazi* were not, it is said, commonly used in Anatolia before the fifteenth century, and even if they were used, the words did not embody a holy and sacred meaning.[17] Indeed, until Ahmedi's chronicle *Iskendername*, written in the beginning of the fifteenth century, the word *ghaza* does not appear in the indisputably authentic sources directly related to the Ottomans. It is suggested that the inscription in the Bursa mosque bearing the date of 1337, given as authentic evidence of an early Ottoman usage by Wittek, was a later interpolation.[18]

Against this, it can be argued that the terms *ghaza*, *harb*, and *jihad* were widely used long before the early Ottomans, and there had been a tradition of *ghaza* and *jihad* among the various Muslim polities from the very beginning, be they empires, beyliks, or emirates. The early Ottomans living in post-Seljukid Anatolia were definitely influenced by both the legacy of early Islamic polities, including the Seljuk empire, and the other beyliks that were contemporary to the Ottomans. Epic collections, oral or written, of the heroic battles against the infidels, such as the *Battalname* (recording and reiterating the battles of the Umayyad warrior 'Abdallah Battal, known as Sayyid Battal Ghazi in Anatolia) and the *Danishmendname* (recording and reciting the activities of Melik Danishmend Ahmed Ghazi, the founder of one of the early Turkic beyliks in Anatolia), predated the early Ottomans and were widely known to the Turkic peoples of Anatolia.[19] The early Ottomans were also familiar with these epic collections. The tomb of Battal Ghazi near Eskişehir was very close to Söğüt (known to be the birthplace of the Ottoman beylik), and the tomb had already become a sort of pilgrimage destination by the end of the twelfth century. Furthermore, various other beyliks, with which the Ottomans were in contact, used the title *ghazi*.

Besides these epic collections, books of the "catechism" (*ilm-i hal*) used in fourteenth-century Anatolia included the terms *ghaza* and *jihad*. These books generally gave the articles of Muslim faith and rules for religious behavior. Some provided definitions of *ghaza* and *jihad* and also explained rules for behavior in *ghaza*. According to the research by Şinasi Tekin, a fourteenth-century catechism contains a section on the rules of *ghaza*, referring to offensive battle, and of jihad, referring to defensive battle.[20] In short, the word *ghaza* and its derivatives were quite common in Anatolia, and we cannot, as pointed out by Cemal Kafadar, assume that the Ottomans were not familiar with and were indifferent to such notions.[21] The idea of *ghaza* was inherited by the Ottomans and the other beyliks from the Seljuks. Even Osman, the eponymous founder of the dynasty, is reported to have said that "Allah has given me the khanate with *ghaza* just as He gave the sultanate to the Seljukid Sultan."[22]

With the beginning of the fifteenth century, we can see references to *ghaza* in the Ottoman chronicles, as in the case of Ahmedi's *Iskendername*. An anonymous chronicle recording the battles of Murad II (r. 1421–1451) bears the title *Ghazavat-ı Sultan Murad bin Mehmed Han*.[23]

As mentioned earlier, the words *ghaza* and *jihad* were imprecisely and often interchangeably used by the Ottomans. Yet, while *ghaza* usually referred to the heroic battles of individuals or groups of individuals, *jihad* usually connoted more of an organized battle with some legal norms that needed to be satisfied. As the Ottomans grew from a small frontier beylik to a large empire, they conceived of *ghaza* and *jihad* differently and emphasized different aspects.

Even during a particular period of time, the notion of *ghaza* was employed with different meanings by different groups within and around the Ottoman beylik and later empire. In the words of Linda Darling, "*ghaza* was not the property of a homogenous group: people advocated or engaged in it from different standpoints and for different reasons."[24] Nevertheless, in what follows, I examine the Ottoman conception of war in the two historical periods mentioned earlier: the early or foundational period from the beginning of the fourteenth century to the mid-fifteenth century, when notions of *ghaza* were dominant; and the period of growth from the mid-fifteenth century to the late seventeenth century, when the influence of European ideas of statecraft became significant, resulting in the decrease—though not the end—of *ghaza* rhetoric.

The Early Period

In popular belief and in much scholarship, the zeal for *ghaza* is the driving force and stimulus of the early Ottomans. Located on the edges of the Byzantine empire in northwestern Anatolia, the early Ottomans adopted, or inherited, *ghaza* as a frontier activity that had been conducted for centuries before them by Muslim warriors whose legendary exploits were recounted in popular ballads. However, as a nomadic or semisettled people, they did not conceive of *ghaza* as a war that was legally prescribed or constrained by some specified rules. It was a heroic activity of various warriors and *akhis* (pious groups) with a religious overtone. This is the essence of the *ghazi*-state view of the Ottomans developed by Wittek and others. Indeed, this idea seems plausible to some extent. When one considers the heterogeneous nature of the early Ottoman warriors, their cooperation from time to time with both Christians and other Muslims in Anatolia, their concentration on expansion and booty rather than proselytizing, and the elements of unorthodoxy in their daily lives and religious practice, it is hardly possible to view the early Ottoman *ghazis* as "Islamic holy warriors." In other words, for the early Ottomans, "*ghaza* was not *jihad* and did not adhere to *jihad*'s legal norms." It was an activity that various people could join in, and it benefited both the individual warrior and the beylik. The epic poems of the period depict *ghazi* warriors as "living for battle and booty, glory and girls." The struggle to spread Islam, for the *ghazis*, did not prohibit alliance and marriage with non-Muslims. "*Ghaza* was inclusive rather than exclusive, aiming at the attachment of new territories and new adherents by whatever means proved successful."[25] From the early period, therefore, the Ottoman conception of *ghaza* and even of jihad did not entail zealous proselytism or forceful conversion. Rather, as İnalcık writes, "Holy War was intended not to destroy but to subdue the infidel world." The idea was to expand the Muslim domain and redirect the profits of non-Muslim lands toward the Muslims.[26] This idea continued throughout the classical period of the empire.

A contrary argument was proposed by Colin Imber. Through analysis of the early incidents and chronicles and by verifying them from the contemporary non-Turkish sources, he posits that shari'a provided the legal underpinning for the empire at the beginning. Based on his study of legal manuals, he suggests that the Ottomans at first believed that they should conduct warfare and organize their territories in accordance with the rules of classical Islamic jurisprudence. The picture of unorthodox tribal *ghazis* was a fifteenth-century reconstruction intended to establish the Ottoman empire as the heir to the Seljuk empire following Timur's incursion into the empire.[27]

The early sources support both views of the early Ottomans: unorthodox *ghazi* warriors and warriors abiding by the strictures of Islam. Common to both views is the claim that there was, to a certain extent, a religious motivation in the wars of the Ottomans. The prevalent discourse of *ghaza* obviously led the Ottoman warriors to view it as a religious duty. Yet religious motivation was not, I think, the main stimulus for war. *Ghaza*, with its religious overtones, was used to justify or sanctify other mundane goals, for *ghaza* could be used to refer to a wide range of activities by the warriors and the central authorities. Quite often, *ghaza* was used to gain legitimacy, prestige, and leverage by various groups. It was frequently deployed as a justification for conquest after the fact, rather than as a stimulus for warfare. This practice, of course, was not confined to the Ottomans. The use of religion to legitimize warfare and territorial acquisition was a common tactic among contemporary small polities, Christian and Muslim.[28] In employing the rhetoric of religiously motivated war to further quite secular ends, the Ottomans were merely conforming to their environment.

When one considers the geopolitical milieu in which the Ottoman beylik emerged, situated as it was next to the Christian Byzantine empire and several rival beyliks, *ghaza* provided the early Ottoman leaders with a ready resource for mobilizing friends and allies and subduing opponents. As İnalcık notes, the disruption of tribal bonds by migration and mercenary service in the Byzantine armies made the idea of *ghaza* as a uniting force and recruiting mechanism appealing to the Ottoman beys.[29] As there was no clear hierarchy at the time among the rival tribal beys, the Ottomans, along with other prominent warriors, made use of *ghaza* to assert their power and legitimacy vis-à-vis one another. This began to change with the consolidation of Ottoman rule begun by Beyazid I (r. 1389–1402). The process was completed only in the mid-fifteenth century with the conquest of Constantinople. Even Mehmed II is said to have used *ghaza* against the powerful vizier Chandarlı Ali Pasha.[30] It is plausible to assume, then, that in the early period, *ghaza* was used not just against the infidels but also against rival *ghazis*.

Similarly, *ghaza* was employed as a means of gaining leverage by one Anatolian beylik over another. With their beylik being situated next to the Byzantine empire and being rather small compared with some other beyliks in Anatolia, the Ottomans probably found it convenient to invoke the spirit of *ghaza* in order to enhance their prestige over the other beyliks.[31] The use of holy war rhetoric was indeed a significant source of power and prestige in the Muslim world. The later Ottoman sultans, for instance, regularly sent *fethnames*, or accounts of their conquests against Christian (and Muslim) enemies, to other Muslim leaders. This practice was common among Muslim rulers and was intended partly to inform and to counter "false" reports. But it was also the continuation of the early Ottoman policy of using *ghaza* to secure the prestige that came with being warriors for the faith.

In addition to religious motives, the need for unity, and being a means of legitimacy and a source of power, another benefit that *ghaza* provided was purely material: booty and slaves. In the catechism *Risaletül-Islam*, written in the first half of the fourteenth century, *ghaza*, along with farming and trade, was stipulated as a proper way of gaining livelihood.[32] Undoubtedly, material gain, pure and simple, drove many, rulers and commoners alike, to pursue *ghaza*.

To sum up so far, in the early period of the Ottoman empire, war was generally understood in terms of *ghaza* as a consequence of the prevalent discourse and practice in Anatolia. *Ghaza* had contested meanings and meant different things to different groups. It encompassed the raids and heroic battles of individual warriors in addition to the organized campaigns of rulers. A variety of motives and aims, from religious to mundane, animated the participants. Yet the "holiness" of *ghaza* remained as an underlying aspect of the concept, the result of religious devotion or the need for legitimacy in the eyes of fellow Muslims. The religious overtones of the Ottoman conception of war continued into the period of growth.

The Period of Growth

In this period, the Ottoman beylik became an empire with extensive territories spread across three continents. Centralization of the principal bodies and warrior groups had already begun in the second half the fourteenth century, and after the conquest of Constantinople, the empire acquired its principal institutions. As a consequence of this development, military campaigns on the western borders of the empire were to a great extent brought under the control of the central administration. A change in the significance attached to the traditional discourse and customs of war also occurred. For example, according to the six-teenth-century historian Neşri, Mehmed II abandoned the traditional *ghazi* custom that involved the sultan standing when the drums of the army were beaten.[33] This does not mean that the Ottomans discarded the notion of *ghaza*, as the raids of the frontier beys were still considered *ghaza* and the sultans con-tinued to use the title *ghazi*. The idea of *ghaza* continued to provide the sultans with a source of legitimacy and mobilization. What changed was a shift in the centrality of *ghaza* in Ottoman discourses. For example, in accounts of the wars of the regular imperial army, the idea of *ghaza* is noticeably not given the prominent place it had occupied earlier. Similarly, soldiers and fellow beys, who, as fellow *ghazis*, had earlier been regarded as the "friends" or comrades of the sultan, came to be viewed as his "subjects."

In this period, war began to be described and carried out in formal terms. It was no longer the incursions or heroic battles of loosely organized groups of indi-viduals. War was now considered a campaign of the regular imperial army carried out with careful planning and long preparations. As an indication of the institu-tionalization of war, justification by legal opinion of the ulema in the form of *fetva* (fatwa) began in the sixteenth century.

From the mid-fifteenth century on, the conception and conduct of wars by the Ottoman empire may be outlined under three categories. The first set of wars was waged and justified by religion. The Ottoman empire publicly declared itself the champion and guardian of Islam, and Ottoman rulers repeatedly made it known that they could go to war when Islam was insulted. A sixteenth-century Ottoman chronicler, Kemalpaşazade Ahmed Şemseddin, wrote that in waging wars, the Ottoman sultans served for the glory of Islam and acted as the commanders of the Muslims.[34] In this conception, war was understood in terms of religious duty, as in the early period. What was new now was that the duty was implemented not only against the non-Muslim infidels but also against the heterodox sects of Islam, especially Shi'ism, which was considered heresy.[35] The wars against the Shi'i empire of the Safavids in Iran were treated as such and justified on the ground of preventing *fitna* (sedition).

Second, the Ottoman empire may be said to have waged wars for humanitarian reasons. According to Kemalpaşazade, saving oppressed people from the rule of tyrants was a just cause of war, and the Ottoman sultans had the duty to relieve such destitute people from the oppressors.[36] This was, I think, a result of the Otto-mans' conception of their empire as a universal empire, a notion that started with Mehmed II and became more visible during the reign of Suleiman the Magnifi-cent. It was also a reflection of the Ottomans striving to combine diverse political and cultural traditions within their administration, most notably the Roman/ Byzantine tradition to which they claimed to be the successors. The Ottoman sul-tans thus appealed to the peoples of the world, not just Muslim peoples. This conception of war and the accompanying propaganda was manifest and proved effective in some of the Ottoman land and naval campaigns. For example,

Kemalpaşazade wrote in his chronicle that one of the reasons for Suleiman's campaign against Rhodes was to relieve the island's inhabitants of the cruel and oppressive rule of the Order of Saint John.[37]

Finally, the Ottoman empire waged wars on the ground of political necessity, namely the interests of the state, similar to the European idea of *raison d'état* and the need to gain political allies. Although this secular and mundane approach to war can be found in the early centuries of the empire, it became prevalent in the sixteenth century. It is reported that in a dialogue between Sultan Murad I (r. 1361–1381) and his grand vizier, besides the religious necessities, the interest of the state was cited as the reason to go to war.[38] In the sixteenth century, political considerations became central to the justification of state policies, especially with the increasing involvement of the empire in the affairs of the newly emerging European states system.[39] The system of alliances in Europe and the Ottoman rivalry with the Hapsburg empire necessitated political allies, and consequently war was used as a means of gaining and maintaining political allies.

By the seventeenth century, war was largely understood in terms of what we nowadays call reason of state. The Ottomans frequently participated in European wars, and their approach to war was influenced by the European states. When one reads, for instance, the memoirs of Osman Aga from Timişoara, who fell prisoner to the Austrians in the wars following the siege of Vienna in 1683, it is apparent that both the Austrians and the Ottomans had common definitions and rules in respect of the meaning, treatment, and exchange of prisoners.[40] According to Géza Pálffy, prisoner exchanges were common practice in the Ottoman-Austrian borderland from the sixteenth century onward. These were either realized through mutual agreement between the two states or frontier authorities or incorporated into peace treaties signed after major wars. For example, in late 1628, after receiving word that the pasha of Buda was willing to exchange six Christian prisoners, the Hungarian border authorities released six Ottoman prisoners of similar ransom value.[41] In the eighteenth century, the impact of Europe increased, and the empire adopted the customs and conventions of war accepted by the European states.

The Idea of Peace in the Ottoman Empire

In the early centuries of the empire, the Ottomans glorified *ghaza*, and we consequently do not find much praise for peace. Given the opportunities to expand toward the Byzantine frontier and the Balkans and the ongoing rivalry with the other beyliks, it is not surprising that war, rather than peace, defined the Ottoman imagination. As the Ottoman polity evolved into a widespread empire made up of diverse peoples, and as its external engagements with different regions and powers grew, the issue of peaceful coexistence within the empire and with other polities had to be addressed. Let us consider first how the Ottoman administration ensured peace within the empire.

The basis of peace both internally and externally for the Ottomans was justice. They held that if justice was done, then peace would be ensured. The internal formula for this is expressed in the famous idea of the "circle of equity" (*daire'yi adliyye*). Based on the cyclical theory of history developed by Ibn Khaldun, the idea was elaborated by sixteenth-century Ottoman writers.[42] The circle runs more or less as follows:

1. There can be no royal authority without the *askeri* (the imperial administration, consisting of the army, court officials, provincial rulers, and ulema).
2. Wealth is required to maintain the *askeri*.
3. The *reaya* (peasantry) produce the wealth.
4. The sultan keeps the *reaya* loyal by making justice reign.
5. Justice necessitates harmony in the world.
6. Harmony is provided by the state, the basis of which is (religious) law.
7. Law is implemented by royal authority.

Whether or not this circle worked in the way Ottoman writers envisioned is outside the focus of this chapter. What is significant for us is that justice formed the basis of the circle, hence the "circle of equity," and if it is implemented properly by the rulers, peace prevails in the society.

Another formula for ensuring justice within the imperial borders was the *millet* system.[43] This was developed for the non-Muslim subjects of the empire. According to this system, subject populations, classified in terms of religion, were given the right to govern their internal affairs with their own law. They were free to practice their own religion and implement their own legal system among themselves. Their immunities and security were guaranteed by the sultan in return for a certain tax. It is widely agreed that the *millet* system worked smoothly and ensured peaceful coexistence among the various subject peoples of the empire until the spread of nationalism in the nineteenth century.

With respect to Muslim peoples of the empire in the outlying regions of the Middle East, North Africa, and Crimea, Ottoman authorities worked with the local rulers and adopted or adapted the local customs that had worked for centuries. The Ottoman formula here was ratification of the equilibrium of the local forces and arbitration when they had disputes. Based on the *millet* system and the formula for the outlying regions, it is fair to conclude that, besides justice, the second principle for ensuring peace, itself derived from the principle of justice, was the recognition of traditional and indigenous rights of the peoples.

The Ottoman conception of peace with respect to the polities outside the empire may be considered in one sense the projection of the internal principles over the external world. We see this projection in the idea of humanitarian war waged against oppressive rulers to save oppressed peoples. Such wars were viewed as just wars and may be considered the projection of the principle of justice beyond the frontiers of the empire.

We also see the projection of the *aman* system. The system of *ahdname*, or capitulations, was a direct result of the extension of the *aman* system to foreign peoples.[44] The *ahdnames* addressed not only the foreign merchant communities within the empire but also the rulers of the home countries of the merchants. It is true that the *ahdnames* were unilateral documents granted by the sultans and valid only during the lifetime of the granting sultan. Hence, they needed to be renewed upon the ascension of a new sultan. Yet in many ways, these were legal documents based on the principle of reciprocity. For example, the *ahdname* granted to the English in May 1580 contains clear provisions for reciprocity.[45] Item 22 stipulates that the sultan will keep his promises as long as the queen keeps and observes terms of "the league and holy peace." Hence, it would not be wrong to infer that for the Ottomans, one of the conditions for the establishment of peace between powers was *ahde vefa*, the principle that agreements made should be kept, known in international law as *pacta sunt servanda*.

A second condition that can be derived from the *ahdname* of 1580 is respect for Islam. Item 11 draws attention to the possibility of false witnesses claiming that Englishmen insulted Islam. The Ottomans had long maintained that insulting Islam was a just cause for war; peace, therefore, required respect for Islam and the sultan. Given the universal claims and pretensions of the Ottoman empire, this may be described as "peace by submission." For the Ottomans, submission meant the recognition of the supremacy of the sultan (and thus the empire), not only by the foreigners inside the empire but also by their states. Furthermore, a strong show of goodwill and friendship was expected, meaning in some cases payment of a certain amount of tribute. Every *ahdname* begins with a statement calling for a show of "goodwill and friendship" by the other party. Respect for Islam was one of the significant conditions for peace in the Ottoman perception.

Two principles that began to be used in the making of peace among European states from the sixteenth century onward were also adopted by the Ottomans. One was a reflection of the notion of *raison d'état*. The interests of the empire could supersede other considerations in the establishment of peace between the Ottoman empire and other polities. According to a fatwa issued by the shaykh al-Islam Ebussuud, peace can be accepted if it is in the interest of the Muslims.[46] The other principle that the Ottomans came to use in making peace was the customary rule of *uti possidetis*, the principle that whoever has actual control should also have legal control. It is suggested that the empire used this customary rule as early as the sixteenth century.[47] The principle was clearly and successfully invoked in the negotiations leading to the Treaty of Karlowitz in 1699. According to Sir Edward Shepherd Creasy, when the English ambassador, Lord Paget, proposed to the Porte in 1696 that England should intervene to effect pacification on the basis of *uti possidetis*, the Ottoman authorities welcomed this offer by stipulating that a peace might be concluded generally on the principle of *uti possidetis.* But they added the further stipulations that the Austrians should abandon Transylvania, that the city of Peterwaradin should be razed, that the Austrians should evacuate all of the fortified places on the Turkish side of the Unna River, and other, similar exceptions.[48] Likewise, the first article of the Treaty of Passarowitz signed between the Ottoman empire and Austria in 1718 stipulated that the borders between the two states should be determined in accordance with the principle of *uti possidetis.*[49]

Whereas in the early centuries of the empire, "holy war" (*ghaza*) and "holy warriors" (*ghazis*) were glorified and peace was not given a prominent place in Ottoman literature, the lengthy wars and signs of decline in the seventeenth century changed the situation. We see the emergence of the idea of "holy peace." The *ahdname* of 1580 to the English referred to "holy peace" (*mübarek sulh*). An earlier, unratified capitulation of 1535 to the French began by pointing out "the calamities and disadvantages which are caused by war" and emphasized "the good, quiet and tranquility derived from peace." It is explicitly declared that "peace is preferable to war."[50] The Ottoman-Hapsburg Treaty of Vasvar (1664) and the later Treaty of Karlowitz were referred to as "holy peace."[51]

In short, the Ottomans started to exalt peace and give it a prominent place in their external relations from the second half of the sixteenth century. This movement led to the emergence in the late seventeenth century of a relatively rare type of classical Ottoman poetry called *sulhiyye*, a poem for the praise of peace.[52] One such poem was written by the celebrated seventeenth-century poet Yusuf Nabi to celebrate the signing of the Treaty of Karlowitz. Although this treaty resulted in significant territorial losses for the Ottoman empire, Nabi hails it as a "great achievement" and praises the preservation of peace. The poem starts: "Thank God that the arena of war and quarrel has closed, the world once more experiences order through peace and tranquility."[53] Another poem was penned by Sabit, an eighteenth-century poet, after the Treaty of Pasarowitz in 1718. It also welcomes the end of war and the emergence of peace, by the grace of God: "Thank God that with the order of the caliph of Islam the drink of war became prohibited and the drink of peace became permitted."[54]

In the seventeenth century, we see that some ideas of peacemaking that prevailed in the European states system began to find their way into Ottoman statecraft. The Ottoman empire long observed the customary principles of *uti possidetis* and *pacta sunt servanda*. In the eighteenth century, the Ottomans began to refer to international law as a means of ensuring peace. References by the Ottoman authorities to international law in their dealings with the Europeans can be found as early as the first half of the eighteenth century. Grand Vizier Koja Ragip Pasha used the arguments of Grotius in his meetings with the European ambassadors in Istanbul, and we see increasing references to the rules of international law from the late eighteenth century onward. Sultan Selim III (r. 1789–1807) is said to have explicitly referred to the rules of international law in 1799 when Russian warships entered the Turkish Straits unannounced.[55]

Conclusion

In this chapter, I have argued that the Ottoman conception of war cannot be confined to a single or simple motivation, either in the foundation period or in the period of growth. I have shown that the Ottomans understood war in both religious and mundane terms. Even in the beginning, when the Ottomans were rather homogeneous and a small beylik, they were animated by a variety of motives in their battles. When its territorial reach grew over three continents, the Ottoman empire became not just more centralized and institutionalized but also more internally diverse and more externally engaged with a range of states. Different conceptions of war and peace logically developed in such a large, heterogeneous empire.

An intensive and to some extent unorganized *ghazi* activity and glorification of *ghaza* in the beginning is understandable given the frontier conditions in which the Ottoman state emerged. In this culture, both glorification of the *ghazis* and recognition of the necessities of their situation played a role. In light of the inherited *ghazi* tradition and the fierce rivalry with the other beyliks, the Ottomans must have felt that they needed to prove themselves in their devotion to the cause of Islam. Located in an area adjacent to the Christian Byzantine empire, they had the opportunity to do so. The necessities, on the other hand, led the Ottomans to wage wars in mundane terms, as seen in the wars waged against the other Muslim beyliks and wars of internal conflict.

The religious discourse and the necessities of the empire went on influencing the Ottoman conception in the period of growth. Increasing engagement with the European states system and the need for political allies brought *raison d'état* to the forefront. Yet the self-image of being a universal Islamic empire, the guardians of Islam and of Muslims, resulted in the high saliency of religious discourse. No doubt, the wars they waged were for them "just wars," fought not only for expanding *dar-al Islam* but also for self-defense, justice, and upholding Islam against insults

I have shown that the Ottoman conception of peace, too, was informed by Ottomans' identification with Islam and the requirements of the case. Even in the early periods, the Ottomans did not hesitate to establish peaceful relations with not only the other Muslim beyliks but also the Byzantines and the Balkan rulers. As a "world empire," the Ottoman state took upon itself the mission of ensuring peace and doing justice. The Ottoman authorities tried to secure this end according to the realities of the period and capabilities available to them, including alliances with European states. They justified peace, like war, on both Islamic and pragmatic grounds and, as the eighteenth century wore on, increasingly with reference to the newfangled notion of international law.

Acknowledgments

This chapter was completed during my research at Kansai University, Osaka, Japan, as a visiting scholar at the Institute of Legal Studies in the summer of 2009. I thank Kansai University for its support and especially Takeshi Tsunoda, who acted as my joint researcher during my stay. In finalizing the text, I received help from Mustafa Serdar Palabiyik, to whom I must express my thanks.

Notes

1. J. C. Hurewitz, "Ottoman Diplomacy and the European States System," *Middle East Journal* 15 (Spring 1961): 145–46.

2. Bernard Lewis, *The Middle East and the West* (London: Weidenfeld and Nicholson, 1964), 30, 32.

3. M. S. Anderson, *The Rise of Modern Diplomacy, 1450–1919* (London: Longman, 1993), 71.

4. Thomas Naff, "The Ottoman Empire and the European States System," in Hedley Bull and Adam Watson, eds., *The Expansion of International Society* (Oxford: Clarendon, 1984), 144.

5. Ibid.

6. Ercüment Kuran, *Avrupa'da Osmanlı İkamet Elçiliklerinin Kuruluşu ve İlk Elçilerin Siyasi Faaliyetleri, 1793–1821* (Ankara: Türk Kültürünü Araştırma Enstitüsü Yayınları, 1988), 10–11.

7. Herbert A. Gibbons, *The Foundation of the Ottoman Empire: A History of the Osmanlis, 1300–1403* (Oxford: Oxford University Press, 1916).

8. Mehmed Fuat Köprülü, *The Origins of the Ottoman Empire*, trans. and ed. Gary Leiser (Albany: State University of New York Press, 1992).

9. Paul Wittek, *The Rise of the Ottoman Empire* (London: Royal Asiatic Society, 1938).

10. Rudi P. Lindner, *Nomads and Ottomans in Medieval Anatolia* (Bloomington: Indiana University Press, 1983).

11. Norman Itzkowitz, *Ottoman Empire and Islamic Tradition* (Chicago: University of Chicago Press, 1972), 6, 11.

12. Halil İnalcık, "The Rise of the Ottoman Empire," in M. A. Cook, ed., *A History of the Ottoman Empire to 1730* (Cambridge, U.K.: Cambridge University Press, 1976), 47–48.

13. For a good summary of these debates, see AbdulHamid A. Abu Sulayman, *The Islamic Theory of International Relations: New Directions for Islamic Methodology and Thought* (Herndon, Va.: International Institute of Islamic Thought, 1987).

14. See Nasim Sousa, *The Capitulatory Régime of Turkey: Its History, Origin, and Nature* (Baltimore: Johns Hopkins University Press, 1933), 16. Article 16 of the agreement reads as follows: "that his lordship of Venice may, if he desires, send to Constantinople a governor (consul), with his suit, *according to existing custom*, which governor (consul) shall have the privilege of ruling over, governing, and administering justice to the Venetians of every class and condition" (emphasis added).

15. See Mehmet İpşirli, "Osmanlı Devletinde 'Eman' Sistemi," in İsmail Soysal, ed., *Çağdaş Türk Diplomasisi: 200 Yıllık Süreç* (Ankara: TTK Yayınları, 1999), 4–5.

16. Dorothy M. Vaughan, *Europe and the Turk: A Pattern of Alliances, 1350–1700* (Liverpool: Liverpool University Press, 1954); Daniel Goffman, *The Ottoman Empire and Early Modern Europe* (Cambridge, U.K.: Cambridge University Press, 2002), 18, 20, 224.

17. See Şinasi Tekin, "Türk Dünyasında Gaza ve Cihad Kavramları Üzerine Düşünceler," *Tarih ve Toplum* 19, no. 109 (1993): 9–18.

18. Şinasi Tekin, "Gazi Teriminin Anadolu ile Akdeniz Bölgesinde İtibarını Yeniden Kazanması," *Tarih ve Toplum* 19, no. 110 (1993): 73–80. See also Ahmedi, *Iskendername*, ed. Ismail Ünver (Ankara: TDK Yayınları, 1983).

19. For Battal Ghazi and *Battalname*, see A. Y. Ocak, "Battal Gazi," *Türkiye Diyanet Vakfı Islam Ansiklopedisi*, 5:204–5; and "Battalname," *Türkiye Diyanet Vakfı Islam Ansiklopedisi*, 5:207. For *Danishmendname*, see Necati Demir, ed., *Danişmend-name* (Ankara: Akçağ Yayınları,

2004). For a recent analysis of these and similar collections as the sources of the Ottoman conception of *ghaza*, see Selahattin Döğüş, "Osmanlılarda Gaza İdeolojisinin Tarihi ve Kültürel Kaynakları," *Belleten* 72, nos. 263–65 (2008): 817–88.

20. Şinasi Tekin, "XIV. Yüzyıla ait bir İlm-i Hal: Risaletül-Islam," *Wiener Zeitschrift für die Kunde des Morgenlandes* 76 (1986): 279–92; "XIV. Yüzyılda Yazılmış Gazilik Tarikası 'Gaziliğin Yolları' Adlı bir Eski Anadolu Türkçesi Metni ve Gaza/Cihad Kavramları Hakkında," *Journal of Turkish Studies* 13 (1989): 139–204. For the sources and examples of the prevalence of the words *ghaza* and *ghazi* in thirteenth- and fourteenth-century Anatolia, see Cemal Kafadar, *Between Two Worlds: The Construction of the Ottoman State* (Berkeley: University of California Press, 1995), 76–78; and Feridun M. Emecan, "Gazaya Dair XIV. Yüzyıl Kaynakları Arasında bir Gezinti," in *Prof. Dr. Hakkı Dursun Yıldız Armağanı* (Ankara: Türk Tarih Kurumu Basımevi, 1995), 191–97.

21. Cemal Kafadar, "Gaza," *Türkiye Diyanet Vakfı Islam Ansiklopedisi*, 13: 427–29.

22. Halil İnalcık, "Osmanlı Devletinin Kuruluşu Sorunu," in *Doğu-Batı Makaleler I* (Ankara: Doğu-Batı Yayınları, 2005), 117. See also Elizabeth A. Zachairadou, "İlk Osmanlılara ait Tarih ve Efsaneler," in O. Özel and M. Öz, eds., *Söğüt'ten Istanbul'a Osmanlı Devleti'nin Kuruluşu Üzerine Tartışmalar* (Ankara: Imge Kitabevi, 2000).

23. See Halil İnalcık and M. Oğuz, *Gazavat-ı Sultan Murad bin Mehmed Han* (Ankara: TTK Yayınları, 1978).

24. Linda T. Darling, "Contested Territory: Ottoman Holy War in Comparative Context," *Studia Islamica* 91 (2000): 134.

25. Ibid., 137.

26. Halil İnalcık, *The Ottoman Empire: The Classical Age, 1300–1600* (London: Leidenfeld and Nicholson, 1973), 7.

27. Colin Imber, *Ebussu-ud: The Islamic Legal Tradition* (Edinburgh: Edinburgh University Press, 1997), 73.

28. See Rudi P. Lindner, "Stimulus and Justification in Early Ottoman History," *Greek Orthodox Theological Review* 27 (1982): 207–24; and Darling, "Contested Territory," 138.

29. Halil İnalcık, "The Question of the Emergence of the Ottoman State," *International Journal of Turkish Studies* 2 (1980): 71–79.

30. See Halil İnalcık, "Ottoman Methods of Conquest," *Studia Islamica* 2 (1954): 103–29. See also Halil İnalcık, *Fatih Devri Üzerine Tetkikler ve Vesikalar* (Ankara: TTK Yayınları, 1954).

31. İnalcık, "The Rise of the Ottoman Empire," 31.

32. Tekin, "XIV. Yüzyıla ait bir İlm-i Hal," 286.

33. Kafadar, "Gaza," 428.

34. Kemalpaşazade, *Tevarih-i Al-i Osman*, transcribed and ed. Şerafettin Severcan (Ankara: TTK Yayınları, 1996), lvi.

35. Ibid., lix.

36. Ibid., lxii.

37. Ibid.

38. M. Serdar Palabıyık, "Türkiye'de Savaş Düşüncesi," *Uluslararası İlişkiler* 4, no. 14 (2007): 188.

39. For the involvement of the Ottoman empire in the European states system, see A. Nuri Yurdusev, "Ottoman Attitude toward Diplomacy," in A. Nuri Yurdusev, ed., *Ottoman Diplomacy: Conventional or Unconventional?* (Basingstoke, U.K.: Palgrave Macmillan, 2004).

40. See Orhan Sakin, ed., *Bir Osmanlı Askerinin Sıra dışı Anıları 1688–1700: Temeşvarlı Osman Aga* (Istanbul: Ekim Yayınları, 2008).

41. Géza Pálffy, "Ransom Slavery along the Ottoman-Hungarian Frontier in the Sixteenth and Seventeenth Centuries," in Géza Dávid and Pál Fodor, eds., *Ransom Slavery along the Ottoman Borders (Early Fifteenth–Early Eighteenth Centuries)* (Leiden: E. J. Brill, 2007), 54–55.

42. See Cornell Fleischer, "Royal Authority, Dynastic Cyclism and 'Ibn Khaldunism' in Sixteenth-Century Ottoman Letters," in Bruce Lawrence, ed., *Ibn Khaldun and Islamic Ideology* (Leiden: E. J. Brill, 1984).

43. See İpşirli, "Osmanlı Devletinde 'Eman' Sistemi."

44. For the system of *ahdname*, see Sousa, *The Capitulatory Régime of Turkey*; and Halil İnalcık, "Imtiyazat," *Encyclopaedia of Islam*, 2nd ed. (Leiden: E. J. Brill, 1971).

45. For the English text, see J. C. Hurewitz, ed., *The Middle East and North Africa in World Politics: A Documentary Record*, 2nd ed. (New Haven, Conn.: Yale University Press, 1975).

46. M. Ertuğrul Düzdağ, *Şeyhülislam Ebussuud Efendi Fetvaları Işığında 16. Asır Türk Hayatı* (Istanbul: Enderun Kitabevi, 1972), 108–9.

47. See Rifa'at Ali Abou-El-Haj, "Ottoman Diplomacy at Karlowitz," in Yurdusev, *Ottoman Diplomacy*.

48. Sir Edward Shepherd Creasy, *History of the Ottoman Turks: From the Beginning of the Ottoman Empire to the Present Time*, vol. 2 (London: Richard Bentley, 1856), s. 99.

49. Laurens Winkel, "The Peace Treaties of Westphalia as an Instance of the Reception of Roman Law," in Randall Lesaffer, ed., *Peace Treaties and International Law in European History: From the Late Middle Ages to World War One* (Cambridge, U.K.: Cambridge University Press, 2004), 235.

50. For the texts, see Hurewitz, *The Middle East and North Africa*.

51. Viorel Panaite, *The Ottoman Law of War and Peace: The Ottoman Empire and Tribute Payers* (Boulder, Colo.: East European Monographs, 2000), 79.

52. See A. Fuat Bilkan, "İki Sulhiyye Işığında Osmanlı Toplumunda Barış Özlemi," in H. C. Güzel et al., eds., *Türkler*, 21 vols. (Ankara: Yeni Türkiye Yayınları, 2002), 12: 598–605.

53. Ibid., 599.

54. Ibid., 603.

55. Naff, "The Ottoman Empire," 160.

10

Islam and Christianity in the Works of Gentili, Grotius, and Pufendorf

JOHN KELSAY

The goal of this chapter is to answer questions about the impact or influence of Islam in some early modern Protestant accounts of the laws of war. Among such accounts, Grotius's treatise on *The Law of War and Peace* is the one most familiar to contemporary scholars. Gentili's *Three Books on the Law of War* and the pertinent sections of Pufendorf's *On the Law of Nature and Nations* are also well known.[1] In particular, scholars of international law and ethics know that Pufendorf's work was read widely throughout Europe in the late seventeenth and eighteenth centuries and was considered by some of his contemporaries as a corrective to what they saw as Grotius's overemphasis on self-preservation in matters of political ethics.

An examination of these authors should provide information that will help us to think about the role of Islam in the development of an international law of war or more generally of just war thinking in the early modern period. I emphasize *should*; as the argument proceeds, readers will come to understand that the evidence suggests that the impact of Islam in this period was not very great. This is so whether one is thinking of the kind of "indirect" influence characteristic of great power politics—that is, in terms of the sort of analysis suggested by Jonathan Israel's landmark study, *Conflicts of Empire*—or in terms of the more "direct" influence exemplified by citations of the Qur'an or texts by Muslim writers.[2] In the end, the impact of Islam on early modern Protestants seems actually to have been a function of certain popular accounts in which Christians returning or escaping from captivity in Muslim lands testified about their experiences—in other words, of stories that were heard or read for their entertainment value and were forged as a mix of fact and fiction.

On my account, then, the short answer to the question "What was the impact of Islam on early modern Protestant thinking about war?" is "precious little." I begin by situating my chosen authors in the context of Protestant ideas about world order and the rule of law. I then move to a discussion of the evidence for Muslim influence in these authors, both indirect and direct, before assaying a brief conclusion regarding the prospects for Christian-Muslim interaction in the development of a contemporary law of war.

Protestant Thought and the Notion of World Order

All three of our authors had Protestant connections. Their texts should be read in relation to these. Gentili, for example, was an Italian Protestant. Born in 1552, his religious affiliation led him, with his extended family, to flee their ancestral home in 1579. After brief sojourns in Slovenia and in Germany, Gentili made his way to England, where he was ultimately appointed the Regius Professor of Civil Law at Oxford in 1587. This biography places him at the heart of events related to the internationalization of Protestantism; his lectures on the law of war (*De jure belli libri tres*, Three Books on the Law of War) were published in 1589, immediately after the grand contest between the British and Spanish armadas. That the former styled itself as defending the Protestant establishment in Britain while the latter advanced claims to defend the rights of Roman Catholics in the island is reflected in Gentili's preoccupation with the "aggressive" power of Spain.

Grotius's career was similarly connected with religious controversy. Born in 1583, the Dutch scholar published the first edition of *De jure belli ac pacis* (On the Law of War and Peace) in 1625; a revised edition appeared in 1631. This work was preceded by the 1609 *Mare liberum* (The Freedom of the Seas), which was itself a section of a 1604–05 work that Grotius titled *De Indis* (On the Indies). This last was never published in Grotius's lifetime, only coming into the public realm in 1868 and then under the title *De jure praedae* (On the Law of Prize). Grotius's advocacy of notions associated with the heterodox Calvinist Jacob Arminius (1560–1609) led to exile from the Netherlands. Interestingly, the first publication of *De jure belli ac pacis* appeared while Grotius lived in Paris, under the protection of the Catholic monarch Louis XIII, and he dedicated the work to Louis. Despite such sponsorship, Grotius's work is best understood as a Protestant version of the humanism associated with Erasmus and with John Calvin. The revised edition of 1631, which appears to have been undertaken in connection with Grotius's brief and unsuccessful attempt at repatriation to his homeland, provides further evidence of this. Grotius ended his days in exile (he died in 1645), though with a long stint as Sweden's envoy to Paris.

While one may speak of a broadly Protestant or Reformation outlook in Gentili and Grotius, they are most easily understood within the framework of Calvinism. By contrast, Samuel Pufendorf (1632–1694) was a German Lutheran. As a result of political instability, much of Pufendorf's career was spent in Sweden, where he taught at the University of Lund and was eventually appointed as the royal historian in Stockholm. Pufendorf returned to Germany at the invitation of the elector of Brandenburg; Pufendorf died in Berlin. His *De jure naturae et gentium* (On the Law of Nature and Nations, 1672) and *De officio hominis et civis* (On the Duty of Man and Citizen, 1675) express standard Reformation ideas, particularly as filtered through the more scholastic strains of Lutheran orthodoxy. It is perhaps worth noting that the scholar most responsible for these, Philip Melanchthon (1497–1560), was the Lutheran intellectual most closely aligned with Calvin. In that sense, the argument advanced by Pufendorf, namely that the created or original nature of human beings was good and that "vestiges" of this original goodness provide a thin but real basis for cooperation in social and political life, seems closer to the Calvinism of Gentili and Grotius than to the views of Luther himself.[3]

Some may wonder why Calvinist and Lutheran traditions would inspire serious reflection on the law of war. After all, the central religious insight of Luther had to do with the notion that salvation comes by grace, through faith, and Luther's meditations on the limits of "the law" are well known. The first use of the law, he writes, lies in the fact that it shows human beings just how far they are from the divine ideal of righteousness. And while the second use of the law does have a political or civil dimension, this is primarily a matter of disciplining evildoers. Good people, says Luther, need no law; they know what to do, and even more, they do it. The political use of the law correlates with Luther's emphasis on the state as a "dike against sin." Especially by means of coercive power, political authorities (or, we might say, the law and its agents) restrain evil.[4]

With much less emphasis, Luther mentions a third—more positive—use of the law, in that in this respect, law functions as a guide for believers.[5] Calvin picks up on this and pronounces it the most important consideration in speaking about the matter. Thus, there is a constructive role for legal norms, and the work of magistrates who promulgate and administer the law is a great calling, second only to the ministry of word and sacrament by which the Gospel is proclaimed.[6]

It is this emphasis on the positive aspects of law that lies behind the work of Gentili and Grotius. And if we take seriously the development of Lutheran thinking about the law through the work of Melanchthon, there is no difficulty in understanding the career of Pufendorf. The constructive work of these early modern developers of the law of war is thus consonant with or even inspired by their religious affiliation. Protestantism in its Calvinist and Lutheran forms is indeed a religion focused on grace, in the sense of an emphasis on the overwhelming love of God for undeserving humanity. But law has its place, too, as our authors show.

Indeed, by the time these writers constructed their arguments about the law of war, Calvinism and Lutheranism were establishment religions, tied into the legal institutions of a number of states. In that connection, the interest in law turned rather naturally to international matters, in connection with the great contests of the day. For example, Grotius's writing is clearly motivated by contests between Protestant and Catholic powers. The struggle for control of Europe (and thus, for the right of Protestants to advance their interests abroad) was such that Spain, and to a lesser extent Portugal, exerted a tremendous impact on his work. As chapter 12 of the early treatise on war prizes indicates, Protestant leaders in the Low Countries understood Roman Catholicism as the legitimizing source for the claims of Spain and Portugal to hold dominion over the open sea, one-third of the entire global network being assigned to Spain and another one-third to Portugal. Similarly for Gentili and Pufendorf, Protestant visions of world order and thus of the law of war developed largely in connection with the contest among Calvinists, Lutherans, and Roman Catholics.

As for any threat posed by the Ottoman empire, Grotius in particular seems uninterested in the expansion of Ottoman power in southern and central Europe. Why this is so is unclear. As I turn to the question of influence later in this chapter, it may be helpful to provide a brief chronology of Ottoman activity in Europe. The Ottoman advance began in the mid- to late fourteenth century. At Kosovo in 1389, the Turks struck an important blow against Serbia, which fell by the end of the fifteenth century. The Bulgarian empire was defeated, for the most part, by the end of the fourteenth century. Constantinople fell in 1453, and Greece was conquered by 1460, Albania by 1480, and most of Bosnia-Herzegovina by 1482. Other Balkan lands would follow. Most of Hungary came under Ottoman domination during the sixteenth century. In southern Europe, Venice was in competition with the Ottomans from 1423 to 1503, when the Spanish provided assistance sufficient to halt the Ottoman forces until the middle of the seventeenth century. From the 1520s on, the Ottomans exerted intermittent pressure on the Hapsburg empire, with the fighting from 1593 to 1606 being fierce enough to be remembered as the "Long War." 1683 marked the end of Ottoman attempts with respect to Austria. In short, we have ongoing military and political pressure exerted by the Ottomans throughout the time our authors worked, so that their lack of attention to this rivalry becomes quite striking. Perhaps one explanation is to be found in the fact that the primary venues for Ottoman activity in Europe were in the southern and central (and hence, Catholic and Orthodox) regions.

The Indirect Influence of Islam

What about Muslim influence? I begin with influence that might be called indirect. A passage from Gentili will serve as a beginning. In book 1, chapter 14 of *On the Law of War*, the topic is wars of defense, specifically those fought on the "grounds of expediency." As the text indicates, Gentili has in mind the type of fighting we would call anticipatory, preventive, or even preemptive:

> I call it a defence dictated by expediency, when we make war through fear that we may ourselves be attacked . . . we ought not to wait for violence to be offered us, if it is safer to meet it halfway . . . One ought not to delay, or wait to avenge at one's peril an injury which one has received, if one

may at once strike at the root of the growing plant and check the attempts of an adversary who is meditating evil.[7]

As the argument continues, Gentili raises the question of timing. When does a threat reach the point where it becomes necessary to strike? In striking contrast to some more recent treatments of the issue, our author writes that there need not be a "great and clear cause for fear" but only one that is "legitimate."[8] By way of explication, Gentili suggests that we think of "ambitious chiefs," whom he describes as "content with no bounds" or, to put it in more straightforwardly political terms, bent on universal dominion. The Turks, along with the Spaniards, provide the most immediate examples:

> Do not all men with complete justice oppose on one side the Turks and on the other the Spaniards, who are planning and plotting universal dominion? True, the Turk does not injure many, nor does the Spaniard; neither one nor the other is able to do so; but they injure some, and he who injures one, threatens many. Shall we wait until they actually take up arms? We have heard about the Turks before and we all have our opinion of them. If any one does not know about the Spaniards, let him learn from Paolo Giovio that their disposition also is lawless and greedy for power; and when they have once crept in, they always secure the supreme control by every kind of artifice.[9]

The discussion that follows is fascinating. As Gentili has it, the cause that makes preemptive strikes just has to do with prevention. Specifically, it is right to keep any single political actor from obtaining power sufficient to silence criticisms of injustice. There must always be alternative centers of power. One thinks of the French critique of American "hyperpower" as a contemporary expression of this worry. At the same time, there is a distinction to be made between cases in which the power of an actor grows by "successions and elections" and those in which power increases by conquest. Gentili's point is thus that anticipatory strikes may be justified when a pattern of behavior suggests an intention to achieve universal dominion. And he believes that the Ottomans, along with the Spaniards, may be considered in this way.

With respect to our interests, this discussion of defense motivated by "expediency" provides a nice example of the "indirect" influence of Islam on early modern Protestant authors dealing with the law of war. For Gentili, the Turks are a rival for world domination. They epitomize the sort of threat with respect to which anticipatory strikes may be justified. And thus, they play a role in the construction of his argument. They do not provide him with "sources," assuming that we mean by that term texts or precepts or precedents intended to guide action. But they do provide him with an example, by which he can describe the contours within which particular kinds of action make sense.

It should be said that among our three authors, Gentili provides the most evidence of such indirect influence. Thus, in a discussion of "divine causes for making war," he notes, "The Turks too [in addition to ancient Israel] always have this reason for their wars, that it is a command of Mahomet to make war upon men of different religion from their own."[10]

Indeed, Gentili is even aware of sectarian strife between Sunni and Shiʻi Muslims, although he puts this in national rather than religious terms: "Thus they themselves [the Turks] and the Persians, each heretics in the eyes of the other, are said to wage an almost ceaseless strife in behalf of their religion."[11]

In an interesting aside, he notes that some say that the Ottomans understand that the war against Christians takes priority over that against the heretical Persians. Among the Christians, by contrast, the fight against heretics takes precedence. In any case, Gentili regards both sides as incorrect, since it is not right to wage war with religion "as the sole motive."[12] One's enemy must pose some threat or do some harm—for example, by denying rights of passage or violating treaties or (as noted above) by demonstrating an intention to attain universal domination by force.[13]

Gentili is thus aware of Islam and has some reports about it. I will return to these in the discussion of "direct" influence. For now, it is enough to note the way in which Gentili deploys his sources as he crafts answers to particular questions regarding war's justice. The Ottomans, and to a lesser extent the Saracens, provide him with cases by which he can speak about the rights and wrongs of war. In this regard, they are like the Spanish—both provide examples as Gentili wields his pen.

By contrast, Grotius and Pufendorf make less use of the example of the Turks (and/or Saracens). They do provide some material of interest, however. And in cases where one finds such appeals, Grotius and Pufendorf place Muslims in the role of a foil, a kind of rhetorical trope by which they can enhance their arguments. In the early treatise on war prizes, for example, Grotius criticizes any Spanish claim against the "East Indians" insofar as it is based on a papal grant or on the notion that the natives fail to acknowledge the sovereignty of the pope or his envoys. In support of his argument, Grotius cites works by well-known Catholic writers and ends with a flourish: "Indeed, and in truth, it may be affirmed that no such pretext as that was ever invoked to despoil even the Saracens."[14]

In *Law of War and Peace*, the role of Muslims is somewhat different. There, in a discussion of the right exercised by those who take and hold prisoners of war, Grotius argues for the justice of "a maxim, universally received among the powers of Christendom, that prisoners of war cannot be made slaves. . . ." As if to add the weight of further examples to the point, he then observes that in "this respect the Mahometans act towards each other in the same manner as Christians do." Thus, one might say that *even the Muslims* act according to certain norms, a point that lends itself to the judgment that the behavior Grotius advocates is in accord with universal law. At this point, the behavior of Muslims, or at least Grotius's understanding of it, serves to reinforce one of the major themes of his work, namely the natural law legitimacy of a law of nations.[15]

This rhetorical use of the category "Muslims" is, if anything, even more pronounced in Pufendorf. In a discussion of the role of arbitration, we read of the value of those who help parties in conflict to avoid war. The duty of Christians in this regard is reinforced by the notion that "even the Koran, so stupid in general, in the chapter *On Doors*, teaches that if two Moslem nations and countries engage one another in war, the rest shall make peace between them, and compel him who committed the injury to offer satisfaction; and when this is done, bring them by fair and good means to friendship."[16]

In other places, Pufendorf makes similar use of the Qur'an in discussions of marriage and remarriage, oaths, and the like—that is, the fact that the Qur'an, despite its many errors, nevertheless confirms the importance of norms in guiding human conduct, reinforces the notion that there is a law that we may describe as "natural" to human beings.[17]

The Direct Influence of Islam

As Pufendorf's citations of the Qur'an indicate, some Muslim sources were available to and known by early modern Protestant writers.[18] Nevertheless, citations of such sources in the works of our authors are few and far between. This is in stark contrast with their copious citations from the Bible and a wide range of classical and Christian sources. This characteristic of our authors' writing is derived from the humanistic tradition of the fourteenth and fifteenth centuries. Thus, they are interested in grounding their arguments in an appeal to antiquity. Indeed, one of the more interesting debates surrounding the interpretation of Gentili, and even more that of Grotius and Pufendorf, has to do with which strands of antiquity do the most work in their writings. By contrast with the Spaniards, Aristotle carries little weight with Pufendorf, who among our three is the most interested in the Stagirite philosopher. Cicero and the tradition of Roman law are certainly significant for our authors, although Tuck argues that the truly distinctive tone in the works of early modern Protestants derives from their debt to Tacitus.[19]

For our purposes, such controversies are really beside the point; our interest is in the almost complete lack of interest in Muslim sources among these writers. It is this lack that leads to the judgment outlined in my introductory remarks: the evidence of direct Muslim influence on early Protestant writers is almost nonexistent, at least in connection with the law of war.

That is not to say, of course, that one does not find parallels, even striking ones, between Muslim authorities and particular judgments advocated by early modern Protestants. Protestant treatments of safe conduct, for example, are really quite similar to those offered in Muslim juridical texts. Similarly, discussions of right authority, rebellion, and the like bear more than a family resemblance. What is going on? Why the formal or even substantive resemblances, without any acknowledgment or citation that would lend itself to the judgment that our authors knew Muslim sources and borrowed from them?

One possibility is that the Protestant writers were afraid to cite Muslim sources—that is, they engaged in borrowing but suppressed or disguised the evidence, on the grounds that Christian readers would be less inclined to take seriously any argument drawing on "foreign" or "infidel" authorities. To evaluate the likelihood of this hypothesis, one would need to look very closely for quotes or half-quotes drawn from Latin translations of Muslim sources, the sort of thing one might expect a translator and editor such as John C. Rolfe to ferret out. Rolfe's marginal notes in the Carnegie translation of Gentili's *On the Law of War* are quite conscientious with respect to identifying the texts from which Gentili quotes. The fact that Rolfe's notes include only a few Muslim sources cited by Gentili in connection with a point of logic (for example, Ibn Rushd's *De primitate praedicatorum* [On the Predicates in Demonstrations; *Al-qawl fi al-mahmulat al-barahin*])[20] would not count against this, in and of itself; it is possible that Rolfe did not know the Muslim sources as well as he knew others.

In the absence of further evidence in favor of scholarly dissimulation on the part of Gentili and others, however, I think we have to favor another line of explanation. Here, such parallels as are present would have to do with the fact of a shared political and economic reality, namely the forms of empire common to both Christendom and Islamicate societies, as these developed in the fourteenth through eighteenth centuries. One would also think of such parallelism as a function of themes shared between the Bible and the Qur'an and, perhaps most important of all, of the legacy of Rome. I would suggest that scholars of Islamic law might do a good deal more to illumine the ways in which the Muslim law of war reflected the remnants of Roman practice present in those territories taken from the Byzantines in the early Islamic conquests.[21]

It is true, of course, that Gentili, Grotius, and Pufendorf had some information about Islam. Otherwise, how could Gentili (for example) write as he did about the threat posed by the Turks in his discussion of the justice of anticipatory strikes? Or, again, how else would Gentili have known about the distinction between Sunni (Turks) and Shi'i (Saracens) forms of Islam? Here we find one of the most interesting features of the ways in which early modern Protestants managed to bring Islam into their discussions. Rolfe's marginal notes refer primarily to two sources whenever Gentili speaks about Islam. The first, Paolo Giovio's *Historiae sui temporis* (History of His Own Times, 1550–1552) was a standard historical work, in which a Renaissance humanist compiled reports from his own and others' experiences regarding a variety of events of interest to his contemporaries. It seems clear that Giovio's sources involved oral reports from statesmen, diplomats, and other observers whose accounts of their experiences with (or of others' experiences with) the Turks and the Saracens provided

Europeans with a source of information regarding their Muslim competitors. Such tales would have been collected for a variety of motives, including the desire not only for information but also for entertainment and edification, the latter in the sense illustrated by the rhetorical use of Islam in our authors' texts. That is, referring to the "other" provides a way of talking about oneself, in addition to providing information about a distinctive group of political and moral agents.

The other source noted by Rolfe further illustrates this tendency. Throughout his treatise, Gentili draws from the *Speeches on the War against the Turks* by Scander-beg, who from the fifteenth through the nineteenth centuries was widely thought of as the Albanian national hero. During those centuries, Scander-beg's story circulated in a variety of forms, not the least interesting being a poem by Longfellow and a historical novel by Disraeli.[22] The story of an Albanian prince taken into captivity when the Ottomans conquered his father's principality fascinated and, no doubt, repelled Europeans. Gjerji Kastrioti (1405–1466) converted to Islam in the court of the sultan and was given the name Iskander Bey, signifying his role as a representative of the Ottoman court. Sent to his ancestral land, he employed deception in order to obtain power, then renounced Islam and led a revolt against the Ottomans. While his forces won several significant victories, Kastrioti died (apparently of malaria), and the campaign he began ultimately failed when the Ottomans took Kruje (1478) and Shkoder (1479). The precise nature and especially the text history of Scander-beg's *Speeches* will have to wait for another day. Its role in Gentili's treatise is suggestive, however, of one very important way in which early Protestant writers gained access to information about Islam and developed their image of it.

So important is this type of source, in fact, that I wish to end with a quote from another Protestant author, who could himself have formed a part of this essay. In *An Essay on Toleration*, John Locke argues that the use of force as a means of compelling belief is not only immoral but also ineffective. Everyone, writes Locke, "in what he believes has so far this persuasion that he is in the right." Indeed, resistance to compulsion in matters of faith or opinion really has little to do even with how well grounded or informed one may be in his or her own religion. And this is shown by the example of "those galley slaves who return from Turkey, who, though they have endured all manner of miseries rather than part with their religion, yet one would guess by the lives and principles of most of them that they had no knowledge of the doctrine and practice of Christianity at all."[23]

We need not spend time parsing the arguments of Locke in this regard. For our purposes, what is important is his reliance on stories identified with Christians taken into captivity by the armies of the sultan. Whatever may be said about the reliability of such sources, they clearly represent a very important way by which early modern Protestant writers "accessed" and formed an image of Muslim tradition. And thus, if we wish to speak about the influence of Islam on early modern Protestant accounts of the law of war, we will have to deal with these stories, admixtures of fact and legend, of real experience and of scandal—if you will, a blend of the *New York Times* and the *National Enquirer*.

Notes

1. The material quoted from Gentili, Grotius, and Pufendorf is from the following editions and translations: Alberico Gentili, *De iure belli libri tres*, vol. 2, trans. John C. Rolfe, with an introduction by Coleman Phillipson (Oxford: Clarendon, 1933). This translation, based on the edition of 1612, is part of the Carnegie Endowment's Classics of International Law Series, ed. James Brown Scott. Hugo Grotius, *Mare liberum*, from *The Freedom of the Seas*, trans. Ralph van Deman Magoffin, with a revision of the Latin text of 1638; ed. James Brown Scott, with an introductory note (New York: Oxford University Press, 1916), also from the Carnegie Endowment Series. Hugo Grotius, *The Rights of War and Peace*, trans. A. C. Campbell, with an introduction by David J. Hill (London: M. Walter Dunne, 1901). Samuel von Pufendorf, *De jure naturae et gentium libri octo*, vol. 2, trans. C. H. Oldfather and W. A. Oldfather (Oxford: Clarendon, 1934); Carnegie Endowment Series translation of the edition of 1688.

2. Jonathan Israel, *Conflicts of Empire* (London: Hambledon, 1997).

3. In this regard, I should note the argument of Richard Tuck, who in *Philosophy and Government 1572–1651* (Cambridge, U.K.: Cambridge University Press, 1993) and also in *The Rights of War and Peace* (Oxford: Oxford University Press, 1999) makes the case that Pufendorf actually imposed his own position on that of Grotius. That is, Pufendorf advances his argument in part by way of rescuing Grotius from the charge that his position ultimately makes power, rather than morality or law, the arbiter of human affairs. Tuck rightly notes the role of Melanchthon's affinity for Aristotle as a factor in Pufendorf's work. Also, his suggestion that Pufendorf's presentation of Grotius more or less elided the latter's actual position goes some way toward making sense of comments attributed to Rousseau and Kant, each of whom expressed puzzlement regarding attempts to separate Grotius from Hobbes (1588–1679) and suggested that the positions of those two authors were, in fact, identical. While I cannot make the case in full in this chapter, my own view is that Tuck's position only makes sense if one ignores Calvinist theology—a tradition of thought that has, in its own career, suffered not infrequently from the charge that its view of fallen human nature makes for a more or less "Hobbesian" notion of the war of each against all.

4. A convenient statement of Luther's position on these matters can be found in his commentary on Paul's letter to the Galatians. See, for example, the selections from this commentary in *Martin Luther: Selections from His Writings*, ed. John Dillenberger (New York: Anchor, 1962), esp. 139–65.

5. Ibid.

6. See John Calvin, *Institutes of the Christian Religion*, ed. John T. McNeill, trans. Ford Lewis Battles (Philadelphia: Westminster, 1960), esp. II.vii–viii (pp. 348–422), III.xix (pp. 833–49), and IV.xx (pp. 1485–1524).

7. Gentili, *De iure belli libri tres*, I.xiv (p. 61).

8. I have in mind Michael Walzer's discussion of preemptive strikes in *Just and Unjust Wars* (New York: Basic, 1977) and in his more recent collection *Arguing about War* (New Haven, Conn.: Yale University Press, 2004).

9. Gentili, *De iure belli libri tres*, I.xiv (p. 64).

10. Ibid., I.viii (p. 36).

11. Ibid.

12. Ibid., I.ix (p. 40).

13. Ibid., I.xix (pp. 86–92). This entire discussion reflects the move toward an understanding of religion as distinct from politics and in some sense also from morality. In I.ix (p. 39), Gentili

writes that religion "is a matter of mind and will, which is always accompanied by freedom . . . the soul has no master save God only, who can destroy the soul . . . Religion is a kind of marriage of God with man. And so, as liberty of the flesh is resolutely maintained in the other wedlock, so in this one freedom of the spirit is granted." A bit later in the chapter, he writes that "since the laws of religion do not properly exist between man and man, therefore no man's rights are violated by a difference in religion, nor is it lawful to make war because of religion. Religion is a relationship with God. Its laws are divine, that is between God and man; they are not human, namely between man and man. Therefore a man cannot complain of being wronged because others differ from him in religion." Gentili extends these notions so as to cut against any enforcement of religious uniformity within a single political community. Difference in religion cannot be cited by a group as a reason to cause civil unrest. Nor can war be waged to make a group of people listen to the Gospel, although once conquered, a people may be compelled to hear (though not to believe; see I.xxv [pp. 122–27]). The one case where religion may serve as just cause of war would seem to involve a group of people who claimed to be atheists, who in some sense "divest themselves of human nature" and are thus like pirates, or even brutes (p. 125).

14. Grotius, *The Freedom of the Seas*, XII (p. 224).
15. Grotius, *The Rights of War and Peace*, III.vii (pp. 1360–73). On the natural law dimension of Grotius's work and the relation of appeals to charity, see James Turner Johnson, *Ideology, Reason, and the Limitation of War* (Princeton, N.J.: Princeton University Press, 1975); and James Turner Johnson, *Just War Tradition and the Restraint of War* (Princeton, N.J.: Princeton University Press, 1981). Also see Tuck, *The Rights of War and Peace* and *Philosophy and Government*.
16. Pufendorf, *De jure naturae et gentium*, V.xiii (p. 831). Pufendorf means chap. 49 of the Qur'an, *Surat al-hujurat* (Private Apartments).
17. A nice example of this rhetorical use of the category "Muslim," albeit from a later period and for more strictly religious or philosophical purposes, is discussed by Jonathan Israel in his massive *Enlightenment Contested* (Oxford: Oxford University Press, 2006). See especially the discussion "Rethinking Islam: Philosophy and the 'Other,'" 615–39. As Israel demonstrates, a "freethinker" such as Pierre Bayle (1647–1706) knew enough about Islam to speak with some accuracy about the life and work of Ibn Rushd. For Bayle, however, the point was to put this information to use in the context of the European argument about the role of religion in public life. Representations of Islam as a pure monotheism, unaffected by superstitions such as miracles or sacraments, thus vie with accounts in which Islamic authorities suppress philosophy and thereby illustrate the universal tendency of religion toward oppression.
18. It is perhaps useful to note that by most accounts, the first translation of the Qur'an into Latin was done at the instigation of Peter the Venerable, abbot of Cluny, in the middle of the twelfth century. The twelfth and thirteenth centuries saw a great deal of activity in translations from Arabic into Latin, mostly of scientific and medical treatises, along with Ibn Rushd's commentaries on Aristotle. Given this availability, it is striking that our authors, all trained in the humanist tradition, did not avail themselves of these sources. I should note that I have not read of more strictly juridical works being translated in this period (that is, of the type that might have provided a direct model for Gentili, Grotius, and Pufendorf in discussions of the law of war).
19. See the works of Tuck cited above.
20. Gentili, *De iure belli libri tres*, 2:254.
21. A line of inquiry suggested by Fred Donner, among others. See Fred Donner, "The Sources of Islamic Conceptions of War," in John Kelsay and James Turner Johnson, eds., *Just War and Jihad* (Westport, Conn.: Greenwood, 1991), 31–70.
22. See Henry Wadsworth Longfellow's "Tales of a Wayside Inn." Disraeli's *The Rise of Iskander* can be found in *The Works of Benjamin Disraeli*, vol. 2, ed. Edmund Gosse (London: M. Walter Dunn, 1904). A simple search of the Strozier Library at Florida State University turned up several other versions of the tale of Scander-beg, including Marghertia Sarrochi [1560–1617], *Scanderbeide: The Heroic Deeds of George Scanderberg, King of Epirus*, trans. and ed. Rinaldina

Russell (Chicago: University of Chicago Press, 2006), and several electronic versions of the tale. In addition, a text published as number 233 in a series of early printed books titled "The English Experience" carries the title *Orations* and includes material introduced as follows: "Orations, of Arsanes against Philip the treacherous king of Macedonia: of the Ambassadors of Venice against the Prince that under crafty league with Scanderbeg, laid snares for Christendom: and of Scanderbeg praying aid of Christian princes against perjourous murdering Mahomet and against the old false Christian Duke, Mahomet's confederate. With a notable example of God's vengeance upon a faithless King, Queen, and her children." The text seems to have been published first in London in 1560; the version available to me is from Amsterdam and New York: Da Capo, 1970.

23. John Locke, "An Essay on Toleration (1667)," in *Locke: Political Essays*, ed. Mark Goldie (Cambridge, U.K.: Cambridge University Press, 1997), 154.

PART FOUR

EUROPEAN IMPERIALISM

Upon landing in Alexandria, Egypt, on July 1, 1798, Napoleon Bonaparte issued a proclamation to the Egyptian people that began by justifying the invasion: "For a long time [the Mamluks] who lorded it over Egypt have treated the French community basely and contemptuously and have persecuted its merchants with all manner of extortion and violence. Therefore the hour of punishment has now come." The proclamation went on to preempt a hostile Egyptian response in the name of religion by making the astounding claim: "The French are also faithful Muslims, and in confirmation of this they invaded Rome and destroyed the Papal See, which was always exhorting the Christians to make war with Islam. And then they went to the island of Malta, from where they expelled the Knights, who claimed that God the Exalted required them to fight the Muslims."[1] The ploy failed. An insurrection broke out in Cairo, provoked in part by ulema who declared jihad against the French invaders. Al-Jabarti, the chronicler of these events, makes his low opinion of the revolt's leaders quite clear: "This deluded one forgot that he was a prisoner in the hands of the French, who occupied the fortress and its walls, the high hills and the low; fortifying them all with forbidding instruments of war; such as cannons on carriages, rifles, carbines, and bombs."[2]

As European imperialism spread in Muslim territories during the nineteenth and early twentieth centuries, the French foray into Egypt proved paradigmatic as far as European rationales and Muslim reactions were concerned. The European justifications for imperialism were manifold, but the rhetoric of just war and crusaderism was prominent. The former is evident in the French proclamation cited above. They were defending their national honor and interests. They were punishing the offenders. These rationales would be repeated time and again. The latter was intrinsic to French perceptions of their mission in Egypt and would figure in Napoleon's subsequent administrative edicts. It was the notion of *mission civilisatrice*, which manifested itself in many forms over the coming century. This civilizing mission could be viewed as a modern version of crusaderism. Jonathan Riley-Smith divides this phenomenon into "paracrusading" and "pseudocrusading":

> Paracrusading had within it some elements drawn from the old movement, although chosen selectively and distorted. Pseudocrusading had

no correspondence to the old reality, but borrowed its rhetoric and imagery to describe ventures—particularly imperialist ones—that had nothing at all to do with the Crusades, as nations already expressing pride in their crusading past became involved in the scramble for empire.[3]

Neither of these forms of crusaderism had a direct religious motivation, at least not explicitly. In the program of many missionaries, however, crusaderism was a means to open lands for peaceful proselytizing, analogous in some ways to the intention behind the expansionist jihad of classical doctrine. As such, this crusaderism could be said to have had indirect religious motivations.

Many Muslims interpreted European imperialism as a new crusade. The first modern history of the medieval Crusades, *Al-Akhbar al-saniyya fi al-hurub al-salibiyya* (Splendid Accounts of the Crusades), was published in 1899 by the Egyptian scholar Sayyid 'Ali al-Hariri. The author prefaces his work by noting: "Our most glorious sultan, Abdülhamid II, has rightly remarked that Europe is now carrying out a Crusade against us in the form of a political campaign."[4]

Muslims responded to imperialism in varied ways. Some opposed imperialism in the name of "enlightened" European principles of liberty, equality, and the rule of law, even in war. Others invoked Islam to argue against opposition, mainly on pragmatic grounds in light of the superior military power of the imperialists. There were also protracted legal debates grounded in the classical Islamic theory of world order, revolving around the question of under what circumstances Muslim territory conquered by non-Muslims ceases to be *dar al-Islam* and becomes *dar al-harb*. Still others invoked the language of jihad in resistance. This was true of anticolonial struggles from Morocco to Afghanistan, from Iran to Indonesia. European imperialism prompted a fundamental shift in jihad doctrine from the expansionist war of the classical theory to defensive war that dominates the tradition today.

Notes

1. Al-Jabarti, *Napoleon in Egypt: Al-Jabarti's Chronicle of the French Occupation*, trans. Shmuel Moreh (Princeton, N.J.: Markus Wiener, 1993), 25–26.

2. Ibid., 83–84.

3. Jonathan Riley-Smith, *The Crusades, Christianity, and Islam* (New York: Columbia University Press, 2008), 54.

4. Cited in Carole Hillenbrand, *The Crusades: Islamic Perspectives* (New York: Routledge, 2000), 592.

11

Just War and Jihad in the French Conquest of Algeria

BENJAMIN CLAUDE BROWER

This chapter examines the moral claims made upon the violence of the first decades of France's occupation of Algeria. This history exemplifies many of the problems of just war and jihad doctrine and anticipates much of the debate surrounding these concepts in the twentieth century. On the French side, these moral claims included the assorted justifications of the Bourbon Restoration that launched the invasion with a combination of references to international order, France's crusader past, and the language of liberation inherited from Napoleon Bonaparte's invasion of Egypt in 1798—all of which were amalgamated into a "just war." These continued after the Revolution of 1830 swept the Bourbons out of power only weeks after their victory in North Africa. The military leaders and politicians of the Orléanist monarchy (1830–1848) justified the campaigns in Algeria in the same sorts of idioms used by the Bourbon figures they had replaced. The Algerian response also contended with the ethicopolitical stakes of the French invasion and its violent consequences. Some Algerians articulated an openly defiant subaltern discourse, which deployed the ideals of the Enlightenment to take to task France's claims of moral superiority in light of the army's misconduct and arbitrary use of force. These were best represented by Hamdan Khodja, who denounced the *vae victis* of French rule when he wrote in 1833, "le mal gouvernait, malheur aux vaincus" (when misfortune governs, woe to the vanquished).[1] Others looked to Islamic traditions such as jihad for the proper response to the French occupation. Most famous is the amir 'Abd al-Qadir, who led a long and partially successful jihad against France. The powerful moral legitimacy of Islamic resistance through military struggle helped the amir make his claim to sovereignty, even as he came to express doubts about his ability to advance a moral agenda through violence.[2]

The Bourbon Restoration and France's
Just War in Algeria: 1827–1830

The role of French violence in the Muslim Mediterranean had been in the public eye since 1798, the year of Napoleon Bonaparte's expedition against Mamluk Egypt. The brutal suppression of the Cairo revolt in October 1798 and the gratuitous violence of French troops in Egypt and Syria drew some negative commentary within France, but the French generally saw the expedition in a positive light.[3] Its violence was the inevitable result of order and modernity confronting the entrenched archaism of an old regime, it was thought. Visual representations, such as Jean-François Lejeune's painting *The Battle of the Pyramids* (1806), reinforced this view. With its bird's-eye view of the solid arrangements of French troops coolly facing a chaotic Mamluk army, Lejeune's painting told viewers that the French-led war was just in intent, execution, and result: the army's efficiency and success pointed to the moral superiority of French society.[4] (In the midst of the 2005 riots in France, a similar message was conveyed in the pages of *Paris Match*, whose editors reproduced Lejeune's *The Battle of Aboukir Bay* [1799] with the caption: "It's beautiful, it's grand, it's glorious, and it's us.")[5]

The artist and scholar Vivant Denon, who accompanied the expedition, gave different articulation to the same argument. His account of the campaign drew a tableau of the role of violence in historical development, a role that he thought was natural and positive. To fix this image in his reader's mind, Denon compared the annual flooding of the Nile to the other "calamities inseparable from revolutions."[6] Such catastrophes were, he implied, both inevitable and fertile, redeeming their violence in the better life that came in their wake. Thus, the Nile served Denon as a metaphor for history as war, exemplifying the same process of stagnation and decay, destruction and rebirth.

In Algeria, a similar view of the violence of French empire came into focus thirty years later, but it had to contend with the contentious politics of the Bourbon Restoration. The idea of sending an army against the Ottoman dey in Algiers had been hatched during the First Empire, when Napoleon commissioned a military engineer to reconnoiter Algiers's defenses in 1808.[7] The plan was suspended by Napoleon, but it became irresistible later as Charles X struggled against his political opponents. The Bourbon king hoped that a decisive victory against the Ottoman regency in Algiers would consolidate his domestic position vis-à-vis the opposition in a wave of enthusiasm, militarism, and national support. These motives did not go unnoticed by the king's enemies. A last-ditch effort by a dying monarchy, the expedition was, as one contemporary clearly saw, the final "resort of despair."[8] Standing on the crumbling edifices of Bourbon power in France, Charles X could not simply invoke *raison d'état* or bluntly claim in the Algerian expedition the omnipotent, mysterious power to which he aspired. After all, this war was about *his* political survival, which the revolution had separated from that of the French state itself. Therefore, around the core of political expediency, Charles X scaffolded the ideals and rationales that would make his war "just."

In this period, it is more useful to speak of just war ideals or discourse than of just war doctrine. The norms of European war making that emerged in the wake of the Thirty Years War (1618–1648) suffered a significant challenge in the course of the Revolutionary and Napoleonic wars. As David A. Bell argues, the years 1792 to 1815 saw the emergence of total war, when European wars went from relatively controlled and rule-governed affairs between states to an all-consuming and unrestrained "race into the abyss."[9] Even if the Congress of Vienna reestablished a semblance of order in Europe in 1815, the norms governing war arguably lacked the conceptual clarity and strength of the old regime. Thus, an ambiguous moral and legal terrain opened around war, where differing ideals converged and competed. When European states made war off the Continent in colonial and imperial contexts, as Isabel Hull shows, these ambiguities redoubled.[10]

France's war on the Ottoman regency of Algiers (1827–1830) is a case in point. A report to the king written in October 1827 by the minister of war, Clermont-Tonnerre, explained how this war was justified.[11] The minister deployed the many different terms of lawful war making that were available to him. First, he stressed that France had *casus belli*. This came in an altercation on April 29 of the same year, when the dey of Algiers, Hussein Dey (al-Husayn ibn al-Husayn), struck the French consul with a fly whisk.[12] "Just wars avenge injuries" was a doctrine enunciated by the earliest just war theorists, including Saint Augustine, and the fly-whisk incident, according to the minister, provided ample injury to French honor.[13] Following this incident, France severed diplomatic relations with the dey, calling the consul home in June, and imposed a naval blockade on Algiers. In response, Hussein Dey ordered the destruction of French trading posts.[14]

The minister of war continued his argument by implying that the war on Algiers upheld the conservative ideals of the Congress of Vienna. The war would contribute to rolling back revolution in Europe by strengthening the French crown. It would also expand the conservative order into the southern Mediterranean and forcibly integrate this area into an international system dominated by the European monarchies. Having acted with Russia and England to break Greece away from the Ottoman empire and bring it into this community in 1827–28, France drew attention to the Algerian dey and his navy—"a handful of bandits"— as the primary threat to the new order in the western Mediterranean. "Algiers lives solely off the war it wages on the commerce of the Christian powers," as Clermont-Tonnerre told the king. "Algiers must perish if Europe wants to be in peace."[15] Here the minister could draw on long-standing politicolegal traditions that viewed sea raiders as "the enemy of all" and the more immediate movement to end piracy that started at the Congress of Aix-la-Chapelle (1818).[16] He repeated this point in 1830: "The very existence of Algiers is a sufficient grievance for all civilized nations, [it represents] a just and permanent reason to destroy this nest of pirates and crooks."[17] In the end, the minister reassured the king, "Sire, you have undertaken a just war."[18]

Thus, Clermont-Tonnerre found an assortment of grounds for the French war against Algeria, allowing military planners considerable scope for creativity in prosecuting it. Proponents of the war anticipated a severe, even violent response from other European powers and concerted resistance from the domestic liberal opposition. The Bourbon monarchy needed a strong rationale to legitimize this war, and just war arguments provided a credible defense. Inasmuch as the just war arguments were diffuse and could be framed in different ways, they were easily adapted to changing circumstances and difficult to refute. The rhetoric of just war allowed France to pose as Europe's policeman in the Mediterranean while minimizing the chances that other European powers would intervene to check its move against Algeria.

Just war arguments were also deployed by the Bourbon monarchy to promote its interests in national politics. For example, Clermont-Tonnerre's report to the king reads: "Sire, you have undertaken a just war—the interest of *your* country, that of *your* own glory, in consequence, *must alone mark the limits* of the satisfaction that you demand."[19] Here we see that Charles X's concerns centered not so much on making the war conform to the legalistic criteria of just war doctrine but on how just war discourse might expand the throne's power. Thus, the key tribunal faced by the struggling French king was the volatile court of domestic public opinion. In such politically conflicted times, there were many different views of a just war, and Charles X's need to rally a broad consensus helps to account for the otherwise confused grouping of rationales and justifications for the Algerian expedition. The conquest of Algiers offered the king an opportunity to rally his supporters on the right by grounding his reign in the Bourbon tradition of defending Christendom. Charles X, the "son of Saint Louis" (the crusading Louis IX), would lead the attack on the dey, one of the worst "enemies of the Christian name," wrote Clermont-Tonnerre.[20] Another war plan of 1827 also stressed this tradition: "What honor for the eldest son of the Church to carry back the sacred fire of Christianity . . . and to make the Catholic religion bloom again where it once shined so brightly."[21] This appeal to the rhetoric of the crescent versus the cross galvanized the support of the monarchist far right behind Charles X's overall claim that his reactionary rule represented an authentic French monarchy. Moreover, the occupation of Algeria would serve to extend Catholicism, a goal that appealed to these supporters still vexed by the setbacks suffered by the church during the revolutionary and Napoleonic eras. While Clermont-Tonnerre thought that "tolerance" toward Islam should be pursued initially in order to placate Algerians, he told the king that maybe "with time, we will have the fortune, in civilizing them, to make them Christians!"[22] Such conversions would be the triumphant culmination of carrying the cross back to Algeria.[23]

Finally, there was a new type of just war discourse born of the French Revolution: the imperial war of liberation inaugurated in Egypt. There, Napoleon

Bonaparte declared righteous intentions by telling Egyptians that France was a benevolent empire, promoting rights and liberation throughout the world.[24] Orientalist discourses of the eighteenth century had prepared this view. For example, the Comte de Volney saw the Ottoman empire as a place ripe for revolution, with the Ottomans and Mamluks as the analogues to the outmoded French aristocracy. In the words of historian Henry Laurens, French observers such as Volney saw a "veritable oriental third estate" in the Ottoman empire's diverse subjects, a revolutionary class of oppressed Arabs, Armenians, and Greeks who waited for France to help them throw off the "Ottoman yoke."[25] Thus, Bonaparte promised Egyptians that he would put his military force at the service of this higher cause. In his "Proclamation to Egyptians" (July 1798), Bonaparte announced that his army had come to "restore to you your rights and to punish the usurpers."[26] That this announcement of emancipation was drafted in poor Arabic did not help rally Egyptians (historian Juan Cole has commented that it was "as though they had conquered England and sent forth their first proclamation in Cockney"),[27] and its appeal to solidarity based on Bonaparte's proclaimed hostility to Catholicism did not convince Cairene notables such as al-Jabarti, who bitterly denounced the French general's pretensions in his famous chronicle of the occupation.[28]

The failure of Bonaparte's rhetoric in Egypt did not deter the Bourbon generals from borrowing heavily from it in their invasion of Algeria. In 1830, French troops boarded ships, with their officers boasting that "the civilized nations of the *deux mondes* have their eyes fixed upon you. . . . The cause of France is that of humanity."[29] They thought that they would be greeted warmly by Algerians: "Far too long oppressed by a greedy and cruel militia, the Arab will see in us their liberators."[30] The same promises of ending a despotic old regime made their way into the Arabic text that announced the arrival of the French army to the people of Algiers: "Our presence among you is not to fight you; our goal is only to make war on your Pacha."[31]

July 5, 1830: A Victory and a Defeat for the Just War

The French response to the Algiers expedition was mixed. While the liberal Parisian press remained skeptical, other constituencies rallied to the invasion, and these supporters fully exploited the discourse of just war to make their case in the summer of 1830.[32] For example, the archbishop of Aix-en-Provence led his congregation in prayer for the expedition by mixing just war language with that of the Crusades:

> If there was ever a just war . . . it is that which is prepared today against the perfidious and cruel enemy of the Christian name in Africa. It is to avenge the repeated insults made on our flag; it is to efface the shame of

the tribute paid until today to the tyrant of Algiers by Christian nations; it is to assure the freedom of the seas to our commerce; it is to deliver from Moslem slavery the unfortunate navigators who frequent these vicinities. [It is for all this] that our august monarch has seized the sword that God has confided him to defend and protect his people.[33]

The archbishop skillfully invoked the key institutions of post-1815 Europe, monarchy and Christianity, and linked them to the European powers' readiness to use military force in the name of causes such as the abolition of slavery and the freedom of the seas. He narrowly aimed his prayer at select followers, but support echoed from other quarters. Even an economist such as Simonde de Sismondi, from a group that preferred free trade to colonies, reasoned that the king had made his case.[34] In May 1830, he wrote: "We firmly believe, and we wish to establish that the war on Algiers . . . is a just war, that it is honorable, that it is useful."[35]

France's just war rhetoric was also heard in Algeria. On July 5, 1830, the French commander received the capitulation of Hussein Dey, only a few weeks after the French army landed in Algeria. Following a five-hour bombardment that destroyed the main defenses of Algiers, the dey agreed to French demands for his surrender. With few military options and pressured by local notables such as Ahmed Bouderba and Hamdan Khodja, who reputedly suggested to the dey that the war was the limited one that the French proclaimed and that they would honor their commitments, the Ottoman leader yielded on the promise of specific protections to persons, property, and religion.[36] These were guaranteed in the Convention of 1830, to which the dey affixed his seal in defeat. In unambiguous terms, it stated: "The liberty of the inhabitants of all classes, their religion, their properties, their commerce, and their industry will experience no harm."[37] The document also outlined how and when the change in power would occur (precisely at ten o'clock in the morning), promising an orderly and nonviolent transition. In all, it expressed values of deliberate planning, organization, and law-based rule implied by the Bourbon monarchy's just war discourse. We do not know if the dey was convinced of French assurances or if he signed the convention merely to avoid a costly to-the-last-man defense of the city. Yet whatever faith the people of Algiers may have had in French promises vanished quickly in the hours after the army entered the city. French troops, not knowing if they had come to liberate oppressed people or to attack the "enemies of the Christian name," decided to line their pockets. Soldiers and officers looted the home of the dey and other prominent buildings in the capital, including those of the foreign diplomatic corps.[38] In their plunder, they even took with them the better part of the dey's treasury, a crime against the French state itself, which claimed the prize of 150 million to 500 million francs as its own.[39]

Philosophers might find logical grounds to separate *jus ad bellum* and *jus in bello*, requiring that war be "judged twice," as Michael Walzer has argued.[40] But for participants, victims, and onlookers in 1830, the looting undercut the claims of just war. Instead of restoring law and order, French soldiers transgressed it. Recognizing this, Hamdan Khodja wrote, "The French thus followed the example of the barbarians."[41] While the French army had established a new political order through the rites of war, the rites of peace it chaotically staged in the streets of Algiers—French troops acting like the "pirates and crooks" they had come to punish—were profoundly problematic. Just as the suppression of the Cairo revolt famously tore the "philanthropic veil" off Bonaparte's expedition, the violence of July 1830 compromised the just war claims of the Bourbons and set the stage for a dangerous turn of events.[42] Historian Charles-André Julien put this as follows: "The disorder harmed the prestige of the army as much in Algiers, where the population witnessed deplorable scenes, as in France where the facts were known and, sometimes, exaggerated."[43] If the morality of France's war was to come from the law and justice that its violence instantiated, as Charles X's just war discourse claimed, then the outcome of events foretold its failure.

Louis-Philippe: Colonial Violence and the Just War of Conquest

This failure anticipated a more dramatic defeat on a different front, the battle for public opinion. A cannon salute at the Invalides announced the news of the fall of Algiers on July 9, and a Te Deum at Notre Dame and illumination of monuments celebrated the triumph.[44] But the opposition did not embrace the victory.[45] Writing in the *Journal des Débats* a fortnight after the seizure of Algiers, Chateaubriand mocked the expedition: "They imagine that a victory, *coûte que coûte*, will alarm France, and give them a majority."[46] As Chateaubriand anticipated, it did not. The glorious victory of the king's army in Algiers was followed at the end of the month by "Three Glorious Days," when workers and the liberal classes joined in the July Revolution of 1830. They succeeded in ousting Charles X, and, like Hussein Dey, he ignobly exited his capital on the path to exile. Signaling their support of the king's overthrow, soldiers in Algiers donned the revolutionary cockade soon after news of the revolution arrived.[47]

The new French king, Louis-Philippe, seemed untroubled by what he had inherited in Algeria. According to his minister, François Guizot, the Orléanist monarch felt "fully resolved, both by honour and instinct, not to abandon what the Restoration had conquered."[48] In this respect, he enjoyed what Jennifer Pitts has called the "liberal volte-face" after 1830, when French liberals enthusiastically endorsed imperial expansion.[49] The liberals' change of heart did not follow from a significant rethinking of French imperialism by the monarchy. Louis-Philippe rallied liberals by simply adapting the main lines of the Bourbon justifications. Even the crusading themes, potentially less appetizing to liberals, received dramatic visual articulation in the newly commissioned Hall of the Crusades at Versailles, while the emancipatory claims passed down nicely to the new regime and its claims of modernity and progress.[50]

The just war could also be used to expand empire. The original war, sparked by the diplomatic incident of 1827, pitted Charles X against Hussein Dey himself. It was not a war against the regency's subjects or against the Ottoman empire, inasmuch as French policy makers chose to see the dey as an independent, rogue leader and thereby obscure Ottoman sovereignty in Algeria. The 1827–1830 war was, in this respect, quite limited, and when the dey surrendered on July 5, the expedition's mission was accomplished. Even if the archives clearly show that France anticipated staying in Algeria, it was not until the end of May 1830 that the Bourbon monarchy firmly embraced a project of colonization as the ultimate goal of the expedition against Algiers, and it did so privately.[51] The threat of an international backlash, led by Great Britain, made it necessary to leave intentions vague. This ambiguity gave the French political cover should Britain use its fleet anchored off Sardinia ("in an almost menacing attitude") to force a French withdrawal.[52] Even General Bourmount, who led the French army, was kept in the dark about the decision to establish a colony until after the fall of Algiers.[53] Therefore, in the weeks following July 5, people did not know "if, after victory, the French flag would continue to fly on the African coast."[54] The king's prime minister and his generals clashed over the future of the expedition, while Algerians were told that the occupation would last only six months.[55]

After the Revolution of 1830, the just war argument helped resolve the question. Despite Guizot's claims cited above, Louis-Philippe's vision for Algeria emerged incrementally. In November 1830, the government announced its intention to expand French sovereignty over all territories of the regency, territories still under the authority of Ottoman-invested beys.[56] This meant either persuading local Ottoman authorities to recognize French sovereignty or making war on them (as happened with Constantine's Ahmed Bey, who saw his city fall to the French army in 1837).[57] To silence critical voices, defenders of the policy used the rhetoric of just war. Accordingly, one deputy wrote that France had conquered Algiers "following a just war, [and] it was up to France alone to do with its conquest according to its interests and honor."[58] And procolonial groups in Marseille used just war discourse when they wrote that France had acquired Algeria "by the sacred right of nations, the right of a just war."[59] Just war claims thus helped expand the mission from a limited war against the dey to broad assertions of French sovereignty in Algeria. From the just war opened the path to empire. As one French deputy declared on the chamber floor in 1834, during a debate on the future of the colony: "It is a matter of a territory occupied by France by the title of conquest, following a just war; it is a matter of a territory that belongs to us by a most uncontestable title; it is a matter of a territory that is French."[60] In the deputy's reasoning, because the initial war against the Algerian regency was a just one (he did not specify in what sense), French claims to its territory were therefore equally just.

As was the case with other Orléanist policies, this argument, too, had been used earlier. When the Bourbon monarchy decided to claim the territory of the Ottoman regency in May 1830, the justification was based on the legal entitlements of war: "The right of war leads to the [right] of conquest," the note to the king's council of ministers put it.[61] This comment demonstrates both how malleable the legal norms of war making were at the time and how easily they could be used to assert control over land and people or simply to justify violence. However, the 1830 note went further. It introduced a new element in the justifications for extending the war in Algeria: "The King would be all the more justified to claim it [the right of conquest] in this circumstance [because] it is a question of a country located outside of civilization."

Talal Asad has recently emphasized some of these dangers lurking in just war theory. Arguing that the just war implies the existence of an unjust enemy, he shows how certain types of violence are legitimized and others are condemned following a simple logic that legitimizes the violence of the strong (rational, remorseful, legal) and delegitimizes the violence of the weak (uncivilized, excessive, illegal).[62] In colonial Algeria, his arguments hold true. Because the French war in Algeria was just, the thinking at the time went, any resistance was unjust and could, or even had to, be crushed by any means available. Moreover, placing Algeria "outside of civilization," as the May 1830 note did, created a space free from the norms of lawful war making. This reasoning created conditions in which a sort of "dirty war" emerged from the politics and semantics of the just war discourse, a war with state-sanctioned terror as a primary tool.

A series of early massacres announced the sort of war France would wage against Algerians, one that would be brutal and unrelenting. In two infamous early incidents, the November 1830 massacre at Blida and the April 1832 slaughter of the Ouffia ('Ufiyya), French soldiers killed entire communities, making none of the distinctions that typically afforded protection to noncombatants in this era. In the case of the Ouffia, the tribe was "destroyed" outright, as the French commander put it, not because it posed a military threat—the Ouffia had not taken up arms in rebellion—but on a spurious account that they had robbed travelers loyal to France.[63] In retaliation, units of the French army attacked Ouffia camps without warning in an early-morning raid that ended in the mass murder of about one hundred people. "All that lived was condemned to death, all that could be taken was removed; there was no distinction made for age or sex."[64] To add to the spectacle of violence, French troops mutilated the dead, cutting heads and ears from victims and displaying them as trophies.[65] Two years earlier at Blida, a town lying just south of Algiers, French troops killed an estimated eight hundred people over the course of several days of slaughter, during which time improvised summary executions of local men gave way to a murderous rampage in which entire neighborhoods were put to death.[66]

The reasoning of those who wished to lift limits on warfare in the name of a just war against an unjust enemy was not accepted by all. Indeed, the military's enthusiasm for extreme forms of force presented significant challenges, and the massacres attracted bad press. Although the worst scandals in Algeria would not come until decades later, when events such as the Dahra asphyxiations (1845) and the Doineau affair (1856) focused negative attention on the army's practices, already in the 1830s, news of French atrocities made their way into the headlines. From abroad, the massacre of the Ouffia prompted a journalist to write in the liberal British newspaper the *Westminster Review*: "These are the kind of things which make the name of Frenchmen hated throughout Europe."[67] While in Leipzig, another author told his German readers details of the "great bloodbath" that had occurred in Blida.[68] American newspapers first published articles generally favorable to the French, who were seen to be continuing a war against the Barbary states that the American republic had begun in 1801. Nevertheless, after the Blida massacre, stories appeared in American newspapers reporting the "melancholy result" of French raids, including summary executions and burning of Algerian corpses.[69] By the 1840s, American public opinion had embraced the Algerian cause, as embodied by 'Abd al-Qadir, a man Americans saw as a patriot.[70]

French figures also denounced the violence. Some, including the civil prefect of Algiers, Baron Pichon, and General Berthezène, commander of the army in 1831, wrote strong denunciations of the military's gratuitous violence.[71] These occasioned sharp polemics. In the early 1830s, a long debate opened in France between a "colonialist party," which advocated the harshest use of military force toward Algerians, and people such as Pichon and Berthezène, who sought noncoercive relations.[72] It was occasioned in 1832 by an anonymous letter that alluded to the desirability of the physical elimination or expulsion of Algerians that was published in the *Sémaphore de Marseille*. The author argued that if Algerians could not be forced to abandon Islam with its "law" of "hate towards Christians," they would have to be exterminated. "We must act in this country as if they do not exist," the letter bluntly proclaimed.[73]

It was a controversial point. Even the procolonial editors at the *Sémaphore* felt compelled to include a note that expressed their disapproval. But the letter was republished in national newspapers, giving it wide exposure and forcing the government to include extermination as one option among others in their policy deliberations. The idea was eventually rejected by officials in Paris and military leaders in Algeria, but pundits continued to embrace extermination as a solution to what was called the "indigenous question" into the second decade of the occupation and beyond.[74] It was taken up most notably by Eugène Bodichon, a leftist doctor from Algiers who linked the extermination of Algerians to racial progress in a series of articles he wrote calling on the army to provoke a demographic catastrophe in Algeria.[75] Bodichon believed that such a war was justified because eliminating an "archaic" population would inaugurate an era of progress and modernity for Algeria, a thought shared by several prominent officers. But few in the upper echelons of power embraced his call for a holocaust in Algeria. Although the wars resulted in a demographic crisis in which the country lost about half of its precolonial population, those responsible for policy making understood that Algerian labor was necessary to build the colony.[76]

This was certainly the thinking of powerful liberal Alexis de Tocqueville, who wrote that "the European needs the Arab to cultivate his land, and the Arab needs the European to have a good salary."[77] A strong defender of the colonial project in Algeria, Tocqueville did not question the legitimacy of French rule, nor did he debate the causes that brought France to North Africa in 1830.[78] His concerns centered on convincing his readers that the colonial project was worth the expense and on setting out a clear plan for how to win the war against 'Abd al-Qadir. In the absence of an argument about the justness of the ongoing war, Tocqueville implied that its moral value was measured simply in terms of France's national interest and national honor, an argument that paralleled the one made in Clermont-Tonnerre's 1827 report. But unlike the Bourbon minister, he did not feel it necessary to make explicit reference to just war doctrine or use its rhetoric to make his case. In his two most important groups of texts written about the colony in the 1840s, Tocqueville narrowly extolled the virtues that came from rallying the national community around the colonial project in a democratically healthy political effervescence, and he warned that a withdrawal would announce France's declining role in world affairs.[79]

The question of violence did, however, concern him. When he weighed in on the debate about the French conduct of war, in a discussion that defended the army's brutality while condemning a policy of outright extermination, he invoked military necessity and the mantra that war was an essentially different undertaking in Algeria from what it was in Europe. The army was justified in using different rules of engagement, he argued, ones that targeted entire populations and their resources and not just men in arms. "For my part, I think that all methods to devastate the tribes must be used. I make exception only for those that humanity and the law of nations condemn," Tocqueville wrote, without ever defining what these exceptions and laws might be.[80] Responding to the critics of the army's most controversial punitive raids, known as *razzias*, notorious for their promiscuous killings and the devastating subsistence crises that their systematic destruction of harvests and herds provoked, he retorted that practices of war in Europe were no more just: "How is it more odious to burn harvests and to make women and children prisoners than to bomb the inoffensive population of a besieged city?"[81] The comment illustrates well the points made by Cheryl Welch in an insightful article that shows how Tocqueville used irony and avoidance as part of broader "strategies of self-deception to avoid weighing the moral consequences of political choices" associated with French rule in Algeria.[82]

While he found violence necessary and even morally justifiable, Tocqueville stopped short of claiming that it served a positive moral function, as had others who made just war arguments. While defending the principle of force as "our first rule," he recognized that "we make war in a manner that is more barbarous than the Arabs themselves."[83] In making this point, Tocqueville showed little concern for the victims of French violence but worried about the potential for blowback of colonial war in the metropole. Most troubling was the threat of moral corruption and Caesarism: "God protect us from ever seeing the day that France is led by one of these officers of the African Army."[84]

The uncomfortable facts coming back from Algeria disturbed assumptions about French colonialism and its just war origin, and they are likely at the heart of Tocqueville's hesitance to engage the moral dimensions of French violence. The justness of France's mission became increasingly vague in the 1840s, and its legitimacy came to rest on ever more bluntly worded expressions of national interest like Tocqueville's, along with the arguments embedded in the "unjust enemy" thinking, which portrayed the Algerian resistance as irrational and fanatical. As early as 1836, this crisis of the just war's moral paradigm and the mounting costs of the war led critics to call for the "decolonization" of Algeria.[85] In the 1840s, as the struggle with 'Abd al-Qadir entered a new round, a vocal opposition in the parliament leveled politically damaging attacks on the "barbarous war" led by the French army in Algeria.[86] The initial argument that colonial war was a morally justifiable civilizing force began to unravel under the intensity of this criticism. A letter of 1862 by a French doctor in Constantine summed up the exhaustion of the just war paradigm for the critics: "By the pretext of a fan whisk, you have committed an odious, iniquitous, and immoral act, you have confiscated a nation and a territory. . . . Why at that moment did you not remember your civilization and the obligations that it imposed upon you[?]"[87]

Algerian Views of France's Just War

Although they were completely ignored by people such as Tocqueville, Algerian voices weighed in on this debate. Two figures in particular stand out: Ahmed Bouderba (Ahmad Abu Darba) and Hamdan Khodja (Hamdan ibn 'Uthman Hujah). Bouderba was a merchant from Algiers who had relocated to Marseille in 1820 at the age of nineteen.[88] There he learned French, married a local woman, and stayed until around 1830, when a business deal gone bad forced him to return to Algiers sometime before the French army arrived.[89] Khodja was from mixed Anatolian-Algerian parents (a *Kuloghlu*) and had also traveled in France.[90] Like Bouderba, Khodja had broad cultural horizons, as can be seen in his polyglotism. He wrote in Turkish and Arabic, conversed in French and English, and could at least read Italian.[91] Part of the Ottoman elite in Algeria, Khodja had served in Hussein Dey's government, following his father and uncle in state service, and he had sizable landholdings in the fertile Mitidja plain outside Algiers.[92]

For many years, a rivalry divided Bouderba and Khodja, but these two representatives of Algiers's urban notable class shared ideas about the future of their country.[93] Both agreed that although the French occupation was dangerous, the end of the Ottoman regime opened a way forward. The problem now was how to direct the French out of the country and thus open the way for an Algerian version of Muhammad 'Ali Pasha, who, as governor-general of Egypt (1805–1848), effectively charted an independent course after the withdrawal of Bonaparte's army. Failing this, the goal would be to redirect French rule toward an equitable governance that would welcome elites like themselves. To these ends, they developed relations with like-minded French politicians and administrators and took their case directly to the government and public opinion, becoming in time two of the best-known Algerians in France. Abdelkader Djeghloul has called these efforts a "resistance-dialogue," or a project to shape events through political lobbying rather than the force of arms.[94]

In their negotiations, Bouderba and Khodja showed themselves to be well versed in European political culture, including France's just war discourses. They were not alone among their compatriots. Even before the expedition to Egypt supposedly first opened the Middle East to Europe's modernity, the world-historical events of the French Revolution attracted the close scrutiny of observers in North Africa. For example, in c. 1794, Ahmad ben Sahnun (Ahmad ibn Muhammad 'Ali ibn Sahnun al-Rashidi) wrote a detailed description of the French Revolution for the bey of Oran.[95] He recounted major events such as the meeting of the Estates-General, the fall of the Bastille, and the king's flight to Varennes and his execution. He also paid attention to the anticlerical and secular policies of revolutionaries (nationalization of church property, people "without belief") and the abolition of the noble ranks and their replacement with new political categories such as "citizen," which he translated as *akh*. Even the formation of a sovereign French assembly (*diwan*) made its way into Sahnun's account. Writing for the bey, Sahnun gave all of this a negative gloss, calling the revolution a period of anarchy (*fudi*). But Sahnun also recounted how French revolutionaries rallied people across Europe to rise against injustice and follow their example, giving the bey an indication of the mass appeal of revolutionary ideology and an implicit warning of the threat of future social upheavals in the region.

As history would have it, it was the forces of reaction that overflowed from France into Algiers in 1830. But as we have seen, the Bourbon government claimed to Algerians that their armies brought emancipation in the revolutionary tradition. For their part, Bouderba and Khodja, like al-Jabarti before them, were likely not long duped by this recycled discourse of liberation, nor did they see themselves as Algerian Jacobins, analogues to the European middle classes who welcomed French armies in their bid to do away with oppressive old-regime monarchs. Instead, seeing the imminent military defeat of the dey in 1830, they may have simply hoped that the French could be held accountable to the Enlightenment's universal ideals. Thus, they participated in the July negotiations that led to the dey's capitulation and succeeded in shaping the actual language of the Convention of 1830, ensuring broad guarantees for Algerian interests after the war.[96]

The success of Bouderba's and Khodja's project hinged on making unfavorable comparisons between the ideals of emancipation announced in 1830 and the destructive colonial practices that followed. Accordingly, they insisted on the injustice and inhumanity of massacres, summary executions, and unlawful requisitions of property, including the 1830 seizure of Islamic pious foundations, or *hubus*.[97] Moreover, both men challenged the terms of the colonial debate that focused on the unsuitability of Algerians for liberation, suggesting instead that it was the French who represented alterity and deviance from civilized norms.

An important moment for political action came in 1833, when Louis-Philippe convoked a special commission to study French policy in Algeria. The commission was made up of two appointed bodies, one of which traveled to Algeria in the fall of 1833 for five months of research and a second, the "Africa Commission" proper, which met in Paris through the spring of 1834 to make proposals.[98] A primary task of the commissions was to decide on policy toward Algerians: what sort of relations to establish, what sort of governance would be effective, or, more brutally, whether it would be "this alternative that we must subjugate them or expel [*chasser*] them."[99]

The commissions had no Algerian members, but Bouderba and Khodja made their views known by drafting reports and testifying in Paris. Bouderba was called before the African Commission on January 20, 1834. Speaking in French, he started by taking to task the particular way French policy linked justice and violence. An "enlightened and severe justice," he told members, does not "exclude moderation."[100] Bouderba was building on ideas that he had outlined in a report previously addressed to the commission. In it, he criticized French governance in the colony, its "force and violence, the regime of the sword and terror."[101] France had violated its own values, Bouderba argued, and only when justice, moderation, and patience determined political practices would "the true civilization" arrive.[102] Of course, "true civilization" was a polyvalent term and had many different guises. Bouderba may have been familiar with radical anti-Enlightenment thinkers such as Louis de Bonald or Joseph de Maistre and their ideas of civilization as violence. Maistre certainly would have been comfortable with the massacres in Algeria, as he had been with the Terror, which he saw as purifying a corrupt and weak French moral fiber.[103] But Bouderba ignored them and put forward a specific, liberal vision of France as the true France. In this vision, he strategically emphasized the humanist dimensions of French political philosophy in his call for reformed rule, in effect reproducing the discourses of liberation that announced the invasion as a just war and using these as standards to measure the occupation.

Writing in French and signing his petitions in Arabic and Latin characters, Bouderba made a straightforward case, free of mimicry, double entendres, misappropriations, or the "sly civility" that characterize other subaltern discourses.[104] Although already in 1834, Bouderba appeared in the eyes of some as an archetype of the "non-Western" modern subject—a colonized Muslim to be dominated and/ or forcibly "liberated"—he could himself look back to a not-so-distant Mediterranean past when, as Fernand Braudel described it, people "lived and breathed with the same rhythms."[105] Bouderba could also take heart in eighteenth-century

European thought that had not yet cast the Maghreb into the realm of "primitive" Africa or "fanatical" Islam, notwithstanding the influential writings of Volney.[106] Thinking that this recent past could be made to intrude on the present, Bouderba did not recognize the new fault line traced across the Mediterranean world by French empire. Thus, it was natural enough for him to take as his own the voice of the rational, progressive actor who adhered to the principles of the Enlightenment. This helped fix a certain meaning to the war in Algeria and its justness, one that opened a powerful critique of French policies. "If you want to introduce civilization in the interior, you have only one method: patience, loyalty on your part—keep your promises—justice and equity, moderation, in short all the good qualities that an honest man [*homme intègre*] possesses."[107] In other words, the just war should not be pleasing stories that the French told to themselves, about themselves, but it had to be confirmed in practices of justice in and after war. The effect of Bouderba's argument was underscored at the Africa Commission hearings after he stepped down and Hamdan ben Amin Secca, who had also worked with the French early on as *agha des Arabes*, took the stand and said: "When the French came, we took them for liberators not conquerors [but] the massacre of the Ouffia has harmed the French [reputation] these acts have destroyed confidence."[108]

Khodja, the third and last Algerian to speak before the commission, did so through an interpreter on January 23, 1834, but his testimony was carefully controlled by the French panel.[109] Khodja was already known as an unyielding critic of French rule, and so the commission's president narrowly limited questions. In particular, he feared that Khodja might expound on the views expressed in his book *The Mirror*, a lengthy and scathing denunciation of the occupation written in October 1833.[110] Published in French, *The Mirror* confronted the government with France's violations of the Convention of 1830 and its unwillingness to extend basic rights to Algerians.[111] "Their [the Algerians'] interests are unknown; their hopes are deceived, for them no indulgence and no justice!" Khodja protested.[112] The universal principles announced in France's just war discourse had been jettisoned, Khodja argued, in the pursuit of narrow national interests along with those of procolonialist groups who saw Algerians at best as a subject population useful only as a potential source of labor or at worst as an impediment to be swept aside. Violence grew out of this dehumanized conception of Algerians, spreading throughout the colonial project and producing "all these horrors committed in the name of a free France."[113] Like Bouderba, Khodja used the political philosophy of the Enlightenment to point out the contradictions and paradoxes of French policy. But Khodja's primary goal was not the liberalization of colonial rule but the outright withdrawal of the army.[114] Thus, he gave a more blunt anticolonial message than Bouderba, and he used France's moral default to call on it to leave Algeria: "Evacuate the country and renounce any idea of conquest by establishing an indigenous government, free and independent, as was done in Egypt."[115]

Ultimately, however, the resistance dialogue of Bouderba and Khodja failed. The Africa Commission recommended that France remain in Algeria and made no substantive proposals to open government to Algerians. Instead, in its concluding arguments, the commission reached into just war discourses once again to say that relations between the French and Algerians—parties named as "conquerors and vanquished"—would be based on "justice."[116] This did not protect Khodja and Bouderba, who were forced out of Algeria in 1836, victims of a campaign within the governor-general's office to rid the colony of dissenting Algerian voices. Khodja, announcing his exile in Istanbul to Bouderba (who himself was trying to get to Marseille from the Balearic Islands), summed up his bitter feelings by appending to his signature "*al-gharib*" (the stranger).[117] And in another letter to Bouderba, Khodja expressed the impossibility of their initial project with a characteristic bit of irony: "God protect us from the *injustice* of the Turks and the *justice* of the French."[118]

'Abd al-Qadir and the Algerian Jihad

Two years before the Africa Commission endorsed the colonial project, the amir 'Abd al-Qadir ('Abd al-Qadir ibn Muhyi al-Din al-Jaza'iri, 1808–1883) was chosen to lead the jihad against the French. Born in the west of Algeria to an influential family of Sufi notables, 'Abd al-Qadir fought against the French with minor interruptions between 1832 and 1837 and again in the years 1839 to 1847. His fortunes varied, but by the terms of the Treaty of Tafna (May 30, 1837), 'Abd al-Qadir claimed the better part of Algeria's western interior and the country's central territories, marking the zenith of his power. The amir's success came from jihad of the sword, a war that was by default holy, just, and obligatory. "Fighting for the sake of God," with its powerful imperatives of solidarity and righteousness, advanced 'Abd al-Qadir's personal authority in Algerian society, a society that reflexively guarded its autonomy.[119] Seeking supporters from the interior of the country, he told people to see the French landings in Algiers and the occupation of Algeria's Mediterranean ports through the optic of jihad. France did not represent a new version of the occasional power of the Ottoman deys and beys—a central state to be ceded to when necessary and ignored when possible—but was a non-Muslim invader that all Algerian Muslims were obliged to resist under his banner.[120]

This was a venture that carried great risks, risks that deterred many potential supporters. To forge support, 'Abd al-Qadir circulated fatwas endorsing his jihad from renowned authorities in Morocco and Egypt.[121] History also helped the amir make his case. The call to jihad had resonated across the Maghreb for centuries. The 'Alawi sultans in particular had used the jihad against Spain to forge an ideological consensus in support of their centralizing project in Morocco.[122] In western Algeria, too, jihad was a strong part of local political culture. Here the struggle against the Spanish, who held Oran as a *presidio* (fortified base) until 1792, left a strong mark.[123] Thus, many who might have otherwise spurned the amir in order to forge their own response to the French menace accepted his leadership and sent troops and taxes.

Although jihad was an effective anticolonial tool, inasmuch as it brought together under a single command a disconnected society that otherwise might have sought local responses to the French occupation, and it gave this resistance a powerful sense of legitimacy that tied it back to the origins of Islam itself, it was less so as a limit on war and its practices. As this book's introduction claims, jihad is arguably an analogue to the just war. Although they are distinctive, both traditions agree that morally desirable goals can be advanced through violence. At the same time, this moral claim is predicated on the limits that these traditions place on the occasion of war and its conduct. Such limits were part of jihad's legal doctrine, which gave more or less clear rules for when, where, and how war could be pursued. Nevertheless, the Algerian example shows cases of excess when jihad's restrictive rules of war did not limit soldiers' conduct in battle. 'Abd al-Qadir's troops certainly knew the warning in the Qur'an, "Do not transgress limits" (*la ta'tadu*) in war (2:190), but they entered vague terrain at several points during the fight with France and chose an understanding of limits that was broadly construed. Examples include the massacre of French prisoners (255 were killed on April 27, 1846); the killing of European settlers, such as occurred in the Mitidja (November 1839); and the frequent mutilation of corpses.[124]

Such practices as the killing of prisoners and civilians occurred in a legal gray zone. As John Kelsay has shown, jurists had censured them or curtailed the situations when they might be permitted, but there were many scholars who did not condemn them outright.[125] For his part, 'Abd al-Qadir chose a conservative and cautious reading of the rules of war. The 1846 massacre of French prisoners, one of the most controversial incidents, occurred when the amir was away from his camp, and it was not undertaken on his order. Indeed, he had previously taken the initiative to ensure that soldiers taken in battle were not killed in 1841, when he opened negotiations with the bishop of Algiers that resulted in a successful exchange of several hundred prisoners.[126] The amir also punished soldiers for mutilating corpses. Nevertheless, his orders proved easy enough to ignore in practice, and the dubious sorts of killing practiced by the amir's troops potentially compromised the jihad's claim to advance moral goals.

Unlike the cases of Bouderba and Khodja, there were not, at this point, many French commentators who stepped forward to condemn the Algerian jihad on these grounds. Typically, jihad was indexed as "fanaticism" or the irrational political behavior of Muslims in general, an irrationality that could be countered only by force. That jihad might have its own rules limiting the conduct and occasion of war was lost on most French observers. But criticism did emerge on the Algerian side. Worth considering in this context is 'Abd al-Qadir's own thinking about jihad, which evolved considerably during his life. In 1832, the amir told Algerians that the only permissible response to the French occupation was military jihad. Afterward, he reflected on jihad's other possibilities. Having ended his combat in 1847, 'Abd al-Qadir spent five years in French prisons until he was released and moved to Ottoman territories, eventually settling in Damascus in 1856. This intellectually rich city was his home during the last three decades of his life, a period of great activity for the amir. His intervention to protect Damascus's Christian community in 1860, which was threatened by the violence spilling over from Mount Lebanon, is most famous.[127] This act endeared him to metropolitan France and established his reputation as a peacemaker. Less well known are 'Abd al-Qadir's teachings on Islam. In Damascus, he undertook a rereading of the Sufi traditions presented in the work of Ibn 'Arabi, and the amir emerged as one of "the most influential interpreters of Ibn 'Arabi in his time," as Itzchak Weismann argues.[128] 'Abd al-Qadir's teachings were situated within the modernist project for the regeneration of Islam, and critically rethinking the place of jihad as a part of an individual's spiritual progress was part of the amir's work. Already during his war with France, 'Abd al-Qadir had had considerable occasion to question his armed struggle. His jihad suffered a particularly stinging rebuke in 1841, when the Baghdad shaykh of the Qadiriyya Sufi order, Sayyid Mahmud al-Kilani, condemned the amir's war as a futile and thus illegitimate jihad.[129] The reproach was all the more bitter because 'Abd al-Qadir, an affiliate of the Qadiriyya, knew the shaykh personally and had been al-Kilani's guest when he and his father visited the tomb of the Qadiriyya founder in the 1820s.

A profoundly religious man, 'Abd al-Qadir is often studied as representative of a pure Algero-Muslim identity.[130] In this reading, his jihad is emblematic of the Algerian refusal of French colonialism *tout court*, and its successes represent the vitality of specifically Islamic forms of military resistance to European imperialism. But 'Abd al-Qadir did not see armed struggle as the only or even the preferable response to the French invasion, particularly after the Treaty of Tafna in 1837 recognized his authority in much of the country. In these years leading up to the second round of war in 1839, he undertook a lengthy correspondence with a variety of French leaders, including personal letters to the king and his wife, wherein he stressed the beneficial qualities of peace and the desirability of nonmilitary options as long as the French respected their obligations toward Algerians.[131]

Moreover, certain texts attributed to 'Abd al-Qadir from the period after 1847 show that he had complex and variable views on the jihad he led, views that limited the moral claims made on the war and instead focused on its hardships and even undesirability. Most notable is the *Sira*, a text drafted in French prisons that did not linger on the morally uplifting and glorious qualities of jihad.[132] This continued in Damascus, where 'Abd al-Qadir taught his students to think about jihad in ways that highlighted its moral dangers.[133] He marked in clear terms the division between the military jihad (*al-jihad al-saghir*, the lesser jihad) and the spiritual jihad (*al-jihad al-akbar*, the greater jihad), giving priority to the latter.

'Abd al-Qadir explained, "The combat against the non-believing enemy is not pure and does not rid one of the sullied failings. [These] are pushed aside only by the combat with the soul, by its correction and its purification."[134] Thus, as a spiritual path pleasing to God, raising arms against the nonbelievers was not a substitute for the more difficult struggle with the self. If they wished to be counted among the spiritual elite, 'Abd al-Qadir's students had to remain focused on the spiritual jihad.[135] Those who chose war, who sought to "physically eliminate the unbe-lievers," did not understand the Prophet's true goal, 'Abd al-Qadir warned.[136]

Conclusion

War is fundamentally about killing people. For this reason, the fit of the pieces of just war doctrine has not always been a firm or easy one. Often, the ambivalences and ambiguities of just war and jihad have provided powerful symbolic spaces to legitimize, vindicate, and promote violence, even violence that would otherwise be understood as excessive and destructive to the very moral norms that it sup-posedly defends or establishes.[137] Sigmund Freud recognized this fundamental fact of war during the First World War. As the author of a provocative hypothesis that the law (i.e., normative restrictions on desire) had a paradoxical origin in primal human violence,[138] Freud saw that later forms of moralized violence, such as the war to end all wars, did not convey the norms that they proclaimed. Instead, war ultimately dissolved the possibility of moral action itself, when it trampled "in blind fury on all that comes in its way."[139]

The case in Algeria bears out Freud's thoughts. In 1830, the French idea of empire was simultaneously undefined and overdetermined, filled to capacity with France's unrealized utopias, the country's failed revolutions and counterrevolu-tions. As a result, it was unpredictable and even unmanageable. To resolve such ambiguities, the French reflex in Algeria was toward violence, and the just war stories that the French told themselves provided ready cover for the atrocities that were part of the war for civilization. Nevertheless, coexisting with the belief in the efficacy of force in achieving dominance over non-European, Muslim people were the countertendencies of Enlightenment thought. Bouderba and Khodja sensed the contingency of French policies, how France was improvising its way to modern empire in the Mediterranean in the guise of a just war. They tried to con-struct a new story for Algeria out of the claims of the just war, which they con-trasted with the hidden details of French policy and the sordid, undisclosed facts of colonial practices. This amounted to a dialogical encounter between Europeans and North Africans wherein Bouderba and Khodja tried to reconnect the practice and theory of France's just war in terms of their historical experiences and polit-ical goals. They failed, of course, and the subsequent path of Algerian history ful-filled their worst fears. French commentators routinely argued that Algerians were not "just enemies" (*justus hostis*) but political outsiders and "out-of-the-laws" (*hors-la-loi*), who might suffer the full impact of the French army's violence.[140] Events such as the Blida massacre and the annihilation of the Ouffia expressed this thinking and set an example for practices of mass murder that reappeared periodically over the course of the next two decades and beyond. Up through the Algerian revolution (1954–1962), Algerians of all sorts were subject to the label "enemy," regardless of their military role or even their political disposition, a fateful move that blurred the distinction between war and peace, greatly expanding the military's privilege to kill.[141]

For his part, 'Abd al-Qadir found in military jihad a powerful response to the French invasion and the radically unequal power relations of colonialism. It gave him the political legitimacy and righteousness that would help him articulate a political future for Algeria in wake of the collapse of the Ottoman province, a future that did not refer to European political idioms to express itself. This sort of just war also had a long impact on Algerian history. Most notably, after its victory against the French in 1962, the Front de Liberation National (FLN) enshrined its war of liberation, a popular but massively costly and confusing struggle, as the fulfillment of 'Abd al-Qadir's aspirations (rearticulated as part of the unceasing combat of the Algerian people to create an independent nation-state). Marked by events such as the 1966 repatriation of the amir's remains from Syria, this helped to secure the FLN's monopoly on political life and gave a reassuring and politically palatable version of the uneven course of Algerian history under French rule. But as we know, 'Abd al-Qadir recognized violent jihad's moral perils. His teachings in Damascus, lauding the primacy of the Sufi's inner striving, show particularly well his critical rethinking of the tradition. And although he tried to wage a war that would advance Islam's principles and norms—or more simply preserve them in face of a colonial occupier that had spoken of the annihilation of Muslims in Algeria—he found that the uncontrollable nature of war itself made such a moral goal profoundly elusive.

Notes

1. Hamdan Khodja, *Le Miroir: Aperçu historique et statistique sur la Régence d'Alger* (Arles: Actes Sud, 1985), 184.
2. The struggle of Ahmed Bey of Constantine against the French is outside the scope of this chapter.
3. Darcy Grimaldo Grigsby's reading of Antoine-Jean Gros's celebrated painting *Bonaparte Visiting the Plague Victims of Jaffa* (1804) opens understanding of French ambivalences about the expedition. Darcy Grimaldo Grigsby, *Extremities: Painting Empire in Post-Revolutionary France* (New Haven, Conn.: Yale University Press, 2002), 65–103. However, the long-standing positive consensus should not be underestimated. For example, it was marked in powerful ways by French president François Mitterrand's annual vacations in Egypt, a tradition that Nicolas Sarkozy tried to rearticulate and renew during a 2007 holiday to Egypt at the beginning of his own presidential term. For example, see special issue, "Egypte—La passion," *L'Express*, 2372 (December 18–26, 1996): 68–145.

4. David O'Brian, *After the Revolution: Antoine-Jean Gros, Painting and Propaganda under Napoleon Bonaparte* (University Park: Pennsylvania State University Press, 2006), 138–41.

5. *Paris Match*, November 10–16, 2005, pp. 32–33.

6. Vivant Denon, *Travels in Upper and Lower Egypt*, vol. 1, trans. Arthur Aikin (New York: Arno, 1973), 168.

7. Vincent-Yves Boutin, *Aperçu historique, statistique et topographique sur l'état d'Alger* (Paris: Picquet, 1830); Jean Marchioni, *Boutin: Pionnier de l'Algérie française* (Nice: Gandani, 2007).

8. François-Alexandre Desprez, *Journal d'un officier de l'Armée d'Afrique* (Paris: Anselin, 1831), 5.

9. David A. Bell, *The First Total War: Napoleon's Europe and the Birth of Warfare as We Know It* (New York: Houghton Mifflin, 2007), 8.

10. Isabel V. Hull, *Absolute Destruction: Military Culture and the Practices of War in Imperial Germany* (Ithaca, N.Y.: Cornell University Press, 2005); Carl Schmitt, *The Nomos of the Earth in the International Law of the Jus Publicum Europaeum*, trans. G. L. Ulmen (New York: Telos, 2006).

11. Paul Azan, ed., "Le rapport du marquis de Clermont-Tonnerre, ministre de la guerre, sur une expédition à Alger, 1827," *Revue Africaine* 70 (1929): 209–53.

12. Thomas Bianchi, *Relation de l'arrivée dans la rade d'Alger du vaisseau "La Provence"* (Paris: Ladvocat, 1830).

13. Philippe Contamine, *War in the Middle Ages*, trans. Michael Jones (New York: Blackwell, 1984), 264.

14. Ministre de la Guerre, *Aperçu historique, statistique et topographique sur l'état d'Alger, à l'usage de l'armée expéditionnaire d'Afrique, avec plans, vues et costumes* (Paris: Picquet, 1830), 75.

15. Ibid., 251.

16. Daniel Heller-Roazen, *The Enemy of All: Piracy and the Law of Nations* (New York: Zone, 2009).

17. Ministre de la Guerre, *Aperçu historique*, 77.

18. Azan, "Le rapport du marquis," 215.

19. Ibid.; emphasis added.

20. Ibid.

21. Laisné de Villévêque, "Expédition d'Alger," July 10, 1827, archives of the Ministre des Affaires Étrangères, Paris (hereafter MAE), Mémoires et documents, Algérie, 11.

22. Azan, "Le rapport du marquis," 241.

23. Sarah A. Curtis, "Emilie de Vialar and the Religious Reconquest of Algeria," *French Historical Studies* 29, no. 2 (Spring 2006): 261–92; Karima Direche-Slimani, *Chrétiens de Kabylie, 1873–1954: Une action missionnaire dans l'Algérie coloniale* (Paris: Bouchène, 2004).

24. Henry Laurens, *L'expédition d'Égypte, 1798–1801* (Paris: Armand Colin, 1989), 329.

25. Henry Laurens, *Orientales I: Autour de l'expédition de l'Égypte* (Paris: CNRS, 2004), 70.

26. J. Christopher Herold, *Bonaparte in Egypt* (New York: Harper and Row, 1962), 69.

27. Juan Cole, *Napoleon's Egypt: Invading the Middle East* (New York: Palgrave Macmillan, 2007), 30.

28. 'Abd al-Rahman al-Jabarti, *Al-Jabarti's Chronicle of the First Seven Months of the French Occupation, 1798*, trans. S. Moreh (Leiden: Brill, 1975). See also André Raymond, *Égyptiens et Français au Caire, 1798–1801* (Cairo: Institut Français d'Archéologie Orientale, 1998), 88–90.

29. Bourmont's Proclamation of May 10, 1830, cited in François-Alexandre Desprez, *Journal d'un officier de l'Armée d'Afrique* (Paris: Anselin, 1831), 55–56.

30. Ibid.

31. "Proclamation en arabe adressée par le général de Bourmont aux habitants de la ville d'Alger et des tribus, en juin 1830," trans. M. Bresnier, *Revue Africaine* 6 (1862): 151.

32. *Sémaphore de Marseille* 677 (March 18, 1830).

33. Mandement of Charles Alexandre de Richery, archbishop of Aix-en-Provence, May 5, 1830, reported in *Ami de la Religion* 74 (May 12, 1830): 53.

34. Marwan R. Buheiry, *The Formation and Perception of the Modern Arab World* (Princeton, N.J.: Darwin, 1989), 13–32.

35. J. C. L. Simonde de Sismondi, "L'expédition contre Alger," *Revue Encyclopédique* 46 (May 1830): 277.

36. Ahmed Bouderba to Minister of War, Paris, June 3, 1833, Archives Nationales d'Outre Mer (hereafter ANOM), 1 H 1.

37. MAE, traités, Alger 18300005, microfilm no. TR117.

38. A. Berenguer, "Documents suédois sur la prise d'Alger (1830)," *Revue d'Histoire et de Civilisation du Maghreb* 4 (1968): 42.

39. Jean-Baptiste Flandin, *Prise de possession des trésors d'Alger* (Paris: Féret, 1835); Jean-Baptiste Flandin, *Notice sur la prise de possession des trésors de la régence d'Alger* (Paris: Chassaignon, 1848).

40. Michael Walzer, *Just and Unjust Wars: A Moral Argument with Historical Illustrations*, 4th ed. (New York: Basic, 2006), 21.

41. Khodja, *Le Miroir*, 177.

42. Vivant Denon, quoted in Edmond Ferry, *La France en Afrique* (Paris: Colin, 1905), 48.

43. Charles-André Julien, *Histoire de l'Algérie contemporaine*, vol. 1: *La conquête et les débuts de la colonisation, 1827–1871* (Paris: PUF, 1979), 57.

44. Minister of Foreign Affairs to General Bourmont, Paris, July 12, 1830, MAE, Mémoires et documents, Algérie, 6.

45. Julien, *Histoire*, 47.

46. *Journal des Débats*, July 17, 1830, cited in Arthur Wellesley, *Dispatches, Correspondence, and Memoranda of Field Marshal Arthur, Duke of Wellington, K.G.*, vol. 7: *April, 1830–October, 1831* (London: J. Murray, 1878), 121–22.

47. Anonymous, "Réfutation aux observations du général Clauzel sur son commandement à Alger," n.d. (ca. 1835), no. 29, MAE, Mémoires et documents, Algérie, 16.

48. François Guizot, *Memoirs to Illustrate the History of My Time*, vol. 3, trans. J. W. Cole (London: Bentley, 1860), 242.

49. Jennifer Pitts, *A Turn to Empire: The Rise of Imperial Liberalism in Britain and France* (Princeton, N.J.: Princeton University Press, 2005), 165–203.

50. Elizabeth Siberry, *The New Crusaders: Images of the Crusades in the Nineteenth and Early Twentieth Centuries* (Aldershot, U.K.: Ashgate, 2000); Claire Constans and Philippe Lamarque, *Les Salles des croisades: Château de Versailles* (Versailles: Gui, 2002).

51. "Note pour le Conseil," May 26, 1830, MAE, Mémoires et documents, Algérie 5.

52. Ibid.

53. Instructions to Bourmont, June 26, 1830, MAE, Mémoires et documents, Algérie 5.

54. *Procès-verbaux et rapports de la commission d'Afrique instituée par ordonnance du roi du 12 décembre 1833* (Paris: L'Imprimerie Royale, 1834), 391.

55. Julien, *Histoire*, 60; Khodja, *Le Miroir*, 183.

56. Minister of War to Minister of Foreign Affairs, November 12, 1830, MAE, Mémoires et documents, Algérie 6.

57. Abdeljelil Temimi, *Le Beylik de Constantine et Hadj Ahmed Bey (1830–1837)* (Tunis: Revue d'Histoire Maghrébine, 1978).

58. Jacques de Milleret, *La France depuis 1830, perçus sur sa situation politique, militaire, coloniale et financière* (Paris: Perrotin, 1838), 555.

59. Claude Fouqué d'Arles, *Histoire raisonnée du commerce de Marseille: Appliquée aux développements des prospérités modernes*, vol. 1 (Paris: Roret, 1843), 213.

60. M. J. Madival et al., eds., *Archives parlementaires de 1787 à 1860*, 2nd series, vol. 89: *17 avril-5 mai 1834* (Paris: Dupont, 1894), 687.

61. "Note pour le Conseil," May 26, 1830, MAE, Mémoires et documents, Algérie 5.

62. Talal Asad, *On Suicide Bombing* (New York: Columbia University Press, 2007).

63. Louis-André (Baron) Pichon, *Alger sous la domination française: Son état présent et son avenir* (Paris: Barrois et Duprat, 1833), 401.

64. Eugène Pellissier de Reynaud, *Annales algériennes*, vol. 1 (Paris: Dumaine; Algiers: Bastide, 1854), 247.

65. Pichon, *Alger sous la domination*, 108–9; Comte d'Hérisson, *La chasse à l'homme: Guerres d'Algérie* (Paris: Ollendorff, 1891).

66. "Expédition de l'Armée française en Afrique contre Blédéah et Médéah," *Le Spectateur Militaire* 10 (1831): 371–90.

67. "Algerine Commission," extract from *Westminster Review*, republished in *Museum of Foreign Literature and Science* 26 (January–June 1835): 356.

68. August Jaeger, *Skizzen und Erinnerungen aus Algier und Algerien* (Leipzig: E. L. Fritzsche, 1840), 229.

69. *Rhode-Island American* 3, no. 15 (September 6, 1831).

70. Nora Achrati, "Following the Leader: A History and Evolution of the Amir 'Abd al-Qadir al-Jazairi as Symbol," *Journal of North African Studies* 12, no. 2 (June 2007): 139–52. The town of Elkader, Iowa, established in 1846, is named after 'Abd al-Qadir.

71. Pichon, *Alger sous la domination*; Le Baron Berthézène, *Dix-huit mois à Alger* (Montpellier: Richard, 1834). I discuss the 1840s debates in Benjamin Claude Brower, *A Desert Named Peace: The Violence of French Empire in the Algerian Sahara* (New York: Columbia University Press, 2009).

72. Charles-Robert Ageron, *Le gouvernement du général Berthezène à Alger en 1831* (Paris: Bouchène, 2005), 75–82.

73. "Colonie d'Alger," *Sémaphore de Marseille* 4, no. 1421 (August 22, 1832).

74. The letter was reprinted in *La Tribune des Départements* 4, no. 242 (August 29, 1832).

75. Eugène Bodichon, *Études sur l'Algérie et l'Afrique* (Algiers, 1847).

76. Kamel Kateb, *Européens, "indigènes," et juifs en Algérie, 1830–1962* (Paris: Éditions de l'INED, 2001); Brower, *A Desert Named Peace*, 24–26.

77. Alexis de Tocqueville, "Rapports sur l'Algérie (1847)," in *Oeuvres complètes*, vol. 1, ed. André Jardin (Paris: Gallimard, 1991), 819.

78. On Tocqueville and Algeria, see Pitts, *A Turn to Empire*, 204–39; and Melvin Richter, "Tocqueville on Algeria," *Review of Politics* 25 (1963): 362–98; Tzvetan Todorov, "Introduction: Tocqueville et la doctrine coloniale," in Alexis de Tocqueville, *De la colonie en Algérie* (Paris: Complexe, 1988), 9–34; Cheryl B. Welch, "Colonial Violence and the Rhetoric of Evasion: Tocqueville on Algeria," *Political Theory* 31, no. 2 (April 2003): 235–64; Olivier Le Cour Grandmaison, *Coloniser exterminer: Sur la guerre et l'état colonial* (Paris: Fayard, 2005), 98–113; Roger Boesche, "The Dark Side of Tocqueville: On War and Empire," *Review of Politics* 67, no. 4 (Fall 2005): 737–52.

79. Alexis de Tocqueville, "Travail sur l'Algérie (1841)" and "Rapports sur l'Algérie (1847)," both in *Oeuvres*, 1:689–759, 797–905.

80. Tocqueville, "Travail," 705.

81. Ibid.

82. Welch, "Colonial Violence," 247.

83. Tocqueville, "Rapports," 819; and "Travail," 704.

84. Tocqueville, "Travail," 712.

85. Marwan R. Buheiry, "Anti-Colonial Sentiment in France during the July Monarchy: The Algerian Case" (PhD dissertation, Princeton University, 1973). See also Todd Sheppard, *The Invention of Decolonization: The Algerian War and the Remaking of France* (Ithaca, N.Y.: Cornell University Press, 2006).

86. Tocqueville, *Oeuvres*, 1:689–759; Deputy Joly, *Le Moniteur Universel*, June 6, 1844.

87. André Nouschi, ed., *Correspondance du Docteur A. Vital avec I. Urbain (1845–1874)* (Paris: Larose, 1959), 60.

88. Ahmed Bouderba to Minister of War, Marseille, May 14, 1837, ANOM, 1 H 1.

89. "Notice sur Abouderbah," not dated, ANOM, 1 H 1.

90. Georges Yver, "Si Hamdan ben Othman Khodja," *Revue Africaine* 57 (1913): 97–98.

91. On the languages of the precolonial Mediterranean, see Jocelyne Dakhlia, *Lingua franca: Histoire d'une langue métisse en Méditerranée* (Arles: Actes Sud, 2008).

92. Tal Shuval, "The Ottoman Algerian Elite and Its Ideology," *International Journal of Middle East Studies* 32, no. 3 (August 2000): 323–44.

93. Mahfoud Smati, *Les élites algériennes sous la colonisation* (Algiers: Dahlab; Paris: Maisonneuve et Larose, 1998), 96–113.

94. Abdelkader Djeghloul, *Éléments d'histoire culturelle algérienne* (Algiers: ENAL, 1984), 51–60, 165–69. Ageron, *Le gouvernement*, 36.

95. Tayeb Chenntouf, *Études d'histoire de l'Algérie (18e et 19e siècle)* (Algiers: OPU, 2004), 77–85.

96. Bouderba to Minister of War, Paris, June 3, 1833; and Bouderba to Minister of War, Marseille, May 14, 1837, ANOM, 1 H 1.

97. The importance of these properties is discussed in Miriam Hoexter, *Endowments, Rulers, and Community: Waqf al-Haramayn in Ottoman Algiers* (Leiden: Brill, 1998).

98. Georges Yver, "La Commission d'Afrique," in *Recueil de mémoires et textes publiés en honneur du XIVe Congres des orientalistes à Alger* (Algiers: Pierre Fontana, 1905), 547–608.

99. *Procès-verbaux et rapports de la commission nommée par le roi, le 7 juillet 1833* (Paris: L'Imprimerie Royale, 1834), 15.

100. *Procès-verbaux et rapports de la commission d'Afrique institué par ordonnance du roi du 12 décembre 1833* (Paris: L'Imprimerie Royale, 1834), 40.

101. Ahmed Bouderba, "Réflexions sur la colonie d'Alger," *Revue Africaine* 57 (1913): 221.

102. Ibid., 238.

103. Joseph de Maistre, *Considerations on France*, trans. Richard A. Lebrun (Cambridge, U.K.: Cambridge University Press, 1994).

104. Homi K. Bhabha, *The Location of Culture*, 2nd ed. (London: Routledge, 2004), 145–74. In other correspondence, Bouderba simply signed his name in Latin characters. Later in the 1830s, he developed a signature that included his name in Arabic characters neatly tucked into two loops that he formed at the end of his name written in Latin characters. See examples in ANOM, 1 H 1.

105. Fernand Braudel, *The Mediterranean and the Mediterranean World in the Age of Philip II*, vol. 1, trans. Siân Reynolds (Berkeley: University of California Press, 1995), 14.

106. Ann Thomson, *Barbary and Enlightenment: European Attitudes towards the Maghreb in the 18th Century* (Leiden: E. J. Brill, 1987).

107. Bouderba, "Réflexions," 244; repunctuated for sense.

108. *Procès-verbaux*, 44.

109. Ibid., 56–59.

110. First edition: Hamdan-Ben-Othman Khoja, *Aperçu historique et statistique sur la régence d'Alger, intitulé en arabe: "Le Miroir,"* trans. Hassuna Daghis (Paris: Goetschy Fils, 1833).

111. An interpreter for the bey of Tunis, Hassuna Daghis was the translator and likely collaborated in writing the *Mirror*; Djeghloul in Khodja, *Le Miroir*, 34.

112. Ibid., 37.

113. Ibid., 38.

114. Following the Treaty of Tafna in 1837, Bouderba embraced the Egyptian solution for Algeria, i.e., turning over sovereign power to 'Abd al-Qadir. Bouderba, "Observations sur la traité de 30 mai avec Abd el Kader et les avantages immenses qui peuvent résulter pour la France et l'Afrique, la civilisation et l'humanité," November 3, 1837, ANOM, F^{80} 1672.

115. Khodja, *Le Miroir*, 262.

116. *Supplément aux procès-verbaux de la commission d'Afrique, instituée par ordonnance royale du 12 décembre 1833* (Paris: Imprimerie Royale, 1834), 5; italics added.

117. Khodja to Bouderba, 1836 (Arabic and numeric code), ANOM, 1 H 1.

118. Khodja to Bouderba, May 26, 1836 (French translation, no original), ANOM, 1 H 1.

119. Michael Bonner, *Jihad in Islamic History: Doctrines and Practice* (Princeton, N.J.: Princeton University Press, 2006), 2. For the varied Algerian responses to French imperialism, see Julia A. Clancy-Smith, *Rebel and Saint: Muslim Notables, Populist Protest, Colonial Encounters (Algeria and Tunisia, 1800–1904)* (Berkeley: University of California Press, 1997).

120. Pessah Shinar, "'Abd al-Qadir and 'Abd al-Krim: Religious Influences on Their Thought and Action," *Asian and African Studies* 1 (1965): 139–74.

121. Rudolph Peters, *Islam and Colonialism* (The Hague: Mouton, 1980), 56–61. Muhammad ibn 'Abd al-Qadir, *Tuhfat al-za'ir fi tarikh al-Jaza'ir wa al-amir 'Abd al-Qadir*, ed. Mamduh Haqqi (Beirut: Dar al-Yaqza al-'Arabiyya li al-Ta'lif wa al-Tarjama wa al-Nashr, 1964). French translation: E. Michaux-Bellaire, "Traduction de la fetoua du fiqîh Sîdi 'Ali et Tsouli contenant le

'souâl' du Hadj Abdelqader ben Mahi ed Din et la réponse," *Archives Marocaines* 11, no. 1 (1907): 116–28; continued in *Archives Marocaines* 11, no. 3 (1907): 395–454.

122. Amira K. Bennison, *Jihad and Its Interpretations in Pre-Colonial Morocco: State-Society Relations during the French Conquest of Algeria* (London: Routledge, 2002). See also Paul L. Heck's discussion of historical context and changing conceptions of jihad, "*Jihad* Revisited," *Journal of Religious Ethics* 32, no. 1 (2004): 95–128.

123. Gregorio Sánchez Doncel, *Presencia de España en Orán, 1509–1792* (Toledo: Estudio Teológico de San Ildefonso, 1991); Mercedes García-Arenal and Miguel Angel de Bunes, *Los españoles y el Norte de Africa, siglos XV–XVIII* (Madrid: MAPFRE, 1992).

124. Maurice d'Irisson, Comte d'Hérrison, *La Chasse à l'homme: Guerres d'Algérie* (Paris: Ollendorff, 1891), 136–65; Julien, *Histoire*, 153; Charles Henry Churchill, *The Life of Abdel Kader, Ex-Sultan of the Arabs of Algeria* (London: Chapman and Hall, 1867), 77.

125. John Kelsay, *Islam and War: A Study in Comparative Ethics* (Louisville, Ky.: Westminster/John Knox, 1993), 57–76; John Kelsay, *Arguing the Just War in Islam* (Cambridge, Mass.: Harvard University Press, 2007), 110–22.

126. Adrien Berbrugger, *Négociations entre Monseigneur l'évêque d'Alger et Abd el Qader pour l'échange des prisonniers* (Paris: Delahaye, 1844).

127. Bruno Etienne, *Abdelkader: Isthme des isthmes (Bazakh al-barazikh)* (Paris: Hachette, 1994), 290–306.

128. Itzchak Weismann, *Taste of Modernity: Sufism, Salafiyya, and Arabism in Late Ottoman Damascus* (Leiden: Brill, 2001), 6. See also David Dean Commins, *Islamic Reform: Politics and Social Change in Late Ottoman Syria* (Oxford: Oxford University Press, 1990), 26–30.

129. The news came back from the Hijaz with Algerian pilgrims who had solicited the shaykh's advice while performing the hajj. Letter of General Bedeau, Mostaganem, November 30, 1841, ANOM, 2 EE 15.

130. Abdelkader Boutaleb, *L'émir Abd-El-Kader et la formation de la nation algérienne: De l'émir Abd-El-Kader à la guerre de libération* (Algiers: Dahlab, 1990); James McDougall convincingly critiques this use of the amir's memory in *History and the Culture of Nationalism in Algeria* (Cambridge, U.K.: Cambridge University Press, 2006).

131. Abdelkader Hani, *Correspondance de l'amir Abdelkader, 1833–1883* (Algiers: Dar el Gharb, 2004); Alexandre Bellemare, *Abd-el-Kader, sa vie politique et militaire* (Paris: Hachette, 1863), 246–62.

132. 'Abd al-Qadir ibn Muhyi al-Din, *Al-Sira al-dhatiyya* (Algiers: Al-Sharika al-Wataniyya li al-Nashr wa al-Tawzi', 1983); partially translated as *L'émir Abdelkader: Autobiographie*, trans. Hacène Benmansour (Paris: Dialogues Éditions, 1995).

133. 'Abd al-Qadir ibn Muhyi al-Din, *Kitab al-mawaqif fi al-tasawwuf wa al-wa'z wa al-irshad*, vol. 1 (Damascus: Dar al-Yaqza al-'Arabiyya li al-Ta'lif wa al-Tarjama wa al-Nashr, 1966–67), 144–46. French translation: 'Abd al-Qâdir al-Djazâ'irî, *Le livre des haltes*, vol. 1, trans. and ed. Michel Lagarde (Leiden: Brill, 2000), 191–94.

134. Ibid., 191.

135. Ibid., 192.

136. Ibid., 193.

137. Dominick LaCapra, *History and Its Limits: Human, Animal, Violence* (Ithaca, N.Y.: Cornell University Press, 2009), 90–122.

138. Tracie Matysik, *Reforming the Moral Subject: Ethics and Sexuality in Central Europe, 1890–1930* (Ithaca, N.Y.: Cornell University Press, 2008), 130–40.

139. Sigmund Freud, "Thoughts for the Times on War and Death," *Standard Edition of the Complete Psychological Works of Sigmund Freud*, vol. 14, trans. and ed. James Strachey (London: Hogarth, 1953–74), 279. See also Anthony Sampson, "Freud on the State, Violence, and War," *Diacritics* 35, no. 3 (2005): 78–91.

140. Schmitt, *The Nomos of the Earth*, 152–71.

141. Sylvie Thénault, *Un drôle de justice: Les magistrates dans la guerre d'Algérie* (Paris: Découverte, 2004).

12

Jihad, *Hijra,* and Hajj in West Africa

DAVID ROBINSON

West Africa, or more specifically the savanna portion that we call western and central Sudan,[1] does not conform very easily to the major themes of this book.[2] In the region, the history of Islam and European imperialism are shallow in several ways—an Islamic presence for one thousand years, certainly, but a sense of belonging to the *dar al-Islam* only in the last two hundred to three hundred years, and then only in selected regions, and we do not yet know very much about how this came about. The emergence of 'Uthman dan Fodio (1754–1817) and the Sokoto caliphate around 1800 certainly had a lot to do with the consolidation of an Islamic identity.

The European presence is much more recent, going back to the late nineteenth century, as France, Britain, and finally Germany competed for interior African territory. Even then, European control was by no means complete, nor was their knowledge very substantial. By and large, the new colonial powers considered themselves to be secular and excluded Christian missionaries from lands that they deemed Muslim or at the very least sharply limited the kinds of activities that missionaries could perform.[3] But the Muslims and the self-consciously Muslim states that West Africans formed in the last three centuries did have to deal with Europeans in an imperial register, a bit later than South Asia and the Middle East, and they employed similar strategies in the face of this threat. They knew little, or believed little, of the distinction touted by the Europeans between Christian and secular or the prohibitions against Christian missionary activity. Their aggressive new opponents were all *al-Nasara* (Christians).

As suggested above, the historiography of Islam and Islamization in West Africa has featured the Sahel, which is to say, the western and central Sudan, and even more, five jihads of the sword that succeeded in establishing and maintaining self-consciously Muslim states in the eighteenth and nineteenth centuries.[4] All five of the jihads were led and constituted to a large degree by Fulbe or Haal-Pulaar (literally, "speakers of Pulaar," one name for the language), communities of pastoralists, farmers, and scholars who had spread across the western and central Sudan over several centuries.[5]

The first two states usually go by the label Almamates (from *al-imam*) and were located in the far western area. Futa Jalon, in the highlands of Guinea Conakry around the watersheds of the Niger, Senegal, and Gambia Rivers, was the first. Futa Toro, the middle valley of the Senegal River, was the second, at the end of the eighteenth century.

The third jihad occurred in Hausaland, which is to say most of today's northern Nigeria and some adjacent areas, in the early nineteenth century. Its leader and initial theologian was 'Uthman dan Fodio, arguably the best-known sub-Saharan African of the precolonial era. 'Uthman's movement resulted in the creation of a new capital at Sokoto and a new federation, commonly called the Sokoto caliphate. The Sokoto caliphate dominated the central Sudan throughout the nineteenth century, from a federal capital (Sokoto) in northwestern Nigeria and state or emiral capitals and city-states, such as Kano, spread across the whole area. It is by far the most extensive, enduring, and well known of the regimes, and the descendants of its ruling classes occupy important positions in Nigeria today. Its response to British imperialism, concentrated in the first decade of the twentieth century, is discussed in the last portion of this chapter.

The fourth of the movements was initially a western extension of the Sokoto phenomenon, but by the 1820s, it had established itself as the independent caliphate of Hamdullahi in the Middle Niger southwest of Timbuktu.

The fifth led to a regime of a different kind. 'Umar Tall, or al-Hajj 'Umar (c. 1797–1864), as he is usually known, hailed from Futa Toro, went on the overland journey to Mecca, and returned with unusual credentials as a pilgrim and "missionary" for the Tijaniyya Sufi order, new to West Africa. After a decade of teaching and writing, he embarked in 1852 on a jihad of the sword to "destroy paganism" in which he used recruits from Futa Toro to wage war not in his home area but in the western portions of today's Mali. The Umarian movement dominated the western Sudan in the early 1860s but was not successful in maintaining its sway. Well before the French conquest of the 1880s and 1890s, it had shrunk to a number of urban centers and settlements in the area of today's Mali. The responses of his descendants and their followers to French penetration is the focus of the first portion of this chapter.

'Umar, the Umarians, and French Imperialism

The Umarian regime, or the "Tokolor empire," as the French were wont to say, takes its name from 'Umar Tall, born into the declining Almamate of Futa Toro at the end of the eighteenth century. He was destined for a role of distinction by his intelligence, study, travel, Sufi affiliation, and ambition. "Tokolor" is the label that the Wolof of Senegal and the French applied to the Haal-Pulaar of Futa Toro. Since these Futanke (residents of Futa Toro) formed the imamate or Almamate in the late eighteenth century, they were deemed to be "fanatical Muslims," distinguished from other Haal-Pulaar, Fulani, and other Muslims in Senegal by the ethnonym "Tokolor."[6] Using "empire" was a useful ploy for the French as they sought to expand their holdings from coastal Senegal to the east in the late nineteenth century.

'Umar, after completing the pilgrimage to Mecca by land and repeating it in three successive years (1828 to 1830), returned to West Africa, visited the existing Islamic states, and settled in the Almamate of Futa Jalon in the 1840s. The journey gave him critical credentials: those of pilgrim, very unusual for West African Muslims in that day, and *muqaddam* (representative) of the Tijaniyya order, the Sufi organization that began in Algeria and Morocco but expanded into other regions and had an important representative in Medina.[7]

On his return, 'Umar spent several years in Sokoto in the 1830s. He fought in some of the recurrent frontier actions (also called jihads) against foes of Sokoto and produced a small Sufi following sharing his allegiance to the Tijaniyya.[8] 'Umar impressed the Uthmanian community with his learning, military prowess, and charisma and was offered the hands of several noblewomen in marriage (including the granddaughter of 'Uthman dan Fodio). One of these women gave birth to Ahmad, 'Umar's main successor in the late nineteenth century, who will be featured later in this chapter. The others gave birth to Ahmad's chief rivals.

The second sojourn of great significance occurred in Masina or the Middle Niger delta. There, 'Umar was the guest of the caliphate of Hamdullahi, a regime established by the fourth of the successful jihads around a capital of the same name. 'Umar's Tijaniyya affiliation and following provoked tension with the caliphal family and also with the Kunta of the Timbuktu area, who saw themselves as the leading commercial and religious authorities in the western and central Sudan and custodians of the Qadiriyya Sufi affiliation. The conflict was portentous for the later history of Masina, the Kunta, and the Umarians.

From his base in Futa Jalon, 'Umar reflected on the role he would play in the western Sudan during a time of considerable ferment and pressure for the extension of Islam. He invested considerable energy in writing and teaching and attracted Muslim students from a wide arc stretching from Freetown, capital of the embryonic British colony of Sierra Leone, to Futa Toro and southern Mauritania. It is tempting to say that he could not resist a more active role, especially after traveling back to Futa Toro in 1847, getting new students and recruits, and establishing a new capital at Dingiray, just east of Futa Jalon. Dingiray was in the not very Muslim state of Tamba, and it was predictable that conflict would ensue between the king and the growing Umarian following. In 1852, the king sought to constrain his new guest community, whereupon 'Umar, after all of the proper consultations and preparations, declared the jihad of the sword.

From 1852 until his death in 1864, 'Umar Tall was consumed by the military effort, to the point of abandoning his more pedagogical role in Islamization and the Tijaniyya. He relied to a considerable degree on those he had recruited and trained in the earlier years. The campaigns took him to the north, into the Upper Senegal valley, and from there he recruited a large following of Haal-Pulaar and others to wage the jihad against non-Muslim regimes. This mission included Mandinka-speaking peoples, such as the ones in Tamba, but focused especially on the Bambara,[9] who had acquired the reputation of being the "arch pagans" of the western Sudan. The traditions paint 'Umar as the "destroyer of paganism," who removed the last obstacles to membership in the *dar al-Islam*.[10]

In the process, 'Umar confronted an early and brief European expansion. The French under Governor Leon Louis Faidherbe (1854–1861, 1863–1865) moved up the Senegal River, into the middle valley (Futa Toro) and beyond. In so doing, Faidherbe's French and African troops confronted 'Umar at the height of recruitment for the Bambara campaigns.[11] The sharpest clash was the unsuccessful siege of the jihadists against the fort of Medine in 1857. It was during this period that 'Umar wrote a letter to the Muslims living in the French base of operations, Saint-Louis, at the mouth of the Senegal River. In general, these Muslims supported or tolerated Faidherbe's efforts, and 'Umar accused them of *muwalat*, "association" with the opponents of Islamization.[12] We will revisit this formulation below.

A brilliant recruiter and military strategist, 'Umar succeeded in attracting tens of thousands of soldiers and families and defeating the two strongest Bambara regimes of the day. In 1855, he entered the capital of one of them, Kaarta, and gave it the name of Nioro, from *al-nur* (light). In 1861, he distinguished himself even more by taking Segu, the capital and state along the Middle Niger. Segu had dominated the region and traded far and wide for almost two hundred years. Its king kept a number of "fetishes" at the palace, and 'Umar soon arranged for a public destruction of the idols to celebrate his victory. Congratulations came in from Muslim leaders, including well-placed Tijaniyya in Morocco. At this point, one might well compare 'Umar's achievement to what 'Uthman dan Fodio had accomplished fifty years before and see 'Umar dominating the western Sudan just as the Uthmanians did the central Sudan. In this scenario, the two complete the consolidation of the *dar al-Islam* of West Africa.[13]

But 'Umar was not finished with his military campaigns. Upon discovering letters of support from the caliph in Hamdullahi and the Kunta leaders for the pagan Segu king, the reformer challenged the authors about their commitment to Islam and the extension of it that 'Umar was undertaking in the western Sudan. He demanded that Hamdullahi turn over the refugee Bambara king and apologize for their errors. When Hamdullahi—with Kunta encouragement—refused, 'Umar declared that they had become apostates (*takfir*), attacked, defeated the Masinanke army, and killed the caliph (1862). One year later, the people of Masina, supported by the Kunta network, revolted, dismantled the Umarian army and regime, and killed 'Umar (1864).[14] Many of the Umarian leaders died in the same revolt, but a nephew, Ahmad al-Tijani, survived and organized a regime on the eastern frontier of the middle delta, at Bandiagara. From there, he conducted a kind of "reconquista" of Masina and by his death in 1887 had succeeded in reestablishing Umarian control over much of the region. I call this phase of the Umarian enterprise (1862–1864) the "destruction of apostasy," as distinguished from the earlier "destruction of paganism" (1852–1861).

This war of Muslim reformer versus Muslim reformer, of Haal-Pulaar versus Haal-Pulaar, was very costly on many levels: to the environment and the agropastoral economy, to the population and the leadership on both sides, and to the cause of Islamization. For some contemporaries, it was a prime example of *fitna*, the discord or civil war that plagued the early Muslims of the Arabian Peninsula and many societies since.[15]

The Hamdullahi campaign and revolt took a huge toll on what we could call the Umarian state and its leadership. Ahmad, the oldest son of 'Umar Tall, remained behind at Segu, which became the capital of the regime. But Ahmad was in his early thirties, inexperienced militarily, politically, and theologically, and he had little support from his surviving brothers. He nonetheless survived for the better part of three decades and presided over the "Tokolor empire," the designation favored by local French officials and their Parisian superiors. I prefer "Umarian regime" and define it as a series of towns and hinterlands dominated by the Umarians, separated from one another by dangerous areas dominated by bandits and indigenous people unsympathetic to the invaders. Most of these areas are in today's Mali.

French Conquest and Umarian Response

All of this prolegomena has been necessary to situate the Umarian regime that the French dismantled in the late 1880s and the 1890s. They defeated the centers of Umarian colonies one by one and took the main capital of Segu in 1890. Ahmad had already left the town to the care of his son Madani and gone to Nioro to deal with another instance of *fitna*, led by his brother Muntaga.[16] He stayed there until 1891, when the French drove him out. He then fled to Bandiagara, the last surviving Umarian center, and took charge of the community there. Two years later, in 1893, the French advanced on Bandiagara, with Ahmad's younger brother Agib in tow as a replacement ruler under the title "king of Macina" (see map 12.1).[17] Ahmad and the Umarian community faced a difficult decision: submission, resistance, or flight. Their experience had shown the futility of resistance against the much better-equipped and -organized enemy. Ahmad, according to the Arabic chronicle we have from this period,[18] wanted to go down fighting, which he deemed the appropriate response of the head of an Islamic community and state.

The core followers persuaded him, however, to lead a *hijra* (migration) to the east, where the European forces had not yet established their control. Not without reason, the Umarian community feared that Ahmad might be captured and executed and possibly even have his body dismembered. This fear persisted as they moved across the western and central Sudan, even to the point where a small core of followers disinterred the body of Ahmad in Hausaland after his death in 1897, on two separate occasions.

Before leaving Bandiagara in 1893, Ahmad wrote letters to the Alawite sultan of Morocco, Mulay Hasan, pleading for his assistance against the Christians who

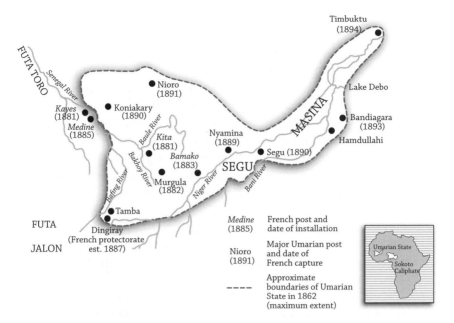

Medine (1885) — French post and date of installation

Nioro (1891) — Major Umarian post and date of French capture

- - - - Approximate boundaries of Umarian State in 1862 (maximum extent)

were invading and desecrating the *dar al-Islam* of the western Sudan. Morocco was a much more widely known Islamic state than the Umarian regime; many contemporaries acknowledged the Sharifian ancestry of its rulers, who traced their lineage back to the Prophet Muhammad, and it had exercised some influence in the Sahara and the western Sudan over the centuries. But it was not an Ottoman empire with effective claims to other territories. While the British paid lip service to Ottoman claims to Egypt and the Nile Sudan, the French gave no credence to Moroccan claims to areas to the south. It was only when the French began their "pacification" of Mauritania in the early twentieth century that the sultan of Morocco mobilized resistance in the region. The French conquests of the western Sudan and Mauritania were preludes to the establishment of their protectorate over Morocco itself in 1912.[19]

The Arabic originals of Ahmad's letters have not been found, nor is there any indication that Sultan Hasan responded or even received them. All I have been able to find is the French translation of the second letter, written on May 30 or 31, 1893, just after the exit from Bandiagara. It is contained in a packet of materials from the archives of the governor-general of Algeria of 1895, and it was presumably sent over from Morocco by French intelligence agents. In this letter, Ahmad summarizes the Umarian relations with the French from the time when he took over (1863–1864) until the deliberations in Bandiagara. The letter concludes as follows:[20]

> And now, O Lieutenant of God on earth, successor to the Prophet for his people, descendant of the chief of the prophets, make haste, make haste! Your friends have been abandoned, your country is ruined and

your subjects are dispersed. Death, captivity and pillage, that is the end which awaits them. The enemy has destroyed mosques, burned Qur'ans, thrown our scientific books into the desert, and has transformed our places of prayer into churches—the church bell has replaced the muezzin [the Muslim prayer caller]. He has kidnapped the daughters of the Shaykh and forced his sons into his service. The children of Muslims have been divided among the chiefs of the army which has taken the whole country (which requires a month to cross).[21]

See then what you must do, because we belong to you, we are yours, we have only you, and it is with you alone that we have relations, because we are descendants of Shaykh al-Tijani, who swore loyalty to your venerable ancestor.[22]

The enemies of your God and the competitors of your ancestors have taken your country. Make them leave and cover them with humiliation, these repugnant people, and make them pay the *jizya*, because they force humiliation [upon us] without a moment's hesitation.

Do not listen to their lying words and do not lend an ear to their false arguments, nor their vain insinuations, because the French are the most perfidious of God's creatures, and the most deceitful and villainous of races.

We have already written numerous letters since this event, and we are still waiting in vain for any response.

It is highly unlikely that Ahmad and the Umarians held out any hope of help from the north, on the other side of the Sahara Desert. The *dar al-Islam* was a reality for the Umarian community and many others in the western Sudan, but it had not been consolidated against its local foes or European-led armies. It is important to note that Ahmad played the Tijaniyya card, which had not been a fundamental part of Islamic practice within his administration. Here, he evokes the close relationship that existed between the Sufi order and the Moroccan court, dating back to the order's founder, Shaykh Ahmad al-Tijani, whose tomb lies in Fez, the intellectual capital of Morocco.

The only option seriously considered by the leadership in Bandiagara was *hijra*, emigration to the east just ahead of the advancing European armies,[23] and this was what they launched in May 1893. The *hijra* document contains no theological formulation but recounts the chronology of movement, west to east, from 1893 to late 1897, when the "commander of the faithful" died near the village of his mother in Hausaland.

Ahmad and his companions survived a range of challenges over those years. Hundreds of his followers deserted back to Bandiagara and the west at different times, where they submitted to French colonial rule. Those who persisted in their eastern journey encountered serious resistance and logistical problems and only occasional support. They communicated with the leaders in Sokoto and received a respectful reception when they entered the territory of the caliphate. After Ahmad's death, the group split into three main sections and settled in different parts of Hausaland.

Uthman, the Uthmanians, and British Imperialism

The Sokoto caliphate, where the second *hijra* was performed ten years later, in 1903, represented a very different situation. 'Uthman dan Fodio, his family, and his close associates were part of the West African Muslim Fulbe community. They carefully crafted their reform movement in the late eighteenth century, moved to a military jihad, and created an embryonic state after 1804. They adopted much of their model from the Prophet Muhammad's life, especially the Medina period (622–632 C.E.), and developed a considerable apologetics about their actions and legitimacy. Former students and associates of 'Uthman carried out successful jihads in most areas of Hausaland and beyond, usually in their areas of origin. They maintained allegiance to Sokoto in a federal arrangement throughout the nineteenth century. Thus, when the British approached the Sokoto domain in the early twentieth century, from bases in what was becoming southern Nigeria, they encountered a relatively cohesive society and state with a common founding memory and a strong sense of belonging to the *dar al-Islam*. The caliph enjoyed considerable prestige. If he led a *hijra* to the east, he might be followed by hundreds of thousands of Muslims, if not more, posing considerable logistical problems— both for themselves and for their European opponents. In all of these ways, Sokoto contrasted with the Umarian situation.

'Uthman dan Fodio was born in the mid-eighteenth century to a distinguished family of Fulbe scholars who had lived in Hausaland for several generations.[24] He traveled to various teachers for his education but never seriously entertained the idea of the pilgrimage. This stemmed in part from his affiliation to the Qadiriyya order, the one dominated by the Kunta in West Africa; it placed little premium on fulfilling the obligation from this extremity of the *dar al-Islam*. 'Uthman began his teaching, preaching, and writing career in his twenties, in the 1770s, mainly in and around Gobir, one of the Hausa city-states governed by a sultan who considered himself Muslim and made some pretense to governing a Muslim society.

'Uthman seems initially to have envisioned a career of teaching and reform, without resort to military action. He placed considerable emphasis on influencing the Gobir court to rule more in accordance with Islam. But over the years, his preaching attracted a growing and increasingly militant community, which, in turn, radicalized his approach to reform. The Hausa court took increasing exception to the growing community on the borders of its territory. In 1804, they attacked an Uthmanian group, enslaved some of its members, and brought on the confrontation that had been brewing for some time. In rapid succession, the community emigrated (they called it *hijra*, of course) to a nearby hamlet, declared themselves an Islamic state, with 'Uthman as the commander of the faithful, and started the jihad of the sword. In 1808, they succeeded in decisively defeating the Gobir army, and in the following year, they created a new and "pure" capital at Sokoto. Meanwhile, students and companions of 'Uthman, sporting his flags of authorization, carried out largely successful efforts at overthrowing the other Hausa regimes across most of today's northern Nigeria. By 'Uthman's death in 1817, a structure of federal and state regimes was in place through most of Hausaland and beyond.[25]

'Uthman's successors reigned over this vast area with considerable success and stability throughout the nineteenth century. The caliphs came from the male descendants of 'Uthman,[26] and they were in place as the British advanced from the south in the 1890s. A *wazir* handled much of the administrative load, both in Sokoto and in relations between Sokoto and the states. These states or emirates, governed by descendants of the flag bearers and students whom 'Uthman sent out in the early nineteenth century, had complex bureaucracies and *wazirs* of their own. Each year, they sent tribute to Sokoto along with levies for an annual jihad, waged primarily against the various *anciens régimes* that had taken refuge in the north, in what became French Niger. The Uthmanian regime obviously had a very different profile from that of the "Tokolor empire." It was more deeply entrenched and posed a much more serious challenge to European conquest and rule.

British Conquest and Uthmanian Response

It was in Sokoto in the late nineteenth century that Caliph 'Abd al-Rahman, his *wazir*, and his court confronted the issues posed by the advance of the British forces and their obvious superiority in armament and organization (see map 12.2). They were certainly knowledgeable about Ahmad's *hijra* from French rule and may well have consulted with the surviving Umarian leaders now living in their midst, but there is no evidence of significant influence.[27] But the court in Sokoto did have, on a larger scale, the same dilemma that had confronted the Muslims at Bandiagara in 1893: submission, resistance, or emigration. They had observed the British advance from south to north for almost ten years and the inability of any indigenous armies to stand up to European firepower and organization. They were also concerned about the French advance, from west to east, moves that soon yielded the territory of Niger.[28]

The caliph had corresponded with Frederick Lugard, the newly appointed British high commissioner of northern Nigeria, for several years.[29] In 1900, Lugard, in the name of Queen Victoria, declared British sovereignty over the area of northern Nigeria, roughly corresponding to Hausaland and the Sokoto caliphate. He realized that it would be impossible to consolidate control without taking over the federal capital, since the emirs continued to show considerable loyalty to the caliph. By the end of 1902, Lugard, his West African Frontier Force, and other

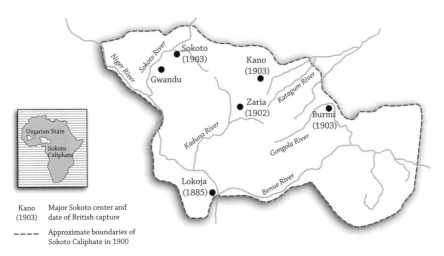

Kano   Major Sokoto center and
(1903)   date of British capture

– – – –   Approximate boundaries of
Sokoto Caliphate in 1900

military units were ready to make their final move. They took Kano, the largest city and emirate of the north, in February 1903. They then moved against Sokoto in March. On the fifteenth of that month, British forces won a decisive battle against the local forces, led by Muhammad Attahiru, usually called Attahiru I, who had succeeded to leadership in late 1902 upon the death of 'Abd al-Rahman. At that point, Attahiru I embarked on a *hijra* to the east, on the basis of an infidel conquest of the *dar al-Islam* and the hope of getting to areas where Muslims might continue to control affairs—whether in the eastern ranges of Nigeria, the Nile Sudan,[30] or the Holy Cities. His retinue, consisting of some of the Sokoto leadership, expanded exponentially as he moved across Hausaland in March, April, and May—precisely the height of the dry season, when resources were scarce.

A few days after the key battle, Lugard moved into Sokoto, appointed a cousin from the caliphal family (Attahiru II) as the new emir of Sokoto,[31] and reaffirmed earlier promises to respect the practice of Islam. A number of people, including some former members of the court, came back to the town in the days after the battle and submitted to the new colonial order. Fatigue, the difficulty of finding food and water, and the problems of organizing an increasingly large exodus during the dry season, along with assurances about religious practice, played a role in their submission. One key returnee was the highly respected *wazir* Bukhari. He consulted scholars and soon issued a *risala*, or treatise, that provided a rationale for accepting non-Muslim rule as long as the practice of Islam was preserved.[32]

Bukhari intended his document for wide dissemination. He put particular emphasis on his consultation with a well-respected local cleric named Ahmad ibn Sa'd and quoted him extensively in his document. Bukhari and Ahmad examined the obligations of Muslims toward infidel rulers and the conditions under which submission was legitimate. They examined *muwalat*, association or friendship, the same term that 'Umar Tall had used in his earlier letter to the Muslim companions of the French but with a very different interpretation.[33] They also emphasized preserving the Islamic character of the region; massive emigration would remove the area from the *dar al-Islam* and undo the achievements set in motion by 'Uthman dan Fodio.[34] I suspect that the document had little immediate impact until the British forces finally succeeded in stemming the movement of emigration of Attahiru I in July 1903. From that point on, the *Risala* may have become an important justification for submission to colonial rule.

What follows are some key extracts from the *Risala*:

> I [Bukhari] wrote [this treatise] that they [everyone among the people of knowledge and reflection] may know that I did not act in the affair with the Christians . . . in pursuance of selfish passions but that I acted on the guidance of our learned men. Thus when we stopped at Marnona [not far outside of Sokoto] the people gathered around me to take counsel together. They consulted among themselves but they saw no way of making a *hijra* from this land owing to the scarcity of water along the roads or the total lack of it . . . as well as the severity of the heat and the presence of the Christians camped along all the routes. . . . They [the learned men] read to me the book of our Shaikh and our Imam, Uthman b Fudi, . . . where he [wrote][35] about befriending the unbelievers. . . . The first category of friendship is that which is unbelief according to consensus and that is having relations with unbelievers, befriending and loving them because they are unbelievers and because of hatred for the religion of Islam. . . . The second category of friendship is that which is disobedience and not unbelief according to consensus. It is having relations with unbelievers as a means of acquiring the wealth in their hands. . . . The third category of friendship is that which is permissible by consensus. It is having relations with unbelievers and befriending them, out of fear of them, with the tongue but not with the heart.

Bukhari then makes some citations from the fifteenth-century Egyptian jurist al-Suyuti. He mentions his own letter to Lugard to determine British attitudes toward Islam and Muslims. He says that he received assurances that the British would respect the practice of Islam, in the form of the five pillars of the faith, and then quotes extensively from Ahmad ibn Sa'd. Ahmad begins his response to Bukhari by citing the destruction of Baghdad in 1258 C.E. by the Mongols and the Qarmatian sack of Mecca in 930 C.E. He goes on to say:

> This deed of yours [to submit] is definitely the right thing, and God knows best, because this our land is a land of Islam and if we emigrate from it, it becomes a land of unbelief. . . . It is incumbent on the individual to emigrate from a place where unbelievers prevent him from the practice of the five foundations of Islam or turn him into a slave. However, those [Christians] do not impede religion and the rites of Islam

established in our land. Their goal is seeking territory and overlordship in worldly matters. As regards Islam, they do not hinder any one from it from Futa[36] to here. Thus the best thing for you is to negotiate a truce with them and to seek settlement with them since negotiation is permissible to the Imam and his deputy when Muslims are too weak to fight.

Bukhari ends his letter expressing relief at Ahmad's confirmation of his own interpretation of what Muslims should do.

Scarcely had Lugard dispatched self-congratulatory messages to London about his victories over Kano and Sokoto than he recognized the menace posed by the growing following of Attahiru I for the new colonial regime. Thousands of people joined the procession, while others who ostensibly had accepted European control sent supplies of food and clothing. Attahiru headed for the region of Burmi, where a lot of Mahdist sentiment had been expressed in the late nineteenth century. A British column was driven back in May 1903, and only in July did reinforcements finally conquer and destroy Burmi, kill the caliph and most of his closest supporters, and effectively end active resistance to conquest. In this Burmi phase, the *hijra* of Attahiru had clearly turned into a defensive jihad of what remained of the *dar al-Islam*.[37]

A number of Umarians joined in the emigration, usually with their Fulbe patrons. Some were killed, some submitted to British rule, and a few continued their flight to the east. Bashir, the son of 'Umar Tall appointed as Ahmad's successor by the remnant community, was captured, whereupon he submitted to the colonial regime. The most famous Umarian of this period was Alfa Hashim, the probable author of the *Hijra Ahmad b. Shehu* and grand-nephew of 'Umar. Hashim crossed the Sudan and settled in Medina in 1904. The French and the British were concerned about his attitudes and influence among West African pilgrims, but by World War I, they were reassured that he accepted European colonial rule.[38]

Conclusion

What can one extract from these accounts? The jihad to defend the *dar al-Islam* was the first impulse of Umarians and Uthmanians. Both groups were committed to defending the *dar al-Islam*, only a few generations deep in West Africa, and both deemed that the Fulbe or Haal-Pulaar had played the critical role in the extension of Islam. Their efforts to fight failed in a range of costly defeats against the French and the British. Submission was the course adopted, as elsewhere, by the overwhelming majority of subjects—out of necessity. It can be equated with *taqiyya* (dissembling) or, in some more recent literature, with the idea of "creating Muslim space" within the colonial setting. This is the idea of Murray Last in his article on the "colonial caliphate" of northern Nigeria.[39] Wazir Bukhari's *Risala* was an important effort to create a Muslim rationale for this action around the *muwalat* of necessity.

The emigration option remained theologically attractive for the heads of state and elites that surrounded them, but it posed significant problems for the Umarians after 1893 and overwhelming ones for the much larger group of Uthmanians in 1903. The possibility of losing the Islamic character of the western and central Sudan, especially in the northern Nigeria case, weighed heavily in the thinking of theologians and subjects. Massive departures were not only potentially suicidal, but they might also undo the work of 'Uthman dan Fodio and his contemporaries in creating the *dar al-Islam*.

But some Muslims were determined to continue the *hijra* after Burmi, albeit with much smaller numbers, more comparable to those of the Umarians who moved out of Bandiagara. Here, the idea of *hijra* began to meld with the obligation of hajj, as shown most clearly in the trajectory of Alfa Hashim Tall, who established himself in Medina after 1904 and became a kind of host and counselor to West African pilgrims (*takruri*). Most of the *muhajirun* (emigrants) settled in the Nile region, in places such as Mai Wurno, where they worked out their own terms of accommodation with the British in the Sudan. The overwhelming majority of Muslims stayed behind and submitted to colonial rule, but they accorded considerable prestige to emigrants and pilgrims who sustained their "resistance" by continuing on to the east.[40]

Notes

1. Extending roughly from Lake Chad in the east to the Atlantic Ocean in the west and from the Sahara down to the woodlands.
2. Nor is the historiography of real interest to historians of Islam and the Middle East. A recent case in point is Michael Bonner's *Jihad in Islamic History* (Princeton, N.J.: Princeton University Press, 2006), a fine work but one that gives slight and distorted mention to 'Uthman dan Fodio and even slighter to al-Hajj 'Umar, the two main founders of regimes treated in this chapter. Bonner uses a very old bibliography.
3. Evangelical and Pentecostal missionaries have come in, but mostly since the mid-twentieth century and the independence of the former colonial territories. Predictably, they have come into conflict with established Muslim interests but more particularly with the radical Muslim groups that emerged in the same period, best exemplified by the Yan Izala and most recently by the Boko Haram in Nigeria , and the so-called Wahhabis of francophone West Africa (especially Mali and Guinea). See Barbara Cooper, *Evangelical Christians in the Muslim Sahel* (Bloomington: Indiana University Press, 2006); and Louis Brenner, *Controlling Knowledge: Religion, Power and Schooling in a West African Muslim Society* (Bloomington: Indiana University Press, 2001).
4. The main author of the "vulgate" of Islam and Islamization in Africa, with a special emphasis on West Africa and its jihads, was John Spencer Trimingham, who came out of a British missionary background. Oxford University Press published his *Islam in West Africa* (1959) and *A History of Islam in West Africa* (1962), in addition to his works on Islam in the Sudan and Ethiopia. The French equivalents of this work were Alphonse Gouilly, *L'Islam dans l'Afrique occidentale française* (Paris: Larose, 1952), and J. C. Froelich, *Les musulmans d'Afrique noire* (Paris: Éditions de l'Orante, 1962). For a recent revision of this historiography, see my article, David Robinson, "The *Jihads* of the Western Sudan," in Nehemia Levtzion and Randal Pouwels, eds., *The History of Islam in Africa* (Athens: Ohio University Press, 2000), 131–52.

The traditional version also ascribes the main Islamization of the western and central Sudan to the precolonial phase or pre-1900 period, whereas we now know that, with the exception of northern Nigeria or Hausaland, the creation of the majority of Muslim societies came during the colonial period or twentieth century.

5. "Pulo," plural "Fulbe," is the name that the people give themselves. An alternative, especially in the western Sudan, is "Haal-Pulaar," speakers of Pulaar. The Hausa term for the Fulbe is "Fulani," while the Bornu term is "Fellata."

6. *Toucouleur* in French, undoubtedly derived from Takrur, the name given to a Muslim city and state in the eleventh century situated somewhere in or near the Senegal River valley. *Takruri* became the name for West African pilgrims in the Holy Lands. See Umar al-Naqar, *The Pilgrimage Tradition in West Africa* (Khartoum: Khartoum University Press, 1972).

7. Some Umarian sources claim that he was appointed *khalifa* (caliph) for the Tijaniyya in the western Sudan, but this is not a very strong tradition in West Africa. The claim did strengthen 'Umar's prestige in West Africa for his followers and probably suggested a political in addition to a Sufi role. For 'Umar's pilgrimage and his jihad, see David Robinson, *The Holy War of Umar Tal* (Oxford: Oxford University Press, 1985), chap. 3. My book remains the major study of 'Umar and his movement.

8. Some Umarian traditions claim that he "converted" caliph Bello ('Uthman's son and successor) to the order as the caliph lay dying and that Bello even appointed him as his successor, in preference to members of Bello's own family. There is little confirmation of this. Discussed in Robinson, *The Holy War*, 102–8; and John Paden, *Religion and Political Culture in Kano* (Berkeley: University of California Press, 1973), 76–79. For the Sokoto caliphate in the nineteenth century, the principal work is still Remi Adeleye, *Power and Diplomacy in Northern Nigeria, 1804–1906: The Sokoto Caliphate and Its Enemies* (London: Longman, 1971).

9. See the fictionalized account in Maryse Condé, *Segou: A Novel* (New York: Viking, 1987, translated from the French original of 1984).

10. One of the best examples is the *'ajami* text (in this case, a Pulaar *qasida* or poem written in Arabic characters and approximating twelve hundred verses) of Mohammadou Aliou Tyam, *La vie d'El Hadj Omar, Qaçida en Poular*, transcrib., trans., and ed. Henri Gaden (Paris: Institut d'Ethnologie, 1935).

11. See Robinson, *The Holy War*, chap. 5. The image of resistance to French expansion has been magnified in the historical memory, especially by Umarians and Senegalese Muslims in general. In the process, they have obscured the main mission of their hero. See David Robinson, "D'empire en empire: L'empire toucouleur dans la stratégie et mémoire impériales françaises," presented at the colloquium "Mémoires d'empires," at the Ecole des Hautes Etudes en Sciences Sociales, Centre d'Histoire Sociale de l'Islam Méditerranéen in Paris in May 2000, to be published in a festschrift in honor of Jean Boulègue in 2012.

12. See Robinson, *The Holy War*, chap. 4. See John Hanson and David Robinson, *After the Jihad: The Reign of Ahmad al-Kabir in the Western Sudan* (East Lansing: Michigan State University Press, 1993), 108–11, 328, for translations and a photocopy of the Arabic letter, which was actually written in 1855 to the Muslims of the French colonial center of Saint-Louis. I have not put this in the text, since 'Umar and the Umarians were working from a position of strength at the time and demanding that the French pay *jizya* in recognition of their subjection to an Islamic authority. One passage, however, is worth quoting here in relation to arguments later in the chapter: "Sons of Ndar, God forbids you to be in relations of friendship [*muwalat*] with them. He made it clear that whoever becomes their friend becomes an infidel, and one of them, through His saying: 'Take not the Jews and Christians for friends. They are friends of each other. And whoever amongst you takes them for friends, he is indeed one of them'" (Qur'an 5:51). Umarians and Senegalese Muslims in general have magnified these episodes and made them into a tradition of resistance to European invasion and rule. See the conference and publication held on the occasion of the bicentennial of 'Umar's birth, *Bicentenaire de la naissance du Cheikh El Hadj Oumar al-Futa Tall, 1797–1998* (Rabat: Publications de l'Institut des Etudes Africaines, 2001).

13. In Robinson, *The Holy War*, chap. 9, I suggest that this analogy is superficial and that 'Umar had in no sense prepared his areas of conquest for a process of Islamization and incorporation into an Islamic state. I use the expression "imperial" jihad to contrast 'Umar's work with the "revolutionary" and primarily internal, reform-minded jihad of 'Uthman (and indeed also those that emerged in Futa Jalon, Futa Toro, and Masina).

14. For the document that 'Umar prepared on the sins and apostasy of Masina and the Kunta, see Sidi Mohamed Mahibou and Jean-Louis Triaud, eds., *Voilà ce qui est arrivé: Bayan ma waqa'a d'al-Hagg 'Umar al-Futi* (Paris: Editions du CNRS, 1983). For the Masina campaigns, see Robinson, *The Holy War*, chap. 8. Many Umarians claim to this day that 'Umar disappeared in 1864, with the unspoken implication of availability to return or at least inspire his successors and followers.

15. A pronounced criticism of 'Umar's efforts came from Muhammad al-Fadhil and the Fadhiliyya Qadiriyya tradition. See Dedoud ould Abdallah, "Guerre sainte ou sedition blâmable: *Nasiha* de Shaykh Sa'd Buh contre le *jihad* de son frère Shaykh Ma' al-'Aynayn," in David Robinson and Jean-Louis Triaud, eds., *Le Temps des Marabouts* (Paris: Editions Karthala, 1997), 119–53. Fadhiliyya traditions contain a number of references to encounters with 'Umar, set in the late 1850s and early 1860s, when he controlled Karta and was moving against Segu and Masina. In one tradition, 'Umar offered a command post to Sidi Buya (also called Sidi 'Uthman), one of Muhammad al-Fadhil's sons. Sidi refused or refused after a brief participation. See Amar Samb, trans. and ed., "La condamnation de la guerre sainte de Cheikh Moussa Kamara," *Bulletin de l'IFAN* B (1976): 174. In another, 'Umar sought to impose tribute payments on the Fadhiliyya, who promptly migrated farther west. See J. Gros, ed., *Soleillet en Afrique* (Paris: A Picard et Kaan, 1888), 131.

16. Ahmad's first struggle came in the 1870s, against his brothers Habib and Moktar, sons of the daughter of Muhammad Bello of Sokoto. The confrontation with Muntaga occurred in 1885. For the struggles of Ahmad and his brothers, see John Hanson, *Migration, Jihad and Muslim Authority in West Africa* (Bloomington: Indiana University Press, 1996); and Hanson and Robinson, *After the Jihad*. These bitter struggles among the brothers are a source of great embarrassment for the custodians of the Umarian heritage.

17. See David Robinson, "Between Hashimi and Agibu," in David Robinson and Jean-Louis Triaud, eds., *La Tijaniyya: Une confrérie musulmane à la conquête de l'Afrique* (Paris: Editions Karthala, 2000), 101–24.

18. *Hijra Ahmad b. Shaikh* ['Umar]. An Arabic version and an English translation appear in Hanson and Robinson, *After the Jihad*, 251, 400. The author, according to the Umarian traditions, was Alfa Hashim ibn Ahmad al-Tijani, the son of 'Umar's nephew who effected the "reconquista" of the Masina area from his base in Bandiagara. Hashim settled in the Missau area of Hausaland with the largest surviving Umarian group, after the death of Ahmad al-Kabir at the end of 1897. He and many of his relatives joined in the *hijra* of the Sokoto caliph in 1903, the second event sequence of this chapter (see below). He survived the struggles with the British in that year and emigrated to the east; he apparently arrived in Medina in 1904. For an analysis of the emigration, along with an English translation of *Hijra Ahmad b. Shaikh*, see David Robinson, "The Umarian Emigration of the Late 19th Century," *International Journal of African Historical Sources* 20, no. 2 (1987): 245–70.

19. See David Robinson, *Paths of Accommodation: Muslim Societies and French Colonial Rule in Senegal and Mauritania, 1880–1920* (Athens: Ohio University Press, 2000), especially chaps. 3 and 4 on the conquest of Mauritania and the Moroccan connection.

20. Contained in the archives of the Gouverneur Générale, Algerie, 22 H 36. The passage here is taken from Hanson and Robinson, *After the Jihad*, 247–48. I have translated from the French. No Arabic original has been found.

21. All of what Ahmad cites is true except for the transformation of mosques into churches. This phrase may have come from the memory of Muslims subjected to Christian rule in other situations.

22. A reference to al-Tijani's move to Fez, Morocco, in the late eighteenth century and his allegiance to the sultan. It is interesting that Ahmad cites this as the basis of a claim of Moroccan

intervention rather than any of the forays of Morocco, from the fifteenth century on, into the Sahara and the western Sudan, including the well-known expedition of 1591, which destroyed the army and empire of Songhay.

23. Colonel Louis Archinard, the Commandant Supérieur for the campaign, put Ahmad's younger brother Agib on the throne of Bandiagara in a thinly veiled attempt at indirect rule. For a French account based on archives and memoirs, especially those of Archinard, see Jacques Méniaud, *Les pionniers du Soudan*, 2 vols. (Paris: Société des Publications Modernes, 1931).

24. The best account of 'Uthman and the founding of the regime is Murray Denis Last, *The Sokoto Caliphate* (London: Longman, 1967). Last gives a full treatment of the apologetics that 'Uthman, his brother 'Abdullah, his son Muhammad Bello, and other leaders created around their movement. A valuable biography of 'Uthman is Mervyn Hiskett, *The Sword of Truth* (Oxford: Oxford University Press, 1973).

25. Indeed, the founder of the caliphate of Hamdullahi began to correspond with 'Uthman before his death and thought of himself initially to be creating a western extension of the Sokoto regime. See David Robinson, "Breaking New Ground in 'Pagan' and 'Muslim' West Africa," *Canadian Journal of African Studies* 2–3 (2008): 300–313.

26. There was a period of disputation in 1817–1821 between 'Abdullah, the younger brother of 'Uthman, and Muhammad Bello, his oldest son. This was resolved in favor of the son, who reigned from Sokoto and had special jurisdiction over the eastern zones of the caliphate. 'Abdullah and his descendants held forth at nearby Gwandu and had responsibility for the less extensive western zones. On the dispute and its resolution, see C. C. Stewart, "Frontier Disputes and Problems of Legitimation: Sokoto-Masina Relations, 1817–1837," *Journal of African History* 19, no. 4 (1976): 497–514. Sokoto remained the caliphal capital, and the descendants of 'Uthman constituted its leadership, assisted by *wazirs* whose roles often passed down also from father to son. For the nineteenth-century history of the Sokoto caliphate, including the British conquest in the early twentieth century, see Adeleye, *Power and Diplomacy*, in addition to Last, *The Sokoto Caliphate*. For the social and economic dimensions of the caliphate in the nineteenth century and the considerable expansion of slavery, see Paul Lovejoy, *Transformations in Slavery* (Cambridge, U.K.: Cambridge University Press, 1983). For a full treatment of Muslim responses to British colonial rule, see Muhammad Sani Umar, *Islam and Colonialism: Intellectual Responses of Muslims of Northern Nigeria to British Colonial Rule* (Leiden: Brill, 2006).

27. Last, *The Sokoto Caliphate*, 139.

28. Called by a number of other names before the French settled on Niger, which occupies the northern fringe of Hausaland and a considerable portion of the Sahara. For the conquest, in addition to Adeleye, *Power and Diplomacy*, see D. J. M. Muffett, *Concerning Brave Captains* (London: A. Deutsch, 1964).

29. Frederick Lugard (1858–1945) was born in Madras, India, to a British army chaplain. He served in several military campaigns in Asia before participating in British expansion in areas of eastern and southern Africa in the late 1880s. In 1897, he was called to West Africa to organize the West African Frontier Force (WAFF), an African and largely Hausa unit that played a decisive role in creating British dominions in the Gold Coast and Nigeria. From 1900 to 1906, he was high commissioner for the protectorate of northern Nigeria. He returned in 1912 as governor-general of Nigeria to preside over the amalgamation of the northern and southern regions. From 1922 to 1936, he was the British representative on the Permanent Mandates Commission of the League of Nations. He was married to the prominent writer Flora Louise Shaw. Lugard published *Dual Mandate in British Tropical Africa* (London: W. Blackwood, 1923), in which he laid out his understanding of indirect rule, on the basis of his background in India, his vast experience in Asia and Africa, and his recent work in northern Nigeria. Not surprisingly, he saw the Muslim Fulbe as a superior group of people who should be kept in place under the supervision of British residents. Administrators often sought to apply his understanding in other parts of British Africa during the interwar period. For biographical details on Lugard, including his understanding of Islam and the Fulbe, see Margery Perham, *Lugard* (New York: Archon, 1968).

30. The Sokoto leaders were aware of the British conquest of the Nile Sudan and the Anglo-Egyptian Condominium that was in place but apparently saw that area as a more fluid and attractive situation than the one they faced in Nigeria. The dominant position of the Arabic language and the proximity to the Holy Lands were other factors.

31. The position of caliph was abolished. Lugard and the colonial authorities regarded the Sokoto leader as an emir, first among equals.

32. A translation and commentary on this document can be found in Remi Adeleye, "The Dilemma of the Wazir: The Place of the *Risalat al-Wazir ila ahl al-'ilm wa'l-tadabbur* in the History of the Conquest of the Sokoto Caliphate," *Journal of the Historical Society of Nigeria* 4, no. 2 (1968): 285–311. Adeleye does not give a date for this document, but we can assume that it was probably written in April 1903.

33. In some respects, the acceptable form of *muwalat* resembles *taqiyya* (dissembling).

34. This was the opposite argument to flight from infidel control and reflected the enormous logistical problems associated with migration, problems that were not involved in the much smaller Umarian movement of 1893. Murray Last reflects on the question of keeping the Islamic character and status of Hausaland under British rule in "The 'Colonial Caliphate' of Northern Nigeria," in Robinson and Triaud, *Le Temps des Marabouts*, 67–82.

35. From *Masa'il muhimma*, written in 1803 just before the jihad and creation of the Sokoto state. 'Uthman also wrote about these issues in *Bayan wujub al-hijra 'alaal-'ibad*, ed. E. H. el-Masri (Khartoum: Khartoum University Press, 1972).

36. Presumably, a reference to Futa Toro, the area from which 'Uthman's ancestors reputedly came, well before the birth of 'Umar. Ahmad ibn Sa'd then would be referring to the whole western and central Sudan (and the Fulbe Muslim leadership), which the French and the British were conquering at the time.

37. Adeleye, *Power and Diplomacy*, chap. 6, treats the emigration and battles of Burmi as a valiant effort at resistance to infidel rule. The British, in their determination to stem the hemorrhage of emigration, were undoubtedly influenced by the difficulties of repopulating and creating a viable system of law and order in the Anglo-Egyptian Sudan after their conquest in 1898. For relations with the Nile Sudan and British and French anxieties, see C. J. F. Tomlinson and G. J. Lethem, *History of Islamic Political Propaganda* (London: Waterlow, 1927).

38. Robinson, "The Umarian Emigration," 260–64.

39. See note 34 above. Cheikh Anta Babou used the formulation of "Muslim space" to describe the thinking of Amadu Bamba as he accommodated to the French regime of Senegal. See Cheikh Anta Babou, *Fighting the Greater Jihad: Amadu Bamba and the Founding of the Muridiyya* (Athens: Ohio University Press, 2007).

40. For an example of Muslim attitudes in the early colonial period, see the encounter in the Holy Lands between Alfa Hashim and an important Umarian cleric of the early twentieth century who had become a *qadi* under French rule in Mauritania. Ibrahima-Abou Sall, "Cerno Amadu Mokhtar Sakho, *Qadi* Supérieur de Boghe (1905–34)," in Robinson and Triaud, *Le Temps des Marabouts*, esp. 238–39.

13

Jihads and Crusades in Sudan from 1881 to the Present

HEATHER J. SHARKEY

The first jihad of modern Sudanese history began in 1881, when a northern Sudanese Muslim scholar named Muhammad Ahmad (1844–1885) declared himself to
be al-Mahdi—"the Rightly Guided One"—who would restore justice in an age of
chaos before the Day of Judgment. Muhammad Ahmad, the Mahdi, then declared
jihad against the Turco-Egyptian regime that had been ruling the region since
Muhammad ʻAli, the Ottoman governor of Egypt, had ordered a conquest in
1820.[1] Tapping into popular Muslim millenarian beliefs and into widespread
grievances against this regime, the Mahdi amassed followers, who defeated Turco-
Egyptian forces in a series of battles. The regime collapsed in 1885, when Mahdist
armies overtook the colonial capital, Khartoum, and killed Charles Gordon, the
British military careerist and devout Christian whom authorities had appointed
as governor-general. Gordon's death, in turn, galvanized evangelical Christians in
Britain and helped to fuel a burgeoning movement among Protestant missionaries who were adopting the militant rhetoric of the British government in its age
of "New Imperialism."[2] Some of these missionaries indeed described their evange-
lism as a modern crusade.[3]

The Mahdi died from a sudden illness shortly after the fall of Khartoum in 1885,
so the task of organizing the Mahdist state fell to his successor, known as al-Khalifa
Abdullahi (r. 1885–1898) or simply the Khalifa.[4] Meanwhile, British authorities
eyed Sudan from the distance of Egypt, which Britain had occupied in 1882.
Drawing on British popular support for retaliation against the Mahdists and
responding to the "Scramble for Africa," Britain launched a "Reconquest" of Sudan
in 1898 while using new technologies such as railways and Maxim guns to crush
Mahdist armies. After contriving a government known as the Anglo-Egyptian Condominium (which reflected an ostensible partnership with Egypt), Britain went on
to rule Sudan until 1956. Throughout the Anglo-Egyptian period, British fears of

Muslim "fanaticism" influenced colonial policies toward education, administration, and public health, while arguably also shaping assumptions about Islam among members of the Christian (Protestant and Catholic) missions that streamed into the country on the heels of the colonial conquest.

At decolonization in the mid-1950s, Britain passed control of Sudan—by then consisting of a territory far larger and more culturally diverse than anything the Turco-Egyptians or Mahdists had ruled—to a small group of highly educated and socially elite Muslim Arabic-speaking nationalists, many of whom were sons and grandsons of the Mahdi's supporters. In 1955 (just months before formal independence), concerns about the transfer of power set off a conflict that many historians retrospectively called the "first civil war" (1955–1972), in relation to what became known as the "second civil war" (1983–c. 2005). Meanwhile, in 1958, following a brief period of parliamentary rule in which factions followed Muslim sectarian lines, a military junta seized power in a coup d'état. Military-backed regimes went on to rule Sudan for most of the half-century that followed. At the same time, postcolonial conflicts variously simmered and boiled, with "rebels" in Sudan's southern, western, and eastern peripheries resisting the policies of the Khartoum regimes. So complex, long-running, and geographically diffuse were Sudan's civil conflicts that one historian later argued convincingly for a plurality of Sudanese "civil wars."[5]

Sudan's civil conflicts have been complex and multifaceted. Yet in the postcolonial period, foreign media often portrayed them simplistically, as a single war between a Muslim Arab North and a Christian African South. This portrayal was misleading insofar as it emphasized a kind of religious and ethnic or racial antipathy while minimizing the battles over power and resources that lay at the root of the conflict. Meanwhile, jihadist rhetoric periodically surfaced amid the fighting. Successive regimes in Khartoum, though most notably the ideologically Islamist regime of 'Umar al-Bashir (r. 1989–present), invoked jihadist discourses to justify central-government attacks on dissidents in the country's peripheries.

If one thing stands out from this history, it is that jihads and crusades have been self-constitutive acts.[6] They have been more about affirming or defining the self than about striking at enemies. They have entailed assertions of power and sometimes calls for change, both between and within religious communities. Neither Muslims and Christians within Sudan nor observers outside the country appear to have appreciated fully these aspects of the "holy" wars of modern Sudan.

Jihad, Anti-Christian Sentiment, and the Mahdist Revolution

Contrary to the insinuations of late-Victorian-era British writers, the anti-Christian dimension of the Mahdist jihad was minimal. When Na'um Shuqayr, a Syro-Lebanese official in the Intelligence Department of the Anglo-Egyptian regime, published

Jughrafiyya wa tarikh al-Sudan (an Arabic survey of Sudanese history, culture, and geography) in 1903, he listed the factors that had inspired the Mahdist movement and its call to arms. Above all, Sudanese Muslims resented the Turco-Egyptian regime's oppressive and mounting taxation, its efforts to restrict the slave trade (which Sudanese Muslims regarded as part of the Islamic social order and on which many relied for agricultural labor), its crushing of early dissidents, and its favoritism toward particular groups.[7] Economic distress among small-scale farmers and traders, along with dislocations caused by government monopoly systems and the introduction of cash currencies, also contributed to dissatisfaction.[8] Still others objected to what they perceived as the irreligiosity and debauchery of Turco-Egyptian (Muslim) administrators. For example, one writer claimed in 1901, twenty years after the start of the Mahdist revolution, that "Muhammad Ahmad [al-Mahdi] was among the group of religious notables in al-Obeid who were outraged by a marriage ceremony between a man and a young boy, but when they protested to the local Egyptian official they received insulting treatment."[9]

It made matters worse, in the eyes of Sudanese Muslims, that in the 1870s, the Turco-Egyptian administration had begun appointing European Christian (and Jewish)[10] officers to positions of importance.[11] This policy marked a sharp departure from conventions of Islamic statecraft, which had barred Christians and Jews from bearing arms in Muslim societies.[12] The Turco-Egyptians appointed men such as the Briton Charles Gordon, first as governor of Equatoria province and later as governor-general of the whole territory.[13] In Equatoria alone, Gordon's staff included "two Americans, an Italian, a Frenchman, and three (later five) Englishmen."[14] Elsewhere in Sudan, the Turco-Egyptians appointed several Americans who had fought for Confederate forces during the American Civil War and who found themselves unemployed afterward.[15] Sudanese Muslims regarded these appointments as further evidence of the mismanagement of the Turco-Egyptian regime.

There is no evidence that the Mahdi had grievances about Charles Gordon in particular or that he even knew much about him. And in fact, Gordon appears to have done a good job as a Sudan administrator. According to one historian, when Gordon was serving as the Turco-Egyptian governor-general from 1877 to 1880, he reversed long-standing Turco-Egyptian policies that had marginalized Sudanese Sufi leaders, adopted a more tolerant attitude toward Sudanese Islam, and included more Sudanese Muslims in his administration. Symbolically, in an effort to make the Turco-Egyptian government more responsive, Gordon even affixed a suggestion and complaint box to the gates of his palace in Khartoum so that the people could express their concerns.[16]

Nevertheless, the appearance of non-Muslims in the Turco-Egyptian regime during the 1870s disturbed Sudanese Muslims insofar as through these men, the acceleration of Western imperialism was becoming visible. By the time Muhammad Ahmad declared himself Mahdi in 1881, fifty-one years had passed since the French invasion and conquest of Algeria, while just six years had passed since an

Anglo-French banking consortium had seized control of Ottoman and Egyptian finances and public debts. A mere four years had passed since Queen Victoria had declared herself empress of India. Meanwhile, Britain was intent on safeguarding the Suez Canal (opened to traffic in 1869) along with maritime routes to India. European powers were calling the Ottoman empire "the Sick Man of Europe," and the empire was certainly struggling to hold on to its fringes: Greece had been independent since the 1820s, while other Christian populations (such as the Armenians) were becoming more restive. Disquieting news from Muslim traders and pilgrims crossing the Sahara, traversing the Nile Valley or the Red Sea corridor, and returning from Mecca contributed to the flow of information into Sudan on all of these aspects of European expansion. Such news added to the sense of anxiety and malaise that made Sudan a ripe field for millenarianism.[17]

Even the war that the Mahdists began with Christian Abyssinia (Ethiopia) does not support the idea that the Mahdist jihad was explicitly anti-Christian. To be sure, in 1889, when the Mahdists fired a volley that killed Yohannes IV, the Abyssinian emperor, on the battlefield, the Khalifa Abdullahi hailed the emperor's death as a great victory for Islam against Christianity. Yet the Mahdist victory against Abyssinia had practical purposes that transcended ideology: it drew more firmly what had been until then a shaky Sudanese-Ethiopian border while maintaining commercial exchanges and did so at a time when the Mahdists were trying to assert the bounds of their territory vis-à-vis "Muslim" Egypt.[18] Indeed, the Mahdists called all of their opponents infidels (*kuffar*), both Muslims (such as the Turco-Egyptian authorities) and Christians. Invoking jihad against "infidels" justified the seizure of booty and helped to build up the Mahdist treasury at a time when the Mahdist state was increasingly isolated, restricted in trade, and desperate for income.[19]

Watching from the distance of Mecca as the Mahdist revolution unfolded, a Shafi'i Muslim scholar named Ahmad Zayni Dahlan (d. 1886)—a man who was neither Sudanese nor a believer in the Mahdi—voiced support for its battles. Dahlan expressed hope that the Mahdi and his supporters would strike Western, Christian forces that were beginning to exert themselves in the region and thereby help to bolster the Ottoman empire. But Dahlan was misinformed about the movement.[20] Opposition to an incipient Western imperialism was one source of Mahdist activism but only one: at least in the early years of the movement (1881–85), opposition to Turco-Egyptian imperialism was far more important in triggering and sustaining jihad.

The Nature, Goals, and Impact of the Mahdist Jihad

The overarching goal of the Mahdist movement was to reform Islam from within, by purging popular customs and practices deemed "un-Islamic," and to establish an Islamic government. In this regard, the Sudanese Mahdist movement belonged to a series of reformist jihad movements that swept through Islamic Africa during the nineteenth and early twentieth centuries.[21] Like the earlier jihads of 'Uthman dan Fodio and 'Umar Tall in West Africa (discussed by David Robinson in chapter 12 above), the Mahdi's jihad largely entailed a battle among Muslims over the direction that Muslim culture and statecraft should take. It also had a strong nativist dimension, insofar as it emphasized the primacy of local Muslim rule.

Sudanese Islam had been evolving for centuries and, like religious cultures everywhere, was a work in progress. Arab Muslim conquerors had reached Nubia, roughly along the present-day Sudanese-Egyptian border, as early as 651—the same year when Arab Muslim armies overthrew the last Sassanian shah of Iran. But compared with Islam in Iran, Islam in Sudan took centuries longer to spread. Christianity persisted in Nubia until the early fourteenth century, that is, until around 1315, when the first Muslim seized the Nubian throne.[22] Two centuries later, around 1500, a Muslim sultanate known as the Funj emerged near the junction of the White and Blue Niles, followed shortly thereafter, around 1600, by another sultanate, led by the Kayra dynasty, in Darfur to the west. The emergence of these two Muslim states helped to foster what historians have described as the consolidation of Sudanese Muslim culture. During the Funj era, this Muslim culture centered on Sufi holy men, who often functioned as amulet writers, healers, fortune-tellers, and even rainmakers.[23] The Funj and Kayra sultanates also provided the kind of political stability that enabled new Muslim pilgrimage and trade routes to flourish. Instead of crossing the Sahara to North Africa's Mediterranean coast and from there heading by sea to Arabia, West African pilgrims began taking a route across the interior Sudanic belt of Africa, which brought them past Lake Chad through Sudan to its Red Sea port at Suakin, which was just two hundred miles from Jiddah.[24] Indeed, West African pilgrims from the Sokoto caliphate probably transmitted the millenarian ideas and Mahdist expectations that caught on in Sudan.[25]

The reforms that developed out of the Mahdist jihad emphasized the more rigorous implementation of Islamic law, practice, and administration. Important evidence for this change appears in the proclamations (*manshurat*), fatwas, letters, and warnings (*indharat*) that the Mahdi (and to some extent the Khalifa) issued in writing. The Mahdi and Khalifa used these texts to justify their leadership, announce appointments, or make stipulations for the functioning of the military, treasury, and other branches of government. Several of the Mahdi's proclamations also set social guidelines. For example, he issued orders about marriage and divorce (including limits on dowries and bride wealth), musical performance (for example, by forbidding the use of certain instruments but allowing, within limits, the use of copper drums), and social infractions (by specifying punishments for offenses as minor as swearing, for example, by calling a fellow Muslim believer [*akh mu'min*] a "dog," a "pig," or a "Jew," with the first two of these slurs also connoting a Jew or a Christian).[26] Given the Mahdist state's attempts to pronounce and enforce matters of Islamic law governing the details of everyday life, it is no accident that some observers of contemporary Sudan have drawn parallels between the Mahdist state and Sudan's post-1989 regime, the government of General Bashir.[27] The latter touted its Muslim credentials and commitment to Islamic law, while enforcing rules on mundane behavior, for example, by forbidding women from wearing trousers and requiring them to wear a particular style of *hijab* that covered more hair than the sari-like *tobe* (*thawb*) had conventionally done.[28]

The Mahdist jihad also entailed an internal war for Muslim authority and leadership and posed a direct threat to local Sufi orders (*tariqas*) that had developed clear structures of power.[29] Thus, the staunchest opponents of the Mahdi were the Sudanese Muslim Sufi leaders, who refused to offer fealty (*bay'a*). Among these were members of the Mirghani family, leaders of the Khatmiyya Sufi *tariqa*, who had close ties to Egypt and the Hijaz and who were interested in the kind of Muslim reform that some scholars have described as "neo-Sufism."[30]

Tribal and regional differences, along with economic rivalries, also came into play, complicating the Mahdist movement's internal politics. Divisions were visible within the ranks of Mahdist supporters, notably between the *awlad al-balad* families of the riverine north (some of whom were relatives of the Mahdi) and the Baqqara Arab nomads of western Sudan (some of whom were relatives of the Khalifa). The Mahdi and the Khalifa pursued two strategies to curb their enemies and to stifle dissent. First, the Mahdi declared Sufi *tariqas* null and void (though this had limited effect, and indeed Sufi organizations persisted and later rebounded). The Mahdi also established specific rituals for devotion, notably by promoting an authoritative prayer book (*ratib*), that made Mahdist practice somewhat distinct from other Sufi *tariqas*.[31] Second, the Khalifa tried to erase tribal differences through policies of forced migration (*tahjir*), urban resettlement (in the new capital, Omdurman), and intermarriage.[32]

In the late twentieth century, Sudanese historians were still debating the success of the latter policies. Some argued that the Khalifa's policies successfully generated unity through amalgamation and muted tribal consciousness. Others maintained that his policies left Sudanese Muslim communities more divided and more mutually hostile than ever and that they helped to foster a culture of Muslim sectarianism.[33] Certainly, the Khalifa's occasional use of brutal collective punishments signaled his own continuing recognition of clans and tribes, rather than individuals, as social units.[34]

In an age when literacy rates were minimal and when movable-type printing and railways had not yet reached the country, how did the Mahdi and the Khalifa spread their messages of jihad and reform at the grassroots to rally popular support?[35] It appears that panegyric poetry, recited and sung, was the Mahdist movement's mass medium.[36] The Mahdi and the Khalifa sponsored panegyrists, and while a few wrote their compositions down, most appear to have recorded them in their own heads.[37] Some of these praise poets passed their Mahdist compositions down to sons and grandsons, whose continuing commitment to Mahdist faith arguably represented its own form of Sufi "*tariqa* loyalty."[38] In the mid-twentieth century, a Sudanese scholar named Qurashi Muhammad Hasan interviewed the grandsons of Mahdist praise poets and recorded their compositions. Qurashi Muhammad Hasan later suggested that Mahdist praise poetry in the 1880s had entailed a "jihad of the pen" and that it had been just as important as the "jihad of the sword" in accomplishing revolution.[39] He recognized, in other words, that the Mahdist jihad had had a strong rhetorical dimension.

After Jihad: The British in Sudan

In 1898, a joint British-Egyptian army overthrew the Mahdist state. At the battle of Karari just outside Omdurman, eleven thousand Sudanese Mahdist soldiers died, and sixteen thousand were wounded, compared with just 49 dead and 382 wounded among the Anglo-Egyptian forces. In *The River War*, Winston Churchill, who had been a young war correspondent covering the invasion, noted the technological supremacy of British weapons and called the battle of Karari "the most signal triumph ever gained by the arms of science over barbarians."[40] However, it took nearly a year for Anglo-Egyptian soldiers to catch up with the Khalifa Abdullahi, who had retreated. Later, British sources publicized a photograph of his corpse, which was splayed on the prayer mat where soldiers had killed him.[41] In 1932, one writer called the Khalifa's death "the end of Mahdism," but history was already proving that claim wrong. After 1898, Mahdist faith persisted among humble families that had supported the movement, while in the years following World War I, some sons and grandsons of the Mahdist elite came to lead a mainstream political movement that sought to negotiate Sudanese independence from Britain and Egypt. Often called neo-Mahdism, this twentieth-century movement became a central player in Anglo-Egyptian-era nationalist activities and in postcolonial Sudanese politics.

Initially, after 1898, British authorities pursued a strategy of quarantine vis-à-vis the surviving family members of the Mahdi, the Khalifa, and their emirs (leading military commanders). They exiled many sons of these Mahdist elites into a kind of prison-cum-house arrest in Egypt and kept the two surviving sons of the Mahdi under close watch in Khartoum.[42] But within a few years, they were revising their policy, by providing the sons of Mahdist elites (including sons of the Khalifa) with modern educations and hiring them into the Anglo-Egyptian colonial bureaucracy as agricultural inspectors, civil engineers, district officials, and the like. The policy of co-opting elites had already served Britain well in India, and it became highly effective in Sudan, too.[43]

The greatest fear of British officials in Sudan was that they might do something to stimulate Muslim "fanaticism" and to provoke a new jihad. So they took special pains to cultivate Muslim elites, particularly those, such as members of the Mirghani family, that had resisted the Mahdist movement. Meanwhile, British authorities set out to cultivate a new quiescent class of ulema who could keep a system of Islamic law courts running. Worried that al-Azhar, in Egypt, would introduce Sudanese students to Egyptian-style, anti-British nationalism, the authorities founded in 1912 a new Sudanese institute for Islamic education, called al-Ma'had al-'Ilmi, in Omdurman. At the same time, at Gordon College in Khartoum (named in honor of General Charles Gordon and founded in 1902), British authorities trained some elite Muslim boys for a future as moderate *qadis* (while training others as accountants, schoolteachers, and the like).[44]

World War I prompted the British to accelerate their efforts at co-opting elites. When the Ottoman government of the Young Turks sided with Germany and declared the war against the Entente powers to be a jihad, Britain feared that Muslims throughout the British empire would rise up in waves of resistance. British fears were compounded when leaders of the Sanusiyya movement in Libya staged an attack on Egypt's western flank in 1915–16 and when 'Ali Dinar, sultan of the quasi-autonomous region of Darfur, sensed an opportunity and declared jihad against the British in 1916 (prompting British authorities in Sudan to invade, conquer, and annex Darfur in return).[45]

Rather than confirming fears of widespread Muslim hostility, World War I provided an opportunity for Britain to cultivate new alliances with powerful Muslim individuals and groups. Britain countered the Ottoman invocation of jihad, most famously, by wooing Sharif Husayn of Mecca and orchestrating the Arab Revolt from the Hijaz to Syria. In Sudan, the British made new overtures to Sayyid 'Abd al-Rahman al-Mahdi (1885–1959), the posthumous son of the Mahdi, who agreed to declare support for Britain and its allies. In return, as a demonstration of their goodwill, the British enabled Sayyid 'Abd al-Rahman to build up large cotton plantations in the budding Gezira Scheme, with some officials calculating that by making him rich, they might also make him complacent. Sayyid 'Abd al-Rahman used the opportunities wisely and benefited from the free farm labor of the Mahdist faithful who settled on his land and paid him alms in return for his *baraka* (blessings). In fact, many of his faithful laborers were "Fellata," or Hausa-speaking immigrants from northern Nigeria, who headed toward Sudan with the goal of fulfilling millenarian expectations, performing the pilgrimage to Mecca, and finding economic opportunities.[46]

By the time World War I ended, Sayyid 'Abd al-Rahman al-Mahdi was beginning to sponsor early nationalist activities among young elite literati. One of his most important ventures was funding *Hadarat al-Sudan*, a weekly newspaper started in 1919. This newspaper consciously supported "modernization" programs such as the extension of piped water systems in Omdurman and the opening of new schools, but it also took two approaches that reflected the evolution of a Mahdist worldview. First, it attacked "un-Islamic" or superstitious customs and called for their reform through education. Second, it supported the idea of Sudanese independence from both Britain and Egypt and became associated with the nationalist slogan of "Sudan for the Sudanese" (*Sudan li al-Sudaniyyin*).[47]

Sayyid 'Abd al-Rahman was charismatic, politically astute, and unflaggingly hospitable to British guests; he also proved skillful at organizing the Ansar (followers of the Mahdi) behind him while insisting to the British that his intentions were peaceful. By some accounts, Sayyid 'Abd al-Rahman transformed the Mahdist movement into a twentieth-century Sufi organization; certainly, the Ansar contributed to a political and social landscape of Muslim sectarianism.[48] Before and after World War I, Sayyid 'Abd al-Rahman also voiced steadfast support for the Anglo-Egyptian government in the face of a series of rural protests that evoked the Mahdi. These protests were called Nabi 'Isa (Prophet Jesus) movements, because their leaders claimed to be 'Isa, or Jesus, returning after the Mahdi but just before the Day of Judgment in the face of the "Antichrist" (*al-Dajjal*), which they interpreted to mean the British government. In the words of one historian, "With the exception of the war years, hardly a year passed during the first generation of Condominium rule without a Mahdist rising" or Nabi 'Isa movement, and yet these rural uprisings failed to rally much support.[49] These revolts, which were the closest the British came to facing the popular jihad that they feared, proved to be very local and easily suppressed.

Colonial Crusades?

Did jihadist discourses in modern Sudan inspire reciprocal colonial crusades? Bernard Lewis has argued that the late-nineteenth-century translation of European history books into Arabic inspired new Muslim interest in the Crusades (c. 1096–1271) and thereby kindled an oppositional interest in jihads.[50] However, within the specific local context of Sudan, it may be possible to argue the reverse, namely that the assertion of Muslim holy war discourses within the Mahdist movement encouraged the articulation of Christian equivalents, particularly within British missionary circles.

Certainly, in the 1880s, around the time Britain occupied Egypt, British and, to some extent, American evangelicals were beginning to place a strong emphasis on the evangelization of Muslims worldwide, from Morocco to Southeast Asia. In this period, British missionaries were adopting the kind of strong-arm rhetoric that mirrored the aggressive language of British imperialism, while in Britain itself, popular imperialism and popular nationalism both maintained strong evangelical Protestant dimensions.[51] In responses to the Mahdist revolution, missionaries adopted particularly strident tones and did so at a time when some were envisioning a contest for souls between Islam and Christianity. By 1898, British and American missionaries were cheering on the advance of Anglo-Egyptian forces into Mahdist Sudan, while British missionaries of the Church Missionary Society (CMS) expressed a desire to evangelize Muslims as a way of avenging the death of Charles Gordon many years earlier.[52] In sum, although British colonial authorities never declared an official crusade in the manner that the Mahdi declared a jihad, some Britons in Sudan, particularly missionaries of the CMS, freely invoked crusader discourses at the turn of the century. They did so, in large part, to rally support among evangelical Christians in the home churches who provided missions with the bulk of their funding.

Perhaps it was an awareness of this militant Christian rhetoric that prompted anthropologist Janice Boddy to argue that British policies in Sudan after 1898 amounted to a series of "colonial crusades." Boddy attributes a spirit of crusaderism not only to Christian missionaries but also to all British colonial functionaries in Sudan and suggests that Christian agendas shaped the regime. She argues that British efforts began with a crusade against Mahdism and evolved in the early twentieth century into crusades against Sudanese customs, among them the widespread practice of female genital cutting. Equating Christianity with civilization, British officials in Sudan fancied themselves as "knight-administrators," Boddy contends. They engaged in a struggle that amounted to a "clash of moralities" and deployed workers, such as government educators and midwives, as if they were "secular missionaries."[53] Boddy's arguments are too sweeping, however, insofar as they ignore the divergent views and mixed motives of British protagonists in Sudan.

In fact, high-ranking British colonial authorities, including Lord Cromer and Sir Francis Wingate, regarded Christian missionaries as a nuisance and believed that their evangelical agendas toward Muslims would stimulate popular resistance. Thus, they were often lukewarm or skeptical toward missionary claims, even if deference to domestic British opinion inhibited them from airing their views in public.[54] In the end, British officials after the Reconquest officially forbade Christian missionaries to proselytize among Sudanese Muslims. They allowed them to remain in northern towns with the understanding that they would either cater to Christian expatriates (notably Copts, Greeks, and Ethiopians) or provide social services to Muslims without trying to convert them.[55] CMS missionaries resented this curtailment and did their best to evade it on the ground in Sudan. Meanwhile, as early as 1910, at the World Missionary Conference in Edinburgh, their supporters criticized British policies toward missionaries in Sudan and in northern Nigeria.[56] CMS missionaries in the Nile Valley were also annoyed that British officials approved only the teaching of Islam at Gordon College and that they approved the use of "grammar books [that] deny the Christian faith."[57]

However, British authorities such as Wingate had other plans for Christian missionaries. They diverted them south, pointing to wide-open fields of endeavor, and "urged a mission to the Pagans."[58] Through another neat maneuver, British authorities managed to get missionaries to shoulder costs and responsibilities for providing southern Sudanese peoples with some schooling.[59] At the same time, in remote and thinly governed areas of southern Sudan, British officials were able to use missionaries as proxies and relied on them for training southern Sudanese men for employment as government clerks.

Missionaries were already describing southern Sudanese conversion to Christianity as a "mass movement" in 1932, with one CMS missionary recalling how at

Yei, "Huge crowds surged round the car demanding books, baptism, confirmation and more teachers."[60] Yet even in the south, British officials occasionally found missionaries to be a nuisance. Around 1938, they deported one CMS missionary, Richard Jones, who held very fiery revival meetings where he urged sinners and backsliders to repent. British officials apparently deemed his style too inflammatory, but some southern Sudanese borrowed and adapted this "Jones Revival" style, with its ecstatic worship and faith healing, so that its impact persisted for years afterward.[61]

Relative to the total southern Sudanese population, Christian conversions appear to have been demographically minute during the colonial period. Nevertheless, the southern Sudanese products of mission schools became political organizers when civil conflict broke out in 1955, after an army mutiny at Torit, months before Britain staged its official ritual of decolonization by lowering the Union Jack in Khartoum. Mission converts also functioned as the nucleus of a Christian community that expanded dramatically in the late twentieth century, leading some to argue in the 1990s that Christianity in war-torn southern Sudan had indeed become a mass movement and a vehicle for collective resistance.[62]

During the Anglo-Egyptian period in northern Sudan, British missionaries had persisted in evangelizing among Muslims, covertly and as opportunities arose, notwithstanding the colonial government ban. By 1956, the CMS northern Sudan mission claimed to have "won" just one convert from Islam in its half-century of work in the region.[63] Yet its mission still made an impact, in social if not religious terms, by providing models for the earliest formal girls' schools in northern Sudan, including some schools that welcomed girls of slave origins.[64]

Occasionally during the interwar period, rumors surfaced suggesting that missionaries may have converted orphan Muslim children to Christianity. Such stories galvanized northern Sudanese Muslims in three ways. First, Sudanese Muslims began by the 1920s to establish independent, community-supported popular (*ahliyya*) schools as an alternative to Christian mission schools (since British government schools were very limited in number and often restricted to Muslim elites). Second, Sudanese Muslim women began to establish neighborhood "Needlework Homes," where girls could learn the art of homemaking before getting married. One Sudanese writer also claimed that opposition to Christian mission education prompted Muslim women to organize a public protest in 1946, a protest that helped to inspire the foundation of the Sudanese Women's Union, an important feminist and women's advocacy organization, in 1952.[65] Third and finally, such stories confirmed among some Muslim thinkers the belief that British colonial rule allowed and therefore abetted Christian missionary efforts to evangelize among Muslims.[66]

Here is where the discussion of "colonial crusades" arises again. Colonial policies and missionary activities sometimes stimulated Muslim resistance, with the case of female genital cutting, and missionary- and government-supported efforts to eradicate it, offering a good example. Beginning in the late 1920s, British authorities had funded the establishment of a midwifery training college in Omdurman under the leadership of two British sisters, Mabel and Gertrude Wolff. These two women taught hygienic techniques and encouraged the modification of an operation of genital cutting that was almost universally practiced among northern Sudanese Muslim women at the time. This operation (sometimes called "infibulation" in English) entailed excision of the clitoris and labia and restriction of the vaginal opening, and it required surgical intervention at childbirth.[67]

In 1946, the Anglo-Egyptian government, urged on by the wife of the British governor-general, declared a ban on the operation of infibulation, known in Arabic as "Pharaonic circumcision" (al-khitan al-fir'awni).[68] Muslim leaders, such as Mahmud Muhammad Taha (who went on to found the organization known as the Republican Brothers), organized an antigovernment rally to protest this ban on an accepted practice. His resistance, which appears to have enjoyed considerable popular support, landed him in prison.[69] Yet it is worth noting that prominent Muslim scholars and leaders at the time issued opinions or published statements supporting the ban and calling for the reform of female genital cutting as it was usually practiced. In a newspaper statement, for example, Sayyid 'Abd al-Rahman al-Mahdi declared that "Pharaonic circumcision is a shame and a degradation to women apart from being contrary to the authenticated sunna [practice of the Prophet Muhammad]." The mufti of Sudan published a statement that went further, suggesting that even the custom of clitoridectomy had dubious Islamic grounds.[70] Were Muslim leaders like these pressured by Britons into supporting the ban, did they support the ban to curry British favor, or did they genuinely believe in its aims as they related to the pursuit of Islamic practice? Historians should not discount the possibility that these prominent Muslim critics of female genital cutting genuinely supported the ban, since Sudan has furnished ample evidence in its modern history to indicate the diversity of Muslim opinion.

The Lingering Discourse of Jihads and Crusades

When the conflict that later became known as the first civil war erupted with a military mutiny at Torit in southern Sudan in 1955, northern Sudanese politicians in Khartoum looked upon missionaries as enemies who had undermined national cohesion by propagating Christianity among southern "pagans." Thus, in 1957, the Khartoum government began to nationalize mission schools, and in 1964, it deported all foreign missionaries. A government memorandum issued at the time described missionaries as an obstacle to national integration and accused them of sheltering, supplying, or otherwise abetting southern "mutineers" and "outlaws."[71] These measures forced the rapid indigenization of southern Sudanese church leadership and confirmed the assumption among political analysts that Muslim-Christian conflict would either become or remain a perennial theme in modern Sudanese history.

This first civil war abated in 1972, with the signing of the Addis Ababa Agreement, but it flared up again, more intensely, after 1983, when President Ja'far Numayri proclaimed shari'a law. During the second civil war, as the post-1983 conflict became known, Muslim ideology played an important role in the central government's discourses. To rally popular support and justify military drafts among northern Muslims, Khartoum regimes portrayed the civil war as a jihad and proclaimed that its war dead were martyrs. By the mid-1990s, the government had set up large murals of "martyrs" along major streets in the capital and was inculcating militant Islam even in girls' elementary schools, where uniforms were made out of camouflage fabric.[72]

After 1983, Khartoum politicians found jihad to be politically expedient in other ways, too. Jihadist rhetoric enabled the regime to draw more support from other Muslim states, such as Saudi Arabia, which helped the government with its Islamization programs by offering money to construct mosques and Islamic schools in remote and largely non-Muslim regions.[73] More generally, northern politicians gave lip service to shari'a law and Islamic values as a way of appealing to Muslim populations who were otherwise disillusioned with the corruption, mismanagement, and factional infighting of successive postcolonial regimes.[74]

After its rise to power in the coup of 1989, the Bashir regime proved willing to invoke jihad for internal wars, not only against assumed non-Muslims in the south (where many Muslim families also lived, particularly in towns) but also against Muslims elsewhere. The latter proved true in 1992, when government forces bombed dissident Muslim communities in the Nuba Mountains of Kordofan and apparently sold thousands of survivors as slaves to the Arab tribal militias that backed the regime. According to French analyst Gérard Prunier, the Bashir regime's readiness to invoke jihad against Nuba Muslims presaged policies that it would later pursue in Darfur following the outbreak of war there in 2003.[75]

By emphasizing the religious dimensions of civil conflicts, the Sudanese government tried to distract attention from the deep economic and political grievances that had been propelling these wars from the start. Many southerners, along with other non-Arab Sudanese peoples (including Muslims from Darfur, the Nuba Mountains, and the Red Sea Hills region), resented the way Arabic-speaking Muslims of the northern riverine Sudan had monopolized power and resources. They were disgusted, in other words, with a history of underdevelopment and neglect in the country's peripheries (a history that went back to the Anglo-Egyptian period).[76] By 1983, many southerners opposed the regime's Jonglei Canal project, which proposed to drain the south's White Nile tributaries in order to feed the main Nile going into northern Sudan and Egypt. They feared the local environmental consequences that the canal would have. Demand for Nile water, spurred by the development of agricultural industries and the Aswan Dam's hydroelectric power plant, was growing, so that "hydropolitics" functioned as an important issue for Sudanese-Egyptian diplomacy.[77] Much the same later applied to "petropolitics," which centered on the oil that the Khartoum government began to extract from the southern Sudan (with help from Chinese, Malaysian, Canadian, and other companies) in 1999. On top of this environmental and economic exploitation, the regime's attempts to foist Arabic and Islamic culture onto non-Arabs or non-Muslims amounted to what some dissidents described as a new, internal colonialism.[78]

After 1983, the Sudan People's Liberation Army and Movement (SPLA/M), which was the main southern opposition force, called for secular government and official recognition of Sudanese pluralism. The SPLA/M, which spread its organization into the Nuba Mountains and included both Muslim and Christian supporters (including Nuba Muslim commanders such as Yousif Kuwa Mekki),[79] did not resort to crusader discourses even though Christianity was becoming increasingly influential as a cultural force among much of its rank and file.[80] Amid war and displacement, international Christian organizations claimed to detect the rapid expansion of Christianity among refugees and even among soldiers, citing, for example, a sharp rise in the number of SPLA Christian chaplains by 2000.[81] One anthropologist ascribed the dramatic spread of Christianity to two things: first, Christianity helped southern Sudanese to overcome ethnic divisions, which had led to intense internecine fighting; and second, it offered them a "sturdy ideological opponent" against the official Islam of the Khartoum regimes.[82] Yet the SPLA/M retained both Muslim and Christian supporters, and this internal diversity reinforced the movement's commitment to cultural pluralism.

The so-called second civil war was brutal. In 1998, some fifteen years after this bout of war had begun, the U.S. Committee for Refugees was estimating that some 2 million southern Sudanese people had died from war-related causes and more than 80 percent of the southern population had experienced displacement.[83] However, this second civil war appeared to end in 2005, when the government of Sudan (representing the Bashir regime in Khartoum) and the SPLM (representing southern interests) met in Naivasha, Kenya, to sign a Comprehensive Peace Agreement (CPA). After so many years of strife, southern Sudanese people—both in Sudan and in the diaspora—drew hope from the CPA's claim that following a transitional period of government partnership, southerners would have the chance to vote in a referendum on national unity in 2011.

In 2003, a new Sudanese civil war broke out in the western Sudanese region of Darfur, pitting "rebels" and settled civilian populations on the one hand against government forces and nomadic Arab militias on the other. By 2005, at the peak of the violence against Darfurian civilians, some analysts were suggesting that the westward shift of war toward Darfur was no accident, insofar as the Khartoum regime was using war as a machine for survival in the aftermath of signing the CPA with southerners. Regardless, the war in Darfur illustrated that peace for southern Sudan was and could only be a partial resolution of Sudan's civil conflicts, since popular grievances extended into the Muslim-majority regions of the country's eastern and western peripheries. The Darfur war also illustrated the limits of using religion—and in this case, the ostensible Islamic ideology of the Bashir regime—as an explanatory device for political behavior. Indeed, Sudanese and non-Sudanese analysts alike agreed with reference to the Darfur war that notions of race and ethnicity (involving Arab rather than Islamic ideology) were intensifying and complicating the conflict.[84]

Conclusion

In 1974, the Sudanese folklorist Qurashi Muhammad Hasan argued that praise poetry—which he called the "jihad of the pen"—had been more important to the success of the Mahdist revolution than the "jihad of the sword" involving soldiers in combat. Yet historians of Sudan have remembered the "sword fights" more than the "pen fights," by emphasizing the importance of battles such as the "Fall of Khartoum" in 1885, the Battle of Karari (Omdurman) in 1898, or the Torit Mutiny in 1955 (the event that by many accounts set off the "first" Sudanese civil war). Fewer have examined the discursive evidence of conflict, found in proclamations, panegyrics, memoranda, personal letters, memoirs, newspaper articles— the list goes on and on. Such discursive evidence can tell us how, amid the claims for jihads and crusades, Muslims and Christians in Sudan have mobilized supporters, attacked opponents, and justified proposals for change, even while defining themselves.

Fulfilling provisions that the CPA of 2005 had set out, southern Sudanese people had the opportunity to vote in a referendum on national unity that occurred in January 2011. The referendum yielded clear and dramatic results: nearly 99 percent supported southern secession. Secession occurred in July 2011, and a new country, the Republic of South Sudan, was born. With South Sudan now a state apart from Sudan, possible conflicts still loom large, conflicts involving natural resources (oil and water) and the treatment of religious minorities (Christians in Sudan and Muslims in South Sudan). However—to a degree much greater than in earlier periods of Sudanese history—external powers are likely to intervene in these disputes for the sake of advancing their own diverse interests. These external powers will include Egypt, China, the United States, Saudi Arabia, Kenya, and Uganda.[85] As this chapter's study of Sudanese history suggests, for better or worse, jihadist or crusader discourses may well continue to provide a vehicle and a flexible vocabulary for advancing agendas, claims to power, and calls for change.

Notes

1. The best overview of the Turco-Egyptian period remains Richard Hill, *Egypt in the Sudan, 1820–1881* (London: Oxford University Press, 1959).
2. Regarding the British missionary movement and its relationship to British imperialism in this period, see Jeffrey Cox, *The British Missionary Enterprise since 1700* (New York: Routledge, 2008), 9.

3. Illustrating this trend, for example, is W. A. Rice, *Crusaders of the Twentieth Century, or the Christian Missionary and the Muslim: An Introduction to Work among Muhammadans* (London: Church Missionary Society, 1910).

4. Use of the title *khalifa* to mean "successor" indicated an awareness of and a sense of continuity with Islamic history, insofar as the Prophet Muhammad's successors had used this title. Yet Abdullahi's use of the title also reflected his bid for political legitimacy.

5. Douglas H. Johnson, *The Root Causes of Sudan's Civil Wars* (Bloomington: Indiana University Press, 2003).

6. On this idea of religious activism as self-constitution, see Simon Coleman, "Continuous Conversion? The Rhetoric, Practice, and Rhetorical Practice of Charismatic Protestant Conversion," in Andrew Buckser and Stephen D. Glazier, eds., *The Anthropology of Religious Conversion* (Lanham, Md.: Rowman & Littlefield, 2003), 15–27.

7. Na'um Shuqayr, *Jughrafiyya wa tarikh al-Sudan* (Beirut: Dar al-Thaqafa, 1967), 631–36. By the 1870s and largely as a result of a slave trade that had burgeoned during the Turco-Egyptian era, northern Sudanese landowners had come to rely heavily on slave labor on farms, particularly as many free men migrated out in search of economic opportunities. See Jay Spaulding, "Slavery, Land Tenure, and Social Class in the Northern Turkish Sudan," *International Journal of African Historical Studies* 15, no. 1 (1982): 1–20; and Heather Jane Sharkey, "Domestic Slavery in the Nineteenth- and Early Twentieth-Century Northern Sudan" (MPhil thesis, University of Durham, 1992).

8. Anders J. Bjørkelo, *Prelude to the Mahdiyya: Peasants and Traders in the Shendi Region, 1821–1885* (Cambridge, U.K.: Cambridge University Press, 1989).

9. Ibrahim Fawzi, *Kitab al-Sudan bayna yaday Ghurdun wa Kitshinir* (Cairo, 1901), 1:73–74; cited in John Obert Voll, "A History of the Khatmiyyah Tariqah in the Sudan" (PhD dissertation, Harvard University, 1969), 1:217.

10. Rudolf von Slatin and Eduard Schnitzer (a.k.a. Emin Pasha) had Jewish mothers and fathers but were baptized as Christians. Both had ambiguous religious identities and were said to be Muslims at different points in their lives.

11. P. M. Holt, *The Mahdist State in the Sudan, 1881–1898: A Study of Its Origins, Development, and Overthrow* (Oxford: Clarendon, 1970), 35. Holt's account remains the most detailed analysis of the Mahdist revolution.

12. Claude Cahen, "Dhimma," in *Encyclopaedia of Islam*, 2nd ed. (Leiden: E. J. Brill, 1983), 2:227–31.

13. Alice Moore-Harell, *Gordon and the Sudan: Prologue to the Mahdiyya, 1877–1880* (London: Frank Cass, 2001).

14. Holt, *The Mahdist State*, 35. Some of these men, such as Rudolf von Slatin, Eduard Schnitzer (a.k.a. Emin Pasha), and Romolo Gessi, later left memoirs or inspired biographers.

15. Richard Hill, *A Biographical Dictionary of the Sudan*, 2nd edition (London: Frank Cass, 1967). These men included, for example, William P. Campbell of Tennessee, Charles Chaillé-Long of Maryland, and Raleigh Edward Colston of Virginia.

16. Moore-Harell, *Gordon and the Sudan*.

17. One of the best surveys to connect events in Sudan to the rest of the Muslim world in this period is John Obert Voll, *Islam: Continuity and Change in the Modern World* (Boulder: Westview, 1982).

18. Iris Seri-Hersch, "Transborder Exchanges of People, Things, and Representations: Revisiting the Conflict between Mahdist Sudan and Christian Ethiopia, 1885–1889," *International Journal of African Historical Studies* 43, no. 1 (2010), 1–26; and Navin Fu'ad 'Abd al-Khaliq, *Al-Tatawwur al-tarikhi li mushkilat al-hudud al-Sudaniyya al-Athyubiyya* (Cairo: Al-Dar al-'Arabiyya li al-Nashr wa al-Tawzi', 2006).

19. Ahmad Ibrahim Abu Shouk and Anders Bjørkelo, eds. and trans., *The Public Treasury of the Muslims: Monthly Budgets of the Mahdist State in the Sudan* (Leiden: E. J. Brill, 1996). See also Yitzhak Nakash, "Fiscal and Monetary Systems in the Mahdist Sudan, 1881–1898," *International Journal of Middle East Studies* 20, no. 3 (1988): 365–85.

20. Heather J. Sharkey, "Ahmad Zayni Dahlan's *Al-Futuhat al-Islamiyya*: A Contemporary View of the Sudanese Mahdi," *Sudanic Africa* 5 (1994): 67–75.

21. See B. G. Martin, *Muslim Brotherhoods in Nineteenth-Century Africa* (Cambridge, U.K.: Cambridge University Press, 1976).

22. Yusuf Fadl Hasan, *The Arabs and the Sudan, from the Seventh to the Early Sixteenth Century* (Edinburgh: Edinburgh University Press, 1967).

23. Neil McHugh, *Holymen of the Blue Nile: The Making of an Arab-Islamic Community in the Nilotic Sudan, 1500–1850* (Evanston, Ill.: Northwestern University Press, 1994), 57–95.

24. R. S. O'Fahey and J. L. Spaulding, *Kingdoms of the Sudan* (London: Methuen, 1974).

25. M. A. al-Hajj, "The Thirteenth Century in Muslim Eschatology: Mahdist Expectations in the Sokoto Caliphate," *Research Bulletin, Centre of Arabic Documentation* (Ibadan) 3, no. 2 (1967): 100–15.

26. Muhammad Ibrahim Abu Salim, ed., *Manshurat al-Mahdiyya* (Khartoum: Khartoum University Press, 1969), regarding marriage and divorce, 196–98, 300; musical instruments, 165–68; punishment for "he who calls his brother believer 'you dog, you pig, or you Jew,'" 185–87. On the latter slurs, see Bernard Lewis, *The Jews of Islam* (Princeton, N.J.: Princeton University Press, 1984), 33; and Heather J. Sharkey, *American Evangelicals in Egypt: Missionary Encounters in an Age of Empire* (Princeton, N.J.: Princeton University Press, 2008), 52.

27. See, for example, Gabriel Warburg, "Mahdism and Islamism in Sudan," *International Journal of Middle East Studies* 27, no. 2 (1995): 219–36.

28. Ann Mosely Lesch, *Sudan: Contested National Identities* (Bloomington: Indiana University Press, 1998), 129–47 (chap. 8, "Indoctrination and Control").

29. The literature on modern Sudanese Sufism is extensive. See Ali Salih Karrar, *The Sufi Brotherhoods in the Sudan* (Evanston, Ill.: Northwestern University Press, 1992); Mark Sedgwick, *Saints and Sons: The Making and Remaking of the Rashidi Ahmadi Sufi Order, 1799–2000* (Leiden: E. J. Brill, 2005); and Albrecht Hofheinz, "Internalizing Islam: Shaykh Muhammad Majdhub: Scriptural Islam and Local Context in the Early Nineteenth-Century Sudan" (PhD dissertation, University of Bergen, 1996). Taking the study of Sudanese Sufism into the post-1989 period is Noah Salomon, "In the Shadow of Salvation: Sufis, Salafis, and the Project of Late Islamism in Contemporary Sudan" (PhD dissertation, University of Chicago, 2010).

30. Voll, "A History"; and R. S. O'Fahey, *Enigmatic Saint: Ahmad ibn Idris and the Idrisi Tradition* (Evanston, Ill.: Northwestern University Press, 1990).

31. Muhammad Ibrahim Abu Salim, ed., *Al-Athar al-kamila li al-Imam al-Mahdi*, vol. 6: *Al-Ratib wa al-ada'iyya wa al-khattab* (Khartoum: Khartoum University Press, 1993).

32. Robert S. Kramer, *Holy City on the Nile: Omdurman during the Mahdiyya* (Princeton, N.J.: Markus Wiener, 2010).

33. A strong case for the Khalifa as a divisive figure appeared in Muhammad Mahjub Malik, *Al-Muqawama al-dakhiliyya li harakat al-Mahdiyya* (Beirut: Dar al-Jil, 1987). On Sudanese divergences over history in general, consider Gabriel Warburg, *Historical Discord in the Nile Valley* (Evanston, Ill.: Northwestern University Press, 1992).

34. Consider the experience of the Batahin (a Baqqara tribe), "sixty-seven of whose kinsmen had been publicly hanged or mutilated in Omdurman [in 1888] by the Khalifa because of their subordination." Holt, *The Mahdist State*, 177.

35. On Sudanese print culture, see Heather J. Sharkey, "A Century in Print: Arabic Journalism and Nationalism in the Sudan, 1899–1999," *International Journal of Middle East Studies* 31, no. 4 (1999): 531–49.

36. This suggests, in turn, that Arabic oral culture exceeded the movement's literary (written) culture in importance even if historians have generally privileged the latter. Of course, the tangibility of written sources and the near irretrievability of oral sources make this tendency understandable. A compendium of Arabic sources, including those from the Mahdist period, appears in R. S. O'Fahey, ed., *The Arabic Literature of Africa*, vol. 1: *The Writings of Eastern Sudanic Africa to c. 1900* (Leiden: E. J. Brill, 1994).

37. For an important example of a written text, see Haim Shaked, *The Life of the Sudanese Mahdi: A Historical Study of Kitab sa'adat al-mustahdi bi-sirat al-Imam al-Mahdi* (New Brunswick, N.J.: Transaction, 1987). The author of this text was Isma'il ibn 'Abd al-Qadir al-Kurdufani.

38. This phrase comes from Voll, "A History," 1:302–3.

39. Heather J. Sharkey, "Mahdist Oral Poetry as a Historical Source: Qurashi Muhammad Hasan's *Qasa'id min shu'ara al-Mahdiyya*," *Sudanic Africa* 5 (1994): 95–110; and Qurashi Muhammad Hasan, *Qasa'id min shu'ara al-Mahdiya* (Khartoum: Al-Majlis al-Qawmi li Ri'ayat al-Adab wa al-Funun, Wizarat al-Thaqafa wa al-I'lam, 1974).

40. Winston Spencer Churchill, *The River War: An Historical Account of the Reconquest of the Sudan* (London: Longmans, Green, 1900), 2:164; and P. M. Holt and M. W. Daly, *A History of the Sudan*, 5th ed. (London: Longman, 2000), 96. A powerful rejoinder to accounts such as Churchill's, and a fine work of military history, is 'Ismat Hasan Zulfo, *Karari: The Sudanese Account of the Battle of Omdurman*, trans. Peter Clark (London: F. Warne, 1980).

41. Richard A. Bermann, *The Mahdi of Allah: The Story of the Dervish Mohammad Ahmed*, intro. Winston S. Churchill (New York: Macmillan, 1932), frontispiece, labeled "The End of Mahdism." Another report had earlier explained, more sympathetically, "The Khalifa met his fate like a man, and, seeing that all was lost, seated himself upon a sheep-skin with his chief Emirs, and with them fell riddled with bullets." E. A. Wallis Budge, *Cook's Handbook for Egypt and the Sudan* (1906), 1:269.

42. Hasan Ahmed Ibrahim, "The Policy of the Condominium Government towards the Mahdist Political Prisoners," *Sudan Notes and Records* 55 (1974): 33–45.

43. Heather J. Sharkey, *Living with Colonialism: Nationalism and Culture in the Anglo-Egyptian Sudan* (Berkeley: University of California Press, 2003).

44. Gabriel Warburg, "Religious Policy in the Northern Sudan: Ulama and Sufism, 1899–1918," *Asian and African Studies* 7 (1971): 89–119; John O. Voll, "The British, the 'Ulama, and Popular Islam in the Early Anglo-Egyptian Sudan," *International Journal of Middle East Studies* 2, no. 3 (1971): 212–18.

45. John Paul Slight, "British and Muslim Perceptions of and Responses to Jihad in the British Empire, 1914–1924" (MPhil thesis, Cambridge University, 2007).

46. M. W. Daly, *Empire on the Nile: The British in the Anglo-Egyptian Sudan, 1898–1934* (Cambridge, U.K.: Cambridge University Press, 1986); and C. Bawa Yamba, *Permanent Pilgrims: The Role of Pilgrimage in the Lives of West African Muslims in Sudan* (Edinburgh: Edinburgh University Press, 1995), 46.

47. Sharkey, "A Century in Print."

48. Peter Woodward, "In the Footsteps of Gordon: The Sudan Government and the Rise of Sayyid Sir Abd al-Rahman, 1915–1935," *African Affairs* 84, no. 334 (1985): 39–52; Gabriel R. Warburg, "British Policy towards the Ansar in Sudan: A Note on a Historical Controversy," *Middle Eastern Studies* 33, no. 4 (1997): 675–92; Daly, *Empire on the Nile*; and Hassan Ahmed Ibrahim, *Sayyid 'Abd al-Rahman al-Mahdi: A Study of Neo-Mahdism in the Sudan, 1899–1956* (Leiden: Brill, 2004).

49. Hassan Ahmed Ibrahim, "Mahdist Risings against the Condominium Government in the Sudan, 1900–1927," *International Journal of African Historical Studies* 12, no. 3 (1979): 440–71.

50. Bernard Lewis, *The Crisis of Islam: Holy War and Unholy Terror* (New York: Modern Library, 2003), 50–51.

51. Cox, *The British Missionary Enterprise*; Linda Colley, *Britons: Forging the Nation, 1707–1837*, 2nd ed. (New Haven, Conn.: Yale University Press, 2005); Deborah Cohen, *Household Gods: The British and Their Possessions* (New Haven, Conn.: Yale University Press, 2006); Andrew Porter, *Religion versus Empire? British Protestant Missionaries and Overseas Expansion, 1700–1914* (New York: Manchester University Press, 2004); Brian Stanley, *The Bible and the Flag: Protestant Missions and British Imperialism in the Nineteenth and Twentieth Centuries* (Leicester, U.K.: Apollos, 1990); and David Bebbington, "Atonement, Sin, and Empire, 1880–1914," in Andrew Porter, ed., *The Imperial Horizons of British Protestant Missions, 1880–1914* (Grand Rapids, Mich.: Eerdmans, 2003), 14–31.

52. Heather J. Sharkey, "Christians among Muslims: The Church Missionary Society in the Northern Sudan," *Journal of African History* 43 (2002): 51–75; Thomas Prasch, "Which God for Africa? The Islamic-Christian Missionary Debate in Late Victorian England," *Victorian Studies* 33 (1989): 51–73; and Heather J. Sharkey, "A New Crusade or an Old One?" *ISIM*

Newsletter 12 (2003): 48–49. There are few studies of the CMS in northern Sudan. An unpublished study is Renate Lunde, "Between Tradition and Modernity: Girls' Education in Northern Sudan, 1899–1956" (master's thesis, University of Bergen, 2001).

53. Janice Boddy, *Civilizing Women: British Crusades in Colonial Sudan* (Princeton, N.J.: Princeton University Press, 2007), 2, 5, 24, 54, 106.

54. For the parallel situation in Egypt during this period, see B. L. Carter, "On Spreading the Gospel to Egyptians Sitting in Darkness: The Political Problem of Missionaries in Egypt in the 1930s," *Middle Eastern Studies* 20 (1984): 18–36.

55. Sharkey, "Christians among Muslims," 51–75. For a solid overview of British policy in the pre-World War I period, see Gabriel Warburg, *The Sudan under Wingate: Administration in the Anglo-Egyptian Sudan, 1899–1916* (London: Frank Cass, 1971).

56. Brian Stanley, "Church, State, and the Hierarchy of 'Civilization': The Making of the 'Missions and Governments' Report at the World Missionary Conference, Edinburgh 1910," in Porter, *The Imperial Horizons*, 58–84; see p. 74.

57. Church Missionary Society archives, University of Birmingham (henceforth CMS), G3/E/P1/1898/79 (p. 102): F. F. Adeney, December 9, 1898.

58. Ibid., G3/E/P1/1899/9 (p. 122): F. F. Adeney, January 2, 1900.

59. Lilian Passmore Sanderson and Neville Sanderson, *Education, Religion and Politics in Southern Sudan, 1899–1914* (London: Ithaca, 1981); David Sconyers, "British Policy and Mission Education in the Southern Sudan, 1928–1946" (PhD dissertation, University of Pennsylvania, 1978).

60. Grace Riley, *No Drums at Dawn: A Biography of the Reverend Canon A. B. H. Riley, Pioneer Missionary in the Sudan* (Victoria, Aus.: Church Missionary Historical Publications, 1972), 21.

61. Roland Werner, William Anderson, and Andrew Wheeler, *Day of Devastation, Day of Contentment: The History of the Sudanese Church across 2000 Years* (Nairobi: Paulines Publications Africa, 2000), 335–38.

62. Ibid.

63. Sharkey, "Christians among Muslims."

64. Heather J. Sharkey, "Chronicles of Progress: Northern Sudanese Women in the Era of British Imperialism," *Journal of Imperial and Commonwealth History* 31, no. 1 (2003): 51–82; and Lunde, "Between Tradition and Modernity." See also the fascinating memoirs of a British girls' school inspector: Ina Beasley, *Before the Wind Changed: People, Places, and Education in Sudan*, ed. Janet Starkey (London: Oxford University Press for the British Academy, 1992).

65. Sharkey, "Chronicles of Progress"; and Heather J. Sharkey, "Women, Gender, and Missionary Education: Sudan," in Su'ad Joseph, ed., *Encyclopedia of Women and Islamic Cultures* (Leiden: Brill, 2007), 4:287–88.

66. Consider, for example, Ahmad 'Abd al-Rahim Nasr, *Al-Idara al-Baritaniyya wa al-tabshir al-Islami wa al-Masihi fi al-Sudan* (Khartoum: Wizarat al-Tarbiyya wa al-Tawjih, 1979).

67. Boddy, *Civilizing Women*.

68. See the Sudan-related essays in Rogaia Mustafa Abusharaf, ed., *Female Circumcision: Multicultural Perspectives* (Philadelphia: University of Pennsylvania Press, 2007).

69. Abdullahi Ahmed an-Na'im, intro. to Mahmoud Mohamed Taha, *The Second Message of Islam* (Syracuse, N.Y.: Syracuse University Press, 1987), 1–30.

70. Sudan Archive, Durham University, SAD 657/4/26, 658/5/15: Ina Beasley Papers, trans. of Sayyid 'Abd al-Rahman al-Mahdi's speech against female circumcision, reported in *Al-Nil* (Khartoum), July 22, 1944; and SAD 582/8/39–52: Mabel and Gertrude Wolff Papers, foreword by the mufti of the Sudan, Sheikh Ahmed El Taher, in E. D. Pridie et al., *Female Circumcision in the Anglo-Egyptian Sudan* (1945).

71. Republic of the Sudan, Ministry of the Interior, *Memorandum on Reasons That Led to the Expulsion of Foreign Missionaries and Priests from the Southern Provinces of the Sudan*, March 1964, p. 3, appendix B ("List of Contraventions Committed by Some Missionaries"); and Heather J. Sharkey, "Missionary Legacies: Muslim-Christian Encounters in Egypt and Sudan during the Colonial and Postcolonial Periods," in Benjamin F. Soares, ed., *Muslim-Christian Encounters in Africa* (Brill: Leiden, 2006), 57–88.

72. I witnessed the martyrs' murals and the camouflage uniforms during a visit to Khartoum in October 1995.

73. Discussion by Douglas H. Johnson after a lecture he gave at the University of Pennsylvania in February 2005. See also Wendy James, *War and Survival in Sudan's Frontierlands: Voices from the Blue Nile* (Oxford: Oxford University Press, 2007); and Wendy James, *The Listening Ebony: Moral Knowledge, Religion, and Power among the Uduk of Sudan* (Oxford: Clarendon, 1988), about this process in the village of Chali on the Sudan-Ethiopian border.

74. Abdullahi Ali Ibrahim, *Manichaean Delirium: Decolonizing the Judiciary and Islamic Renewal in the Sudan, 1898–1985* (Leiden: Brill, 2008).

75. Gérard Prunier, *Darfur: The Ambiguous Genocide* (Ithaca, N.Y.: Cornell University Press, 2005), 161.

76. Tim Niblock, *Class and Power in the Sudan: The Dynamics of Sudanese Politics, 1898–1985* (Houndsmills, U.K.: Macmillan, 1987).

77. The best explanation of this issue appears in Robert O. Collins, *The Waters of the Nile: Hydropolitics and the Jonglei Canal, 1900–1988* (Oxford: Clarendon, 1990).

78. Heather J. Sharkey, "Arab Identity and Ideology in Sudan: The Politics of Language, Ethnicity, and Race," *African Affairs* 107, no. 426 (2008): 21–43. See also Deng D. Akol Ruay, *The Politics of Two Sudans: The South and North, 1821–1969* (Uppsala: Nordiska Afrikainstitutet, 1994).

79. Yousif Kuwa Mekki (1945–2001): Obituary, *Independent* (London), April 4, 2001.

80. For how the regime's Islamist ideology surfaced in peace talks and how the SPLA/M responded, see the fascinating account in Steven Wöndu and Ann Lesch, *Battle for Peace in Sudan: An Analysis of the Abuja Conferences, 1992–1993* (Lanham, Md.: University Press of America, 2000).

81. Marc R. Nikkel, "Aspects of Contemporary Religious Change among the Dinka," in *Papers of the Second International Sudan Studies Conference*, University of Durham, April 8–11, 1991 (Durham, U.K.: University of Durham, 1991), 1:90–100; and Sharkey, "Missionary Legacies."

82. Sharon Elaine Hutchinson, "Spiritual Fragments of an Unfinished War," in Yusuf Fadl Hasan and Richard Gray, eds., *Religion and Conflict in Sudan* (Nairobi: Paulines Publications Africa, 2002), 136–61.

83. U.S. Committee for Refugees, *World Refugee Survey 1998* (Washington, D.C.: Immigration and Refugee Services of America, 1998), 95–96.

84. Prunier, *Darfur*, 162; Julie Flint and Alex de Waal, *Darfur: A New History of a Long War*, 2nd ed. (London: Zed, 2008); Amir H. Idris, *Conflict and Politics of Identity in Sudan* (New York: Palgrave Macmillan, 2005).

85. Heather J. Sharkey, "The Ninety-Nine Percent Referendum: Southern Sudan Votes to Secede," *Berfrois*, February 16, 2011, at http://www.berfrois.com/2011/02/heather-sharkey-southern-sudan (accessed April 1, 2011).

14

The Trained Triumphant Soldiers of the Prophet Muhammad

Holy War and Holy Peace in Modern Ottoman History

MUSTAFA AKSAKAL

Historians have little trouble finding religious rhetoric in the encounters and exchanges between Ottomans and Europeans, including appeals to holy wars and crusades.[1] Such appeals seem to reflect a universal connection between war making and religious meaning. For the armed forces of the People's Republic of China, for example, the prevention of Taiwanese independence is inscribed as a "sacred responsibility."[2] The religious and civilizational language that has accompanied the so-called U.S. war on terror since September 11, 2001, or President William McKinley's prayerful sinking to his knees in the decision to annex the Philippines in 1898 are instances that suggest a universal linkage of war and religion. Rather than examining historically the role of religion in Ottoman wars from the eighteenth to the twentieth centuries, one might simply shrug and say, "All wars are wars of religion."[3]

A study of the Ottomans in the age of European imperialism with attention to religion can reveal, however, the extent to which geopolitical and strategic concerns, and not religious motives, underlay calls for jihad. It also suggests that religion generally and jihad as holy war in particular accompanied the conduct of war and peace during this period in significant if often counterintuitive ways. Sultan Mahmud II's (r. 1808–1839) military reforms, for instance, took European armies as their model. His creation of a European-style troops system in 1826, in which some five thousand members of the old troops, the Janissaries, were massacred for their opposition, was perhaps the single most radical reform measure implemented. And yet this measure, which is often characterized as "Westernization" and which earned Mahmud II the sobriquet "infidel sultan," at the time was cast as a "religious obligation" and was backed by several fatwas, or religious rulings. In the ceremony that celebrated the creation of the new troops, speakers kissed the banner of the Prophet Muhammad, which had been displayed in reverence for the occasion.[4] The new European-style troops were named, without the slightest hint of irony, "The Trained Triumphant Soldiers of the Prophet Muhammad" (*Muallem Asakir-i Mansure-i Muhammediye*). At the same ceremony, the sultan's speech, delivered by the court historian Mehmed Esad, explained that the Ottoman victories of the past had been accomplished thanks to the spreading of the "pure religious law" and the power of "the sword of jihad" (*seyf-i cihad*), which regrettably had slipped away as a result of the Janissaries' corruption.[5] Islam and jihad, therefore, could be invoked right in the midst of renewing military institutions along European lines.

Jihad (*cihad* in Ottoman Turkish) as a term to describe a fight against all sorts of challenges occupied a prominent place in the cultural register of Ottoman society at large. *Jihad* carried many meanings, and its usage therefore varied accordingly. To get an idea of the term's range in the Ottoman context, we may turn to the storied seventeenth-century traveler Evliya Çelebi. Describing the marital life of a grand vizier in whose retinue Evliya had served for many years, the wily adventurer characterized his patron's most intimate moments spent with his strong-willed wife, Kaya Sultan, "for the propagation of the species" as resembling a "greater jihad," a reminder of both the term's chameleon-like nature and its presence in the daily social fabric.[6] One did not even have to be Muslim to "wage jihad" in the Ottoman context. When Maronite Christians in Mount Lebanon felt threatened by the increasing activity of Protestant missionaries from the United States in the 1820s, the Maronite patriarch saw his church locked in a "continuing struggle [jihad] with all our power against those Biblemen."[7] Thus, the designation *jihad* was not a doctrinal concept with a legal-theological definition but a call for marshaling an all-out effort in the face of formidable challenges. Such a broad understanding explains, for example, why the new coins minted in the crisis years under Sultan Mahmud II were called *cihadiye*.[8]

The Ottoman state waged wars against both Christian and Muslim powers throughout its six-hundred-year existence (1300–1922), just as it also concluded formal peace treaties and military alliances with both Christian and Muslim powers alike. In the late eighteenth century, Ottoman diplomats sought alliances with European states in the quest for a firm footing in the international order then reemerging after the Seven Years War, a European war with deep global dimensions and fought as far away as North America and the Indian subcontinent. Like sultans before him, Selim III (r. 1789–1807) cultivated relations with European powers, concluding alliances with Prussia in 1790 and Britain and Russia in 1798. At first glance, it may appear strange that as an Islamic state whose sovereign was also the caliph, the Ottoman state attempted to join an international society known in earlier times as the *respublica Christiana* (or Christendom) and whose political writings frequently referred to the Ottomans as the "eternal enemy of Christianity against which Christianity has to fight in unity."[9] On closer inspection, however, this is not at all surprising, for as Nuri Yurdusev shows in chapter 9 above, the Ottoman state had been part of the European power balance since at least the sixteenth century, and the Ottomans had a tradition of dubbing not only wars as "holy" but also peace. In the Ottoman-Hapsburg treaty of 1664, for example, the sultan's statesmen called the peace treaty a *mübarek sulh*, or "holy peace."[10]

By the nineteenth century, however, new technologies had begun to give European armies clear military supremacy, not just in the Middle East but throughout the world. The Ottomans were clearly on the defensive, a dynamic that would intensify as European states (and their settler offshoots) could draw on economies increasingly powered by the forces of industrialization.

In almost every decade from the 1760s to the 1920s, Ottoman soldiers took up arms against Christian foes, either in wars against sovereign Christian powers or in the suppression of popular uprisings and independence movements of mostly—though with important exceptions, as we shall see—Christian subject populations in the Balkans. Throughout these one hundred fifty years, the Ottoman state lost more than half of its territory, including some of the empire's most productive and densely populated regions, absorbed millions of Muslim refugees, and several times nearly disappeared altogether. In 1770, for instance, a Russian fleet entered the Mediterranean through the Straits of Gibraltar and sank a large portion of the Ottoman navy in the Aegean, inspiring rebellion among Christian subjects on Crete in the so-called Orloff uprisings.[11] Defeated by Russian forces again in 1774, this time on land, the Ottomans received reports of the Russian empress Catherine II (the Great) parading through victory arches boasting the inscription "The Road to Byzantium," that is, to Istanbul.[12] Later, Catherine II's successors not only supported revolutions against Istanbul among Ottoman Serbs (1804) and Greeks (1821), but the Russian army also closed in no farther than sixty miles from the Ottoman capital in 1829, crushing the sultan's forces so severely that Hüsrev Pasha, the Ottoman commander, pleaded desperately for international support: "We [have been] so beaten, we cannot be beaten more."[13] In 1877–78, Russian troops camped ten miles—a day's march—outside the capital, and Bulgarian units advanced within forty miles in 1912 during the First Balkan War. In a recent book, Virginia Aksan characterized the Ottomans as "an empire besieged" and referred to the entire 1760–1830 period as "a do-or-die moment for the Ottoman house."[14]

Ottoman observers often cast the empire as a victim of the international system. As a result, we see the tropes of victimhood and self-defense running prominently through contemporary Ottoman sources. Since the greatest threats to the empire's future came from Christian powers—and since religion became part of the official ideology of the Ottomans' imperial rivals, the Hapsburgs and the Romanovs—it is perhaps not surprising that Islam became politicized in important new ways throughout the long nineteenth century. This politicization became pronounced during the reign of Sultan Mahmud II and that of Sultan Abdulhamid II (r. 1876–1909), who revived and then championed the title of caliph and cast himself as the head of all Muslims worldwide. Thus, like their neighbors and in the absence of a usable nationalism based on ethnic lines, the Ottomans utilized religion in the effort to strengthen the ties between the state and its subjects. In addition, because Islamism could speak only to the empire's Muslim subjects, Ottoman statesmen simultaneously promoted a second ideology, Ottomanism (*osmanlılık*), which was directed primarily toward the empire's non-Muslim subjects (and, in an attempt to appease them, toward their great power protectors). The political and military leadership, therefore, employed religion strategically, including, as we shall see, an ideology of jihad as holy war. Over the long nineteenth century, the military underwent a gradual process of Islamization by which a particular "image of Islam," as an "invented tradition," became a central "agent of social change" by blending religion with resistance to European imperialism.[15]

A portion of the Ottomans' lost territories were incorporated into neighboring Christian powers, such as the Hapsburg empire in the Balkans and Russian lands in the Caucasus and the Crimea, or they were seized by western European powers as part of their growing overseas colonial empires, as was the case in the French occupation of Algeria beginning in 1830 or the British takeover of Egypt in 1882. Other areas of Ottoman territory, those along the borderlands and with majority Christian populations, became independent states, such as Greece in 1832, Serbia in 1878, and Bulgaria in 1908. Some of these regions had been inhabited by sizable and at times, as in the case of the Crimea, majority Muslim populations. Dislocated by Ottoman military defeat, as many as 5 million to 7 million of these Muslim subjects arrived in the empire's shrunken borders as refugees, to be resettled and housed by the state at tremendous cost and with far-ranging social and political implications. Often, such refugees brought with them little more than stories of personal tragedy, stories that over time could mutate into deep resentment against not only the growing military and political influence of European powers but also their own Christian neighbors within the empire.[16]

Eventually, these seismic shifts in demography were mirrored by the ethnic cleansing of Asia Minor and the destruction of its Christian population: the percentage of non-Muslims plummeted from roughly 20 percent in 1912 to less than 2 percent in 1923.[17]

Looking forward from the vantage point of the late eighteenth century, however, this tragedy was by no means a foregone conclusion.[18] Karen Barkey, Linda Darling, Molly Greene, and Cemal Kafadar, among others, have shown—without concealing the violence that accompanied imperial conquest—how the empire's expansion between the thirteenth and the sixteenth centuries and its subsequent longevity and administration of far-flung populations were made possible by the state's capacity to integrate into the Ottoman ruling strata a diverse mix of ethnic and religious groups. In this process of integration, the state employed various methods of accommodation without the constant use or threat of force. Once the smoke of conquest settled, the state succeeded in establishing stable center-periphery relations.[19]

The greatest challenge to this imperial order resulted from the connections between the empire's subject populations and an outside, international rival. Such a challenge emerged most clearly in the early modern period with the rise of the Safavid state in Iran. The Safavids traced back their origins to Turco-Shi'i groups in eastern Anatolia, territory that by now had been conquered by the Ottomans but was inhabited by populations with loyalties to the Safavid state nonetheless. Some of these declared the Iranian shah and the Shi'i Safavids to be the "real *ghazis*," referring to Muslim warriors who had dominated the hybrid frontier culture between the Byzantine state and the Muslim principalities in Anatolia out of which the Ottomans emerged.[20] To break these ties, the Ottomans not only waged war against the Safavids in long campaigns, but the state also dealt harshly with its own Shi'i border populations. In addition, the Ottoman dynasty fully embraced Sunni Islam in the effort to demarcate itself from its neighbors.[21]

By the nineteenth century, however, the challenges presented by Ottoman subjects linked to foreign powers became all-pervasive. As a result, religion became intensely politicized at the state level. Muslim-Christian relations lay at the very heart of Ottoman state policy. How could the state maintain the empire's regions with large Christian populations in the Balkans and parts of Anatolia under the Ottoman umbrella? Co-opting their allegiance by granting autonomous rights could result in independence, while curbing rights tightly was equally risky and could bring about strong opposition, if not fierce clashes, and provoke great power intervention.

The state's answer was a wide-ranging reform movement, the *Tanzimat* (Reordering), changes intended to centralize the empire by modernizing the institutions through which it ruled. At the same time, the state utilized religion in the attempt to win the loyalty of its subjects. This ideological mobilization never managed to resolve a central paradox. While the state established legal equality of all subjects regardless of religion in the attempt to win the support of its non-Muslim subjects within an inclusive Ottomanism, it also accorded Islam an increasingly prominent role, intended, in turn, to win the loyalties of its ethnically diverse Muslim populations from Bosnia to Kurdish populations in eastern Anatolia to Arab populations in Syria, Iraq, and the Hijaz. As Christian Balkan populations broke away or gained autonomous status under European great power aegis and Muslim refugees arrived in Anatolia, Ottomanism increasingly gave way to policies that identified the Ottoman state and Ottomans with Islam. This new ideological shift portrayed the European Christian powers and their imperialist ambitions as Istanbul's enemies, a portrayal that over time came to be extended to the empire's Christian (and, later, Jewish) population, too. Islam as state policy became most developed in the reign of Abdulhamid II. Thus, centralization and modernization, on the one hand, and a renewed Islamization, on the other, together eventually constituted the strategic policy for the empire's survival and regeneration in the nineteenth century.

The Young Turks who came to power in 1908 and more firmly in 1913 also understood the power of this ideology, and they went on to capitalize on it in 1914, when they entered World War I on the side of Germany and Austria-Hungary and—despite the apparent contradictions that alliance with the Christian powers entailed—declared jihad on November 14, 1914. By this time, they had embraced the belief that the empire could not be salvaged by reforms, diplomacy, or "those old books of international law, but only by war."[22]

Religion at the Intersection of International and Domestic Politics

Over the course of the long nineteenth century, the empire never succeeded in becoming part of the European Concert. The primary reason for this exclusion should be seen in the empire's continued military vulnerability and its own domestic insecurities; as an ally, the Ottomans did not bring much to the table. Rather than becoming party to European diplomacy, the Ottomans became subject to it. Constructing railway lines in eastern Anatolia near the Russian border or lines connecting Anatolia and Syria, purchasing modern battleships for its fleet, increasing import custom duties from 11 percent to 15 percent in order to protect domestic manufacturers and industries, and taking out loans from private European banks were all actions dependent on European great power approval.[23]

The expanding influence in the region played by European consuls and businesses fed the image of the empire's non-Muslim subjects as allies of Western imperialism and thus as undermining Ottoman sovereignty and security. One such example from the mid-nineteenth century was the doubtful news that American missionaries had offered to pay off the debts of the Greek Orthodox village of Hasbayya in Damascus province if all of its inhabitants converted to Protestantism. The scandalous rumor infuriated the general population, but it had serious consequences for the governor of the province, Ali Pasha. The British consul threatened to have the governor removed if he did not permit the village of Hasbayya to do as it saw fit.[24]

In the Balkans, the onset of nationalist independence movements among Christian populations, which depended for their success on the international support of the European great powers, further alienated the empire's Muslim and non-Muslim populations from each other. Segments of European public opinion, moreover, pressured their own governments to look out for the well-being of their coreligionists. As calls for humanitarian intervention intensified on the one side, fears and hostility against imperialist interference solidified on the other, rendering increasingly precarious the situation of Christian Ottomans in the empire.

Thus, the loss of territory to European, Christian states brought about not only the major redrawing of the empire's external boundaries—in the Balkans and along the Black Sea, in the Caucasus, in the Aegean and Cyprus, and in North Africa—but also the redrawing of the empire's internal ethnoreligious boundaries, this time reconfiguring also Christian-Muslim relations at home. Such internal boundaries were being redrawn precisely at a time when Christian populations along the border-lands strove for independence and Muslim refugees arrived in the empire with "bag and baggage" (as the British Liberal Party's statesman William Gladstone had put it in 1876 in reference to the Bulgarian Eastern Crisis). In addition to the growing European economic interests, charitable and church organizations provided mis-sionary and educational aid to non-Muslim communities by building schools and hospitals, thereby forging relations that were viewed by many Muslim Ottomans as disloyal and intrusive. This new politicization of religion is illustrated, for example, in the relabeling of Greek Orthodox Ottomans from Ortodoks or Rum (i.e., descen-dants of the Romans/Byzantines) to Yunan following the establishment of the Greek nation-state, Yunanistan, in 1832, which had the effect of establishing an ex-plicit link between a Christian Ottoman population and a foreign European power.[25]

From the European perspective, the Ottoman empire represented clearly an "anomaly"; it was a defunct empire ruling over Christian populations in an age when European Christian powers and their colonial offshoots in North America and Australia controlled much of the world.[26] The European Concert justified re-strictions on Ottoman sovereignty by pointing to unstable relations between the empire's Christian and Muslim subjects. The Ottoman empire and other non-Christian states were not considered members in the emerging European-centered international society. This principle was made explicit in the work of the American diplomat Henry Wheaton, whose *Elements of International Law*, published in Phila-delphia in 1836 and followed by numerous subsequent editions, became the stan-dard work in the field. In Wheaton's view, international law "prevail[ed] between the states of Christendom" and was the product of "Christianity and civilization."[27] Throughout the nineteenth century, Ottoman statesmen and diplomats sought to undermine this premise, by sending military officers and students to European capitals, hiring European technical experts, participating in international conven-tions, and, when possible, concluding alliance treaties. In his codification of shari'a rulings, the *Mecelle*, published in 1876, Ahmed Cevdet Pasha remarked that the need for such a work arose from the fact that "civilized and advanced countries" always had such law codes.[28] Ottoman elites pursued the state's territorial and military security primarily by becoming part of the European-based international system, not by fighting it, either by holy war or by any other means.

Mahmud II and the Trained Triumphant Soldiers of the Prophet Muhammad (1808–1839)

Scholarship of the last decade has linked the military defeats of the late eigh-teenth century to the new debate surrounding Ottoman subjecthood and citizen-ship. These works contend, convincingly, I think, that the reforms engendered by military defeats launched the question of universal conscription, which, in turn, raised questions about the military service of non-Muslims—exempt until the nineteenth century through a special tax—and, to a lesser degree, the role of non-Turks in the Ottoman military.[29]

Sultan Mahmud II came to the throne in 1808 following rebellion and counter-rebellion and only after escaping a death order issued by the previous sultan. The rebellion had overthrown Selim III, who had sought to reform the Janissary corps, the powerful infantry that dominated the military, but encountered opposition that resulted in his murder. With the memory of Selim III's bloody overthrow still fresh, Mahmud II understandably approached the issue of reform cautiously, and when he did, he secured the support of religious leaders and gave the new measures he introduced the greatest legitimizing cloak possible; he not only dressed his policies in religious language but also backed them up with fatwas issued by high-ranking ulema and calls for jihad.

While religion and even the call for jihad as holy war had always been a part of Ottoman warfare, it was never the cause of war. In its confrontation with Russia in the early 1770s, for instance, the state issued an official declaration that jihad had become an "individual obligation" (*farz-ı ayn*), as opposed to the standard, peacetime "communal obligation" (*farz-ı kifaye*). The declaration acknowledged that non-Muslims were not expected to participate in holy war on behalf of the Ottoman state: in the current situation, "jihad is an obligation on all Muslims" residing in the border districts.[30] Non-Muslims, however, supported the state financially during times of war, making special payments of "holy war duties" (*rüsumat-ı cihadiye*) and "holy war donations" (*iane-i cihadiye*). Complicating the meaning of *jihad* once again, non-Muslims made such payments even during times of "regular" wars, that is, during wars that had not been declared jihad by the state, as in the case of the Crimean War.

With the chaos surrounding his accession hardly settled, Mahmud II faced a major uprising among the empire's Serbian Christian population in 1808. Here, the Ottoman state decreed that because "Serbs are attacking the Ottoman domains from all sides . . . the duty of jihad . . . has become an individual obligation on each person [*farz-ı ayn*]."[31] In addition, eight banners to be "unfurled for jihad" were sent out to local troops.[32]

And yet the use of religion during the reign of Mahmud II was highly ambiguous, even contradictory, and can only be explained by the fact that the state issued different messages, messages that were at odds to one another, to different audiences. In 1809, Mahmud II's grand vizier, Alemdar Mustafa Pasha, announced a decree that Christians, as people who believed in the same god as Muslims, should not be referred to as *gavur*, or "infidels."[33] In order to counter the criticism of his modernization efforts—he had been nicknamed "infidel sultan," as noted earlier—Mahmud II and his advisers secured the backing of ulema and leaders among the Janissary corps itself before pushing through in 1826 the most far-reaching package of reforms up to that point.

Meeting with fierce resistance nonetheless, he gave orders to massacre the Janissary corps, replacing it with a new army, the Trained Triumphant Soldiers of the Prophet Muhammad. More than one hundred imams, individuals trained to lead worship, were assigned as chaplains to the new troops.[34] With the power of the Janissaries broken, the center of opposition to Mahmudian reforms had also been shattered. The state saw it necessary to justify its bloody suppression of the Janissaries by claiming that the massacre had been the result of the corps's Christian infiltration; the palace spread rumors that the Janissaries had disfigured copies of the Qur'an with knives[35] and that the "cross of the *gavur* (infidel)" had been discovered tattooed on the bodies of some of its members.[36]

At the same time, the Greek War of Independence (1821–1829) continued to rage on. While the state appears not to have declared holy war against the Orthodox revolutionaries that would succeed in establishing a Greek nation-state in 1832, Russia's support for Greek independence was a different matter: "Because the Russians have incited the Greek Orthodox [*rum milletine*] to wage war [against us] in pursuit of independence and because this war has thus been caused by hostility towards the Islamic faith and therefore is a religious struggle, jihad has become an obligation for all those between the ages of twelve and seventy of the people of Islam."[37] The state did not declare jihad against the Christian "rebels" themselves for fear that this would antagonize Orthodox Christians in other parts of the empire.

As if the blow-up with the Janissaries in 1826, the ongoing uprising for Greek independence that had begun in 1821, the defeat of the Ottoman-Egyptian fleet at Navarino by a European coalition fleet in 1827, and the highest rate of inflation the Ottomans had ever faced were not sufficient problems, Mahmud II declared war and jihad on Russia after Russian troops had moved into Ottoman territory in 1827. The distinction between Ottoman Christians—even those in rebellion—and foreign powers remained, however. In 1829, Mahmud addressed those fighting for Greek independence directly: "There will in the future be no distinctions made between Muslims and [non-Muslims] and everybody will be ensured the inviolability of his property, life and honour by a sacred law and my sublime patronage." On a tour of Bulgaria about a decade later, the sultan delivered the same message personally.[38] In addition, the principle of equality of all subjects became enshrined, at least on paper, in the century's major legislative reform edicts, the Tanzimat declarations of 1839 and 1856 and Article 8 of the 1876 constitution.[39]

In 1828, roughly around the time Mahmud sent his conciliatory letter to the Greek independence fighters, the government also confiscated the possessions of the three wealthiest Jewish bankers in Istanbul, executed them, and expelled some twenty thousand Catholic Armenians from the capital.[40] Thus, until the second half of the nineteenth century, both policies, tolerance and persecution, were options linked to tangible rather than religious motives.

A consistent policy of jihad could never emerge, because from the perspective of the Ottoman state, the world never simply divided into two halves of Christian foes and Muslim friends. Serious threats also came from Muslim power centers within the empire itself, from regional rulers such as Ali Pasha of Ioannina (the "Muslim Bonaparte" in what later became Greece)[41] and Muhammad 'Ali of Egypt. Muhammad 'Ali had first put out one fire of rebellion on the sultan's behalf, the Wahhabi revolt in Arabia, but had been beaten back by an allied European force in 1827 when putting out a second, the Greek uprising. Eventually fed up with playing the role of Mahmud II's fireman, Muhammad 'Ali sent his soldiers within 220 miles of Istanbul, fully intending to overthrow the sultan's rule and install his own. The Egyptian grab for power pitted Muhammad 'Ali's *Jihadiye* troops against Mahmud II's Trained Triumphant Soldiers of the Prophet Muhammad. Both men, through their ulema, issued fatwas and counterfatwas, declaring each other respectively "rebel" and "deviant from the Faith."[42] Waiting nervously in his palace, Mahmud was saved in 1833 only by—of all saviors—Russia, the Ottomans' longtime international rival and nemesis. In 1839 to 1841, a coalition of European powers again threw back the same Egyptian challenger, Muhammad 'Ali, this time to defend Mahmud II's successor, Sultan Abdulmecid I (r. 1839–1861).

Religion and jihad during the reign of Mahmud II had thus been employed to mobilize soldiers in wars against Russia in 1768–1774 and again in 1827–1829 and against Serbian rebels in 1809. In contrast, the state did not attempt to use jihad against Ottoman Christians fighting in the Greek War of Independence. We have seen that the state also employed jihad against the Janissaries in the effort to legitimize military reforms based on European models.[43] The new taxes put in place to pay for these military reforms, moreover, became known as *rüsumat-ı cihadiye* (holy war duties), and special wartime donations were collected as *iane-i cihadiye* (holy war donations),[44] establishing further explicit links between territorial defense and cultural and religious survival.

Having suffered a series of military defeats and internal upheavals from the Balkans to Arabia to Egypt, the Ottoman state sought to consolidate the empire through policies of administrative centralization and military reform. While in earlier times the state may have sought to mobilize an all-Muslim army with a call to holy war, in the mid-nineteenth century, it could no longer afford to alienate its non-Muslim subjects through such an action. Utilizing jihad as holy war in a systematic, widely publicized manner would have contradicted the central objectives of the state's domestic and foreign policy: keeping non-Muslim subjects in the empire and European imperialists out.

The Tanzimat (1839–1876)

Until the reign of Abdulhamid II, the empire sought to play down religious differences in its international relations. Islam and the state were *not* mutually reinforcing, as they were more clearly in the case of the Romanovs' Orthodoxy or the

Hapsburgs' Catholicism, where religious and imperial ideology could blend without the danger of provoking international intervention in support of minority populations.

In the effort to defuse the potential divisiveness of both religion and nationalism at home, the state undertook major legislative reforms. In the Tanzimat decrees of 1839 and 1856, the sultan's government boldly guaranteed to all of "our subjects" perfect security of life, honor, and property. These reforms promised a standardized system for the conscription of troops from all subject populations regardless of religion or class. The 1856 decree emphasized the importance of local representative government, reinvigorating "the provincial and communal councils in order to insure fairness in the choice of the deputies of the [Muslim], Christian, and other communities and freedom of voting in the councils."[45] Article 8 of the 1876 Constitution stated that "everyone who is within the Ottoman state, whatever his religion or sect, is without exception to be labeled an Ottoman."[46]

The writings of the Ottoman diplomat and statesman Mehmed Sadık Rifat Pasha reflect the political outlook shaping these reforms. Sent to Vienna in 1837 as ambassador, Sadık Rifat worked closely with Mustafa Reşid Pasha, the foreign minister and later grand vizier. While Reşid Pasha has become known as the Tanzimat's "architect" and "foremost proponent of Ottoman accession to the European concert,"[47] Sadık Rifat's reports written from Vienna (published first in 1840 and reprinted several times subsequently) served as an important source for Reşid Pasha's thinking.[48] Far from fighting Christian Europe, the key to saving the Ottoman empire, according to the reformers, was to ensure territorial security and peace through the "European system of the Law of Nations."[49] In the words of Cemil Aydın, "it was the appeal of joining a stable and prosperous family of states, a new international society, that shaped the early formulation of Ottoman Westernism."[50] The superiority of the new international legal system, according to Sadık Rifat, lay in the fact that its participants now acknowledged that war between states no longer was an option because it proved too costly even for the victorious side, and therefore diplomatic solutions should always prevail.[51]

The Ottomans came closest to membership in this international society during the years of the Crimean War (1853–1856), when they were joined in their war against Russia by Britain, France, and Sardinia as their allies. The war's immediate cause was the rivalry between Catholic (read French) and Orthodox (read Russian) control over Christian holy sites in Jerusalem.[52] Even though the Ottoman state had declared the duty of jihad to be operative for the Russian wars of 1768–1774 and 1827–1829, no such declaration was made in 1853. Instead, with Christian powers on their side, the Ottomans asserted that "Even more care and attention than previously will be taken to defend and protect the Christian subjects of the Exalted State."[53] Such a declaration put an exclamation mark behind the Ottomans' protests against European interventionism on behalf of Christian minorities. To top it off, speeches by Ottoman Christian leaders published in the official state gazette affirmed their love and support for the state during this time of war.[54]

The Crimean War's longer-term causes were rooted in the intensifying international rivalry in the empire as the great powers staked out territories and cultivated regional populations as interest groups, primarily through the utilization of religious links. The Tanzimat years reveal that this is not simply the story of European military and economic expansion entangling with Ottoman religious reaction. Often what mattered most to the Ottomans was military and economic security, while religion frequently played an important role for European leaders and organizations, not to mention the thousands of missionaries who came to the Ottoman empire during this period. The Ottoman empire, after all, ruled not only over the holy sites of Mecca and Medina but also over the Jewish and Christian holy land. Lord Aberdeen, the British prime minister during the Crimean War, declared that he would "as soon think of preferring the Koran to the Bible, as of comparing the Christianity and civilization of Russia to the fanaticism and immorality of the Turks."[55] His ambassador at Istanbul, Lord Stratford Canning, worked ardently to open a Protestant church in Jerusalem.

Even though there had been only a small Protestant population in Jerusalem, Britain and Prussia together succeeded in establishing the first Protestant cathedral in the region, Christ Church, in 1849. A London Society for Promoting Christianity among the Jews had been established as early as 1809, and a number of charities, religious organizations, and some industrialists eventually began to issue calls for a British protectorate over Palestine. While the rate of conversion to Protestantism was minimal among Jews, the Anglo-Prussian Episcopate achieved greater success among the Christian Orthodox population of Greater Syria. In 1850, the British government succeeded in gaining the Ottoman state's legal recognition of Protestant Ottomans as constituting a religious community analogous to the other recognized religious communities (*millets*).[56] Thus, in an interesting twist, the European powers were supporting confessional rights and a confessional organization of the empire's population while the Ottoman state through its legislative reforms promoted equal citizenship among all subjects.

Even before the outbreak of the Crimean War, St. Petersburg had moved troops into the Ottoman provinces of Wallachia and Moldavia, especially once the revolutionary movements of 1848 threatened to spill inside Russia. In such times of military threat, the empire's various provinces and regional notables remitted to the state a special "jihad assistance" (*iane-i cihadiye*), including from primarily Christian areas such as Crete in 1849–50.[57] Thus, from the state's perspective, evoking jihad allowed the mobilization of financial resources in addition to the mobilization of recruits. From the people's perspective, for both men and women, wartime could mean presenting oneself to the state, ready to participate in jihad for its defense. During the years of the Crimean War, for example, a woman by the name of Ayşe traveled to the Ottoman capital to join the "jihad," even though, as noted, the state did not declare holy war during this conflict. Ayşe's initiative leaves us wondering about the meanings and function of jihad, but it also demonstrates its evidently strong popular appeal. Whether she intended to take up arms or expressed her willingness to serve, for example, in a medical unit remains unclear. She may simply have expected the state to reward her support and loyalty monetarily and to send her home, which is how the episode ended.[58] Even though the documentation lacks detail, we can say at least that her case was not unique; a woman by the name of Nazıma, in the same year, declared similarly her intentions to serve on the state's behalf.[59]

Abdulhamid II, Europe, and the Specter of Global Jihad (1876–1909)

Sultan Abdulhamid II's rule is perhaps best known for its projection of Islamic authority in the attempt to foster support for the Ottoman state among Muslims at home and worldwide from Africa to India to Southeast Asia. At the center of this Pan-Islamism stood Abdulhamid II's "reinvention of tradition" that arrogated to himself the role of sultan-caliph. It could be said, however, that he did not so much choose this direction as it was set for him by the prevailing conditions when he came to power. These included massive interreligious violence in the Balkans followed by war with Russia in 1877–78, the Austro-Hungarian occupation of Bosnia and Herzegovina in 1878, the British occupation of Egypt in 1882, large-scale massacres of Armenian Christians in 1894–1896, and war with Greece in 1897.[60]

Abdulhamid II ascended the throne on the heels of major uprisings that broke out first in Bosnia and Herzegovina. These uprisings had been supported by neighboring Serbia and Montenegro and, most important, Russia.[61] In April 1876, revolt also erupted in the Bulgarian Panagjurishte region, where the first wave of violence produced some one thousand Muslim dead.[62] The region had seen revolts before, but their internationalization meant that local tensions now could escalate into much bloodier clashes than in earlier times. In this case, "Russian arms and agents encouraged fellow Slavs to rise up against the symbols of the Ottoman state—or, in their absence, the local Muslim population."[63] The Ottomans' reprisal campaign in Bulgaria resulted in further bloodshed, this time with mostly Christian victims. The reprisals' "severity was then exaggerated beyond proportion" in the European press and in the United States, where the reprisals became known as the "Bulgarian atrocities"[64] and Abdulhamid II as "the Red [i.e., bloody] Sultan."[65] The immediate cause for the uprisings included opposition to taxation in the aftermath of a series of poor harvests. Studying the economic history of the Balkans under Ottoman rule from the region's own local sources, Michael Palairet concludes that the longer-term causes behind the April 1876 insurrection were rooted, ironically, in an "impressive economic advance" that had been fostered by the "strengthening of Ottoman institutions" there.[66]

With Britain focused on the southern Mediterranean after the opening of the Suez Canal in 1869, Russia and Austria-Hungary moved to divide up the Balkans into spheres of influence. In early 1877, the former attacked Ottoman territory along the western Black Sea shore, while the latter seized Bosnia and Herze-govina. By the time the Treaty of Berlin settled the crisis, the Ottoman empire had lost 230,000 square kilometers of territory and more than 5 percent of its population.[67]

The role that international powers played in this politicization of ethnicity and religion in the Balkans coupled with the territorial losses and military defeats that the Ottomans suffered formed a vicious pattern in the minds of Istanbul's states-men. Commenting both on the involvement of foreign powers and on the interna-tional reporting of the crisis, Abdulhamid II observed, "We are accused in Europe of being savages and fanatics. [Yet] unlike the Czar, I have abstained till now from stirring up a crusade and profiting from religious fanaticism, but the day may come when I can no longer curb the rights and indignation of my people at seeing their co-religionists butchered in Bulgaria and Armenia."[68]

In line with this sentiment, the Ottoman state did not declare the 1877–78 war against Russia a holy war but employed religion in quieter ways nonetheless. It provided financial support—and Abdulhamid II's personal blessings—for a jihad in the Russian Caucasus fought there by Russian Muslims.[69] The state also ramped up its support for the distribution of treatises and pamphlets, in public and among the military, emphasizing the importance of waging jihad as holy war, the model of the Prophet Muhammad as a warrior, and the spiritual rewards of warfare for soldiers—types of publications that had begun to appear in the reign of Mahmud II.[70] In 1876, the year of Abdulhamid II's accession, these included Mehmed Emin Efendi's *Umdet ül-cihad* (The Principle of Jihad) and Halid Efendi's *Risale-i cihad* (The Book of Jihad).[71]

This politicization of religion confirmed for European and American observers long-entrenched views. Earlier in the century, English missionary William Jowett had put it this way: "Holy War and Consecrated Licentiousness are peculiar to the Mahomedan Creed—foes, implacable to the entrance of our pure and peaceful Religion." Pliny Fisk, his American colleague, expressed his view of Muslims much the same: "[Islam] was first propagated, and is still defended by the sword. Cruelty and blood are among its most prominent characteristics."[72] While Christian mis-sionaries did not contemplate the use of force in winning converts, of course, and while they denounced the historical Crusades of the medieval period, they under-stood their own endeavors for converts in the Ottoman empire as a form of "holy violence," as one missionary put it.[73]

From the other side, Abdulhamid II saw in the activities of European and American missionaries "the most dangerous enemies to social order."[74] For the sultan, religion lay at the heart of international relations:

> In England, Russia, and France there exist Bible Societies which become exceedingly rich through the donations of rich and fanatical Christians who bequeath all their wealth to them in their wills. . . . Although the English, Russian and French governments seem not to be involved in

their activities, they secretly aid and abet them in sending missionaries into darkest Africa. In this way they spread their beliefs among the local population. By increasing the numbers of their followers this religious influence is then transformed into political leverage. . . . Although it is obviously desirable to take firm measures against them, if open opposition is brought to play, the Sublime Porte will suffer the vexing interventions of the three powers' ambassadors. Thus the only way to fight against them is to increase the Islamic population and spread the belief in the Holiest of Faiths.[75]

These words from May 1892 illustrate the conviction that Christian missionaries, backed by great power diplomats directly or indirectly, could be confronted by polarizing local Muslim populations against them. In Selim Deringil's words, this encounter represented "nothing less than ideological war, a war that challenged the very basis of Ottoman legitimacy among Christian and Muslim."[76] Deringil also reminds us that this response was by no means a uniquely Muslim reaction, quoting the Chinese dowager empress Tzu Hsi (d. 1908) as saying: "These Christians are the worst people in China. . . . They rob the poor country people of their land and property, and the missionaries, of course, always protect them, in order to get a share for themselves."[77]

Abdulhamid II's regime employed Islam both domestically and internationally. At home, left with a shrunken empire after 1878 that was demographically more Muslim than before, the sultan consolidated the empire by presenting himself as the defender of the faith and through projects such as the Hijaz Railway, whose construction was financed entirely with "Muslim money" (including from Muslims as far away as India) and whose avowed purpose was to provide more efficient and safer transport for the pilgrimage to Mecca. The allegedly religious purpose of the railway, completed in 1908, also permitted the Ottomans to keep European involvement to a minimum.[78] Internationally, Islam provided leverage over millions of Muslim subjects in British Egypt and India, French North Africa, and Russian Central Asia and the Caucasus. But Abdulhamid II and later perhaps also the Young Turks were well aware of the limits of Pan-Islamism and jihad as an international policy. The sultan-caliph believed that "the threat of *cihad* was more effective than the call itself."[79] During his long reign (1876–1909), Abdulhamid II refrained from declaring holy war, even though he invoked religious feeling whenever he addressed soldiers directly.[80]

As the state cultivated an Islamic official identity, it also extended this Islamization to the armed forces. The imperial war college resumed the teaching of religion in its regular curriculum, and students who did not fast during the month of Ramadan or skipped prayers were disciplined.[81] The state declared these practices necessary because "the survival of the Sublime State depends on the preservation of the Islamic faith." All civil and military servants of the state had to be taught "the sacredness of their duty."[82]

Kaiser Wilhelm II's Faith in Jihad in 1914

The call for holy war by Sultan Reşad Mehmed V (r. 1909–1918) is the most prominent instance of any state-declared jihad in the modern period. Once the Ottomans entered the war on the side of Germany and Austria-Hungary in late October 1914, they proclaimed jihad against the Entente two weeks later. Most have seen in this jihad a "jihad made in Germany," a linchpin of a German plan to revolutionize the Muslim populations of Berlin's enemies, in British Egypt and India, in French North Africa, in the Russian Caucasus and Central Asia.[83] While some have also pointed to the 1914 proclamation as proof that the Ottomans pursued the formation of a Pan-Islamic and Pan-Turkic empire,[84] we have come to think of it as a German invention, alien to the usual practice of Ottoman statecraft.

The 1914 jihad, however, was neither the product of German coercion nor the result of an Ottoman drive for global Muslim empire. There are reasons to suggest that the German emperor Wilhelm II, backed by a group of German scholars and politicians, put more faith in jihad and its military impact than the sultan or his war minister, Enver Pasha, did. For some leaders in Berlin, the idea that Pan-Islamism and jihad could bolster German military efforts in the event of war had played a persistent role in German strategic thinking since the late nineteenth century.[85] Wilhelm II—cheekily referred to by critics as Hajji Wilhelm Muhammad after visits to Jerusalem and Saladin's tomb—was sold on the idea that the sultan's call to holy war could incite Muslims worldwide against Berlin's enemies. In Istanbul, Enver Pasha held out the potential of jihad to his German allies on several occasions. But once Berlin pressed for the declaration after the war's start in Europe, Enver registered his doubts. He argued that a declaration of holy war as urged by the kaiser was implausible; a jihad would be directed against all "infidel" powers, including Germany. Rather than declaring jihad, Enver suggested, the sultan could "call upon all Muslims to take up arms against the powers of the Triple Entente."[86] Berlin deemed this gesture insufficient and snubbed it. Over Enver's apparent objections, however, the call for holy war eventually went out nonetheless, and the jihad fatwas were read in a public ceremony to a large cele-bratory crowd gathered outside the mosque of Fatih Sultan Mehmed (the Con-queror) on November 14, 1914, followed by similar festivities in Medina.[87]

How do we make sense of Enver's back-and-forth? Did he really object to the declaration of jihad, consenting only in the face of German pressure? Could he, in fact, decide on jihad, single-handedly, one way or the other? And were Kaiser Wil-helm II and his so-called experts unaware of all the other failed jihad movements of the nineteenth century, from Africa to Indonesia?

Despite the fact that the jihad proclamation at first sight appears to be an ad hoc decision, prompted only by the July crisis and by Berlin's tactical consider-ations in waging "war by revolution," we have noted a much longer-term, *Ottoman* history of jihad. The declaration of jihad as holy war in 1914 cannot simply be explained as a move dictated by Berlin in the context of the German-Ottoman alliance and the Ottoman entry into World War I. The use of jihad rhetoric by the resistance movement—though not proclaimed by the state—against Italy in Libya in 1911–12, in which Enver himself fought, calls such a view into question.

Rather than seeing the declaration as Berlin's work or Enver's vision for a Muslim empire, the call to holy war in 1914 should be seen as the wartime extension of Ottoman domestic policies aimed at consolidating the empire. While the state did not call for holy war during the Balkan wars—a somewhat puzzling move since the small Balkan states themselves utilized religious rhetoric in their war propaganda—it did step up its use of Islam to mobilize society behind the state. This intensified Islamist policy was aimed especially at its Arab provinces in the attempt to knit them more tightly into the sultan-caliph's domains. In Hasan Kayalı's words, "the call for jihad was the culmination of the Islamic propaganda carried out by the Ottoman government since 1913."[88] Thus, jihad was "not meant to pit the Muslims of the world against the Christian European powers, but rather to achieve more limited aims consistent with and supported by the ideological and political circumstances preceding it. It was, first of all, designed to increase domestic support for the government's war effort."[89] The calculations of Kaiser Wilhelm's orientalists and military advisers may have rested, in part, on an "essentialist image of Muslims" which portrayed them "as fundamentally guided by the norms of the scripture."[90] But Gottfried Hagen's careful study also has shown that the same German believers in jihad thought it would succeed as an anticolonial and not simply as a religious movement.[91]

Conclusion

Throughout much of the nineteenth century, the state employed jihad in limited ways, as Ottoman statesmen believed that employing jihad broadly would be effective neither in their international nor in their domestic politics. On the international stage, they could achieve the empire's territorial security only through membership in the European Concert; at home, the Ottoman state ruled over too many non-Muslim citizen-subjects. State and jihad, in other words, were not mutually supportive, and the politicization of religion appeared self-destructive. By the twentieth century, however, this perspective began to change. Abdurrahman Cami, a prominent member of the Ottoman chamber of deputies observed in *The Ottoman Future: Its Enemies and Its Friends* that "only Europe stands in the way of the Turk's Europeanization,"[92] an allusion to the Ottomans' hope of joining the European-based international state system. For Cami, the European great powers had rejected the Sublime Porte's bid for cooperation and friendship, preferring instead to follow a policy of undermining the empire's integrity and controlling its geostrategic and economic resources.

Pan-Islamism, the idea that Muslim populations worldwide join forces politically, even militarily, played only a small role in Cami's outlook. He considered Pan-Islamism (İttihad-ı İslam) a fabrication of European imperialist powers, a ghost invented to manipulate domestic public opinion back home and to justify continued aggressive schemes of expansion into Muslim territories. Perhaps eventually, Cami believed, a kind of global Muslim union might appear after all as a self-fulfilling, European prophecy but not in the manner imagined in the West: "This union, however, will not be the result of the caliph's politics, but of the Europeans' oppression in the colonies: Pan-Islamism is not a positive result of Muslim politics, but it will be the negative result of Christian oppression."[93] This Pan-Islamism, in other words, could lead to the formation of an anticolonial, defensive league of Islamic states, a united front against, as he saw it, Anglo-French-Russian aggression.

The new, younger leadership that seized power in 1908 as the Committee of Union and Progress had given up on international diplomacy, and they had decided that the only way they could join the European state system was through an alliance with Germany, even if—in one of those historical twists of irony—this came at the cost of entering a war against three European great powers. This new attitude also meant that the leadership of the CUP put aside concerns about the disastrous impact that waging jihad could have on relations between Muslims and non-Muslims within the empire.

Finally, it should be noted that the call for jihad had not lost all of its resonance once the empire came crashing down at the end of World War I. This continued appeal is illustrated by the Turkish Grand National Assembly's bestowing on Mustafa Kemal Atatürk, the new republic's president, the title of *ghazi*, or warrior, which retained some of its religious connotation and registered the presence of religious identity in political and military affairs.

Notes

1. For a nonmilitary call, see Florence A. Fensham, Mary I. Lyman, H. B. Humphrey, *A Modern Crusade in the Turkish Empire* (Chicago: Women's Board of Missions of the Interior, 1908). Others, such as Charles Dickens, bemoaned this attitude and the policies behind it; see Charles Dickens, "The Eastern Question as It Was," *All the Year Round: A Weekly Journal*, new series no. 478 (January 26, 1878): 9–14.
2. People's Republic of China, National Defense Policy, issued December 28, 2004, http://english. pladaily.com.cn/site2/chinanationaldefense/2004-12/28/content_98517.htm (accessed January 30, 2012).
3. Jacques Rivière, a prisoner of war in Germany during World War I, made this statement in 1915. See Jacques Rivière, *À la trace de Dieu* (Paris: Gallimard, 1925), 37; quoted in Annette Becker, *War and Faith: The Religious Imagination in France, 1914–1930*, trans. Helen McPhail (New York: Berg, 1998), 7.
4. Virginia H. Aksan, *Ottoman Wars, 1700–1870: An Empire Besieged* (New York: Pearson Longman, 2007), 319, 321.

5. Tobias Heinzelmann, *Heiliger Kampf oder Landesverteidigung? Die Diskussion um die Einführung der allgemeinen Militärpflicht im Osmanischen Reich, 1826–1856* (New York: Peter Lang, 2004), 48, 47–66, more generally, quotes the document at length.

6. Robert Dankoff, *An Ottoman Mentality: The World of Evliya Çelebi* (Leiden: Brill, 2004), 121.

7. Patriarch Yusuf Hubaysh, quoted in Ussama Makdisi, *Artillery of Heaven: American Missionaries and the Failed Conversion of the Middle East* (Ithaca, N.Y.: Cornell University Press, 2008), 131.

8. Şevket Pamuk, "The Great Ottoman Debasement, 1808–1844: A Political Economy Framework," in Israel Gershoni, Hakan Erdem, and Ursula Woköck, eds., *Histories of the Middle East: New Directions* (Boulder, Colo.: Lynne Rienner, 2002), 28–29.

9. Éva Bóka, "In Search of a Stereotype: 'The Turkish Question,'" *Südost-Forschungen* 55 (1996): 1. See also Brinda Charry, chapter 8, and John Kelsay, chapter 10, above.

10. Viorel Panaite, *The Ottoman Law of War and Peace: The Ottoman Empire and Tribute Payers* (Boulder, Colo.: East European Monographs, distributed by Columbia University Press, 2000), 79.

11. Molly Greene, *A Shared World: Christians and Muslims in the Early Modern Mediterranean* (Princeton, N.J.: Princeton University Press, 2000), 206–9.

12. Aksan, *Ottoman Wars*, 160–61.

13. Quoted in ibid., 393, n. 22.

14. Ibid., 7.

15. Gottfried Hagen, "The Prophet Muhammad as an Exemplar in War: Ottoman Views on the Eve of World War I," *New Perspectives on Turkey* 22 (Spring 2000): 147, 156, and passim.

16. Donald Quataert, *The Ottoman Empire, 1700–1922*, 2nd ed. (Cambridge, U.K.: Cambridge University Press, 2005), 112, 117.

17. Erik-Jan Zürcher, "Griechisch-orthodoxe und muslimische Flüchtlinge und Deportierte in Griechenland und der Türkei seit 1912," in Klaus J. Bade et al., eds., *Enzyklopädie Migration in Europa: Vom 17. Jahrhundert bis zur Gegenwart* (Munich: Ferdinand Schöningh and Wilhelm Fink, 2007), 623, 627.

18. See also Nuri Yurdusev, chapter 9 above.

19. Karen Barkey, *Empire of Difference: The Ottomans in Comparative Perspective* (Cambridge, U.K.: Cambridge University Press, 2008), 1–191; Linda Darling, "Contested Territory: Ottoman Holy War in Comparative Context," *Studia Islamica* 91 (2000): 133–63; Molly Greene, "The Ottoman Experience," *Daedalus* 134 (Spring 2005): 88–99; Greene, *A Shared World*; Cemal Kafadar, *Between Two Worlds: The Construction of the Ottoman State* (Berkeley: University of California Press, 1995).

20. Kafadar, *Between Two Worlds*, 93, demonstrates the difficulties involved in defining *ghazi* and *ghaza*. See also Yurdusev, chapter 9 above.

21. Barkey, *Empire of Difference*, 85; Kafadar, *Between Two Worlds*, 73, 75–76, 145.

22. Zeki Arıkan, "Balkan Savaşı ve Kamuoyu," in *Bildiriler: Dördüncü Askeri Tarih Semineri* (Ankara: Genelkurmay Basımevi, 1989), 176, citing the Ottoman newspaper *Ahenk*, September 13, 1912. For a broader discussion, see Mustafa Aksakal, *The Ottoman Road to War in 1914: The Ottoman Empire and the First World War* (Cambridge, U.K.: Cambridge University Press, 2008), 1–41.

23. Aksakal, *The Ottoman Road to War*, 83.

24. Elizabeth Thompson, "Ottoman Political Reform in the Provinces," *International Journal of Middle East Studies* 25 (1993): 457–75.

25. Bruce Masters, *Christians and Jews in the Ottoman Arab World: The Roots of Sectarianism* (Cambridge, U.K.: Cambridge University Press, 2001), 108–11 and, more generally, 130–68.

26. Selim Deringil, *The Well-Protected Domains: Ideology and the Legitimation of Power in the Ottoman Empire, 1876–1909* (New York: I. B. Tauris, 1998), 4.

27. Henry Wheaton, *Elements of International Law*, 8th ed., ed. Richard Henry Dana (Boston: Little, Brown, 1866), 327 and passim; on this point, see also the excellent article by Richard S. Horowitz, "International Law and State Transformation in China, Siam, and the Ottoman Empire during the Nineteenth Century," *Journal of World History* 15 (December 2004): 452–54.

28. Deringil, *The Well-Protected Domains*, 50.

29. Aksan, *Ottoman Wars*, 485–86; Heinzelmann, *Heiliger Kampf*, 269–339; Hakan Erdem, "Recruitment for the 'Victorious Soldiers of Muhammad' in the Arab Provinces, 1826–1828," in Gershoni, Erdem, and Woköck, *Histories*, 189–206.

30. Başbakanlık Osmanlı Arşivi (hereafter BOA), Turkish Prime Ministry's Ottoman Archives, Istanbul, C.HR 90/4492, no month, no day, 1773.

31. Ibid., C.HR 52/2567, May 10, 1809.

32. Ibid., C.AS 414/17121, 14 Cemaziyelahir 1224 (1810).

33. Aksan, *Ottoman Wars*, 360.

34. Heinzelmann, *Heiliger Kampf*, 52–53.

35. Ibid., 50, 52.

36. Aksan, *Ottoman Wars*, 322.

37. BOA, C.HR 38/1864, no month, no day, 1244 (1829).

38. Aksan, *Ottoman Wars*, 360.

39. For English translations of the 1839 and 1856 documents, see J. C. Hurewitz, ed., *The Middle East and North Africa in World Politics: A Documentary Record*, vol. 1: *European Expansion, 1535–1914*, 2nd ed. (New Haven, Conn.: Yale University Press, 1975), 269–71, 315–18. For the English text of the Ottoman Constitution of 1876, see http://www.anayasa.gen.tr/1876constitution.htm.

40. Aksan, *Ottoman Wars*, 325, 325, n. 53.

41. K. E. Fleming, *The Muslim Bonaparte: Diplomacy and Orientalism in Ali Pasha's Greece* (Princeton, N.J.: Princeton University Press, 1999).

42. Khaled Fahmy, *Mehmed Ali: From Ottoman Governor to Ruler of Egypt* (Oxford: Oneworld, 2009), 84, 86.

43. For Mahmud II's explanation for the need to adopt the military techniques of "our enemies," see Heinzelmann, *Heiliger Kampf*, 48.

44. Aksan, *Ottoman Wars*, 380, 382; A. Uner Turgay, "Iâne-i Cihâdiyye: A Multi-Ethnic, Multi-Religious Contribution to Ottoman War Effort," *Studia Islamica* (1986): 115–24.

45. From the English translation in Hurewitz, *The Middle East*, 1:317–18.

46. This translation from Masters, *Christians and Jews*, 140.

47. M. Şükrü Hanioğlu, *A Brief History of the Late Ottoman Empire* (Princeton, N.J.: Princeton University Press, 2008), 73.

48. Şerif Mardin, *The Genesis of Young Ottoman Thought: A Study in the Modernization of Turkish Political Ideas* (Syracuse, N.Y.: Syracuse University Press, 2000), 175–78; Mehmed Sadık Rifat, *Müntahabat-ı Asar* (Istanbul: Tatyos Davitçiyan, 1870). But see Heinzelmann, *Heiliger Kampf*, 126, who urges caution concerning Sadık Rifat's influence on Reşid Pasha.

49. Rifat, *Müntahabat-ı Asar*; quoted in Mardin, *The Genesis*, 186.

50. Cemil Aydın, *The Politics of Anti-Westernism in Asia: Visions of World Order in Pan-Islamic and Pan-Asian Thought* (New York: Columbia University Press, 2007), 18.

51. Heinzelmann, *Heiliger Kampf*, 127.

52. Hanioğlu, *A Brief History*, 76–85; Aksan, *Ottoman Wars*, 437–45.

53. Ali Fuat Türkgeldi, *Mesail-i Mühimme-i Siyasiyye*, 4 vols., ed. Bekir Sıtkı Baykal (Ankara: Türk Tarih Kurumu, 1960), 1:321; quoted in Aksan, *Ottoman Wars*, 442.

54. Aksan, *Ottoman Wars*, 443.

55. Ibid., 440.

56. Alexander Schölch, "Britain in Palestine, 1838–1882: The Roots of the Balfour Policy," *Journal of Palestine Studies* 22 (1992): 39–56; Masters, *Christians and Jews*, 147–49.

57. BOA, İ.DH 221/13141 (1266).

58. Ibid., A.MKT.MHM 58/97, 15 Zilhicce 1270 (September 8, 1854).

59. Ibid., İ.DH 306/19416, 1270 (1853).

60. For a poignant overview of Abdulhamid's reign, see Benjamin C. Fortna, "The Reign of Abdülhamid II," in Reşat Kasaba, ed., *Turkey in the Modern World*, vol. 4: *The Cambridge History of Turkey* (Cambridge, U.K.: Cambridge University Press, 2008), 38–61. For full

treatments, see François Georgeon, *Abdülhamid II: Le sultan calife (1876–1909)* (Paris: Fayard, 2003); Kemal H. Karpat, *The Politicization of Islam: Reconstructing Identity, State, Faith, and Community in the Late Ottoman State* (Oxford: Oxford University Press, 2001); and Deringil, *The Well-Protected Domains*.

61. Norman Rich, *Great Power Diplomacy, 1814–1914* (New York: McGraw-Hill, 1992), 221.

62. Michael Palairet, *The Balkan Economies: c. 1800–1914* (Cambridge, U.K.: Cambridge University Press, 1997), 173.

63. Fortna, "The Reign of Abdülhamid II," 45.

64. Palairet, *The Balkan Economies*, 173.

65. Briggs Davenport, *A History of the Great War, 1914–* (New York: Putnam's, 1916), 49.

66. Palairet, *The Balkan Economies*, 163.

67. Fortna, "The Reign of Abdülhamid II," 47.

68. Quoted in Deringil, *The Well-Protected Domains*, 46.

69. Karpat, *The Politicization of Islam*, 86–87.

70. Hagen, "The Prophet Muhammad."

71. BOA, MF.MKT 40/102, for Mehmed Emin Efendi's work; BOA, MF.MKT 45/66, for Halid Efendi's.

72. Makdisi, *Artillery of Heaven*, 65–66.

73. Ibid., 67.

74. Deringil, *The Well-Protected Domains*, 114.

75. Ibid., 114.

76. Ibid., 115.

77. Ibid., 113.

78. Eugene L. Rogan, *Frontiers of the State in the Late Ottoman Empire: Transjordan, 1850–1921* (Cambridge, U.K.: Cambridge University Press, 1999), 65–66.

79. Karpat, *The Politicization of Islam*, 234.

80. There does not seem to have been a formal declaration of holy war during the Ottoman-Greek War of 1897, as Karpat states in *Politicization*, 256. For examples of Sultan Abdulhamid II addressing troops in 1897, see Vecihi, *Musavver Tarih-i Harb* (Dersaadet: İkdam, 1898), 300–301.

81. Deringil, *The Well-Protected Domains*, 94–97.

82. Ibid., 97.

83. For the most recent use of the phrase, see the impressive study by Tilman Lüdke, *Jihad Made in Germany: Ottoman and German Propaganda and Intelligence Operations in the First World War* (Münster: Lit, 2006); also Gottfried Hagen, "German Heralds of Holy War: Orientalists and Applied Oriental Studies," *Comparative Studies of South Asia, Africa and the Middle East* 24 (2004): 145–62; Wolfgang G. Schwanitz, "Djihad 'Made in Germany': Der Streit um den Heiligen Krieg, 1914–1915," *Sozial. Geschichte* 18 (2003): 7–34; Gerhard Höpp, *Muslime in der Mark als Kriegsgefangene und Internierte in Wünsdorf und Zossen* (Berlin: Das Arabische Buch, 1997).

84. Şevket Süreyya Aydemir, *Makedonya'dan Ortaasya'ya Enver Paşa* (Istanbul: Remzi Kitabevi, 1971), 2:11–21, 505–6; Jacob M. Landau, *Pan-Turkism: From Irredentism to Cooperation*, 2nd ed. (Bloomington: Indiana University Press, 1995), 51–56. See also the earlier, more balanced presentation in Jacob M. Landau, *The Politics of Pan-Islam: Ideology and Organization* (New York: Oxford University Press, 1994), 94–103.

85. Wilhelm van Kampen, "Studien zur deutschen Türkeipolitik in der Zeit Wilhelms II" (PhD dissertation, University of Kiel, 1968), 57–68; Herbert Landolin Müller, *Islam, ğihād ("Heiliger Krieg") und Deutsches Reich: Ein Nachspiel zur wilhelminischen Weltpolitik im Maghreb, 1912–1918* (New York: Peter Lang, 1991), 173–85; Donald M. McKale, *War by Revolution: Germany and Great Britain in the Middle East in the Era of World War I* (Kent, Ohio: Kent State University Press, 1998), 17–96; Hagen, "German Heralds"; Lüdke, *Jihad Made in Germany*.

86. Quoted in Aksakal, *The Ottoman Road to War*, 17.

87. Hagen, "German Heralds," 145; Stanford J. Shaw, *The Ottoman Empire in World War I*, vol. 2: *Triumph and Tragedy, November 1914–July 1916* (Ankara: Türk Tarih Kurumu, 2008), 752–54.

88. Hasan Kayalı, *Arabs and Young Turks: Ottomanism, Arabism, and Islamism in the Ottoman Empire, 1908–1918* (Berkeley: University of California Press, 1997), 187.

89. Ibid., 187.

90. Hagen, "German Heralds," 152.

91. Ibid.

92. Cami [Abdürrahman Cami Baykut], *Osmanlılığın Âtisi: Düşmanları ve Dostları* [The Ottoman Future: Its Enemies and Its Friends] (Istanbul: İfham Matbaası, 1331 [5 Kanunisani 1328/ January 18, 1913]), 21–29.

93. Ibid., 44–45.

15

Muslim Debates on Jihad in British India

The Writings of Chiragh 'Ali and Abu al-A'la Mawdudi

OMAR KHALIDI

This chapter examines the views of two influential Indian writers on jihad, Maw-lawi Chiragh 'Ali (1844–1895) and Mawlana Abu al-A'la Mawdudi (1903–1979). Both lived and worked for a time in Hyderabad, the nizam's dominion of the Dec-can in southern India. But that is where their similarity ends. The two understood the idea and practice of jihad in very different ways. Chiragh 'Ali wrote his treatise *A Critical Exposition of the Popular "Jihad"* in English and Mawdudi his principal work on jihad, *Al-Jihad fi al-Islam* (Jihad in Islam), in Urdu, indicative of their different intellectual backgrounds and intended audiences. In this chapter, I sit-uate the two men within the intellectual, social, and political milieus in which they wrote, discussing who their respective audiences were and how these factors shaped their views on jihad. I consider whether the two writers were aware of just and holy war ideas in other religions and modern secular thought and, if so, to what degree that awareness influenced their own views on jihad. Finally, I discuss the impact of their work on contemporary Muslim debates on war and peace.

The decline of the Mughal empire, beginning in the eighteenth century, and the advance of the British East India Company culminated in the Indian revolt, or Sepoy Mutiny (as the British called it) of 1857. The revolt failed, leading to the ban-ishment of the emperor Bahadur Shah Zafar and the end of the empire. The histor-ical accounts are not clear about whether the Muslim participants in the revolt perceived it as a jihad. Given that many upper-caste Hindus were among the leaders of the revolt—the Rani of Jhansi, Nana Sahib, and Tantiya Tope, for example—the revolt cannot have been motivated entirely by notions of jihad. Moreover, the fact that some prominent Muslim rulers, including the nizam of Hyderabad, backed the British diminishes from the claim that it was a jihad. Regardless, most colonial au-thorities characterized the mutiny as a Muslim revolt against the British.

The failure of the uprising left the Muslim elite prostrate, with little more than imperial memories to sustain itself. This episode created the conditions for Indian

Muslim thinkers to reexamine many aspects of their Islamic intellectual heritage, including the sources of jurisprudence. A new kind of leadership—a leadership of adjustment—was needed to find a modus vivendi with the British rulers and their resurgent Hindu supporters.[1] For more than three decades immediately after the mutiny, Sayyid Ahmad Khan (1817–1898) provided this leadership. He attributed the revolt to the distrust created by the sweeping social change initiated by the British. Indians feared that the changes presaged an attempt by the British to convert the people to Christianity. This fear was exploited by those who had been displaced from power to rally support for one last desperate effort to regain what they had lost. The failed revolt and the dire situation of Indian Muslims afterward convinced Sayyid Ahmad that Islam must come to terms with the West if it was not to remain permanently in a state of social and political backwardness. He stressed the commonality of fundamental Islamic and Christian teachings and values. He also emphasized both civilizations' indebtedness to the classical Greek intellectual heritage. Reason, alongside revelation, he argued, was basic to both Western and Islamic intellectual systems, leading him to stress the importance of modern scientific and technological education for Muslims. Finally, he advocated political loyalty to the British Raj. In short, Sayyid Ahmad and the school of thought he epitomized sought to redefine Islam in a manner compatible with modern sensibilities and rational sciences.[2] When presenting this view of Islam to the British colonial authorities, missionaries, and intelligentsia, Sayyid Ahmad and his protégés were compelled to question conventional understanding of a number of vital issues: women's status, slavery, and jihad, among others.

Chiragh 'Ali

The most prominent member of Sayyid Ahmad's circle to reexamine critically the classical Islamic jurisprudence of jihad was Chiragh 'Ali, a civil servant in Hyderabad state, a notable modernist thinker, and an influential author. Chiragh 'Ali wrote during the peak of the Raj in the 1880s, when the nizam's dominion, although semiautonomous, was entirely under the sway of British authorities.

Chiragh 'Ali's family had Kashmiri origins, but his grandfather had migrated to Punjab and then to the United Provinces during the early nineteenth century, where his father, Muhammad Bakhsh (c. 1821–1856), was born and raised. Because of his knowledge of English, a rare skill at that time, Bakhsh found employment as a clerk in the district administration of Saharanpur. Chiragh 'Ali, born in 1844, was the eldest of Muhammad Bakhsh's four sons and was educated privately at home by his parents and grandmother. If he acquired any additional formal education, no information exists about it, but competence in his native Urdu, Persian, and English landed Chiragh 'Ali a job as a subordinate clerk in the district treasury in Basti. This led to a higher post, as deputy *munsarim*, or junior land settlement officer, in Lucknow's Court of the Judicial Commissioner in 1872, when he was twenty-eight years old.

During the early 1870s, Chiragh 'Ali encountered Sayyid Ahmad Khan, then presiding over the movement to advance modern, scientific education centered in Aligarh, which would lead to the founding of the Mohammedan Anglo-Oriental College (later Aligarh Muslim University) in 1875. Finding the young man bright and capable, Sayyid Ahmad entrusted Chiragh 'Ali with a translation project, financed by Hyderabad state authorities. Impressed with Chiragh 'Ali's successful execution of the project, Sayyid Ahmad recommended the young man to Salar Jang I, prime minister of Hyderabad, for a high post in the nizam's administration. Armed with the offer of the lucrative post of assistant to the commissioner of revenue, Chiragh 'Ali arrived in Hyderabad in 1876. Thus, he joined an elite group associated with the Aligarh movement, which Salar Jang I had begun in cooperation with Sayyid Ahmad to bring about Hyderabad's bureaucratic and financial modernization. This group included such icons of the Aligarh movement as Muhsin al-Mulk, Wiqar al-Mulk, "Deputy" Nazir Ahmad, Sayyid Husayn Bilgrami, Justice Khuda Bakhsh, and Fath Nawaz Jang.[3] Within a decade, Chiragh 'Ali received rapid promotions: to *subahdar* (district commissioner) of Warangal and Gulbarga, followed by secretary to the board of revenue, a very powerful post. The nizam conferred on Chiragh 'Ali the title of *nawab azam yar jang*, "the brave knight in war," during the royal birthday awards in 1887. Five years later, he rose to the powerful position of secretary to the political and finance department of Hyderabad. He was serving in this office when he died in 1895, barely fifty-one years old.[4]

Chiragh 'Ali was a prolific writer, with publications starting in 1871. His two most frequently cited works in English are *The Proposed Political, Legal, and Social Reforms in the Ottoman Empire*[5] and *A Critical Exposition of the Popular "Jihad," Showing That All the Wars of Muhammad Were Defensive; and That Aggressive War, or Compulsory Conversion Is Not Allowed in the Koran.*[6] He also published two seminal works on Hyderabad's economic and administrative history: *Hyderabad (Deccan) under Sir Salar Jung* and *History of Some of the Important Jagirs.*[7] As secretary to the board of revenue, Chiragh 'Ali prepared and published the state budget, a novelty at the time. In addition to his English writings, he published extensively in Urdu, contributing frequently to Sayyid Ahmad Khan's journal *Tahdhib al-akhlaq* (The Cultivation of Morals). Some of his works remain unpublished.[8]

Chiragh 'Ali was a voracious reader; he read while dining, during travel, in the toilet, in bed, and while at his desk.[9] Bureaucratic positions in India were associated then (as they still are today) with cajoling, scolding, and managing struggles over promotions and demotions, leaving little time for scholarly pursuits. Chiragh 'Ali, however, was truly an exception among the bureaucrats of his time.[10] Despite his lack of a formal, modern education, he learned English in addition to some Latin, French, Chaldean, and Hebrew. A veritable bibliophile, he collected books from far and wide, and his intellectual interests ranged across many fields. Muslim scholars and particularly the ulema of his time were generally unfamiliar with and uninterested in the comparative study of religions.[11] Some learned about other religions in order to refute them in polemics, or *manazira*. In contrast, Chiragh 'Ali studied the Old and New Testaments and read widely in Christian theology not to refute Christian teachings but to find similarities between the Bible and the Qur'an. At his death, the Asafiyya State Central Library in Hyderabad acquired his large collection of books. It has not been properly maintained, though, and today most of the books are in an advanced state of disrepair and decay.

Although he never traveled abroad, "modernist trends from other parts of dar al-Islam converged in Chiragh 'Ali's writings. In an article written in 1880, he cites works of the Egyptian traveler to the West and educationist Rifa'a Rafi al-Tahtawi, of Sayf Efendi of Beirut, of the Tunisian modernist and statesman Khayr al-Din Pasha, and of the Syrian journalist and literary critic Ahmad Faris al-Shidyaq."[12] His own modernist approach led him to criticize strongly the historical develop- ment of Islam and what he saw as the Muslims' divergence from the ideal religion as expounded in the Qur'an. His critical examination of classical Islamic jurispru- dence led to some conclusions that put him in conflict with many ulema. Respond- ing to his request to help translate one of his works into Urdu, Chiragh 'Ali's admirer and facilitator Sayyid Ahmad Khan wrote: "In my opinion, it is not proper to publish it in Urdu. The people would not understand your objective in writing this work. . . . It has already caused hostile feelings against you at Aligarh, and if published in Urdu, it would cause an unprecedented enmity in Hyderabad, where people are even more ignorant than Aligarh."[13] The identity of the work in ques- tion is unclear from the correspondence between the two, but it may very well have been Chiragh 'Ali's most controversial and lengthy work, *A Critical Exposition of the Popular "Jihad,"* published in 1885 and dedicated to Sayyid Ahmad Khan. It was, in fact, translated into Urdu by Khwaja Ghulam al-Saqalayn (d. 1915) of Panipat and published in 1913.[14]

Chiragh 'Ali clearly hoped that his *A Critical Exposition* would be read by and influence the thinking and conduct of his fellow Indian Muslims. In the vein of Sayyid Ahmad's and other reformers' writings, Chiragh 'Ali's work was intended to demonstrate the Islamic basis for the modernist policy of accommodation with the British, in this case by undermining the position of those Muslims who still harbored hopes of overthrowing British rule through a renewed jihad.

But the primary audience Chiragh 'Ali had in mind were European orientalists, missionaries, and colonial officials who saw Muslims as a continuing threat to Brit- ish rule. On the Muslim side, it was British rule and the intellectual justifications that missionaries and orientalists gave it that were seen as a threat to Muslim so- ciety in the subcontinent and, indeed, also in other regions. Some of the mission- aries, orientalists, and colonial officials described Islam in their writings as a religion spread by the sword that sanctioned slavery and the servitude of women. Explicitly or implicitly, these writings lent credence to the view that the British came as liber- ators and civilizers of backward peoples. Modernists such as Sayyid Ahmad Khan, Chiragh 'Ali, and Sayyid Amir 'Ali (1849–1927) took it upon themselves to write rejoinders to such British writers as Edward Sell (1839–1932), Malcolm MacColl

(1831–1907), Samuel Green (1822–1905), William Muir (1819–1905), and William Robertson Smith (1846–1894). Chiragh 'Ali opens *A Critical Exposition* by declaring: "In publishing this work, my chief object is to remove the general and erroneous impression from the minds of European and Christian writers regarding Islam, that Mohammad waged wars of conquest, extirpation, as well as of proselytizing against Koreish, other Arab tribes, the Jews, and Christians; that he held the Koran in one hand, the scimitar in the other, and compelled people to believe in his mission."[15] His book is sprinkled throughout with quotations from British and other European writers, sometimes to support his position, sometimes to refute theirs. His main contention was that missionaries and orientalists judged Islam on the basis of the Islamic law devised by ulema, not on the principles enunciated in the Qur'an.

Although Chiragh 'Ali had read both Jewish and Christian scriptures and an examination of his personal library at Asafiyya Library reveals a good deal of literature on Semitic religious traditions and European history, he surprisingly makes no references in *A Critical Exposition* to the war traditions of other religions. He does, however, refer to "natural law," "international law," or the "law of most civilized countries" but only sporadically and briefly.[16] Instead of drawing comparisons, Chiragh 'Ali pursues single-mindedly his goal of correcting false views propagated by both Muslims and non-Muslims on the nature of jihad and of the wars that Muhammad fought.

Chiragh 'Ali's central argument on jihad is that all of the wars[17] that the Prophet Muhammad fought were defensive and none was aimed at the forcible conversion of Arabs.[18] There is not a single instance in the life of Muhammad, he asserts, that shows that the Prophet made anyone become a Muslim by holding the sword to the neck.[19] According to Chiragh 'Ali, any war fought in pursuit of one's legitimate rights may be called a defensive war. In his opinion, facing force with force, dispelling oppression, safeguarding one's own rights that are in jeopardy, retaking property lost to the hands of the enemy, or taking steps to ensure one's safety do not fall into the category of oppression or go against the idea of tolerance.[20] The Prophet Muhammad used force only when all else failed, including sincere attempts at peaceful negotiations.[21]

In order to establish his claim that Muhammad and his followers were the oppressed and the Quraysh of Mecca the oppressors, Chiragh 'Ali cites some of the activities of the Quraysh against the Prophet and the first Muslims. He says that the followers of the Prophet endured many tortures at the hands of the Quraysh. The enormity of torture and oppression increased to such an extent that some Muslims pretended allegiance to the Quraysh, although at heart they remained faithful to Islam. The Quraysh personally targeted the Prophet in many ways, but he endured with remarkable patience. In the end, when he saw his life at risk, the Prophet and his followers emigrated to Medina. Yet even after the Hijra, the Quraysh did not relent but rather increased the torture of the emigrants' kin who had remained behind. They also banned the emigrants from visiting Mecca, their native place, even to perform the hajj or pilgrimage to the Ka'ba.

Under these circumstances, Chiragh 'Ali postulates, had the Prophet initiated war against his enemies, he would have been acting in conformity with the morals and customs of the land. Resorting to force was his right, but he did not take this action until other circumstances forced him to do so. These circumstances compelled him to fight against his enemies more than once. According to Chiragh 'Ali, the Prophet's involvement in each war (more accurately, battle) had its own justification. The Prophet took up the sword against his will and wish.[22]

For Chiragh 'Ali, the first and foremost proof of the defensive nature of the Prophet's wars is found in the Qur'an. It states, categorically or by implication, that the wars were defensive, and for a believer, that is sufficient. Chiragh 'Ali quotes verse after verse with the aim of demonstrating that nothing in the Qur'an teaches Muslims to fight non-Muslims without instigation or provocation from the latter.

Chiragh 'Ali then mentions verses 2:189 (193), 8:40 (39), and 9:5, which appear to command aggressive war or imply forcible conversion. Qur'an 9:5, the "sword verse," requires particular attention: "And when the sacred months are passed, kill those who join other gods with God wherever ye find them; and seize them, and besiege them, and lay wait for them with every kind of ambush; but if they repent and observe prayer and pay the obligatory alms, then let them go their way. Verily, God is Gracious, Merciful."[23] Chiragh 'Ali rejects the claim that this verse commands an aggressive war. In his opinion, it must be read in the context of the verses preceding and following it, specifically Q. 9:1–15, which were revealed when the people of Mecca broke the Treaty of Hudaybiyya and attacked the Muslims' allies in the tribe of Banu Khuza'a.[24] The injunctions found in these verses were not carried out, however, because Mecca came under Muslim control without fighting.

As for Q. 2:189 (193), which reads, "And do battle against them until there be no more persecution [fitna], and the worship be that of God: but if they desist, then let there be no hostility, save against wrong-doers," Chiragh 'Ali claims that it also cannot be read as an unconditional declaration of war. In the context of other verses before it, Q. 2:189 (193) justifies only a defensive war. The same is also true for Q. 8:40 (39), which reads: "Fight then against them till civil strife be at an end, and the religion be all of it God's; and if they desist, verily God beholdeth what they do." Chiragh 'Ali derives the defensive nature of this verse from the word for persecution or civil strife, fitna. According to him, fitna refers here to the aggressive and abusive activities of the Quraysh. Hence, God only commands war in response to violence being received and only until the fitna is stopped. Putting an end to torture and oppression is inherently a defensive war for Chiragh 'Ali.[25]

Apart from the Qur'an, the historical accounts of Muhammad's military campaigns also confirm that he fought only in self-defense, Chiragh 'Ali writes. First, he takes issue with both the Muslim and the European biographers of Muhammad for exaggerating the number of expeditions that took place during the Prophet's lifetime. The numbers they give range from nineteen to more than one hundred. These numbers reflect, according to Chiragh 'Ali, a confusion of military engagements with sundry, nonviolent activity, including missions sent to rulers calling them to Islam, missions to prepare alliances or pacts, and missions to reconnoiter enemy positions or other types of espionage. He concludes that the number of expeditions in which actual fighting occurred may be reduced to only five: Badr, Uhud, Ahzab, Khyber, and Hunain. "Even these five scarcely deserve the name of battle," he writes. "From a military point of view, they were but petty skirmishes in their results."[26]

Chiragh 'Ali reviews the Prophet's battles mainly to repudiate European historians who narrated them in such a way that Muhammad appears to be the aggressor. With respect to the battle of Badr, the first fought by Muslims, he avers that the Prophet left Medina only after the Quraysh had left Mecca with the intention of attacking Medina. Most European writers, basing their accounts on some of the earliest Muslim histories,[27] held that the Qurayshi force left Mecca not to attack Medina but to defend a Meccan caravan returning home from Syria that they feared would be attacked by Muhammad. Chiragh 'Ali argues that if this view is correct, the Ansar (the Muslim converts native to Medina) would not have marched out with Muhammad and the Muhajirun (the immigrants from Mecca) because they had pledged to fight only in defense of Medina. In addition, Chiragh 'Ali claims that the battle of Badr occurred on January 13, 624. The Quraysh left Mecca on January 4, while the Muslim force left Medina four days later, on January 8. In Chiragh 'Ali's view, this chronology establishes that Badr was fought by the Muslims in self-defense, "as in terms of historical sequence, the offensive had already been taken by the hostile Meccans by torturing and humiliating the followers of the Prophet. Military strategy demanded initiative against the enemy and its Bedouin allies after the Prophet's migration to Madina."[28]

Chiragh 'Ali's argument that all of the battles of the Prophetic era were defensive provides the basis for his thesis that the only permissible motive for jihad is self-defense. There is no injunction in the Qur'an, he argues, that requires Muslims to declare an unconditional war against unbelievers for the purpose of imposing Islam. In advancing his thesis, he excludes a number of Qur'anic verses containing "jihad" or other derivatives of the Arabic root *j-h-d* from his list of verses dealing with war. Making full use of Edward Lane's *Arabic-English Lexicon* to examine linguistic terms related to, derived from, or cognate with "jihad," Chiragh 'Ali postulates that the root *j-h-d* and its third form, *jāhada*, do not mean fighting or quarreling with the enemy. Rather, they mean "to strive, labor, or toil" toward some goal with one's utmost capacity and strength.[29] Certainly, Chiragh 'Ali could have added that millions of Indian Muslims understood it as such in Urdu.

As Chiragh 'Ali writes, the root *j-h-d* and its third-form derivatives are found in both the Meccan and the Medinan verses of the Qur'an. He claims that in all of these verses, the only appropriate reading of "jihad" is the one held by pre-Islamic Arabs, in which there is no implication of religious war. Jihad became a religious war only after the exegetes and jurists of later generations interpreted many of the occurrences of *j-h-d* in the Medinan verses that way. Chiragh 'Ali then proceeds to refute this interpretation by examining these Medinan verses. He concludes that when the context of each verse is taken into account, each and every occurrence of *j-h-d* can be read in the broad sense of "striving" or "toiling," not waging war.[30] For example, Q. 2:215 (218) was revealed in connection with the Hijra. Hence, in his opinion, the phrase *jāhadu fi sabil Allah* that occurs in this verse refers to the pain and hardship the Muslims endured in fleeing from Mecca.[31] Likewise, the association of *jāhadu* with *sabirin* (those who are patient) in Q. 3:136 (142) and with *nafs* and *mal* (life and property) in Q. 8:73 (72) provides no reason to interpret the word in any other way than its conventional meaning at the time of "striving" and "laboring."[32]

But Chiragh 'Ali does not deny that the Qur'an accepts some types of fighting as legitimate. When it treats war and fighting, it does so using words derived from the roots *h-r-b* and *q-t-l*. Nevertheless, Chiragh 'Ali maintains, the Qur'an does not countenance an aggressive religious war. He defends this contention by positing that only two Qur'anic verses, 2:245 (244) and 9:124 (123), contain an "absolute or non-conditional injunction for making war against the unbelievers." The other Qur'anic verses dealing with fighting or warfare are all "limited or conditional." When faced with both general and conditional verses on the same subject, Chiragh 'Ali posits, the rules of exegesis require that "the conditional is to be preferred, and the absolute should be construed as conditional, because the latter is more expressive of the views of the author than the general which is considered as vague in its expression." Classical Muslim jurists derived their ideas of aggressive war only by violating this exegetical principle and by drawing on non-Qur'anic sources. In his opinion, they did so in order to support the expansionary policies of the later caliphs.[33]

Second, Chiragh 'Ali declares that the Qur'anic sanctions for war against unbelievers are all temporary and a response to the specific conditions of the Prophet's time. They have no bearing on modern times. In order to sustain this position, Chiragh 'Ali needed to refute two hadiths attributed to the Prophet, which are often quoted by classical and modern exponents of the idea that jihad is an open-ended war to bring all the world under Islamic sway: "Jihad will last up to the Day of Resurrection," as narrated by Abu Dawud; and "I have been enjoined to fight the people until they profess that there is no god except God," as narrated by Bukhari. With reference to the first hadith, Chiragh 'Ali notes that "jihad" here is ambiguous and may be read without any imputation of war. Moreover, he rejects the hadith's authenticity on the grounds that one of the narrators in its chain of transmission, Yazid ibn Abi Shayba, is considered a *majhul* narrator, one whose life (and hence credibility) is not well documented. Chiragh 'Ali contests the second hadith, narrated by Bukhari, because it is contrary to such clear Qur'anic verses as 2:189 (193) and 8:40 (39) that command the believers to fight the infidels only in self-defense until persecution and civil discord are ended.[34] In short, Chiragh 'Ali's view is that the defensive action taken by Muhammad and the

Qur'anic injunctions regarding them were all "transitory in their nature, and are not to be considered positive injunctions for future observance or religious precepts for coming generations."[35]

A Critical Exposition of the Popular "Jihad" has generated controversy since its release. Many modernist Muslim authors were inspired by it and produced books, articles, and pamphlets in Arabic, English, and Urdu or spoke out in public forums about jihad in the spirit of Chiragh 'Ali's work. More broadly, Chiragh 'Ali's argument that only the Qur'an has normative value in determining Islamic law and ethics has become a hallmark of Muslim modernism. Others, Muslims and non-Muslims, were extremely critical of the book. Less than two decades after the publication of *A Critical Exposition*, in December 1901, Dutch Reformed minister Herman T. Obbink (1869–1947) defended a thesis in Utrecht titled *De heilige oorlog volgens den Koran* (Holy War according to the Qur'an), in which he showed that Chiragh 'Ali's views were well outside the mainstream Islamic tradition as formulated in the classical expositions of Muslim scholars.[36] Many Muslim scholars of Chiragh 'Ali's time leveled the same charge, as Ghulam Mohammad Jaffar notes.[37] A scholar of our time, Mustansir Mir, criticizes Chiragh 'Ali as an apologist who was trying to "prove that Islam and pacifism are synonymous" and consequently whose writing had "not much to commend itself."[38] In response, Ayesha Jalal recently wrote that labeling Chiragh 'Ali and like-minded reformers as apologists "accords precious little attention to the historical context" in which they were writing. "Their partiality to Islam was intended to offset brazen attacks by Christian authors and cannot be judged by the standards of latter-day critical scholarship."[39]

Abu al-A'la Mawdudi

Nearly three decades after Chiragh 'Ali died, Abu al-A'la Mawdudi emerged as a second important interpreter of jihad in the Indian subcontinent. His first major work, the one that established him as a rising star among Indian Muslim intellectuals, was *Al-Jihad fi al-Islam*. But Mawdudi wrote on a wide range of topics relating to religion, politics, economics, and society during his long and prolific career. He is rightly considered one of the most influential Islamic thinkers of the twentieth century, and his ideas have shaped Islamic revivalism in Muslim societies throughout the world.

Mawdudi was born in 1903 in Awrangabad, Deccan, then a part of Hyderabad state.[40] After formal education in a government school in Awrangabad, he entered the field of journalism. Mawdudi went back and forth between various cities—Bhopal, Jabalpur, and Delhi—until he finally moved from Hyderabad to Punjab in 1938. Between 1925 and 1928, he was a columnist for *Al-Jami'at*, an Urdu newspaper published in Delhi by the Jami'at al-Ulema-yi Hind, an organization of Muslim divines aligned with the Congress Party. In early 1927, he serialized a column in *Al-Jami'at* on jihad. It was titled *Al-Jihad fi al-Islam*, and unsuspecting readers may well have thought it was written in Arabic, not Urdu. The serialized column earned him recognition from some of the prominent scholars of the time and the public at large. Dar al-Musannifin, an Islamic academy located in Azamgarh published it in book form in 1930. In a short preface to the second printing written on July 31, 1974, Mawdudi stated that "the book was unavailable for some time. Firstly, it was hard to reprint such a voluminous book during the Second World War [perhaps because of paper rationing]; secondly, I held back from reprinting as I wanted to include changes [in] international law during the Second World War. But I fell ill, rendering writing and reading difficult, so this book is now being republished with minor changes."[41]

By the close of the twentieth century, *Al-Jihad fi al-Islam* had gone through several editions in India and Pakistan, selling nearly one hundred thousand copies, certainly a record for any Urdu book. The book's circulation would be far larger if it had been translated into other languages, but as of yet, there are no translations of the full work available.[42] It consists of seven chapters. The first five are devoted to Mawdudi's understanding of Islamic precepts of war and peace. They are titled "Truth about Islamic Jihad," which is mostly about combative jihad (pp. 23–50); "Defensive War" (pp. 53–82); "War for the Common Good" (pp. 85–149); "The Spread of Islam and the Sword" (pp. 153–75); and "Islamic Laws concerning Peace and War" (pp. 179–324).

One of Mawdudi's aims in this work is to compare jihad with the just and holy war traditions of other religions and secular ideologies; this is his task in the last two chapters. In the sixth chapter, he devotes considerable space (pp. 327–456) to the concept of war in Hinduism, Judaism, Buddhism, and Christianity. In his last chapter, he presents an extended discussion (pp. 459–600) of the idea and practice of war among modern states and in international law.

Characteristically, Mawdudi writes flawless Urdu prose: clear, coherent, logical, assertive, authoritative, systematic, even persuasive. Qur'anic and hadith quotations are given both in the Arabic original and in Urdu translation. A number of primary and secondary sources are cited in the discussion of other religious traditions and international law. The extensive citations from European authors confirm his biographers' claims that Mawdudi had mined a significant library of Western scholarship on theology, philosophy, and law.[43]

Mawdudi opens his treatise by asserting that one of Islam's cardinal principles is respect for human life. He cites Qur'an 5:32, which affirms the biblical principle that "whosoever kills a human being, if not retaliation for a murder, nor for causing corruption in the land, must be accounted to have killed all mankind; and whosoever saves a life, it will be as if he had saved the life of all mankind."[44] At the same time, he continues, Islam permits killing when needed for the good of society. In Mawdudi's interpretation, "causing corruption [*fasad*] in the land" and fomenting dissension, rebellion, or oppression (*fitna*) are the two capital political sins against which jihad is directed.[45] Before the advent of the Prophet, Arab society was mired in the moral corruption of paganism, and the people were in open rebellion against the divine order. The Prophet proclaimed jihad in order to eliminate *fasad* and *fitna*.[46] God employed Muslims to make the world a better place by means of jihad, calling on them to "enjoin the right and forbid the wrong" (see Q. 3:110). There are times when jihad by the tongue or the pen is not sufficient, and in such situations, resort to arms is necessary and justified. God uses jihad to protect one set of people from another. Freedom of all religions is secured by way of jihad, as clearly stated in Q. 22:40:

> Those who have been expelled from their homes unjustly only because they said: "Our Lord is Allah." For had it not been that Allah checks one set of people by means of another, monasteries, churches, synagogues, and mosques, wherein the name of Allah is mentioned much would surely have been pulled down. Verily, Allah will help those who help His [cause]. Truly, Allah is All-Strong, All-Mighty.

Mawdudi interprets this verse to mean that God uses the just to fight the oppression and persecution of the unjust.[47]

Following the exegesis of numerous classical commentators (discussed by Asma Afsaruddin in chapter 2 above), Mawdudi believes that Q. 22:39 was the first verse to link jihad with *qital*, or fighting, and that it establishes the reason for war: "Sanction is given unto those who fight because they have been wronged; and Allah is indeed able to give them victory."[48] The people against whom Muslims are permitted to war are not those who possess fertile lands or great wealth, nor are they simply believers in a different faith. Instead, it is those who oppress people for their faith and expel them from their homes without right. Against such oppressors, not only is a war of self-defense permissible, but believers are enjoined to rush to defend others who are being persecuted and liberate them. Mawdudi invokes Q. 4:75: "And what is wrong with you that you fight not in the cause of Allah, and for those weak, ill-treated and oppressed among men, women, and children, whose cry is: 'Our Lord! Rescue us from this town whose people are oppressors; and raise for us from You one who will protect, and raise for us from You one who will help.'"[49]

In his chapter on defensive war, Mawdudi writes that the Qur'an preaches patience and acceptance in all matters, except for any attack to wipe out Islam and any attempt to impose an alien system. If anyone attempts to violate the Muslims' human rights, properties, freedom of faith and conscience, the believers must repel the aggression with their fullest might.[50] For Q. 2:191–94 state: "Fight against those who fight against you. . . . Kill them wherever you confront them and drive them out from where they drove you out. [For though killing is sinful] wrongful persecution is even worse than killing."[51] Mawdudi draws on classical legal texts, such as al-Kasani's *Al-Bada'i' wa al-sana'i'*, which prescribe that if a Muslim territory is attacked, it is the duty of every Muslim individual to obey the call of the trumpet (*nafir*).[52] But the call to join the jihad has to reach the individual through his government. Those outside the directly threatened territory must obey the call to help when officially sent. If Muslims living in a non-Islamic state are attacked by that state and it has a treaty of nonaggression with the Islamic state, the Muslims cannot be rescued by jihad, unless the treaty is first revoked through diplomatic channels. Mawdudi bases this position on Q. 8:72, a verse that Muslim scholars have traditionally cited as the basis for the principle of *pacta sunt servanda*, "agreements must be kept." From the purview of jihad, internal enemies of Islam, the hypocrites, are not exempt; Mawdudi cites Q. 9:73: "O Prophet! strive hard against the unbelievers and the hypocrites, and be firm against them."[53]

Turning to the question of war for the common good, Mawdudi postulates that the evils of *fitna* and *fasad* stem from false, unprincipled, disobedient-to-God systems of government.[54] Even if a government does not directly bring about evils, the evils' persistence results from the government's bad influence and inaction. A government such as this becomes the fountainhead of all evils; through its agency, wrongdoers and tyrants will find power to carry out evil deeds. It will enact laws that corrupt morality and destroy social justice. Therefore, in order to eradicate evil and to prevent wrong, Islam has prescribed that by organized effort—jihad—all such governments should be wiped out, by war if necessary. In their place, a just and equitable system of government should be founded, based on fear of God and divinely ordained rules (*hukumat-i ilahiyya*).[55] Such a government would serve not personal, class, or national ambitions but human interests. Its purpose would be to implement the Qur'anic injunction that Muslims promote good and prevent evil (*amr bi al-ma'ruf wa nahi 'an al-munkir*).

Unlike Chiragh 'Ali, who, despite his familiarity with Jewish and Christian traditions, made no reference to just and holy war concepts in them, Mawdudi devotes considerable attention to other religious traditions after advancing his ideas on what jihad entails. He prefaces this discussion with three points. First, it is unnecessary to "disprove" the authenticity of others' beliefs in order to prove one's own. Second, he who claims that truth is in his own and no one else's religion is unfair not only to the others' faith but also to his own. Actually, the light of truth is more or less found everywhere. Finally, one should avoid studying any religion through the lens of either its detractors or its uncritical followers. Ideally, one should study a particular religion through its own sources.[56]

Mawdudi's comparative study includes Hindu and Buddhist views on war, peace, violence, and nonviolence; since our focus here is on Muslim, Christian, and Jewish views, I will leave these sections aside. When he turns to look at Christian conceptions of just and holy war, Mawdudi prefaces the discussion by alerting readers that he is talking not about the Qur'anic prophet 'Isa but about Jesus as presented by Pauline Christianity. He finds the New Testament ethics of how to gain the kingdom of heaven incapable of handling issues of war and peace. Pauline Christianity does not shed any light on how to acquire the power that Mawdudi considers essential to repel and prevent oppression or how to use the power if it is, in fact, acquired. He also finds many other serious lacunae in Christian teachings. If there is to be peace among nations, on what principles should it be founded? How should enemies on the battlefield be treated? How should conquered enemies be treated? According to Mawdudi, because of the absence of clear guidelines regarding war, Pauline Christianity must be held responsible for the excesses committed by Christians, whether or not they claim that they are acting in the name of their faith.

To Mawdudi, if all people were to follow Jesus's advice, "To him who strikes you on one cheek, offer the other also" (Luke 6:29), and "But I say to you, do not resist one who is evil" (Matthew 5:39), chaos would result, and the unjust would be emboldened. At best, Mawdudi suggests, one could interpret Jesus's remarks as part of an effort to build the moral fiber of his followers, in preparation for his jihad against the Romans. Along these lines, Mawdudi interprets "Think not that I am come to send peace on earth. I came not to send peace, but a sword" (Matthew 10:34) and "They said, Lord, behold, here are two swords. And he said to them, 'It is enough'" (Luke 22:38) as glimpses of what Jesus may have had in mind but did not get a chance to pursue further.[57]

As far as Judaism is concerned, Mawdudi starts by making (in a lengthy footnote) the same disclaimer that he makes about Christianity: His source for Jewish views on justified war is the Hebrew Bible, not the *Taurat* (Torah) as revealed to the prophet Musa (Moses) of the Qur'an. Mawdudi quotes a number of passages from the Pentateuch, which demonstrate, he claims, that the aim of war in the Hebrew Bible is conquest of land. As for limits on war, he writes that very few details are enumerated in the scriptures. He proceeds to discuss the twofold division of the Israelites' enemies found in Deuteronomy: those over whom God has given the Israelites discretion and those over whom he has not. If the first refuse to surrender their land, Mawdudi writes, the males may be killed and the women and children enslaved. The second category is doomed to utter annihilation, allegedly according to God's command. Mawdudi concludes that the Hebrew Bible's view of the Israelites as a "chosen people above all others" is responsible for the exclusion of contemporary Palestinians from their homeland through unjust warfare.[58]

Why did Mawdudi compose *Al-Jihad fi al-Islam*, and what audience did he have in mind? It is well documented that his immediate provocation for starting his column in *Al-Jami'at* was the murder in 1925 of Swami Shradhananda, an Arya Samaji preacher. The swami was murdered by a young Muslim angered by what he thought were the swami's insulting remarks against the Prophet Muhammad and Islam. The slaying unleashed a spate of writing and speeches denouncing Islam as a religion of the sword. Mahatma Gandhi was troubled by the murder, and though he was a staunch advocate of Hindu-Muslim tolerance and cooperation, he made remarks deemed disparaging by some Muslims.[59] Mawlana Muhammad 'Ali, in the great Jama Masjid of Delhi, cried, "Is there not a *banda-yi Khuda* [servant of God] who would get up and respond to the calumny against our faith?"[60] Shortly thereafter, Mawdudi feverishly wrote the series of articles presenting what jihad meant in Islam and also firmly rejecting the charge that jihad was nothing more than a religious license to kill innocent non-Muslims simply because they were not Muslim.

But there is also evidence that Mawdudi had been thinking of writing about the subject well before the incidents described above. He felt the need to correct what he deemed the apologetic approach to jihad of earlier writers such as Chiragh 'Ali. Mawdudi told Abu al-Nasr Muhammad Khalidi (d. 1985) of Osmania University that in conversations with Chiragh 'Ali's son, Mahbub 'Ali (d. 1970), he had expressed his dissatisfaction with the defensive arguments in *A Critical Exposition of the Popular "Jihad."*[61] Further evidence that Mawdudi was responding to Chiragh 'Ali comes from the publisher's preface in Mawdudi's book. It submits that "a century and a half of servitude to the West has imposed such a conception of jihad that we immediately apologize when we hear the word 'jihad' by putting our hands over our ears [the Indian gesture for apology]. Before independence even the best educated persons used to be terrified when merely hearing the word 'jihad.' In an age characterized by the dual condition of both physical and mental slavery, Mawlana Mawdudi wrote on this topic with great courage."[62]

Mawdudi, like Chiragh 'Ali before him, was concerned solely with understanding the theory of jihad. Despite their divergent views on jihad, both writers held the Qur'an to be the only authoritative source for this theory. Neither writer discussed the practice of jihad beyond the Prophetic era in any significant way. One searches in vain for their views on the practice of jihad in their native India, including nineteenth-century jihad movements such as that of Sayyid Ahmad Shahid (d. 1831) or even such a transformative event as the uprising of 1857.

After the publication of *Al-Jihad fi al-Islam* and as leader of his own political party, the Jama'at-i Islami, Mawdudi did express his views on jihad in relation to contemporary political events. The first instance was in 1947–48, when conflict broke out in his native Deccan over the future of Hyderabad state in the postcolonial political order. The Muslim ruler, the nizam, wanted to retain his dynastic rule independent of India over a population that was overwhelmingly Hindu. He couched his ambitions to retain power in secular, nondenominational terms, and at the same time, he lent support to a right-wing organization, the Majlis-i Ittihad al-Muslimin (Assembly of Muslim Unity), which sought to maintain Muslim domination, through paramilitary action if necessary. Once it was in power, the Congress Party government in New Delhi pressed for the immediate merger of Hyderabad with India. During the futile negotiations between New Delhi and the nizam, Mawdudi wrote to the Majlis's chief, Sayyid Qasim Rizwi, advising him to come to a peaceful settlement with India rather than press any exclusivist claims in the name of Muslims. But Rizwi disregarded Mawdudi's advice, and the Majlis used the idiom of jihad to rouse young Muslim men to fight against the Indian army, resulting in their total defeat amid much bloodshed in September 1948.[63]

Shortly after the absorption of Hyderabad into the Indian federation, the Indian government moved to incorporate the Muslim-majority princely state of Kashmir, setting off a protracted conflict with Kashmiris and Pakistan that continues still. From Pakistan, where he had decided to settle when partition of India became inevitable, Mawdudi endorsed the Kashmiris' fight against India as jihad and advocated that Pakistan openly and with full determination help the fighters. If the Pakistani government meant truly to support the Kashmiris' jihad, all relations with India, including diplomatic ties, must be severed, he argued. But on this and many other issues, the government found Mawdudi's pleas to be politically subversive and moved to limit his and his party's activities in the country.[64]

In contrast, when the Pakistani military moved in 1971 to quash the rebellion in East Pakistan that led to the creation of Bangladesh, the government welcomed Mawdudi's support. The Jama'at-i Islami members in East Pakistan fought in paramilitary organizations along with the Pakistani army to suppress what Mawdudi condemned as an illegitimate move to tear apart Pakistan. Indian military intervention confirmed for Mawdudi that this was a religious conflict, one between Muslims who cherished the idea of an Islamic Pakistan and communists, secular nationalists, and Hindus who sought to destroy that ideal.[65]

Conclusion

Chiragh 'Ali came to maturity in the wake of the collapse of Muslim rule in India and its replacement by the rule of a Christian nation. Accompanying and supporting the political domination were, in his mind, the brazen attacks on Islam of Christian missionaries, colonial officials, and orientalists. These motivated him to come to the defense of his faith. But his defense of Islam went far beyond the arguments put forth by traditional Muslim scholars. He gave an interpretation of the Qur'an radically different from that of the authoritative exegetes of the classical era. Chiragh 'Ali also questioned the authenticity of much of the hadith, deeming it to be mostly spurious and thus unfit as a source of law. Islam and Islamic ideas on just and holy war, Chiragh 'Ali argued, must be judged not by the man-made shari'a of the *fuqaha* (jurists) but by the ethical principles of the Qur'an.

Mawdudi's view of jihad is much closer to classical views, but his work is clearly informed by a modern sensibility and written in a distinctly modern idiom. He understood jihad as having simultaneously offensive and defensive characteristics. In both instances, he argued that jihad's main purpose is to preserve and perpetuate an Islamic value system. *Fitna* and *fasad*, oppression and injustice, in Mawdudi's understanding, cannot be confronted and overcome except through armed struggle.

Mawdudi wrote in the period between the two world wars, when British (and European) supremacy—political, economic, and moral—was badly tarnished by the bloodletting of World War I. It was also a time when Indian nationalism, heavily tinged with Hindu symbolism, was on the rise, alienating many Muslims and sometimes leading to violence, as exemplified by the murder in 1925 of a Hindu preacher by a Muslim youth. Mawdudi seized the occasion to write on the subject of jihad with the aim of giving a "true" picture of it and contrasting it with other religious and secular approaches to war and peace. His book still remains one of the very few comparative studies by a Muslim author.

Notes

1. Aziz Ahmad, *Studies in Islamic Culture in the Indian Environment* (Oxford: Clarendon, 1964), 54.
2. For overviews of Sayyid Ahmad Khan's life and thought, see Aziz Ahmad, *Islamic Modernism in India and Pakistan, 1857–1964* (London: Oxford University Press, 1967), 31–56; and Wilfred Cantwell Smith, *Modern Islam in India: A Social Analysis* (London: Victor Gollancz, 1946), 15–28.
3. Omar Khalidi, ed., *An Indian Passage to Europe* (Karachi: Oxford University Press, 2006), xiii.
4. 'Abd al-Haq, *Chand ham 'asr* (Aligarh: Anjuman-i Tarraqi-i Urdu, 1968), 64.
5. Bombay: Education Society, 1883.
6. Calcutta: Thacker, Spink, 1885; reprint Karachi: Karimsons, 1977. All references below are to the 1977 reprint.
7. The history of Hyderabad under Salar Jang was published in four large volumes (Bombay: Education Society, 1886). The history of important *jagirs* (estates) was published privately in Hyderabad in 1884.
8. Munawwar Husayn, *Mawlawi Chiragh 'Ali ki 'ilmi khidmat* (Patna: Khuda Bakhsh Library, 1997), 31–83, 91–95.
9. 'Abd al-Haq, *Chand ham 'asr*, 48.
10. Manikrao Vitthalrao, *Bustan-i Asafiyya*, vol. 7 (Hyderabad: n.p., 1909–32), 188.
11. An exception is the translation of Wilfred Cantwell Smith's article, "Comparative Religion," in Mircea Eliade and Joseph Kitigawa, eds., *The History of Religions: Essays in Methodology* (Chicago: University of Chicago Press, 1959), 31–58, by Abu al-Nasr Muhammad Khalidi and Mubariz al-Din Rifat, "Mazahib ka taqabuli mutala'a: Kyon aur kis tarah," *Burhan* 49 (April 1962): 142–56.
12. Aziz Ahmad, *An Intellectual History of Islam in India* (Edinburgh: Edinburgh University Press, 1966), 58.
13. Sayyid Ahmad Khan, *Maktubat* (Lahore: Majlis-i Tarraqi-i Adab, 1976), 370.
14. The Urdu translation was published under the title *Tahqiq al-jihad* (Lahore: Rifah-i Am, 1913; reprint Hyderabad: Ahmad Husayn Ja'far 'Ali Tajir-i Kutub, 1950; reprint Karachi: Nafis Academy, 1967).
15. Chiragh 'Ali, *A Critical Exposition*, i.
16. Ibid., ii, xxv, xxx, 41, 103, 117.
17. Chiragh 'Ali uses "war" loosely and sometimes in connection with military engagements that are more accurately labeled "battles" or "skirmishes"; see, for example, ibid., ii, 25, 41.
18. Ibid., xxxi–xxxii, xlvii–xlviii, lix.
19. Ibid., xxxii.
20. Ibid., ii, vii–viii.
21. Muhammad attacked three Jewish tribes of Medina after they broke their agreement with him; likewise, he marched against Mecca when the Quraysh violated the Treaty of Hudaybiyya. Ibid., xxv–xxvi, 15–16, 34–35.
22. Ibid., 25–35.
23. Ibid., 17–25, 123. Chiragh 'Ali relies on J. M. Rodwell's translation of the Qur'an, first published in 1861, and follows the Flügel edition (1834) numbering of verses, which varies from the standard Cairo edition (1925) numbering commonly used today. I have retained Chiragh 'Ali's citations and given the standard number, where different, in parentheses.
24. Ibid., 51–55, 123.
25. Ibid., 41–43.
26. Ibid., xx–xxiii.
27. See, for example, the narrative in Ibn Ishaq, *The Life of Muhammad*, trans. Alfred Guillaume (Karachi: Oxford University Press, 1990), 291–94.
28. Ahmad, *An Intellectual History*, 62.
29. Chiragh 'Ali, *A Critical Exposition*, 163–64.
30. Ibid., 171–92.

31. Ibid., 181–82.
32. Ibid., 182–83.
33. Ibid., 117–20.
34. Ibid., 133–34.
35. Ibid., 116.
36. Herman T. Obbink, *De Heilige Oorlog volgens den Koran* (Leiden: Brill, 1901).
37. Ghulam Mohammad Jaffar, "The Repudiation of Jihad by the Indian Scholars in the Nineteenth Century," *Hamdard Islamicus* (Autumn 1992): 93–100.
38. Mustansir Mir, "Jihad in Islam," in Hadia Dajani-Shakeel and Ronald A. Messier, eds., *Jihad and Its Times: Dedicated to Andrew Stefan Ehrenkreutz* (Ann Arbor: University of Michigan, Center for Middle Eastern and North African Studies, 1991), 117.
39. Ayesha Jalal, *Partisans of Allah: Jihad in South Asia* (Cambridge, Mass.: Harvard University Press, 2008), 159.
40. Omar Khalidi, "Mawlana Mawdudi and Hyderabad," *Islamic Studies* 41, no. 1 (Spring 2002): 35–68.
41. Abu al-A'la Mawdudi, *Al-Jihad fi al-Islam* (New Delhi: Isha'at-i Islam Trust, 1988), 20.
42. Charles J. Adams translated brief excerpts in Aziz Ahmad and Gustave E. von Grunebaum, eds., *Muslim Self-Statement in India and Pakistan 1857–1968* (Wiesbaden: Otto Harrassowitz, 1970), 156–57. Excerpts of the book were translated into Arabic and published along with writings of the two leading figures of the Muslim Brotherhood, Hasan al-Banna (1906–1944) and Sayyid Qutb (1906–1966), in *Al-Jihad fi sabil Allah* (Cairo: Ittihad Tullab Misr, 1977).
43. Naim Siddiqi, "Sayyid Abu al-A'la Mawdudi," *Nuqush*, Shakhsiyat Number (1956): 1186; and the author's conversations with Abu al-Nasr Muhammad Khalidi, who knew Mawdudi during the 1920s through the 1940s.
44. Mawdudi, *Al-Jihad fi al-Islam*, 24.
45. Ibid., 39–40.
46. Ibid., 42; Siddiqi, "Sayyid Abu al-A'la Mawdudi," 1187.
47. Mawdudi, *Al-Jihad fi al-Islam*, 38.
48. Ibid., 39.
49. Ibid., 40.
50. Ibid., 53–56.
51. Ibid., 56–57.
52. Ibid., 57.
53. Ibid., 70.
54. Ibid., 114–17.
55. Ibid., 117.
56. Ibid., 327–30.
57. Ibid., 407–54.
58. Ibid., 381–88.
59. Mahatma Gandhi, *Collected Works*, vol. 37 (New Delhi: Ministry of Information and Broadcasting, 1999), 457.
60. Communicated to the author by Abu al-Nasr Muhammad Khalidi.
61. Ibid.
62. Publisher's preface to Mawdudi, *Al-Jihad fi al-Islam*, 14.
63. For Mawdudi's letter, see Khalidi, "Mawlana Mawdudi," 57–62; and for the 1948 massacres, see Omar Khalidi, ed., *Hyderabad: After the Fall* (Hyderabad: Hyderabad Historical Society, 1988), 95–115.
64. Abu al-A'la Mawdudi, *Masalah-yi Kashmir aur uska hal* (Lahore: Idara-i Matbu'at-i Talaba, 1980), 7.
65. See Masudul Hasan, *Sayyed Abul A'ala Maududi and His Thought* (Lahore: Islamic Publications, 1986), 2:393–416.

PART FIVE

INTERNATIONAL LAW
AND OUTLAWS

The evolution of the international law of armed conflict is, in many ways, the culmination of centuries of evolution of the just war tradition. The emergence of positive international law has not, however, led to the demise of just war thinking. Indeed, if anything, the just war tradition has seen a revival and significant growth during the twentieth century through the normative work of Paul Ramsey, Michael Walzer, James Turner Johnson, Jean Bethke Elshtain, and a number of other important contributors. Just war theorists continue to push beyond the confines of current international law in such areas as humanitarian intervention, transitional justice, and the response to terrorism.

International law has similarly challenged and revitalized Christian, Jewish, and Muslim thinking on just war and peace. Unlike the just war tradition, Muslim and Jewish theorists not only have had to adapt to a different cultural and intellectual framework, but they have also had to close the gap created by centuries of neglect and desuetude—both practical and intellectual—of their own traditions. The challenge is, therefore, formidable, but the response has been vibrant. The broad mainstream of both traditions shows every indication of reconciling Muslim and Jewish theory with just war and international law.

The "triumph of just war theory" is tempered, however, by the lingering presence—indeed, resurgence—of holy war rhetoric and justifications over the past four decades. The creation of Israel in 1948 led to renewed charges of Western crusaderism by Muslims. Israel's capture of East Jerusalem in 1967 sharpened holy war rhetoric among Muslims, Jews, and Christians. In the wake of the September 11, 2001, attack on the United States and the American-led wars in Afghanistan and Iraq, the rhetoric of crusade has resurfaced in the West and in the Muslim world, challenging interpreters of just war and jihad to respond.

16

Jihad and the Geneva Conventions

The Impact of International Law on Islamic Theory

SOHAIL H. HASHMI

The advent of an international legal regime governing war and peace has had an obvious and profound impact on Muslim articulations of jihad. As postcolonial Muslim states acceded to the United Nations Charter, the Geneva Conventions, and other treaties that make up this legal regime, they contributed to the claim that public international law is a universally accepted set of principles and procedures, the first such in history. This claim of universality threatened to make Islamic theories of world order, articulated in the classical jurists' works on *siyar*, completely obsolete. In practice, Muslim states had never fully conformed to the principles of *siyar* even at the time of its development, long before European penetration fundamentally altered their behavior. Yet now, with the rise of international law, the *siyar* was threatened not just by desuetude but also by supersession, if not outright renunciation. International law was something that no Muslim statesman, jurist, or activist could ignore.

This chapter explores the different reactions that the rise of international law elicited among Muslim theorists. I divide the responses into three broad categories. The first group I call the assimilationists. They treat the *siyar* largely as a historical and now obsolete theory of world order. The assimilationists accept the universality of public international law and argue that through the accession of Muslim states to the international legal regime, most Muslims also do so. The second group is the accommodationists, who coalesce around the claim that while international law appropriately governs the conduct of Muslim states in international society as a whole, Islamic law could and should have a role in the mutual relations of Muslim states. In other words, they see the potential for an Islamic international law alongside public international law. Potential conflict of laws is minimal, in the accommodationist view, because the basic Islamic principles governing international relations are fundamentally compatible with those underlying modern international law. The third group is the rejectionists, who view international law as an alien code imposed on Muslims by Europeans. The rejectionists affirm the superiority of Islamic law over public international law and call for its application by Muslim states, not just in their relations with each other but also in their relations with non-Muslim states. These three categories are ideal types; there are, of course, nuances within each of these general positions, and few writers fit perfectly into one camp or another. Still, the three groups do represent, I believe, an accurate expression of the spectrum of Muslim responses to the advent of international laws on war and peace.

Development of International Law

International law on war and peace consists of a diverse set of principles, expectations, and aspirations stipulated in treaties, declarations, legal rulings, and custom. This complex and growing body of law deals with both the legal grounds for war (*jus ad bellum*) and the restraints governing the conduct of war (*jus in bello*). The latter are generally termed the laws of war or the laws of armed conflict.

The legitimate grounds for war is, of course, a topic with deep roots in Western just war theory, but until the twentieth century, little effort was made by states to codify principles governing their resort to war. In the nineteenth-century Concert of Europe, war was viewed as an instrument of power politics, a "continuation of politics by other means," as famously described by Clausewitz.[1] Resort to war was tempered by the prudence of statesmen pursuing ideally an enlightened notion of their national interests.

The Hague Convention for the Pacific Settlement of International Disputes (1899, revised in 1907) signaled the development of a new perception of war. It called on states to resolve conflicts through diplomacy, commissions of inquiry, and ad hoc arbitration tribunals. It established the Permanent Court of Arbitration, which has evolved today into an institution that, unlike the better-known International Court of Justice, mediates disputes involving both state and non-state parties.

The carnage of World War I gave impetus to the strengthening of laws and institutions for the nonviolent resolution of international conflicts. Article 12 of the Covenant of the League of Nations (1920) required member states to submit international conflicts for "arbitration or judicial settlement or to enquiry by the [League] Council." States that launched wars in contravention of the covenant's procedure for resolving disputes were threatened under Article 16 with war against all league members. The Kellogg-Briand Pact (1928) went further than the covenant in renouncing war altogether as a legitimate instrument of national policy.

Neither the covenant nor the pact prevented the outbreak of World War II, but the UN Charter (1945) reaffirmed their essential principles while creating a putatively more effective collective security mechanism in the Security Council. The charter retained the principle of renunciation of threats or use of force against any state (Article 2), qualified only by the legitimacy of self-defense against armed aggression (Article 51). The framers of the charter left "aggression" undefined, and a number of legal scholars have argued for the value of such an approach.[2] Nevertheless, the UN General Assembly has adopted resolutions specifying what constitutes aggression. The assembly's Declaration on Principles of International Law concerning Friendly Relations (1970) legitimizes armed struggles for decolonization and, in making the colonial power the aggressor state, sanctions third-party support for national liberation struggles. On December 4, 1974, the General Assembly adopted the Definition of Aggression Resolution, which lists such "traditional" acts as cross-border invasion, bombardment, and blockade but also includes violations of the terms under which the armed forces of a state are allowed by another state to enter or operate in its territory. Because both of these resolutions were adopted by the General Assembly and not the Security Council, their status as international law is disputed, and they are generally treated as "soft" or customary law.

Thus, during the past century, international law has made strides toward curtailing the legitimate use of force and thereby expanding the possibilities for peaceful resolution of international disputes. Its focus has largely been on interstate rather than intrastate conflicts, the type of wars that have proved the most frequent and destructive since World War II. The debate on the right of humanitarian intervention that gained ground in the 1990s and led to UN endorsement in 2005 of a "responsibility to protect" evinces international recognition that resort to force may be legitimate in circumstances quite different from traditional cross-border aggression.

International law governing the conduct of war dates back to the mid-nineteenth century, when the onset of industrial warfare dramatically increased the level of destruction that modern armies could wreak. This technological development occurred simultaneously with the increase of wars of nationalism, which blurred distinctions between combatants and noncombatants. The laws of armed conflict that developed in response to the upsurge of total war restrict the ways belligerents engage each other on the battlefield, the weapons and tactics that may be employed, and the treatment of prisoners of war and civilian populations. The first two areas are the focus of the so-called Hague Law, because the bulk of initial agreements restricting actual combat emerged out of conferences held at The Hague. The treatment of prisoners of war, including those wounded and disabled, and the protection of civilian populations form the substance of international humanitarian law (IHL), or Geneva Law, as it is often called, because many of the conventions on these issues bear the name of this city.[3]

The St. Petersburg Declaration (1856) marks the beginning of formal international efforts to impose limits on the conduct of war. The declaration opens by stating a principle that would guide the subsequent development of the law of armed conflict: "The only legitimate object which states should endeavor to accomplish during war is to weaken the military forces of the enemy." Seven years later, the International Committee of the Red Cross (ICRC) was founded in Geneva, creating an organization dedicated to gaining international recognition for the rights of combatants, prisoners of war, and civilian populations. Its first achievement was the 1864 Convention for the Amelioration of the Condition of the Wounded in Armies in the Field, now known as the First Geneva Convention. The Second Geneva Convention, for the Amelioration of the Condition of Wounded, Sick and Shipwrecked Members of Armed Forces at Sea, followed in 1906. And in 1929, the Third Geneva Convention was adopted to provide for the humane treatment of prisoners of war.

The Hague Convention of 1899 expanded dramatically the scope of treaty law concerned with the conduct of war. It included the Convention with Respect to the Laws and Customs of War on Land (Hague II) and an adaptation of the First Geneva Convention to the conditions of maritime warfare (Hague III). In addition, the conference adopted a convention and three declarations banning certain types of weapons, namely, projectiles launched from balloons, projectiles that diffuse "asphyxiating or deleterious gases," and hollow-point bullets. The Hague Convention of 1907 elaborated on and adapted many of the provisions of the 1899 convention, focusing particularly on the conduct of naval warfare. Following World War I, which saw the extensive use of chemical warfare, the Geneva Protocol for the Prohibition of the Use in War of Asphyxiating, Poisonous or Other Gases and of Bacteriological Methods of Warfare was adopted in 1925 as an addendum to the Hague Convention.

The atrocities of World War II led to the prosecution of German and Japanese war criminals by international tribunals at Nuremberg and Tokyo, the adoption of the Genocide Convention (1948), and, in 1949, the revision of the first three Geneva Conventions and the addition of a fourth convention regulating the treatment of civilians in war zones and in occupied territory. Two additional protocols were adopted in 1977, the first elaborating on rules governing international conflict and the second focusing, for the first time, on the conduct of internal wars.

The post-World War II era has also witnessed significant developments in efforts to outlaw or curtail the use of certain types of weapons. Weapons of mass destruction have received the greatest attention. The development, production, and stockpiling of biological weapons were banned under the Biological Weapons Convention of 1972 and likewise for chemical weapons under the Chemical Weapons Convention of 1992. Although the testing and proliferation of nuclear weapons have been restricted by a number of agreements, including the Partial Test Ban Treaty (1963), the Nuclear Nonproliferation Treaty (1968), and the Comprehensive Test Ban Treaty (1996, not yet in force), no treaty yet exists banning their use. The UN General Assembly has passed a number of resolutions to this effect, and in 1996, the International Court of Justice issued an advisory opinion that could be read as effectively outlawing the use of nuclear weapons. Other agreements deal with more ordinary yet highly lethal weapons: the UN

Convention on Prohibitions or Restrictions on the Use of Certain Conventional Weapons Which May Be Deemed to Be Excessively Injurious or to Have Indiscriminate Effects (1980, with later protocols) and the Convention on the Prohibition of the Use, Stockpiling, Production and Transfer of Anti-Personnel Mines and on their Destruction (1997).

The most recent milestone in the evolution of an international legal regime governing military conduct is the creation of the International Criminal Court under the Rome Statute of 1998. It establishes the first permanent international institution to prosecute individuals for genocide, crimes against humanity, and war crimes.

As this body of international law evolved, Muslim involvement in its formulation was sporadic and minor until after World War II. The Ottoman empire acceded to the First Geneva Convention in 1865, and Qajar Persia followed in 1874. Ottoman and Persian delegations were present at the 1899 and 1907 Hague Peace Conferences. The delegates—"westernized and westernizers," as James Cockayne characterizes them—made little attempt to inject Islamic rulings on the conduct of war into the deliberations, but "as a result of the Islamic delegations' interventions, the Hague Peace Conferences officially confirmed the principle of religious non-discrimination as a central tenet of IHL."[4]

Rather than the substance of IHL, it was the red cross symbol adopted in 1864 that emerged as the most contentious issue for the Ottoman empire and later other Muslim states. The Ottomans, during their war in 1876 with Serbia and later Russia, declared that they would display a red crescent emblem instead of the red cross, because the latter evoked the Crusades and thus was offensive to their soldiers. The Russians initially challenged the Ottomans' move but eventually agreed to respect the red crescent emblem as long as the Ottomans reciprocated for the red cross. This proved to be merely the opening round of a prolonged controversy over the emblem.

Once the red crescent had been tacitly accepted as an alternative emblem, other states also moved to have their own distinctive emblems recognized, including Persia, which proposed a red lion with sun, based on the Qajar insignia. Realizing that a Pandora's box had been opened, the ICRC mobilized efforts, official and unofficial, to reinstate the red cross as the unique symbol of the movement. The 1906 conference that drafted the Second Geneva Convention unanimously adopted a resolution denying any religious origins or connotation to the emblem. Likewise, numerous ICRC spokesmen gave accounts of how the red cross symbol was adopted in attempts to establish its purely secular origins and significance. These efforts proved in vain. Upon the insistence of Turkey, Persia, and Egypt, the 1929 conference that drafted the Third Geneva Convention formally approved the red crescent and the red lion with sun for use only by those national societies already using them, hoping thereby to limit their use. This effort also failed. As new Muslim-majority states gained independence and acceded to the Geneva Conventions, they adopted, with very few exceptions, the red crescent symbol for their own national societies. Iran dropped the use of the red lion with sun and adopted the red crescent soon after the Iranian Revolution.[5]

Muslim engagement in efforts to broaden the scope of the laws of war would not be prominent until the negotiations for the 1977 Geneva Protocols. At that time, a number of Muslim states, motivated primarily by the Palestinian conflict against Israel, pressed for the adoption of the second protocol elaborating the rights of irregular fighters. But again, they did so without recourse to any specifically Islamic injunctions.

International Law and *Siyar*

As a result of international law's distinctively Western origins and the generally peripheral role played by Muslims in its development, international law's relationship to the jihad tradition is fundamentally different from its relationship to the just war tradition. As Ann Elizabeth Mayer observes: "The West today deals with international law as a familiar and integral component of Western civilization that has evolved pari passu with Western culture and religion over centuries." This is certainly not to say that the laws of war and peace are fully embraced by just war theorists, but the objections are more along the lines of refinements and not fundamental challenges. "In contrast," Mayer continues, "the Islamic doctrines of war and peace have been part of a juristic culture that has remained closer to its premodern roots."[6] In other words, when Muslims engage with international law as Islamic scholars or jurists, their point of reference is the *siyar*, the theory of world order developed more than a millennium ago that was never fully implemented but never fully rejected or revised, either. For many Muslims, therefore, international law is not an outgrowth of their own culture's previous discourses and practices; it is a rival system to the authentically Islamic system.[7]

This is not to say that the classical Islamic laws of war and peace are essentially incompatible with modern international law. As argued in the introduction to this book, the classical theory of jihad shares many substantive points with just war theory, and inasmuch as these just war principles underlie the evolution of modern international law, the principles of jihad are also compatible with international law. But the jihad tradition evinces far less creative rethinking and adaptation in the modern period than does the just war tradition. The difference between the two traditions is seen in the fact that few modern international lawyers would feel bound by the writings of Hugo Grotius, whereas expositors of Islamic laws of war and peace ineluctably turn to the eighth-century jurist Muhammad al-Shaybani as an authority. Even those Muslims who embrace or accommodate international law cannot ignore the legacy of *siyar*. Their task is to reconcile or otherwise deal with certain basic conflicts between *siyar* and modern international law.

At the broadest conceptual level are basic epistemological differences. International law, whether it is seen as derived from natural law, as much of humanitarian and human rights law is, or from positive law, expressed in treaties among states, is firmly secular in foundation. By contrast, the shari'a, of which *siyar* was one branch, was conceptualized as divine law, as revealed in God's dispensation, the Qur'an, and expounded by God's messenger, Muhammad, through the hadith literature compiled centuries after his death. The Qur'an and hadith present no systematic or, some might argue, consistent theory of world order in general or laws of war and peace in particular. Thus, it was left to the jurists to develop such a theory through interpretation of the Qur'an and the *sunna*, or example, of the Prophet. Some scholars were more willing than others to undertake creative legal reasoning (*ijtihad*) than others. Nevertheless, all saw their jurisprudence (*fiqh*) not as human lawmaking but as an exercise in trying to discern God's law.

International law, or specifically public international law, regulates the interactions of states with one another. The *siyar*, on the other hand, established rules of behavior for the Muslim state (which in the classical theory was envisioned as a single, unified entity) and Muslim individuals in their interaction with non-Muslim political groups and individuals or with Muslim rebels, apostates, and criminals. It was conceived as a unilateral legal system binding only on Muslims, with no assumptions of reciprocity or accountability from those outside the Muslim *umma* (community). It was thus not "international" law at all. The *siyar* did validate diplomacy, treaties, and truces with non-Muslims, but by engaging in such activity, non-Muslims did not come within the legal framework of Islamic law, unless they agreed to *dhimmi* status, through which they accepted Islamic sovereignty while retaining a degree of communal autonomy. Those who did not accept *dhimmi* status remained outside of Islamic law, and both they and the Muslims were bound only by the specific provisions of their mutual agreement. If there were any assumptions at all about a "law of peoples" on the part of Muslim jurists, they were what might be called a rudimentary notion of natural law.

The principal sources of international law are treaties and custom. The *siyar* is primarily "jurists' law"; it is contained in the intellectual output of scholars working more than a millennium ago. Since custom, or state practice, was never accepted as a legitimate source of *siyar*, Islamic laws of war and peace were more theoretical than practical from their origins. The problem was compounded not just by dramatic changes in the international system and the technology of war but also by the intellectual conservatism that set in after the collapse of the Abbasid empire in the mid-thirteenth century. The generations of jurists who followed busied themselves with preserving their legal heritage rather than revising it.

This approach is evident even among twentieth-century Muslim commentators on Islamic international law. The earliest extended treatises in Western languages by Muslim authors date from the period between the two world wars. In 1929, Najib Armanazi, a Syrian, published his doctoral dissertation titled *L'Islam*

et le droit international (Islam and International Law), written at the University of
Paris.[8] The Indian scholar Muhammad Hamidullah (d. 2002) published in 1935
his doctoral dissertation submitted to the University of Bonn on neutrality in
Islamic law. Hamidullah published a greatly expanded English edition of the work
titled *The Muslim Conduct of State* in 1942. This book underwent several revisions
in the following decades and became a standard reference for students of Islamic
international law.[9] Ahmed Rechid, a Turkish legal scholar, published *L'Islam et le
droit des gens* (Islam and the Law of Nations) in 1937.[10] Armanazi and Hamidullah
focus almost exclusively on classical works of *siyar* as they elucidate Islamic laws
of international relations. Their references to Muslim practice are confined mainly
to the era of the Prophet and the first four caliphs. Rechid, however, does devote
considerable space to Ottoman practices, particularly in the field of conflict of
laws, reflecting no doubt his prior experience as a legal adviser to the Turkish
Ministry of Foreign Affairs.

For their part, Muslim states adapted to their changing circumstances and
adopted various extra-shari'a norms in their statecraft. As Nuri Yurdusev shows
in chapter 9 of this book, the Ottomans began to accommodate themselves to
European custom by the mid-fifteenth century. In the twentieth century, all postcolonial Muslim states readily acceded to the modern international legal regime.
All are members of the United Nations; seven are charter members, including the
kingdom of Saudi Arabia. All are signatories to the Geneva Conventions. This
leads to the fundamental question: Through their practice, have not Muslim states
all but renounced any place for a distinctively Islamic international law? The
answer would seem to be yes, especially as far as relations between Muslim states
and non-Muslim states are concerned. But this answer must be qualified by the
observation that not infrequently, and especially in their mutual relations with
one another, Muslim statesmen still invoke Islamic values and doctrines, including jihad, as if they are still relevant. Moreover, as I discuss in the conclusion
of this chapter, Muslim states have taken a tantalizing step toward the creation of
an institution that would give substance to the claim that Islamic international
law is more than just a historical artifact.

Moving from the broad conceptual level to the specific rulings on war and
peace, modern Muslim commentators again face a number of important differences between *siyar* and international law. Under *jus ad bellum*, the first issue they
must grapple with is the classical theory's bifurcation of the world into two opposing spheres: *dar al-Islam* and *dar al-harb*. *Dar al-Islam* was ideally a single political entity, governed by a single ruler, the imam/caliph. In reality, *dar al-Islam* was
not united even at the time the classical theory was being developed, and as the
centuries passed, Muslim jurists found ways to rationalize the existence of separate Muslim states. Most Muslim scholars and activists are reconciled today to the
legitimacy of multiple Muslim states, but the principle of state sovereignty that
lies at the heart of international law remains to be fully reconciled with the Islamic
ethical ideals of Muslim unity and fraternity.[11]

Dar al-harb was defined as territory where the shari'a was not enforced, and as such, the classical theorists conceived of it as populated by benighted peoples. Muslims were called upon by God to bring the light of Islam to them, through peaceful proselytizing, if possible, and, if not, through war. The residents of *dar al-harb* could elect to submit to Muslim sovereignty as *dhimmis*, upon which their territory was considered absorbed into *dar al-Islam*. The expansionist jihad to which the classical jurists devoted so much attention is an obvious and glaring problem for modern Muslim theorists who would accommodate the *siyar* to international law.

Under *jus in bello*, Islamic injunctions do enjoin discrimination and proportionality. But as we delve deeper into the specific opinions of the different legal schools, we find a number of provisions that dilute the force of these principles. Discrimination in war meant refraining from the intended killing of women and children. Many jurists added various categories of males to this list, including the elderly and infirm, farmers and merchants, monks, and others removed from society. But this notion of discrimination is not equivalent to the modern principle of noncombatant immunity. All able-bodied, adult male prisoners, whether they were previously engaged in fighting or not, could be executed upon the decision of the Muslim commander, unless they had surrendered with an explicit guarantee of security (*aman*). All of the enemy population, military and civilian, could be held for ransom or sold in slavery.[12]

Classical jurists also gave Muslim commanders wide latitude in terms of the weapons and tactics they could employ in overcoming the enemy. They could besiege towns with large numbers of civilians trapped inside, cut off the water supply, fire incendiary devices, and flood the enemy.

Finally, the classical Islamic theory contains no formal provisions for punishing Muslim commanders or troops who violate restrictions on the proper conduct of jihad. Under Islamic law, a Muslim who kills a fellow Muslim is both morally and legally accountable. But a Muslim soldier who violates the rules of war against a non-Muslim enemy, either military or civilian, is at most morally accountable, meaning that he will be judged and punished by God in the hereafter, not by humans in this life.[13]

These are merely some of the most prominent conflicts between the *siyar* and modern international law. All Muslim theorists, if they are to be intellectually credible, must address these basic concerns, whether their goal is to assimilate, accommodate, or reject international law.

The Assimilationists

Muslim proponents of assimilationism are few in number, at least as far as theorists are concerned. The reason may have to do with the fact that assimilationism treats the Islamic theory of world order as a historical artifact, one with no real applicability in the modern age. Pragmatically, it has no applicability because the conditions of international relations today are fundamentally different from those in which the theory was elaborated. Morally, it has no applicability because it is grounded in neither the Qur'an nor the *sunna* but on unidentified, non-Islamic sources that influenced the classical jurists who developed it. Thus, for the assimilationists, the impetus to comment on the *siyar* is not great; they assume that public international law is practically and normatively binding on Muslims. Muslim jurists who have contributed to the development of international law during the past century have most often done so without invoking Islam in their profession.

Majid Khadduri (d. 2007) is the best-known and most influential scholar of the Islamic laws of war and peace in the West. He was an Iraqi Christian, not a Muslim, but this fact seems to be unknown or unimportant to a number of Muslim and non-Muslim commentators on his work. His impact on the study of the Islamic theory of international relations is certainly comparable to that of any contemporary Muslim scholar, so he merits inclusion in this discussion. Khadduri was not only a scholar of Islamic law and philosophy and Middle Eastern history and politics, but he was also a lawyer and diplomat who participated in the drafting of the UN Charter as a member of the Iraqi delegation. He wrote a number of articles and books on Islamic theories of international relations, including the survey *War and Peace in the Law of Islam* and a translation of one of the seminal works in *siyar*, a treatise by the jurist al-Shaybani.[14] There is a paradox here: Through his scholarship, Khadduri revived interest in classical Islamic theory, among both Muslims and non-Muslims, but through his career as a diplomat and his reflections on the place of Islamic theory in the modern age, he consigned this theory largely to the past.

Two articles published by Khadduri during the 1950s, "Islam and the Modern Law of Nations" and "The Islamic System: Its Competition and Co-Existence with Western Systems," outline most clearly his views on the role of Islamic law in the modern age. Both essays open with the claim that Christendom and Islam had developed historically as two opposing civilizations, "each advocating a world order sharply in conflict with the other. . . . The world orders of the two opposing ideologies were at the outset so exclusive and inflexible that each deemed the destruction of the other as absolutely necessary for its survival."[15] Such an intractably hostile stance could not be maintained for long, Khadduri continues, and so, "after a long period of competition and warfare by virtue of which each came to the inevitable conclusion that its moral and political principles could not be imposed on the other," both civilizations began to adapt to the necessities of coexistence.[16]

The triumph of pragmatism over ideology, Khadduri writes, resulted in a "thorough re-examination" by Muslims of their earlier "legal theory of foreign relations." He cites three changes embraced by Muslim powers, in particular the Ottoman empire: the separation of religious doctrine from the conduct of foreign relations; acceptance of the possibility of peaceful intercourse among nations of different religions; and the territoriality of law, which undergirds the idea of sovereign states.[17] Still, despite the thorough revision in Islamic principles of statecraft, "neither Islam nor Christendom [was yet] prepared to meet on a common ground and modify their religious principles for the purpose of developing a law of nations based on equality and reciprocity." Had the Ottoman empire been integrated into the European system during the formative period of the law of nations (by which Khadduri means the sixteenth century), this law might have become universal much earlier in time, he suggests.[18]

"Twentieth-century Islam found itself completely reconciled to the Western secular system," Khadduri concludes. "The active participation of Muslim states in international councils and organizations demonstrates Islam's willingness to take active part in the promotion of international peace and security and its support of the development of the modern law of nations."[19] In particular, jihad has become "an obsolete weapon."[20] By this Khadduri means the notion of expansionist jihad, for elsewhere he clarifies: "Even those publicists who objected to the secularization of the internal law of Islam have accepted marked departures from the traditional Muslim law governing Islam's foreign relations. Almost all of them, who often invoked the *jihad* against Western encroachment on Islam, repudiated the idea that the *jihad* is offensive in character."[21]

Khadduri ends one of his essays by acknowledging that some Muslim jurists (those I have labeled accommodationists) maintain that the modern law of nations, in order to meet the needs of "an expanding world community," should incorporate elements of Islamic law. They often base their claims, Khadduri notes, on Article 38 of the Statute of the International Court of Justice, which "permits the adoption of new maxims of law from the legal systems of 'civilized nations.'"[22] What principles might Islamic civilization contribute to the further development of international law? Khadduri suggests two: (1) recognition of the individual as a subject of international law; and (2) that moral principles should not be divorced from law, for "the historical experiences of Islam, indeed the historical experiences of all mankind, demonstrate that any system of law, whether municipal or international, would become meaningless if divorced completely from moral principles." He hastens to add, however, that the moral principles he has in mind are not based on specific religious doctrines. "Religious doctrine as a basis for the conduct of the state created friction and continuous warfare with other nations; but religion in terms of moral principles prompted the Muslims to observe humane principles embodied in their law during their hostilities with other nations."[23]

The Accommodationists

The accommodationist strand of Muslim response is characterized by the acknowledgment that most aspects of the *siyar* are incompatible with modern international relations but that through renewed interpretive activity (*ijtihad*), the moral values of Islam could provide the basis for a new and distinctive Islamic international law. This Islamic law might then be enforced as a form of "regional law" among Muslim states. A number of distinguished Muslim jurists have espoused some form of this accommodationist line, including 'Abd al-Razzaq al-Sanhuri, Subhi Mahmassani, Muhammad Abu Zahra, Muhammad Tal'at al-Ghunaimi, and Wahba al-Zuhayli. I will focus here on the arguments of the Algerian diplomat and former judge of the International Court of Justice, Mohammed Bedjaoui.

Bedjaoui contributed a lengthy analysis of the Iran-Iraq War in light of the principles of Islamic law to an anthology titled *The Gulf War of 1980–1988: The Iran-Iraq War in International Legal Perspective*.[24] He concludes this essay by asking two pertinent questions. First, does an Islamic legal order even exist today, "when that order not only appears to have undergone no evolution since the seventh century but also transpires in practice to have found little favour with Muslim States in their respective relations"? And second, how might an Islamic legal order, "were it to be recognized, updated and applied . . . co-exist with the universal legal order, in accordance with the relevant provisions of the United Nations Charter"?[25]

The answer Bedjaoui gives to the first question is no—Islamic law has no modern relevance. "More particularly, Islamic international law still remains, regrettably, a law of speculation pursued for purely academic purposes." He blames the stagnation of Islamic law partly on Western scholars and jurists, who historically denied Muslim contributions to the development of their own legal system. Thus, Islamic law was treated as an alien system of law when European states disseminated their own law of nations in the tracks of imperialism.[26] Muslim jurists by and large accepted the European interpretation of Islamic law, according to Bedjaoui, and it is these Muslims to whom he assigns principal responsibility for the "decadence" of Islamic law. "With a few rare exceptions, jurists from the newly independent Muslim countries have succumbed to the easy temptation of lazily imitating the West instead of meeting the more demanding needs of creativity."[27]

But instead of resigning himself to the complete obsolescence of Islamic law, Bedjaoui declares that Muslims can and should find a place for Islamic law in international relations. He writes: "I can restrain myself no longer from *appealing to all jurists in the Muslim world to take greater personal responsibility and mobilize more efficiently in a decisive effort of creativity, instead of confining themselves to an attitude of slavish imitation which often results in strapping lifeless artificial limbs of foreign legal origin on living human communities*" (emphasis in original).[28]

Finally, Bedjaoui turns to his second question on how a revived Islamic law might coexist with international law. He observes that by becoming parties to the UN Charter, Muslim states did not foreclose the possibility of establishing "their own regional organs within which Islamic law could have enjoyed every opportunity of a revival." Muslim states have, in fact, moved to create such "regional" organizations, the most prominent being the Organization of the Islamic Conference, founded in 1969 and today consisting of fifty-seven members. Yet, as Bedjaoui notes, "so far that Organization does not appear to have produced any clear undertaking to ensure the development and modernization of Muslim public international law by adapting it to the new structure of the international community and having it applied in inter-Islamic relations."[29] Should it ever do so, Bedjaoui is confident that no fundamental incompatibility will arise between the newly framed Islamic international law and public international law. In the case of the Iran-Iraq War, for example, "one arrives at virtually the same legal analysis . . . whatever the 'key' be used, whether that of public international law or that of Islamic law."[30]

The Rejectionists

At the forefront of Muslim opinion rejecting international law are, of course, the spokesmen of militant Islamic groups. Not just the leaders of al-Qaeda but most extremist groups have long expressed their contempt for the United Nations and for international law, which they dismiss as tools for Western hegemony. In 1993, the same cell that planned and executed the bombing of the World Trade Center was plotting to bomb the UN headquarters. In 2003, one of the first targets of al-Qaeda in Iraq was the newly established UN office in American-occupied Baghdad. Osama bin Laden addressed international law directly in his so-called Letter to America, released on October 6, 2002. In it, he does not condemn or reject international law directly, perhaps a reflection of the Western audience to which the message is aimed. What he rails against are the double standards and hypocrisy that the United States demonstrates with respect to international law. He cites four cases: The United States touts policies to prevent nuclear proliferation, but it exempts Israel. The United States pays lip service to the UN and UN resolutions, but it supports Israel despite its refusal to comply with UN resolutions. The United States demands the censure and prosecution of individuals it labels war criminals while at the same time demanding that its troops be granted immunity from prosecution. The United States claims that it supports human rights while it flouts international law in its treatment of Muslim prisoners. "What happens in Guantanamo is a historical embarrassment to America and its values, and it screams into your hypocritical faces: What is the value of your signature on any agreement or treaty?"[31]

Perhaps the most detailed and sophisticated treatment of the international law of war penned by a skeptical Muslim writer is that of Abu al-A'la Mawdudi (d. 1979) in *Al-Jihad fi al-Islam* (Jihad in Islam). Mawdudi began this work in 1926 as a series of articles in the Urdu-language newspaper *Al-Jami'at*, and the complete book was first published in 1930.[32] At the end of his book, Mawdudi included a lengthy essay on the development and content of the modern law of war. Here, he takes the reader through the main points of the Hague Conferences of 1899 and 1907, the Covenant of the League of Nations, and the post-World War I conferences on arms control. Turning from international law to state practice, he contends that World War I had demonstrated the abject failure of Western humanitarian principles, but in spite of the catastrophe of that conflict, Western nations showed no signs of altering their behavior. International law, for Mawdudi, is nothing more than rhetorical camouflage for great power politics.[33]

Mawdudi's intent in *Al-Jihad fi al-Islam* is to demonstrate the distinctiveness and superiority of the Islamic laws of jihad, which are of divine origin, over all other systems, including international law. He concludes with the following gist of his comparison between Islamic law and international law: First, international law cannot be defined as "law" in any true sense. It is entirely subject to the whims and self-interests of states, in particular the great powers. Under such circumstances, how can one establish any objective standards for determining the lawfulness of state behavior? Second, if international laws generally have little relevance to interstate behavior, the laws of war are especially irrelevant. States constantly resort to the notion of military necessity to set aside the military conventions they have previously signed. Third, since international law is not based on transcendent moral principles, as is the case with Islamic law, and it binds only those states that consent to be bound by treaty, the laws of war are speedily cast aside when war breaks out. One state withdrawing from its treaty obligations is enough to bring about the collapse of the entire edifice of international law, as the law of reciprocity dictates that states match the deeds of their opponents lest they lose the strategic advantage. Fourth, even though Islamic law predates Western law by more than thirteen centuries, international law has not added in any notable way to the humanitarian principles that Islam legislated in the conduct of war. Fifth, Western laws of war limit only the means, not the ends, of war. Thus, they do not prevent wars of conquest and plunder. Islamic law, in contrast, strictly limits both the means and the ends of war.

Having charted the differences between the two legal systems in sharp relief, Mawdudi concludes: "Compared to Western laws, Islam's law of war is more correct, beneficial, logical, and solid."[34] He never explicitly rejects Muslim adherence to international law, but we can infer that he would ask why, after his analysis, any Muslim of sound mind would choose international law over Islamic law.

Conclusion

The advent of international law has yielded divergent responses from Muslim theorists. Nevertheless, I believe that the trend is overwhelmingly in favor of the assimilationist or accommodationist view. The rejectionist position is propounded by a limited number of the most conservative scholars and activists. Even rejectionist theoreticians who bitterly criticize international law in their writings fail to effect or even advocate radical changes in state policies when they are in a position to do so. The Jama'at-i Islami, the party that Mawdudi led for nearly thirty years in Pakistan, never demanded that its nation withdraw from the United Nations or the international legal regime in general or the treaties specifically governing the laws of war that Pakistan had signed. The same is true of Khomeini in Iran and the Taliban leadership in Afghanistan. They may have been rejectionist theoreticians, but they were also politicians. As such, they accommodated themselves to the reality that their states operated in an international political and legal system far removed from what they considered ideal.

Despite the evidence indicating that Muslims accept the authority of international law, either begrudgingly or wholeheartedly, it would be a mistake, I think, to dismiss altogether any role for Islamic values or legal principles in contemporary international relations. The most concrete manifestation of the continuing vitality of the accommodationist position is the decision by the Organization of the Islamic Conference (OIC) in 1981 to create the International Islamic Court of Justice (IICJ). This institution emerged out of popular concerns about the inability of the OIC to resolve the Iran-Iraq War. But trouble arose soon after the OIC adopted the resolution to create the court. The statute of the IICJ was not approved until 1987. According to it, the court has jurisdiction over disputes referred to it by the OIC member states. It is also to render advisory opinions, or fatwas, on legal questions referred to it by the other organs of the OIC. To all intents and purposes, it is to operate as an Islamic version of the International Court of Justice. The defining characteristic of this court, however, is that its sole source of law would be the shari'a. Its eleven judges are envisioned as being the leading experts in shari'a provisions on international law.[35]

Everything is in place for this court to begin its operations, even its headquarters in Kuwait. Yet it has never convened because the court's statute has not been ratified by the requisite two-thirds majority of OIC member states. The failure of most states to ratify, the very decision to set the ratification number so high, and the earlier disputes over the statute itself all point to a stark reality of the OIC. It is an intergovernmental organization founded on the rhetoric of Islamic universalism but mired ever since in the politics of its squabbling and ideologically divided member states. So, unfortunately, because the IICJ is not likely to meet anytime soon, we lack the presence of an authoritative body that may resolve such basic questions as whether a modern Islamic law of war and peace is possible and how this law relates to public international law.

Acknowledgments

The author thanks Mohammed Jiyad and Caroline Quinn for assistance during the preparation of this chapter.

Notes

1. Carl von Clausewitz, *On War*, ed. and trans. Michael Howard and Peter Paret (Princeton, N.J.: Princeton University Press, 1976), 87.

2. W. Michael Reisman and Chris T. Antoniou, eds., *The Laws of War: A Comprehensive Collection of Primary Documents of International Laws Governing Armed Conflict* (New York: Vintage, 1994), 9.

3. François Bugnion, "Droit de Genève et droit de La Haye," *International Review of the Red Cross* 83, no. 844 (December 2001): 901–22.

4. James Cockayne, "Islam and International Humanitarian Law: From a Clash to a Conversation between Civilizations," *International Review of the Red Cross* 84, no. 847 (September 2002): 608.

5. In 2005, a third protocol to the Geneva Conventions relating to the Adoption of an Additional Distinctive Emblem was approved. The move came after continuing controversy over the red cross symbol, particularly in Israel, where the emblem used is a red Shield (Star) of David. The third protocol adopts a third symbol, the red diamond, inside which distinctive national insignia may be displayed. See François Bugnion, "Towards a Comprehensive Solution to the Question of the Emblem," 2nd ed., *International Review of the Red Cross* 85, no. 838 (November 2003): 427–78; Jean-François Quéguiner, "Commentary on the Protocol Additional to the Geneva Conventions of August 12, 1949, and Relating to the Adoption of an Additional Distinctive Emblem (Protocol III)," *International Review of the Red Cross* 89, no. 865 (March 2007): 175–207; Jonathan Benthall and Jerome-Bellion Jourdan, *The Charitable Crescent: Politics of Aid in the Muslim World* (London: I. B. Tauris, 2003), 47–53.

6. Ann Elizabeth Mayer, "War and Peace in the Islamic Tradition and International Law," in John Kelsay and James Turner Johnson, eds., *Just War and Jihad* (Westport, Conn.: Greenwood, 1991), 195.

7. For a sustained argument of this view and a critique of Muslim theorists who challenge it, see David A. Westbrook, "Islamic International Law and Public International Law: Separate Expressions of World Order," *Virginia Journal of International Law* 33, no. 4 (Summer 1993): 819–97.

8. Najib Armanazi, *L'Islam et le droit international* (Paris: Librairie Picart, 1929).

9. Muhammad Hamidullah, *The Muslim Conduct of State*, 5th ed. (Karachi: Sh. Muhammad Ashraf, 1996).

10. Ahmed Rechid, "L'Islam et le droit des gens," Académie de Droit International, *Recueil des Cours* 60, no. 2 (1937): 371–650.

11. I have discussed these issues in Sohail H. Hashmi, "Islam, the Middle East, and the Pan-Islamic Movement," in Barry Buzan and Ana Gonzalez-Pelaez, eds., *International Society and the Middle East: English School Theory at the Regional Level* (London: Palgrave, 2009), 170–200.

12. John Kelsay, "Islam and the Distinction between Combatants and Non-Combatants," in James Turner Johnson and John Kelsay, eds., *Cross, Crescent, and Sword* (Westport, Conn.: Greenwood, 1990), 197–220; Sohail H. Hashmi, "Saving and Taking Life in War: Three Modern Muslim Views," in Jonathan Brockopp, ed., *The Islamic Ethics of Life: Abortion, War, and Euthanasia* (Columbia: University of South Carolina Press, 2003), 129–54.

13. Ella Landau-Tasseron, "'Non-Combatants' in Muslim Legal Thought," *Hudson Institute Research Monographs on the Muslim World*, Series 1, Paper No. 3 (October 2006): 2–3.

14. Majid Khadduri, *War and Peace in the Law of Islam* (Baltimore, Md.: Johns Hopkins University Press, 1955); *The Islamic Law of Nations: Shaybani's Siyar* (Baltimore, Md.: Johns Hopkins University Press, 2001).

15. Majid Khadduri, "The Islamic System: Its Competition and Co-Existence with Western Systems," *Proceedings of the American Society of International Law* 53 (1959): 49.

16. Ibid., 50.

17. Ibid., 51.

18. Majid Khadduri, "Islam and the Modern Law of Nations," *American Journal of International Law* 50 (1956): 364.

19. Khadduri, "The Islamic System," 51.

20. Khadduri, "Islam and Modern Law," 371.

21. Ibid., 370.

22. Khadduri, "The Islamic System," 51–52.

23. Ibid., 52.
24. Mohammed Bedjaoui, "The Gulf War of 1980–1988 and the Islamic Conception of International Law," in Ige F. Dekker and Harry H. G. Post, eds., *The Gulf War of 1980–1988: The Iran-Iraq War in International Legal Perspective* (The Hague: Martinus Nijhoff, 1992), 277–99.
25. Ibid., 293.
26. Ibid., 294–96.
27. Ibid., 296.
28. Ibid.
29. Ibid., 297.
30. Ibid., 298–99.
31. Osama bin Laden, *Messages to the World: The Statements of Osama bin Laden*, ed. Bruce Lawrence and trans. James Howarth (London: Verso, 2005), 169–70.
32. See Seyyed Vali Reza Nasr, *Mawdudi and the Making of Islamic Revivalism* (New York: Oxford University Press, 1996), 22–23, for the background to Mawdudi's writing of *Al-Jihad fi al-Islam*. Also see Omar Khalidi's discussion in chapter 15 above.
33. Abu al-A'la Mawdudi, *Al-Jihad fi al-Islam* (Lahore: Idara Tarjuman al-Qur'an, 1988), 459–591.
34. Ibid., 596–600.
35. Noor Ahmad Baba, *Organisation of the Islamic Conference: Theory and Practice of Pan-Islamic Cooperation* (Dhaka: University Press, 1994), 214–15; Mohammad Amin al-Midani, "Presentation of the Islamic International Court of Justice: A Muslim Judiciary Court," at http://www.acihl.org/articles.htm?article_id=8 (accessed August 11, 2011).

17

The Jewish Law of War

The Turn to International Law and Ethics

SUZANNE LAST STONE

In contrast with Islam's long and continuous history of statehood, Judaism developed as a decentralized, semisovereign entity in exile. In place of the biblical presentation of Jewish law as the law of the nation of Israel living on its land—engaged in conquest and wars—the rabbis constructed a transnational legal culture known as the halakha. In a situation of exile and absent a sovereign state, the halakha developed few practical laws and no comprehensive theory of war and warfare. Instead, Jewish sources concentrated on historical and theological reflections about war, often framing their comments as biblical commentary.[1]

The establishment of the state of Israel and the Israeli reality have generated, for the first time, a developed literature addressing both *jus ad bellum*, that is, when a Jewish state may go to war, and *jus in bello*, how such a war should be conducted. While this literature reflects, as one would expect, deep division over the details and even overall contours of the Jewish laws of war, it also reveals a far more fundamental division over the basic question whether Jewish law and Jewish ethics apply at all in situations of modern-day warfare engaged in by the Jewish state. Needless to say, the secular state of Israel does not view itself as bound by traditional Jewish law. Nevertheless, certain segments of Israeli society, such as religious soldiers, the religious public square, and that segment of the secular public square wishing to infuse so-called Jewish values into public life, look to contemporary halakhic elaboration of the laws of war as a source of norms and of identity. Within the halakhic community, opinions range from viewing war as outright forbidden for Jews; to viewing it as an issue that fell into desuetude during exile and now must be elaborated from within, despite the paucity of sources; to viewing war as a category governed by the same laws applicable to non-Jews and, therefore, delimited primarily by international conventions, laws, and ethics. While the first polarity affirms a Jewish ethic of peace and devotion to study so exquisite as to make war impossible for a Jew, the second polarity implies that there is no distinctive Jewish ethics of war and warfare at all. In short, the subject of war raises profound questions about both the nature of contemporary collective Jewish identity and the role of halakha in the modern Jewish state. These larger questions will frame my analysis of the debate over the turn by several Jewish law decisors and thinkers today to international law and to ethics.

The Problem of War as a Jewish Legal Category

According to the traditional sources of halakha, there are two kinds of wars: commanded wars and discretionary wars. All other wars are impermissible, and therefore any killings that ensue would be analyzed solely in terms of the laws forbidding individuals to murder, including self-defense and the laws of the pursuer. These justifications for killing, however, are far narrower than those associated with the laws of war. For example, individual self-defense does not allow the taking of one life to save two, the justification of pursuit requires imminent danger, and the person killed in self-defense must be the actual aggressor. At the same time, the category of discretionary wars does not apply in the contemporary age, because the Jewish king, the Sanhedrin, and the *urim ve-tumim* (the oracular breastplate worn by the high priest) are charged with declaring these wars. While the first institution arguably has modern successors, the other two institutions no longer exist. Accordingly, the only potentially operative contemporary halakhic category of analysis is that of commanded wars, which, according to Maimonides, do not require prior declaration by the Sanhedrin or oracular consultation.[2] As discussed by George Wilkes in chapter 7 above, Maimonides's commanded wars include the war against Amalek and the Seven Nations—also categories not operable today—and also defensive war.[3] Thus, following Maimonides, contemporary wars of self-defense by the Jewish state are potentially governed by the halakhic category of war. Whether a preemptive strike is a defensive war and, if so, what actions on the part of an enemy justify the strike are debated. The consensus appears to be that such strikes are within the category of discretionary wars and thus inoperable today, although some argue that responses to prior armed attacks that are designed solely to prevent future attack fall within the rubric of defensive and, hence, commanded wars.[4]

Halakhic rules governing the conduct of war are equally contested and rudimentary. Maimonides codifies several laws applying to the conduct of war, such as first seeking peace before going to war;[5] not surrounding a town on all four sides (one side must be left open for those who wish to depart the battlefield);[6] and not waging war if doing so will destroy more than one-sixth of the population, a rule that modern jurists have noted has implications for the use of nuclear weapons.[7] But, for the most part, Jewish law developed few rules of battle.

By far the most contested issues regarding the conduct of war, given the contemporary Israeli reality, is reprisals, that is, imposing collective punishment on enemy civilian populations in response to terrorist acts by a few individuals. The topic of reprisals first engaged the serious attention of modern Jewish jurists and thinkers after the Israeli raid on the Palestinian village of Qibya in October 1953. The Israel Defense Forces launched the raid in response to persistent terrorist attacks but in the operation killed more than sixty civilians in the village. The event stirred numerous and conflicting responses by religious Zionist jurists and thinkers and laid the groundwork for the terms of the ongoing debate revived by the Second Intifada.

One can divide the responses into three broad schools of thought, which I have termed variously diasporists, collectivists, and cosmopolitans. These terms do not and are not intended to describe an actual school or group; rather, they are intended to describe common patterns of legal thought. Each of these groups reaches a different substantive conclusion about the permissibility of collective punishment in warfare. Underlying these different substantive conclusions, however, is a deep division over which sources to use in constructing a response: halakhic doctrines regulating aggression and self-defense, which are developed but are framed around the individual and not the collective; the sparsely developed indigenous sources about war; or international law and conventions.

For example, the diasporist school turns not to war as a halakhic category but rather to already well-developed categories within the halakha to analyze killings: self-defense and aggression or pursuit. Self-defense provides a very limited warrant to kill. It is confined to situations of imminent danger when no better alternatives exist and does not permit more force than minimally needed. Moreover, self-defense does not permit killing an aggressor after his or her evil act is over as a form of punishment or reprisal. Although some decisors have attempted to stretch these categories so as to cover situations where civilians have conspired to aid terror or even merely extended support through words, the sources do not lend themselves easily to this direction.[8] Using the analogy of self-defense for analyzing responses to terrorism may arguably yield a genuinely just and ethical result. Reprisals and collective punishment in the context of terror have proved one of the most difficult topics for moral philosophers and just war theorists. At the same time, the turn to the legal analogy of individual self-defense and pursuit also implies a rejection of collective state action as a distinct analytic category and concrete reality within halakha, in addition to a deep commitment to using the traditional sources of Jewish law consistently developed over the centuries. With rare exceptions, these sources did not elaborate on the legal category of war, since there were no wars conducted by a Jewish state from the Bible until the modern era.

The collectivists, on the other hand, recognize war as a distinct halakhic category and would, in theory, analyze the question of reprisals and responses to terrorist activity as a question to be decided under the analytic category of war, free of the restrictions imposed by the rules surrounding self-defense and aggression. The dilemma this school of thought faces, however, is the paucity of preexisting halakhic rules on the conduct of war. In the absence of specific rules addressed to this precise question, the collectivists are prepared to develop rules of war by engaging indigenous sources that are exceedingly ancient, with no intervening development, such as biblical sources; or sources that are not conventionally viewed as "legal," such as biblical commentaries, aggadic narratives, or more open-ended, fluid, and ambiguous principles as opposed to rules.

On the one hand, the very openness and ambiguity of these sources allow for the creative development of a Jewish law of war in light of ethical ideals drawn from the tradition as a whole. Thus, for example, Rabbi Shlomo Goren (1917–1994) cites biblical passages that suggest that the collective punishment of the city of Shechem by Jacob's sons in retaliation for Dinah's rape was morally, if not legally, suspect as sources for constructing an ethics of warfare that would prohibit reprisals, collective punishment, or retaliation against innocent civilians.[9] Similarly, Rabbi Hayyim David HaLevi (1924–1998) cites a famous Talmudic narrative describing Jews as merciful and contrasting this trait to the cruelty of the Gibeonites who demanded the slaughter of King Saul's innocent sons in retaliation for Saul's crimes against them. According to HaLevi, the treatment of hostile civilian populations must therefore be shaped by the ethical ideal of mercy.[10] Still others have argued that the few rules regarding conduct of war that do exist, such as ensuring avenues of escape, evidence an underlying ideal, around which the concrete rules revolve, of mercy and minimization of cruelty to the enemy.[11] And still others have invoked open-ended principles such as *hillul hashem*, avoiding desecration of the Name, as yet another basis for constructing an ethically informed, aspirational set of Jewish laws of war.[12]

Yet precisely because the sources within the tradition dealing with the category of war are so sparse and open-ended, they are equally capable of yielding precisely the opposite conclusion. Thus, jurists associated with the more militant segments of religious Zionism have cited the very same example of Shechem as a warrant for collective punishment and the very same principle of *hillul hashem*, but giving it a militant twist, in which God's name is profaned by a display of weakness.[13]

In contrast with the diasporic and collectivist schools, the cosmopolitans contend that wars conducted by the Jewish state are to be governed not by discrete and particular rules of the halakha—whether self-defense or the halakhic rules of war—but, rather, by international law and conventions. Responses to terrorism and reprisals would therefore follow the practice of the nations and of international conventions. The legal rationales for this conclusion are various: war is a universal and not particular category of experience;[14] or the cessation of development of laws of war in the Jewish legal tradition creates a gap in the rules which may be filled by turning to non-Jewish norms.[15] Underneath the differing rationales, however, is a common assumption: that the halakha recognizes war as a legitimate activity of statecraft designed to reduce social conflict permitted to the rest of the nations and that the Jewish state qua state merely must conduct itself "like all other nations."[16]

At the deeper level, the divisions among these three schools of thought over the proper sources to use to analyze the legitimacy of war and warfare turn on far larger jurisprudential and ideological disagreements about the nature of halakha itself and of the meaning of Jewish history.[17] Is the halakha an ethics, a politics, or autonomous law? Is it addressed only to individuals, or does it also address collectivities such as the Jewish state? Is it comprehensive, or does it have gaps? What is the relationship of the universal domain it posits to the particular? Thus, my aim here is to show how contemporary responses to fashioning laws of war, especially those of the cosmopolitans, are related to numerous long-standing arguments within the Jewish legal tradition over the proper description of halakha itself. In the next section, I offer some necessary historical background to the main arguments in the chapter by tracing the transformation of the biblical view of collectivist law to the classical rabbinic diasporic model and then by outlining the tensions inaugurated within Jewish thought with the rise of the modern nation-state of Israel.

The Return of the Repressed: From the Bible to the State of Israel

Pursuant to its story of origin, the Jewish legal system came into being through a historical covenant at Sinai. The covenant was made with a particular people, the people of Israel, orienting Jewish collective life in a particularist direction. Moreover, the story tells of the founding of a nation organized for practical political action, including war. The destruction of this national political and religious order culminated with the destruction of the Second Temple in 70 C.E. Thereafter, religious, social, and rabbinic elites formulated an alternative concept of collective identity: a collective dedicated to the observance of the law. The Bible became relegated to Judaism's canonical national history and only the starting point of the Jewish legal system (halakha), which is composed of the written law (the first five books of the Bible describing the law received by Moses) and the oral law (recorded in the Mishna and the Talmud, the rabbinic legal product of the first millennium C.E.). Indeed, the biblical picture of a unified religious polity was to a large extent transferred over to the halakha even though it was operating and developing in exile without a state, official institutions, a supreme court, or a national center. The halakha was thought to create all of the political institutions necessary for continued self-governance across the globe. As Eliezer Schweid put it, the halakha functioned as "a portable political entity."[18] At the same time, the rabbinic concept of law reverses the biblical image: the law itself constitutes the nation, and without the law, there would be no nation.

The national-collective orientation of the Bible was also transformed. The biblical conception of national law portrays rewards and punishments for performing the law in national-collective terms: The nation as a whole performs the law and reaps material blessings or punishment. In late antiquity, however, religious orientations arose that were more focused on the individual and on individual salvation. The rabbis, too, transformed the national-collective orientation of the law into a far more individualized conception. As Shlomo Fischer points out, "observance of Jewish law in exile became incumbent on the individual Jew, or in regard to a number of cases, on the local community, which was conceived as being constituted by individual Jews."[19] While "the obligations upon the individual Jew derive from his membership in the primordial community," nonetheless, "the legal-behavioral implications of this membership are worked out in regard to the individual."[20]

The rabbinic conception of the law as the sole locus of national identity and as a fully functional, albeit portable, political entity succeeded in no small part because the imperial corporatist models in which Jews were situated cooperated. Contrary to what Salo Baron labeled the "lachrymose" view of Jewish history, the legal and political autonomy that Judaism enjoyed under Roman rule, feudal Europe, and the Ottoman empire was remarkable. Jews maintained their own court system throughout this time and possessed sufficient legal autonomy to enforce traditional Jewish law fully. To be sure, foreign rule occasionally intruded on autonomy, and the tradition developed early on, in the fourth century, a Jewish version of "render unto Caesar what is Caesar's." The Babylonian *amora*[21] Samuel is credited with formulating the principle "the law of the kingdom is the law." In terms of duties owed to foreign rulers, the principle originally had limited practical application. It is fair to speak during this long period of a total halakhic society as a way of life.

The rise of the modern nation-state put an abrupt end to this era. Large parts of the halakha fell under the nation-state's commitment to the unity of law and its monopolization of legal subjects formerly left to subgroup elaboration and enforcement. The standard history of Jewish legal transition to the new political formation of the modern nation-state tells a story of modern rupture and pragmatic accommodation. These accounts emphasize the post facto legitimization of the ideology of the modern nation-state, made possible because the halakha, like any rich legal tradition, had something available "to hang necessity and opportunity on."[22] According to this standard history, at the dawn of the Jewish emancipation, the old principle "the law of the kingdom is the law" was seized upon in order to justify the trading of Jewish sovereignty over governmental, communal, civil, and domestic matters for equal citizenship rights. The principle thus facilitated and legitimized the reorganization of Judaism from a semisovereign entity into a voluntary organization. The principle figured prominently in the responses of the Assembly of Notables to Napoleon I's questions about the suitability of Jews to fulfill the obligations incumbent upon them as French citizens. From then on, Judaism took its shape as a private religious faith, concentrating mainly on the performance of private rituals, with the retention of overlapping sovereignty with the state only in issues relating to marriage and divorce. Thus, the principle became Judaism's corollary for the division of the secular and religious realms of life and, in the process, was responsible for the modern demise of the halakha from a distinctive, all-encompassing system governing all aspects of life—the social, civil, communal, political, and religious—to a religion. Yet the conceptual basis for life as citizen within a host nation already had been laid down by the Talmudic abandonment of the biblical national-collectivist conception of identity in favor of an individualist orientation. Debate over the value of religious coercion as opposed to freely chosen observance could, indeed, be found within the Talmudic tradition, and even the contraction of the sphere of halakha primarily to ritual matters had genuine halakhic purchase.

From Moses Mendelssohn on through the rise of Zionism, modern Jewish thought has engaged in a rich dialogue about the changes that needed to be made in the traditional Jewish vision of halakha as total society to adjust to the new reality of the modern nation-state and, with it, the new phenomenon of a secular Jewish identity.[23] With the modern separation of domains of life into separate spheres, argument centered for the first time on whether halakha was a politics, law, or religion. Intertwined with this argument was renewed attention to an age-old question about the relationship of the universal and particular elements of Judaism. And underlying both was the persistent issue of a national-collective Jewish identity apart from halakha. The participants in this debate differed primarily over whether the Jewish community should give up its collective national identity, retaining only the sacral or, conversely, only its universal parts, or whether it should seek to retain a national identity by "arriving at some sort of compromise with the modern state."[24] The more traditionally minded Jews asserted that, after exile from the land, the exclusive organizing principle of continued Jewish collective identity was continued obedience to the halakha. No other Jewish national expression is required. These eighteenth- and nineteenth-century debates set the stage for the contemporary contests over modern Jewish nationalism.

Zionism, even before the establishment of the state of Israel, posed a major crisis to the traditional mind-set. One issue was its identification as a secular, modern movement and, as such, inimical to religion. The second was the reclamation in the historical present, and not the messianic future, of the biblical national-collective worldview, including territorial sovereignty and national-collective institutions such as state and military ones. Most of the Jewish religious movements current in Israel are modern utopian movements. They differ markedly in how they interpret the meaning of history, however, and this ideological division brings with it radically different approaches to the legal process, particularly in fashioning norms bearing on the subject of war.

The ultrareligious, or those of the diasporist school, do not relate to the state as a religious vehicle or as any means for perpetuating Jewish collective national identity. For them, "Jewish collective identity has become 'bracketed'; relegated to the distant biblical past or messianic future" and perpetuated in the present only through the community of the faithful.[25] In short, the halakha remains the sole national expression of Jews. Moreover, the diasporic school of thought attempts to perpetuate a particular post-Talmudic conception of transnational halakha as autonomous law—a normative framework independent of any philosophic, political, or mystical ideologies, whether religious or secular. This approach essentially treats the nation-state and its institutions and policies—whether a host state or the state of Israel—as external conditions or circumstances, new political formations, in which the transnational halakha is objectively applied.[26] Pursuant to this approach, a variety of halakhic principles and doctrines are canvassed and marshaled to assess whether discrete and particular acts, such as war, are compatible with preexisting halakhic rules, traditionally developed throughout the ages, governing such matters as self-defense and aggression.

The religious Zionist movement, from which the collectivist school emerges, understands the establishment of the state of Israel both as religiously significant and as a vehicle for reviving halakha as national law in the nation. Some wings of this movement see it in vivid messianic terms, as the beginning of the fulfillment of the redemption. For them, the state provides the opportunity to resuscitate the original biblical ideal of law in the nation and to resacralize the secular. Halakha, in this vision, is a means to achieve the spiritual and political perfection of the nation. The non-messianically-oriented wings see it as an opportunity to revive halakha as a religio-national law and Jewish national-cultural-spiritual expression. Both return to the original biblical conception of law as the law of a sovereign nation whose identity is defined in collective, national terms. Law is deeply political in this school of thought and often ideologically saturated. Indeed, halakha is a politics, which integrates what we now call state, law, and religion or philosophy, and in this sense, the school harks back to Maimonides's conception of the halakha as a politics aimed at perfection of the body and the intellect.[27]

Ideological divisions aside, the chief jurisprudential division between the collectivists and the diasporists, as Shlomo Fischer has astutely observed, is the question of whether the law recognizes only the rights and duties of individuals or also recognizes the Jewish state as a separate corporate embodiment of the nation, with collective rights.[28] Nowhere is this shift more evident than as applied to the issue of war, which exposes acutely the tension between a collectivist versus an individualist framework. For example, as Arye Edrei has analyzed at length, one of the key representatives of the collectivist school, Rabbi Goren,[29] argued that there are "two planes to Jewish law," that of individual conduct, which is governed by classic halakhic norms such as saving lives wherever possible unless the right of self-defense is immediately activated, and that of national existence and institutions, bound by national-collective obligations and rights, including the right to conduct war and peace in the national interest without regard to the lives of its individual citizens.[30] It is this construction, at the normative level, of a national-collective plane in which different halakhic rules apply that the more traditional adherents of the diasporic school of thought are at pains to deny. Instead, they are intent on preserving the traditional construction of halakha as a set of obligations addressing only individuals, whose adherence to these norms is the exclusive legitimate national expression.

What both the diasporists and the collectivists have in common, however, is a commitment to a total halakhic society, in which particularist Jewish norms govern every aspect of life, and to preserving a transcendent element in the law in both the domestic and international arenas. As Edrei argues, traditionalists have often asserted that halakha is seamless and comprehensive. There is a halakhic answer to every question, for halakha addresses every facet of human experience, from the private to the public. A supposed gap in the law—such as rules of war—is merely apparent, not real. The gap either signals that the conduct is forbidden to the individual or that the rule must be extrapolated by analogy from other, developed areas of the law, such as the criminal law. It is precisely by reasoning through the spiral of precedent that the transcendent dimension of halakha, embedded in the tradition, is retained.[31]

A commitment to halakha as total way of life is also the position of the collectivist school, Edrei shows. Rabbi Goren, for example, rejected the idea of halakhic indifference to any area of life; rather, as a normative system, halakha is able and required to relate to all areas of life, including areas such as war, of which it had no experience for two thousand years.[32] Indeed, as Edrei explains, he claimed that this was merely the logical extension of the traditional idea that Jewish nationalism is defined by its law rather than by territory or other sociological categories. He fashioned a separate normative system for war from biblical sources and even noncanonical ones, rather than rely on the developed criminal law precedents, because he was himself a military man who viewed the criminal law as an inadequate analogy for war. He hoped to retain a transcendent dimension to the newly fashioned rules by joining law with ethics and a sensitivity to a uniquely "Jewish worldview."[33] Accordingly, for Goren, international standards of war were inadequate because they failed to reflect a particularist Jewish viewpoint.

It is precisely this idea that the halakha is all-encompassing, covering every aspect of human life under a single, unified sacred framework and forming a total society governed by Torah law that the cosmopolitan school disputes.

The Cosmopolitan Halakha

By far the most fascinating and underexplored model is that of what I have termed the cosmopolitans, who turn to international law as the standard governing war in the Jewish nation on the theory that war is a universal experience and category permitted to all nations, including the Jewish state, by the halakha itself. The mundane aspects of statehood, occasionally and obliquely addressed by the halakha, are not particular to halakha or its essence; they reflect its universal and therefore conventional aspect. Accordingly, international law or the custom of the nations govern the state of Israel—from the halakhic perspective—and not indigenous, particularist, national-collective norms or realistic-ethical norms such as halakhic standards of individual self-defense. Thus, war is emptied of independent, concrete, and specifically halakhic content.

Technically, however, halakha may only incorporate international norms of war if war is viewed as a realm of discretion, a halakhic gap where concrete and particular legal rules have run out, or a sphere conceptually subject to a different set of legal rules from halakha proper. The cosmopolitan school arrives at this conclusion through an innovative reading of three related and complex bodies of doctrine: the one pertaining to the rights and duties of the Jewish king, the second to the rights and duties of non-Jewish societies, and the third to the rights and duties of Jews to incorporate the foreign law of the non-Jewish kingdom under the halakhic principle that "the law of the [non-Jewish] kingdom is the law." This is not the place for an extended analysis of these doctrines.[34] Instead, I would like to focus, first, on the seminal opinion of the chief representative of the cosmopolitan school, Rabbi Shaul Yisraeli (1909–1995), on the vociferous criticism that has surrounded it, and, finally, on the fascinating counterreaction it has evoked.[35] For while many within this school agree with the foundational premise that affairs of state operate pursuant to a different law and logic from the particularist rules of halakha, the abdication of responsibility for developing an indigenous ethic of just war is deeply troubling to them. For these critics, halakha is not solely autonomous law but also ethics. And they argue for a return to Jewish ethics informed, although not necessarily governed, by halakha.

The Turn to International Law

Rabbi Yisraeli's opinion was authored immediately after the Qibya raid and was motivated by the wish to defend the actions of the Israel Defense Forces in the face of public outcry within Israel. Thus, he undertakes a retrospective examination of whether the killing of civilians in response to terrorist activities was permissible under Jewish law. Indeed, Yisraeli attempts to apply all three schools discussed in this chapter.[36] He first turns to the preexisting legal analogies of self-defense and aggression, per the diasporists, and concludes that neither will afford a defense. He then turns to the legal category of war, contending that reprisals such as Qibya may be viewed as part of an ongoing war. Finally, he offers a third alternative: incorporating international law by applying the mechanisms contained within the halakha itself for filling gaps in the law or for displacing specific halakhic rules.

Yisraeli apparently bases his view that the rules of war are those agreed to by the global community of nations on two legs. The first is that war is a part of statecraft, an activity committed to the Jewish king and its successor institutions such as the modern Jewish state. He cites Deuteronomy 17:14, in which the people ask for a king "like all the nations." And he couples this with the view, most clearly articulated by the Netziv[37] in the nineteenth century, that war is a universal activity permitted to all societies and therefore should be waged by universal rules. Deuteronomy 17:14 is ordinarily not viewed as a legal source.[38] Yet Yisraeli is compressing here a long tradition of legal and political discourse about the universal dimension of Jewish kingship, which merits unpacking.

Deuteronomy 16:18 through 18:22 lists the officials of the polity—judge, king, priest, prophet—and assigns each a role, although there is considerable overlap of functions. In Deuteronomy 17, the king has only one positive duty: to write out a scroll of the law, read it every day of his life, and obey its commands. At the same time, the king is described as a monarch "like all the other nations."[39] The text thus immediately sets up a tension between a model of kingship that is culturally specific and one that is universal. In theory, juristic reconciliation could take a variety of forms—that lawless kings reigned in Israel for much of the monarchy but this did not sever the relationship of ruler to subjects or give rise to a right of resistance, that kings held legally defined emergency powers to administer royal courts, or that they had political discretion to depart from Torah law in times of need, to name a few solutions that later emerged. A far more radical reading views the textual phrase "like all the nations" as a warrant for interpreting the powers of the Jewish king in light of a universal and not a particular concept of kingship.

The groundwork for this view was laid by Maimonides, although he adhered strictly to a view of Jewish kingship as firmly integrated with religious law. The Torah's commandments relating to governmental structures are part of the perfection of the body because they aim at securing social order, which is a necessary condition for achieving perfection of the soul.[40] All governmental structures—not only the king but also the court—are obligated to secure social order. From a technical legal perspective, Maimonides solves the question of the judicial powers of the Jewish king by codifying emergency powers held by the king to depart from Torah law in order to maintain social order.[41] These emergency powers are only theoretically temporary, and they entail the power to punish free of the biblical procedural restrictions of two witnesses and forewarning.[42]

In the Maimonidean system, however, the only actor who truly can be entrusted to exercise discretion is the jurist-sage. Maimonides's king has very little actual discretion. This is a realm not of politics or wisdom but of law. Rather, as Gerald Blidstein points out, Maimonides appropriated for the king a more lenient legal model whose initial Talmudic context is the obligations incumbent upon non-Jews.[43] With so-called Noahide law, the Talmud begins a sustained reflection on the legal and political model ordained for other civilizations. In addition to six substantive commands, Noahide law includes a command of justice, *dinim*.[44] Maimonides understands the Talmudic commandment of *dinim* as intending to preserve social order by establishing a judiciary that will enforce the other substantive commands. The Talmud had already noted that "Noahides" punish in accordance with the testimony of one witness and without forewarning.[45] In Maimonides's Code, the Jewish king, like non-Jewish government, is authorized to punish on the basis of the testimony of one witness and no forewarning. "Maimonides' entire edifice of monarchic powers identified Jewish and gentile governance as a single structure possessing similar goals and utilizing similar instruments."[46] The biblical language to appoint a king "like all the other nations" now becomes a warrant for resorting to universal norms of governance to define the powers of the Jewish king. Of course, these non-Jewish norms of governance are themselves offshoots of Talmudic jurisprudence.[47] Nevertheless, they are universal and not particular norms (from the Jewish point of view). They operate, however, as a kind of indigenously "Jewish" universalist fall-back or residual law, which can be drawn on when the particular law requires supplementation or adjustment

A century later, another member of the Spanish royalist school, Solomon Ibn Adret, invoked similar ideas to legitimize medieval punishment practice.[48] But the most far-reaching articulation of this view is in the Eleventh Homily of Rabbi Nissim Gerondi, the great fourteenth-century scholar. Gerondi posits a central gap in the halakha: the lack of conventional modes of governance able to preserve social order. Torah law, with its requirements of judging in accordance with the testimony of two witnesses and forewarning, cannot accomplish this end. Thus, it is deficient by comparison with other political systems. Yet the Torah itself provides the means for correcting this deficiency. The king, who is concerned only with guilt or innocence, may punish without resort to the Torah methods of criminal adjudication. Like Maimonides, Gerondi links the king's authority to a general religious command to preserve social order, *tikkun olam*. This term cannot be found in the Pentateuch and is cited by the early rabbis, not as a rule but as an explanation for enacting a variety of social legislation. But both Maimonides and Gerondi are using the Talmudic term as a generative legal "principle." Gerondi, at least, takes the Bible's instruction about kingship as the source of this command.[49]

Gerondi goes far beyond Maimonides, as Gerald Blidstein elaborates. First, power, not institution, is the key for him. Thus, the religious command is not to appoint a monarch per se but, rather, always to embed monarchical power somewhere in the Jewish polity.[50] Indeed, the monarch is merely the site of social order historically chosen by the people, who may consent to another institutional form if they so desire. Second, the language about the need for public order and social welfare is so broad that it is virtually impossible to confine the "power" Gerondi is describing to punishment.[51] Third, Gerondi does not place the king's powers within the more conventional emergency jurisdiction model, although he cites the phrase once or twice. Moreover, the political domain is stripped of any aura of the sacred. Although there is a vague bow to the Jewish king upholding the religion, there is no attempt to integrate the king within the rest of the system, as Maimonides labored to do, nor is there any attempt to coordinate state power with religious law and institutions. This is a separate jurisdiction legitimately operating under its own rules. Although Gerondi is largely silent on what these rules are and whether there are any inherent limits to them, I believe that we must read him against the background of the earlier discussion as implicitly incorporating any rules permitted to non-Jewish societies.

In short, Gerondi's theoretical discussion and Maimonides's codification of the laws of the Jewish king have become core elements of contemporary religious Zionist political and legal thought. They have served as the justification for essentially separating state functions of social order from religion and legitimizing a secular government run in accordance with nonhalakhic norms. The underlying rationale—that government and preserving social order are a universal Noahide norm incumbent on all societies, Jewish and non-Jewish alike and in the same way—also underlies Yisraeli's approach to war. Thus, Yisraeli relies on earlier precedent holding that war is not only permitted to non-Jewish societies but is a logical outgrowth of the Noahide command of *dinim*, because war in present times is a means to reduce social conflict and therefore to preserve social order.

The second leg of Yisraeli's opinion relies on a more familiar halakhic principle: *dina de-malkhuta dina* (the law of the land is the [legitimate] law; henceforward DDM), which is first articulated in the context of the power of foreign rulers to tax and expropriate land. On the face of it, then, no principle would seem to symbolize more visibly the loss of Jewish sovereignty than this one, which appears four times in the Babylonian Talmud. Several scholars have already noted how far this appearance is from reality[52] once one focuses closely on how the principle is actually deployed in the Talmudic discussion. In none of these cases is it operating as a concession to foreign rule or an expression of powerlessness. On the contrary, in its original uses, the principle serves to make the halakha fully functional in exile. This postulate took on a life of its own as the jurists begin to theorize in the Middle Ages about the conceptual basis for the principle. And in a chain of logical progression, these conceptual bases begin to undermine the conception of halakha as an all-encompassing system. Instead, the sphere of halakha becomes more and more contracted.

The Talmud already hints at a close association between the principle and the custom of the people, and many of the medieval theories revolve around one or another form of popular consent or social contract theory. As Shmuel Shilo notes, the theories also attest to the rich interpenetration of the medieval discussions of the rights of kings taking place in the European Middle Ages.[53] Portions of halakha become theoretically optional and not mandatory as the principle is extended through a series of logical progressions and in tandem with the extension of the rights of kings in Europe far beyond the concrete context from which it sprang—taxes and land—and far beyond what is necessary to resolve actual, rather than theoretical, cases.

The twelfth-century Talmudic commentator Rashi potentially shifts the paradigm, however, by building a bridge between the principle and the by now familiar idea of a universal, divinely ordained law, which played so critical a role in the discussion of the Jewish monarchy. Rashi focuses on the one instance in the Babylonian Talmud where DDM functions not as a duty-imposing rule but as a power-conferring rule to Jewish litigants in an intra-Jewish dispute to take advantage of non-Jewish validation of deeds even though the signatories are non-Jews and the method contrary to Jewish law.[54] Here, DDM is allowing non-Jewish law to penetrate into Jewish law as an alternative norm.[55] Rashi draws on the familiar Jewish legal principle that only one who is himself under a divine obligation to perform an action can be an effective legal agent for others. He explains the Talmudic permission as resting on the notion that non-Jews are commanded to "institute justice," citing the Noahide norm of *dinim*. Accordingly, they can be effective agents for all matters subsumed under that command. Recall that from the internal perspective of rabbinic Judaism, this command obligates humanity to preserve social order by enacting systems of law.[56] The kingdom's law is rooted ultimately in divine command and therefore has legal and moral legitimacy equal to that of Jewish law. As the product of divine command, it is, in a sense, sanctified. Accordingly, non-Jewish legal activity can serve here as an alternative norm even for Jews and even when it is at variance with Jewish law. Conversely, he notes, with respect to matters not subsumed under the command of *dinim*—Jewish marriage and divorce bills—DDM cannot be invoked as a power-conferring rule to utilize alternative norms. The implication of Rashi's rationale is that large portions of the halakha are, in fact, replaceable by the law of other civilizations, thus shrinking the scope of halakha to matters of ritual and religious prohibition.[57]

According to this pluralist conception, the function of DDM is to arbitrate which norms generated by diffuse jurisdictions are relevant in different circumstances. In this light, Rabbi Yisraeli ruled that the Jewish state was obligated by—and only by—international standards of war.[58] From a technical perspective, he relies on the Talmudic dictum "the law of the kingdom is the law," but he gives it a radically innovative meaning. Where formerly the dictum governed the obligations and privileges of individual Jews relative to their host states, it now, in the elaboration by Yisraeli, governs the obligations and privileges of the Jewish nation acting in the international context. And where formerly, the dictum extended only to the laws of a sovereign ruler, such as king or state, it now, in the rabbi's elaboration, extends to international law on the theory that the non-Jewish kingdom could be defined in global terms, as long as the collective will of the world's citizens ratified the global kingdom's law. Yisraeli's opinion, moreover, seems to blend the underlying rationales of the DDM consent school and of Rashi's turn to Noahide *dinim*. Jews can consent to be governed by international norms, just as they can consent to be governed by the civil laws of host states. Consent to laws pertaining to war is legitimate even though war involves the religious prohibition of bloodshed. War, however, is a chosen means to settle disputes in contemporary life and, as such, fulfills the goal of civilizing the world and securing social order, even if such wars are not undertaken for the sake of enforcing Noahide norms.[59]

The upshot of this innovative use of DDM is the treatment of the modern Jewish state as merely one member of the global community of nations. International codes of war, treaties, and so on, govern the state of Israel—from the halakhic perspective—and not indigenous, national-collective norms or particular, aspirational norms developed to govern relations of members within a covenantal community. In his analysis, Yisraeli makes clear that halakhic norms pertaining to use of force developed within the context of individual self-defense could not countenance the manner of conducting warfare acceptable within the international community. But rather than view halakha as a ground for ethical critique, he sees halakha as allowing the incorporation of looser standards of behavior when the nation acts beyond its border. Should international society adopt more stringent norms than halakha, these, too, would be binding on the nation acting in the international arena. The Jewish nation-state is no longer modeled on a concept of exceptionalism; instead, it is merely a member of international society whose norms should converge.

Already in the medieval period, Rabbi Menachem Meiri had observed that the doctrine of the Jewish king and that of "the law of the kingdom" are merely two facets of a single concept: conventional political institutions or government "like all the other nations." Both doctrines ultimately can be traced back to the tense coexistence within Judaism of the universal and the particular—of two normative systems, the one consisting of universal obligations binding all humanity and the other of commandments particular to Jews. The Bible first launched this complex internal structure by describing the pre-Sinai world as one filled with law given to humanity, including Israel's forefathers. This account is transformed in the Talmud into a full-fledged description of two normative orders. The Talmud primarily focused on the universal law as an explanatory model for the law that existed before "the law"—the law given at Sinai—and used the model as a contrasting image of a conventional society, unlike the covenantal one forged at Sinai, in order to explore the differences between the two and to construct identity.[60] Although it left open the relationship between the two legal orders, it largely presented that relationship as a historic progression, with the universal law superseded for Jews by the particular obligations revealed at Sinai. It was left to the medieval period to construct a far more complex relationship between the two, with the universal law serving in the eyes of some jurists, as I have claimed elsewhere, essentially as an alternative source of norms even in a national Jewish context. Discretion can only exist as long as law does not exist to fill the space. And pursuant to this interactive model, gaps in halakha disappear once valid law appears, whether the law is generated by the non-Jewish state, the Jewish state, or even the international community.[61]

Still, the existence of this universal legal system within a particular legal system opens a deep fissure in Jewish thought. From an internal perspective, the Noahide system is the law that humanity was commanded to follow, including Israel's forebears, and is binding on everyone. The giving of the Torah at Sinai imposed additional obligations only on Jews. But if the universal Noahide law is God-sanctioned—and developed in detail by Jewish jurists—and a reflection of the moral and political law, what precisely is the point of Sinai? The question "Why Sinai?" haunted the rabbis. As noted, in the Talmudic period, Noahide law and its juristic development served as a site for bolstering self-identity and for laying the groundwork for a theory about the duties of members of covenantal as opposed to conventional political societies. Indeed, the two-witness rule itself was thought to symbolize the covenantal community. Maimonides sought to solve the issue by integrating the political structures with religious norms and stitched the Jewish king into the religious fabric, portraying him as a sage or king messiah. The philosopher Hermann Cohen (1842–1918) and various nineteenth-century reform movements sought to solve it by reconstituting Judaism into the Noahide, moral, universal religion, in which ritual is secondary, at best. Conversely, one could view the added particularist obligations of Sinai as the essence and the universal, political law as necessary but insignificant. In short, this is the halakhic underpinning for the debate in the eighteenth and nineteenth centuries after the Jewish emancipation about which is the core and which the periphery of halakha.

Indeed, Gerondi's sermon, which forms a critical background text for the license of the modern Jewish state to govern pursuant to conventional norms of social order, explicitly deals with the question "Why Sinai?" In the course of outlining the Jewish king's powers, he also reconceives the purpose of the halakha. For Gerondi, the sphere of Sinai law is the sacred and the numinous and the sphere of true justice. Thus, certain biblical laws, such as judging in accordance with two witnesses, were never intended as a practical means to govern society. Rather, they were intended to bring on the divine effluence. In addition, they are truly just precisely because they focus solely on the rights of the individual and do not take into account the needs of society. Thus, Gerondi rejects out of hand Maimonides's entire project of embedding divine law in society and integrating the two. The realm of the political may be inaugurated by divine command, but it does not partake of the divine thereafter.

If we speak of Christian influences, by far the most important here is the Gelasian doctrine of two powers: pope and king. Yet Gerondi is certainly working off earlier rabbinic sources in addition to extending the doctrine of Noahide law to one logical conclusion. He is following, as Gerald Blidstein pointed out, Yehuda Halevi, who wrote about "the social–ethical law given to humanity (Noahide law) to which the spiritual-ceremonial law is added at Sinai," and decisively splitting the two into the realm of the sacred and particular, where true justice is possible, as opposed to the realm of the profane and universal, where the needs of society are irreconcilable with the rights of individuals.[62]

It is precisely this splitting of halakha into two—with particularistic religious-ethical norms governing Jewish individual obligations and universal Noahide norms governing affairs of state and especially war—that is so troubling to Rabbi Yisraeli's critics.

A Revived Jewish Ethics?

Rabbi Yisraeli's position was revived recently by Michael Broyde in two symposium issues on the topic of Jewish law and war. The responses it invoked are telling. Even those thinkers who are sympathetic to the idea that the laws of the Jewish king and Noahide law bear a "family resemblance" were deeply troubled both by the complete "surrender to comparative law"[63] and by "the suspension of the normative ethics of Jewish law."[64] The gist of both objections is that in turning to international law, Yisraeli left no standard for ethical critique or reason to contribute a distinctively Jewish ethical voice. What is at stake is the role of the halakha as an ethics and not solely law. For those who rely on doctrines permitting Jews to agree to be governed by international law, under the rubric of *dina de-malkhuta dina*, there is no further role for halakha. International law sets the standard of behavior even if it diverges from the norm that the halakha would supply, were it to be developed. International law might set a lower or higher standard of humanitarian behavior than would be the case under halakha, but in either case, the international rule would govern, because from a technical legal perspective, halakha permits its incorporation. This view leaves no room for halakha to function as an aspirational set of norms. For many, however, including those who read the sources relied on by Rabbi Yisraeli as also permitting the separation of religious and many state functions, this is precisely the role of halakha vis-à-vis the state: to guard against the excesses of secular nationalism and function as ethical critique. This was the position of the Israeli philosopher Yeshayahu Leibowitz (1903–1994), who published a scathing critique of the Qibya reprisal and later became an outspoken critic of Israel's retention of territories conquered during the Six-Day War.

In an essay on how major schools within religious Zionism viewed the Israeli army and military action, Ellie Holzer describes one school that perceives certain totalizing characteristics of political nationalism as idolatry.[65] The nation-state is essentially seen as idolatrous, either because nationalism demands that religious conceptions of holiness be extended to mundane—or even evil—acts of statecraft, such as war and international confrontation, or because nationalism fails to give precedence to the individual as an autonomous human being, subordinating the human being to society. This group, like Gerondi, sees the essence of the halakha as first and foremost a sacred religion, defining the essence of divine worship, and also as an ethics guarding the status of the individual as against society, including the state. Perhaps the best-known proponent of this view was Yeshayahu Leibowitz, who initially sought the revival of the halakha in areas of public, national life and then changed his mind and became the foremost proponent for the radical separation of halakha from state. The role of halakha and religion vis-à-vis the state within this school of thought is ethical critique. Halakha becomes a source of criticism of nationalist-political ideology when the latter becomes total and radical and tramples the status of the individual. Religion is essential in this model to prevent the degeneration of secular political nationalism into nationalism as an ideology. Thus, this position is sharply distinguishable from that of the collectivists who seek precisely to resacralize the body politic and for whom the concept of Jewish kingship should be culturally specific, not universal.

This discourse over incorporating foreign law anticipates several themes raised by the United States Supreme Court's decision in *Roper v. Simmons* debating the role of foreign norms in interpreting American constitutional provisions.[66] As with *Roper*, the discussion divides along models of resistance, convergence, and engagement.[67] Resistance is the familiar problem of the loss of national distinctiveness, which many medieval jurists raised as an objection to DDM.[68] Yet other rabbinic authorities, especially in the modern age, saw incorporation of non-Jewish law into the halakha not as a threat to Jewish distinctiveness and particularity but rather as a method of correcting the halakha. The assumption that drives this approach, already found in the Talmud, is that one of the purposes of the universal law preceding Sinai must be to set a floor on ethical obligations, and this notion, as Shilo put it, "became incorporated into the discussion of DDM." If Jewish law allows ethically inferior conduct that other legal systems forbid, the ethically superior norm should displace Jewish law so that the two converge. Thus, as Shilo points out, the progress forward in the self-correction of the halakha in light of the laws of other civilizations was made in the modern era with exposure of halakha to democratic systems.[69] Rabbi Yisraeli and his followers claim that this relationship now needs to be reversed. They argue that halakha should converge with international law, even if the latter sets an ethically inferior standard. Those who view the halakha as a source of ethical critique, by contrast, seek to engage the state. Indeed, this is the true goal of even some of the collectivists. Efforts such as Goren's to craft an indigenous law of war from the sparse sources on the subject, one that emphasizes the ethical contributions that halakha could make to the topic, do not, in the end, aim to bind the state; rather, they aim to engage it.

Notes

1. On Jewish perspectives on war generally, see Michael Walzer, "War and Peace in the Jewish Tradition," and Aviezer Ravitzky, "Prohibited Wars in the Jewish Tradition," in Terry Nardin, ed., *The Ethics of War and Peace* (Princeton, N.J.: Princeton University Press, 1996), 95–127. See also Lawrence H. Schiffman and Joel B. Wolowelsky, eds., *War and Peace in the Jewish Tradition* (New York: Yeshiva University Press, 2007).
2. Cf. Ramban, "Supplement of Nahmanides to Maimonides's Book of Commandments," Positive Commandment no. 17; Noam Zohar, "Can a War Be Morally Optional?" *Journal of Political Philosophy* 4, no. 3 (1996): 229–41; J. David Bleich, "Preemptive War in Jewish Law," in *Contemporary Halakhic Problems* 4 (New York: KTav, 1989), 251.
3. Maimonides, *Mishneh Torah*, Laws of Kings 5:1.
4. See Michael J. Broyde, "Just Wars, Just Battles, and Just Conduct in Jewish Law: Jewish Law Is Not a Suicide Pact!" in Schiffman and Wolowelsky, *War and Peace* , 14–15.
5. Maimonides, *Mishneh Torah*, Laws of Kings 6:1.

6. Ibid., 6:5.
7. Babylonian Talmud, Tractate Shevu'ot, 35b. See generally J. David Bleich, "Nuclear Warfare," *Tradition* 21, no. 3 (Fall 1984): 84–88.
8. See discussion in Broyde, "Just Wars," 9–17; see also Shaul Yisraeli, "Military Action in Defense of the State," in *Amud ha-Yemini*, rev. ed. (Jerusalem, 1991), 168–205; discussed extensively in Arye Edrei, "Law, Interpretation, and Ideology: The Renewal of the Jewish Laws of War in the State of Israel," *Cardozo Law Review* 28, no. 1 (2006): 101.
9. Edrei, "Law, Interpretation, and Ideology," 221–22.
10. See Broyde, "Just Wars," 5–6. See also discussion by Ehud Luz, "Jewish Ethics as an Argument in the Public Debate over the Israeli Reaction to Palestinian Terror," *Israel Studies* 7, no. 3 (2002): 134–56.
11. Broyde, "Just Wars," 26.
12. Luz, "Jewish Ethics," 149–53.
13. Yaakov Ariel, "Self-Defense (The Intifida in Halakha)," *Tehumin* 1 (1988): 13–26. See discussion in Broyde, "Just Wars," 5–6, 10, 24.
14. Broyde, "Just Wars," 10–11.
15. Edrei, "Law, Interpretation, and Ideology," 216–17.
16. As Michael Broyde summarizes, this is the view of Rabbi Berlin and the Netziv, and it is followed by Rabbis Ariel, Yisraeli, Lior, and others. See discussion in Broyde, "Just Wars," 11. See also R. Lior, "Gishat ha-Halakha le-Sichot ha-Sahlom bi-Zmanenu," *Shvilin* 33–35 (1984): 146–50; Gerald Blidstein, "The Treatment of Hostile Civilian Populations: The Contemporary Halakhic Discussion in Israel," *Israel Studies* 1, no. 2 (1996): 27–44.
17. See Edrei, "Law, Interpretation, and Ideology"; Shlomo Fischer, "Excursus: Concerning the Rulings of R. Ovadiah Yosef Pertaining to the Thanksgiving Prayer, the Settlement of the Land of Israel, and Middle East Peace," *Cardozo Law Review* 28, no. 1 (2006): 229.
18. Eliezer Schweid, "The Attitude toward the State in Modern Jewish Thought before Zionism," in Daniel J. Elazar, ed., *Kingship and Consent: The Jewish Political Tradition and Its Contemporary Uses* (Washington, D.C.: University Press of America, 1983), 134.
19. Fischer, "Excursus," 229, 236.
20. Ibid, 236.
21. The *amoraim* (pl. of *amora*, "interpreter") were Torah scholars who, over the course of three centuries (c. 200–500 C.E.) argued and reconciled the discussions of the *tannaim*, or scholars of the Mishnaic era (c. 70–200 C.E.). These commentaries make up the text of the Talmud Bavli. See Suzanne Last Stone, "In Pursuit of the Countertext: The Turn to the Jewish Legal Model in Contemporary American Theory," *Harvard Law Review* 106 (1993): 813, 816.
22. Bernard Susser and Eliezer Don Yihyeh, "Prolegomena to Jewish Political Theory," in Daniel J. Elazar, ed., *Kinship and Consent* (Washington, D.C.: University Press of America, 1983), 91–111.
23. Schweid, "The Attitude toward the State," 186.
24. Leora Batnizky, "From Politics to Law: Modern Jewish Thought and the Invention of Jewish Law," *Diné Israel* 26 (2009): 19
25. Fischer, "Excursus," 236. Fischer identifies their utopian orientation in terms of the wish to recapture the transhistorical, objectively true divine law "as it exists in the mind of God." For this reason, they base their rulings on the most stringent interpretation, lest actual practice fail to conform to divine halakhic truth. This is a departure from the more modest and skeptical epistemology of the Talmud, which emphasizes procedural validity rather than metaphysical truth.
26. For a theoretical overview of this method, see Suzanne Last Stone, "Formulating Responses in an Egalitarian Age: An Overview," in Marc D. Stern, ed., *Formulating Responses in an Egalitarian Age* (Lanham, Md.: Rowman & Littlefield, 2005), 53–81.
27. See Maimonides, *Guide for the Perplexed* 3:31, 26–27.
28. Fischer, "Excursus," 229, 232.
29. Shlomo Goren was the founder and head of the rabbinate of the Israel Defense Forces. He later served as the chief rabbi of Tel Aviv and the chief rabbi of the state of Israel. He is considered an authority on Jewish military law.

30. See Edrei, "Law, Interpretation, and Ideology."
31. Ibid.
32. Ibid., 218.
33. Ibid., 219.
34. Suzanne Last Stone, "Religion and State: Models of Separation from within Jewish Law," *International Journal of Constitutional Law* 6 (2008): 631.
35. Yisraeli was a prominent halakhic authority within the Israeli religious Zionist community. He served as a member of the Chief Rabbinic Council and was one of the heads of Yeshivat Mecaz Harav Kook.
36. See Shaul Yisraeli, "Pe'ulat Kibiyeh le'or hahalakha" [The Qibya Raid in Light of Halakha], *HaTorah Vehamedina* 6 (1953–54): 113; republished in expanded form as "Pe'ulot tagmul le'or hahalakha" [Retaliation in Light of Halakha], in Yehudah Shaviv, ed., *Betzomet ha-Torah vehamedina*, vol. 3 (Jerusalem: Ma'aleh, 1991), 253–89.
37. Rabbi Naphtali Berliner, a Russian rabbi who lived from 1816 to 1893. He served as the head of the Volozhin Yeshiva in Lithuania.
38. Broyde, "Just Wars," 10–11.
39. Deuteronomy 17:4.
40. See Maimonides, *Guide for the Perplexed* 3:31, 26–27.
41. See Maimonides, *Mishneh Torah*, Laws of Kings 3:8–10; Laws of Killing 2:4.
42. Maimonides purports to be codifying Talmudic law, and there are scattered statements in the Talmud reporting a tradition that the court meted out punishments not according to law "in order to safeguard the law" (Babylonian Talmud 46a and parallels). The two cases attached to the statement tell of impositions of the death penalty by the court for highly public violations of the law. These cases emerge as rare exercises of judicial discretion to depart from biblical rules, although they do attest to a Talmudic distinction between law as an aspect of individual justice, entitling the individual to full due process of the law, and law as an aspect of political or social governance, which may require relaxation of the rigors of the law in times of extreme breakdown of social order. See Gerald Blidstein, "'Ideal' and 'Real' in Classical Jewish Political Theory," *Jewish Political Studies Review* 2 (1990): 43–66; but see also Hanina Ben-Menahem, *Judicial Deviation from Talmudic Law: Governed by Men, Not by Rules* (New York: Hardwood Academic, 1991), who argues that Talmudic judges had power to disregard norms and exercised broad judicial discretion. The Talmud also depicts the court as authorized to "correct" the law, by relaxing or tightening it, through rabbinic legislation addressing social needs, applicable to everyone. Maimonides conflates the two and reinterprets the Talmudic tradition about a few judges exercising discretion in the sphere of punishment as a report of the passing of positive law: a power-conferring rule authorizing judges to exercise discretion when sitting in formally temporary but actually permanent emergency jurisdiction.

    This radical transformation of the Talmudic materials can be explained by Maimonides's near-Hobbesian predilection for centralized order and for severity toward murderers (above any other category of sinner) and by his rationalist assessment of the biblical procedural protections of two corroborating witnesses and forewarning as not any sort of truth-guarding mechanism necessary to protect the innocent. Talmudic law is known for its skepticism about definitively ascertaining the truth, whether of facts or of law. Yet the Talmud does not evince a particularly skeptical attitude toward the two-witness rule. One gets the sense that the Talmudic jurists viewed it as no better or worse than any other mode of truth acquisition. Indeed, for those who abhorred the death penalty, it was a highly convenient way to circumvent the law.

43. Blidstein, "'Ideal' and 'Real,'" 53.
44. See Suzanne Last Stone, "Sinaitic and Noahide Law: Legal Pluralism in Jewish Law," *Cardozo Law Review* 12 (1991): 1157.
45. Babylonian Talmud, Sanhedrin 56a–58b.
46. Blidstein, "'Ideal' and 'Real.'" Traditional jurists commenting on Maimonides note this connection; see Meir Simhah Cohen, *Ohr Sameah*, Laws of Kings 3:10.

47. Indeed, as a historical matter, their real origin may well lie in Talmudic observation of Roman practice just as much as in legal dissection of the Genesis narratives "attesting" to the universal law that God commanded. For Maimonides, surely, it did not matter. He most likely thought that the whole topic of universal Noahide law was based on natural law thinking on the part of the jurists from the beginning.

48. Thus, Ibn Adret, in a series of responses dealing with handing over informers to the Spanish government for capital punishment, draws on a variety of precedents for departing from the criminal law strictures. He cites the powers of the community (acting in lieu of the king) and of the rabbinic courts exercising emergency jurisdiction. Ibn Adret remarks that whereas the Torah's procedural laws are largely theoretical and are thus impractical in their evidentiary demands, those of the king are aimed at producing verdicts and punishing offenders. He comments: "If you issue decisions based exclusively on the law as given in the Torah, why then society would be destroyed." Cited in Joseph Karo, *Beit Yosef* (Commentary on Tur), Choshen Mishpat, Rules of Judges, Section 2.

49. Nissim Gerondi, "Eleventh Homily," *Homilies of the Ran*.

50. Gerald Blidstein, "On Political Structures—Four Medieval Comments," *Jewish Journal of Sociology* 22 (1980): 47–58.

51. See Gerald Blidstein, "On Lay Legislation in Halakha: The King as Instance," in Suzanne Last Stone, ed., *Rabbinic and Lay Communal Authority* (New York: Yeshiva University Press, 2006).

52. See Shmuel Shilo, *Dina de-malkhuta dina* [The Law of the State Is Law] (Jerusalem: Hotsaata Defus Akademi, 1974).

53. Thus, one sees DDM as a subspecies of personal contract law in that Jews are assumed to have implicitly contracted to obey the kingdom's customary, established laws and to have waived their rights under Jewish law. From the thirteenth century onward, the distinction between custom and new legislation begins to disappear, probably under the influence of the rise of positive law in Latin Europe. See Amos Funkenstein, *Perceptions of Jewish History* (Berkeley: University of California Press, 1993), 158. The subject is fully explored in Shilo, *Dina de-malkhuta dina*.

54. Babylonian Talmud, Tractate Gittin 9b.

55. This usage of DDM may reflect the general predisposition of the Babylonian Talmud toward legal pluralism and decentralized law, which Rashi's localized comments illuminate. Ben-Menahem, *Judicial Deviation*, 93.

56. Exactly what is included in this command—whether to institute criminal enforcement jurisdiction alone or to develop a legal system—is, as one would expect, a subject of juristic debate. See Stone, "Sinaitic and Noahide Law."

57. Jewish law maintains that with respect to financial matters, as opposed to religious matters, it is possible for parties to contract out of the law in any event, despite the fact that these norms originate in divine law. But the rationale that links the validity of Gentile law to the Noahide command of *dinim* would suggest that it could extend to all laws subsumed under the Noahide command, including criminal law and punishment, traditionally categorized as "religious." Rashi elsewhere assumes that it is permissible to hand Jews over to the criminal processes of the non-Jewish government, even though this entails bypassing Jewish evidentiary and penal law. Babylonian Talmud, Tractate Niddah 61a. Rashi's theory has very few internal limits, except that subjects unique to Jewish law cannot be displaced.

58. Yisraeli, "Military Action," 187.

59. For additional discussion of the halakhic issues surrounding the incorporation of international laws of war, see Jeremy Wieder, "International Law and Halakhah," in Schiffman and Wolowelsky, *War and Peace*, 239–64.

60. I explore this at length in Stone, "Sinaitic and Noahide Law."

61. See ibid. and also Wieder, "International Law and Halakhah," applying this idea to the question of whether the halakhic polity is bound by international law.

62. Halevi also speculated about whether certain social laws were really religious commands with no social function except to bring on the divine overflow.

63. Gerald Blidstein and Michael Broyde, "Ethics and Warfare Revisited" *Meorot* 6, no. 2 (November 2007): 1–11.

64. David Shatz, introduction to Schiffman and Wolowelsky, *War and Peace*, xvii.

65. See generally Ellie Holzer, "Attitudes toward the Use of Military Force in Ideological Currents in Religious Zionism," in Schiffman and Wolowelsky, *War and Peace*, 341–414.

66. *Roper v. Simmons*, 543 U.S. 551 (2005).

67. Vicki C. Jackson, "The Supreme Court, 2004 Term: Comment: Constitutional Comparisons: Convergence, Resistance, Engagement," *Harvard Law Review* 119 (2005): 109.

68. The thirteenth-century Provençal jurist Menahem Ha-Meiri placed the issue squarely on the table. Meiri held that non-Jewish society was an enlightened civilization and, singularly among rabbinic thinkers, argued that they were brothers within the meaning of scripture to whom full legal and juridical equality under Jewish law was owed. Yet he vigorously opposed the conclusion that Jews can use non-Jewish law when the two conflict: "The laws of their ancient sages, which oppose our laws, are not included in the scope of DDM. For, if they were, all the laws of Israel would be cancelled." Menahem Meiri, Beit Ha-Behira, Bava Kamma, 113b. Various consent advocates also tried to limit what is properly deemed a law of "the kingdom" to core governmental functions such as taxes or matters pertaining to land, in order to keep the doctrine confined.

69. See Shmuel Shilo, "Equity as a Bridge: Between Jewish and Secular Law," *Cardozo Law Review* 12 (1990–91): 743–51.

18

Fighting to Create the Just State

Apocalypticism in Radical Muslim Discourse

DAVID COOK

Classical Apocalyptic Prophecies and Achieving the Just State

Muslim apocalyptic literature is a vast mine of material that gives us insight into the social and religious critique of Muslim societies as if those societies were living at the end of the world. The apocalyptic mind-set behind this literature depends on the feeling that society—both Muslim and non-Muslim—should radically change before the end of the world. Employing an interpretation of history that posits a continuous downward slide in society from the time of the Prophet Muhammad, through the first caliphs, to the later caliphs, and finally to the present day, the ideal is to confront whatever corruption has been allowed to fester, excise it, and ultimately establish the just state under the leadership of the Muslim messianic figure, the mahdi. This longing for justice and the ideal that earthly justice will be achieved is encapsulated in one of the most common traditions (hadiths) concerning the mahdi: "If there were only one day left in the world, God would lengthen it to send a man from my [Muhammad's] family who will fill the earth with justice and righteousness just as it has been filled with injustice and oppression."[1] It is interesting that the duration of the just state is irrelevant; its fact before the end of the world is all that truly matters. Even if there is only one day of true righteousness in this world, it is important that it be realized, as if to say that while the earth has only known one state (of injustice) for its existence, this final day would be a transition period into the next world.

Justice stands at the heart of so much Muslim political and religious thought and practice.[2] But how to achieve it? Although there were many different methods chosen by various Muslim political and religious groups, the discourse of apocalypse stands out as extremely common. Apocalypse, being a prophetic narrative of events that are due to occur before the end of the world, is a convenient literary form for critique of society. In general, these narratives begin with a list of the moral or social evils of society, which are at least tacitly juxtaposed with the idealized just state of the mahdi. In some cases, the social forces enabling the evils are described in depth, with the implication that these groups must be combated. Often, the second section of the apocalyptic narrative will detail how these groups will be fought in the apocalyptic future, by different messianic or semimessianic figures. By semimessianic I mean religious reformers whose mission of social purification is revolutionary and transformative but not necessarily with the goal of establishing a state or through the method of taking the title of mahdi.[3]

Apocalyptic prophecies then describe the messianic state, although usually not in any detail. Many of these idealized descriptions are taken from similar messianic aspirations in the book of Isaiah (11:6–8) or the New Testament book of Revelation (21):

> They will worship God truthfully [*ya'buduna Allaha haqq al-'ibada*], and the mahdi will enjoin justice between people upon the rest of his governors. The sheep will pasture with the wolf in the same place, and the boys will play with vipers and scorpions, with nothing harming them. Evil will disappear and good will remain; a man will sow a bushel and reap 700 bushels, as God said: "like a grain which produces seven ears, in each of which are a hundred grains" [Qur'an 2:261]. Hypocrisy, taking of interest, and drinking of alcohol will disappear and fornication too, and people will advance with worship, lawful [actions], the faith and group prayer. Lives will be lengthened, trust will be given, the trees will bear [fruit], blessings will be redoubled, the evil people will perish and the good people will remain. None will remain who hate the People of the House [of the Prophet].[4]

Messianism has a number of different ramifications in the classical Islamic period. Some of them are revolutionary and political in nature, such as those connected with the Shi'is and the Abbasids dating from the eighth and ninth centuries C.E. This type of messianism has a close connection to either successful or failed political-religious movements, and the apocalyptic narratives circulated by these groups are useful as historical sources (with some caution). Once in power, the Abbasid dynasty made great effort during the first century of its rule (747–833) to present itself as the realization of Muslim messianic hopes. Many traditions (hadiths) supporting this idea were circulated and continue to be cited in later times, although reinterpreted into the apocalyptic future.

A second type of messianism has to do with reform. This type of messianism holds to a continuous cyclical process of an idealized Muslim society that degenerates and then is reformed by a chosen figure usually known as the *mujaddid* (renewer). The key tradition supporting this idea is the following: "God will send to this community [Muslims] at the turn of every century someone who will renew the religion for it."[5] This hadith was very useful, especially to the ulema and formal religious establishment, as a sanction for socially corrective measures.[6] We will return to this hadith when discussing contemporary radicals' use of apocalyptic traditions.

Both of these two types of messianic categories are closely connected to establishments, either political or religious. However, beyond them exists a third category divorced from *necessary* connection with establishments. This third category contains popular expectations of messianic figures that do not correspond to the accepted apocalyptic narratives as mandated by normative Islam (Sunni or Shi'i) and includes attempts to date the end of the world (forbidden by Qur'an 7:187) and apocalypticism based in astrology. Both of these tendencies were strongly resisted by all Muslim elites during the classical period. Dating the end of the world or making predictions of its imminence held the potential for riots and social upheavals. Astrologers were beyond the control of the religious establishment and did not derive their authority from any obvious religious text or message, nor did apocalypses stimulated by astrology have any obvious moral imperative.

It is this last point that helps us bridge the gap between apocalypse and jihad. In religiously based apocalypses or messianic narratives—despite the inherently divisive nature of the material—the basic goal of the genre is repentance. Repeatedly, there are connections made between the moral failings of Muslim society and the judgment of God (as in Q. 8:51–53 and many other citations), and the basic goal of the mahdi and other apocalyptic figures is to correct these failings. Even though the apocalypse is always "near" (Q. 6:31, 12:107, 15:85, 20:15), there is always time to repent, and God is always willing to delay a date for the end if there is hope that society will repent. Apocalyptic writers were not purveyors of violence itself; they viewed violence merely as an eventual means by which the messianic state would be established.

Is Jihad Part of the Apocalypse?

Jihad, or "divinely sanctioned warfare," is not usually thought of as being part of the apocalypse, if only because the idealized opponent fought in jihad is typically a non-Muslim enemy. Traditionally, jihad is associated with the warfare of the Prophet Muhammad against his pagan and Jewish opponents or with the great Islamic conquests during the first century after his death which transformed the Middle East. Although jihad has been proclaimed many times since that early classical period, frequently that proclamation has been contested because of the sectarian nature of the enemy (namely other Muslims) or the fact that the leader calling for jihad is not an ideal Muslim.

According to the classical definitions, jihad has a very strong spiritual aspect. It is not unrestricted warfare but one in which there are very set rules. The manner of its proclamation, the authority of the proclaimer, the identity of the enemy to be fought, the categories of the enemy that can be slain (legitimately), the types of spoils that can be taken, and the manner in which the warfare is brought to an end are all proscribed by the hadith literature and codified in the

legal literature. Although there is a great deal of discussion concerning these issues, there was general agreement that not every type of violence or warfare
would or could constitute jihad.

One of the more interesting aspects of jihad, however, was its presentation as
a purification process from sins. From the early *Kitab al-jihad* of 'Abdallah ibn al-
Mubarak (d. 797), we read:

> The slain [in jihad] are three [types of] men: a believer, who struggles
> [*jahada*] with himself and his possessions in the path of God, such that
> when he meets the enemy [in battle] he fights them until he is killed. This
> martyr [*shahid*] is tested [and is] in the camp of God under His throne; the
> prophets do not exceed him [in merit] except by the level of prophecy.
> [Then] a believer, committing offenses and sins against himself, who strug-
> gles with himself and his possessions in the path of God, such that when
> he meets the enemy [in battle] he fights until he is killed. This cleansing
> wipes away his offenses and his sins—behold the sword wipes [away]
> sins!—and he will be let into heaven from whatever gate he wishes. [Then]
> a hypocrite, who struggles with himself and his possessions in the path of
> God, such that when he meets the enemy [in battle] he fights until he is
> killed. This [man] is in hell since the sword does not wipe away hypocrisy.[7]

This tradition is interesting because it makes such stringent demands on the
fighter and points to a spiritual transformation inherent in the fighting process
and either culminating in it (as part of a prebattle spiritual purification) or resulting from it (in the sense of desiring nothing of this world as a result of battle and
ultimately winning the battle over oneself).[8] The first two categories of fighters
are lauded for their transformation, which could be viewed on a macro level as
paralleling the transformation that is effected in the society by their fighting. Just
as they win a battle over themselves and enter paradise, so does the larger community gradually transform either in victory or in martyrdom (Q. 9:52) from a
society of this world to a society of the next (the messianic kingdom).

Ibn al-Mubarak's *Kitab al-jihad* gives us more than that, however. It presents
the Muslim community as a whole as one that is eternally fighting until the Day
of Judgment:

> Behold! God sent me [Muhammad] with a sword, just before the Hour [of
> Judgment], in order that they would worship God alone—without any
> partner!—and placed my daily sustenance beneath the shadow of my
> spear, and humiliation and contempt on those who oppose me, and who-
> ever imitates a group is [numbered] among them.[9]

In such a tradition, we have the portrayal of the Muslim community, led by its
Prophet, as one closely tied to the sword and the spear. In such a presentation, the

salvific function of the weapons is clear—no mention is made of any aspect of sedentary Islam. Only those who carry the weapons could expect to enter paradise. The picture of the Muslims that is implied in such a tradition is one of constant movement. They do not have time to eat formal meals or construct formal camps, only to eat what is placed under the shadow of one's spear. Victory will be the result of this movement, as God has mandated in order to validate the truth of Islam.

But for our purposes, most important is the timing of the tradition. Muhammad is sent just before the Hour of Judgment. In other words, there is a strong sense of urgency to the fighting and an implied limit to its duration. Juxtaposed with the numerous dated apocalyptic traditions, especially from the first centuries of Islam, it seems clear that this type of tradition does reflect the early fighting mind-set of the Muslims that led to the success of the conquests.[10] In other words, apocalypse, not victory, supplied the energy for the conquests. Because there was believed to be only a limited amount of time before the end of the world, it was necessary to fight and conquer. Conquest, as mandated by the laws of jihad above, was not merely for conquest's sake alone. It also had a proclamatory and a demonstrative aspect to it. Without the conquest, the structural barriers to the spread of Islam (in the sense that people would not have had easy access to it) would have precluded people from adhering to it. But with the conquest, and with the sense of eternal victory granted by God to the Muslim community, conversion and social transformation were possible.

Another similar major tradition, given in many variants, along those same lines is the following: "A group of my [Muhammad's] community will continue fighting for the truth, victorious over those who oppose them, until the last of them fights the Dajjal [the Antichrist]."[11] But whereas the first tradition purports to speak for the entire Muslim community and present it as one based on warfare, this second one has a very different attitude. It presents jihad as also a salvific action, mandates an eternal sense of victory, and gives us a sense of duration (as well as the identity of an end-times opponent) but indicates that only part of the Muslim community will be saved. This part of the community, sometimes called *al-ta'ifa al-mansura* or *al-firqa al-najiya*, will be the ones who will be in heaven. Other traditions in the general ideological field rely on the "seventy-three sects" tradition, in which one learns that there will be a multiplicity of sects in Islam but that only one will be saved.[12] How will one know the "saved sect" from the other ones? They will be the ones fighting.

This worship of the fighting process as a distinguishing characteristic between truth and falsehood goes back to the Qur'an. In Q. 33:18–19, we read about the so-called hypocrites who were unwilling to fight for the early Muslim community and are described thus:

> Allah would surely know those of you who hinder the others and those
> who say to their brothers: "Come over to us"; and they do not partake of

fighting, except a little. They are ever niggardly towards you, but if fear overtakes them, you will see them look at you, with their eyes rolling like one who is in the throes of death. But when fear subsides, they cut you with sharp tongues.[13]

Fighting is very useful in telling the true believers from the false believers. This ideal produces the necessity for there to be a *ta'ifa al-mansura* that constitutes a Muslim elite. This group is characterized by a willingness to fight and risk itself for the sake of Islam (jihad) and a willingness to judge other Muslims, most especially the rulers, on their failings.

Probably the best-known tradition that indicates judgment of the rulers states, "What type of jihad is the best? He [Muhammad] said: Speaking a word of truth in front of a tyrannical ruler."[14] Far from being the leader of jihad as one would expect from normative Muslim literature, the ruler is one who is the object of jihad according to this tradition. 'Abdallah ibn al-Mubarak purportedly acted on this tradition when he confronted the Abbasid ruler Harun al-Rashid (r. 786–809) with the latter's unwillingness to fight.[15] Later radical Muslims would make extensive use of this tradition and the heritage of antigovernmental activism that surrounds it in order to justify their confrontation with contemporary Muslim governments. Their ideal is a hierarchy in which the jihadists, whose locus of power is outside the establishment, arrogate to themselves the right to judge the establishment because of its failing to defend Islam.

Although the classical tradition of jihad is not inextricably intertwined with that of apocalypse, the two genres do touch in a number of points. Both seek to establish an ideal society (one governed by a caliph, the other by a mahdi or similar messianic figure). Both narratives involve fighting to achieve this goal. In both genres, there is an ambiguous attitude toward elites and establishments that could either be utilized by the latter or turned against them. There are also differences, however. One is the determinism that is inherent in the apocalyptic materials. If God has mandated how and when the apocalypse will occur, human action to bring it about or in anticipation of it could be counter to his will or plan. This is in contrast with the obvious activist attitude of the jihad materials, in which, although God has mandated victory, there is much more room for human action in determining how that victory will be achieved.

Contemporary Apocalyptic Prophecies

Contemporary Muslim apocalyptic materials are taken to a large degree from their classical forebears, but in contradistinction to the traditional practice (after the first centuries of Islam), there is much more of an interpretive effort. In some cases, this interpretive effort will take the traditional materials and make them applicable to contemporary events and even try to prophesy what will happen in the immediate future. This tendency is heavily influenced by similar tendencies in evangelical Christianity, and there is a surprising amount of cross-pollination between Muslims and Christians in this regard.

Conversation between Muslims and Christians concerning apocalyptic predictions has been a constant all the way back to the classical period. For example, the apocalyptic figure of the Sufyani, the messianic hero of Syria, appears in the ninth-century Christian Apocalypse of Bahira.[16] Contemporary Muslim apocalyptic writers frequently have recourse to the Bible and especially to the evangelical Protestant interpretation of Christian eschatology popularized during the 1970s and 1980s (which will be discussed below). Reacting to the interpretations of the Bible that have led to widespread support of Israel on the part of American evangelical Christians, the Saudi radical intellectual Safar al-Hawali in 2001 penned his *Yawm al-ghadab*. In an attempt to reach an American audience and influence its attitude toward Israel, the work was quickly translated into English under the title *The Day of Wrath* and made available for easy downloading on the Internet.[17] Many other contemporary Muslim apocalyptic writings cite biblical verses or use exegesis that is based on the idea that contemporary events are closely prophesied by revelation.

For the most part, contemporary Muslim apocalyptic writers use classical apocalyptic prophecies as their source base but add a great deal of biblical exegesis (from a Muslim point of view) and materials from anti-Semitic conspiracy literature. The state of Israel is central to the apocalyptic narrative popular in Arabic today, which presents a problem, because there is little in the classical apocalyptic narrative concerning Jews, other than the tradition that states, "The Hour will not arrive until the Muslims fight the Jews, until the Jew will take refuge behind the rocks and the trees, and they will say to the Muslims: O 'Abdallah, servant of God, there is a Jew behind me, come and kill him."[18] Because this tradition is usually cited within the context of Muslims fighting the Dajjal, there is an opening to assimilate a large body of anti-Semitic materials in which the Jews are described as followers of the Antichrist (variously described as a hidden personality, as a prominent political leader, as a country such as the United States or Israel, or as a diffuse political-cultural construct such as "the West").

Anti-Semitic conspiracy theories give contemporary Muslim apocalyptic literature much more of a malevolent tinge than do the classical apocalyptic prophecies, in which the Dajjal is usually portrayed as a ridiculous being rather than one whose attractive exterior conceals monstrous hatred. These conspiracy theories are also useful for understanding the problematic position of the Muslim world vis-à-vis the rest of the world throughout the latter part of the twentieth century. If there were a Jewish conspiracy to defeat and destroy the Arabs or the Muslims as a whole or to keep them from fully developing, that would explain a number of uncomfortable realities. Hence the popularity of this material.

Biblical exegesis, with the way paved by Christian evangelicals such as Hal Lindsey and Billy Graham, provide a context. Of course, the evangelicals are overwhelmingly pro-Israel in their exegesis of the Bible, but it is perfectly possible to reinterpret their materials radically and come up with something that approximates the anti-Semitic conspiracy theory. For example, Bashir Muhammad 'Abdallah, a mid-1990s Egyptian writer, in his exegesis of Daniel 7:27 ("Then the sovereignty, power and greatness of the kingdoms under the whole heavens will be handed over to the saints, the people of the Most High. His kingdom will be an everlasting kingdom and all rulers will worship and obey him"), says:

> The "saints" are the Muslims, the believers and fighters in the path of God, since they are described in the present-day antichrist media as fundamentalists, terrorists, and extremists. His word "the sovereignty will be handed over [to the saints]" refers to the continuing victory they will have in the establishment of the Islamic caliphate at the hands of the Ancient of Days (the Mahdi) first of all, and then their victory over crusader [Christian] Europe second of all, and then their final victory under the leadership of the true messiah, Jesus the son of Mary, over the antichrist and his armies of Masonic and hypocritical followers thirdly, and after that the purification of the earth from Gog and Magog.
>
> Daniel then continues speaking of the present and continuous struggle taking place between the human kingdom under the leadership of the Secret World Government, headed by the antichrist, and the Muslims, the believers and fighters in the path of God in every place in the world, in groups and as individuals: "As I watched, this horn (which is Israel on the outside and the Secret World Government on the inside)[19] was waging war against the saints and defeating them" [Daniel 7:21], in other words slaughtering them and annihilating them by making slaughters of them in Palestine, Afghanistan, India, Kashmir, Bosnia and Herzegovina, Azerbaijan, and Tajikistan, and in every place where they hold onto the confession that "There is no god but God and Muhammad is the messenger of God."
>
> The angel then interprets the tribulation falling upon the believers and the martyrs, and clarifies that it is from the leaders and the Secret World Government, meaning the Zionists mounted upon the crusaders [i.e., Western Christians] and deceiving them as the jinn deceive [people] using human bodies, and the angel says about this hidden government, the antichrist: "He will speak against the Most High and oppress his saints and try to change the set times and the laws. The saints will be handed over to him for a time, times and half a time" (*sic!*) [Daniel 7:25].[20]

These passages help us understand how biblical exegesis can be read through the anti-Semitic conspiracy theory. Identification of the "saints" of the verses with the Muslims and of the "Ancient of Days" with the mahdi opens up new possibilities for an apocalyptic writer. 'Abdallah preserves the universality of the original verse, Daniel 7, and its intense sense of persecution. Indeed, it is not at all unusual for contemporary Muslims to compare themselves to the persecution that the early Christians suffered under the Romans.[21] This sense of persecution and the idea that the entire world is conspiring to destroy Islam are elements that apocalyptic writers share with contemporary jihadi radicals. But beyond the persecution, there is a sense of exaltation because of the fact that the prophecies indicate that victory will soon be at hand. These types of wild prophecies, indulged by even such well-known figures as Shaykh Yusuf al-Qaradawi,[22] are typical of the apocalyptic mind-set. They also constitute a common field with jihadi groups. However, as in the classical prophecies, there is no imperative to actually "conquer" anything, only the assurance that at some point in the apocalyptic future, these regions will be conquered. This type of deterministic mind-set is problematic for transferring prophecies into activist groups.

Another problem, as mentioned above, is the use of exact dates. Probably the best example of this tendency is within the Palestinian group Hamas. Hamas in general is an offshoot of the Egyptian Muslim Brotherhood and is extremely cautious about associating itself with apocalyptic prophecies that are not connected closely to jihad. It cites the tradition of the "rocks and trees" mentioned above in its charter[23] but in general is quite cautious about associating itself with any prophecy that does not have practical value and might lead to fatalism among its cadres and supporters.

Still, one of its leading members, Shaykh Bassam Jirrar, started in 1995 to issue works dedicated to gematrical calculations of the Qur'an and most especially (and successfully) to a gematrical exposition of Q. 17:4–8, which give a thumbnail sketch of the fall of the two temples in Jerusalem.[24] From this exposition, he was able to calculate that the state of Israel will come to an end in the year 2022. This date was later modified under pressure from Shaykh Ahmad Yasin, the spiritual leader of Hamas, to 2026. Jirrar utilizes virtually no Muslim apocalyptic sources; his exegesis is almost entirely Qur'anic. In fact, his work is among the first to squeeze an apocalypse narrative out of the Qur'an without recourse to the hadith literature at all. Although on a popular level, Jirrar's work was received quite well in the mid-1990s, the leadership of Hamas has always treated his calculations with some caution. If one takes them seriously, there is little need for exertion in fighting Israel; and if that were the case, then the raison d'être of Hamas would be open to question.

The apocalyptic literature in Arabic reaches a wide audience and is more likely to have entertainment value than practical or spiritual value. While the claims made for sales of apocalyptic books are high, it is still very much an open question how many people truly believe what they read. In my opinion, the most influential aspect of apocalyptic literature has been that it highlights the sense of conspiracy that is so commonly felt in the Muslim world and makes the common Muslim aware of such figures as the mahdi, the Dajjal, and the apocalyptic battles. The material could possibly activate people at a more distant period or if some mass hysteria occurs, but for the present, its influence does not seem to be very apparent in society.

This is not the case, however, inside Shi'i apocalyptic expectations. Shi'i messianism is centered around the figure of the twelfth imam, Muhammad al-Mahdi, who, according to Twelver Shi'i beliefs, never died but went into "occultation" around the year 874. His return from occultation will herald the beginning of the messianic age. Because the identity of this figure is dependent on historical sources, the control of which is in the hands of the religious elite, there is not as much chance in Shi'ism as in Sunnism of random mahdis appearing and generating mass movements. Messianism in general is of a governmentally sponsored or establishment-sponsored variety, such as the recent upswing in interest in the return of the mahdi sponsored by the Ahmadinejad regime in Iran. This messianism has been propagated by the Mahdaviyyat Society, headed by Ayatollah Misbahi-Yazdi (Ahmadinejad's spiritual adviser). It has taken the form of increased focus on the shrine of the mahdi located at Jamkaran (close to the holy city of Qom in Iran), where a massive mosque is being built. Ahmadinejad himself has repeatedly declared that the appearance of the mahdi is near, even in such public forums as the UN General Assembly.[25]

Occasionally, however, there appear popular messianic manifestations that are antiestablishment. One such phenomenon is the Jund al-Sama' group in southern Iraq, which is led by a mahdi claimant and which sponsored violence in 2007 and 2008 during the month of Muharram. Its original mandate appears to have been ecumenical, spanning both the Sunnis and the Shi'is of Iraq, and antiestablishment. It apparently took quite seriously some prophecies that among the signs of the mahdi will be that he will destroy the beautiful mosques and kill the ulema and consequently attempted to assassinate Ayatollah 'Ali al-Sistani, the leading clerical figure among Iraqi Shi'is. Although much about this group remains obscure, its ideology appears to be highly eclectic, and it is certainly one of the most interesting messianic manifestations in the Middle East during the past thirty years. So far, however, its appeal appears to be limited to the unstable conditions in Iraq.

Radical Jihadi Movements and the Apocalyptic Temptation

The desire to reform society radically and to achieve a just state is also one that the apocalyptic writers and radical jihadis share. The former are able to communicate within the context of mainstream Islam and publish their ideas freely because they are generally perceived by governments as lacking any activist agenda. Jihadis, on the other hand, are hampered in their communication because of their commitment to active reform of Muslim societies, bringing about pan-Islamic unity, and eventually electing a caliph. This type of messianic vision is not always openly espoused, but it appears to be one of the driving forces behind their recruitment.

Another would have to be the sense of persecution and worldwide conspiracy to destroy Islam already noted above. Probably the most common tradition cited by writers is the so-called hadith of Thawban, which reads:

> The Messenger of God said: "The nations are about to flock against you [the Muslims] from every horizon, just as hungry people flock to a kettle." We said: "O Messenger of God, will we be few on that day?" He said: "No, you will be many as far as your number goes, but you will be scum, like the scum of the flash-flood, since fear will be removed from the hearts of your enemies, and weakness [*wahn*] will be placed in your hearts." We said: "O Messenger of God, what does the word *wahn* mean?" He said: "Love of this world and fear of death."[26]

This tradition encapsulates the essence of the message that radical Muslims want to communicate to their audiences. First, it is placed in the apocalyptic future. Second, it portrays the Muslims as being numerically strong but practically weak. Third, there is a worldwide conspiracy to fall upon Islam and the Muslims and devour them just as hungry people devour a bowl of food. This view is affirmed by recourse to numerous conspiracy theories that are present in the Arab and Muslim worlds.

But even more important than these three points, there is a strong contempt for Muslims that is obvious from the text. They are "scum," which is the message that radical Muslims need. It is not the heritage of empire and imperialistic self-congratulation so common in Muslim literature to which they look but the sense of failure, of defeat, of despair that they feel when they contemplate the position of Islam in the present world. They need the Muslims collectively to feel that sense of humiliation and lowliness in order to get the masses to act. It is not sufficient for the radicals merely to communicate the realities of the Muslim situation or to wallow in self-pity; they need to act to change the situation.

And the tradition promptly supplies radicals with the answer to the problem. Fear of fighting and fear of death are the cause of present-day Muslim misery and humiliation. Love of this world has sunk into the masses to the point where they are unwilling to fight for the sake of Islam. Radical Muslims offer the jihad as a collective expiatory action that will lead Muslims back to their predominant position and allow them to reclaim their self-esteem. Rejection of fear (*wahn*) is the method by which that can be achieved.

Just as with the classical literature, the tradition implies that only part of the Muslim community is truly Muslim. Again, this attitude is in stark contrast to the classical Sunni attitude, which did not usually demonize (*takfir*) other Muslims, even during periods of disagreement. But harking back to the heritage of such jihad-scholars as 'Abdallah ibn al-Mubarak, contemporary jihadis see themselves as the *ta'ifa al-mansura*, or the "victorious party," set apart from all other Muslims.[27] Only they deserve to enter heaven, because they have been willing to fight and die for Islam. Only they have the ability and the right to judge Muslim societies and their political leaders and religious establishments.

Essentially, the violence that radical Sunni Muslims employ is directed against the establishments, primarily the political and secondarily the religious. Although the attacks are leveled (for the most part) against non-Muslims (Americans, Israelis, Europeans, Russians, Indians, and others), the real battle that radical Muslims are fighting is one for spiritual prestige. As Abu Mus'ab al-Zarqawi, the leader of al-Qaeda in Iraq until he was killed in 2006, stated:

> O nation of Islam, come to the rescue of the jihad in Iraq before the infidel majority besieges the *mujahidin*. O by God, who holds my soul, if the torch of jihad is extinguished, if the breath of jihad weakens, and if the pockets of jihad in Iraq are closed, the Islamic nation will not rise until God wills it to rise. The noose around the entire nation will be tightened and humiliation and submission will be forced upon the nation. It will then receive God's punishment. Then our conditions will be an embodiment of what Ibn Kathir said in his book, *al-Bidaya wa al-nihaya* [The Beginning and the End],[28] namely, that when people abandoned jihad they were surprised to find the Tatars at their homes. A Tatar woman would pass by groups of men. She would tell them: "Stop, do not go." Then she would bring a knife and slay them all, one by one. They never showed any resistance. Thus the punishment will be followed by further punishments and the disobedience is followed by further disobedience. The punishment will not be lifted unless by full repentance. Repentance means a return to your religion, namely, jihad.[29]

Just as with apocalypse writers, the goal of al-Zarqawi is repentance, by which he implies that the vast majority of Muslims who are not fighting in Iraq are actually in a state of sin as long as they do not participate in the jihad.

In general, radical Muslims who fight are cautious about the use of apocalyptic themes. Probably the most obvious case is that of Osama bin Laden, who in the wake of September 11, 2001, was frequently mentioned as a possible mahdi candidate[30] and did occasionally allude to apocalyptic themes in his writings (for example, the use of "Khurasan" for Afghanistan, knowing that one of the optional places for the mahdi to appear is from Khurasan).[31] However, despite the use of many of the apocalyptic-jihad traditions cited in the first section of this chapter, mainly from 'Abdallah ibn al-Mubarak, bin Laden was always careful to portray himself as a reformer or as one who paves the way for the messianic figure and not as the messianic figure himself. This fact is best illustrated by his ritual adherence to the caliphal pretensions of the Taliban leader Mullah 'Umar Mujahid, who in

1997 took the caliphal title of *amir al-mu'minin* (commander of the faithful). This action was taken as a joke by most in the wider Muslim world, but for radical Muslims, the taking of such a title represented one of the supreme manifestations of their egalitarian, pan-Islamic appeal, as Mullah 'Umar was not an Arab and achieved his spiritual prestige mainly by virtue of his leadership in the multinational jihad in Afghanistan against the Soviet Union and its clients. Recognizing the caliphal claims of Mullah 'Umar was also a strike against the spiritual authority of mainstream Muslim establishments.

Numerous apocalyptic prophecies about the Taliban were circulated on the Internet, mainly those connected with the "black banners will come from the east," a tradition originally circulated to benefit the Abbasid revolution centered in Khurasan. The radical Muslim thinker and strategist Abu Mus'ab al-Suri ridiculed these prophecies, especially those that appeared in the last days of the Taliban regime.[32] However, his massive 2004 work *Da'wat al-muqawama al-Islamiyya al-'alamiyya* (A Call to Worldwide Islamic Revolution) concludes with seventy-five pages of apocalyptic traditions.[33] Al-Suri is probably one of the most harshly self-critical of all contemporary radical Muslim jihadis. His *Da'wa* gives its reader a good sense of the failures of these groups (including al-Qaeda but also a large number of ideological affiliates) in gaining popular support. The apocalyptic traditions indicate that al-Suri sees hope in a final victory and that he is laying out for his audience a method by which the messianic pan-Islamic state can still be achieved. However, he, like Osama bin Laden, is careful not to interpolate anything. He leaves it to his readers to gain a sense of what needs to be done: fighting non-Muslims, destroying the influence of Muslim elites, and building up purely Muslim societies that will not be led by "apostates." The method by which these objectives will be realized over the long haul is not always clear, although al-Suri does offer a number of short-term strategies, such as the creation of small Islamic societies (*jama'at*), which ideally over a period of years will combine to form an Islamic state.

In contradistinction, al-Zarqawi is a very interesting case of a jihadi who went from being almost completely ignorant of the apocalyptic side of jihad to being a primary proponent of apocalyptic warfare. Reading his early works,[34] one sees the reformer of Islamic society, very much in the tradition of bin Laden during the early 1990s. But gradually, as the Iraq War progresses, al-Zarqawi becomes more and more apocalyptic, until finally, during the sieges of Falluja (April and November 2004), his pronouncements are almost completely dependent on an apocalyptic worldview. He sees American forces as the Rum (the Byzantines) that are portrayed in the apocalyptic literature as invading the lands of Islam and himself as the righteous avenger of the honor of the community. He compares contemporary Shi'is, who are the primary beneficiaries of the U.S. invasion of Iraq, with Muslim allies of the Mongols, who came into Islamic lands in the mid-thirteenth century and destroyed Baghdad, killing the last Abbasid caliph in 1258. He refers to the Shi'is as the "descendants of Ibn al-'Alqami," the vizier of the last Abbasid caliph, who, according to Sunni sources, allegedly betrayed him. The demonology here is clear. The destruction of Baghdad, viewed as one of the crowning horrors of medieval Muslim history (in terms of loss of political and religious prestige but also in terms of loss of culture), is recurring at the hands of Americans and their Shi'i allies.

Because the present-day conflict between Islam and its enemies is total war and so much rides on its outcome, one is permitted to use any and all weapons against the demonic enemy. This type of mind-set is characteristic of the apocalyptic jihad. Primary among these weapons has been the suicide attack or martyrdom operation (*al-'amaliyyat al-istishhadiyya*). From the first usage of suicide attacks by Palestinians against Israel, they were applauded by most of the mainstream religious establishment[35] as a tactic that could overcome the material strengths of the Israeli opponent and equalize the struggle. For example, Shaykh Sulayman ibn Nasir al-'Ulwan of Saudi Arabia stated:

> The sacrificial operations that are taking place in Palestine against the Jewish usurpers and in Chechnya against the Christian aggressors are martyrdom operations and legitimate [*shar'i*] forms of fighting. They have stunned the aggressors, proven their effectiveness, and caused the usurpers to taste the bitterness of their crime, and the evil of what they have done such that the infidels have become afraid of everything and expect death from every direction. Some of the papers have mentioned that the criminal [Ariel] Sharon has demanded the stopping of these operations. Thus these operations have become a woe and destruction upon the Israelis, who have usurped the lands, violated honor, spilled blood, and killed the innocent. The Most High said, "And make ready for them whatever you can of fighting men and horses, to terrify thereby the enemies of God and your enemy . . ." (Qur'an 8:60), and also, "Fight the polytheists with your wealth, yourselves, and your tongues."[36]

Fatwas like this one in support of suicide attacks abound[37] and are equally intellectually sloppy.[38] Because all of the qualities that al-'Ulwan so blithely ascribed to the Israelis in Palestine and the Russians in Chechnya are also ascribed by radical Muslims to their own regimes,[39] it is clear that there was a large opening for the vast expansion of the range of suicide attacks following the September 2000 (Second) Intifada.

No one illustrated that better than al-Zarqawi during his impressive career as the leader of al-Qaeda in the Land of the Two Rivers (from 2003 to 2006). Because al-Zarqawi was able to demonize the Shi'is as non-Muslims and as allies of the U.S. and Coalition forces, he systematically attacked their civilians and holy sites using suicide attacks.[40] Eventually, these mass-casualty suicide attacks caused first the Muslim world to turn against him and then even prominent leaders of the radical Islamic movement such as his former mentor Abu Muhammad al-Maqdisi and the second-in-command of al-Qaeda, Ayman al-Zawahiri. They remonstrated with him that Shi'is are also Muslims, however misguided, and that killing them in such large numbers, especially when women and children were included, was giving the jihad a bad name.[41] And indeed, repeated use of suicide attacks by radicals in Morocco, Saudi Arabia, Iraq, Jordan, Egypt, Uzbekistan, Indonesia, Algeria, Afghanistan, Pakistan, and Turkey has caused significant opposition to their movement. It is clear that radicals need to rethink carefully their strategy before proceeding on the route of al-Zarqawi.

While Shi'is have been the primary targets of Sunni radical violence, they have also been changing their use of messianism in jihad. It is interesting that Hizbullah in its published hagiographies of the 2006 war against Israel emphasizes the role of the mahdi. This emphasis was not the case during its earlier fifteen-year-long battle with Israel (1985–2000), where one does not find any examples of visions of the mahdi fighting alongside the Shi'is. From the 2006 conflict, we find the following example of a vision that took place as three Hizbullah fighters approached the Israeli outpost town of Metula:

> One of us began to pray the ordained mid-day prayer when a man giving off rays of light appeared to him. The fighter said to him in surprise and fear, "Who are you? How did you get here?" The man said, "I am the Imam al-Hujja, your master. I appear by the permission of God to our supporters whenever I wish and in whatever place, and I would like to speak with you." He said, "My master, I am not alone; there are other fighters in position."

So the man guided the mahdi to the other fighters. "Just at that moment the Zionists approached with their tanks and bulldozers," and Israeli missiles began to rain down on the three fighters. The mahdi pointed with his hand, and one of the missiles fell on an Israeli tank instead. Then the three fighters began to attack the other tanks, and one of them succeeded in firing a rocket-propelled grenade right at it and destroyed it. "Then the imam called out to the fighters, saying to them, 'Now, retreat,' and the fighters retreated, but they were victorious with his divine help."[42] It seems clear with stories like these being circulated about the mahdi that his transformation from a purely religious reference point to a more religious-nationalistic icon is complete.

Conclusion

Apocalyptic jihad is part of the Muslim heritage of warfare. The Qur'an speaks of the coming of the Hour of Judgment quite extensively, and it remains an open question how much of the early Muslim conquests were influenced by beliefs that the world was about to end. Certainly, the available evidence allows one cautiously to surmise that these beliefs were at least one of the contributing factors in the expansion of Islam. This type of apocalyptic warfare was one in which the Muslims were supplied with a considerable amount of energy because of the shortness of the time they had to accomplish the conquests. But the apocalyptic warfare probably made them stretch themselves too far and conquer more territory than they could easily hold, such as regions in southern France, Italy, and the Byzantine empire. Although there is some evidence that other Muslim conquests around the year 1000 in the Islamic calendar (1591–92 C.E.) were also of an apocalyptic jihad nature (such as the Ottoman conquests, those of Ahmad Grañ in Ethiopia, and those of Mai Idris Alooma in Bornu), the pattern of extreme exertion has never repeated itself.

But currently in radical Islam, there is a movement that can harness the apocalyptic heritage of classical Islam. From the point of view of major strategists and thinkers among the radicals, Islam is in a critically perilous situation as a result of a concerted attack by all of the non-Muslim countries together, in addition to a systematic betrayal from within by Muslim establishments—both political and religious. This is a situation that has led to the humiliation of Muslims, the occupation of their lands, the systematic despoiling of their resources, and the desecration of their sanctities. The only way this situation can be confronted and reversed, in their analysis, is through jihad.

The problem they face is the fact that the elites and establishments that the radicals see as having betrayed Islam are themselves in control of the power to declare jihad, at least according to the classical strictures. In general, radical Muslims are outsiders, not part of the establishment, and see themselves locked in mortal combat with it. The best method for them to wrest control from the apostate Muslim establishments is to delegitimize them by defending Islam better than they are capable of doing. Muslim elites hold out to their populations the (tacit) promise of modernization and parity with the West at some undefined period in the future—a somewhat messianic promise. This promise, however, has been repeatedly delegitimized, first, by the establishments' inability (or in some cases unwillingness) to carry through with it and, second, through miserable failures in confronting perceived enemies of the Muslim world such as Israel and, in some cases, the United States, Russia, or India.

Therefore, the radicals have an opening. They can promise a future that the establishments cannot, which is essentially a return to the past—the past of Muslim conquest and domination. It is difficult to know whether to take seriously the maximalist radical Muslim goals, such as those stated by 'Abdallah 'Azzam, which would involve eternal jihad and conquest of all regions ever occupied by Muslims.[43] These goals are so fantastic that they make one wonder whether the person who made them lived in the world of reality. Yet there is a certain exaltation to proclaiming them, especially to a religious group that feels strongly a sense of humiliation, oppression, and injustice as a result of its position in the contemporary world. The radicals have not been able to engender widespread support for their maximalist goals, but those they do attract to their ranks are willing to give everything for the cause.

Where radicals part ways from most Muslims is in the methods by which they seek to fight their apocalyptic jihad. Clearly, the indiscriminate use of violence initially against civilian non-Muslims and then quickly (since 2003) against civilian Muslims (either Sunni or Shi'i) has decisively turned large numbers of Muslims against the radicals. It is not because the latter do not expound their reasoning for using indiscriminate violence. Countless treatises along with video and audio recordings have been published, usually on the Internet, establishing the Qur'anic, Prophetic, and shari'a justifications for such violence and killing. No matter how they are packaged, these justifications have not been accepted by the Muslim masses. The callous disregard for human life has proved to be impossible for them to accept.

Notes

1. David Cook, *Studies in Muslim Apocalyptic* (Princeton, N.J.: Darwin, 2002), 137.
2. See Abdulaziz Sachedina, *The Just Ruler in Shi'ite Islam* (Oxford: Oxford University Press, 1988), 120–27.
3. Following Mercedes Garcia-Arenal, *Messianism and Puritanical Reform: Mahdis of the Muslim West* (Leiden: Brill, 2006), chap. 4.
4. Al-Sulami, *'Iqd al-durar fi al-mahdi al-muntazar*, ed. Muhib ibn Salih ibn 'Abd al-Rahman al-Burayni (Al-Zarqa': Maktabat al-Manar, 1993), 267–68 (no. 309), paraphrasing the material in al-Dani, *Al-Sunan al-warida fi al-fitan wa ghawa'iliha wa al-sa'a wa ashratiha*, ed. Riza'allah ibn Muhammad Idris al-Mubarakfuri (Riyadh: Dar al-'Asima, 1995), 3: 1103–4 (no. 596).
5. Abu Da'ud, *Sunan* (Beirut: Dar al-Jil, 1988), 4: 106–7 (4291).
6. For discussion of its usage, see Ella Landau-Tasseron, "The 'Cyclic' Reform: A Study of the *Mujaddid* Tradition," *Studia Islamica* 70 (1989): 79–113; and a critique by Yohanan Friedman, *Prophecy Continuous* (Berkeley: University of California Press, 1989), 95–97, 106–9.
7. 'Abdallah ibn al-Mubarak, *Kitab al-jihad* (Beirut: Nazih Hammad, 1971), 30–31 (no. 7).
8. For example, al-Bukhari, *Sahih* (Beirut: Dar al-Fikr, 1991), 3:272 (no. 2810).
9. Ibn al-Mubarak, *Kitab al-jihad*, 89–90 (no. 105), cited in many collections; see David Cook, "Muslim Apocalyptic and *Jihad*," *Jerusalem Studies in Arabic and Islam* 20 (1996): 75.
10. See Suliman Bashear, "Muslim Apocalypses," *Israel Oriental Studies* 13 (1993): 75–99.
11. Abu Da'ud, *Sunan*, 3:4 (no. 2484); see Cook, "Muslim Apocalyptic," 71–72, for additional references.
12. See Uri Rubin, *Between Bible and Qur'an: The Children of Israel and the Islamic Self-Image* (Princeton, N.J.: Darwin, 1999), chap. 7; and Steven Wasserstrom, *Between Muslim and Jew* (Princeton, N.J.: Princeton University Press, 1995), chap. 3.
13. Majid Fakhry, trans., *The Qur'an: A Modern English Version* (London: Garnett, 1997).
14. Al-Nasa'i, *Sunan* (Beirut: Dar al-Fikr, n.d.), 7:161; variants in A. J. Wensinck, *Concordance et indices de la tradition musulmane* (Leiden: Brill, 1936–62), s.v. *kalima, haqq*.
15. Deborah Tor, "Privatized Jihad and Public Order in the Pre-Seljuq Period: The Role of the Mutatawwi'a," *Iranian Studies* 38 (2005): 555–73.
16. See Cook, *Studies in Muslim Apocalyptic*, 125, n. 154, 143, n. 208.
17. Safar ibn 'Abd al-Rahman al-Hawali, *The Day of Wrath*, at http://www.freshwap.net/forums/ e-books-tutorials/171855-day-wrath-safar-ibn-abd-al-rahman-al-hawali.html.
18. See Wensinck, *Concordance*, s.v., *shajara, hajar*; and David Cook, *Contemporary Muslim Apocalyptic Literature* (Syracuse, N.Y.: Syracuse University Press, 2005), 35–36.

19. The addition to the verse is 'Abdallah's.

20. Bashir Muhammad 'Abdallah, *Zilzal al-ard al-'azim* (Cairo: n.p., 1993), 165.

21. For example, Safar al-Hawali in his "An Open Letter to President Bush" (October 2001), at http://www.sunnahonline.com/ilm/contemporary/0025.htm; and personal correspondence with Pakistani academics, October 9, 2008.

22. "Leading Sunni Sheikh Yousef al-Qaradhawi and Other Sheikhs Herald the Coming Conquest of Rome," Memri.org, "Special Dispatch Series," no. 447 (December 6, 2002).

23. See Khaled Hroub, *Hamas: Political Thought and Practice* (Washington, D.C.: Institute for Palestine Studies, 2000), art. 7, p. 272.

24. Bassam Jirrar, *Ziwal Isra'il 2022* (Beirut: Maktabat al-Biqa' al-Haditha, 1995); trans. Mohammad Yasin Owadally, *The End of Israel in 2022* (Kuala Lumpur: A. S. Nooreddin, 2002).

25. See, for example, Ahmadinejad's speech at the UN on September 19, 2006, at http://www.npr.org/templates/story/story.php?storyId=6107339.

26. Sulaym al-Silafi, *Al-Fawa'id al-hisan min hadith Thawban (tada'i al-umam)* (Casablanca: Dar Ibn 'Affan, 2001), 7–14, brings all of the variants; cited in such sources as Osama bin Laden, *Messages to the World: The Statements of Osama bin Laden*, ed. Bruce Lawrence, trans. James Howarth (London: Verso, 2005), 59 (February 23, 1998); and Yusuf al-'Ayyiri, *Dawr al-nisa' fi jihad al-'ada'*, 3, at http://www.e-prism.org/images/nesaa.pdf.

27. Hamid Ahmad Ba Bakr, *'Aqidat ahl al-sunna wa al-jama'a aw al-firqa al-najiyya wa al-ta'ifa al-mansura* (Khartoum: Dirasat Minhajiyya, n.d.); Abu Basir, *Sifat al-ta'ifa al-mansura*, at http://www.altartosi.com/book/book07/index.html; and Abu Qatada al-Filistini, *Ma'alim al-ta'ifa al-mansura*, at http://www.e-prism.org/images/Maalim_al-Taifah_al-Mansurah.doc.

28. A medieval apocalyptic history of the world.

29. Statement of Abu Mus'ab al-Zarqawi, April 6, 2004.

30. See Ihab al-Badawi and Hasan al-Zawwam, *Usama bin Ladin: Al-Mahdi al-muntazar um al-masih al-Dajjal?* (Cairo: Madbuli al-Saghir, 2002); and the analysis of Camille al-Tawil, *Al-Qa'ida wa akhwatuha qissat al-jihadiyyin al-'Arab* (Beirut: al-Saqi, 2007), 273.

31. See Usama bin Ladin, *Declaration of War*, trans. Abu Umama (London: Khurasan Press, n.d)

32. Abu Mus'ab al-Suri, *Ru'y wa ahlam am tamanniyyat wa takhayyulat wa awham* (dated 2001), at http://anonymouse.org/cgi-bin/anon-www.cgi/http://tawhed.ws/r? i=3908&;a=p&;PHPSESSID=5174f526a6412baeaf30944432542c03; and see my analysis in David Cook, "The Recovery of Radical Islam after the Fall of the Taliban," *Terrorism and Political Violence* 15 (2003): 31–56.

33. Abu Mus'ab al-Suri, *Da'wat al-muqawama al-Islamiyya al-'alamiyya*, at http://www.ctc.usma.edu/am-suri.doc; details in Brynjar Lia, *Architect of Global Jihad: The Life of al-Qaeda Strategist Abu Mus'ab al-Suri* (New York: Columbia University Press, 2007), esp. chaps. 2–4, 6, 8; see also the biography at http://anonymouse.org/cgi-bin/anon-www.cgi/http://tawhed.ws/a?PHPSESSID=5174f526a6412baeaf30944432542c03&;i=78.

34. Al-Zarqawi, *Kalimat mudi'a: Al-Kitab al-jami' li khutab wa kalimat al-shaykh al-mu'tazz bi dinihi Abi Mus'ab al-Zarqawi* (dated 2006), at http://www.e-prism.org/images/AMZ-Ver1.doc.

35. Notable exceptions were Nasir al-Din al-Albani, Ibn 'Uthaymin, and Hasan Ayyub.

36. Forsan.net (2002); the hadith citation is from Abu Da'ud, 3: 10 (no. 2504).

37. Most of them are collected by Nawaf al-Takruri, *Al-'Amaliyyat al-istishhadiyya fi al-mizan al-fiqhi* (Damascus: Al-Takruri, 2004), 102–79.

38. As are those that oppose suicide attacks; see "Clerics Conference in Lahore Issues Prohibition against Suicide Attacks in Pakistan," Memri.org, "Special Dispatch Series," no. 2093 (October 28, 2008), at http://memri.org/bin/articles.cgi?Page=archives&Area=sd&;ID=SP2 09308; and see also the Indonesian *Fatwa Majles Ulama Indonesia* (Jakarta, 2005), which is equally intellectually incoherent.

39. As can be seen in the numerous justifications of mass-casualty suicide attacks: for example, al-'Ayyiri's *Haqiqat al-harb al-salibiyya al-jadida*; the anonymous *Ghazwat al-hadi-'ashara min Rabi' al-Awwal: 'Amaliyyat sharq al-Riyad*; the response to Abu Basir al-Tartusi's denunciation of the July 7, 2005, suicide attacks in London, *Al-Ta'sil li mashru'iyyat ma jara fi Lundun min tafjirat wa al-radd 'ala al-bayan al-mashu'um li Abi Basir al-Tartusi*; and Imam Samudra's

defense of the Bali suicide attacks (October 2002), *Aku Melawan Teroris* (Solo: Jazera, 2004), in which he actually cites al-Takruri.

40. Mohammed Hafez, *Suicide Bombers in Iraq: The Strategy and Ideology of Martyrdom* (Washington, D.C.: United States Institute of Peace, 2007), esp. chaps. 3–5.

41. For example, Abu Muhammad al-Maqdisi, cited at Memri.org, Inquiry and Analysis (no. 239), September 11, 2005; and Ayman al-Zawahiri, *His Own Words*, trans. Laura Mansfield (Old Tappan, N.J.: TLG, 2006), 250–79 (dated October 11, 2005).

42. Majid Nasir al-Zabidi, *Karamat al-wa'd al-sadiq: Tawthiq al-nasr al-ilahi li al-muqawama al-Islamiyya fi Lubnan* (Beirut: Dar al-Mahajja' al-Bayda', 2007), 191–92.

43. He specifically notes Spain, southern France, southern Italy, the Balkans, all of southern Russia and the Ukraine, most of China and India, the Philippines, and large sections of Africa.

19

How Has the Global Salafi Terrorist Movement Affected Western Just War Thinking?

MARTIN L. COOK

I think the important thing here, Tim, is for people to understand that, you know, things have changed since last Tuesday. The world shifted in some respects. Clearly, what we're faced with here is a situation where terrorism has struck home in the United States. We've been subject to targets of terrorist attacks before, especially overseas with our forces and American personnel overseas, but this time because of what happened in New York and what happened in Washington, it's a qualitatively different set of circumstances.

> —U.S. Vice President Dick Cheney, interview with Tim Russert,
> *Meet the Press*, September 16, 2001

In the immediate aftermath of the September 11, 2001, attacks, the Bush administration frequently asserted that fundamental changes would be necessary in how the United States approached its security in light of the potential for future attacks by al-Qaeda. Further, as the two terms of this administration unfolded, we witnessed unprecedented departures from previously accepted norms in a wide range of areas—from permissible interrogation techniques when dealing with prisoners, to the civil liberties of American citizens, to claims regarding necessary changes in international law on the legitimate uses of military force.

This chapter evaluates these developments in three stages. First, it articulates the general understandings of justified war as they have evolved over recent centuries and as they were understood before the attacks of September 11, 2001. Second, it lays out the specific claims and changes offered by the Bush administration regarding the *jus ad bellum* requirements of just war.[1] This phase of analysis will be descriptive in intent. What did the administration say and do that departed from earlier norms, and what rationales did it offer for those departures?

The third section of the chapter is normative rather than descriptive. In this section, I attempt to offer some critical assessments of the responses and rationales offered in the second section and to make some judgments about how the Western tradition should adapt itself to the new realities of an indefinite future of engagement with global Salafi terrorist movements.[2] The general argument will be that given the kind of adversary that al-Qaeda represents, some modifications to the particular instantiation of the Western just war tradition as it has been codified in international law is indeed necessary. These modifications can be validly grounded in the deeper religious and ethical traditions of just war in the West and require thinking about the current world situation in ways more typical of the earlier, pre-Westphalian just war tradition. I will argue that the modifications largely do not support the policies advocated and pursued by the Bush administration. Nevertheless, the administration was correct to assert that the conceptual and legal models that we have inherited from the twentieth century are maladapted to the realities of the current world environment. Last, I will argue that an approach more likely to address the new challenges effectively can emerge, grounded in the deep traditions of Western just war and pointing to evolutionary directions in both customary and perhaps eventually codified international law.

The Pre-9/11 Norms

Before we can usefully explore the ways in which the Bush administration departed from existing just war standards, we must articulate what those standards are. As is commonly known, for the past four hundred years, the baseline of the Western understanding of just war has been the understanding of the global system that emerged in the aftermath of the Protestant Reformation and the Wars of Religion that it precipitated in Europe. As a shorthand term for this system, we often refer to the Westphalian international system, taking its name from the 1648 Peace of Westphalia.

The central feature of the Westphalian system is that it is made up principally of sovereign states. Further, it sees world politics in terms of the relations among those states. Despite the widespread deference to this system resulting from its long-standing prevalence in modern politics, it is important to recall that the system is not grounded essentially in ethical or political ideals. In fact, when the system emerged in the seventeenth century, it was considered very much a suboptimal compromise for all of the European states. Ideally, what each power in Europe would have preferred at the time was to restore the religious unity of European Christendom. The difficulty was that there were competing versions of the Christian religion. None had the political or military power to force that unity, as the previous century and a half of religious warfare had demonstrated.

The "solution" that Westphalia proposed was that individual states would be seen as "sovereign" (at liberty to conduct themselves entirely as they saw fit in their domestic affairs), and their borders would be treated (in theory, in any case) as sacrosanct. These two principles, if respected by all states, would bring, it was hoped, a more or less durable peace to Europe.

The twentieth century witnessed some rather dramatic developments in the generally agreed-upon understanding of the Westphalian system. Perhaps the most important was the 1928 Kellogg-Briand Pact which for the first time spelled out explicitly an absolute prohibition of any and all wars of aggression. Although one might argue that prohibition was pretty clearly implicit in the hoped-for stability that Westphalia offered from the outset, Kellogg-Briand removed any possible ambiguity about the matter. Indeed, the Kellogg-Briand Pact provided the legal foundation for the prosecution of the war crime of planning aggressive war or "crimes against peace" at the Nuremberg War Crimes Tribunal.

Furthermore, the principle that military force may only be used by a state in response to "wrong received" from an aggressor state is enshrined as a central principle in the Charter of the United Nations. The charter intends that "collective security" action by the member states, authorized by the Security Council, should replace national self-defense as the ideal response to all acts of aggression. This, of course, has remained a largely unfulfilled expectation.

There are important qualifications to the apparent clarity of the Westphalian standards of sovereignty, territorial integrity, and military response to aggression. These qualifications arise from a legitimate exception for "anticipatory self-defense" or preemption and also from more recent claims against an absolute notion of sovereignty in order to justify international intervention to prevent genocide or other crimes against humanity. Concerns about protecting human rights in the face of brutally repressive states culminated in the UN's adoption in 2005 of a "responsibility to protect."[3] I will consider the relevance of these qualifications below. For now, however, let us stick to the "simple case" of the Western understanding of legitimate *jus ad bellum*, which, in Michael Walzer's words, is that "nothing but aggression can justify war."[4]

There was a major ethical flaw in the Westphalian system from the outset. The issues dividing Europe were largely religious (and, of course, political but to a large extent in the guise of religious questions). Yet the Westphalian solution consigned the fate of religious minorities entirely to the tender mercies of the sovereign state within whose borders individuals and communities found themselves. In other words, and to use an anachronistic phrase for the time, the Westphalian system sacrificed the idea of human rights (which was not a major political concept for another century or more) on the altar of hoped-for political stability among states.

This decision created a major gap, which in the twentieth century, would lead to various attempts to diminish the power of state sovereignty from its initial "black box" understanding in which internal affairs of sovereign states were entirely removed from cross-border scrutiny. Most strongly after the Holocaust, the international system attempted to ensure the protection of the rights and lives of individuals and groups. These efforts began in earnest with the Genocide Convention adopted by the UN General Assembly in 1948 and were recently further codified in the UN's adoption in 2005 of the concept of a "responsibility to protect" incumbent on all states.[5]

The U.S. Response and Proposed Modifications of the International System

This understanding of the normative international system helps us see immediately how the attacks by al-Qaeda make any response by the United States difficult to justify or even to conceptualize within this framework. To begin with the most obvious: al-Qaeda is not a state, and its agents do not represent the policies, interests, or instructions of a state. Insofar as the legal version of just war theory is taken as definitive, its state-centric structures and assumptions are to a large degree inapplicable to the problem posed by the 9/11 attacks (and the earlier attacks on U.S. embassies in Africa, the USS *Cole*, and even the Khobar Towers bombings in Saudi Arabia—all seen now as earlier acts of al-Qaeda).

Nevertheless, there was never a serious question that the 9/11 attacks warranted a military response, if feasible, both to retaliate against those responsible for planning and funding them and to attempt to eliminate continuing capabilities to mount future attacks against the West. There were certainly plenty of reasons to wonder how well the Bush administration understood the nature, goals, purposes, and grievances that motivated al-Qaeda's actions. President Bush's speech to the nation on September 20, 2001, did not inspire confidence in the depth of his understanding. He said on that occasion, "They hate what they see right here in this chamber: a democratically elected government. Their leaders are self-appointed. They hate our freedoms: our freedom of religion, our freedom of speech, our freedom to vote and assemble and disagree with each other." Bush's unscripted remarks on September 16, 2001, in which he referred to an extended war on terrorism as a "crusade," reflected a profound historical and cultural insensitivity. It implicitly endorsed the most austere "clash of civilizations" analysis of the threat possible and inevitably evoked the nadir of Muslim-Christian relations in minds around the world. Such a Manichaean interpretation of the struggle before us arguably appeared to license responses that would, because of their unsubtle understanding of the nature of the problem and the threat, lead to unnecessary and ultimately ineffective actions. Furthermore, such language would inevitably be heard by a significant portion of the Evangelical Christian population of the United States in terms of their own well-developed apocalyptic thinking in which the cosmic conflict between good and evil, culminating in the return of Christ to reign on earth, is widely expected to occur in the near future.[6] In other words, the language of crusade and clash of civilizations would lead some to a reading of the conflict with al-Qaeda in terms of Christian holy war thinking, perhaps even framed in terms of the final battles of the end of time.

Although Secretary of State Colin Powell often echoed President Bush's language on these points, he did occasionally reveal a more nuanced and correct understanding of the nature of al-Qaeda's grievances. He correctly noted on *Meet the Press* in late September 2001, "They hate our presence in parts of the world that they think we should not be in." Yet Powell's better grasp of the issues only foreshadowed his role as the administration's Cassandra, accurately foreseeing much but influencing the course of affairs little.

Misunderstood though the threat may have been in those early days (and perhaps during most of the Bush administration's tenure), that al-Qaeda posed a threat to the United States and its interests abroad is indisputable. Further, given the scale of the destruction caused by the 9/11 attacks, some type of American military response was inevitable. It had been well known for a number of years that the center of al-Qaeda's planning, training, and funding lay within the borders of Taliban-governed Afghanistan. Although the Taliban government was widely condemned and considered illegitimate by most Western governments, there was nevertheless no question of its de facto governing status. So the situation presented a nonstate actor, responsible for the attacks, located within the sovereign territory of a state whose de facto government, despite its widely condemned character, was unquestionably distinct from the attackers. To strike al-Qaeda within the borders of Afghanistan was therefore an act of aggression against Afghanistan—if we take the legalist paradigm as our model—and therefore an illegal act.[7]

The theoretical possibility existed that the Taliban government might choose to cooperate in locating and eliminating al-Qaeda centers, or, failing that, it might even allow the United States, NATO, and other forces to operate freely within its territory for that purpose. But this was never really a practical possibility given the close intermingling of ideology and finances between the Taliban and al-Qaeda.

This left the obvious reality that if there were to be an attack on al-Qaeda in Afghanistan, it would necessarily be an attack on the state of Afghanistan. Despite this obvious violation of the existing legal instantiation of just war principles, few Western states seriously questioned the legitimacy of such an attack. The attack proceeded and by many measures was a stunning success both in terms of the outcomes sought and in terms of the creative means employed by U.S. forces. The wisdom of hindsight, to be sure, reveals major flaws in the operational plan, especially the failure to use U.S. forces, rather than rely on Pakistani and Afghan forces, to close the "back door" into Pakistan for the retreating al-Qaeda. Those failures greatly complicated the U.S. relationship with Pakistan and led to increased violence in the tribal areas of northwest Pakistan and in parts of Afghanistan. Even with the death of Osama bin Laden, there is no end in sight for this continuing violence.

Still, the decision to use force in Afghanistan unquestionably marked an implicit reworking of the accepted understandings of international law and just war. Insofar as the action was accepted as legitimate by the international community, it established a standard for international conduct. According to that standard, nonstate actors who have demonstrated a sufficient level of threat cannot expect existing protections of state sovereignty to shelter them from outside attacks; neither can the states that harbor such nonstate actors on their territory. America's NATO and other allies made it clear that they accepted this principle of action. Indeed, some NATO allies would have agreed to participate in the military operation had the United States requested their assistance pursuant to Article 5 of the NATO charter.[8]

So here we see one de facto modification of just war in response to the global Salafi terrorist threat: the weakening of the concept of state sovereignty when used as a cover for the actions of nonstate actors, when those actions rise to a level of definite and imminent threat to other states. Since the legitimacy of the attack on al-Qaeda in Afghanistan was widely accepted by the major powers, one may safely assert that this action constituted a revision of international law inasmuch as general acceptance of state actions that might not have been clearly legal before they were carried out constitutes a change in customary international law.[9]

Shortly after the Afghanistan action, the Bush administration articulated formally what it argued were novel principles of international conduct required by the threat of international terrorism. It did so in the 2002 National Security Strategy of the United States of America (NSS). Published periodically, the NSS is the most comprehensive overview of an administration's estimate of global security threats and opportunities. The Pentagon is responsible for responding to the NSS with its own document, the National Military Strategy of the United States of America, which articulates the military posture, equipment, and size of the armed forces that it deems necessary to meet the NSS's goals. The 2002 NSS laid out as a matter of general principle a reworking of the international system in which the United States would act unilaterally and not only in response to "wrong received" by an aggressor state or a nonstate actor. One supposes, if these modifications were indeed offered as necessary reinterpretations of international law in response to the global Salafi terrorist threat, that the actions espoused for the United States were also considered legitimate for all other states.

The crux of the argument, as far as existing international law is concerned, is an already accepted exception to the legalist paradigm (again, that "nothing but aggression can justify war"). This exception is the concept of "legitimate anticipatory self-defense" (as the lawyers refer to it) or "preemptive war" (as it is more commonly called in the philosophical literature). This principle recognizes that a strict adherence to the legalist paradigm's requirement that a state must already have been the object of an attack fails to capture our genuine moral intuitions in a narrow range of cases. In those cases, a state may legitimately use force first against another state that is planning or threatening an attack. This traditional exception involves three elements:

1. Capability: the potential adversary has the capability to do the state in question grave harm if its military attack is allowed to be carried out.
2. Intent: the potential aggressor manifests unambiguously its intention to use those capabilities to mount such an attack.
3. Risk: the level of risk must be unacceptably high so as to counsel against waiting to find out whether one's assessment of capability and intent are indeed correct. In other words, if waiting for the first blow to fall is not likely to be devastating beyond recovery or to constitute defeat all by itself, it may be both prudent and morally preferable to wait for the blow and then respond to the manifest aggression.

To their credit, the authors of the NSS take on the legal and ethical arguments explicitly and directly:

> For centuries, international law recognized that nations need not suffer an attack before they can lawfully take action to defend themselves against forces that present an imminent danger of attack. Legal scholars and international jurists often conditioned the legitimacy of preemption on the existence of an imminent threat—most often a visible mobilization of armies, navies, and air forces preparing to attack.
>
> We must *adapt the concept of imminent threat* [emphasis mine] to the capabilities and objectives of today's adversaries. Rogue states and terrorists do not seek to attack us using conventional means. They know such attacks would fail. Instead, they rely on acts of terror and, potentially, the use of weapons of mass destruction—weapons that can be easily concealed, delivered covertly, and used without warning.[10]

The crux of the argument here is that by its very nature, the threat from international terrorist organizations makes the application of reasonably settled understandings of legitimate preemption impossible. Small, covert terrorist cells do not mobilize armies or navies or otherwise signal their capabilities and intentions. Yet as 9/11 and other attacks clearly demonstrate, the terrorists pose a significant risk. With their known intent to acquire and use weapons of mass destruction (WMD), the threat from terrorists grows dramatically. Faced with this new enemy, the NSS argues, terrorists' capability must be eliminated wherever it can be found, even absent the indications of specific intent to attack:

> The United States has long maintained the option of preemptive actions to counter a sufficient threat to our national security. The greater the threat, the greater is the risk of inaction—and the more compelling the case for

taking anticipatory action to defend ourselves, even if uncertainty remains
as to the time and place of the enemy's attack. To forestall or prevent such
hostile acts by our adversaries, the United States will, if necessary, act pre-
emptively.[11]

This line of argument was soon extended beyond the Afghanistan case to justify an attack on Iraq. The administration claimed that Saddam Hussein's government had or was developing WMD, had close ties to al-Qaeda, and would certainly
make WMD available to terrorist groups. The nexus between the government of a
"rogue" state and international terrorists, it was argued, would permit nonstate
actors to attack the United States and its allies, wreaking enormous devastation,
and under circumstances where the ultimate source of their WMD capability was
at least ambiguous. This ambiguity made it difficult, if not impossible, to deter a
state from making this capability available to terrorist groups. It would also make
retaliation against the proliferators difficult to justify in the eyes of the international community.

Although couched in the logic of established principles of preemptive war, the
strategy actually espoused by the Bush administration was effectively, as many
critics have noted, one of preventive war. The distinction is this: preemption (or
anticipatory self-defense) focuses on something one has good evidence that an
adversary is planning to do; preventive war, by contrast, is focused on ensuring
that the potential adversary never has the capability even to contemplate doing
anything against one's state.[12]

The immediate application of what came to be known as the Bush Doctrine was
the decision to attack Iraq in order to locate WMD and change the regime to one
that would no longer harbor the alleged intentions to develop such weapons. It is
now obvious that at a minimum, a number of the beliefs and claims on which the
decision was based were mistaken. The important question to which we will return
below is whether the flawed American occupation of Iraq was the result merely of
inept application of legitimately transformed principles in light of the global
Salafi terrorist challenge or of more fundamental problems in the administration's logic that modifications to the international system were necessary in the
first place.

The systemic changes argued as being necessary by the Bush administration
can be summarized in the pithy phrase from the 2002 NSS: "The greater the
threat, the greater the risk of inaction." It was this claim that served as the basis
of the assertion of moral and legal right for U.S. action against Iraq, including
unilateral action if international cooperation was not available, forthcoming, or
timely.[13] To quote the NSS once more:

It has taken almost a decade for us to comprehend the true nature of this
new threat. Given the goals of rogue states and terrorists, the United
States can no longer solely rely on a reactive posture as we have in the

past. The inability to deter a potential attacker, the immediacy of today's threats, and the magnitude of potential harm that could be caused by our adversaries' choice of weapons do not permit that option. We cannot let our enemies strike first.[14]

The unilateralism of the early Bush administration eventually came to look considerably less attractive—even to the administration. This is most clearly seen in the strenuous efforts to get more NATO allies involved in serious counterinsurgency and even combat operations in Afghanistan, at the same time that anything resembling real coalition operations in Iraq were quickly diminishing. Indeed, in President Bush's final speech to the UN General Assembly on September 23, 2008, we can detect the change in the administration's emphasis and tone: "The United Nations and other multilateral organizations are needed more urgently than ever. . . . In the decades ahead, the United Nations and other multilateral organizations must continually confront terror."[15]

Such concerns point the way to the next section of this chapter, which suggests possibilities for adjusting the international system to accommodate better the genuinely new realities of a global terrorist threat from nonstate actors. Clearly, such accommodations are needed, and clearly, the state-centric model of international relations that has dominated since Westphalia is inadequate to the task. On the other hand, the Bush administration's specific proposals for modification were excessive and unsustainable if they are to be taken for what they purport to be: normative changes of the international system to be accepted as legitimate principles of action for all nations. I offer, therefore, some alternative proposals for the kinds of modifications that the threat of global terrorism requires and that may legitimately be built on the foundation of the deeper, pre-Westphalian roots of the Western just war tradition.

Toward a Normative Revision of Just War Doctrine

Thus far, I have argued two major points. First, the nature of al-Qaeda and other similar Islamic terrorist groups and the threat they represent necessitate various forms of military response. These responses will not fall clearly within current legal understandings of the legitimate grounds for war. Second, the Bush administration's explicit articulations of how the criteria must be modified were too sweeping in their assertion of unilateralism. The criteria articulated in the 2002 NSS would be too radically destabilizing to the international system if they were universally claimed by and applied to all states. They would, in effect, allow each state, on its own authority and without the requirement to meet publicly agreed standards, choose unilateral actions and justify them by unverifiable claims that it "knew" of threats to its security. Given what we know now about the seriously flawed intelligence used to back up the justifications for invading Iraq—intelligence that was questioned even before the invasion—the need for caution and skepticism about classified intelligence is all the greater.

In what follows, I propose some reasonable modifications to the norms of the international system that would make it possible to address the global Salafi terrorist challenge without unduly destabilizing the international system. Furthermore, I attempt to ground these modifications in the full historical depth of the Western just war tradition. Doing so requires us to reach back behind the specific evolution of the tradition as a legal standard that has evolved since the Peace of Westphalia to the much deeper religious and moral traditions that ground just war theory's core principles. Finally, I show that the modifications necessary to craft principles sufficient to address the global Salafi terrorist threat are consonant with modifications already being suggested from another set of concerns entirely, those pertaining to the Genocide Convention and the Responsibility to Protect.

One useful place to begin this discussion is at the origins of the Western Christian just war tradition, specifically with the situation faced by Augustine of Hippo in the late fourth and early fifth centuries. In important ways, the threats posed by al-Qaeda and other similar groups today bear a closer resemblance to the threats that the Roman empire of Augustine's day faced than to examples from post-Westphalian interstate conflict.

In Augustine's time, the Roman empire was battling incursions of various tribal groups that are in some ways analogous to al-Qaeda. They were not "conventional" actors as the Romans understood them. The threat they posed was an existential threat to *tranquillitas ordinis*, the stability and "tranquility of order" that the effective governance of the empire provided. Augustine feared that the success of the tribal invasions would result in the collapse of civilization itself, the civilization built on Roman power, law, and administration. Since, in fact, Rome was ultimately destroyed by these attacks, resulting in a severe cultural decline in Europe that lasted for centuries, Augustine's dire prognostications seem prophetic.[16]

Augustine inherited from the earlier Christian tradition a deep suspicion of the military and of government service generally. For much of the first two centuries of the church's existence, it took the presence of the Roman empire for granted and generally realized that it benefited from the security and order that the empire provided. But since that order ultimately rested on conquest and violence, Christians in general were counseled to stay removed from government and military service. Historians have noted that the reasons for this attitude were complex and included at least the following elements: the New Testament's rejection of the use of force and violence, the fact that government service necessarily involved one in pagan religious rites, and the morally corrupting aspects of military camp life.

The prospect of the total collapse of Roman civilization forced Augustine to develop his complex and nuanced endorsement of the defense of tranquility of order.[17] With the older and more sectarian Christian tradition, Augustine maintains the strong sense that no earthly and human organization or structure (including the Christian church) should ever be thought of as unambiguously pure and holy. The Kingdom of God remains in all earthly time an eschatological vision rather than an institutional reality. Moral ambiguity runs through all human creations and institutions. They vary only in degree of relative justice and peace.

But, Augustine argues strenuously, one should not allow appreciation of these ambiguities to blind one to the fact that the degrees of variation in justice and peace are great and significant. The closest approximations to peace and order in human society will require the proper use of coercion and perhaps even lethal force if order is to be restored after it has been disrupted by the invader, the criminal, the bandit. It is in this context that Augustine counsels the conscientious Christian to take up arms. The need to do so is indeed a "sad necessity,"[18] but it is a necessity nonetheless, and the conscientious warrior driven to resist evil is, Augustine claims, a "peacemaker" who, in the words of the Gospel, is "blessed."[19]

This Augustinian way of thinking about the nature and roots of the use of military force has great relevance to our age, even if one does not share the theological framework in which it rests. To put it more precisely, one can accept the sober analysis of world affairs even if one does not share Augustine's confidence in the eschatological vision of a future state in which absolute good and justice will be manifest. It is especially helpful, I suggest, in attempting to locate in the Western just war tradition a proper framework for dealing with Salafi terrorist movements.

There are clear parallels between Augustine's military and political situation and our own, and there are clear divergences from the conditions that shaped just war thinking in the West since Westphalia. The primary threat to Augustine's civilization, as with our own, comes from what might be called irregular fighters. Conventional wars fought between states—or in the case of the Roman empire, with parallel empires such as the Sassanid in Persia and Mesopotamia—are the exception rather than the norm and are generally confined to brief border skirmishes. In both cases, the nature of unconventional warfare means that the customs and norms governing traditional warfare apply poorly, if at all.

Furthermore, the goals of the attackers are not traditional goals of acquisition of territory, capture of goods, or replacement of governments with new ones that in most respects would carry on business as usual. Rather, both the barbarian invaders of Rome and the Salafi terrorists of today seek a major change not just of governments but of the entire international system. In the case of Rome, defeat holds the prospect not merely of new rulers but also of the loss of an integrated administrative, economic, transportation, technological, and educational base built up over centuries. In the case of the present conflict, the stated goal of Salafi terrorist movements is, in the near term, the retreat of American military power from Muslim countries and the overthrow of the allegedly corrupt and un-Islamic regimes in Muslim states. This will pave the way for an end to the hegemony of

Western civilization and the creation of an order based on conservative interpretations of shari'a law and the restoration of the Islamic caliphate in the Muslim world. Once this initial phase is complete, the Salafis' stated mission is to expand Islamic hegemony throughout the world. Of course, one might argue that these broader goals are recognized, even by al-Qaeda, as more aspirational than realistic—or, perhaps, even eschatological rather than temporal.[20] But it is clear that in trying to realize even their short-term goals, al-Qaeda and its affiliates see the United States, its allies, and much of the world as their enemies. Salafi terrorism is not aimed simply at one or more nations that it wishes to destroy; rather, its target is the international system itself. Should these extremists succeed in coming to power in only a few Muslim countries, the implications would be consequential for all countries; what is at stake is the entire structure of democratic polity, human rights, liberal citizenship, gender and religious equality, noninterference and peaceful relations among states, and other values developed in the West but now championed under international law.

This way of framing the problem is helpful in at least two ways. First, it dramatically highlights why the existing state-centric form of Western just war theory corresponds so poorly to the threat environment that we now face. While the power to make decisions and the military forces to respond to threats all reside with individual sovereign states, they are not threatened as discrete states. The concept of "collective security" applies in ways far more powerful than in the more conventional idea of collective security as the proper response to interstate aggression. In contrast with interstate aggression, the framework under which the UN Charter's provisions for collective security were framed, the Salafi terrorist threat is global and diffuse; it therefore demands a collective response. The UN's collective security machinery needs to be adapted and strengthened in order to combat effectively this common threat.

Second, it provides some useful pointers for ways in which like-minded states that have a common stake in the defense of the essential tenets of their civilization might work together to develop a common understanding of the rules governing military action in this new environment. Because collective action is clearly required in response to a fundamental threat to our civilization, a collective security framework allows us at least to outline some of the ways we should move forward, building on the older and deeper roots of Western just war tradition before the principles of the Westphalian state system became codified. Because the full scope and nature of the challenge posed by Salafi terrorism became clear only after the 9/11 attacks and is still evolving, my proposals are inevitably programmatic and sketchy. They provide only general directions for the further development of just war thinking.

The central value of the Westphalian system, as noted above, is state sovereignty. But sovereignty as initially understood was morally ambiguous at best. On the positive side, it did bring a degree of peace to Europe that could not be attained as long as the desire to rebuild some form of Christendom drove military and political actions. Further, it had the salutary effect of removing religion from statecraft to a large degree.

On the other hand, the international system created by Westphalia entirely subsumed individuals within states; international politics stopped, at least according to theory, at the jealously guarded borders of sovereign states. This normative development, while perhaps unavoidable and salutary in the seventeenth century, gave states almost unfettered leeway in how they treated those living within their borders. It took the genocides of the twentieth century to spur a fundamental questioning of how far sovereignty should be privileged above all other norms in international relations. Since World War II, a steady stream of declarations, from the Genocide Convention to the Responsibility to Protect, has in principle reduced the valence of sovereignty in favor of safeguards for individual human rights. Unfortunately, the history of this same time period illustrates plainly and painfully that despite the declarations, states have generally been reluctant to act in ways that challenge the norms of sovereignty, even when the conditions manifestly justified international intervention. Nevertheless, the point remains that the principle that state sovereignty is not an absolute is one that the world community has accepted, at least since 1948.

This is important because the exigencies of effective military action against al-Qaeda and similar groups will in some cases require violations of previously accepted constraints imposed by sovereignty. Terrorist cells cannot be allowed safe haven even when military action to destroy them would, in traditional terms, be an act of aggression against the states where they reside. In cases where the harboring state is willing and able to cooperate in eliminating the terrorist elements in its territory, no bending of existing sovereignty rules is required. But in cases where the state cannot or will not act, outside intervention against the terrorists will clearly be required, even in the face of objections from the harboring state.

However, I argued above that the normative claims advanced by the 2002 NSS are far too unilateral and sweeping to be acceptable international norms. I therefore now explore some alternatives to that degree of unilateralism, which I believe show some promise of working effectively to deal with the threat.

There is an existing multilateral framework that, in principle, might be sufficient to cope with the challenge: the UN system and, in particular, the Security Council. As is commonly known, any use of military force other than in direct response to an ongoing attack is supposed legally to be managed by the Security Council, as outlined in Chapter VII of the UN Charter. One might hope, therefore, that with sufficient diplomatic effort, the UN's collective security mechanisms might be developed and strengthened. In particular, an international consensus could emerge regarding the threshold necessary to justify the use of military force (and other coercive means) against sovereign states harboring terrorist groups in one way or another.

Indeed, the Security Council's initial responses to the 9/11 attacks were impressive. In a number of Security Council resolutions, starting with Resolution

1368 (September 12, 2001), the international community rallied around the central claim that attacks such as these cannot be permitted, international cooperation on a number of fronts to contain and eliminate groups planning such attacks would be required, and the conventional claims of state sovereignty could not be allowed to shelter these groups while they gathered resources and capabilities. Shortly after the United States launched military operations in Afghanistan, the Security Council adopted Resolution 1377 (November 12, 2001). It declared that "acts of international terrorism constitute a challenge to all States and all of humanity" and affirmed that "a sustained, comprehensive approach involving the active participation and collaboration of all Member States of the United Nations, and in accordance with the Charter of the United Nations and international law, is essential to combat the scourge of international terrorism."[21]

The quick and forceful UN response needs to be highlighted because it has become quite common to disparage or even dismiss the UN system as totally ineffectual. UN resolutions stopped short of implementing a collective international response to the 9/11 attacks, nor did they explicitly sanction the American military action in Afghanistan. Yet the United States did not solicit a collective response under Chapter VII, nor did it ever signal that it sought explicit Security Council authorization for attacking Afghanistan. All that the Bush administration really wanted from the Security Council was its legal imprimatur for the direct military confrontation with al-Qaeda and the Taliban in Afghanistan. The tacit authorization came, in the view of the administration, from post-9/11 Security Council resolutions such as 1368.

Over the long term, this is the main way in which Western just war theory and international law needs to adapt to accommodate itself to the realities of Salafi terrorism: to build on the more than fifty-year movement of the international system to diminish the claims of sovereignty from their strongest Westphalian version. The Holocaust caused the world community to begin a trajectory of diminishing sovereignty in the name of human rights and humanitarian concerns. Still, the ever-growing body of human rights law and international humanitarian law is integrated poorly, at best, with older, sovereignty-focused international law. Consequently, humanitarian law is invoked and used as a basis of state and international action only fitfully. Similar problems will arise in integrating new counterterrorism legal standards with the claims of state sovereignty. Applying the lessons learned by the international community in developing humanitarian law to the future development of counterterrorism measures is the central challenge facing the Western just war tradition in response to international terrorism.

Furthermore, how best to respond is more a diplomatic than a military question. Since al-Qaeda and similar groups are visibly challengers to many states, and not just to the United States, a strong basis exists to start the hard work of diplomatic clarification of the main issue: when and in what manner it is legitimate to use military force against a sovereign state harboring terrorist groups plotting attacks against other states.

To pursue this line of argument, we must engage in a bit of counterfactual history. The fact that the Bush administration demonstrated a distrust and dislike of diplomacy led it to engage in (largely) unilateral actions in its "war on terror," including most significantly the invasion of Iraq. Most of the international community did not consider the broadening of the war on terror to be warranted. The widespread support that the United States enjoyed in the Security Council immediately after 9/11 turned into deep opposition, including from key allies such as France. Had the administration demonstrated greater interest in diplomacy and multilateralism, as it had done before the intervention in Afghanistan, it would have placed the world on a clearer path to effective and coordinated international responses to the Salafi threat when the moment was most propitious for such diplomatic initiatives.

The fact that the Bush administration failed to pursue this diplomatic course and the resulting divergence between U.S. policy and international opinion damaged the mechanisms through which an international consensus will have to be developed. The diplomatic challenges are probably more daunting now than they would have been had the United States exercised leadership consistently in this direction after 9/11. Russia, China, and many other states are less disposed to cooperate with the United States now than they would have been in 2002 or 2003.

The leadership in Washington, D.C., has changed, but Salafi terrorism remains a threat to the United States and its allies and to the international system itself. The institutions of the international system have not changed, so the centrality of the Security Council on these questions remains the same. In the early stages of the Obama administration, it seemed clear that the new president intended to approach many world issues with a far more internationalist bent, including (as evidenced by the appointment of Susan Rice as UN ambassador and the reelevation of that position to cabinet status) a revitalized commitment to reform the UN. As the administration's policies evolved, however, the contrast with the previous administration became more ambiguous. By choosing to morph the Afghanistan campaign into a full-scale counterinsurgency and nation-building effort, Obama put the focus on strengthening the Afghan state, which may prove futile and certainly commits resources there when terrorist threats are now clearly centered elsewhere. While NATO's effort in Afghanistan has, in some respects, been impressive (at least politically), it has also shown, as Secretary of Defense Robert Gates pointed out fairly sharply at the end of his tenure, the severe challenges that NATO continues to face as an effective military alliance.[22] The U.S.-Pakistan relationship has deteriorated because of increased drone strikes that have killed civilians and special-forces raiding parties, including most dramatically the operation that killed bin Laden thirty-eight miles from the capital of Islamabad. This strained bilateral relationship is a testament to the fact that the problem of using military force for counterterrorism within sovereign territories is still far from resolved and has become, if anything, more complicated. In short, the Obama administration advocates internationalism and multilateralism but has not shied away from unilateral action at crucial junctures in its foreign policy.

What if, in the years ahead, the diplomatic efforts that I advocate are unsuccessful or the movement toward an international consensus is too slow? Obviously, the United States and others will not stand idle if they acquire information regarding future terrorist attacks just because Security Council authorization is not forthcoming. Insofar as preemptive strikes can be justified retroactively by a clear showing to the international community that the threat was real, we may reasonably expect such action to be approved as justifiable though irregular. If subsequent actions based on this precedent are also generally accepted, new standards have been added to customary international law. But for this course of evolution to occur, it is vital that the intelligence backing such decisions be correct nearly 100 percent of the time. The sobering lesson of American intelligence failures leading up to the Iraq War is that any developing international consensus for the legitimacy of preemptive action, especially unilateral action, can erode overnight.

Besides customary international law, we may expect further developments in treaty law. Security Council Resolution 1377 "calls on all States to become parties as soon as possible to the relevant international conventions and protocols relating to terrorism, and encourages Member States to take forward work in this area." Yet again, under Obama, the United States has done little to lead diplomatic efforts in this area.

Conclusion

Since the struggle against Salafi terrorism promises to be decades long, the effort to respond to it will require sustained and international cooperation along the lines that I have suggested. As the response evolves, the military component will be an occasional and, one hopes, specifically targeted aspect of the overall effort. The challenge for the Obama administration is to coordinate diplomatic, economic, law-enforcement, informational, and military aspects of the overall effort. As the threats to the United States are no longer in Afghanistan and have now metastasized to Pakistan, Yemen, and many other places, one hopes that the administration will think deeply about the most effective use of resources—a requirement all the more urgent as significant reductions in defense spending, and therefore military capability, loom on the horizon. Whatever one thinks of the wisdom of committing the bulk of American military power to the wars in Iraq and Afghanistan, resources of that order of magnitude are not going to be available as we move forward. This will force much more careful and focused decisions about the best use of those limited resources.

Moreover, an effective response will have to be multilateral and comprehensive. The Salafi terrorist threat cannot be dealt with by individual states or in isolation from other issues of justice and good governance. Indeed, combating this terrorist movement joins the list of other issues demanding internationally coordinated responses, including stopping genocides, responding to global warming, and stabilizing the global economy. Ultimately, this may prove to be the lasting impact of the war on global Salafi terrorism, that it gave the international system another impetus to develop the internationalism that has been evolving in fits and starts since World War II.

These necessary changes to the international system are considerable. But, as I have argued, they are not so much a break with the West's understanding of just war as they are a retrieval of its deep history. Viewed from the extremely long perspective of the whole of the tradition, the state-centric Westphalian and international-legal way of formulating that tradition is increasingly becoming apparent for what it really is: a period piece. It was a way of trying to preserve some, but not all, of the richness of the just war tradition at a very specific moment in the historical evolution of the West, namely the collapse of even notional Christendom.

The kinds of attacks that al-Qaeda and other terrorists are making or planning place us in a situation more analogous to the Roman empire's in the late fourth and early fifth centuries, when what was at issue was the survival of an entire integrated pattern of civilization. The genius of the Augustinian response to those historical circumstances was to find a way to think clearly about the importance and legitimacy of vigorous defense of that pattern, which provided a "tranquility of order" essential for the maintenance of many important human goods. But equally important, Augustine was able to provide that defense without idealizing the moral foundations of the civilization that he wished to defend or denying the many morally questionable bases on which it rested.[23]

This nuanced view is necessary to avoid unreasonably denying the legitimacy of some of the anger, resentment, and criticism from other cultures toward Western attitudes and actions. But it also provides the moral space within which to justify a spirited and firm defense of Western civilization and to modify its understanding of just war in ways to make that defense possible. Like Augustine, we must find ways to articulate the view that although the integrated global civilization that the West has made is less than the "Kingdom of God," nevertheless, serious damage to it would be an incalculable loss for human civilization generally and for millions of human beings individually. In other words, it is important to defend the civilization of the West and to assert its value against the illusion that a restored caliphate, governed by shari'a law, would in any way be a force for human good. But we can do so without cultural triumphalism or unwarranted assertions of absolute moral and political purity, insofar as we genuinely do retrieve Augustinian sobriety regarding all human institutions in making that defense.[24]

Acknowledgments

The views expressed in this chapter are those of the author and do not necessarily reflect the official policy or position of the United States Navy, the United States Department of Defense, or the United States government.

Notes

1. I do not consider in this chapter the whole range of modifications that the Bush administration made and attempted to justify in the realm of *jus in bello*. The rulings regarding the definition of torture, the indefinite detention of "illegal combatants," the establishment of military tribunals, and other issues are all very important to assess in their own right but lie beyond the scope of this analysis.
2. "Salafi" refers to the first three generations of Muslims and reflects the belief held by some Muslims that Islam as practiced by those generations was most pure and normative. Broadly, therefore, it reflects a fairly widespread view among these Muslims (often called fundamentalists) that a restoration or recovery of that original, pristine Islam is normative for all time.
3. See http://www.responsibilitytoprotect.org.
4. Michael Walzer, *Just and Unjust Wars: A Moral Argument with Historical Illustrations* (New York: Basic, 1977), 62.
5. See http://www.responsibilitytoprotect.org/index.php/united_nations/398?theme=alt1.
6. See Martin L. Cook, "Christian Apocalypticism and Weapons of Mass Destruction," in Sohail H. Hashmi and Steven P. Lee, eds., *Ethics and Weapons of Mass Destruction* (New York: Cambridge University Press, 2004), 200–10, for a discussion of this theological framework and its implications for attitudes toward military conflict, especially in the Middle East.
7. My argument is based on the legalist paradigm and as such is philosophical and hypothetical, not legal. For concise summaries of the debates among international lawyers on the legality of U.S. action in Afghanistan, see Thomas M. Franck, "Terrorism and the Right of Self-Defense," *American Journal of International Law* 95, no. 4 (October 2001): 839–43; Steven R. Ratner, "*Jus ad Bellum* and *Jus in Bello* after September 11," *American Journal of International Law* 96, no. 4 (October 2002): 905–21.
8. NATO is now heavily engaged in Afghanistan. The decision for the United States to conduct initial combat operations essentially alone probably reflects difficulties encountered in managing the multinational military operation in Kosovo rather than a principled unwillingness to accept the full support of NATO.
9. To develop a precise understanding of the degree of imminence and the magnitude and character of the threat that does indeed justify overriding sovereignty would require explicit diplomatic agreement. A general understanding may be claimed under customary international law but only after a number of precedents (some accepted and some rejected by the international community) are available.
10. National Security Strategy of the United States of America, September 2002 (NSS 2002), sect. V, at http://georgewbush-whitehouse.archives.gov/nsc/nss/2002 (accessed July 30, 2011).
11. Ibid.
12. See Henry Shue and David Rodin, eds., *Preemption: Military Action and Moral Justification* (Oxford: Oxford University Press, 2007), for a collection of excellent articles exploring the distinction between preemption and prevention.
13. Witness, for example, the great efforts required of Secretary of State Powell to persuade President Bush, in the face of opposition from Vice President Cheney, to engage the United Nations in advance of the decision to invade Iraq. See the *Frontline* documentary, "Bush's War," at http://www.pbs.org/wgbh/pages/frontline/bushswar/view; Bob Woodward, *Plan of Attack* (New York: Simon & Schuster, 2004), 151, 176–85.

14. NSS 2002, sect. V.

15. See http://www.whitehouse.gov/news/releases/2008/09/print/20080923-5.html.

16. See Augustine, Letter 189, "To Count Boniface"; and Augustine, *The City of God*, bk. XIX, chap. 12, for an extended discussion on the requirements for civil order, which barbarian triumph will destroy.

17. See Augustine, *City of God*, bk. XIX, chaps. 12–13, for his classic discussion of tranquility of order.

18. See ibid., chap. 6, for his discussion of the conscientious judge who, knowing that he will make mistakes and condemn innocent people, nevertheless shoulders the responsibility of judging as part of his responsibility to make the society he serves as peaceful and law-abiding as possible.

19. This application of the concept of "peacemaker" to the conscientious soldier occurs famously in Augustine, Letter 195, "To Count Boniface."

20. See Sohail H. Hashmi, "9/11 and the Jihad Tradition," in Daniel J. Sherman and Terry Nardin, eds., *Terror, Culture, Politics: Rethinking 9/11* (Bloomington: Indiana University Press, 2006), 149–64, for a very nuanced presentation of al-Qaeda's self-understanding in terms of realistic goals versus theologically informed aspirational goals.

21. At http://www.un.org/News/Press/docs/2001/sc7207.doc.htm (accessed July 29, 2011).

22. Thom Shanker, "Defense Secretary Warns NATO of 'Dim' Future," *New York Times*, June 10, 2011, at http://www.nytimes.com/2011/06/11/world/europe/11gates.html (accessed August 1, 2011).

23. One sees this balancing of goods most clearly in Augustine's Letter 189, "To Count Boniface." In this letter, he addresses a Christian military commander engaged in defending Carthage against barbarian invasion. Since "peace" in the earthly sense means, for Augustine, a kind of tranquility of order that is necessary for human flourishing, the barbarians are responsible for disrupting the antecedent peace. Because of that understanding, Augustine can apply (admittedly, improbably) Jesus's "Blessed are the peacemakers" to Boniface and his soldiers, who struggle to restore that antecedent peace. But, Augustine argues, it is essential not to confuse the kind of peace achieved and sustained by military force with any true and complete peace. That, he insists, is a kind of ideal peace only attainable in the "Kingdom of God," or to put it in less overtly religious terms, a transhuman reality of perfection.

24. Samuel Huntington's provocative *The Clash of Civilizations and the Remaking of World Order* (New York: Simon & Schuster, 1996) concludes with some excellent observations that bear on this issue. He notes the tendencies of civilizations to imagine that they are destined to endure forever when, in fact, they do not. But more important, he offers a number of helpful suggestions about how the West will need to adapt if it is indeed to persist. Among the most important of these is the suggestion to continue to affirm the core Western values of democracy, individualism, and rights within the sphere of our own civilization while simultaneously accepting the multicultural and multipolar global civilization now emerging as the dominance of the West declines. More recently, Fareed Zakaria has made a quite similar argument very cogently in his book *The Post-American World* (New York: W. W. Norton, 2008). These arguments help point the way to the kinds of diplomatic effort that will be required: a simultaneous recognition of global multiculturalism and an attempt to bridge those cultural divides in ways that focus on the common threats to those connected to the international system. Thomas P. Barnett's *The Pentagon's New Map: War and Peace in the Twenty-First Century* (New York: G. P. Putnam's, 2004) lays out a very interesting conceptual model for doing precisely that. He discusses the "connected core" of states and civilization that, while culturally perhaps distinct, have common interests in the globalized system of communication, trade, and economics. Those, he suggest, have enough common interests that they can be expected to find common cause on many questions. Here, for example, is an area where the threat of Salafi terrorism constitutes a common threat to that "core." Thinking about the problem in this way may help ameliorate the tendency to frame the issue as if it were "the West versus Islam"—a particularly unhelpful and dangerous way of looking at the problems.

Conclusion

A Look Back and a Look Forward

JAMES TURNER JOHNSON

When reflecting on the contributions made by each of the chapters above and by this book as a whole, it is good to realize not only how important it is to try to identify and explore links, influences, commonalities, and differences across major cultural divides but also how very difficult this is to do at all and how much more difficult it is to do well. Such work must not only reach across divides between and among cultures regarding fundamental values, interests, and ways of conceiving them but also bridge the lines of division between and among scholarly disciplines. Both are challenging tasks. They are made more difficult, but at the same time more important to do and do well, by an atmosphere sometimes present in the sphere of public policy that regards cultural factors as ultimately irrelevant and practices an institutional blindness toward them. The work engaged in by this book and the project that led to it matters not only for scholarship; it also holds policy implications. This is yet another reason to approach it with the greatest seriousness. Doing it well requires looking backward into the history of each of the understandings of war being examined, their development as distinct traditions, and the interactions and influences across cultural lines that appear there. But this look backward is not only important in itself; it also provides a starting point for new understandings of each of these traditions and the potential for dialogue among them. Hence the title of this concluding chapter.

It is useful to set this book in a larger context. The subject it treats, the major Christian, Jewish, and Islamic traditions on war and the place of war in the affairs of political communities, is an old one but one on which focused study is comparatively recent. For the just war tradition of Western culture, contemporary attention reaches back only to the 1960s, when Paul Ramsey's two books on the subject appeared.[1] For Islamic tradition, the comparable benchmarks are two books by Majid Khadduri from 1940 and 1966.[2] But while Ramsey's breaking of the ground was followed by other work on the just war idea—including Michael Walzer's 1977 book[3] developing a version of just war in the frame of political philosophy, the United States Catholic bishops' 1983 pastoral letter[4] that simultaneously defined the position of a major American religious body and inserted the just war idea into the attention of military and policy circles, my own historical studies,[5] and my own and many others' contributions exploring the application of just war thinking to issues in contemporary warfare—it required the emergence of radical Islamic thinking and political action to bring about concerted attention to the idea of jihad and its place in Islamic thought and culture. While a particular, highly politicized version of the idea of jihad continues to be central to the rhetoric and practices of radical Islamism and while a critical literature has emerged focused largely on this, there remains a dearth of serious historical study of the development and use of the jihad tradition and the larger conception of Islamic political society and its relation to other societies within which the tradition on war is set. John Kelsay's recent book stands out as a scholarly work providing a longitudinal study of the idea and practice of jihad within the frame of development of Islamic shari'a.[6] Critical study and reconstruction of the treatment of war in Jewish and Byzantine Christian tradition remain in the beginning stages, as compared with the cases of the traditions of just war and jihad.

Comparative study of the sort undertaken here is relatively new. As recently as two decades ago, there was none. Two collections of essays edited by John Kelsay and me, based on a series of seminars held in 1988–89 and published in 1990 and 1991,[7] constitute the first substantial comparative effort to bring the traditions of just war and jihad of the sword into a focused dialogue. Several recent collections have cast their net more broadly, with chapters on the treatment of war in all of the major religions.[8] What such efforts gain in breadth, though, comes at the sacrifice of depth, for no single essay, however good, can cover everything that a complex religious tradition may have said, and may be saying, on a subject as many-faceted as war and its relation to political life. Nor do these books aim at exploring influences and common themes among the religions treated. The present volume, with its sustained historical focus and its explicit purpose of seeking out commonalities and forms of interaction, has a quite different aim and purpose, and it provides a far deeper perspective.

I mention these recent comparative collections and Kelsay's and my project of twenty-odd years ago because they help to mark, in different ways, both how far scholarship has come on religious and cultural treatments of the subject of war and how far it still has to go. This book's introduction holds out the promise that it will explore and shed light on "evidence that Christians, Jews, and Muslims were influenced in their views on the ethics of war and peace through their mutual interaction." But as the organization of this project and the topics treated by its participants show, this is not a simple two-way pattern of interaction. In terms of the cultures involved, there has been at least a three-cornered interaction, with the third corner represented by the Byzantine empire's guiding concept of war and of international relations, its understanding of the relation between religion and temporal rule, and its interactions with Islamic cultures and Islamic military power, on the one hand, and with western European cultural (including religious) differences and western European military power, on the other. So the current

volume goes substantially beyond the old pattern of Middle Eastern studies scholarship in which the scope was understood as bipolar, with Israel and the West, and
their institutions and political interests, lumped together on one side and the
Arab world, with its institutions and political interests, on the other.

In suggestive respects, the conception of the Islamic *umma* as a community
defined both religiously and politically and the definition of the nature and place of
jihad of the sword within that conception—achievements associated particularly
with the early Abbasid jurists al-Shaybani and al-Shafi'i—reflect the internal conception and ordering of the Byzantine empire, and this remained obscure until
more began to be clarified about the latter. And in addition to the question of interaction between just war and jihad, there is also the matter of the interaction between
Latin Christendom and the Byzantines over religion, culture, and practice of war
throughout the Middle Ages and until the fall of Byzantium.

When one thinks more closely about the specific religions involved in this interaction across cultural boundaries, the three-cornered dialogue among the major
cultures becomes one with as many as six participants: both Protestant and Catholic
forms of Western Christianity, the Orthodox Christianity of the Byzantine world,
Judaism, and both the Sunni and Shi'i forms of Islam. These have been involved
with one another at different times, in different places, in different ways, and with
different effects, but the reality of this complicated six-way interaction serves as a
reminder of how intricate the relationships are.

A further level of complexity is introduced by the terms in the title of this
book—*just war*, *jihad*, and *holy war*—in themselves. As discussed in the introduction, the first two of these terms refer to well-defined traditions, each of which
has its own specific historical origin in time and place, its original purpose, its
function relative to the conduct of the affairs of the political communities involved,
and its specific core content. Even so, there is an extensive contemporary literature that employs these terms in ways often very different from their historically
rooted meaning, sometimes reshaping them for particular political purposes, and
at other times these historical traditions and their contents are ignored altogether.
A further issue is that the two terms do not "travel" well across cultures, as each
culture tends to reinterpret the position of the other according to its own lights.
Thus, the ideas of both just war and jihad have been represented as forms of "holy
war" from the perspective of the other culture.

As noted in the introduction, the term *holy war* is deeply problematic, often used
loosely and imprecisely and applied to quite diverse phenomena. The treatment in
this volume serves the useful purpose of setting this term in historical context
rather than treating it as a tradition of similar strength to those of just war and
jihad or as a reductive category to apply to either of these.

A central issue that runs throughout the chapters of this book is the conception of the relation between the religious and the secular or temporal. In the West,
these have been understood as separate from very early on, and the just war tradition from the first, though dependent significantly on religious sources, defined

the matter of just war as belonging securely to the temporal sphere, to the authority of temporal rulers with no temporal superiors. In the Byzantine and Islamic traditions, though, no such sharp distinction is made, and the religious and the secular are understood as aspects of a single reality in ways not easily understood from the perspective of those used to the distinction made in the West. The essays in this volume individually and collectively provide a more fine-grained understanding of the relation of the religious and the secular or temporal in the traditions under consideration.

The conception and description of the present project raises the question of whether, and if so, in what ways, there has been a cross-cultural conversation across the whole period in which the cultures of the West, of Byzantium, and of Islam have existed at the same time. Some of the chapters above focus squarely within one or another of the three cultural frames of the West, Byzantium, and the Islamic world, developing their subjects within those frames in detail but not attempting to work cross-culturally. While not themselves comparative in nature, they provide a useful contribution to the project as a whole, because to have serious and insightful recognition of interactions and possible influences across major cultural boundaries requires detailed historical and thematic work aimed at understanding and depicting each of the cultures involved. Serious comparative work requires a significant depth of understanding of both (or all, in the case of multipronged comparisons) subjects being compared. Because of the nature of scholarly training and the differences among scholarly disciplines, most critical scholars develop expertise in only one subject, and perhaps only a narrow portion of it at that; so those seeking comparative understandings must depend on one another to provide understanding of the cultures in which some are trained and others are not, so that all can hope to recognize parallels, connections, distinctions, and differences and come to identify possible lines of relationship or influence. In the course of work on particular cultures, possible connections and lines of investigation across cultural boundaries may be missed; yet close-grained study by specialists in their own fields enables those well grounded in study of other cultures to recognize important issues that reach across the cultural divides and may open up innovative and fruitful new lines for scholarly investigation and collaborative interaction.

Let me illustrate how this may develop, using examples from the three chapters in part I. Early in Paul Stephenson's chapter, there is a brief discussion of "the imperial theology of victory" in late Roman practice and, in particular, of the use of the concepts of *felicitas* and *virtus* by the emperor Constantine I. While these ideas were older than Constantine, his identification of them as gifts from the Christian God, described by him as the "greatest god" (*summus deus*), initiated an understanding of the relation of Christian religion to the Roman state that remained in later Byzantine thought and practice. Stephenson uses the idea of divine blessing to lead into the discussion of spiritual rewards understood as gained by fallen warriors, the main thrust of his chapter. But his reference to *felicitas* and *virtus* also suggests another line of inquiry. An emperor, by his behavior in battle and particularly by his military success against the state's enemies, showed not only his own *virtus* (which Stephenson translates for the case in question as "manly aggressiveness") but also the divine gift of *felicitas* (literally, "blessedness"). In Byzantine Rome, the Latin *felicitas* became the Greek *makarios*—both terms meaning blessed. The use of this concept reveals something important about the Byzantine understanding of war and the relation of religion to warfare. But anyone who knows the *ghazi* concept in Islamic tradition, from its first appearance in the Abbasids' effort to solidify their rule over the Umayyads through military success on the *thugur*, the frontier with the Byzantine empire, to the use of this same concept by the Turks on their westward movement, to the adoption of *ghazi* as an imperial title by the Ottoman sultans, to the practice of the Ottoman state (on which a window is opened by Yurdusev's chapter), should recognize something strikingly familiar, for the success of the *ghazi*, the warrior, is conceived of as a direct sign of God's *baraka*, the divine blessing and approval of the warrior's action. Speaking of such blessing is far from a conception of "holy war" in either case; the Byzantine usage suggests the importance of a pious dependence on God, and Islamic usage employed it as a mark of legitimacy for the leader who received it. Nonetheless, there seems to be a parallel here in the idea that the successful warrior-ruler should be understood as one who has received divine blessing. It remains for this similarity to be explored, regarding whether it shows influence or a common set of broader beliefs across the two cultures or something else, in addition to meaningful differences between the two sets of concepts. Stephenson's reference plays the valuable role of raising this matter to view—although much remains to explore this theme in Byzantine and Islamic examples and to relate what seems at first look to be a common theme to the distinctively different approach found in the West, where (although desire for God's blessing in war appears again and again in popular thought and in prayers during wartime) the idea of justified war was put not in terms of the need for such blessing but, rather, in terms of the demands of natural justice and the responsibility of the temporal prince, acting in the stead of God on earth, to serve such justice.

Asma Afsaruddin's chapter opens the door to new investigative issues in a different way. Focused closely on passages from the Qur'an and their early interpretation, this chapter provides an important corrective to the argument made by radical Islamists that the understanding of jihad of the sword that they employ expresses a conception unchanged since the time of the Prophet Muhammad and his companions. Afsaruddin's analysis, examining the permission given to Muslims to fight in order to protect houses of worship and the people who worship in them, paints a picture of development in thinking about the central passage in question, Qur'an 22:39–40, shaped by historical events and context from the earliest commentators to the period of the magisterial jurists. Afsaruddin points the way for herself and other scholars capable of doing so to investigate the nature and implications of such shifts in meaning more broadly and to extrapolate the investigation to include the experience of the Islamic community through the early caliphs, the *fitna* (civil) wars, the Umayyad expansion, and the Abbasid revolution, when the juristic conception of jihad was solidified.

A third example is provided by Michael Penn's examination of the Syriac Christian response to the Islamic conquests of territory in the area that is present-day northern Lebanon, Syria, and Iraq. The study of these Syriac sources is an important recent development in historical work on the period and the area in question. While Penn's chapter sheds important light on the Syriac-speaking Christians' reactions to the Muslim conquests in their area, it also cracks open the door on the new perspectives that this literature offers on the Islamic movement as it was developing at the time. Existing interpretations of this early period in the spread and development of Islam have relied heavily on Muslim sources, often written later by authors looking back with particular agendas to further. Although the Syriac Christian sects had their own axes to grind, especially with reference to one another, their more immediate reaction to the new Muslim political and military order, and what this may tell us about contemporaneous Muslim conceptions of such order, looks like an especially promising line for future research.

The chapters in the remaining parts of this book deal with historical contexts in which some form of cross-cultural or interreligious interaction took place; central here is how this affected thinking on war and the practice of war. Yet they, too, open up new potential lines for further research and efforts at developing deeper understandings.

The first of these contexts, treated in part II, is that of the Crusades, viewed in this book (via the chapters by Birk and by Mourad and Lindsay) from two points of view: that of the West and that of Islam. Davis's and Wilkes's chapters extend the view by examining the particular case of religiously related warfare in medieval Spain. Western scholarly writers on the Crusades, even the most highly regarded ones, have not done well by the idea of just war. While elements of just war thinking can be traced to theologians including Ambrose, Augustine, and Isidore of Seville, there was no systematic, coherent statement defining just war until the completion of Gratian's *Decretum* half a century after the call to the First Crusade. Although in the debates after Gratian, some canonical writers held out for religious authorization of some wars, in the end, the just war consensus developed very differently, focused around the requirements of the authority of a temporal sovereign, a just cause having to do with maintaining the temporal good of the political community, and an intention focused on avoiding immoral behavior and achieving the end of temporal peace. As noted in the introduction, the relation between just war and holy war doctrine in this historical context is at best analogical; the normative just war idea, as it developed, was not a doctrine of holy war.

Birk's chapter provides a valuable look at the Crusades not from the perspective of the developing canonical and theological thought on war but from that of southern Italian figures of high knightly rank who became crusaders. As Birk describes these, giving important attention to the context out of which they came, including their responsibilities as temporal rulers and their interactions with Muslim inhabitants, governing authorities, and warriors, a picture emerges that is not at all inconsistent with the conception of just war as it came together beginning with the work of Gratian: that of the use of armed force as a tool that the temporal ruler may use if needed to protect or provide a just and peaceful order in the community for which he, as ruler, has responsibility. That this community could include Muslims and involve them in the establishment and preservation of such an order was not in itself a problem for this conception of just war; rather, the problem that justified resort to armed force was some form of concrete evildoing that threatened or disordered the public good, and this might come from persons of any religious faith—or none. But for Western participants in the Crusades from farther north, where there was no established history of interaction with Muslims as inhabitants of a ruler's domain or as officials or warriors who contributed to the good of the ruler's community, the interaction with Muslims in and around the Holy Land could easily take on a more hostile coloration—and did. Birk's chapter demonstrates that conflict across major cultural and religious divides can be different from this.

When we turn to the concept of jihad of the sword, we encounter different sorts of conceptual and chronological problems from those that present themselves in the West. The earliest systematic conception of such warfare in the context of the welfare of the Islamic community is that defined by the jurists of the early Abbasid caliphate, particularly al-Shaybani and al-Shafi'i and others after them, including al-Tabari and al-Mawardi. As described in the introduction, these scholars depicted the world as divided into two parts, the *dar al-Islam* and the *dar al-harb*, which are understood as being in perpetual conflict because of the disorder and threat associated with the *dar al-harb*, the abode or territory of war. The *dar al-Islam*, by contrast, is depicted as a unity, the political community of all Muslims and those who have accepted submission to their rule, governed by a ruler who bears the same unified religiopolitical authority as the Prophet Muhammad and ordered according to divinely given law, shari'a, interpreted through *fiqh* (that is, juristically). Jihad of the sword is defined within this conceptual frame, so that it is a duty of the ruler and of the community as a response to the disorderliness and threat of the *dar al-harb*. Its normative form is the jihad of communal duty, *fard kifaya*, but emergencies may evoke another form, that of individual duty, *fard 'ayn*.

So far, so good. This is what we may call the standard conception. The picture thus described is that of the magisterial jurists of the early Abbasid period. But this picture in itself does not tell us everything that is worth knowing, and it tends to obscure some of that.

Mourad and Lindsay's chapter shows how this rather ideal conception of jihad was adapted—and changed—in the context of Muslim reaction to the Crusades. Three points stand out: first, the shift in responsibility for engaging in jihad from the distant and relatively unengaged caliph to local authorities and individual Muslims fighting under their lead; second, the depiction of the conquests by the crusaders as evidence that Muslims had fallen away from the true faith, so that only religious purification would make possible the repulse of the crusaders; and third, the success of Nur al-Din as an example of a military leader who also undertook to purify Islamic practice in his domains. All of these are themes that surface later in Muslim anticolonial warfare (as we see in part IV) and in present-day radical Islamist militancy. Nonetheless, all are in tension with the understanding of jihad defined by the magisterial jurists of the early Abbasid period. This underscores the point made in the introduction, that while this juristic model had definite normative value, it was never, in fact, a descriptive account of the Islamic world, for local interpretations and practices varied considerably according to circumstance.

The emphasis on local rule that Mourad and Lindsay identify as a response to the stresses of the Crusades can be thought of more broadly as exemplified in the phenomenon of multiple caliphates and Shi'i imamates that developed in various regions of the Islamic world (including eventually the rivalry between the Ottoman sultans and the Persian shahs). As far as the juristic concept of legitimate rule did, in fact, become universally accepted, it did not take the form of a genuinely universal religiopolitical Islamic entity ruled over by a single ruler carrying the authority of the Prophet but, rather, served as a vehicle for the claims of particular rulers in particular places to be bearing the mantle of religious destiny.

In addition to Mourad and Lindsay's chapter on the Muslim reaction to the Crusades, the chapters by Brower, Robinson, Sharkey, and Khalidi in part IV offer perspectives on this phenomenon in a later historical period in terms of four regions—Algeria, West Africa, Sudan, and India—where local Islamic rule developed in a context of colonialism; those by Yurdusev, Aksakal, and David Cook offer additional perspectives on this issue. In historical and regional terms, jihad is a much more variegated phenomenon than is suggested by the early Abbasid jurists' conception, despite the normative role that this conception plays in Islamic juristic thought.

All of these examples show in different ways how, despite such diversity, the "standard" juristic conception has historically proven to be a powerful framework for a common identity: it provided an ideal model that has always functioned ideologically. What should we make of this as we attempt to examine cross-cultural interactions and possible influences? What does this imply for how to deal with the present-day arguments of radical Islamists, who work from a version of the juristic "standard" account mediated by Ibn Taymiyya and claim that it offers the only right way to think about the world, about the course of history, the ideal Islamic society, and the implications of all of this for the individual Muslim who would be faithful?

Gaining a larger perspective on these questions requires looking back into the pre-Abassid period, as exemplified by Afsaruddin's and Penn's chapters, in addition to considering the course of Islamic history after the framing of the "standard" juristic conception of the *dar al-Islam*, its rule, and jihad of the sword, as exemplified by Mourad and Lindsay's and the other chapters just mentioned. The Abbasids and their supporters criticized the Umayyads for acting too much like kings, not giving religion a prominent enough role in their practice of government. The Umayyad rulers did, in fact, act this way; we see this, for example, through the reactions of the Syriac Christians that Penn discusses. But what if theirs was a more correct reading of the core sources of Islam than the one the Abbasids and their supporters put in place? Does that open up opportunities for a different form of political theory from that centered on the caliphate as defined by the early Abbasid jurists? In the absence of the caliphate, that would seem to be an important question to address.

Within the juristic "standard" conception, there are also important issues to look at more closely, which all of these chapters draw attention to in different ways. Of particular importance for present-day understanding is the conception of the jihad of individual duty, described in a particular way by contemporary radical Islamists as a means of justifying religiously motivated warfare against the West and everything associated with it. But the truth is, as several of these chapters show, that the conception of the jihad of individual duty has been developed somewhat variably in different contexts. Contemporary radical Islamists, as in *The Neglected Duty*[9] and various statements from al-Qaeda spokesmen,[10] regard this as imposing an obligation of individual action on each faithful Muslim. On this interpretation, the circumstances of emergency justifying such undertaking of jihad on one's own authority abrogate the rules of restraint governing the jihad of communal duty, so that an all-out form of warfare is allowed. My sense is that even contemporary critics of the actions of this contemporary radical Islamist conception of jihad tend not to question the main line of their interpretation of the idea of the jihad of individual duty, although they may challenge the radicals' rather vague and open-ended rendering of the emergency to which they are responding or the idea that the rules for fighting are abrogated. But examples from Islamic history show, in fact, that there is by no means consensus that this is the right, or the only, understanding of the idea of the jihad of individual duty.[11] In addition to the historical approaches taken in this volume, it might be informative to examine the understanding of elements of the "standard" model through the lenses of the several schools of Islamic jurisprudence, including the Ja'fari school of Twelver Shi'ism. Such a study would need to be both longitudinal and comparative, and it would need to take account of the different cultural contexts in which each of the schools became established.

In short, there remains much work to be done. But a lesson of this volume is that we need to think of each of the ideas and practices examined not only in itself but as part of a multicornered interaction. Scholars whose primary expertise is in one of the three cultural systems involved should seek to learn from the others, without pressing any into a common mold.

An implication of recognizing variations in how the idea of jihad has been understood and applied in different historical contexts is that reactions to it in the West themselves need to be set in their historical contexts. Wilkes's chapter on Maimonides on war is fascinating in this regard. As Wilkes shows, Maimonides's description of war in three categories linked to biblical references did not build on precedent in rabbinical thought, and other contemporary Jewish thinkers, living in other contexts, found it problematical. This argues for revisiting the matter of the substantial normative role assigned to Maimonides's thinking in present-day depictions of Judaism's position on war.[12] But it also, by being used reflectively as a lens on Maimonides's own cultural surroundings, suggests a closer examination of the relation between Maimonides's understanding of war and the understanding of war prevalent in Andalusian Islamic thinking of his own time.

Something of the same might be hypothesized for the case of Spanish Christians a bit later, after their encounter with Islam via the Reconquista. Davis's chapter stands as a warning not to push such reasoning too far, arguing that "the more rigorous we make our standards for attributing influences, the less credible [claims for such influences] become." Yet at the same time, he suggests three possible lines of inquiry for further exploration into cross-cultural influence, one of which begins by noting that the "distinctively Maliki approach to jihad in al-Andalus" emphasizes the secular authorization and purpose of warfare, as opposed to the religious, similar to the later Christian canonical and theological description of just war in terms of the responsibilities and purposes of secular government, and another of which suggests examining the possible influence on Aquinas and subsequent just war thinkers of the emergence in some Dominican circles of a more positive attitude toward Islam and a rejection of crusading. Nonetheless, the evidence at this stage is of the traditions on just war and jihad developing separately in their own cultural contexts.

Elsewhere in the West, and especially as the historical focus shifts to the early modern period, it is better to speak of perceptions rather than understandings of Islam. This shows through in both Charry's and Kelsay's discussions in part III. Charry's focus is on two figures, John Foxe and Francis Bacon, who lived and wrote in Protestant England in the late sixteenth and early seventeenth centuries, respectively. Neither knew Islam directly; both knew it at second hand. They wrote in a context in which "holy war" discourse was commonplace, although this term carried different content for different writers. It was directed in the first place to the Catholic enemy, for Foxe lived during the reign of the Catholic Queen Mary and the persecution of English Protestants and during the French Wars of Religion, while Bacon was writing during the Thirty Years War, the last great European conflict fed by Protestant-Catholic differences, and his work reflects the fear of a possible war between England, then experiencing the rise of Puritanism, and staunchly Catholic Spain. But these two writers also knew of Islam via conflict with Muslim powers—for Foxe, the Ottoman military and political pressure in southeastern Europe and the Mediterranean; for Bacon, the raiding of English shipping in the Mediterranean by Muslim corsairs from North Africa—and they turned their conceptions of holy war also against Islam. For Foxe, whose work offered a theological reading of English history as a way of explaining the tribulations suffered by English Protestants and their triumph represented by the accession of

Elizabeth I to the English throne, the Ottoman threat becomes apocalyptic in character, and the struggle against it is, in Charry's words, "mythical, ahistorical, and eternal." But the struggle against the pope of Rome and his followers was depicted similarly, and as Charry notes, Foxe was "hard put to decide who is the greater foe," the Muslims or the Catholics. In either case, for Foxe, there was no question of learning from such foes or of compromising in any way with them, even though in the world of politics, England might find advantage in working with the Ottomans against powerful Catholic Spain. Bacon's thinking is similarly three-cornered (Protestant England versus Catholic Spain versus the Muslim corsairs from Algiers and other North African ports), and he, too, employs the language of "holy war" directed toward both enemies. But his purpose is to use this discourse to a secular end—an effort to influence the English king—rather than any sort of theological or religious one. Employing the format of a dialogue, Bacon puts different lines of argument in the mouths of his various speakers, all to the end of addressing the question of military action in response to the threat represented by the corsairs. The value of this method is that it allowed Bacon to present in sympathetic form all of the major lines of discourse regarding war that were in use in England in his time, particularly the discourse of holy war, traditional natural-law-based just war thinking, and the emergent reasoning that would shortly become the background for the Westphalian settlement. As with Foxe, there is no question here of seeking to understand Islam or learn from its tradition on politics and war; rather, the actions of the Muslim actors are fitted into frames that made sense to Englishmen of various sorts in Bacon's time.

Of the three figures on whom Kelsay focuses, Gentili was a direct contemporary of John Foxe, Grotius of Francis Bacon, and Pufendorf from a generation after Grotius, the first post-Westphalian generation. All were Protestants; all contributed in important ways to the emergence of the modern conception of international law. Gentili, though Italian by birth, did his major work as Regius Professor of Civil Law at Oxford. Grotius, having come of age in the context of the Dutch war for independence against Spain, knew Protestant-Catholic religious war at first hand and sought to find a way to define an order of nations in which religious difference would not be a cause of conflict. Pufendorf lived in an era in which, after the great religious conflicts of the previous hundred years (Protestant versus Catholic warfare in Europe, Ottoman Muslim versus European Christian warfare in southeastern Europe and the Mediterranean), religion had receded as a factor affecting rivalries and conflicts among states. Like Foxe, Gentili pairs the Turks with the Spaniards as enemies—for Gentili, enemies intent on universal dominion. But political dominion is the problem for Gentili, not religious difference. Like Vitoria before him, he rejects war with religion as the "sole motive." Holy war discourse has no place in his thought, even though he had suffered religious persecution. As Kelsay argues, Gentili uses the Ottomans and the Saracens (his term for the Persians) the same way he uses the Spaniards, as providing "cases by which he can speak about the rights and wrongs of war." For him, working out of a particular understanding of the just war tradition but also, like Grotius after him, refocusing the meaning of that tradition, natural law is the guide, and the effect of religion is judged by the standard of nature, not the other way around.

Grotius and Pufendorf, argues Kelsay, take a further step in placing Muslims "in the role of a foil, a kind of rhetorical trope by which they can enhance their arguments." For both, as with Gentili, the natural law is the basic norm, and religion's additions to this can be judged regarding their worth by referring back to the law of nature. Kelsay notes that for Grotius, this means that "even the Muslims" act according to certain basic norms, and this draws them closer, in principle, to the Christians and makes it possible to conceive a law of nations independent of religious difference that builds on commonality. Pufendorf makes a similar argument. Kelsay's judgment on these three fathers of modern international law is that there is no evidence in them of direct Muslim influence, although parallels are noted, and overall, there is something "more than a family resemblance," which Kelsay traces to "a shared political and economic reality," "themes shared between the Bible and the Qur'an," and "perhaps most important of all, the legacy of Rome." So the issue is not really one of influence across the cultural borders but rather one of different, though similar, reactions to common factors.

The picture drawn by Charry and Kelsay, then, is one of complexity, not simplicity. This is certainly also an appropriate characterization of the relations described in the chapters in the final two parts of this book, which discuss events and issues from the nineteenth and twentieth centuries to the present. One important issue from this period is the adaptation and use of jihad language as a focus for identity and struggle against European colonial presence and influence, a phenomenon that leads directly into the adaptation and use of jihad language by contemporary radical Islamists. The chapters by Brower, Robinson, Sharkey, and Khalidi in part IV discuss the emergence of jihad as part of the reaction against European imperialism in four different contexts, while David Cook's chapter in part V examines the emergence of apocalypticism as an element of jihad advocacy in contemporary radical Muslim discourse, and that of Martin Cook in the same section of the book looks at the influence of Salafi terrorism, including its conception of jihad and advocacy for jihad, on Western just war thinking. These are all distinct studies in their own right, but taken together, they provide valuable insights into the way in which a historical tradition, formed in one context and applied for centuries as an ideology for powerful states in their operations on the world stage (including, as Brower's chapter demonstrates, the corruption of just war thinking into an ideology for cross-cultural domination), has been reconceived in other regions of the world and applied as an ideology for the underdog engaged in a struggle for identity and self-expression against perceived oppression from non-Muslims. Mustafa Aksakal's chapter in part IV, by contrast, examines the last serious effort to use the language of jihad as part of the war effort of a major state, the Ottoman empire, through the nineteenth century and into the era of World War I. This discussion compares directly with Brower's on the French use of just war language to justify France's conquest of Algeria. It is ironic that in the Ottoman case, Christian populations subjected to imperial conquest and domination by the state's jihad experienced it as the vehicle of oppression, while the Muslim populations who turned to the idea of jihad in their own resistance to European imperial conquest and domination experienced it as a vehicle of liberation. The same phenomenon, mutatis mutandis, can be seen in the colonial powers' argument for conquest of Muslim lands for the purpose of bringing "civilization," sometimes—as in the case of France in justifying war to subdue and annex Algeria—making explicit use of just war language. Possibly no other single fact illustrates so well the problem of speaking about influence across the divide between the cultures of the West and of the world of Islam: each side has in different ways at different times experienced the other as a threat, and each has turned to its own cultural resources to counter that threat. There may have been dialogue, but the more sustained pattern is one of opposition and conflict.

The development of thinking about international law in the modern period and the emergence of positive international law beginning in the late nineteenth century provide a final illustration of the complexity of the interactions among the cultures of the West and the world of Islam and of those between and among Christianity (especially in its Western forms), Islam, and Judaism. Two chapters in this book, Stone's and Hashmi's, address the question of the relationship to international law from the perspectives, respectively, of Judaism and Islam. The situations treated are quite different, and this is reflected in these two chapters. For Judaism, the context is a system of religious law, halakha, developed, in Stone's phrase, as "a transnational legal culture" by a people who had no sovereign state of their own, and the central issues are how to relate this to "the biblical presentation of Jewish law as the law of the nation of Israel living on its land" and to the present reality of the state of Israel with its own laws existing in the context of a system of international law. Islamic law, by contrast, developed in a community understood as at once religious and political. The normative form of Islamic juristic thinking (*fiqh*) first took its distinctive shape in the early years of the Abbasid caliphate, and it included a conception of world order under the term *siyar*, referring to the relations between the Muslim community, the *dar al-Islam*, and the entities making up the non-Muslim world. The conception of jihad as the warfare undertaken by the *dar al-Islam* against *dar al-harb* was set within the context of *siyar*. Hashmi observes of *siyar* that it "was never fully implemented but never fully rejected or revised either," continuing, "For many Muslims, therefore, international law is not an outgrowth of their own culture's previous discourses and practices; it is a rival system to the authentically Islamic system." For Judaism, then, the problem is how to deal with the world of domestic and international law and politics from the perspective of a religion that developed without a political entity of its own and in reaction to this fact, while for Islam, the problem is how to deal with domestic and international politics and law from the perspective of a religious community deeply involved in political life from the first and whose own legal tradition developed a very different conception of political community and world order.

It should be no surprise, then, that the contemporary arguments that have emerged within each of these perspectives have very different characters and that in treating them, Stone and Hashmi go in quite different ways. Yet central to both of their discussions is the question of what the religious tradition in each case should mean for contemporary thinking about the state and an international order founded on states as autonomous political entities. It is important for reflection on their discussions to note that in addition to the internal debate in each of these two religious traditions, there is also one in Western societies over just what international law is and what it is about and how, if at all, religious tradition should be conceived as relating to it.

The chapters in this book, both individually and as a whole, provide informative and useful looks back on the conception and practice of just war, holy war, and jihad in various historical, political, religious, and cultural contexts. They add important content to what is known about these ideas and practices and the shape of their interaction. But by doing so, they also provide perspective for a new look forward in thinking about these ideas and practices and the possibilities for commonality, not conflict, in the future.

Notes

1. Paul Ramsey, *War and the Christian Conscience* (Durham, N.C.: Duke University Press, 1961), and *The Just War: Force and Political Responsibility* (New York: Charles Scribner's, 1968).
2. Majid Khadduri, *The Law of War and Peace in Islam* (London: Luzac, 1940), and *The Islamic Law of Nations: Shaybani's Siyar* (Baltimore, Md.: Johns Hopkins University Press, 1966).
3. Michael Walzer, *Just and Unjust Wars* (New York: Basic, 1977).
4. National Conference of Catholic Bishops, *The Challenge of Peace: God's Promise and Our Response* (Washington, D.C.: United States Catholic Conference, 1983).
5. James Turner Johnson, *Ideology, Reason, and the Limitation of War* (Princeton, N.J.: Princeton University Press, 1975); *Just War Tradition and the Restraint of War* (Princeton, N.J.: Princeton University Press, 1981); and *The Quest for Peace: Three Moral Traditions in Western Cultural History* (Princeton, N.J.: Princeton University Press, 1987).
6. John Kelsay, *Arguing the Just War in Islam* (Cambridge, Mass.: Harvard University Press, 2007).
7. James Turner Johnson and John Kelsay, eds., *Cross, Crescent, and Sword: The Justification and Limitation of War in Western and Islamic Tradition* (Westport, Conn.: Greenwood, 1990); and John Kelsay and James Turner Johnson, eds., *Just War and Jihad: Historical and Theoretical Perspectives on War and Peace in Western and Islamic Traditions* (Westport, Conn.: Greenwood, 1991).
8. In chronological order, these include Perry Schmidt-Leukel, ed., *War and Peace in the World's Religions* (London: SCM, 2004); Torkel Brekke, ed., *The Ethics of War in Asian Civilizations* (London: Routledge, 2006); Richard Sorabji and David Rodin, eds., *The Ethics of War* (Aldershot, U.K.: Ashgate, 2006); and Vesselin Popovski, Gregory M. Reichberg, and Nicholas Turner, eds., *World Religions and Norms of War* (Tokyo: United Nations University Press, 2009). See also my review essay treating the first three of these, together with other relevant recent books, in James Turner Johnson, "Thinking Comparatively about Religion and War," *Journal of Religious Ethics* 36, no. 1 (March 2008): 157–79.

9. *The Neglected Duty (Al-Farida al-gha'iba)*, by Muhammad 'Abd al-Salam Faraj, is available in English in Johannes J. G. Jansen, *The Neglected Duty: The Creed of Sadat's Assassins and Islamic Resurgence in the Middle East* (New York: Macmillan, 1986).

10. The best-known and still arguably the most important of the statements from the future leaders of al-Qaeda is the "World Islamic Front Statement against Jews and Crusaders" from 1998, signed by Osama bin Laden and Ayman al-Zawahiri (available at http://www.library. cornell.edu/colldev/mideast/wif.htm).

11. One such example is provided by John Kelsay's discussion of the Syrian author al-Sulami (also treated for other purposes by Mourad and Lindsay in chapter 5 above); see Kelsay, *Arguing the Just War*, 115–17.

12. For example, see the chapters by Michael Walzer and Aviezer Ravitzky on war in the Jewish tradition in Terry Nardin, ed., *The Ethics of War and Peace: Religious and Secular Perspectives* (Princeton, N.J.: Princeton University Press, 1996), 95–127.

INDEX